D1030714

WATERGATE INVESTIGATION INDEX

House Judiciary Committee Hearings and Report on Impeachment

THE WATERGATE INVESTIGATION INDEX

House Judiciary Committee Hearings and
Report on Impeachment

Compiled by
Hedda Garza

Scholarly Resources Inc.
Wilmington, Delaware

Scholarly Resources Inc.
104 Greenhill Avenue
Wilmington, Delaware 19805

Library of Congress Cataloging in Publication Data

Garza, Hedda.
  The Watergate investigation index.

    1. United States. Congress. House. Committee on
the Judiciary—Indexes. 2. Watergate Affair, 1972–1974—
Indexes. 3. Nixon, Richard M. (Richard Milhous),
1913– —Indexes. 4. Impeachments—United States—
Indexes. 5. United States—Politics and government—
1969–1974—Indexes. I. Title.
KF27.J8 1974e Suppl. 4   364.1′32′0973   85–2040
ISBN 0-8420-2186-8

PREFACE

The President, Vice President, and all Civil Officers of the United States shall be removed from Office on Impeachment for, and Conviction of, treason, bribery, or other high crimes and misdemeanors.

Article II, Section 4

The House of Representatives . . . shall have the sole power of impeachment.

Article I, Section 2

The Senate shall have the sole power to try all impeachments. When sitting for that purpose, they shall be on oath or affirmation. When the President of the United States is tried, the Chief Justice shall preside: and no person shall be convicted without the concurrence of two-thirds of the members present.

Article I, Section 6

The proceedings of the Constitutional Convention show that the Founding Fathers labored over the impeachment clauses. Clearly, impeachment was not intended as a political weapon nor was it to be used frivolously. But yet, while treason and bribery can be readily defined, exactly what is a "high crime" and a "misdemeanor"? Nevertheless, the Founding Fathers did their work well because impeachment has been used but thirteen times in almost 200 years: President Andrew Johnson (1868), Secretary of War William Belknap (1876), Supreme Court Justice Samuel Chase (1804), Appellate Judge Robert Archibald (1912), Senator William Blount (1797), and against eight federal District Court judges. And now in 1974, the House of Representatives, through the Judiciary Committee, was being asked if President Richard Nixon had committed any impeachable offenses.

On 24 July 1974, the Committee on the Judiciary of the House of Representatives began public deliberations on Articles of Impeachment of Richard Nixon. As millions watched on television, the committee, after ten weeks of closed hearings, presented its findings to the American people. The final chapter of the Nixon presidency had begun.

On the very same day, the Supreme Court in a unanimous decision ordered President Nixon to surrender sixty-four tape recordings of presidential conversations to John Sirica, judge of the District Court in the District of Columbia. Judge Sirica was empowered to give all relevant portions of the tapes to the Watergate Special Prosecutor who could then turn them over to Congress. The Court rejected the president's claim of Executive privilege for all of his documents, the exception being military and diplomatic material. Since the tapes did not deal with national security, President Nixon had to surrender the tapes so the courts could base their decisions on all possible evidence. It is these tapes which would reveal the "smoking gun"—that is, President Nixon had attempted to obstruct justice by planning a cover-up of the Watergate burglary—an accusation that he had steadfastly denied.

The end of the Nixon presidency now came swiftly. The president's counsel announced that Nixon would comply with the Court's order. Almost simultaneously, the Special

Counsel for the Judiciary Committee presented a lengthy and powerful brief for impeachment. The evidence—tapes, testimony, and documents—was compelling. On 27 July, the first Article of Impeachment was adopted by a 27 to 11 vote. It recommended impeachment because President Nixon's actions formed "a course of conduct" to obstruct justice in the investigation of the Watergate break-in and to cover up other illegal activities of his subordinates through false statements, payment of "hush money" bribes, withholding evidence, interference with investigations, and lying in addresses to the American people. Two days later, the committee voted for the second article, charging a general abuse of power by the president through a misuse of the FBI, CIA, and the Internal Revenue Service to spy on the American people. Efforts by Nixon's aides, who acted under his instructions, to intimidate Americans with burglaries and wiretaps were included in this article. And on 30 July, the committee voted to adopt the third article which accused the president of failing to comply with the committee's subpoenas to turn over evidence to Congress. The committee's work was done. The House of Representatives now scheduled debate on these Articles of Impeachment, but President Nixon did not wait to find out whether Congress would agree with the committee. He resigned on 9 August 1974.

In retrospect, the Judiciary Committee handled its assignment extremely well. It had the most difficult task of handling through law the great conflict between loyalty to a president and loyalty to the Constitution, between the arrogance of power and the rule of law. The deceptions of President Nixon made millions of Americans cynical about their government and their leaders. The impeachment hearings were the first step in the long process of national healing.

This index of the thirty-nine volumes of the *Hearings Before the Committee on the Judiciary* is indeed a monumental work: an index of more than 25,000 pages of supporting evidence for the Articles of Impeachment. The hearings went beyond the Watergate burglary and include presidential misuse of power, the misuse of governmental agencies for personal financial gain, and illegal wiretapping; even the bombing of Cambodia was covered in the hearings, as the illegal bombing was included in the original impeachment charges but not in the final articles, not for lack of evidence but because the other articles seemed virtually unassailable. Any person who is interested in the Nixon presidency, especially in the crisis of credibility, will find this index an indispensable research tool.

Fred L. Israel

City College of New York
January 1985

Indictments Brought by the Special Prosecutor

	Position	Role in Watergate	Sentence	Amount of Sentence Served
Richard Nixon	President of the United States	Unindicted coconspirator	Pardoned	
Dwight Chapin	Presidential appointments secretary	Convicted of lying to a grand jury	Sentenced to 10 to 30 months	Served 8 m
Charles Colson	Special counsel to the president	Pleaded guilty to obstruction of justice	Sentenced to 1 to 3 years; fined $5000	Served ⁻
John Dean, III	Counsel to the president	Pleaded guilty to conspiracy	Sentenced to 1 to 4 years	Serv
John Ehrlichman	Domestic Council chief	Convicted of conspiracy to obstruct justice, and perjury	Sentenced to concurrent terms of 20 months to 8 years	Served 18 months
H. R. Haldeman	Chief of the White House staff	Convicted of conspiracy and perjury	Sentenced to 30 months to 8 years	Served 18 months
E. Howard Hunt	White House aide	Pleaded guilty to conspiracy, burglary, and wiretapping	Sentenced to 30 months to 8 years; fined $10,000	Served 33 months
Herbert Kalmbach	Personal attorney to the president	Pleaded guilty to violation of Federal Corrupt Practices Act and promising federal employment as a reward for political activity	Sentenced to 6 to 18 months; fined $10,000	Served 6 months
Richard Kleindienst	Attorney general of the United States	Pleaded guilty to refusal to answer questions before a Senate committee	Sentenced to 30 days; fined $100	Sentence suspended

	Position	**Role in Watergate**	**Sentence**	**Amount of Sentence Served**
Egil Krogh, Jr.	White House aide	Pleaded guilty to conspiracy	Sentenced to 2 to 6 years (all but 6 months suspended)	Served 4½ months
Frederick LaRue	Assistant to John Mitchell	Pleaded guilty to conspiracy	Sentenced 1 to 3 years (all but 6 months suspended)	Served 5½ months
G. Gordon Liddy	White House aide	Convicted of conspiracy, burglary, and wiretapping	Sentenced to serve 6 years and 8 months to 20 years; fined $40,000	Served 52 months
Jeb Magruder	White House aide	Pleaded guilty to conspiracy, wiretapping, and fraud	Sentenced to 10 months to 4 years	Served 7 months
John Mitchell	Attorney general of the United States	Convicted of conspiracy and perjury	Sentenced to 30 months to 8 years	Served 19 months
Herbert Porter	Chief of scheduling for Nixon campaign	Pleaded guilty to making false statements to FBI agents	Sentenced to serve 15 months	Served 30 days
Donald Segretti	"Dirty tricks" specialist	Pleaded guilty to campaign violations and conspiracy	Sentenced to 6 months	Served 4½ months
Maurice Stans	Financial director of the Committee to Re-Elect the President	Pleaded guilty to misdemeanor violations of the Federal Elections Campaign Act	Fined $15,000	
Bernard Barker	Watergate burglar	Pleaded guilty to conspiracy, burglary, wiretapping, and unlawful possession of intercepting devices	Sentenced to 18 months to 6 years	Served 12 months

	Position	Role in Watergate	Sentence	Amount of Sentence Served
Virgilio Gonzalez	Watergate burglar	Pleaded guilty to conspiracy, burglary, wiretapping, and unlawful possession of intercepting devices	Sentenced to 1 to 4 years	Served 15 months
Eugenio Martinez	Watergate burglar	Pleaded guilty to conspiracy, burglary, wiretapping, and unlawful possession of intercepting devices	Sentenced to 1 to 4 years	Served 15 months
James McCord, Jr.	Watergate burglar	Pleaded guilty to conspiracy, burglary, wiretapping, and unlawful possession of intercepting devices	Sentenced to 1 to 5 years	Served 4 months
Frank Sturgis	Watergate burglar	Pleaded guilty to conspiracy, burglary, wiretapping, and unlawful possession of intercepting devices	Sentenced to 1 to 4 years	Served 13 months

GUIDE TO THE USE OF
THE WATERGATE INVESTIGATION INDEX

The *Hearings and Report of the House Judiciary Committee* on the resolution to impeach President Richard Nixon comprises several multivolume categories including the Report of the Committee of the Judiciary, Minority Memorandum on Facts and Law, Testimony of Witnesses, Statement of Information and Appendices, Summary of Information, Transcripts of Eight Recorded Presidential Conversations, and Statement of Information Submitted on Behalf of President Nixon. This short guide to the Watergate Investigation Index will make it easier for the user to find the specific information he is seeking and will provide a long-awaited key to these historically important events.

Volume and Page Number: All of the numerical references are to volume and page number. The volume number is set in boldface (heavy) type in order to set it apart in a series of page references. The volumes are numbered consecutively within each category. Abbreviations for the volumes are as follows:

Report of the Committee of the Judiciary	**RHJC**
Minority Memorandum on Facts and Law	**MMFL**
Testimony of Witnesses	**TW**
Statement of Information and Appendices	**SIAPP**
Statement of Information	**SI**
Summary of Information	**SUMM**
Transcripts of Eight Recorded Presidential Conversations	**NT**
Statement of Information Submitted on Behalf of President Nixon	**NSI**
Impeachment Inquiry	**II**

Example: Oswald, Lee Harvey **SUMM I** 19; **II 3** 1940–1941

This would indicate that the subject can be found in Summary of Information, Volume I, page 19; and in Impeachment Inquiry, Volume 3, pages 1940 through 1941.

Alphabetization: The entries are arranged in alphabetical order by the word-by-word system. Most readers are familiar with this method, where, for example, "West Virginia" is placed before "Western." An exception to this rule is that names always take priority over places. When headings have the same first word, alphabetical order is determined by the second word. A comma stops this process.

Example: New, Henry S.
       New, Zelda
       New Jersey
       New York
       Newark
       Newton, Sir Isaac
       Newton Beach

Prepositions and conjunctions (of, by, in, to, and, etc.) are ignored in the alphabetization process.

Example: Committee of Human Rights
         Committee for Preservation of Landmarks

However, if two entries are identical except for a preposition, their order is decided by the preposition.

Example: Committee for Human Rights
         Committee of Human Rights

Subentries: The same basic rules of alphabetization hold for subentries. Prepositions are ignored and are alphabetized word by word.

Example: Jones, John
         trip to Europe
         and visitors to White House

When several listings by date occur in subentries, however, they are not alphabetized by the spelling of the month but are arranged by the actual chronological sequence.

Example: Mitchell, John N.
         log for January 14, 1970
         log for February 12, 1970
         log for July 6, 1972
         log for August 7, 1972

Hyphenated compound words are treated as two separate words.

Cross References: These are indicated by the word *see* and refer the reader from one heading to a more frequently used alternative form.

Example: Bribes *see* Hush money

See Also References: These are listed at the end of a given entry and direct the user to related entries.

Special Cases: Because of the nature of these hearings, the names of some people are treated in a special way. For their prior testimony before the Senate Select Committee the heading reads:

    Mitchell, John N., cited testimony of

However, when they are discussed by other people, the entries look like this:
    Mitchell, John N.
      Dean on meeting with
      relationship with Haldeman

For people who testified directly before the House Judiciary Committee, the heading reads:

    Mitchell, John N., testimony before House Judiciary Committee Impeachment
      Inquiry

Members of the House Judiciary Committee Impeachment Inquiry itself are listed under their names alone, or with the additional words "questioning by" when they are asking witnesses questions.

Often the two different categories have very similar (or even identical) subentries, but their separation will provide Index users with a valuable tool for sifting out differences in the listed person's own versions of an event and the versions of other people.

General Notes: Subentries under particular names also may bear important clues to other entries that might throw further light on a particular topic. For example, the following might lead the user to entries under Immunity, Nixon, or Dean:

> Petersen, Henry E., cited testimony of
>   on conversations with Nixon on immunity for Dean

Important general topics often have been divided into more specific categories. For example, "Financial matters" is cross-referenced to "Hush money" and "Campaign contributions," since they have very special significance for these hearings and deserve separate categories of their own.

Care has been taken to index many names and subjects that only occur once or twice in the long hearings, since the Indexer realizes that any one of these single- or double-mention items might be the sole reason for a painstaking researcher's consulting the work.

A & A Fence Co. **SI12** 145-148

ABC network
memos from McLaren for Ehrlichman on ITT attempted take-over of **SI5-1** 146, 153-162

Abel, Alice SI5-2 789, 793

ABM
"front" organizations supporting Administration policies on **SI6-1** 199, 203

Abplanalp, Robert H.
location of home at Key Biscayne, Fla. **SI12** 156
purchases 23 acres of Nixons' San Clemente property **SI12** 96

Abrams, Creighton W.
statements on bombing of Cambodia **SI11** 51-52, 58-59, 66, 271-272, 300-304, 330

Abzug, Bella II 2 945

Academic freedom
and restrictions on intelligence activity on campuses, Huston plan on **SI7-1** 422

Acheson, Dean SI7-1 365

Acker, Marjorie SI8 69, 115

Acree, Vernon D. (Mike)
and Caulfield's efforts to obtain IRS audit of Greene **SI8** 16, 165, 166-174
as Caulfield's source of tax information on Goldberg **SI8** 142, 143
as Caulfield's source of tax information on Graham **SI8** 151-152
as Caulfield's source of tax information on Wayne and other entertainers **SI8** 15, 155, 156-163
as Dean's source of tax information on Graham **SI8** 14, 145, 146-154
investigates leak of IRS information on Wallace administration **SI8** 41
and IRS audit of Greene **II 2** 1281
and IRS information to Caulfield on politically active people in entertainment industry **II 2** 1279-1281
legal aspects of his giving Caulfield IRS information **II 2** 1271-1272, 1273
obtains IRS information on Goldberg for Caulfield **II 2** 1271
and White House requests for IRS audits **SI8** 17, 175, 176-182

Adams, Kenneth L. TW 3 184-528
See also Colson, Charles, testimony before House Judiciary Committee Impeachment Inquiry

Adams, Sherman SI3-2 1158

ADEPT (Agriculture and Dairy Education Political Trust) SI6-1 87
loan from SPACE to **SI6-2** 706-707, 712-714, 715-717
memo from Hanman on campaign contributions and favorable Administration decisions **SI6-2** 480, 784, 818

Administration on Aging
Todd's recommendations on **SIAPP4** 78

Adult Education Act of 1966
impoundment of funds for **SI12** 24

Adverse inference rule MMFL 41-44

Advertising
campaign budget and **SIAPP4** 136
by Democratic intellectuals on McGovern campaign **SIAPP4** 136
by front groups in Nixon re-election campaign **II 2** 1054-1056
in Nixon re-election campaign **SI1** 87; **SIAPP4** 115
placed by public relations firm in name of fictitious groups supporting Administration policies **SI6-1** 12, 197, 198-211
in Political Matters Memoranda **SIAPP4** 127-128, 138-139, 146-147
by Tell it to Hanoi Committee **SI1** 97-98

Advertising Advisory Group SI1 50

Advisory Panel on the White House Tapes
Report of **SUMM I** 110
Report on a Technical Investigation on EOB Tape of June 20, 1972 by **SI9-2** 552, 558, 578, 581, 867, 869-874, 925, 926-929, 1037, 1038-1044, 1059, 1061-1069
states erasures on June 20, 1972 tape were manually produced **SUMM I** 38

Agenda for the Nation **SI8** 85

Agnew, Spiro T. II 2 1002, 1003; **SIAPP4** 108
appearance at California Republican Assembly **SI1** 85
cancellation of appearance before Southern GOP Conference **SI1** 34
Dent informs New York Conservative Party that he will be on ticket in 1972 **SIAPP4** 25, 46-47
legal proceedings against **II 1** 61
letter from Gerrity on antitrust suits against ITT **SI5-1** 143, 163-165; **SI5-2** 508-509, 513-514, 674-676, 710-712, 803-804, 813-815, 863-864, 897-899, 937-938
in Richardson-Nixon discussion **SI9-2** 533, 737, 738-740
role in Nixon re-election campaign **SIAPP4** 59
in Ryan memo to Merriam **SI5-1** 186; **SI5-2** 672, 708

"Agreement of Merger and Plan of Reorganization," **SI6-1** 4, 58, 83-86

Agricultural Act of 1949
on advance announcement of price support levels **SI6-1** 26, 389, 390-391

Agricultural programs
impoundment of funds for **SI12** 16-19

Aibel, Howard J. NSI2 84-85; **SI5-1** 405

Aibel, Howard J., cited testimony of
on destruction of documents by ITT after disclosure of Beard memo **SI5-2** 491, 613, 629-630

Air Force
Nixon on **SIAPP3** 4-5

Aircraft
in Liddy plan **SI1** 59

Alabama Independent party
National Convention **SIAPP4** 59
platform and National Convention **SI1** 34

Alagia, Damian Paul
at meeting between Nixon and dairy industry leaders on March 23, 1971 **SI6-2** 599-601
meeting with AMPI officials on immediate contributions **SI6-2** 475, 703, 704-721

anti-trust investigation of, *see* Antitrust suit against AMPI
Colson memo to Nixon on $2 million pledge to re-election campaign from **II 2** 1049-1050
Connally denies political or professional connection with **SI6-1** 427
contribution offer to Kalmbach **SI6-1** 3-4, 57-58, 59-87
contribution to Special White House project for Congressional candidates administered by Gleason and Kalmbach **SI6-1** 8, 127, 130-152
contribution to unopposed Democratic Congressional candidates **SI6-1** 13, 213, 214-216
contribution used for Fielding break-in **SI6-2** 481, 821-840
contributions to Nixon campaign through political committees between March 30 and August 5, 1971 **SI6-2** 479-480, 783-784, 785-820
contributions to Republican Congressional campaign committees **SI6-2** 487, 951, 952-963
contributions to Republican Congressional campaign committees transferred to other Republican committees **SI6-2** 489, 965, 966-984
delivery of $100,000 in cash to Kalmbach by Semer **SI6-1** 5, 89, 90-98
discussions on nonpublic additional contributions with Kalmbach **SI6-2** 486, 895, 896-943
Ehrlichman on discussions with Kalmbach on **SI6-1** 6, 99, 106-108
and financing of Fielding break-in **SI7-3** 1184, 1247, 1265-1268
and Hillings' letter to Nixon on dairy import quotas and $2 million pledge of **NSI3** 8, 75, 76-110
informs Colson of $2 million pledge for Nixon's 1972 re-election campaign **SI6-1** 9, 153, 154-160
and meeting between Nixon and dairy industry leaders on March 23, 1971 **SI6-2** 471, 473, 565, 566-620, 627, 628-671
meeting with Nixon **SI6-1** 10, 168-169, 186
and memo from Colson to Dean on limitations on campaign contributions **SI6-1** 11, 191, 192-194
memo from Gleason assigning Colson to matters relating to **SI6-1** 7, 8, 119, 120-125, 127, 128-129
and milk price-support decision **SI6-1** 10, 161, 162-180
Nixon invites dairy leaders to meet with him **NSI3** 3, 29, 30-34
Nixon speech at 1971 convention of **SI6-2** 482, 841, 842-845
payments to Wagner & Baroody **SI6-1** 18, 273, 274-298
and press coverage on connection between milk price-support increase and campaign contributions by **SI6-2** 483, 847, 848-861
press release on Nixon's proclamation on dairy import quotas **SI6-1** 17, 263, 271, 272
reaffirmation of $2 million pledge to Nixon campaign **SI6-2** 476-477, 727-728, 729-766
in Rice memo on pressures for milk price-support increase **SI6-1** 372-373
and Semer-Dent meeting **SI6-1** 6, 99, 103-105
Whitaker memo to Nixon on upcoming meeting with officials of **SI6-1** 26, 389, 396-397; **SI6-2** 469, 545, 546-553

See also Colson, Charles, testimony before House Judiciary Committee Impeachment Inquiry, on his involvement in dairy industry contributions; House Judiciary Committee Impeachment Inquiry, presentation of evidence on dairy industry campaign contributions; *U.S.* v. *David Parr*; *U.S.* v. *Harold Nelson*; *U.S.* v. *Ashland Petroleum Gabon Corporation and Orin Atkins*

Associated Press (AP)
wires for March 26, 1973 **SI4-1** 325-329
Associated Press Managing Editors Association
Nixon's comments at convention of **SI2** 308-309; **SI6-1** 26, 398-399; **SI7-1** 521-522; **SI10** 33-34
question-and-answer session with Nixon at Annual Convention of 1973 of **SIAPP1** 62-67
Atkins, Orin E. SIAPP2 227-230
admission of illegal contribution by Ashland Oil to FCRP **SI9-1** 31, 397, 398
See also U.S. v. *Ashland Petroleum Gabon Corporation and Orin Atkins*
Attorney-client privilege
Bittman on Hunt's refusal to waive **TW 2** 5
House Judiciary Committee Impeachment Inquiry discussion on O'Brien's testimony on Mitchell and **TW 1** 129-131, 133-134
Segretti-Dean relationship and **SI7-3** 1544
Aurelio, Richard SI8 124
Austin, Judge SI5-2 555-556
and antitrust suits against ITT **SI5-1** 169
Automatic sprinkler systems industry SI5-1 3, 4, 69, 94-101, 120-129
See also Grinnell Corporation
Automobile industry
in Nixon-Mitchell-Haldeman discussion on possibility of Republican victory in Michigan **SIAPP3** 30
Ayer, Eugene
and boundary survey at Nixon's San Clemente property **SI12** 126-127, 128
Ayer, William
and GSA payment for structural investigations at Nixon's San Clemente property **SI12** 133
B & C Investment Company SI12 96
Babbe, George SIAPP4 7
Bacon, Donald II 2 1251; **SI8** 38
in Dean and Caulfield briefing memo on IRS **SI8** 199
Bail money for Watergate defendants II 2 718-719
Dean's efforts to obtain from CIA **SI3-1** 8, 129, 130-142; **SI2** 2, 44, 427, 428-441
Hunt's request for, Mitchell-Mardian-LaRue discussion on **II 2** 718-719
LaRue and Mardian inform Mitchell of Liddy's requests for **SI3-1** 4, 97, 98-106
Liddy discusses with Mardian and LaRue **SI7-3** 1200, 1513, 1514-1521
Liddy informs LaRue and Mardian that Hunt believes CRP is responsible for **SI3-1** 3, 87, 88-95
Mitchell instructs Mardian to tell Liddy it is not forthcoming **SI7-3** 1201, 1523, 1524-1531
Mitchell, Mardian, LaRue and Dean discuss CIA providing **SI3-1** 7, 121, 122-127
See also Hush money

Bailey, Consuelo **SI5-2** 587
Bailey, F. Lee **SI3-2** 1022
Baker, Howard H., Jr.
  discussed by Haldeman and Nixon **SI4-1** 115-117,
    119-120, 124-127
  on Executive privilege **SI7-4** 1872
  on Hunt's withdrawal of guilty plea **SI1** 110
  Nixon's instructions to Kleindienst on **II 2** 834;
    SUMM I 87
  Nixon's instructions to Mitchell on **SUMM I** 7
  quotations from Bible by **SI1** 121
  and Stennis Plan **SIAPP1** 53-54
  telephone call from Nixon to Kleindienst on con-
    tacting re Senate Select Committee on Presiden-
    tial Campaign Activities hearings **SI4-1** 4,
    123-127, 213, 214, 215,
Baker, Howard H., Jr., questioning by
  Barker **SI1** 221-222, 227
  Dean **NSI1** 47-48; **SI3-1** 587-589; **SI4-1** 237; **SI8**
    167, 176-177, 215
  Ehrlichman **SI2** 2, 118, 130, 152-153
  Haldeman **SI9-1** 437-438, 441-442
  Hunt **SI3-1** 412
  Kleindienst **SI4-2** 870-871
  LaRue **SI2** 2, 107-108, 109
  Leeper **SI1** 260-261; **SI2** 73, 81
  Magruder **NSI1** 70; **SI3-1** 301
  McCord **SI3-1** 478-480; **SI1** 217-218, 229; **SI7-3**
    1496, 1497-1498
  Porter **SI3-1** 163
  Strachan **SI1** 96-97
  Ulasewicz **SI7-1** 349
Baker, James L. **TW 3** 42
Bakes, Philip **SIAPP2** 12-17
  See also *U.S.* v. *Ehrlichman, et al*
Balaguer (President of Dominican Republic)
  Donald Nixon and **SI7-1** 509
Baldwin, Alfred C., III
  identification of Hunt as one of Watergate bur-
    glars by **SUMM I** 45
  monitoring of Oliver's and Lawrence O'Brien's
    telephone by **SI1** 23, 223, 224-231
Baldwin, Alfred C., III, cited testimony of
  on first unsuccessful break-in attempts **SI1** 22,
    201, 212-213
  on intelligence activities in preparation for Demo-
    cratic National Convention**SI1** 26, 245, 250-251
  on monitoring of tapped telephones at DNC head-
    quarters **SI1** 24, 223, 224-228
Ball, Joseph **SI7-2** 611
Ball, Lucille
  tax information on **SI8** 157
Banowski, William **SIAPP4** 120
Barkan, Alexander E.
  on enemies list **SI8** 73, 107
Barker, Bernard L. **SIAPP2** 67-70
  address book of **SI2** 2, 51, 483, 490-491
  CIA memos to FBI on **TW 3** 19-21
  guilty plea of **SI3-1** 41, 483, 485
  indictment for Fielding break-in **SI9-2** 564, 963,
    964
  intelligence activities prior to Democratic Nation-
    al Convention **SI1** 26, 245, 246-253

payment for Fielding break-in **SI7-3** 1307
recruited by Hunt for Fielding break-in **II 2** 1174
role in Fielding break-in **SI7-3** 1185, 1275, 1276-
  1299
Segretti and **SI7-3** 1484
and unsuccessful break-ins at DNC and McGovern headquarters **SI1** 22, 201, 202-213
See also Mexican checks; *U.S.* v. *G. Gordon Liddy, et al*; *U.S.* v. *John Ehrlichman, et al*
Barker, Bernard L., cited testimony of
  on break-in at DNC headquarters and wiretapping
    of Lawrence O'Brien's and Oliver's telephones
    SI1 23, 215, 221-222
  on Fielding break-in **SI7-3** 1185, 1275, 1276
  on first unsuccessful break-in attempts **SI1** 22,
    201, 202-205
  on recruitment by Hunt for Fielding break-in **SI7-
    2** 561, 1095, 1108, 1110
Barker, Desmond J. **SIAPP4** 96; **TW 3** 259
Barker, Robert W., cited statement of
  on Stans' appearance before Select Committee and
    his constitutional rights **SI2** 2, 58-59, 561-562,
    572
Barnes, Ben **SIAPP3** 27, 32
Barnes, Richard **SI5-1** 437
Barnet, Jackie **SI7-2** 1023
Barnhardt, James D. **SI7-2** 683-684
Baroody, Joseph **SI3-2** 811
  affidavit on AMPI funds used for Fielding break-
    in **SI7-3** 1184, 1247, 1265-1268
  affidavit on AMPI relationship with Wagner &
    Baroody **SI6-1** 18, 273, 294-297
  affidavit on receiving money from Colson for ad-
    vertising projects in support of Administration
    SI6-1 12, 197, 207-210
  affidavit on use of TAPE contribution for Field-
    ing break-in **SI6-2** 481, 821, 825-828
  and financial arrangements for Fielding break-in
    RHJC 165; **TW 3** 235-236; **SI7-3** 1184, 1247,
    1248-1274
Barrera, Roy, questioning by
  Nelson **NSI3** 52, 193; **SI6-1** 458
Barrett, John Bruce **SI1** 260
Barrick, Paul E. **SI1** 85
Barth, Roger Vincent
  and Ehrlichman's dealings with IRS on investiga-
    tion of O'Brien **SI8** 221-222
  and IRS audit of Lawrence O'Brien **II 2** 1287
  memo from Huston requesting report on Special
    Service Group activities on ideological organiza-
    tions **SI8** 45
  memo to Morgan answering Ehrlichman's ques-
    tions on Nixon's 1969 income tax **SI10** 9, 180-
    183, 429-432
  and Newman's appraisal of Nixon's pre-Presiden-
    tial papers in November 1969 **SI10** 9, 184-196
  telephone call to DeMarco informing him that
    Nixon's 1969 income tax return was approved
    and refund check was being issued **SI10** 17,
    365-366
  and termination of IRS investigation of O'Brien
    SI8 24, 227, 228-235

Bartlett, Charles **SIAPP4** 5
Bartlett Construction Co. **SI12** 158
Bartlome, Robert E. **SIAPP2** 323
  *See also U.S. v. George Steinbrenner III, and the
    American Shipbuilding Company*
Basic Water and Sewer Facilities Program
  impoundment of funds for **SI12** 16
Bates, Charles W. **SI2** 2, 95
  and FBI memo from Bolz on investigation of Se-
    gretti **SI7-3** 1203, 1541, 1551-1552
  memo to Bolz on FBI Watergate investigation
    SI2 2, 34, 337, 342-345
Baumhart, A. David **SIAPP2** 323
  *See also U.S. v. George Steinbrenner III, and the
    American Shipbuilding Company*
Bay of Pigs
  and Barker **SI1** 204
  and CIA relationship to FBI Watergate investiga-
    tion **SI2** 2, 457
  Hunt and, in Colson memo to Haldeman **SI7-2**
    699, 701-702
  Hunt's and McCord's involvement in **TW 3** 16
  Hunt's involvement in **II 2** 1126-1127
  Nixon-Haldeman discussion on **SIAPP3** 54-55, 75
Bayh, Birch
  Colson on impact of Pentagon Papers publication
    on **SI7-2** 666
  letter to Eastland requesting ITT files from SEC
    SI5-2 514, 864, 865
Bayh, Birch, questioning by
  Jaworski **SI9-2** 843
  Kleindienst **NSI2** 78-79, 101, 119-121; **SI5-2** 680,
    732
  Richardson **SI9-1** 275
Beard, Dita **NSI2** 119; **SI2** 2, 27, 277, 280, 281-282,
  292
  Anderson on memo to Merriam from **SI5-2** 491,
    613, 618, 628
  FBI locates in Denver hospital **SI5-2** 498, 719,
    725
  in Gerrity memo to Ryan **SI5-1** 185
  Hume contacts Rohatyn on memo to Merriam
    from **SI5-2** 658, 694
  Hume on investigation of memo to Merriam from
    SI5-2 491, 613, 619-625
  Hunt memo on meetings with **SI5-2** 505, 777,
    787-794
  Hunt's interview with **II 2** 1035-1036; **SI5-2** 505,
    777, 778-794
  illness and admission to Denver hospital
    II 2 1029-1030; **SI5-2** 498, 719, 720-728
  LaRue on **SI2** 2, 286
  Liddy informs LaRue and Mardian about connec-
    tion between Watergate break-in and **SI2** 2, 27,
    277, 280, 286, 295
  medical report on **SI5-2** 498, 719, 726-728
  meeting with Gerrity on Anderson memo **SI5-2**
    722
  memo from Hughes to Ehrlichman on conversa-
    tion on antitrust suits against ITT with **SI5-1** 6,
    141, 142
  memo to Merriam on Republican National Con-
    vention **SI5-2** 491, 493, 613, 614-617, 633-636,
    646-647, 682-683, 935-936

Mitchell and **II 2** 1025
Mitchell on contacts with **SI5-1** 180, 181
Mitchell on memo of **SI5-2** 774
Mitchell statement denying discussion of ITT an-
  titrust suits with **SI5-2** 492, 631, 632
in Ryan memo to Merriam **SI5-1** 187
statement on meeting with Gerrity on Anderson
  memo **SI5-2** 498, 719, 720-721
United Air Lines passenger ticket issued to for
  March 2, 1972 flight **SI5-2** 498, 719, 723
United Air Lines stewardess report on illness dur-
  ing March 2, 1972 **SI5-2** 498, 719, 724
Wilson and **SI5-2** 530
  See also Dita Beard matter; ITT matter
Beard, Lane **SI5-2** 789
Beatty, Warren **SIAPP4** 121
Becktel, Stephen D. **SI8** 83
Beecher, William A. **NSI4** 122; **SI7-1** 218; **SI7-2** 891-
  894, 1006
  article on bombing of Cambodia by **SI7-1** 299-
    300, 327; **NSI4** 23, 161, 162-163
  article in *New York Times* on SALT talks **II 2**
    1143, 1147; **NSI4** 24, 167, 168-172; **SI7-2** 864-
    866
  Halperin's resignation from National Security
    Council and articles written by **NSI4** 27, 183,
    184-190
  Plumbers unit and **SI7-2** 891-894, 1006
  See also SALT leaks
Belknap, William W.
  impeachment case against **II 3** 2207-2208
Bell, George T.
  Colson on reasons for enemies list of **SI8** 76-77
  memo to Dean, Warren, and Shumway with list
    of political opponents **II 2** 1268-1269; **SI8** 7, 65,
    72-75
  and "Opponent Priority Activity" list **SI8** 10,
    103, 104-109
  role in circulating enemies list **SI8** 68
Bell, Thomas D. **II 2** 732
  biography of **II 3** 2147
Bellino, Carmine **RHJC** 438-439
Belter, Ernest H. **SI7-2** 683
Benham, Thomas **SIAPP4** 137
Bennett, David **II 2** 1304
Bennett, Donald V. **SI7-1** 23, 383, 384-431
  appointed to ad hoc committee to study domestic
    intelligence **SI7-1** 22, 375, 377, 381, 382
  attitude toward Hoover's objections being includ-
    ed in Huston plan **SI7-1** 433
  See also Huston plan
Bennett, John C.
  cited testimony on bringing subpoenaed Nixon
    tapes to Bull **SI9-2** 528, 607, 611-612
  notes on preparations for Nixon's review of sub-
    poenaed tapes **SI9-2** 528, 529, 607, 613-614,
    619, 646-647
Bennett, Robert **SI2** 2, 303
  deposition on Hunt's actions after Watergate **SI2**
    2, 20, 203, 217-221
Benton, Nelson **SI11** 260-262

Ben-Veniste, Richard NSI1 142-143
on Dean shredding material from Hunt's safe **SI2** 2, 43, 52, 415, 424-426, 511-512
on Dean's testimony on contents of Hunt's safe **SI7-3** 1206, 1575, 1586-1587
on materials in Hunt's safe **SI2** 2, 43, 415, 422-423; **SI7-3** 1204, 1557, 1566-1568
objects to hearsay evidence **SI9-2** 675-676
Ben-Veniste, Richard, questioning by
Bull **SI9-2** 645, 676, 678, 679, 680-685, 722-728; **SI4-3** 1496-1498, 1566
Buzhardt **SI9-1** 250-255, 296-297
Haig **SI9-2** 853-858
Haldeman **SI9-1** 360-365; **SI3-2** 1129-1132; **SI4-3** 1568-1574
Hunt **SI3-2** 916-922
Krogh **SI3-2** 1278-1279
LaRue **SI3-2** 1188-1197
O'Brien, Paul **SI3-2** 903-905
Petersen **SI4-2** 978-988; **SI4-3** 1535-1544, 1546
Unger **SI3-2** 1210-1215
Weiss **NSI4** 221-222
Benz, Robert Melton SIAPP2 320-321; **SI7-3** 1390, 1485
See also U.S. v. Donald Segretti
Bernstein, Leonard
on enemies list **SI8** 119
Berrigan brothers SI5-1 325
defense fund for **TW 2** 102; **SI4-2** 689
Berry, Loren M. SI5-1 137
letter to Nixon attempting to set up Nixon-Ge-neen meeting **NSI2** 5, 35, 36-42
Bible quotations
by Baker **SI1** 121
Bickel, Alexander M. II 3 1821-1822; **SI7-2** 594
argument before Supreme Court on Pentagon Papers **NSI4** 7, 75, 76
Bierbower, James J. SI4-3 1626
retained by Magruder **SI4-1** 28, 393, 487, 496
Big Sky project SI8 122
Bipartisanism
Doar-Hogan discussion on Minority of House Judiciary Committee Impeachment Inquiry representation during interviews with witnesses and **II 1** 96-97
and Garrison distributing separate Minority of House Judiciary Committee Impeachment Inquiry brief on impeachable offenses **II 1** 153-159
House Judiciary Committee Impeachment Inquiry and **II 1** 2
of Impeachment Inquiry staff, Garrison on **II 3** 2036-2038
Latta on **II 1** 299-301
Railsback on **II 1** 290-291
and Wiggins' amendment on right of Minority of House Judiciary Committee Impeachment Inquiry to subpoena witnesses **II 1** 23-32
Bishop, William Paul
biography of **II 3** 2147
memo from Hoover on leaks in government information **SI7-1** 3, 141, 142-145

Bittman, William O. II 3 1626-1627; **SI4-3** 1641-1642
arranges meeting between Paul O'Brien and Hunt **II 2** 786; **TW 1** 125-127, 137-138; **SI3-2** 902-903, 905, 906
arranges for Shapiro to see Hunt **TW 3** 322-323
Colson denies discussing Executive clemency with **TW 3** 472-474
Colson on meetings with **TW 3** 302-315
Colson reports to Dean and Ehrlichman on his meeting with **TW 3** 313-314
Colson reports to Haldeman on his conversation with **II 2** 757-758
Colson's memos to file on dealings with **SI3-1** 38-39, 455-456, 465-474
Dean on **SI3-2** 1023
Dean tells Colson he should meet with **TW 3** 300-302
deliveries of funds for Watergate defendants to **SI3-1** 16, 32, 33-34, 207, 208-219, 385, 386-389, 425-426, 427-454; **TW 1** 224-228
and deliveries of money for Hunt **SUMM I** 52; **SI3-2** 715, 1187, 1188-1237
in Doar's presentation of summary of evidence to House Judiciary Committee Impeachment Inquiry **II 3** 1964-1967
and efforts to determine date of last payment to Hunt **TW 3** 356-359, 362-363
and Executive clemency offers to Hunt **SUMM I** 63-64
House Judiciary Committee Impeachment Inquiry discussion on subpoenaing **II 2** 981-992
and Hunt's demands for money **SI3-1** 202
and Hunt's letter to Colson **SI3-1** 38-39, 455-456, 457-474
LaRue delivers money for Hunt to **SUMM I** 60
LaRue on last delivery of money to **TW 1** 259-260
and LaRue's arrangement for delivery of cash for Hunt to **II 2** 815-821
meeting with Colson **II 2** 757
memo from Dorothy Hunt on funds received and disbursed for Watergate defendants **SI3-1** 17, 22, 31, 221, 233, 281, 290, 378, 383
Nixon asks Colson about his demand for one million dollars **TW 3** 334, 335
O'Brien on his involvement with Hunt **TW 1** 164-166
O'Brien reports on his conversation with Hunt to **TW 1** 126
payments from LaRue from White House campaign contributions **SI3-1** 45, 517, 518-519
Petersen on his motion to suppress related to breaking in to Hunt's safe **TW 3** 75-78, 122
role in distribution of hush money **II 2** 736, 737-738, 751, 755
See also House Judiciary Committee Impeachment Inquiry, discussion on calling witnesses
Bittman, William O., testimony before House Judiciary Committee Impeachment Inquiry TW 2 2-113
on arranging Hunt's meeting with Paul O'Brien **TW 2** 25-27, 47-49, 50-52, 70, 79-80, 86-87, 88-89, 103-105, 111
on being retained by Hunts **TW 2** 5, 31, 84, 87
on being used in conspiracy to obstruct justice **TW 2** 95-96

on belief that money from "Rivers" was raised by defense fund **TW 2** 12-13, 39, 78-79, 96-98, 101-102, 103-105

on commutation of Hunt's sentence **TW 2** 90, 93-94, 105

on contacts with LaRue **TW 2** 14-16, 79, 88

on current legal status of Hunt **TW 2** 5

on date of last delivery of money for Hunt **TW 2** 69-70, 71-72, 75-77, 90-91, 93

on deliveries of envelopes to Hunt **TW 2** 28-29, 45-46, 69-70, 71-72, 74-75, 88

on deliveries of money from "Rivers" **TW 2** 7-12

denies contact with Moore, Ehrlichman, Haldeman, Strachan, or Higby **TW 2** 92, 100

denies having any conversations on Executive clemency for Hunt **TW 2** 68

denies knowledge of threats made by Hunt **TW 2** 70-71, 89-90, 93-94

on discussions with Colson **TW 2** 6-7, 13-14, 20-22, 23-25, 90

on discussions with other members of his law firm on dealings with Hunts **TW 2** 43-44, 60-63, 81-82, 84

on Dorothy Hunt's flight insurance **TW 2** 44, 86, 95

on efforts to obtain information on Hunt's safe **TW 2** 6-7, 21-22, 32-33

on escrow fund set up by his law firm for Hunt **TW 2** 84, 89, 107-108

on first knowledge about commitments to Hunt **TW 2** 49-50, 76, 103-105

on his professional background **TW 2** 2-4

on Hunt's concerns over legal fees **TW 2** 30, 31, 38-39, 83-84, 95, 99, 112

on Hunt's employment at White House **TW 2** 21, 33-37

on Hunt's financial status **TW 2** 95

on Hunt's guilty plea **TW 2** 24, 41-42, 56-58, 82

on Hunt's handling of funds he received **TW 2** 99

on Hunt's meeting with Shapiro **TW 2** 52-53, 89

on Hunt's testimony before Ervin Committee and Watergate Grand Jury **TW 2** 53-55, 59-60, 66-67, 73-74, 98-99, 100, 106-107

on legal fees received from Hunts **TW 2** 5, 7-19, 30, 38-39, 40-41, 42-44, 53, 55, 60-64, 79-80, 105-106

on meeting at Mardian's office at CRP after being retained by Hunts **TW 2** 5-6, 7-10, 32

on memos from Dorothy Hunt on accounts for money received **TW 2** 16-19, 46-47, 63-66, 68-69

on newspaper story that he is unindicted coconspirator in Watergate coverup **TW 2** 72, 109-110

on opinion of Hunt **TW 2** 87

on Parkinson asking him to request postponement of Patman Committee hearings **TW 2** 110

on reasons for accepting Hunt's legal fees in unorthodox fashion **TW 2** 109

on reasons for Hunts coming to his home instead of his office **TW 2** 93

on relationship with Hunt **TW 2** 39-40, 50

on showing Dorothy Hunt's accounts to Parkinson **TW 2** 64-66, 77

on terminating representation of Hunt **TW 2** 80-81, 106-107

Black, Eugene R. SI5-1 381; **SI5-2** 654, 690; **SI8** 83

Black, Hugo
statement in *New York Times Co.* v. *U.S.* **SI7-2** 595

Black, Jeremiah SUMM I 165

Black advance SI1 126-127
See also Liddy plan

Black Americans
and CRP funding of fourth party project **SIAPP4** 17

in Dent's reports **SIAPP4** 83

fourth party campaign and **SIAPP4** 46

and Magruder's activities against Muskie campaign **SIAPP4** 13

Malek and **SIAPP4** 123

Nixon on **SIAPP3** 24

in Political Matters Memoranda **SIAPP4** 6

preservation of democracy and, Rangel on **RHJC** 314

See also Black voters

"Black bag" capability
in Sandwedge plan **SUMM I** 29

Black bag operations SI7-3 1188-1189, 1339-1340,1372-1376
in Huston plan **SI7-1** 420-421
See also Sandwedge plan

Black extremist groups
in Huston plan **SI7-1** 397-401

Black Panther Party II 2 1001; **SI8** 44
Huston memo to Haldeman on use of surreptitious entry against **SI7-1** 440
in Huston plan **SI7-1** 397-398
IRS Special Service Group and **SI8** 47

Black voters
and Dent **SI1** 80
in Louisiana gubernatorial race **SI1** 86

Blair, Joan Curtis SIAPP2 12-17
See U.S. v. *Ehrlichman, et al*

Blake, Eugene Carson
on enemies list **SI8** 119

Blandford, Russ
recommended by Colson for investigation of Pentagon Papers publication **SI7-2** 678

Blanton, Paul E., questioning by
Mallory **SI5-2** 927-928

Blech, Arthur
and attachment of Newman's appraisal of Nixon's 1969 gift of pre-Presidential papers to Nixon's tax return **SI10** 14, 315-317
letters from Drumm on subdivision of Nixon's San Clemente property **SI10** 523-537
telephone conversation with DeMarco in May 1969 on Nixon's future deductions for gift of pre-Presidential papers **SI10** 7, 140-141, 142-143, 144-145

Bliss, Ray SIAPP1 105

Blommer, Michael W. SUMM I 1

Blout, William
impeachment case against **II 3** 2199-2200

Boese, Jean McG. SI5-1 467, 469

Boggs, Lilburn E.
and construction of block wall at Nixon's San Clemente property **SI12** 152
and construction of redwood vs. chain link fence at Nixon's San Clemente property **SI12** 145
and handrails at Nixon's San Clemente property **SI12** 143
and installation of den windows at Nixon's San Clemente property **SI12** 123-125
and restoration of "point" gazebo at Nixon's San Clemente property **SI12** 138
Boggs, Patrick SI2 2, 144, 153
telephone call to Ehrlichman on Hunt's connection with Watergate burglars **SI2** 2, 8, 117, 118
Bolt, Richard H. SI9-2 552, 578, 867, 869-874, 1037, 1038-1044
Bolz, Charles
and FBI memo to Bates on investigation of Segretti **SI7-3** 1203, 1541, 1551-1552
memo from Bates on FBI Watergate investigation **SI2** 2, 34, 337, 342-345
Bombing of Cambodia SI1 4
additional views of Sarbanes and Seiberling, joined by Donohue, Eilberg, Mann, Danielson, Thornton, Smith, and Hogan **RHJC** 301-302
admission of secrecy of bombing operations prior to May 1970 **SI11** 24-26
advertisements supporting **SI6-1** 209
classified report to Senate Armed Services Committee denying prior to May 1, 1970 **SI11** 21, 174
Command organizational structure and officials **SI11** 81-84
Conyers on **RHJC** 289-296
and court opinions in *Holtzman* v. *Richardson* and *Holtzman* v. *Schlesinger* **SI11** 408-442
declassified version of Richardson's Report to Senate Armed Services Committee on **SI11** 186-193
Defense Department answer to House Resolution requesting information on pre-May 1970 period **SI11** 57, 63, 295-297, 319-321
dissenting views supporting Article of Impeachment on **RHJC** 323-328
Drinan on **RHJC** 307-312
in FBI summary of letters reporting on surveillance of State Department employee **SI7-1** 302
glossary of terms used in Senate Armed Services Committee hearings on **SI11** 85-87
Hungate's additional separate views on reasons for joining in dissenting views in support of Article of Impeachment on **RHJC** 329
Impeachment Inquiry staff memo to Committee on Judiciary on focus of investigation and information sources **SI11** 1-3
investigation in House Judiciary Committee Impeachment Inquiry **II 1** 266, 270, 368-373
Laird statement of January 20, 1971 on continuation of **SI11** 48, 266
leaks on **SI7-1** 14, 23, 161, 162-165, 291, 292-300; **NSI4** 23, 161, 162-165
list of sources on **SI11** 112-124
maps of **SI11** 389-392

McCloskey denies change in orders on March 26, 1970 **SI11** 31, 209-210
McCloskey reaffirms U.S. respect for neutrality of Cambodia on April 16, 1970 **SI11** 31-32, 211-214
Moorer supplies information indicating no air strikes prior to May 1970 **SI11** 23, 180-181
Nixon announces plans for on April 30, 1970 **SI11** 33-35. 218-224
Nixon denies necessity for apology to American people on **SI11** 76, 378-379
Nixon's letter of August 3, 1973 warning of hazards of ending **SI11** 69, 340
Nixon's report of June 30, 1970 on **SI11** 41-45, 241-252
Nixon's statement of February 17, 1971 on continuation of **SI11** 48-49, 267
Nixon's televised address of June 3, 1970 on **SI11** 39-40, 237-240
number of sorties and tons of bombs during **SI11** 9
Owens on **RHJC** 333
proposed Article of Impeachment on concealment of information on **RHJC** 217-219
public statements after Schlesinger's letter of July 16, 1973 acknowledging prior to May 1970 **SI11** 68-77, 337-383
public statements of government officials on period from March 1969 to July 1973 **SI11** 28-50, 194-270
public statements on extent of **SI11** 76-77, 375-383
public statements on purpose of **SI11** 68-70, 337-342
public statements on reasons for false documentary submission to Congress **SI11** 75, 369-374
Rangel on **RHJC** 316-317
and report on U.S. aerial attacks in Indochina submitted by Defense Department to Senate Armed Services Committee **SI11** 88-104
Richardson report indicates no air strikes prior to May 1970 **SI11** 22-23, 177-179
Rogers admits prior to May 1970 **SI11** 37, 231-232, 233-235
selected copies and index of "Official Letters of Protest" filed with United Nations **SI11** 443-597
Sihanouk's attitude toward **SI11** 52-54, 275-279
statement of statutory law relating to **SI11** 393-406
statements following Schlesinger's letter of July 16, 1973 acknowledging pre-May 1970 **SI11** 51-77, 271-383
statements on Defense Department data submitted to Senate Armed Services Committee concealing **SI11** 64-68, 323-336
statements to Congress from 1969 to 1973 on **SI11** 10-27
statements to Congress on purpose of **SI11** 51-55, 271-285
in status report of House Judiciary Committee Impeachment Inquiry staff **II 3** 2231-2232, 2247
Stevenson denies prior to May 1970 **SI11** 38, 236
suspected leaks on **SI7-1** 218

television interview with Rogers on May 4, 1970
on **SI11** 35-36, 225-226

termination of **SI11** 9

Waldie on **RHJC** 298

Wheeler admits on May 4, 1970 **SI11** 15-16, 149-153

White Paper on purpose of **SI11** 54-55, 283-285

wiretapping of government employees in connection with leaks on **II 2** 1107

and wiretapping of Halperin **SI7-1** 327

and wiretapping of Kraft **SI7-1** 317

Bombing of Laos SI11 188

Bombings SIAPP1 17, 78-79

of North Vietnam, Nixon on **SIAPP1** 17, 78-79

by Puerto Rican nationalists, in Huston plan **SI7-1** 409

See also Bombing of Cambodia; Bombing of Laos

Bonafede, Dom SIAPP4 2

Boone, Richard

tax information on **SI8** 157

Bork, Robert H. SI5-2 957

appoints Jaworski as Watergate Special Prosecutor **SI9-2** 549, 845, 846-848

assigned by Nixon to appoint new Watergate Special Prosecutor **SI9-2** 546, 831, 832-834

and Cox's firing as Watergate Special Prosecutor **SI9-2** 544, 815, 816-825

files amendment to Watergate Special Prosecutor's charter and writes explanatory letter to Jaworski **SI9-2** 551, 861, 862-866

and Jaworski's letter to Eastland summarizing arrangement made on independence of Watergate Special Prosecutor **SI9-2** 557, 923, 924-925

letter to Cox discharging him as Watergate Special Prosecutor **SI9-2** 544, 815, 824

news conference of November 1, 1973 on appointment of Jaworski as Watergate Special Prosecutor **SI9-2** 549, 845, 847-848

remarks on appointment of Jaworski **SI9-2** 549, 845, 846

Bork, Robert H., cited testimony of

on agreeing to fire Cox **SI9-2** 544, 815, 822

on continuing work of Special Watergate Prosecutor office after Cox's firing **II 2** 1417

on filing amendment to Watergate Special Prosecutor's charter and writing letter to Jaworski on **SI9-2** 551, 861, 865-866

Boston, Mass.

demonstration against Tricia Nixon at **SIAPP3** 66

Boston Globe

on Kleindienst confirmation hearings and Flanigan's testimony **NSI2** 16, 189, 201-202

Boudin, Kathy SI7-2 1129, 1133

Boudin, Leonard B. SI5-2 780; **SI7-4** 1647, 1995, 1998-2013

Colson on releasing derogatory information to press on **TW 3** 212-213, 456, 481-482, 488-490, 493-494, 495-496, 517-518

Colson receives Hunt memo on **SI7-2** 563, 1125, 1128-1136

Colson releases Hunt memo on **SI7-2** 563, 1125, 1126-1149

Colson's release to press of information on **II 2** 1235

and Fielding break-in **SI7-2** 977-978

Hunt memo on **II 2** 1175

memo from Ehrlichman to Colson on **TW 3** 215-222

terHorst article on **SI7-3** 1219

See also Ellsberg case

Boudin, Louis SI7-2 1131

Boudin, Michael SI7-2 1130-1131

Bourke (Solicitor General) SI4-3 1545

Bowles, W. Carter, Jr. SI6-2 852

Boyd, Huck SI5-2 584

Bradford, William TW 2 61

See also Hogan & Hartson

Bradshaw, Dave

and effect of Pentagon Papers on Nixon campaign **SI7-2** 672

Brady v. *The United States* **TW 3** 99, 147-148

Brandeis, Justice

in McLaren speech on antitrust policies **SI5-1** 197-200

Brandt, Willy

Nixon on upcoming visit from **SIAPP1** 17

Braniff Airways, Inc. SIAPP2 231-234

See also U.S. v. Braniff Airways, Inc. and Harding Lawrence

Brayden, Walter E. TW 3 42

Breitbard, Robert SI5-1 444

Bremer, Arthur

Colson denies discussing investigation of **TW 3** 457

Brennan, Charles D. II 2 1134; **SI7-2** 690, 783, 927; **SI7-4** 2061

FBI interview on Sullivan's delivery of FBI files and logs of wiretaps on Kraft to White House **SI7-2** 552, 925, 927, 934-936

memo from Hoover on Haldeman's request for wiretapping National Security Council staff member **SI7-1** 7, 191, 198

Brennan, Major (White House Military Aide) SI12 118

Brewer, Albert II 2 1252, 1253; **SI6-1** 5, 89, 90-98

Kalmbach on money given to **TW 3** 664-666, 669-670

money from Kalmbach's fund for campaign of **II 2** 1048

See also Brewer campaign

Brewer campaign, funding of SI6-1 5, 66, 89, 95, 109

See also Brewer, Albert

Breyer, Charles SIAPP2 12-17

See U.S. v. *Ehrlichman, et al*

Brezhnev, Leonid I.

Nixon's summit meeting with, as excuse for delays in responding to Cox's requests **SI9-1** 30, 399, 400-401

Brickley, James SIAPP4 25

British intelligence

and communist activity on college campuses in 1930's, in Huston plan **SI7-1** 402

Brock, Bill SIAPP1 19

Broder, David S.

article in *Washington Post* on public demand for Watergate investigation **SI9-1** 136

Brokaw, Tom SIAPP1 82

Brooke, Edward W. SIAPP3 31

Brooke, Edward W., questioning by
Laird SI11 159

Brookings Institution II 2 1283
Buchanan advises major public attack on SI7-2 710
Colson's plan for theft at SI7-2 539, 739, 740-753; II 2 1132
compensation of officers, directors and trustees SI8 89-90
Dean tells Nixon about planned robbery of SI3-2 1022
in memo from Dean to Krogh on IRS investigations II 2 1263-1265; SI8 85-88
New Program of Foreign Policy Studies SI7-2 539, 739, 741-745
White House action on SI8 8, 79, 80-94

Brooks, Jack SUMM I 1
on access of House Judiciary Committee Impeachment Inquiry to materials of legal staff II 1 86-87
on appeal from Sirica's ruling on turning Grand Jury materials over to House Judiciary Committee Impeachment Inquiry II 1 202
on calling witnesses before House Judiciary Committee Impeachment Inquiry II 3 1622, 1623, 1669-1670
on Doar, Jenner, and St. Clair meeting II 1 99
on Doar-St. Clair correspondence II 1 177
on Doar's and Jenner's appearance before Sirica II 1 163-164
on elimination of investigation of tax fraud from House Judiciary Committee Impeachment Inquiry II 1 363-364
on Government expenditures on Nixon's properties as impeachable offense II 3 2000-2001
on House Judiciary Committee Impeachment Inquiry issuing subpoena to Clerk of House of Representatives for records of dairy industry campaign contributions II 3 1573
on House Judiciary Committee Impeachment Inquiry issuing subpoenas to Nixon II 1 666-667; II 3 1532-1533, 1547, 1556
on leaks from House Judiciary Committee Impeachment Inquiry II 3 1855-1856
on mail on impeachment II 1 75
motion for letter from Rodino to Sirica requesting materials from Watergate Grand Jury II 1 164
motion on Nixon's noncompliance with House Judiciary Committee Impeachment Inquiry subpoena II 2 946
on need for Jaworski's material by House Judiciary Committee Impeachment Inquiry II 1 60-61
on Nixon's gift of Presidential papers II 3 1465-1466, 1502-1503, 2005-2006
on Nixon's income tax II 3 2014, 2015
on Nixon's noncompliance with House Judiciary Committee Impeachment Inquiry subpoenas II 1 413, 433, 445, 446
on obtaining materials from Jaworski II 1 110-111
on obtaining Nixon's tax returns and audits from IRS II 2 1243-1244, 1246-1247, 1248-1249
on opening evidentiary presentations of House Judiciary Committee Impeachment Inquiry II 2 960-961
on opposing St. Clair's participation in House Judiciary Committee Impeachment Inquiry II 1 212-213
on presentation procedures for House Judiciary Committee Impeachment Inquiry II 1 261
on procedural rules for handling House Judiciary Committee Impeachment Inquiry material II 1 123, 128
on procedures for House Judiciary Committee Impeachment Inquiry II 1 4-5
proposes informing Senate Judiciary Committee of House Judiciary Committee Impeachment Inquiry discussion on Silbert II 2 1229-1231
on relationship between House Judiciary Committee and Joint Committee on Internal Revenue Taxation II 1 95-96
on release of House Judiciary Committee Impeachment Inquiry evidentiary material to public II 2 975-976
on releasing remaining House Judiciary Committee Impeachment Inquiry executive session materials including statement of information on Political Matters Memoranda II 3 2053-2068
on right of Minority of House Judiciary Committee Impeachment Inquiry to subpoena witnesses II 1 25, 28-29
on rules of evidentiary procedures for House Judiciary Committee Impeachment Inquiry II 1 471-472, 488-489
on setting completion date for House Judiciary Committee Impeachment Inquiry II 1 16-17
on Sirica's invitation to Doar and Jenner II 1 134-135, 136, 144
statement of additional views on Report of House Judiciary Committee Impeachment Inquiry RHJC 283-286
on submission of written interrogatories to Nixon II 3 1617-1618
on subpoena powers of House Judiciary Committee II 1 35-36, 68
on use of transcripts for refreshing witnesses' memories TW 3 122-123
on Waldie's motion on Nixon's noncompliance with House Judiciary Committee Impeachment Inquiry subpoenas II 2 942-943
on White House leaks to press on House Judiciary Committee Impeachment Inquiry proceedings II 1 193
on Wiggins' amendment to subpoena to Nixon II 2 951-952

Brooks, Jack, questioning by
Dean TW 2 288-292
Kalmbach TW 3 693-695, 696-697
Petersen TW 3 122-123

Browder, Earl SI7-2 1131

Brown, Gary SI2 2, 631-632
letter to Kleindienst on Patman Committee hearings SUMM I 51
letter to Kleindienst on Stans' testimony TW 3 165-169
in Nixon-Dean-Haldeman discussion on Patman Committee hearings SI8 325-326

Bunting, Reeves **SIAPP4** 47

Burch, Dean
remarks before Republican National Committee on April 26, 1974 **SIAPP1** 105-110

Burdick, Quentin N. SI5-2 865

Bureau of the Budget
Memorandum to the President on "Authority to Reduce Expenditures" **SI12** 7-8

Burgener, Clair W. SI5-1 437

Burger, Warren E. SI5-2 904

Burgess, Guy SI7-1 402

Burglary SI7-1 440-441
See also Surreptitious entry

Burn, Matt SI4-3 1546

Burns, Dr. Arthur SI5-1 132, 133
and antitrust policy proposals **SI5-1** 394
at meeting with President on economy **SI6-1** 384-385, 386-387

Burns, James SIAPP3 71

Burns, John
Nixon-Haldeman discussion on **SIAPP3** 47-48

Burr, Aaron SIAPP1 66-67

Burress, Richard T.
memo to Ehrlichman with routing memo to Whitaker on reaction to Hardin's announcement of March 12, 1971 on not raising milk price supports **NSI3** 12, 127, 128-120
memo to Whitaker on dairy import quotas and dairy industry attitude toward modifications of Tariff Commission's recommendations **NSI3** 9, 111, 115

Bush, George SIAPP1 19; **SI4-1** 463
on public reaction to Watergate **SI9-1** 136

Busing issue SIAPP4 1, 50

Butler, M. Caldwell SUMM I 1, 10
additional views on Article of Impeachment III **RHJC** 503-505
amendment on subcommittees of House Judiciary Committee Impeachment Inquiry **II 1** 40-41
on calling witnesses before House Judiciary Committee Impeachment Inquiry **II 3** 1645-1647, 1703
on depositions from reluctant witnesses for House Judiciary Committee Impeachment Inquiry **II 1** 275
on Easter recess **II 1** 302-303
on Greenspun matter **II 2** 1292
on House Judiciary Committee Impeachment Inquiry interviews of witnesses **II 1** 98-99
on House Judiciary Committee Impeachment Inquiry issuing subpoenas to Nixon **II 1** 317, 325-326, 653-654, 655, 656, 657-658, 660; **II 3** 1536, 1540
on House Judiciary Committee Impeachment Inquiry procedures for taking depositions **II 1** 8-9, 12-13, 228-230
on House Judiciary Committee Impeachment Inquiry receiving two versions of Ehrlichman's handwritten notes **II 3** 1887
on judicial review of impeachment articles **II 1** 69
on legal questions involved in White House staff members obtaining IRS information **II 2** 1274-1275

on legal staff of House Judiciary Committee Impeachment Inquiry **II 1** 68-69
on Nixon tapes taken to Camp David **II 2** 1374
on Nixon's alleged approval of Fielding break-in **II 2** 1164-1165
on Nixon's noncompliance with House Judiciary Committee Impeachment Inquiry subpoenas **II 1** 429-430; **II 2** 913
on Nixon's noncompliance with House Judiciary Committee Impeachment Inquiry subpoenas and lack of evidence on milk fund **II 3** 1981
on procedures for House Judiciary Committee Impeachment Inquiry **II 1** 5-6, 7-8, 40-41
on redated memo from Whitaker to Nixon on his meeting with dairy leaders **II 2** 1084
statement of concurring views with Report of House Judiciary Committee Impeachment Inquiry **RHJC** 281
on testimony of witnesses **II 2** 896
on using subpoena powers of House Judiciary Committee **II 1** 189

Butler, M. Caldwell, questioning by
Bittman **TW 2** 86-87
Dean **TW 2** 328-329
Kalmbach **TW 3** 724

Butterbrodt, John
on Nixon's proclamation on dairy import quotas **SI6-1** 271, 272

Butterfield, Alexander Porter II 3 1626-1627; **SIAPP3** 51, 52, 68; **SI1** 95
disclosure of existence of White House taping system by **SUMM I** 103-104
and Hoover's letter to Nixon **II 2** 1114
and Hunt's termination from White House staff **SIAPP3** 265-266
information on White House staff organization submitted by **SUMM I** 25-26
Kehrli and **SIAPP3** 265
and knowledge of White House taping system **SI1** 163
memo to Magruder on Hoover's letter to Nixon re Clifford **SI7-1** 20, 359, 362-363
money from Strachan to **SI1** 11, 77, 96, 97, 98
organizational chart of White House staff by **RHJC** 18-19
reasons for revealing existence of White House taping system **II 2** 765-766
reveals existence of White House taping system **II 2** 1351, 1358-1359; **RHJC** 123
role in Nixon Administration **RHJC** 13
role on White House staff **II 1** 555-556
and Strachan **SI4-2** 889
takes custody of $350,000 from White House **SI1** 95-96, 97, 98
See also House Judiciary Committee Impeachment Inquiry, discussion on calling witnesses

Butterfield, Alexander Porter, cited testimony of
on Haldeman never acting without knowledge of Nixon **SUMM I** 26
on Nixon's decision-making method **RHJC** 20-21; **SUMM I** 28
on Nixon's interest in grounds of his properties **SI12** 171
on taping system in White House **SI9-1** 28, 379, 380-383

Buzhardt, J. Frederick *(Continued)*
information to Thompson on substance of Dean's calls and meetings with Nixon on Segretti matter **SI7-4** 1777, 1778
informed by Haig that dictabelt of Nixon's recollections of April 15, 1973 conversation with Dean could not be located **SI9-2** 550, 849, 850-860
informs Cox that Nixon will make public statement as response to his request for answer to Dean's testimony **SI9-1** 36, 419, 420-424
informs Richardson that he agreed to give Cox Fielding's ITT file **SI9-1** 15, 269, 275
informs Sirica that June 20, 1972 tape contains erasure **SI9-2** 552, 867, 868-874
informs Sirica two subpoenaed tapes had never been made **SI9-2** 547, 835, 836
instructs Richardson to refuse to give dairy industry campaign contributions documents to Cox **SI9-1** 40, 475, 476-480
Krogh-Young memo to Ehrlichman on meeting with **SI7-2** 553, 951, 961-862
letter from Cox complaining about lack of progress in obtaining access to papers in White House files **SI9-1** 24, 347, 348-350
letter from Cox requesting certain Nixon tapes **SI9-1** 29, 389, 390-392
letter from Cox requesting Nixon statement on Dean's testimony before Ervin Committee **SI9-1** 19, 317, 318-320
letter from Cox requesting specific White House records **SI9-1** 26, 371, 372-373; **SI9-2** 527, 597, 603-606
letter to Cox expressing regret for delays in responding to Cox's requests **SI9-1** 30, 399, 400-401
letter to Jaworski attaching subpoenaed logs **SI9-2** 554, 883, 884-885
listens to tape of Nixon-Dean telephone conversation and reports to Nixon on **SI9-1** 17, 289, 290-312
meeting with Richardson, Haig, Garment, and Wright on Cox's rejection of Stennis Plan **SI9-2** 540, 787, 788-796
meets with sub-committee of Foreign Intelligence Advisory Board on publication of Pentagon Papers **SI7-2** 635-637
on parties responsible for Pentagon Papers affair **SI7-3** 1216
and preparations for Nixon's review of subpoenaed tapes **SI9-2** 529, 619, 620-648
refuses to turn over April 15, 1973 tape of Nixon-Dean conversation to Cox **SI9-1** 12, 243, 244-255
role in investigation of Pentagon Papers affair **SI7-3** 1217
sends logs to Jaworski of meetings and telephone conversations with Nixon of six individuals requested by Cox **SI9-2** 554, 883, 884-890
tells Cox that tapes are under Nixon's personal control **SUMM I** 105
turns over Howard memo to Kehrli to Cox and informs him that only Nixon has authority to control documents held by White House employees **SI9-1** 42, 485, 486-487

turns over records of wiretaps on White House staff members to FBI **SI7-1** 287
and wiretapping records **SI7-1** 201
Buzhardt, J. Frederick, cited testimony of
on Cox's requests for Nixon tapes and Nixon's responses to **SI9-1** 12, 243, 250-255
on Haig informing him about missing dictabelt of Nixon's recollections of April 15, 1973 Nixon-Dean conversation **SI9-2** 550, 849, 850-852
on informing Sirica of erasure on June 20, 1972 EOB tape **SI9-2** 552, 867, 868
on listening to tape of Nixon-Dean telephone conversation and reporting to Nixon **SI9-1** 17, 289, 295-299
on Nixon tape of June 20, 1972 Haldeman-Nixon meeting **SI2** 2, 24, 236, 249-250
on preparations for Nixon's review of subpoenaed tapes **SI9-2** 529, 619, 624-629
on Young's investigation of leak on U.S. position on India-Pakistan War **SI7-3** 1193, 1421, 1425-1429
Byrd, Harry SIAPP4 50, 58
Byrd, Robert SIAPP3 48; **SI3-2** 837
Byrd, Robert, questioning by SI2 2, 335-336
Ford **SUMM I** 116-117
Freidheim **SI11** 323, 324, 326-327
Gray **SI2** 2, 423, 496; **SI4-1** 238
McConnell **SI11** 11-12
Richardson **SI4-3** 1652
Ryan **SI11** 325
Wheeler **SI11** 59
Byrne, William Matthew, Jr.
actions on material on Fielding break-in filed *in camera* by prosecutors of Ellsberg case **SI7-4** 1647, 1995, 1996-2013
discloses meetings with Ehrlichman to Ellsberg defense attorneys **SI7-4** 1649, 2019, 2020-2026
discussions with Ehrlichman on possible appointment as FBI director **SI7-4** 1636, 1879, 1880-1889
dismisses indictment in Ellsberg case **II 2** 1239-1240, 1241; **SI7-4** 1654, 2075, 2076-2083
Doar-Jenner interview with **II 2** 1219-1221, 1222-1223, 1241
Ehrlichman, Haldeman, and Kleindienst discussion as potential nominee for FBI director **SI7-4** 1635, 1867, 1868-1877
Ehrlichman's handwritten notes on **SIAPP3** 244-246
Ehrlichman's meeting with on FBI directorship **II 2** 1206-1209
and exposure of wiretapping of Ellsberg **SUMM I** 135-136
and FBI investigation to locate Kissinger tapes **II 2** 1158
and information on Fielding break-in **II 2** 1233-1234, 1236
informed of Fielding break-in **SUMM I** 138
Kleindienst-Nixon meeting on informing of Fielding break-in **SI9-2** 554, 883, 887-890
Kleindienst and Petersen agree to disclose Fielding break-in information to **SI7-4** 1645, 1975, 1976-1982
meetings with Ehrlichman **II 2** 1218-1225

Chapin, Dwight L. *(Continued)*
 indictment against **II 2** 1416; **SI4-3** 1103, 1443, 1449
 instructed by Haldeman to develop recommendation for political-intelligence plan **SUMM I** 29
 and Kalmbach's payments to Segretti **SI7-2** 580
 letter to Hardin on arrangements for March 23, 1970 meeting between Nixon and dairy leaders **NSI3** 16, 143, 149
 logs of meetings and telephone conversations with Nixon turned over to Jaworski **SI9-2** 554, 883, 884-890
 meeting with Segretti after termination of his activities **SI7-3** 1207, 1589, 1590-1594
 meeting with Segretti after Watergate break-in **II 2** 749; **SI3-1** 26, 327, 328-340
 memo to Dean on Segretti's activities **SI7-3** 1197, 1481, 1488-1492; **SI3-1** 26, 327, 328-335
 memo to Ehrlichman on White House involvement with Segretti **SI7-4** 1619, 1681, 1684-1691
 memo to Flanigan advising him that no appointment has been set up between Nixon and Geneen **NSI2** 5, 25, 44
 memo to Flanigan on proposed appointment with Nixon for Geneen **SI5-1** 5, 131, 138
 and Moore's preparation of report on Segretti matter **SI7-4** 1794-1810
 and newspaper stories on relationship with Segretti **SI7-4** 1617, 1657, 1658-1675
 Nixon-Dean discussion on possibility of felony charge against **SI3-2** 1039
 in Nixon-Dean discussion on Segretti's activities **SI7-4** 1782
 Nixon-Dean discussion of Watergate hearings and **SI8** 416-422; **SI3-2** 806, 861-863
 and Nixon's contacts with dairy industry leaders **II 2** 1062
 perjured testimony before Watergate Grand Jury on White House involvement with Segretti **II 2** 1225-1226
 reasons for leaving White House staff **SI7-4** 1621, 1709, 1710-1717
 report to Ehrlichman on White House involvement with Segretti **SI7-4** 1619, 1681, 1692-1696
 role in Nixon Administration **RHJC** 13; **SUMM I** 25N
 and schedule proposal for Nixon's meeting with dairy industry leaders **SI6-1** 324-325
 Segretti and **II 2** 1184; **SI4-1** 517; **SI7-3** 1190, 1377, 1378-1390, 1543
 Segretti and, Nixon refuses to comment on **SIAPP1** 9-10
 and Segretti matter **SI6-1** 307-308
 and Segretti matter, discussed by Nixon and Dean **SI3-2** 813, 814, 820
 and Segretti's Grand Jury testimony **SI7-3** 1598-1599
 and Sloan's payments to Liddy **II 2** 749
 Ziegler's announcement on his leaving Nixon Administration **II 2** 1200
 See also U.S. v. Dwight Chapin
Chapin, Dwight L., cited testimony of
 on contacts with Segretti **SI7-3** 1203, 1207, 1541, 1553-1555, 1589, 1593-1594
 on false testimony to Watergate Grand Jury on White House involvement with Segretti **SI7-4**

1638, 1897, 1898-1914
 on Haldeman's knowledge of Segretti's hiring **SI7-2** 526, 575, 586-587
 on meeting with Segretti after Watergate break-in **SI3-1** 26, 327, 339-340
 on memo to Ehrlichman on White House involvement with Segretti **SI7-4** 1619, 1681,1692-1696
 on reasons for leaving White House **SI7-4** 1621, 1709, 1715-1717

Chappaquiddick incident
 material in Hunt's safe on **SI2** 2, 43, 415; **SI7-3** 1559
 in Nixon-Dean discussion **SI3-2** 873-877; **SI7-4** 1782, 1789-1792; **SI8** 429-432
 Ulasewicz's investigation of **SI7-1** 18, 335, 350-352, 354

Chase, Samuel
 impeachment case against **II 3** 2201-2203

Chatham, Hugh SIAPP4 83; **SI1** 80

Chenow, Kathleen SI2 2, 474-475
 Dash review of FBI interview of **SI2** 2, 51, 483, 495
 delay of FBI interview of **SI7-3** 1205, 1569, 1570-1574
 and FBI Watergate investigation **SI2** 2, 51, 483, 484-500
 preparations for FBI interview of **II 1** 681-684, 689; **SI2** 2, 54, 517, 518
 telephone records of **SI2** 2, 51, 483, 497-499

Chicago, Illinois
 Nixon-Mitchell-Haldeman discussion as site for Republican National Convention of 1972 **SIAPP3** 15-16
 as proposed site for Republican National Convention **SI5-1** 474, 449, 450

Chicago Tribune
 on Senate Judiciary Committee recommendation of Senate confirmation of Kleindienst as Attorney General **SI5-2** 612

Child Nutrition Act
 impoundment of funds for **SI12** 17-18

Chile
 overthrow of Allende in **SI7-4** 1734

Chilean Embassy, Washington, D.C.
 burglary at **TW 2** 318; **SI2** 2, 674; **SI7-4** 1734

Chisholm, Shirley SIAPP4 46

Chomsky, Noam SI7-2 711

Chotiner, Murray M. SIAPP4 46, 59, 70-71, 108; **TW 3** 364-381
 advises presidential appointment for Governor Petersen of New Hampshire **SI1** 34
 Colson memo on AMPI contributions to unopposed Democratic Congressional candidates **II 2** 1055-1057
 and dairy industry campaign contributions **SI6-2** 678
 death of **SI6-2** 688

deposition of, on contacts with White House urging reversal of March 12 milk price-supports decision **SI6-1** 27, 401, 415-423

deposition of, denies quid pro quo between milk price-support increase and dairy industry campaign contributions **NSI3** 24, 167, 168-173; **SI6-2** 477, 728, 751-754

and Hillings' deposition on letter to Nixon **NSI3** 97-106

letter to Parr with list of political committees for AMPI contributions **SI6-2** 479, 783, 794-801

and list of McGovern campaign staff members **II 2** 1269

and list of McGovern supporters **TW 2** 331

meeting with Colson on March 23, 1971 **SI6-2** 474, 673, 677-689

meeting with Nelson and Kalmbach **SI6-2** 476, 727, 735-740

and meetings with Kalmbach and dairy leaders **SI6-2** 679, 684-685

memo from Colson on AMPI's contribution to unopposed Democratic Congressional candidates **SI6-1** 13, 213, 214

memo from Colson complaining about Harrison and Hillings **SI6-1** 16, 259, 260, 261

memo from Sanders on interview on Hillings letter with **NSI3** 8, 75, 107-110

in Political Matters Memoranda **SIAPP4** 17

and reaffirmation of AMPI $2 million pledge **SI6-2** 476, 727, 729-734

and repayment of Baroody from milk fund **TW 3** 236

resigns as Special Counsel to Nixon and retained by AMPI **II 2** 1067

Weitz affidavit accompanying interview of **SI6-2** 688-689, 749-750

See also Colson, Charles, testimony before House Judiciary Committee Impeachment Inquiry, on his involvement in dairy industry contributions

Chotiner, Murray M., interview with

on Colson's reaction to Hillings' letter **SI6-2** 678-679, 683

on meeting with Nelson and Kalmbach **SI6-2** 476, 727, 741-750

on milk fund **SI6-2** 474, 673, 677-687

Christie, Julie SIAPP4 121

Christophilos, Nicholas SI5-1 205

Church, Frank

Nixon-Haldeman discussion on **SIAPP3** 47-48

Church, Frank, questioning by

Laird **SI11** 166-168

CIA II 2 1118; **SI2** 2, 36, 38-39, 355-357, 361, 375-395; **SI7-3** 1192, 1399, 1400-1420

aid given to Hunt by **II 2** 1128-1131; **SI2** 2, 4, 79, 86, 457; **SI7-2** 547, 843, 844-861

aid to Plumbers unit from **SI7-2** 549, 887, 888-895

aid to Plumbers unit from, in Minority of House Judiciary Committee Impeachment Inquiry views on Articles of Impeachment **RHJC** 461-462

assistance to Hunt, in Doar's presentation of evidentiary material to House Judiciary Committee Impeachment Inquiry **II 1** 631

Colson-Bast discussion on **TW 3** 508-509

Colson discusses its role in Watergate with Nixon and Haig **TW 3** 360-362

coverage of Americans traveling or living abroad **SI7-1** 422, 424, 440-441

and coverup of Fielding break-in **II 2** 711-717

and creation of Plumbers unit **SI7-2** 654

Cushman asks Ehrlichman to restrain Hunt's demands for further assistance from **II 2** 1179

Cushman's identification of person requesting aid to Hunt from **SI7-4** 1622, 1719, 1720-1730

Dean-Petersen meeting on documents sent to Justice Department by **SI7-4** 1623, 1731, 1732

Dean's efforts to obtain bail money for Watergate defendants from **SI3-1** 8, 129, 130-142

Dean's efforts to retrieve materials sent to Justice Department by **SI7-4** 1624, 1733, 1734-1739

delivers psychological profile of Ellsberg to Krogh and Young **II 2** 1168-1169

Director of Security affidavit on psychological profile of Ellsberg **SI7-2** 557, 1007, 1008-1010

Director of Security memo on Cushman's call re Hunt's appointment as Security Consultant to White House **SI7-2** 558-559, 1029-1030, 1040-1041

documents sent to Justice Department on Watergate break-in **TW 3** 3-4, 5-46, 47-70

effort to link to Watergate break-in **SI2** 2, 34, 38-39, 337, 339, 341, 342, 375-395

Ehrlichman memo to Nixon on meeting with Helms on Presidential access to certain documents of **SIAPP3** 204-205

Ehrlichman requests assistance to Hunt from **SUMM I** 91; **SI7-2** 538, 727, 728-738

Ehrlichman states that Nixon authorized all of his dealings with **II 2** 1130, 1131

employee affidavit on aid to Hunt **SI2** 2, 47, 450, 460-466; **SI7-2** 547, 843, 854-859, 564, 1151, 1156-1161

employee affidavit on Hunt's requests for additional aid **SI7-3** 1182, 1225, 1232-1238

employee affidavit on notes summarizing Cushman-Ehrlichman telephone conversation on aid to Hunt **SI7-2** 538, 727, 729-731

employee affidavit on preparation of psychological profile of Ellsberg **SI7-2** 550, 897, 900-904

employee affidavit on taped telephone conversation between Ehrlichman and Cushman on aid to Hunt **SI2** 2, 47, 450, 468-470

and expanded psychological profile of Ellsberg **SI7-3** 1192, 1399, 1400-1420

FBI liaison with **SIAPP1** 22

and FBI Watergate investigation **SI2** 2, 36, 40, 355, 356-362, 397, 398, 399, 400, 401, 402

and FBI Watergate investigation, in Doar's presentation of evidentiary material to House Judiciary Committee Impeachment Inquiry **II 1** 680-695

Gray conversation with Helms on involvement in Watergate of **SI2** 2, 107-108, 109

Gray-MacGregor conversation on White House staff use of **SUMM I** 45

helps Plumbers unit obtain polygraph equipment **II 2** 1144

Hunt on background with **SI7-2** 679

CIA *(Continued)*

Hunt restrained from making further requests to SI7-3 1182, 1225, 1226-1238

Hunt's background in **II** **2** 1125-1126, 1127

and Hunt's interview with Beard **SI5-2** 783

Hunt's pension from **TW** **2** 23, 37, 87

and Hunt's preparations for Fielding break-in **SI7-2** 564, 1151, 1152-1177

and Hunt's survivor benefits **TW** **3** 253-254

instructed by Krogh and Young to do psychological study of Ellsberg **NSI4** 127

interagency coordination and, in Huston plan **SI7-1** 430-431

involvement in Watergate **SI2** 2, 36, 38-39, 95, 355-357, 361, 375-395, 457

Kissinger says Congressional leaders were informed about activities in Laos of **SI11** 62-63, 317-318

Krogh and Young memo to Ehrlichman on article in *New York Times* endangering life of agent of **NSI4** 19, 133, 134-136

letter from Hunt to Houston requesting change in annuity benefit option **SI2** 2, 18, 166, 185

material sent to Department of Justice by **SI2** 2, 67, 673, 674-680

McCord at **SI1** 217

McCord states it was not involved in Watergate break-in **SI4-1** 223, 224; **SIAPP2** 85

in McCord's letter to Caulfield **II** **2** 758-759

McCord's letter to Caulfield on danger of blaming for Watergate break-in **SI3-1** 40, 475, 476-482

meeting of staff psychiatrist with Young **II** **2** 1174

memo from Hunt to Colson requesting aid in changing annuity benefit option from **SI2** 2, 18, 166, 178-179

memo and routing slip on Hunt's requests for additional aid **SI7-3** 1182, 1225, 1228-1230

memos among employees on expanded psychological profile of Ellsberg **SI7-3** 1192, 1399, 1408-1411

and Mexican checks, in Article of Impeachment I **RHJC** 48-50, 53-54

Mitchell on lack of domestic intelligence role for **SI7-1** 466

Mitchell, Mardian, LaRue, and Dean discuss possibility of aid to Watergate defendants from **SI3-1** 7, 121, 122-127

Nixon denies efforts to implicate in Watergate matter **SI1** 39

Nixon explains concern over Watergate investigation uncovering covert operations of **SIAPP1** 24

Nixon-Haldeman discussion on Watergate and **SIAPP3** 41-43, 45, 75, 77-79

Nixon's concern over FBI Watergate investigation and exposure of covert operations of **NSI1** 16, 17, 125, 126-127, 129, 130-135

Nixon's misuse of, in Article of Impeachment II **RHJC** 177, 178

origin of theory of involvement in Watergate break-in **II** **3** 1736; **NSI1** 15, 121, 122-123

Plumbers unit and **SUMM I** 129, 130-133

and Plumbers unit investigation of Ellsberg **SI7-2** 553, 951, 963-966

Plumbers unit meetings with officials of on Pentagon Papers matter **II** **2** 1158

Plumbers unit use of, in Article of Impeachment II **RHJC** 162-163

preliminary psychological study of Ellsberg **SI7-2** 557, 1007, 1012-1019

preparation of psychological profile of Ellsberg **II** **2** 1145-1146

and psychological profile of Ellsberg **SI7-2** 550, 557, 897, 898-909, 912-913, 914, 1007, 1008-1028

refusal to pay bail money for Watergate burglars **SUMM I** 40

refuses to conduct physical surveillance of Donald Nixon **SUMM I** 127

relationship with FBI, in presidential statement on 1970 intelligence plan **SI7-1** 377

reports to Intelligence Evaluation Committee **SI7-1** 500

sends photographs of Fielding break-in to Justice Department **TW** **3** 71-72

on Soviet and bloc intelligence services and dissent in U.S., in Huston plan **SI7-1** 392

staff psychologist meets with Young, Hunt, and Liddy on Ellsberg psychological profile **SI7-2** 560, 1081, 1082-1093

statement of employee on deletion of Hunt's name from White House telephone list **SI2** 2, 28, 297, 298-299

and Watergate coverup **II** **2** 1195; **SUMM I** 39-40

and Watergate coverup, in Doar's presentation of evidentiary material to House Judiciary Committee Impeachment Inquiry **II** **2** 619-631

White House efforts to obtain money for Watergate defendants from **II** **2** 723-727

Young's meeting on leaks with officials of **NSI4** 12, 18, 103, 104-107, 129, 130-131

See also Helms, Richard M.; Walters, Vernon A.

Circumstantial evidence

in Articles of Impeachment against Nixon **SUMM I** 11-12

Citizens for Muskie

Segretti and falsified letter on stationery from **SI7-3** 1379

Citizens Groups SIAPP4 150

Civil rights

of Watergate burglars, Nixon-Dean-Haldeman discussion on **SI8** 315-316, 320-321

Clark, Chris SIAPP1 79

Clark, Matthew E., Jr. SIAPP2 323

See also U.S. v. *George Steinbrenner III, and the American Shipbuilding Company*

Clark, Roger A. SI7-2 594

Classified information

House Judiciary Committee Impeachment Inquiry handling of **SI1** 7

Clawson, Ken SIAPP4 26, 133; **SI2** 2, 150

at meeting to discuss Hunt's White House status **SI2** 2, 17-18, 165-166

taped telephone conversation with Ehrlichman on Hunt's safe **SI2** 2, 20, 203, 212-213

telephone conversation with Ehrlichman on Dean's allegations **SI4-3** 1095, 1317, 1320-1324

in *Washington Post* story on Segretti's activities **SI7-4** 1658

Clayton Act SI5-1 4, 101, 106-119
  and ITT-Canteen merger SI5-1 70-75, 76, 86
  See also ITT, antitrust suits against
Cleaver, Eldridge SI7-2 1132
  in Huston plan SI7-1 398
Clements, William SI11 274, 282, 323
  Freidheim blames for false documentary submission to Congress on Cambodian bombings SI11 75, 372-373
  statement agreeing with Abrams that recommendation for bombing of Cambodia did not include intent to deceive Congress SI11 66, 331
  statement claiming Members of Congress were briefed on MENU operations SI11 61-62, 315-316
  statement claiming Richardson knew about MENU operations but did not review Defense Department report submitted to Senate Armed Services Committee SI11 65, 328
  statement denying those who submitted Defense Department data on Cambodian bombings to Senate Armed Services Committee intended to deceive SI11 66-67, 333-335
  statement on date of his awareness of falsification of Defense Department report on Cambodian bombings SI11 66-67, 333-335
  submits White Paper on Cambodian bombing SI11 54-55, 283-285
Clifford, Clark RHJC 149-150
  in Butterfield's memo to Magruder on Hoover's letter to Nixon on TW 1 57-62
  on enemies list SI8 119
  in Hoover letter to Nixon on wiretapped information SI7-1 20, 359, 360-361, 362-363
  memo from Magruder to Haldeman and Ehrlichman on forthcoming article on Administration Vietnam policy by SI7-1 20, 359, 365
  planned response to forthcoming article on Administration Vietnam policy SI7-1 20, 359, 366-368
  political use of wiretapped information on II 2 1113-1114; SUMM I 125
Cline, Garner J. SUMM I 1
Coast Guard
  expenditures in connection with Key Biscayne since 1969 SI12 156-157
  expenditures in connection with San Clemente since 1969 SI12 100
Cohen, Daniel L. SUMM I 1
  on rules of House on presence of media II 1 473
Cohen, Edwin S.
  memo to Flanigan on sections of proposed Tax Reform Act of 1969 eliminating charitable deductions for gifts of private papers SI10 10, 243-252
Cohen, William S. SUMM I 1
  additional views on Article of Impeachment III RHJC 515-517
  on calling witnesses before House Judiciary Committee Impeachment Inquiry II 3 1644, 1697
  on Ehrlichman's note of approval of Fielding break-in II 2 1172
  on enforcement of subpoenas II 1 113-114

on FBI report to Justice Department on wiretapping of Ellsberg II 2 1134-1135
on first amendment and Kraft wiretapping II 3 1978
on Haldeman listening to Nixon tapes II 2 1357
on House Judiciary Committee Impeachment Inquiry issuing subpoenas to Nixon II 3 1557
on House Judiciary Committee Impeachment Inquiry procedures for taking depositions II 1 232-234
on House Judiciary Committee Impeachment Inquiry recommendations on grounds for impeachment II 1 72-73
on House Judiciary Committee Impeachment Inquiry staying in session during quorum calls II 2 707
House Judiciary Committee Impeachment Inquiry vote on amendment on letter to Nixon on his noncompliance with House Judiciary Committee Impeachment Inquiry subpoenas II 1 454-458
on House Judiciary Committee Impeachment Inquiry's requests for materials from White House II 1 262
on issuing subpoenas to Nixon II 1 317-318, 647, 660
on Kleindienst recommendation of Byrne for Attorney General post II 2 1223
on leaks from House Judiciary Committee Impeachment Inquiry II 1 168-169
on legal basis for domestic surveillance II 2 1093-1094
on Mollenhoff affidavit on IRS investigation of Gerald Wallace II 2 1251-1252
on Nixon-Petersen relationship II 3 2027
on Nixon's conversations with Hardin on school lunch program II 2 1063
on Nixon's noncompliance with House Judiciary Committee Impeachment Inquiry subpoenas II 1 418-419, 440-443, 444, 453-454; II 2 926-927, 950-951
on Nixon's right to excise material from tapes II 1 263, 278
on opening evidentiary presentations of House Judiciary Committee Impeachment Inquiry II 2 965-966
on presentation procedures for House Judiciary Committee Impeachment Inquiry II 1 263
on procedures for House Judiciary Committee Impeachment Inquiry II 1 384-385, 392, 396-397, 400
on references to Bittman in Doar's presentation of summary of evidence to House Judiciary Committee Impeachment Inquiry II 3 1966
on release of House Judiciary Committee Impeachment Inquiry evidentiary material to public II 3 1592, 1602-1603
on right of judicial review in Impeachment Inquiry II 1 12-13
on rules of evidentiary procedures for House Judiciary Committee Impeachment Inquiry II 1 515-516
on Semer's fundraising for Muskie campaign II 2 1052
on setting completion date for House Judiciary Committee Impeachment Inquiry II 1 16

Cohen, William S. *(Continued)*
statement of concurring views with Report of House Judiciary Committee Impeachment Inquiry **RHJC** 281
on subpoena powers of House Judiciary Committee **II 1** 34-35
on suit by Center on Corporate Responsibility **II 2** 1299
on transcripts of Nixon tapes used by St. Clair in his presentation of evidence in behalf of Nixon **II 3** 1746

Cohen, William S., questioning by
Bittman **TW 2** 88-90, 93-94
Butterfield **TW 1** 103-104
Colson **TW 3** 471-474, 505-506
Dean **TW 2** 331-333, 338-340
Kalmbach **TW 3** 705-707, 725-727
LaRue **TW 1** 260-262
Mitchell **TW 2** 193-196
O'Brien **TW 1** 158-160, 162-163
Petersen **TW 3** 152-155

Colby, William E. SI7-4 1735, 1736
and CIA employee affidavit on taped telephone conversation between Ehrlichman and Cushman on aid to Hunt **SI2** 2, 468
identifies Ehrlichman as person arranging for Hunt to get assistance from CIA **II 2** 712-713
meeting with Ehrlichman, Helms, and Dean **SI2** 2, 64, 651, 652-658

Colby, William E., cited testimony of
on CIA dealings with Hunt **SI2** 2, 64, 651, 653-656

Cole, Kenneth R., Jr. SIAPP4 29, 50, 54, 69, 86
in Political Matters Memoranda **SIAPP4** 1-2
role in Nixon re-election campaign **SI1** 83
and Sloan's payments to Liddy **II 2** 722

College students
black extremists, in Huston plan **SI7-1** 399
communist intelligence services and, in Huston plan **SI7-1** 402-403
"New Left" groups and, in Huston plan **SI7-1** 389-396
Trotskyist groups and, in Huston plan **SI7-1** 408

Colleges and universities
Huston memo to Haldeman on intelligence activities in **SI7-1** 440-441
Nixon's approval of Huston plan for intelligence activities in **SI7-1** 455
restrictions on intelligence activities in, in Huston plan **SI7-1** 422-424

Colson, Charles II 2 1123-1147; **II 3** 1626-1627; **SIAPP2** 7-28; **SIAPP3** 77; **SIAPP4** 50; **SI2** 2, 157; **SI5-1** 132; **SI7-2** 918-920
activities discussed by Nixon, Ehrlichman, and Haldeman **SI4-2** 795-796
advice on Watergate discussed by Nixon, Ehrlichman, and Haldeman **SI4-2** 665-674
affidavit on meeting with Bittman **TW 3** 305-312
affidavit on meetings with Nixon after publication of Pentagon Papers **SI7-2** 529, 619, 624-632
affidavit on reasons for establishing Plumbers unit **NSI4** 4, 43, 47-55
and AMPI relationship with Wagner & Baroody **SI6-1** 18, 273, 283-290, 295-296

and antitrust suits against ITT **SI5-1** 164, 185
and approval of Shumway replacement **SIAPP4** 65
assigns Hunt to collect information on Ellsberg and origins of Vietnam war **SI7-2** 717, 720
assigns Hunt to interview DeMotte **SI7-2** 853
assigns Hunt to Pentagon Papers investigation for White House **NSI4** 6, 71, 72-74
calendar for March 15, 1972 **SI5-2** 777, 778, 779
calendar for March 18, 1972 **SI5-2** 506, 795, 796
campaign assignments **SI1** 35
and campaign mailings **SIAPP4** 93
Chotiner and **SI6-1** 416, 417
Chotiner on meetings with **SI6-2** 677-678
cited meetings between Nixon and **SI5-2** 508-509, 803-804, 839
complains to CBS about Schorr's news coverage **SI7-2** 1114
contribution pledged by dairy industry leaders to **NSI3** 55, 57
and dairy industry campaign contributions **II 2** 1048, 1061-1062
in Dean memo on "Dealing with Our Political Enemies" **SI8** 99
in Dean memo to Ehrlichman on *Nader* V. *Butz* **SI6-2** 890
Dean on discussion about Hunt with **TW 2** 308-309, 349-350
Dean plays his recorded conversation with Hunt for Mitchell **TW 2** 134-135
and Dean's testimony to Watergate Grand Jury **SUMM I** 93
and decision that Hunt should interview Beard **SI5-2** 505, 777, 780-781, 784-786
denies knowledge of Watergate break-in to Dean **SI2** 2, 144-145
deposition of, on Diem cable **SI7-2** 558-559, 1029-1030, 1052-1056
deposition of, on learning about Watergate break-in **SI2** 2, 8, 117, 119-120
and Diem cables **SI2** 2, 162
and discrediting of Ellsberg **II 2** 1124-1125
discusses telephone conversation with Magruder on Liddy plan with Haldeman **II 2** 838-839
discussion with Nixon on Executive clemency for Hunt **SUMM I** 64-65; **SI3-2** 892-893
discussions with Bittman **TW 2** 6-7, 13-14, 20-22, 23-25, 90
disputes with Magruder **SIAPP4** 92; **SI1** 89
document freeing from Executive privilege during testimony **TW 3** 445-449, 524
in document from Plumbers unit file **SI7-2** 834
Ehrlichman tells Nixon he had no prior knowledge of Watergate **NSI1** 29, 195, 196-198
Ehrlichman testifies that he hired Hunt **SI7-2** 723
encounter with Hunt after Fielding break-in **II 2** 1182
and enemies list **SUMM I** 141-142; **SI8** 70
excused from Watergate Grand Jury testimony **SI2** 2, 564, 569
and Executive clemency offers to Hunt **SUMM I** 63-65
FBI investigation of **SI2** 2, 33, 329, 330-331, 332-333
and FBI investigation of Schorr **SI7-2** 1115-1116

and Fielding break-in report **SI7-3** 1186, 1301, 1302-1332

and financial arrangements for Fielding break-in **SI7-3** 1184, 1247, 1248-1274

and Geneen **SI5-1** 145

in Gerrity memo to Ryan **SI5-2** 671, 707

guilty plea of **II 2** 1147, 1175, 1434; **SI9-2** 580, 1053, 1054-1058; **SI7-2** 551, 911, 921-923

guilty plea of, in St. Clair's presentation of evidence in behalf of Nixon **II 3** 1896

Hall's notes on conversation with Hunt for **TW 3** 275, 276, 278-285

and Hillings' letter to Nixon on dairy import quotas **NSI3** 8, 75, 76-110

and hiring of Hunt as Plumbers unit member **II 2** 1125-1128

House Judiciary Committee Impeachment Inquiry discussion on subpoenaing **II 2** 981-992

House Judiciary Committee Impeachment Inquiry subpoena to Nixon on May 30, 1974 for specified materials related to conversations between Nixon and **SI9-2** 577, 1031, 1032-1036

Hunt and **SI3-2** 904, 912, 916

Hunt on activities of **SI5-2** 780-782

Hunt believes he is abandoned by **SI3-2** 1030-1031

and Hunt's demands for money **SUMM I** 52

and Hunt's meeting with Shapiro **II 2** 792; **TW 2** 52-53, 89

and Hunt's proposal for creation of file on Ellsberg **SI7-2** 551, 911, 912-923

and Hunt's termination from White House staff **SIAPP3** 265-266

and immunity for Dean **SI4-3** 1350-1352, 1355, 1357

indictment of **II 2** 1425, 1426-1427; **SI9-2** 563, 564, 959, 960-961, 963, 964

informed of AMPI $2 million pledge for Nixon's 1972 campaign **SI6-1** 9, 153, 154-160

informs Ehrlichman on probable testimony by Hunt and McCord before Watergate Grand Jury **II 2** 865

informs Nixon that Hunt was not White House employee at time of Watergate break-in **SUMM I** 37

instructed by Nixon to publicize something on Pentagon Papers project **SI7-2** 563, 1125, 1126-1149

and investigations of Brookings Institution **SI8** 80

and ITT matter **II 2** 1002, 1036, 1037, 1038-1040

joins Mardian and Jaworski in motion for trial subpoena directing Nixon to produce specified tapes and documents **SI9-2** 570, 987, 988-990

and Kalmbach's handling of milk producers' contributions **SI6-1** 19, 299, 300-315

Lambert and **SI7-2** 558-559, 1029-1030, 1070-1075

letter from Casey on antitrust suits against ITT **SI5-1** 7, 143, 169-176; **SI5-2** 513-514, 663-665, 699-701, 863-864, 886-893, 944-946

letter from Hunt **SI3-1** 38-39, 455-456, 457-474

in letter from Merriam to Ehrlichman **SI5-1** 257

letter to Thompson and Dash explaining enemies list **SI8** 7, 65, 76-77

letters from Harrison on political results of March 12 milk price-supports decision **SI6-1** 27, 401,

407-408, 409-413

and Liddy plan **SI4-1** 378-379

and Lofton **SI1** 87

and Magruder's information to U.S. Attorneys **SI4-2** 848, 885

Magruder's telephone call on Watergate to **SI4-1** 255-256

McCord testimony on prior knowledge of Watergate of **SI4-1** 22, 431, 432-443

meeting with AMPI representatives and Kalmbach **SI6-1** 14, 217, 218-233

meeting with Bittman **II 2** 757

meeting with Dean and Ehrlichman on Hunt's letter to Colson **II 2** 757

at meeting to discuss Hunt's White House status **SI2** 2, 17-18, 165-166

meeting with Ehrlichman on March 23, 1971 **SI6-2** 474, 673, 675-676

meeting with Haldeman and MacGregor on Kleindienst confirmation hearings and ITT case **SI5-2** 508-509, 803-804, 805

meeting with Liddy and Hunt on Liddy plan **SUMM I** 31

meetings and conversations between Nixon and **SI5-2** 500, 506, 735, 741, 795, 798

meetings with Geneen **SI5-1** 258

meetings with Nixon from June 14 through July 20, 1971 **SI7-2** 529, 619, 638-642

meets with Shapiro on Hunt's demands **SUMM I** 54

memo about contacts with Hunt **SI2** 2, 160

memo for file on Hunt **SI1** 12, 101, 104-109

memo for file on Magruder's telephone conversation on Watergate **SI4-1** 9, 262-264

memo for file on telephone conversation with Haldeman on Executive clemency offer to Hunt **SI4-1** 8, 9, 249, 257-259, 262-264; **TW 3** 337-339

memo from Ehrlichman on Hunt/Liddy game plan **SI7-3** 1181, 1213, 1220, 1222-1223

memo from Ehrlichman with Hunt memo on Boudin **SI7-2** 563, 1125, 1128-1136

memo from Gleason assigning him responsibilities re milk producers **SI6-1** 7, 8, 119, 120-125, 127, 128-129

memo from Haldeman assigning him as coordinator for Special Campaign Project **SI6-1** 12, 197, 198

memo from Haldeman on milk producers' contributions **SI6-1** 19, 299, 302; **SI6-2** 498

memo from Hall on Hunt's status at White House **SI2** 2, 18, 166, 172

memo from Hunt on Diem coup **SI7-2** 558-559, 1029-1030, 1059-1062

memo from Hunt on "Neutralization of Ellsberg" **SI7-2** 551, 911, 914

memo from Hunt requesting aid in obtaining survivorship benefits from CIA **SI2** 2, 18, 166, 178-179

memo from Krogh and Young on Hunt's memo on "Neutralization of Ellsberg" **SI7-2** 551, 911, 917

and memo on Middle Ameria **SI1** 36

memo from Parker on Hardin's proposal for meeting between Nixon and dairy industry leaders **SI6-1** 21, 319, 320, 321

Colson, Charles *(Continued)*

memo to Chotiner on AMPI's contribution to unopposed Democratic Congressional candidates **SI6-1** 13, 213, 214; **II 2** 1055-1057

memo to Chotiner complaining about Harrison and Hillings **SI6-1** 16, 259, 260, 261

memo to Dean on group wanting information on limitations of campaign contributions **SI6-1** 11, 191, 192-194

memo to Dean on Hunt's status at White House **SI2** 2, 18, 166, 170-172

memo to Dean on ITT matter **NSI2** 16, 189, 194-197

memo to Dean on post-Watergate letter from Hunt **TW 3** 274

memo to Dean on prioritization of names on enemies list **SI8** 10, 103, 104-109

memo to Dean requesting IRS audit of Gibbons **SI8** 22, 213, 214-216

memo to Ehrlichman on briefing of Howard K. Smith on Pentagon Papers case **SI7-2** 529, 619, 633-634

memo to Ehrlichman on Brookings Institution study on Vietnam War **SI7-2** 539, 739, 740-745

memo to Ehrlichman on Buchanan and Hunt recommendations for Pentagon Papers investigation **SI7-2** 536, 703, 706

memo to Ehrlichman on Casey letter **SI5-1** 7, 143, 177

memo to Ehrlichman on FBI investigation of Ellsberg's connection to leak at Rand Corporation **NSI4** 10, 97, 98

memo to Ehrlichman on funding of Senate investigation on Pentagon Papers matter **SI7-2** 526, 829, 841

memo to Ehrlichman on Ichord hearings **SI7-2** 526, 829, 835-836

memo to Ehrlichman on *ITT-Grinnell* litigation **SI5-1** 9, 189, 193-211

memo to Ehrlichman on "rekindling Pentagon Papers issue" **SI7-2** 558-559, 1029-1030, 1066-1069

memo to Ehrlichman recommending affidavit action on cheese imports **SI6-1** 382

memo to Ehrlichman recommending study of leaks appearing in *New York Times* **NSI4** 15, 119, 120

memo to Gleason with article on AMPI contribution to unopposed Democratic Congressional candidates **SI6-1** 13, 213, 215-216

memo to Haldeman on continuation of support or withdrawal of Kleindienst nomination **SI5-2** 508-509, 803-804, 805-809

memo to Haldeman on ITT matter **TW 3** 483-487; **SI5-2** 834-836

memo to Haldeman on political impact of publication of Pentagon Papers and advantages of prosecuting Ellsberg **SI7-2** 532, 663, 664-673

memo to Haldeman on recommendations of investigator of Pentagon Papers publication **SI7-2** 533, 675, 678

memo to Haldeman on Special Project for advertisements sponsored by "front" organizations **SI6-1** 12, 197, 203-206

memo to Haldeman with Bickel's argument before Supreme Court **NSI4** 7, 75, 76

memo to Haldeman with taped telephone conversation with Hunt on Pentagon Papers matter **SI7-2** 535, 697, 699-702

memo to Higby on milk producers' contributions **SI6-1** 20, 317, 318; **SI6-2** 468, 495, 523, 529

memo to Krogh with Hunt memo on "anti-Diem coup post mortem" **SI7-2** 558-559, 1029-1030, 1057-1058

memo to Nixon on AMPI's $2 million pledge to re-election campaign **II 2** 1049-1050; **SI6-1** 9, 10, 153, 161, 181-183

memo to Price on points Nixon wanted included in Presidential statement on Pentagon Papers matter **NSI4** 8, 81, 82-84

memo to Strachan assigning him to responsibility for milk producers' contribution **SI6-2** 465, 493, 494-499

memos to file on dealings with Bittman **SI3-1** 38-39, 455-456, 465-474

memos to Haldeman on locating outside person to handle fundraising from certain groups **SI6-1** 19, 299, 301, 303

memos to Haldeman on milk producers' contributions **SI6-2** 497, 499

Merriam and **SI5-2** 814

and monitoring of Democrats **SIAPP4** 9

Nixon asks Haldeman to ask him if Hunt was offered clemency **SI4-1** 8, 249, 251-252

Nixon asks Petersen if there is evidence against **SUMM I** 69

Nixon-Dean discussion on Hunt and **NSI1** 219-220

in Nixon-Dean discussion on Watergate hearings **SI3-2** 806-808, 864, 865, 1066-1070, 1075-1076

in Nixon-Dean-Haldeman discussion on Watergate **SI8** 361-364

in Nixon-Ehrlichman discussion **SI4-2** 913, 917-918

in Nixon-Haldeman discussion on Dean's working through IRS **SI8** 289

in Nixon-Haldeman discussion on Watergate **SIAPP3** 45; **SI4-3** 1310

in Nixon memo on Watergate **SUMM I** 7

Nixon-Petersen discussion of **SI4-3** 1408

Nixon re-election campaign responsibilities of **SUMM I** 27

Nixon on role in political intelligence-gathering **NSI1** 120

Nixon on testimony of **SIAPP1** 74

Nixon wants him to read *Six Crises* **SIAPP3** 61

Nixon's involvement with perjured testimony of **SUMM I** 85, 89

and Nixon's possible lack of knowledge of Watergate coverup, in Minority of House Judiciary Committee Impeachment Inquiry views on Articles of Impeachment **RHJC** 392-394

notes on FBI interview with **SI2** 2, 33, 329, 334

and O'Brien's meeting with Hunt **TW 1** 154-155

and opening of Hunt's safe **SI2** 2, 19, 189, 200-201

"Opponent Priority Activity" memo to Dean **SI8** 10, 103, 105-109

on organizational chart from files of Special Investigations Unit **SI7-2** 814

and Pentagon Papers matter **II 2** 1121

personal relationship with Hunt **TW 2** 23-24, 27-28

in Petersen's report to Nixon on Watergate Grand Jury testimony **SI4-3** 1299, 1300-1301, 1303

plan for fire and theft at Brookings Institution **SI7-2** 539, 739, 740-753

plays tape of conversation with Hunt for Dean **TW 2** 232-233

in Political Matters Memoranda **SIAPP4** 1, 3

questioning by Doar **TW 3** 184-224, 230-231, 233-241

questioning by Jenner **TW 3** 241-397

reaction to Hillings' letter **SI6-2** 678-679, 683

as recipient of political enemies project memos **SI8** 21, 211, 212

recommendation on handling of Dean **SUMM I** 97-98

recommends Hunt for Plumbers unit **SI7-2** 533, 675, 676-679, 797

relationship with Harrison **SI6-2** 742, 743

removed from milk fund assignment **SI6-2** 896

and replacement for Shumway **SI1** 48-49

report on anti-trust investigation of AMPI **SIAPP4** 16

report to Ehrlichman on White House policy on Watergate investigation **SI4-3** 1308

reports to Haldeman on his conversation with Bittman **II 2** 757-758

Republican platform for 1972 and **SIAPP4** 2

responsibilities with Plumbers unit **II 2** 1141-1142; **SI7-2** 546, 829, 830-841

role in Nixon Administration **RHJC** 14; **SUMM I** 25

role in Nixon re-election campaign **II 2** 1054-1056

role on White House staff **II 1** 557

in Ryan memo to Merriam **SI5-1** 186

and Special Project on use of "front" organization for advertisements supporting Administration policies **SI6-1** 12, 197, 198-211

statement on relationship with Hunt after Watergate arrests **SI3-1** 34-35, 38-39, 405-406, 413-417, 455-456, 465-470

statement to Court before sentencing **SIAPP2** 19-28

tape recorded conversation with Hunt on need for more funds for Watergate defendants **SI3-1** 34-35, 405-406, 407-423

taped conversation with Hunt, in Doar's presentation of summary of evidence to House Judiciary Committee Impeachment Inquiry **II 3** 1963

taped telephone conversation with Conein and Hunt **SI7-2** 558-559, 1029-1030, 1035-1039

taped telephone conversation with Hunt on money for Watergate defendants **II 2** 752-759

taped telephone conversation with Hunt on Pentagon Papers matter **SI7-2** 535, 697, 698-702

telephone call from Ehrlichman on Hunt's connection with Watergate break-in **SUMM I** 36

telephone call from Haldeman on commitments to Hunt **II 2** 836-838

telephone call to Magruder for approval of Liddy plan **SI2** 2, 107; **SI3-2** 1001-1002

telephone call to Magruder on Hunt and Liddy plans **SI1** 12, 101, 102-103, 105, 110-111, 112, 113-114

telephone conversation with Casey on ITT material **SI5-2** 919

telephone conversation with Ehrlichman on his forthcoming Watergate Grand Jury testimony **SI4-3** 1103, 1443, 1447-1448

telephone conversation with Nixon on Watergate break-in **SI2** 2, 15, 155, 156-160

telephone conversations with Mitchell and meeting with Nixon on March 18, 1972 **SI5-2** 506, 795, 796-798

telephone conversations with Mitchell on March 19, 1972 **SI5-2** 506, 795, 797

tells Magruder to get approval for Liddy plan **SI4-1** 356

told by Dean that Hunt had been ordered out of country **SI2** 2, 158

and use of AMPI contribution for Fielding break-in **SI6-2** 481, 821-840

and *Wall Street Journal* article on milk money **SI6-2** 848

Watergate coverup and, in Article of Impeachment I **RHJC** 96

White House record of contacts with Nixon on March 23, 1971 **SI6-2** 472, 621, 625

and White House task force on Kleindienst hearings **SI5-2** 503, 759, 760

See also House Judiciary Committee Impeachment Inquiry, discussion on calling witnesses; Plumbers unit; *U.S.* v. *Colson*; *U.S.* v. *John Ehrlichman, et al*; *U.S.* v. *John N. Mitchell, et al.*

Colson, Charles, cited testimony of

on arranging for meeting between Hunt and Shapiro **SI3-2** 925-926

on Buchanan's belief that he was not the man for Pentagon Papers project **SI7-2** 536, 703, 704-705

on Ehrlichman's decision to hire Hunt as White House consultant **SI7-2** 537, 713, 721-722

on Ehrlichman's instructions on setting up of Plumbers unit **SI7-2** 544, 815, 824-825

on events after Fielding break-in **SI7-3** 1186, 1301, 1331-1332

on FBI interview **SI2** 2, 33, 329, 330-331

on formation of support groups **SI6-1** 12, 197, 211

on Haldeman's telephone call asking about offers of clemency to Hunt **SI4-1** 8, 249, 254-255

on Hunt's interview with Beard **SI5-2** 505, 777, 784-786

on Hunt's safe and Liddy telling Hunt to leave country **SI4-3** 1328-1329

on Hunt's status at White House **SI2** 2, 19, 189, 200-201

on investigation of Schorr **SUMM I** 127

on ITT matter **SUMM I** 146, 148

on meeting regarding Hunt's status at White House after Watergate arrests **SI2** 2, 18, 166, 174-177

on memo from Ehrlichman on Hunt-Liddy Special Operation Number 1 **SI7-3** 1181, 1213, 1222-1223

on memo from Hunt on "Neutralization of Ellsberg" **SI7-2** 551, 911, 915-916

on need to determine authenticity of Beard memo **NSI2** 16, 189, 190

on his guilty plea **TW 3** 364

on his involvement in dairy industry contributions **TW 3** 364-381

on his involvment in foreign affairs **TW 3** 410-412

on his legal relationship with St. Clair **TW 3** 185-186

on his professional background **TW 3** 184-185

on his reasons for consulting with Dean on letter from Hunt **TW 3** 477-478, 495

on his relationship with Hunt **TW 3** 416-417

on his relationship with Nixon **TW 3** 185

on his suspicions of Dean's Watergate involvement **TW 3** 417-418, 449

on his Watergate Grand Jury testimony **TW 3** 526

on Hughes-Rebozo matter **TW 3** 507-508

on Hunt's interview with Beard **TW 3** 250-253

on information disseminated on Boudin **TW 3** 456, 481-482, 488-490, 493-494, 495-496, 517-518

on information given to Watergate Prosecutors **TW 3** 469

on information he released on Ellsberg **TW 3** 500-502

on informing Nixon of Shapiro's recommendations for strategy on Wategate **TW 3** 333-335

on ITT matter **TW 3** 381-398, 400-402, 465-466, 482-488, 506-507

on keeping things from Nixon **TW 3** 505

on learning about Fielding break-in **TW 3** 503-504

on letter from Hunt after death of his wife **TW 3** 296, 297-300

list of points for Hall to make to Hunt **TW 3** 278

on meeting with Hunt and Liddy on approval for intelligence plan **TW 3** 504-505

on meeting with Hunt and Liddy on their efforts to get approval for their plans **TW 3** 244-249

on meeting with Hunt on importance of meeting with Bittman **TW 3** 300-302

on meeting with Nixon on information-gathering on Democratic party candidates **TW 3** 254-255

on meeting with Nixon on June 20, 1972 **TW 3** 267-270

on meeting with Shapiro and Ehrlichman on recommendations for Watergate strategy **TW 3** 342-344

on meetings with Bittman **TW 3** 302-315

memo for file on meeting with Hunt and Liddy **TW 3** 246-248

on memo from Hunt on "Neutralization of Ellsberg" **TW 3** 208, 209

on milk fund **TW 3** 403-409, 460, 471, 479, 496-497

on Mitchell's press release after Watergate break-in **TW 3** 506

on Nixon asking him to write down his recommendations on Watergate strategy **TW 3** 341

on Nixon's attitude toward Ellsberg case **TW 3** 475-476

on Nixon's mention of Bittman's demand for one million dollars **TW 3** 334, 335

on Nixon's other responsibilities during Watergate problem **TW 3** 409-412

on Nixon's reaction to his suggestion that Mitchell take responsibility for Watergate **TW 3** 498

on Nixon's withdrawal of Kleindienst nomination **TW 3** 525

on not attending Dorothy Hunt's funeral **TW 3** 459-460

on obtaining money for Fielding break-in **TW 3** 234-236

opening statement before Senate Select Committee on Presidential Campaign Activities **TW 3** 423-439, 439-441, 483-487, 524

on organization of Plumbers unit to investigate Pentagon Papers matter **TW 3** 196-207

on Pentagon Papers matter as national security issue **TW 3** 415-416

on Plumbers unit projects related to discrediting of Ellsberg **TW 3** 209-229

on political strategy meetings on Democratic party candidates **TW 3** 255-256

questioning by House Judiciary Committee Impeachment Inquiry members **TW 3** 449-527

questioning by St. Clair **TW 3** 399-419, 439-442, 444-446

on reasons for discussing Watergate with Shapiro **TW 3** 474-475

on reasons for not giving Nixon all the information he had **TW 3** 498-500

on reasons for pleading guilty **TW 3** 458-459, 477, 481-482, 490, 493-494, 515

on receiving memo from staff member raising legal and moral objections to his strategy on Ellsberg **TW 3** 476, 522

on recommendations given to Ehrlichman for Nixon on handling of Watergate matter **TW 3** 441-442, 444-445

on relations with rest of White House staff **TW 3** 466-468

on relationship betwen White House and CRP **TW 3** 470, 494-495, 500

on releasing derogatory information on Boudin to press **TW 3** 212-213

on reporting to Dean and Ehrlichman on his meeting with Bittman **TW 3** 313-314

on reporting to Nixon on Beard interview **TW 3** 252

on second meeting with Bittman **TW 3** 314-315

on senior staff meeting after Watergate break-in **TW 3** 260

on senior staff meetings at White House **TW 3** 494-495

on subjects discussed with Nixon **TW 3** 452

on suspicions that CRP was involved in Watergate **TW 3** 315

on taped telephone conversation with Ehrlichman on Dean **TW 3** 344-353

on taped telephone conversation with Hunt **TW 3** 291-296

on telephone call from Nixon on Hunt's status at White House **TW 3** 263-264

on telephone conversation with Haldeman on his dealings with Hunt **TW 3** 336-340

on telling Dean about Dorothy Hunt's telephone call **TW 3** 454-455

on telling Ziegler Ehrlichman and Haldeman should resign **TW 3** 354-355

on Vietnam Veterans for a Just Peace **TW 3** 456-457

Colson, Charles, testimony before House Judiciary
Committee Impeachment Inquiry *(Continued)*
  on White House staff keeping information from
    Nixon TW 3 478-479, 491-492
Comegys, Walker B. NSI2 85; SI5-1 405; SI5-2 553,
  596
  and letter from Walsh to Kleindienst SI5-1 284,
    286
  and request for extension of time to appeal *ITT-
    Grinnell* case SI5-2 753-754
COMINT
  in Huston plan SI7-1 415
Commander in Chief in the Pacific (CINCPAC) SI11
  84
Committee to Re-Elect the President (CRP) SIAPP4
  121-123
  American Airlines Corp. acknowledgment of ille-
    gal contributions to SI9-1 22, 333, 324-325
  Baldwin delivers logs and summaries of tapped
    telephones at DNC to SI1 24, 223, 225
  Bittman on his belief that it was not source of
    money for Hunt TW 2 13
  budget SIAPP4 57, 105, 151
  budget committee SIAPP4 88
  budget staff SI1 85
  Butterfield on Haldeman's relationship with TW 1
    52-53, 111
  Butterfield on Nixon running TW 1 111
  campaign briefing planned for SI1 88
  Colson on relationship between White House and
    TW 3 470, 494-495, 500
  and Corrupt Practices Act SI1 173
  court suits after Watergate SI8 329-330
  Dean informs Haldeman of fundraising for Water-
    gate defendants by SI3-1 14, 199, 200-202
  Haldeman's relationship with SUMM I 26-28;
    SI1 90
  and Hunt SI1 105
  illegal practices of, in Minority of House Judiciary
    Committee Impeachment Inquiry views on Arti-
    cles of Impeachment RHJC 468-470
  and infiltration of Muskie, Humphrey, and
    McGovern campaign staffs SI7-3 1190, 1377,
    1378-1390
  LaRue on his transfer to TW 1 178-180
  Liddy becomes General Counsel to SI1 7, 31, 34;
    SI7-3 1194, 1441, 1442-1448; SI8 20, 205, 206-
    209
  Liddy informs Dean Watergate break-in was oper-
    ation of SUMM I 37
  Liddy informs LaRue and Mardian that Hunt be-
    lieves it should provide bail money for Water-
    gate defendants SI3-1 3, 87, 88-95
  Liddy plan designed to be untraceable to SUMM
    I 31-32
  Liddy's assignment to II 1 557-558; SUMM I 30
  Liddy's transfer from White House to, in memo
    from Strachan to Haldeman SI1 8, 45, 46-51
  linked to Segretti's activities SI7-4 1678-1680
  Magruder asks Porter to lie to FBI on reasons for
    payments to Liddy by SI3-1 10, 157, 158-164
  Magruder reports it has "sophisticated political-
    intelligence gathering systems" SUMM I 31
  Magruder's perjury before Watergate Grand Jury
    on purpose of payments to Liddy from SI3-1

24, 297, 298-309
  memo from Strachan to Haldeman on budget of
    SI1 32
  memo from Strachan to Haldeman on political in-
    telligence-gathering system at SI1 14, 147, 148-
    154
  Mitchell on becoming consultant to TW 2 124-
    125
  Mitchell denies any connection between Watergate
    arrests and SUMM I 35
  Mitchell on Nixon's role in decision-making on
    TW 2 191, 202
  Mitchell on resignation as director of TW 2 135-
    136, 137-138, 173-175, 203
  Mitchell tells Nixon he regrets not controlling
    people at SI2 2, 30, 305, 306-310
  Mitchell's resignation as director of, in Article of
    Impeachment I RHJC 50-54
  Nixon-Dean discussions on Haldeman's knowl-
    edge about and legality of political intelligence-
    gathering operations of NSI1 11, 77, 78-80
  Nixon denies Watergate involvement of any per-
    sonnel of SI2 2, 63, 648, 650
  Nixon and false statements under oath made by
    officials of SUMM I 78-85
  Nixon-Haldeman discussion of transfer of cash
    from White House to SI4-3 1217-1221
  Nixon's knowledge of activities of SUMM I 27-28
  O'Brien's reasons for leaving TW 1 167
  officials interviewed by Watergate Prosecutors or
    called before Watergate Grand Jury II 2 886
  organizational link to White House staff II 1 558-
    559
  organizational structure and decision-making
    methods of RHJC 21-24
  and Political Matters Memoranda on political in-
    telligence-gathering by NSI1 12, 81, 82-84
  press policy SIAPP4 7, 13
  relationship of White House staff to SUMM I 26-
    28
  retains O'Brien TW 1 124-125
  salaries at SI1 50
  salaries and expense accounts at SIAPP4 44-45
  Sedan Chair II activity and NSI1 10, 67, 68-75
  Select Committee hearings and SIAPP1 10
  staff of SI1 95
  transfer of campaign contributions from White
    House for payments to Watergate defendants
    SI3-1 33-34, 425-426, 427-454
  transmission of FBI reports to SI1 58
  use of political-intelligence plan including elec-
    tronic surveillance by SUMM I 29-32
  and Watergate break-in discussed by Dean and
    Nixon SI3-2 701, 803, 804-880
  youth vote and SIAPP4 41
  See also Political Matters Memoranda, on CRP
    activities
Commodity Credit Corporation
  notice from Department of Agriculture Livestock
    and Dairy Division on 1971-72 milk price sup-
    port program NSI3 211-217
Common Cause SIAPP4 118; SI8 119
  and Halperin's name on enemies list SI8 74, 108
  in Political Matters Memoranda SIAPP4 9

suit against CRP, O'Brien on **TW 1** 158, 162-163

Communist Party, U.S.
assessment of current internal security threat of, in Huston plan **SI7-1** 408
Soviet intelligence and, in Huston plan **SI7-1** 403

Community Mental Health Centers Act
termination of **SI12** 21

Compass Systems, Inc. SIAPP4 2, 118

Comprehensive Alcohol Abuse Act of 1970
impoundment of funds for sections of **SI12** 22

Conein, Lucien SI7-2 955
Diem cables and **SI7-2** 1042-1045, 1047
Hunt obtains telephone number and address of **SI7-2** 1041
taped telephone conversation with Hunt and Colson **SI7-2** 558-559, 1029-1030, 1035-1039

Congress SI12 9-11
actions dealing with impoundment of funds during Nixon Administration **SI12** 34-40
bills on dairy price supports **II 2** 1063-1065, 1069-1070; **SI6-1** 175-178, 334-336
and Constitutional arguments for impoundment of funds as grounds for Presidential impeachment **SI12** 43-54
and lobbying efforts of dairy industry for increased milk price supports **NSI3** 10, 117, 118-121
Nixon's statement on impoundment of funds to **SI12** 29
pending legislation to increase milk price supports discussed in March 23, 1971 meeting between Nixon and Administration officials **NSI3** 19, 155, 157, 159
Plumbers unit's efforts to encourage hearings on Pentagon Papers matter by **SI7-2** 546, 829, 830-841; **SI7-3** 1214
in Political Matters Memoranda **SIAPP4** 20
public statements on knowledge of secret bombings of Cambodia **SI11** 73-74, 360-368
public statements on reasons for false documentary submission on bombings of Cambodia to **SI11** 75, 369-374
role in federal funding processes **SI12** 3-4
statements following Schlesinger's letter of July 16, 1973 acknowledging pre-incursion bombing of Cambodia **SI11** 51-68, 271-336
statements on bombing of Cambodia made from 1969 to 1973 in **SI11** 10-27
See also Court cases on Presidential impoundment of funds

Congressional Budget and Impoundment Control Act of 1974 SI12 2, 40

Congressional elections
in Political Matters Memoranda **SIAPP4** 24-25
special White House project funded by AMPI contribution on **SI6-1** 8, 127, 130-152
talking paper from Strachan to Mitchell on **SIAPP4** 38-39

Congressional Record
on confirmation of Kleindienst as Attorney General **SI5-2** 901, 902-903
letter from Jaworski to Percy on failure of White House to produce evidence needed for Mitchell trial and other Watergate Grand Jury investigations **SI9-2** 589, 983, 984-985

resolution establishing Senate Select Committee on Presidential Campaign Activities **SI3-1** 46, 521, 522-525
response of Defense Department to House Resolution requesting information on pre-May 1970 bombings of Laos and Cambodia **SI11** 57, 63, 295-297, 319-321
on Senate confirmation of Richardson as Attorney General **SI9-1** 8, 151, 156
on Senate consideration of Richardson's nomination for Attorney General **SI9-1** 8, 151, 154-155
text of Report of Nixon Task Force on Productivity and Competition **NSI2** 26-30

Congressional Rural Caucus v. *Ash* **SI12** 19

Connally, John B. SIAPP2 350-360; **SIAPP3** 77; **SIAPP4** 38; **SUMM I** 149-150
advises Nixon at March 23, 1971 meeting to raise milk price supports **NSI3** 18-22, 153-161
alleged meeting with Lilly **II 2** 1067
at meeting on milk price supports of March 23, 1971 **SI6-2** 473, 627, 628-671
at meeting with President on economy **SI6-1** 384-385, 386-387
and Dairy industry campaign contributions and milk price-support issue **II 2** 1067, 1068
in Dean memo to Ehrlichman on *Nader* v. *Butz* **SI6-2** 890
directed by Nixon to attack foundations and other tax-exempt organizations **SI8** 87
fundraising and **SIAPP4** 135
Haldeman on discussions of dairy industry campaign contributions with **SI6-2** 465, 493, 510-511
letter from Merriam on antitrust suits against ITT **SI5-2** 508-509, 513, 803-804, 863, 881-882
letter from Merriam on delay of *ITT-Grinnell* appeal **SI5-1** 22, 270, 280, 377, 386-387
letter from Merriam on ITT antitrust cases **SI5-2** 658-659, 694-695
log for March 19, 1971 **SI6-2** 467, 519, 520
log for March 23, 1971 **NSI3** 15, 139, 140; **SI6-2** 470, 474, 555, 561, 673, 698
logs showing meetings with AMPI representatives **SI6-1** 453-456
meeting with AMPI officials **SI6-2** 709-710
meeting with Nixon on March 23, 1971 **SI6-2** 474, 673, 674
meetings with Jacobsen on milk price supports **SI6-1** 27-28, 401-402, 424-426, 427-435; **SI6-2** 467, 519, 520
Mehren on meeting with **SI6-2** 934, 936
memo from Ehrlichman on antitrust policy review **SI5-1** 23, 393, 401
memo to from Merriam on *ITT-Grinnell* **SI5-2** 942-943
Nixon on **SI4-3** 1308
Nixon-Ehrlichman discusssion on **SI5-1** 335
in Nixon-Mitchell discussion on antitrust policy **SI5-1** 372
in Nixon-Mitchell-Haldeman discussion on Presidential election of 1972 **SIAPP3** 27-28, 32
and Nixon's efforts to prevent Patman Committee hearings **SUMM I** 49-51
Page Airway meeting with dairy representatives **SI6-1** 28, 402, 438-440, 441-447

Connally, John B. *(Continued)*
Patman and, in Nixon-Dean-Haldeman discussion **SI8** 315, 317
recommendations to Nixon on milk price-support issue **II 2** 1070
role in Nixon re-election campaign **SIAPP4** 138
telephone conversation with Jacobsen **SI6-2** 474, 673, 698
telephone conversations with Nixon on milk price-support issue **NSI3** 15, 139, 140-142; **SI6-2** 467, 470, 519, 521, 555, 556-563
White House record of contacts with Nixon **SI6-2** 470, 474, 555, 560, 673, 674
See also Milk price-support issue; *U.S.* v. *Jake Jacobsen*; *U.S.* v. *John Connally, and Jake Jacobsen*

Connally, Mrs. John B. SIAPP4 77

Connell, Gerald SI5-1 166-167
and settlement of ITT antitrust cases **NSI2** 82-93

Connerton, Carl SIAPP1 80

Conrad,
memo from Downing on Mitchell's signatures on documents authorizing wiretaps on government officials and newsmen **SI7-1** 4, 157, 168

Conservative movement SIAPP4 108, 25, 46-47
in Political Matters Memoranda **SIAPP4** 3, 7, 19
See also New York Conservative Party; Political Matters Memoranda, on McWhorter's activities

Consolidated Farm and Rural Development Act
mandatory spending language in **SI12** 37

Conspiracy law
and Nixon's involvement in Watergate coverup **MMFL** 47-52

Constitution
and alleged immunity of Presidents from criminal prosecution **RHJC** 304
and arguments for impoundment of funds as grounds for Presidential impeachment **SI12** 43-54
Article II of, Fish on Articles of Impeachment and **RHJC** 355-358
as basis for Nixon's Executive privilege statement of March 12, 1973 **SIAPP1** 6-7
Doar on Presidential subversion of **SUMM I** 4-5
executive power in **SUMM I** 9
grant of "executive power" to President and impoundment of funds **SI12** 76-80
on impeachment **RHJC** 349-350; **TW 1** 2-3
on impeachment, in Minority of House Judiciary Committee Impeachment Inquiry views on Articles of Impeachment **RHJC** 362-372
and improvements to Nixon's Key Biscayne and San Clemente properties **SUMM I** 152
and item veto power **SI12** 51
Jenner on awesomeness of impeachment proceedings and **SUMM I** 15-16, 18
Jenner on Nixon's actions and **SUMM I** 17-18
Jenner on task of House Judiciary Committee Impeachment Inquiry and **II 3** 1938-1940
in Jenner's presentation of summary of evidence to House Judiciary Committee Impeachment Inquiry on Nixon's abuse of powers and **II 3** 1977-1979
Nixon on grounds for impeachment in **SIAPP1** 70

and Nixon's refusal to comply with subpoenas for Presidential tapes **SIAPP1** 31; **SUMM I** 167-169
and Nixon's refusal to testify before Select Committee or allow access to Presidential papers **SIAPP1** 26-27, 45
and Nixon's refusal to turn over Presidential tapes to Select Committee **SIAPP1** 51
Nixon's statement during news conference on his Constitutional right to impound funds **SI12** 33
and power of House of Representatives in impeachment inquiry **SUMM I** 164-165
and Presidential impoundment of funds **SI12** 89-92
Presidential oath and **SUMM I** 15-16, 18, 23
Report by Staff of Impeachment Inquiry on grounds for impeachment in **II 3** 2159-2185
"take care" clause on duty of President, in Doar's presentation **II 3** 1931-1932
"take care clause" on duty of President related to impoundment of funds **SI12** 68-69

Constitutional Convention of 1787
Proceedings of **II 3** 2187-2198

Contract authority, failure to allot
Nixon Administration eliminates from "impoundment" reports **SI12** 5
use by Nixon Administration **SI12** 2-3

"Conversation with the President on Foreign Policy" (television interview) **SI11** 253-255

Conway, Michael M. II 2 732, 1088
biography of **II 3** 2148
on Ruckelshaus' letter to Mitchell on authorization of domestic surveillance**II 2** 1098

Conyers, John, Jr. SUMM I 1
additional views on Nixon's tax evasion as impeachable offense **RHJC** 343-347
additional views on Report of House Judiciary Committee Impeachment Inquiry on proposed Article of Impeachment on secret bombing of Cambodia **RHJC** 289-296
on calling witnesses before House Judiciary Committee Impeachment Inquiry **II 3** 1622, 1633, 1634, 1635, 1638, 1652, 1658, 1661, 1662-1663, 1708
on confidentiality of evidentiary material presented to House Judiciary Committee Impeachment Inquiry **II 1** 545-546, 586
on criteria for excising material from Nixon tapes **II 2** 829
dissenting views supporting proposed Article of Impeachment on secret bombing of Cambodia **RHJC** 323-328
on distinction between deferral and impoundment of funds **II 2** 1308-1309
on elimination of investigation of tax fraud from House Judiciary Committee Impeachment Inquiry **II 1** 364-365
on enemies list **SI8** 74, 108
on exclusion of media from House Judiciary Committee Impeachment Inquiry **II 1** 131-132
on House Judiciary Committee Impeachment Inquiry subpoenas for additional witnesses **II 2** 982
on House Judiciary Committee Impeachment Inquiry's state of confrontation with Nixon **II 1**

Nixon refuses to turn White House tapes over to
SI9-1 34, 43, 407, 408-412, 489, 490-494
Nixon's complaints about activities of SI9-1 33,
403, 404-406
on Nixon's interest in antitrust suits against ITT
SI5-2 957
Nixon's refusal to provide certain documents to in
Article of Impeachment I RHJC 121-132
Nixon's relationship with, in Minority of House
Judiciary Committee Impeachment Inquiry
views on Articles of Impeachment RHJC 414-
424
Nixon's statement on reasons for firing of SI9-2
546, 831, 832-834
Nixon's statement on rejection of Stennis Plan by
SIAPP1 53-54
Nixon's statement to Richardson on getting rid of
II 2 1384-1385
and Nixon's waiver of Executive privilege SI9-1 8,
151, 152-159
in note from Haig to Woods on confusion over
June 20, 1972 subpoenaed tape SI9-2 529, 619,
637
and plea bargaining by Dean II 2 1399
press release on American Airlines Corp. voluntarily acknowledging illegal contributions to
CRP SI9-1 22, 333, 324-325
private conversation with Kleindienst II 2 1030-
1031
receives Stennis Plan from Richardson SI9-2 537,
765, 766-772
receives Strachan's Political Matters Memoranda
file SI9-2 526, 591, 592-595
rejection of Stennis Plan by SI9-2 538, 541, 773,
774-781, 797, 798-800
requests and receives access to ITT file compiled
by Fielding SI9-1 15, 269, 170-176
requests April 15, 1973 tape of Nixon-Dean conversation and is refused SI9-1 12, 243, 244-255
requests records relating to Pentagon Papers matter and Fielding break-in SI9-1 46, 503, 504-516
requests for White House materials prior to learning about Nixon tapes II 2 1346-1351, 1360-
1364, 1366-1367
Richardson ordered by Nixon to direct him to
make no further attempts to obtain subpoenaed
White House materials SI9-2 541, 797, 798
and Richardson's dealings with Haig and Nixon
on his alleged investigation of Nixon's expenditures on his San Clemente property SI9-1 21,
329, 330-332
and Stennis Plan II 2 1385-1387
subpoenaed logs of meetings and telephone conversations of six individuals with Nixon turned
over to Jaworski SI9-2 554, 883, 884-890
See also Fielding break-in, papers from criminal
cases; Illegal campaign activities and contributions; Nixon Administration, attempts to improperly influence; Watergate break-in, papers
from criminal cases related to Watergate Special
Prosecution Task Force
Cox, Archibald, cited testimony of
on Buzhardt's denial of requests for inventory of
White House staff and Plumbers unit files SI9-1
13, 257, 261

on designation by Richardson as Special Watergate Prosecutor SI9-1 7, 145, 149
on efforts to obtain files on Pentagon Papers matter and Fielding break-in SI9-1 46, 503, 511
on efforts to obtain milk producers' campaign
contributions file from Richardson SI9-1 40,
475, 476
on receiving Strachan's Political Matters Memoranda file from Buzhardt SI9-2 526, 591, 592-
593
on removal of White House documents SI9-2 527,
597, 599
on request for access to Fielding's ITT file SI9-1
15, 269, 276
on sending Richardson comments on his proposal
on subpoenaed tapes SI9-2 538, 773, 776
Cox, Edward and Tricia
in questions for Nixon from Joint Committee on
Internal Revenue Taxation on Nixon's income
tax returns SI10 420-421
Cramer, Joan SI7-3 1384
Cramer, Mary Ann SI7-3 1384
Crime
Nixon-Ehrlichman discussion on SI5-1 322-315
Cross-Florida Barge Canal
impoundment of funds for Environmental Impact
Statement on SI12 27
Crossen, Joan SIAPP4 26
Crowe, Kenneth C. SI8 171-172
Cuban-Americans
in discussion by Plumbers unit of Fielding break-
in SI7-2 554, 967, 968-980
reasons for using for Watergate break-in SUMM
I 31-32
Cuban Freedom Committee
Mullen & Company and TW 3 11-12
Cuban government
Boudin and SI7-2 1133
and political asylum for black extremists SI7-1
400
Venceremos Brigade and SI7-1 390
Cuban intelligence
Venceremos Brigade and, in Huston plan SI7-1
390, 403
Cudlip, Chick SI1 88
Cummings, Attorney General
opinion on impoundment of funds SI12 85
Curran, Frank SI5-1 437, 444
Cushenan, Ian SIAPP2 323
See also U.S. v. George Steinbrenner III, and the
American Shipbuilding Company
Cushman, Robert E., Jr.
asks Ehrlichman to restrain Hunt's requests for
CIA assistance II 2 1179
and CIA aid to Hunt II 1 631; II 2 713-714,
1142-1143; TW 3 55; SI2 2, 460-466, 654; SI7-2
547, 843, 844-861
Ehrlichman asks for future aid for Hunt from
CIA SI7-2 538, 727, 728-738; II 2 1128-1131
Ehrlichman denies requesting aid for Hunt from
SI2 2, 457
employee affidavit on taped telephone conversa-
tion between Ehrlichman and SI2 2, 47, 450,
468-470

of March 24, 1971 **SI6-2** 475, 703, 704-726

materials requested by Jaworski and refused by
Nixon related to investigation of **SI9-2** 1050-
1051

and meetings between dairy industry leaders and
government officials prior to increase in levels
of milk price supports **II 2** 1075-1078

memo from Colson to Higby on **SI6-1** 20, 317,
318

Nelson denies discussing with government officials
in connection with milk price-support discussions **NSI3** 51

Nelson and Parr on amounts pledged **NSI3** 5, 53,
54-57

and Nixon's contacts with industry leaders **II 2**
1052-1053

and plans to cancel contributions for tables at
Republican dinner after milk price-supports
decision **II 2** 1068-1069

in Political Matters Memoranda **SIAPP4** 87

reaffirmation of AMPI $2 million pledge to Nixon
campaign **SI6-2** 476-477, 727-728, 729-766

and repayment of Baroody from **TW 3** 236

in St. Clair's presentation of evidence in behalf of
Nixon **II 3** 1744-1814, 1892-1893

Strachan assigned responsibility for **SI6-2** 465,
493, 494-499

in Strachan memo to Haldeman **SI1** 79, 82, 84-85

in talking paper from Strachan to Mitchell
SIAPP4 45

testimony of Colson before House Judiciary Committee Impeachment Inquiry on **TW 3** 364-381

White House refuses cooperation in investigation
of **SI9-2** 560, 935, 936-945

See also AMPI; Dairy import quotas; Kalmbach,
Herbert Warren, testimony before House Judiciary Committee Impeachment Inquiry, on milk
fund; Milk price-support issue; *Nader* v. *Butz*

Dairy industry leaders NSI3 4, 35, 36-52

approval of plan for meeting between Nixon and
SI6-1 21, 319, 320-327

arrangements for March 23, 1970 meeting with
Nixon **NSI3** 16, 143, 144-149

Burress memo to Whitaker on attitude toward
modifications of Tariff Committee recommendations on dairy import quotas **NSI3** 9, 111, 115

Chotiner denies discussing milk price supports in
connection with campaign contributions with
NSI3 24, 167, 168-173

increased lobbying after Hardin's March 12, 1971
announcement that milk price-support level
would not be raised **NSI3** 12, 127, 128-120

list of participants in meeting with Nixon **SI6-2**
548-550

lobbying efforts for increased milk price supports
NSI3 10, 117, 118-121; **SI6-1** 22-23, 329-330,
330-357; **II 2** 1063-1065, 1069-1070

meeting at Louisville airport **II 2** 1076-1077

meeting with Nixon on March 23, 1970 **NSI3** 17,
151, 152

Nixon's invitation to meet with **NSI3** 3, 29, 30-34

See also Nelson, Harold S.; Parr, David L.

Dale, E. Lee II 2 1088

biography of **II 3** 2148

Dale, Francis SIPPA4 13, 122

Daley, Richard J. SIAPP3 15-16; **SIAPP4** 149

Danbury (prison)

Nixon-Haldeman discussion on Liddy's imprison-
ment at **SIAPP3** 35

Dane, Maxwell

on enemies list **SI8** 73, 107, 119

Daniels, Jack SIAPP4 88; **SI1** 85

Danielson, George E. SUMM I 1

on abolishing office of Special Watergate Prosecutor **II 2** 1416-1417

additional views on Nixon's tax evasion as impeachable offense **RHJC** 343-347

additional views on proposed Article of Impeachment on secret bombing of Cambodia **RHJC**
301-302

additional views on Report of House Judiciary
Committee Impeachment Inquiry **RHJC** 303-
306

on alleged immunity of Presidents from criminal
prosecution **RHJC** 304

on calling witnesses before House Judiciary Committee Impeachment Inquiry **II 3** 1623

concurrence with McClory's additional views on
Article of Impeachment III **RHJC** 349-354

on confidentiality of evidentiary material presented to House Judiciary Committee Impeachment
Inquiry **II 1** 579

on delays in White House turning over materials
II 1 265

on discrepancies between transcripts of Nixon
tapes **II 2** 814

on Doar-St. Clair correspondence **II 1** 178-179

on Ehrlichman's second meeting with Byrne **II 2**
1225

on House Judiciary Committee Impeachment Inquiry issuing subpoena to Clerk of House of Representatives for records of dairy industry
campaign contributions **II 3** 1572

on House Judiciary Committee Impeachment Inquiry issuing subpoenas to Nixon **II 1** 643-644;
II 3 1559

on House Judiciary Committee Impeachment Inquiry staying in session during quorum calls **II
2** 707-708

on leaked Dixon memos **II 2** 1327

on legal aspects of impoundment of funds **II 2**
1312-1313, 1320-1321

on listening to Nixon tapes **II 2** 1344

on materials held by Sirica **II 1** 167

on Nixon's discussion on Executive privilege with
Richardson **II 2** 1336

on Nixon's income tax **II 3** 1524-1525

on Nixon's noncompliance with House Judiciary
Committee Impeachment Inquiry subpoenas **II
1** 426-428; **II 2** 907, 926

on Nixon's request for extension of time on answering House Judiciary Committee Impeachment Inquiry subpoena **II 1** 347

on possible Segretti-type activities to discredit
House Judiciary Committee Impeachment Inquiry **II 1** 71-72

Danielson, George E. *(Continued)*
on procedural rules for handling Impeachment Inquiry materials **II 1** 126
on procedures for House Judiciary Committee Impeachment Inquiry **II 1** 381-382, 389, 398, 399
on release of House Judiciary Committee Impeachment Inquiry evidentiary material to public **II 3** 1602
requests availability of applicable statutes for discussion of White House staff members obtaining IRS information **II 2** 1274
on rules of evidentiary procedures for House Judiciary Committee Impeachment Inquiry **II 1** 474, 490-491, 499
on St. Clair's participation in House Judiciary Committee Impeachment Inquiry **II 1** 231-232
statement of additional views on Report of House Judiciary Committee Impeachment Inquiry **RHJC** 283-286
on subpoena powers of House Judiciary Committee **II 1** 37, 67, 68
on television coverage of House Judiciary Committee Impeachment Inquiry **II 1** 102-103, 104
on using subpoena powers of House Judiciary Committee **II 1** 188-189
on White House logs in House Judiciary Committee Impeachment Inquiry's possession **II 2** 839-840

Danielson, George E., questioning by
Bittman **TW 2** 90-92, 110
Butterfield **TW 1** 104-106
Colson **TW 3** 479-481
Dean **TW 2** 329-331
Kalmbach **TW 3** 724-725
LaRue **TW 1** 258-260
O'Brien **TW 1** 160-161
Petersen **TW 3** 150-152, 179

Dash, Samuel
letter from Colson explaining enemies list **SI8** 7, 65, 76-77
review of Chenow's FBI interview **SI2** 2, 51, 483, 495

Dash, Samuel, questioning by
Buchanan **SI9-2** 600-602
Dean **NSI1** 43; **SI2** 2, 429-432, 558; **SI4-1** 276; **SI8** 66-71, 96-98, 114-116, 200-202, 214
Ehrlichman **NSI4** 44-46, 138; **SI3-1** 190-191, 288-289, 308-309, 420, 545-547; **SI2** 2, 150-151, 242, 323-325, 436; **SI3-2** 1269, 1280-1281; **SI7-1** 381; **SI7-2** 723, 733, 748-749, 781-782, 828, 890, 948-949, 1020-1021; **SI7-3** 1214, 1245, 1579-1580; **SI7-4** 1673-1674, 1827-1828, 1857-1858
Haldeman **SI3-1** 200-201; **SI1** 153-154, 195; **SI2** 2, 127, 133, 240-241, 350, 360-361; **SI5-2** 834-836; **SI7-1** 379-380, 434, 446, 478-479; **SI7-2** 813; **SI7-3** 1538-1539
Harmony **SI1** 243
Hunt **SI3-1** 218-219, 411-412; **SI1** 110-111, 246, 256; **SI2** 2, 76-77, 162-163, 485-486; **SI7-2** 698, 717, 853, 912-913, 912-913, 954-955, 1042-1047, 1092-1093, 1126; **SI7-3** 1221, 1571-1572
Kalmbach **SI3-1** 153-155, 166-169, 178-180, 208-209, 229, 259-261, 268-270, 282-283, 378-381; **SI1** 99-100; **SI6-1** 61; **SI7-1** 343

LaRue **SI3-1** 88-91, 98, 176-177, 257-258, 386-387, 436-438, 500, 518-519; **SI1** 112, 118-121; **SI2** 2, 107-108, 278-280; **SI7-3** 1514-1517, 1524
Leeper **SI2** 2, 72, 73-74, 82-85
Magruder **NSI1** 70, 205; **SI3-1** 108-109, 158-159, 246-247, 298-300, 342-344, 513; **SI1** 56-57, 64-65, 113-114, 116-117, 174-175, 180-181, 234-236; **SI2** 2, 106, 126, 186-188, 2, 186-188; **SI4-1** 340-343; **SI4-2** 564, 799, 800-809
McCord **SI3-1** 492-493, 496; **SI1** 216, 230-231, 257; **SI2** 2, 75
Mitchell **NSI1** 8, 57, 58, 183-184; **SI3-1** 101-103, 126-127, 204-206, 304-305, 345, 421; **SI1** 67-68, 122-125, 184-186; **SI2** 2, 291-293; **SI3-2** 1236-1237; **SI4-1** 389-391; **SI7-1** 174-175, 464-465, 475-476; **SI7-3** 1526-1528
Petersen **NSI1** 213; **SI2** 2, 102-103, 122-123, 568-569, 582; **SI4-1** 548; **SI4-2** 989-992, 1014-1015; **SI4-3** 1619-1620; **SI7-3** 1601-1602; **SI7-4** 1934, 1976-1977
Segretti **SI3-1** 395, 397; **SI7-2** 576; **SI7-3** 1389-1390, 1543, 1598-1600
Shoffler **SI1** 262
Sloan **SI3-1** 110, 116-118, 256, 559; **SI1** 93-94, 172-173, 178
Strachan **NSI1** 10, 67, 68-69, 82-83; **SI3-1** 439; **SI1** 37-38, 97-98, 149-152, 164-166, 192-194; **SI2** 2, 132, 262-265, 271-273; **SI7-3** 1387-1388, 1486-1487
Walters **SI3-1** 132-136; **SI2** 2, 378-379, 410-412, 526-527

Daughters of the American Revolution
extension of patent on design of badge of **II 3** 1714-1716

David, Dr. Ed SIAPP4 5, 12

Davidoff, Sidney
on enemies list **SI8** 74, 108

Davidson, John B.
biography of **II 3** 2148

Davis, Angela II 1 298; **II 2** 1001

Davis, Evan A. II 1 552; **II 2** 839-840; **SUMM I** 1
biography of **II 3** 2146
on Nixon-Petersen discussion on immunity for White House aides **II 3** 2026-2027
on Nixon-Petersen relationship **II 3** 2030-2031
and presentation of summary of evidentiary material to House Judiciary Committee Impeachment Inquiry **II 1** 573-577, 587-638; **II 3** 1941-1945
See also House Judiciary Committee Impeachment Inquiry, executive sessions

Davis, Jefferson
and impeachment inquiry on Johnson **SUMM I** 164-165

Davis, Polk (law firm) SI5-2 753-754

Davis, Rennie SI5-1 324

Davis, Robert Thurston TW 3 60

Davis, Sammy, Jr.
tax information on **SI8** 157

De Motte, Clifton SI5-2 780

"Dealing with Our Political Enemies" memo SI8 9, 95, 99-100

Dean, John W., III **II 2** 1259-1263, 1268-1295; **II 3** 1626-1627, 1721-1722; **NSI1** 6, 49, 51; **SIAPP2** 53-60; **TPC** 147-186; **SI3-2** 713, 1135, 1145

advised by Moore to tell Nixon everything he knows **II 2** 797-798

advises Nixon to ask Petersen whether Executive clemency offers to Hunt were lawful **SUMM I** 68

allegations concerning Haldeman's, Ehrlichman's, Mitchell's, Nixon's and his own involvement in Watergate coverup **SI9-1** 18, 313, 316

alleged Watergate investigation of **II 1** 698-701; **II 2** 778-786

and approval of Liddy plan **SI1** 199

asked by Haldeman to return from Camp David to meet with Mitchell and Magruder **II 2** 840

asks Liddy to advise Hunt to leave the country **SI2** 2, 20, 203, 204

asks Walters for audits of McGovern campaign staff members and contributors **SI8** 25, 237, 238-271

asks Walters to request return of materials sent to Justice Department **II 2** 1200

assigned by Ehrlichman to work on Watergate **SUMM I** 37

assigned by Nixon to investigate Watergate break-in **NSI1** 17, 187, 188-191

assigned to "political enemies" project **SUMM I** 30

assigns Kalmbach to raise funds for Watergate defendants **SI3-1** 9, 143, 144-155

attorneys meet with Watergate prosecutors **SI4-1** 27, 483, 484-485

believes he is criminally liable on hush money **SUMM I** 86

Bittman denies contact with **TW 2** 51-52, 67-68, 92

Bittman tells him he is aware of pre-Watergate electronic surveillance activities **SUMM I** 63

briefing paper for Nixon on Kleindienst staying on as Attorney General **SI3-1** 51, 583, 584-595

Butterfield on contacts between Nixon and **TW 1** 86

Buzhardt informs Cox that Nixon will make public statement in answer to charges of **SI9-1** 36, 419, 420-424

and cancellation of Brookings Institution plan **II 2** 1132

"cancer on the Presidency" statement **SI3-2** 995

Caulfield gives him letter from McCord **II 2** 758-759

and Caulfield's offers of Executive clemency to McCord **SI3-1** 42, 487, 488-498

in Chapin's memo to Ehrlichman on White House involvement with Segretti **SI7-4** 1690, 1691

Colson discusses his role in Watergate with Nixon **TW 3** 334

Colson discusses his testimony with Nixon **TW 3** 355-356

Colson on his suspicions of Watergate involvement of **TW 3** 417-418, 449

Colson on his testimony before Senate Select Committee **TW 3** 502

Colson on testimony on enemies list of **SI8** 76-77

Colson plays taped telephone converation with

Hunt for **TW 3** 295-296

Colson reports on his meeting with Bittman to Ehrlichman and **TW 3** 313-314

Colson sends letter from Hunt to **TW 3** 274, 296, 297-300

Colson-Shapiro recommendations to Ehrlichman on **TW 3** 343

Colson tells him about Dorothy Hunt's telephone call **TW 3** 454-455

Colson's reasons for consulting with on Hunt letter **TW 3** 477-478, 495

contacts with U.S. Attorneys **SI4-1** 475

conversation with Colson on his knowledge of Colson-Ehrlichman discussion **TW 3** 344

conversation with Colson on Hunt being ordered out of country **TW 3** 266

conversation with Colson on Hunt's safe **TW 3** 264-266

conversation with Moore on Hunt's demands **SI3-2** 709, 965, 966-968

and coverup of Fielding break-in **II 2** 715-716

Cox requests copy of materials in "miscellaneous intelligence" file of **SI9-1** 26, 371, 372-373

Cox requests statement from Nixon on testimony before Ervin Committee of **SI9-1** 19, 317, 318-320

and Cushman's changed memo to Ehrlichman on identification of person requesting CIA assistance for Hunt **SI7-4** 1622, 1719, 1720-1730

dates of testimony before Ervin Committee **SI9-1** 18, 313, 314-315

and delay of FBI interview of Chenow **SI7-3** 1205, 1569, 1570-1574

and deliveries of funds for Watergate defendants to Bittman **SI3-1** 32, 33-34, 385, 386-389, 425-426, 427-454

delivers portion of materials from Hunt's safe to FBI **SI7-3** 1204, 1557, 1558-1568

denies being instructed to conduct Watergate investigation **SI2** 2, 148-149

and destruction of documents from Hunt's safe **NSI1** 19, 141, 142-143

and discrepancy over April 15, 1973 Nixon tape **SUMM I** 107

discusses refusal to be witness for Ervin Committee **SI8** 408-409

discussion between Nixon, Rogers, Haldeman, and Ehrlichman on testimony of **SI4-3** 1102, 1421, 1427-1428, 1431, 1433, 1435, 1439-1441

discussion with Colson on his draft of statement before Senate Select Committee **TW 3** 439-441, 463

discussion with Colson on his status at White House after resignation or retirement **TW 3** 321-322

discussion with Haldeman on testifying before Watergate Grand Jury without immunity **II 2** 840-841

discussion with Haldeman on use of dairy industry contribution **SI6-2** 480, 784, 808-812

discussion with Mitchell on development of political intelligence capability **SI1** 7, 31, 34

discussion with Nixon and Haldeman on September 15, 1972 of indictment against Watergate defendants **SI3-1** 30, 369, 370-371

Dean, John W., III *(Continued)*

discussion with Nixon on electronic surveillance of Kraft **SI7-4** 1641, 1941, 1942-1945

discussion with Nixon on *Time* magazine disclosure of White House-ordered wiretappings **SUMM I** 135

discussions of clemency for, in Article of Impeachment I **RHJC** 78-80

discussions with Krogh on Hunt's demands for money **II 2** 1202-1204, 1205

discussions with Nixon on relationship with Segretti **SI7-4** 1628, 1775, 1776-1811

discussions with Nixon on wiretapping of Democratic National Committee headquarters **SUMM I** 33-34

domestic intelligence assignment transferred from Huston to **II 2** 1119

draft letter to Nixon requesting leave of absence **SI4-3** 1085, 1141, 1147

draft letter to Nixon tendering his resignation **SI4-3** 1085, 1141, 1146

draft memo on Segretti matter from Moore and **SI7-4** 1628, 1775, 1797-1810

efforts to get CIA to provide bail money for Watergate defendants and stop FBI investigation of Mexican checks **SI2** 2, 44, 427, 428-441

efforts to get CIA to retrieve materials sent to Justice Department connecting Hunt and Liddy to Fielding break-in **SI7-4** 1624, 1733, 1734-1739

efforts to obtain CIA funds for Watergate defendants **SI3-1** 8, 129, 130-142; **II 2** 723-727

efforts to obtain FBI reports on Watergate investigation from Kleindienst **SI2** 2, 57, 555, 560

efforts to obtain IRS information on McGovern campaign staff **II 2** 1293, 1297-1298

efforts to prevent granting of immunity to **II 2** 857, 884-885, 886

efforts to prevent Patman Committee hearings **SUMM I** 49-51, 54

efforts to retrieve CIA material from Department of Justice **SI2** 2, 67, 673, 674-680

efforts to write report on Watergate **II 2** 840

Ehrlichman-Colson discussion on immunity for **SI4-3** 1326-1327, 1330

Ehrlichman directs Fielding to report to him on Dean's dismissal by law firm**SI4-1** 25, 471-472, 474

Ehrlichman discusses deal made between U.S. Attorneys and **SI4-3** 1445, 1447

Ehrlichman-Kalmbach discussion on immunity for **SI4-3** 1548-1549

Ehrlichman's instructions on material from Hunt's safe **SI4-2** 1001

and Ehrlichman's opposition to immunity for White House aides **SI4-1** 541

Ehrlichman's taped telephone conversations with Clawson and Colson on his allegations **SI4-3** 1095, 1317, 1320-1330

and Executive clemency offers to Hunt **SUMM I** 63-64

and exposure of Huston plan **SIAPP1** 22

and FBI interview of Chenow **SI2** 2, 54, 487-488, 484, 495, 517, 518

and FBI interviews of Dahlberg and Ogarrio **SI2** 2, 49, 473, 474-475

and FBI reports on wiretapping of government employees and newsmen **SI7-2** 690

and FBI Watergate investigation **SUMM I** 40-41

first contact with Nixon after Watergate break-in **II 3** 1721-1722

goes to Camp David **II 2** 835-836, 839

Gray gives FBI Watergate files to **SI3-2** 727-728, 772-773

Gray says he probably lied about Hunt's status at White House **SI4-1** 6, 109-111, 113-114, 235, 236, 238

Gray tells Petersen he received Hunt's files from **SI4-3** 1096, 1331, 1332-1339

and Gray's destruction of Hunt's files **SI4-3** 1616

guilty plea of **II 2** 1398-1399

Haldeman arranges for meeting with Ehrlichman, Mitchell and **NSI1** 25, 169, 170-176

Haldeman asks him to write report on Watergate at Camp David **SI4-1** 10, 265, 266-268

Haldeman tells Nixon he believes Mitchell approved Liddy plan **SI4-1** 355

and Haldeman's proposed surveillance of Kennedy **II 2** 1123

House Judiciary Committee Impeachment Inquiry discussion on subpoenaing **II 2** 981-982

House Judiciary Committee Impeachment Inquiry subpoena to Nixon on May 30, 1974 for specified materials related to conversations between Nixon and **SI9-2** 577, 1031, 1032-1036

and Hunt-Colson tape recorded conversation on need for more funds for Watergate defendants **SI3-1** 34-35, 405-406, 407-423

and Hunt's blackmail attempts **SI7-4** 1630, 1821, 1822-1828

and Hunt's demands for money **SUMM I** 52

and Hunt's documents **SI3-2** 780-782

and Hunt's letter to Colson **SI3-1** 38-39, 455-456, 457-474

and hush money **SIAPP1** 49; **TW 1** 259; **II 2** 736, 795-798; **SI3-1** 16, 17, 20, 207, 208-219, 221, 222-233, 253, 254-263

Huston on transfer of responsibilities to **SI7-1** 28, 487, 488

immunity for **SI4-3** 1537-1538

immunity for, Petersen on discussions with Nixon on **TW 3** 113-114

information on Watergate break-in given to Ehrlichman by **NSI1** 7, 53, 55

informed by Gray of FBI theory of CIA involvement in Watergate break-in **NSI1** 15, 121, 122-123

informed by O'Brien about his meeting with Hunt **SUMM I** 54

informed by Strachan of destruction of Haldeman's files **SI1** 166; **SI2** 2, 26, 269, 274-275

informs Chapin he has no legal problems with testimony before Watergate Grand Jury **SI7-4** 1908-1909

informs Haldeman of CRP fundraising for Watergate defendants **II 2** 734-735; **SI3-1** 14, 199, 200-202

informs Haldeman that his attorneys had met with Watergate Prosecutors **II 2** 855; **SI4-1** 30, 501, 502

informs Nixon of details of Watergate **SI3-2** 995-

1009

informs Nixon of first meeting on Liddy plan **SI3-2** 998-1000

informs Nixon of Magruder's and Porter's perjury **SUMM I** 79-81

informs Nixon of original hiring of Liddy **SI3-2** 997-998

informs Nixon of Strachan's perjury **SUMM I** 78-79

informs Nixon that CRP political intelligence-gathering is legal **NSI1** 11, 77, 78-80

informs Watergate prosecutor of Hunt and Liddy participation in Fielding break-in **SI7-4** 1640, 1929, 1930-1939

instructed by Nixon to report directly to him on all Watergate matters **SI3-1** 52, 597, 598-614

instructions to Liddy to get Hunt out of country **SI4-3** 1310

and intelligence-gathering plan given to Sirica **SI1** 40

and interference with Senate Select Committee **II 2** 760-767

interviewed by U.S. Attorneys **SI4-2** 578, 1013, 1014-1019

investigation of Watergate break-in by **SI2** 2, 14, 143, 144-153

involvement in Watergate coverup by Nixon **SUMM I** 13

involvement in Watergate discussed at Paul O'Brien-Ehrlichman meeting **SI4-1** 32-33, 507-508, 509-729

IRS information on Goldberg from Caulfield to **II 2** 1271

and IRS information on Graham **SI8** 14, 145, 146-154

and IRS investigations of Nixon's friends **II 2** 1275-1281

issues public statement declaring he will not become scapegoat in Watergate case **II 2** 887

job offer to Segretti **SI7-4** 1699

joins Nixon-Haldeman meeting of September 15, 1973 **SI8** 27, 287, 291-330

Kalmbach on his relationship with **TW 3** 533-534

in Kalmbach letter to Silbert **SI6-1** 311, 312-314

Kalmbach seeks confirmation from Ehrlichman on his authority to direct fundraising for Watergate defendants **II 2** 741-742

and Kalmbach's assignment as fundraiser for Watergate defendants **II 2** 727-729; **SUMM I** 44

and Kalmbach's resignation from assignment as fundraiser for Watergate defendants **SI3-1** 31, 373, 374-383

Kleindienst briefed by U.S. Attorneys on information furnished by **SI4-2** 569, 863, 864-871

Kleindienst informs Nixon that he is indictable **SI4-2** 942

and LaRue's deliveries of hush money to Bittman **TW 1** 229-231, 236-241, 265-275

and LaRue's payment to Liddy's attorney **SI3-1** 43, 499, 500

learns that McCord's letter to Sirica had been read in open court **SI4-1** 6, 235, 236-237

letter from Sloan with list of political committees for AMPI contributions **SI6-2** 480, 784, 802-807

letter to Nixon requesting leave of absence **SI4-3** 1092, 1266, 1270

Liddy's "confession" to **SI4-3** 1301-1302

list of meetings and conversations with Nixon **SI4-1** 10, 265, 269

list of names of indictable White House personnel **SI4-2** 559, 697, 701, 790-791

and *Los Angeles Times* article on McCord claiming he had prior knowledge of Watergate **SI4-1** 12-13, 311-312, 313-314

and Magruder's appointment to government job after perjured testimony **SUMM I** 80-81

and Magruder's efforts to obtain government post after Watergate **SI3-1** 49-50, 557-558, 559-581

Magruder's perjury before Watergate Grand Jury and **SUMM I** 44-45

Magruder's Watergate Grand Jury testimony on role in Watergate coverup **SI4-2** 819

material from Hunt's safe delivered to FBI agents by **SI2** 2, 43, 415, 416-426

material from Hunt's safe turned over to Gray by **SI2** 2, 52, 501, 502-510; **SI7-3** 1206, 1575, 1576-1587

McCord testimony on prior knowledge of Watergate of **SI4-1** 22, 431, 432-443

and McCord's letter to Caulfield on danger of blaming CIA for Watergate **SI3-1** 40, 475, 476-482

meeting with Colson and Ehrlichman on Hunt's letter to Colson **II 2** 757

meeting on covering up Liddy plan **II 2** 749-750

meeting with Ehrlichman and Haldeman after he meets with Watergate Prosecutors **II 2** 857

meeting with Ehrlichman and Haldeman on April 8, 1973 on his Watergate Grand Jury testimony **SI4-1** 35, 537, 538-542

meeting with Ehrlichman on contents of Hunt's safe **SI2** 2, 32, 317, 318-327

meeting with Ehrlichman, Helms, and Colby **SI2** 2, 64, 651, 652-658

meeting with Ehrlichman on Hunt's demands **SI3-2** 708, 951, 952-956

meeting with Gray on FBI Watergate investigation **SI2** 2, 31, 311, 315

meeting with Gray on Mexican checks **SI2** 2, 34, 337, 338, 339, 340-341

meeting with Haldeman and Ehrlichman on expected indictments of White House staff members **SI4-2** 559, 697, 698-706

meeting with Haldeman, Ehrlichman, and Kleindienst after Watergate arrests **SI2** 2, 127

meeting with Haldeman, Ehrlichman, and Mitchell on March 22, 1973 **SI3-2** 718-719, 1251-1252, 1253-1275

meeting with Haldeman and Ehrlichman on Mitchell's role in Watergate **SI3-2** 713, 1135, 1136-1144

meeting with Haldeman and Nixon on March 21, 1973, Nixon's summary of tape on **SIAPP1** 93-96

meeting with Haldeman on uses for milk fund **II 2** 1078-1079

meeting on June 20, 1972 with Haldeman, Ehrlichman, Mitchell, and Kleindienst to discuss Watergate break-in **SI2** 2, 23-24, 235-236, 237, 238, 239, 240-241, 242

meeting with Hunt on Beard interview **TW 3** 250

Dean, John W., III *(Continued)*
meeting with Magruder and Mitchell to plan Magruder's Watergate Grand Jury testimony **SI3-1** 24, 27, 297, 298-309, 341, 342-352
meeting with Magruder, Mitchell, and Haldeman on Magruder's testimony on Liddy plan **SI4-1** 19, 373, 374-397
meeting with Mitchell, Magruder, and Liddy for first presentation of Liddy plan **SI1** 9, 53, 54, 55, 56-57, 58-60
meeting with Mitchell, Magruder, and Liddy for second presentation of Liddy plan **SI1** 10, 53, 62, 63, 64-65, 66, 67-68, 69-75
meeting with Mitchell, Magruder, Mardian, and LaRue on Watergate arrests **SUMM I** 37
meeting with Mitchell, Mardian, and LaRue to discuss CIA aid for Watergate defendants **SI3-1** 7, 121, 122-127
meeting with Nixon, Haldeman, and Ehrlichman on Hunt's blackmail threats **SI7-4** 1631, 1829, 1830-1836
meeting with Nixon after he meets with Watergate Prosecutors **II 2** 879-882
meeting with Nixon and Haldeman on IRS investigation of O'Brien **SI8** 28-29, 331-332, 333-349
meeting with Nixon and Haldeman on September 15, 1973 on Watergate matter **SI2** 2, 62, 593, 594-656; **II 2** 750
meeting with Nixon on Senate Judiciary Committee vote to call him for testimony at Gray confirmation hearings **SI3-2** 700, 799, 802
meeting with Paul O'Brien on Hunt's demands **SI3-2** 707, 945, 946-949
meeting with Petersen on documents delivered by CIA to Department of Justice **SI2** 2, 66, 671, 672; **SI7-4** 1623, 1731, 1732
meeting with Segretti after Watergate break-in **II 2** 751-752, 1195
meetings and conversations with Nixon on February 27, 1973 **SI3-1** 52, 597, 598-604
meetings with Haldeman, Ehrlichman, and Moore to discuss strategy for Ervin Committee hearings **SI3-1** 48, 535, 536-556
meetings with Mitchell, Magruder, Mardian, and LaRue to discuss Watergate break-in **SI2** 2, 21, 223, 224-229
meetings with Segretti **SI7-3** 1203, 1541, 1542-1555
meets with Liddy after arrests of Watergate burglars **NSI1** 3, 39, 40
meets with Liddy and learns Watergate break-in was CRP operation **SUMM I** 37
meets with Segretti and reports to Haldeman and Ehrlichman **SI3-1** 33, 391, 392-403
memorandum of substance of calls and meetings with the President, February 27, 1973 **SI3-1** 52, 597, 605-607
message to Nixon given to Higby **SI4-2** 579-580, 1021-1022, 1031
and milk fund **II 2** 1054
Mitchell denies recollecting conversation of March 20, 1973 on hush money with **TW 2** 177
Mitchell on role in Watergate **SI4-2** 729
Moore informs Nixon about discussions with **SI4-3** 1107, 1501, 1502-1505

Nixon announces Ehrlichman has replaced him for Watergate investigation **SI4-1** 21, 23-24, 427, 429, 445-446, 448
Nixon announces resignation of **SIAPP1** 13, 15-16; **SI9-1** 5, 131, 132-137
Nixon authorizes Haldeman to listen to several tapes of Nixon-Haldeman-Dean conversations **SI9-1** 25, 351, 352-370
Nixon-Dean discussion of possible resignation of **SI4-3** 73-77, 1294-1295
Nixon discusses with Kleindienst **SI4-2** 943-944
Nixon and Ehrlichman discuss Watergate break-in and **SI4-1** 358
Nixon and Ehrlichman discussion on **SI4-3** 1256
Nixon-Ehrlichman discussion on immunity for **SI4-3** 1393
Nixon, Ehrlichman, and Haldeman discussion on Watergate Grand Jury testimony and immunity for **SI4-3** 1097, 1345, 1350-1386, 1418
Nixon-Ehrlichman telephone conversation on forthcoming Watergate Grand Jury testimony of **SI4-1** 36, 543, 544-545
Nixon-Ehrlichman telephone conversation on preventing him from implicating Haldeman and Ehrlichman **SUMM I** 67
Nixon-Ehrlichman telephone conversation on resignation or leave of absence for **SI4-3** 1084, 1131, 1132-1133, 1134
Nixon fears implication of Petersen by **SI4-3** 1635, 1638-1640
Nixon gives Ehrlichman message of confidence for **SI4-2** 860
Nixon on Gray turning over FBI reports to **SI4-1** 31, 503, 506
Nixon-Haldeman discussion on hush money and **SIAPP3** 36-37
Nixon-Haldeman discussion on immunity for **SI4-3** 1311
Nixon-Haldeman meeting on working through IRS **SI8** 27, 287, 288-330
Nixon on immunity for **SI4-2** 1524-1525
Nixon instructs Ehrlichman on his testimony to Watergate Prosecutor, in Article of Impeachment **I RHJC** 105
Nixon on investigation of Watergate by **SIAPP1** 11
Nixon learns he feels guilty of criminal liability for involvement in fundraising for Watergate burglars **SUMM I** 6-7
Nixon-Petersen discussion on immunity for **SI4-3** 1341, 1640-1641, 1644-1645
Nixon-Petersen-Kleindienst meeting on his information on Watergate coverup **TW 3** 80-85, 105-108
Nixon on reasons for access to FBI files for **SI3-2** 693, 743, 745-746
Nixon on relationship with Gray during FBI Watergate investigation **SIAPP1** 9
Nixon on role played in Watergate investigation **SIAPP1** 45
Nixon statement that he is in charge of White House Watergate investigation **SI2** 2, 61, 587, 589
Nixon states he would object to his appearing at

Gray nomination hearings **SIAPP1** 5

Nixon tells Ehrlichman and Haldeman to urge him to go to Grand Jury **NSI1** 30, 199, 200-201

Nixon tells Petersen he will meet with him **SI4-2** 1033

Nixon on Watergate investigation of **SIAPP1** 3, 5

Nixon's efforts to prevent him from getting immunity **SUMM I** 92-93, 96-99

Nixon's efforts to prevent immunity for, in Article of Impeachment I **RHJC** 106-108, 109-111, 113-115

Nixon's false statements on Watergate investigation of, in Article of Impeachment I **RHJC** 82-83

Nixon's instructions to Ehrlichman on handling **SUMM I** 89

and Nixon's order against immunity from prosecution **SIAPP1** 73-74

and Nixon's order for new Watergate investigation on March 21, 1973 **SIAPP1** 51-52

and Nixon's possible lack of knowledge of Watergate coverup, in Minority of House Judiciary Committee Impeachment Inquiry views on Articles of Impeachment **RHJC** 394-395

Nixon's reaction to his going to Watergate Prosecutors, in St. Clair's presentation of evidence in behalf of Nixon **II 3** 1749-1750

Nixon's reaction to his meeting with Watergate Prosecutors **SUMM I** 74

Nixon's refusal to allow his testimony at Gray confirmation hearings **SIAPP1** 8-9, 10

Nixon's report to Haldeman and Ehrlichman on April 16, 1973 meeting with **SI4-3** 1203, 1204-1211

in Nixon's statement about efforts to uncover facts on Watergate **SIAPP1** 34, 41-42

Nixon's statement on discussion on hush money with **II 2** 1368-1369

and Nixon's suggested IRS investigation of McGovern campaign contributions **SUMM I** 142-143

Nixon's television announcement of resignation of **SI4-3** 1119, 1657, 1658-1659

note from Higby with enemies list **SI8** 11-12, 111-112, 126

note to Hullin with memo on statutes relating to disclosure of intelligence information to newspapers **NSI4** 40-42

notes for Camp David report on Hunt's safe **SI2** 2, 32, 317, 326-327

O'Brien informs him of his discussion with Hunt **TW 1** 127-128, 138-141, 151, 155-157

O'Brien on **TW 1** 146-147

O'Brien on reporting to **TW 1** 160-161, 172-173

obtains FBI report on Watergate investigation from Gray **SI2** 2, 57, 555, 556-559

and opening of Hunt's safe **SI2** 2, 19, 189, 190-201

Operation Sandwedge proposal submitted by Caulfield to **SI7-3** 1188-1189, 1339-1340,1372-1376

opposition to immunity for **II 1** 606

and payment of $75,000 to Bittman for Hunt **SI3-2** 715, 1187, 1193-1196, 1235, 1236-1237

Petersen meeting with Nixon and Kleindienst to report on information received from **SI4-2** 576-577, 973-974, 975-1011

Petersen on discussion with Nixon on immunity for **SI4-2** 1009-1010

Petersen on discussions with **TW 3** 130-131, 153-154, 158-159

Petersen on his destruction of material from Hunt's safe **TW 3** 151-152, 157-158, 179

Petersen on his information on material from Hunt's safe **TW 3** 75-78, 122, 130-131, 140-141, 145-146

Petersen on immunity issue and **TW 3** 116-117, 176-177

Petersen on meeting among Watergate Prosecutors after receiving information from **TW 3** 78-81

Petersen-Nixon discussion on immunity for **NSI1** 35, 223, 224-225

Petersen questions on documents taken from Hunt's safe **SUMM I** 63

Petersen on relationship with **SI2** 2, 123

Petersen reports to Nixon on discussion with **SI4-3** 1400-1401

Petersen tells Nixon he might be indictable **SIAPP1** 45

plays recorded conversation between Colson and Hunt for Ehrlichman, Haldeman, and Mitchell **II 2** 752

pleads guilty and agrees to cooperate with Watergate Special Prosecutor **SI9-2** 542, 801, 802-809

Plumbers unit and **SIAPP1** 23

and "political enemies" project **SIAPP4** 59; **SUMM I** 141-142

and "political enemies" project in memo from Strachan to Haldeman **SI1** 7, 31, 34

possible resignation discussed by Nixon and Petersen **SI4-3** 1235

presence at White House FBI interviews discussed with Nixon **SI3-2** 692, 729, 737-741, 764-765

and prevention of Stans' scheduled Watergate Grand Jury appearance **SUMM I** 45

public statement on not becoming scapegoat in Watergate case **SI4-3** 1106, 1493, 1494-1495

reactions to newspaper disclosure of Segretti's activities **SI7-4** 1617, 1657, 1658-1675

refuses to meet with Ehrlichman on information given to U.S. Attorneys **SI4-2** 579-580, 1021-1022, 1023-1024, 1027, 1031

refuses to testify in Gray confirmation hearings **SI3-2** 702, 703, 881, 882-896, 897, 898-900

relationship with Haldeman **SI1** 38

report on Potential Disruptions at Republican National Convention of 1972 **SIAPP4** 85, 119-120

and Republican National Convention plans **SI1** 88

requests that Caulfield place Edward Kennedy under 24-hour-a-day surveillance **SI7-2** 656-657

and requests from Haldeman for IRS audits **SI8** 17, 175, 176-182

resignation of **II 2** 1333

responsibility for studying Sandwedge plan and other "covert" intelligence activities **SUMM I** 29-30

responsibility for White House domestic intelligence transferred from Huston to **SI7-1** 28, 487,

Dean, John W., III *(Continued)*
488-496
retains attorney **II 2** 854; **SI4-1** 27, 483, 484
returns to Washington after Watergate arrests **SUMM I** 36-37
and Ripon Society suit against Republican National Committee **SIAPP4** 53
role in containment of Watergate from July 1 until elections **SUMM I** 43-44
role in Nixon Administration **RHJC** 14
role in Nixon re-election campaign **SIAPP4** 109
role in Watergate coverup, in Doar's presentation of summary of evidence to House Judiciary Committee Impeachment Inquiry **II 3** 1961
role in Watergate discussed by Nixon, Ehrlichman and Haldeman **SI4-2** 689-691
role on White House staff **II 1** 556
and salary increase for Liddy **SI7-3** 1446
and Segretti's appearance before Watergate Grand Jury **SI7-3** 1208, 1595, 1596-1602
Senate Judiciary Committee votes to request testimony at Gray confirmation hearings **SI3-2** 700, 799, 800-802
and Stans' avoidance of testimony before Watergate Grand Jury **II 1** 695-697
Strachan informs of documents shredded by **SI7-3** 1487
Strachan on reactions to Haldeman's request for 24-hour-a-day surveillance of Edward Kennedy **SI7-2** 531, 655, 658-659
suggests LaRue consult with Mitchell on Hunt's request for money **NSI1** 26, 177, 178-185
suggests that Nixon testify before Watergate Grand Jury **SI4-2** 674
taped conversation with Segretti **II 2** 1200
taped conversation with Segretti on Segretti's activities and involvement with Chapin **SI7-4** 1620, 1697, 1698-1707
taped telephone conversation between Ehrlichman and Colson on **TW 3** 344-353
taped telephone conversation with Ehrlichman **SI3-2** 697,768-769, 777, 778-782
taped telephone conversation with Magruder **II 2** 842; **SI4-1** 15, 331, 332
taped telephone conversation with Nixon on March 20, 1973 **SI3-2** 710, 979, 980-987
telephone call from Nixon at Camp David **SI4-1** 10, 265, 269
telephone call from Nixon instructing him to go to Camp David **SI4-1** 6, 235, 237, 239
telephone call from Nixon to wish him a happy Easter **SI4-3** 1111, 1553, 1554-1555
telephone call to Ehrlichman to inform him about McCord's letter to Sirica **SI4-1** 6, 235, 236-237
telephone conversation between Nixon and Petersen on information given to U.S. Attorneys by **SI4-3** 1083, 1123, 1124-1130
telephone conversation with Ehrlichman on his dismissal by law firm **II 2** 854
telephone conversation with Gray on FBI Watergate investigation **SI2** 2, 46, 449, 451,453
telephone conversations with Haldeman on Camp David report **SI4-1** 12-13, 311-312, 317-318
telephone records of **TW 2** 314-316
tells Colson Hunt has been ordered out of country

SI2 2, 158
tells Haldeman he opposes Liddy plan **SUMM I** 30-31
tells LaRue to get authorization from Mitchell for payment to Hunt **II 2** 815, 817, 879
tells Moore that Nixon has no knowledge of Watergate coverup **NSI1** 8, 57, 58-61
tells Nixon Magruder would probably admit perjury to Special Prosecutor and implicate Mitchell, Strachan, and Haldeman **SUMM I** 6-7
tells Nixon there are things he has no knowledge of **NSI1** 14, 119, 120
tells Silbert and Glanzer about Fielding break-in **II 2** 1226-1228
tells Walters he is handling Watergate investigation **SI2** 2, 39, 376, 395
tells Watergate Prosecutors about Fielding break-in and materials from Hunt's safe **II 2** 815, 817
and *Time* magazine's plan to publish article on White House wiretapping of staff members and newsmen **SI7-4** 1625, 1741, 1742-1748; **II 2** 1201-1202
transcript of taped telephone conversation with Magruder **SI4-1** 15, 331, 333-334
and transfer of campaign contributions to CRP for payments to Watergate defendants **II 2** 738-739
and transfer of ITT material from SEC to Justice Department **SI5-2** 913, 915-916, 932
urges Colson to meet with Bittman about Hunt **TW 3** 300-302
and Walters-Gray meeting **SI2** 2, 40, 397, 398, 399, 400, 401, 402
Walters refuses to attempt to retrieve CIA material on Hunt from Department of Justice **SI2** 2, 67, 673, 678, 680
Watergate coverup and **SUMM I** 39
Watergate coverup and assignments from Nixon to investigate Watergate **SUMM I** 70-74
and White House efforts to obtain IRS audit of Greene **SI8** 16, 165, 166-174
and White House interference with FBI Watergate investigation **II 2** 778-786
and White House task force on Kleindienst hearings **SI5-2** 503, 759, 768-769
and White House use of IRS, in Jenner's presentation of summary of evidence to House Judiciary Committee Impeachment Inquiry **II 3** 1980, 1983-1990
See also House Judiciary Committee Impeachment Inquiry, discussion on calling witnesses; House Judiciary Committee Impeachment Inquiry, presentation of evidence on enemies list and IRS; Nixon tapes; Nixon-Dean meetings; St. Clair, James D., presentation of evidence in behalf of Nixon
See also U.S. v. John W. Dean, III
Dean, John W., III, cited testimony of SI2 2, 60, 575, 581; **SI4-2** 581-582, 1039-1040, 1041-1043, 1044-1046
on attitude toward testifying at Gray confirmation hearings **SI3-2** 835-837
on briefing memo for Haldeman on increasing political responsiveness of IRS **SI8** 19, 195, 200-202

on Caulfield's efforts to obtain IRS audit of
Greene SI8 16, 165, 166-167
on Caulfield's offers of Executive clemency to
McCord SI3-1 42, 487, 497-498
on contacting Mitchell on fundraising for Watergate defendants SI3-2 712, 1117, 1133
on conversation with Moore on Hunt's demands
SI3-2 709, 965, 968
on conversations with Nixon on Executive privilege and Gray turning over FBI materials to
Senate Judiciary Committee SI3-2 698, 783, 791
on creation of independent Warren-type commission on Watergate SI4-1 11, 271, 279
on creation of Interagency Evaluation Committee
and his assumption of Huston's responsibilities
for internal domestic security SI7-1 28, 487,
489-491
on Cushman's memo to Ehrlichman on identification of person requesting CIA assistance for
Hunt SI7-4 1622, 1719, 1720-1721
on dealings with Segretti after Watergate break-in
and reporting to Haldeman and Ehrlichman
SI3-1 33, 391, 392-393
denies advising Nixon on Watergate coverup
NSI1 4, 41, 42-43
denies receiving instructions to conduct Watergate
investigation SI2 2, 61, 587, 590-592
denies that he was assigned to write report on
Watergate NSI1 28, 193, 194
on discussion with Ehrlichman and Haldeman on
Mitchell's role in Watergate matter SI3-2 1142
on discussion with Ehrlichman on his meeting
with Colson and Shapiro recommendations on
Watergate SI4-2 556, 558, 607-608
on discussion with Gray on Watergate break-in
NSI1 15, 121, 123
in Doar's presentation of evidentiary material to
House Judiciary Committee Impeachment Inquiry II 1 589-590, 596-599
on efforts to prepare Camp David report SI4-1
11, 271, 272-279
on efforts to retrieve CIA material on Hunt from
Department of Justice SI2 2, 67, 673, 679-680;
SI7-4 1624, 1733, 1738-1739
on Ehrlichman's efforts to meet with him on his
discussions with U.S. Attorneys SI4-2 579-580,
1017, 1021-1022, 1023-1024
on enemies list SI8 7, 11-12, 65, 66-71, 111-117
on events after newspaper stories on Segretti's activities SI7-4 1617, 1657, 1672
on FBI SI7-4 1817
on FBI files and logs of wiretaps requested by
White House SI7-2 540, 755, 771-773
on FBI interview of Chenow SI2 2, 54, 484, 517,
518; SI7-3 1205, 1569, 1570
on FBI interview of Colson SI2 2, 33, 329, 332,
333
on FBI investigation of Schorr SI7-2 562, 1111,
1124
on FBI reports obtained from Gray SI2 2, 57,
555, 558-559
on first learning about Watergate break-in SI3-2
10051006
on first meeting on Liddy plan SI1 9, 53, 59-60
on first wiretapping of DNC SI3-2 1004-1005

on formation of Intelligence Evaluation Committee SI7-1 29, 497, 500-504
on Gray SI3-2 838-840
on Haldeman calling Mitchell to arrange for
meeting on Watergate NSI1 25, 169, 176
on Haldeman's requests for IRS audits SI8 17,
175, 176-177
on his briefing paper for meeting between Nixon
and Kleindienst SI3-1 51, 583, 586-589
on his efforts to obtain CIA funds for Watergate
defendants SI3-1 8, 129, 137-139
on Hunt's letter to Colson SI3-1 38-39, 455-456,
460-461
on informing Haldeman of CRP fundraising for
Watergate defendants SI3-1 14, 199, 202
on informing Mitchell and Magruder that he will
testify before Grand Jury NSI1 31, 203, 204
on instructions to Liddy to tell Hunt to leave
country SI2 2, 20, 203, 204
on investigation of Watergate break-in SI2 2, 14,
143, 144-146
on Kalmbach's assignment to raise funds for Watergate defendants SI3-1 9, 143, 152
on Kalmbach's resignation as fundraiser for Watergate defendants and burning of his records
SI3-1 31, 373, 382
on Liddy's behavior after Watergate arrests SI3-2
1015-1016
on Magruder's and Porter's Grand Jury perjury
SI3-2 1008-1009
on Magruder's efforts to obtain government post
after Watergate SI3-1 49-50, 557-558, 570-573,
576
on materials from Hunt's safe SI7-3 1204, 1557,
1558-1560
on materials from Hunt's safe given to Gray SI2
2, 52, 501, 507-510
on materials from Hunt's safe turned over to FBI
SI2 2, 43, 415, 416-418
on McCord's letter to Caulfield SI3-1 40, 475,
477
on McCord's letter to Sirica and Nixon's instructions to go to Camp David SI4-1 236-237
on meeting on Hunt's status after Watergate SI2
2, 18, 166, 168-169
on meeting with Ehrlichman on contents of
Hunt's safe SI2 2, 32, 317, 318-319
on meeting with Ehrlichman on Hunt's demands
SI3-2 708, 951, 957
on meeting with Ehrlichman and Gray to turn
over rest of material from Hunt's safe SI7-3
1206, 1575, 1582-1585
on meeting with Ehrlichman and Haldeman on
expected indictments for White House staff
members SI4-2 559, 697, 699-700, 702
on meeting with Gray on FBI Watergate investigation SI2 2, 31, 311, 315
on meeting with Gray on Mexican checks SI2 2,
340-341
on meeting with Haldeman and Ehrlichman on
forthcoming Watergate Grand Jury testimony
SI4-1 35, 537, 538-539
on meeting with Haldeman, Ehrlichman, and
Mitchell on March 22, 1973 SI3-2 1251, 1255-

TW 2 329-331, 352-353

on efforts to obtain immunity from Watergate Prosecutors TW 2 277-279, 323

on FBI Watergate investigation TW 2 351-352

on Haldeman's $350,000 fund at White House and payments to Watergate defendants TW 2 229-234

on Haldeman's role at White House TW 2 334, 344, 346, 349-350

on hiring of Liddy TW 2 222-223

on his conversation with O'Brien about Hunt's demands for money TW 2 238-239, 245, 258-259

on his discussion with Krogh on their legal problems TW 2 247-248

on his discussions with Ehrlichman and Haldeman on Mitchell taking blame for Watergate TW 2 251, 267-268

on his involvement with hush money TW 2 238-239, 245-251, 258-270, 290-297

on his reasons for involvement in Watergate coverup TW 2 326-329, 335-336

on illegal activities at White House TW 2 304-305

on informing Nixon, Haldeman, and Ehrlichman that he had retained counsel and would talk to Watergate Prosecutors TW 2 254-257

on Kalmbach's assignment as fundraiser for Watergate defendants TW 2 306-307

on learning about Watergate break-in TW 2 223-227, 282-283

on misuse of IRS TW 2 300-303, 311, 331-332, 350-351

on Nixon's attitude toward informers TW 2 338

on Nixon's discussion on red box TW 2 337-339

on Nixon's statements on his investigation of Watergate TW 2 298-299

on Nixon's threats against *Washington Post* TW 2 289-290

on obtaining data from FBI TW 2 226-227, 333

on opening of Hunt's safe TW 2 234-236, 287-288

on political-intelligence activities prior to Watergate break-in TW 2 347-348

questioning by St. Clair TW 2 257-288

on reasons for not informing Nixon earlier on his knowledge of Watergate coverup TW 2 258-270, 282-287, 293-297, 299-300, 345-346

on relations with Nixon and other White House staff people after he informs them he is talking to Watergate Prosecutors TW 2 280-282

swearing in at House Judiciary Committee Impeachment Inquiry TW 2 219

on tape of Colson-Hunt conversation TW 2 232-233

on White House concern over Hunt's activities TW 2 317-318

on work relationships with Mitchell, Haldeman, and Ehrlichman TW 2 225-226

See also Nixon-Dean meetings, Dean on

Dean memos

calls and meetings with Nixon on September 15, 1972 SI8 28-29, 331-332, 337-339

"Dealing with Our Political Enemies" SI8 9, 95, 96-102

for briefing Haldeman on increasing political responsiveness of IRS SI8 19, 195, 196-204

from Bell with enemies list SI8 7, 65, 72-75

from Caulfield on actions against producer of *Millhouse: A White Comedy* SI8 18, 183, 184-194

from Caulfield on IRS tax audit information about Graham SI8 14, 145, 146-147

from Caulfield on *Newsday* article on Rebozo SI8 16, 165, 173

from Caulfield with information about tax audits of Wayne and eight other entertainers SI8 15, 155, 156-163

from Chapin on Segretti's activities SI7-3 1197, 1481, 1488-1492

from Colson on group wanting information on limitations of campaign contributions SI6-1 11, 191, 192-194

from Colson on Howard-Kehrli memo on Hunt TW 3 262

from Colson on Hunt's status at White House SI2 2, 18, 166, 170-172

from Colson on ITT matter NSI2 16, 189, 194-197

from Colson on prioritization of names on enemies list SI8 10, 103, 104-109

from Colson requesting IRS audit of Gibbons SI8 22, 213, 214-216

from Ehrlichman on legal aspects of leaks to newspapers NSI4 3, 37, 38

from Fielding on *Millhouse: A White Comedy* SI8 191

from Haldeman on dealing with Ervin Committee hearings SI3-1 47, 527, 528-533, 541, 543

from Higby on dealing with Ervin Committee hearings SI2-1 542

from Hullin asking for information on legal aspects of leaks of secret government information NSI4 3, 37, 39

from Jones on job options for Magruder SI3-1 49-50, 557-558, 577-578

from Strachan with enemies list SI8 11-12, 111-112, 120-125

to Colson on materials relevant to *Nader* v. *Butz* SI6-2 485, 877, 892

to Colson with opponents list memo from Bell II 2 1268-1269

to DeMarco, Evans, and Kalmbach with draft charter for model political committee for milk producers' contributions SI6-2 465, 493, 500-509

to Haldeman and Ehrlichman on *Nader* v. *Butz* SI6-2 485, 877, 879-891

to Haldeman and others with material containing personal information about "enemy" journalist SI8 21, 211, 212

to Higby with enemies list SI8 11-12, 111-112, 118-119

to Krogh on Brookings Institution II 2 1263-1265; SI8 8, 79, 80-90

to Mitchell on creation of interagency domestic intelligence unit SI7-1 28, 487, 493-495

Dean Report SI3-2 714, 1147, 1160-1167, 1171, 1178-1180

conflict of testimony on timing of request for SI4-1 10, 265, 266-268

Dean denies he was sent to Camp David to prepare NSI1 28, 193, 194

Dean denies writing TW 2 250-253, 274-276, 279, 320-321

Presidential papers **SI10** 103-105

mentions deed executed on April 21, 1969 in letter to Coopers & Lybrand but does not mention
re-execution **SI10** 15, 329-331

and Newman's appraisal of Nixon's pre-Presidential papers in November 1969 **SI10** 9, 184-196

and Newman's visit to National Archives to verify
volume of Nixon's pre-Presidential papers for
1969 deduction **SI10** 5-6, 91-94

obtains Nixon's signature on 1969 tax return **SI10**
15-16

telephone call from Barth on checking and approving Nixons' 1969 income tax return and issuing of refund check **SI10** 17, 365-366

telephone conversation with Blech in May 1969
on Nixon's future deductions for gift of pre-
Presidential papers **SI10** 7, 140-141, 142-143,
144-145

See also House Judiciary Committee Impeachment
Inquiry, presentation of evidence on Nixon's income tax; Kalmbach, Herbert Warren, testimony before House Judiciary Committee
Impeachment Inquiry; Nixon's income tax

Democratic National Committee headquarters SI1 22,
201, 202-213

Baldwin delivers logs and summaries of telephone
conversations from tapped telephones at **SI1** 24,
223, 224-231

break-in and bugging of Lawrence O'Brien's and
Oliver's telephones at **SI1** 23, 215, 216-222

first unsuccessful break-in attempts at **SI1** 22,
201, 202-213

Magruder learns about first entry into **SI1** 175,
181

Magruder, Mitchell, and Haldeman receive reports on electronic surveillance of **SUMM I** 33

Nixon-Dean discussions on wiretapping of
SUMM I 33-34

as target of Liddy plan **SI1** 10, 13, 61, 115

targeted for electronic surveillance **SI1** 21, 197,
198-200

wiretapping at **SI1** 25, 233, 243-244

wiretapping at, in Doar's presentation of evidentiary material to House Judiciary Committee Impeachment Inquiry **II 1** 575-576

See also Watergate break-in; Watergate burglars

Democratic National Convention (1968)

in Odle memo to Magruder **SI5-1** 449

Democratic National Convention (1972)

announcement of site for **SI5-1** 465

business exposition at **SI1** 65

intelligence activities of Liddy, Hunt, Barker, and
McCord prior to **SI1** 26, 245, 246-253

Miami as choice of site for **SI5-2** 568

Miami as choice of site for, in memo from Magruder and Timmons to Mitchell and Haldeman
SI5-1 466

Political Matters Memoranda on **SIAPP4** 116

talking paper from Strachan to Mitchell on
SIAPP4 42

Democratic party SIAPP2 294-295

campaigns for presidential nomination, Segretti
hired to disrupt **SI7-2** 526, 575, 576-590

civil suit against Republican party **TW 2** 6

Colson on impact of Pentagon Papers publication
on **SI7-2** 666, 671-672

Colson on motives for continuation of Kleindienst
confirmation controversy by **SI5-2** 806-807

fundraising telethon **SIAPP4** 121

illegal campaign contributions to, *see* Illegal campaign practices and contributions, papers from
criminal cases related to

Nixon on impact of Watergate on off-year elections and **SIAPP1** 73

Plumbers unit activities and **SUMM I** 129

Democratic party primaries

in Nixon-Mitchell-Haldeman discussion **SIAPP3**
19-21

in Political Matters Memoranda **SIAPP4** 20, 21

Segretti and CRP activities during campaigns for
SI7-3 1190, 1377, 1378-1390

talking paper from Strachan to Mitchell on
SIAPP4 41-42

Democrats for Nixon SIAPP4 138

Demonstrations

at appearances of Tricia Nixon, Nixon-Haldeman
discussion on **SIAPP3** 65-68

Dean's report on Potential Disruptions at Republican National Convention of 1972 **SIAPP4**
119-120

expected at Republican National Convention
SIAPP4 85

Nixon on **SI3-2** 1039-1040

Nixon-Mitchell-Haldeman discussion on possibility at Republican Convention **SIAPP3** 7-8, 17-
18

planned for Republican National Convention **SI1**
82

and selection of Republican National Convention
site **SI5-1** 449, 470

in Timmons' report on San Diego as possible
Republican National Convention site **SI5-1** 442

DeMotte, Clifton

CIA provision of material to Hunt for interview
with **SI7-2** 547, 843, 844-861

Colson's authorization of Hunt's interview with
TW 3 454

Hunt's interview with **II 2** 1142-1143

Dennis, David W. SUMM I 1

additional views on Article of Impeachment III
RHJC 503-505

additional views on Articles of Impeachment
RHJC 507-510

on alleged delivery of Pentagon Papers to Soviet
Embassy **II 2** 1140-1141, 1144

amendment to motion to issue subpoena to Nixon
II 1 310-311, 321-323

on atmosphere at time of domestic surveillance **II
2** 1091

on Byrne dismissing indictment in Ellsberg case **II
2** 1240-1241

on calling Hunt as witness before House Judiciary
Committee Impeachment Inquiry **TW 3** 744-746

on calling witnesses before House Judiciary Committee Impeachment Inquiry **II 3** 1637-1639,
1662-1663, 1690-1692, 1694-1695, 1707-1, 1709,
1712

on confidentiality of material from Fielding break-
in grand jury **II 2** 1177-1178

Dennis, David W. *(Continued)*

on Conyers' motion to cite Nixon for contempt of Congress for his noncompliance with House Judiciary Committee Impeachment Inquiry subpoenas **II 1** 460-461

on Doar-Jenner interview with Byrne **II 2** 1222-1223

on Doar's letter to St. Clair requesting materials for House Judiciary Committee Impeachment Inquiry **II 1** 210-211

on dropping some grounds for impeachment of Nixon **II 1** 266-267

on enforcement of subpoenas **II 1** 114

on evidence on date of LaRue's last payment to Hunt **II 3** 1756-1757

on Fulbright's request for House Judiciary Committee Impeachment Inquiry material on Kissinger **II 2** 1324

on hearsay evidence **TW 1** 193-194

on House Judiciary Committee Impeachment Inquiry access to legal staff materials **II 1** 87-88, 91-92

on importance of rules of procedures for House Judiciary Committee Impeachment Inquiry **II 1** 404-405

on interview with Kleindienst **II 2** 1425-1426

on issuing subpoenas to Nixon **II 1** 308, 314-315, 333-334, 336, 641-642, 643, 651, 665-667, 672, 674; **II3** 1533-1534, 1537-1538, 1539, 1559

on Johnnie Walters' responses to Dean's requests **II 2** 1297

on leaked Dixon memos **II 2** 1325-1326, 1330

on leaks from House Judiciary Committee Impeachment Inquiry **II 2** 704, 709

on legal aspects of impoundment of funds **II 2** 1315

on letter from St. Clair to Rodino on leaks from House Judiciary Committee Impeachment Inquiry **II 2** 768

on mail on impeachment **II 1** 74

motion for House Judiciary Committee Impeachment Inquiry issuance of subpoenas for additional witnesses **II 2** 981-982

motion on including St. Clair's oral presentation in House Judiciary Committee Impeachment Inquiry record **II 3** 1913-1914, 1915, 1916

on need for House Judiciary Committee Impeachment Inquiry business meetings **II 1** 265, 405; **II 2** 775-776

on Nixon-Peterson relationship **II 3** 2031-2032

on Nixon tape with gap **II 2** 1410

on Nixon's alleged approval of Fielding break-in **II 2** 1163-1164

on Nixon's gift of Presidential papers **II 3** 1486

on Nixon's income tax **II 3** 1496, 1508, 1527

on Nixon's noncompliance with House Judiciary Committee Impeachment Inquiry subpoenas **II 1** 419-421, 450-451; **II 2** 911, 923-924, 932-939

on Nixon's refusal of tapes to Jaworski **II 2** 935-936

objection to giving back transcripts of Nixon tapes at end of House Judiciary Committee Impeachment Inquiry sessions **II 2** 813

objects to release of draft Articles of Impeachment **II 3** 1924-1925, 1926; **SUMM I** 2, 3-4

on obtaining Nixon's tax returns and audits from IRS **II 2** 1242, 1246

on possibility of Haldeman acting without Nixon's knowledge **II 3** 2022

on power of House Judiciary Committee Impeachment Inquiry **II 1** 84

on presentation of St. Clair's brief **II 2** 1198-1199

on presentation procedures for House Judiciary Committee Impeachment Inquiry **II 1** 268-269

on procedural rules for handling Impeachment Inquiry material **II 1** 124-125

on questions from Minority **II 2** 808

on Rebozo-Hughes contribution **II 3** 1994

on relationship between House Judiciary Committee Impeachment Inquiry and legal staff **II 1** 74

on release of House Judiciary Committee Impeachment Inquiry evidentiary material to public **II 2** 979-980; **II 3** 1584-1585, 1600, 1603, 1608, 1609-1610, 1611

on relevance of evidence on enemies list **II 2** 1260-1261, 1270-1271

on relevancy of discussion on Operation Sandwedge **II 2** 1185

on right of Minority of House Judiciary Committee Impeachment Inquiry to have legal brief **II 1** 303

on right of Minority of House Judiciary Committee Impeachment Inquiry to subpoena witnesses **II 1** 24

on rules for Impeachment Inquiry staff **II 1** 129-130

on rules of evidentiary procedures for House Judiciary Committee Impeachment Inquiry **II 1** 473-474, 501-502, 507-508, 514-515, 530-533, 536

on scheduling St. Clair's presentation of evidence **II 3** 1566

on separate Minority of House Judiciary Committee Impeachment Inquiry brief on impeachable offenses **II 1** 154

on Sirica's invitation to Doar and Jenner **II 1** 138, 146

on St. Clair's participation in House Judiciary Committee Impeachment Inquiry **II 1** 235, 340

on subpoena powers of House Judiciary Committee **II 1** 36, 42-43

on theories of impeachable offenses **II 1** 73-74

on using subpoena powers of House Judiciary Committee **II 1** 187-188

vote on amendment on issuing subpoenas to Nixon **II 1** 328-330

on voting on St. Clair's participation in House Judiciary Committee Impeachment Inquiry **II 1** 303-304

on Waldie's motion on hearing testimony of witnesses in executive session **II 3** 1873-1874

on White House decision-making structure **II 2** 1021-1022

on Wiggins' amendment to subpoena Nixon **II 1** 357

Dennis, David W., questioning by

Bittman **TW 2** 75-77, 80-81

Colson **TW 3** 465-466, 522-523

Dean **TW 2** 307-309

Kalmbach **TW 3** 714-715
LaRue **TW 1** 253-254, 269
Mitchell **TW 2** 179-181, 187-188
O'Brien **TW 1** 147-148
Petersen **TW 3** 142-144
Dent, Frederick
on Watergate **SI9-1** 136
Dent, Harry S. SIAPP4 8-9, 46; **SI5-1** 461
and assignment of Kalmbach to solicit contributions for special White House project on Congressional campaigns **SI6-1** 130, 131
and black voters **SI1** 80
briefing of Ehrlichman on North Carolina **SI1** 33
exclusion from Campaign Strategy Group **SI1** 85
and Gleason memo to Colson on milk producers **SI6-1** 121
Kalmbach informs about AMPI contribution **SI6-1** 102
Kalmbach on arranging for meeting between Semer and **SI6-1** 6, 99, 103-105
memo from Gleason on operating expenses of White House Special Project **SI6-1** 8, 127, 147-152
memo from Haldeman assigning Colson to Special Project **SI6-1** 12, 197, 198
memo from Nelson on invitation to Nixon to address annual meeting of Associated Dairymen, Inc. **SI6-1** 6, 99, 111, 117
in memo from Strachan to Haldeman **SI1** 33
Nelson on meeting with **SI6-1** 6, 99, 114-116
Nixon re-election campaign responsibilities of **SUMM I** 27
and Political Issues Group **SI1** 80
in Political Matters Memoranda **SIAPP4** 1
and replacement for Evans **SIAPP4** 37
at Republican Governors Conference **SI1** 34
role in fundraising **SI6-1** 307
role in Nixon re-election campaign **SI1** 86
Semer on arrangements for meeting with **SI6-1** 6, 99, 109-113
See also Political Matters Memoranda, on Dent
Department of Agriculture
and cheese purchase for school lunch and commodity distribution programs **SI6-1** 365-369
decision of March 12, 1971 on milk price supports **II 2** 1065-1073
House Judiciary staff list of members of Congress contacting in February and March, 1971 **SI6-1** 22-23, 329-330, 350-357
impoundment of funds in 1973 and **SI12** 5
letter from Gleason to Semer on positions on advisory boards or commissions of **SI6-1** 6, 99, 118
and milk price-supports decision of March 12, 1971 **II 2** 1065-1073
notice to Commodity Credit Corporation on 1971-72 milk price support program**NSI3** 211-217
press release announcing price-supports decision and Tariff Commission investigation on cheese imports **SI6-1** 26, 389, 392-395, 397
press release of March 25, 1971 announcing milk price-support increase **SI6-2** 478, 767, 768-769
recommendation against raising milk price supports, White House reaction to **SI6-1** 24-25, 359-360, 361-387

Department of Commerce
Magruder's resignation as Director of Policy Development for **SI4-3** 1114, 1625, 1626
Department of Defense
Appropriations acts, bombing of Cambodia and **SI11** 397, 399, 404
declassified report on bombing of Cambodia **SI11** 21-22, 176
expenditures in connection with Key Biscayne **SI12** 156
impoundment of funds and **SI12** 5, 9
public statements on reasons for false documentary submission on Cambodian bombings to Congress **SI11** 75, 369-374
report on United States aerial attacks in Indochina submitted to Senate Armed Services Committee **SI11** 88-111
response to request from House of Representatives for information on bombing of Cambodia and Laos from January 1969-April 1970 **SI11** 57, 63, 295-297, 319-321
submission of false data concealing Cambodian bombings to Senate Armed Services Committee **SI11** 64-68, 323-336
submits declassified version of Richardson's Report to Senate Armed Services Committee in July 1973 **SI11** 27, 186-193
White Paper on Members of Congress advised of Cambodian and Laotian bombings**SI11** 63, 317-318
White Paper statement on reasons for erroneous information submitted to Congress on Cambodian bombings **SI11** 68, 336
Department of Health, Education, and Welfare (HEW) II 2 1304
court cases on Presidential impoundment of funds for **SI12** 19-26
films for elderly **SI1** 87
See also House Judiciary Committee Impeachment Inquiry, presentation of evidence on impoundment of funds by
Department of Housing and Urban Development (HUD)
and impoundment of funds for federal housing programs **SI12** 12-16
Department of Justice NSI2 26-30; **SI5-1** 70-71
amendment to Watergate Special Prosecutor's charter **SI9-2** 551, 861, 862-864
authorization for lack of records of Halperin wiretaps at **II 2** 1192, 1193
Cox's efforts to obtain milk producers' campaign contributions file from **SI9-1** 40, 475, 476-480
criteria for warrantless wiretaps **SUMM I** 127-128
informed by FBI that no Ellsberg conversations were monitored **II 2** 1134-1139
Internal Security Division, memos to and from Assistant Attorney General on electronic surveillance of Ellsberg and Halperin **SI7-2** 542, 789, 790-794
investigation of Pentagon Papers matter turned over to **SI7-3** 1422
McLaren interviewed by Mitchell and Kleindienst for position with Antitrust Division of **NSI2** 3, 21-24

Department of Justice *(Continued)*
  memo to Timmons on San Diego as site for
    Republican National Convention of 1972 **NSI2**
    12, 127, 145
  Mitchell's press release denying discussion of ITT
    antitrust suits with Beard or Nixon **SI5-2** 492,
    631, 632
  Nixon instructs Petersen not to investigate Field-
    ing break-in **SI7-4** 1643, 1949, 1950-1966
  Nixon on Watergate investigation of **SIAPP1** 3
  Nixon tells Petersen it should not investigate
    Fielding break-in **II 2** 1228-1229, 1231, 1232
  Nixon's interference with, in Article of Impeach-
    ment I **RHJC** 98-115
  Nixon's misuse of, in Article of Impeachment II
    RHJC 178-179
  Petersen on reporting to Nixon on Watergate
    investigation of **TW 3** 86-105, 110-117, 128-130,
    146-147
  Petersen on responsibility of representing Presi-
    dency **SI4-3** 1544-1546
  Petersen orders report on information in Ellsberg
    trial emanating from Fielding break-in **II 2**
    1226-1228
  position on impoundment of funds in 1973 **SI12**
    88
  reports from FBI on wiretaps involving Ellsberg
    SI7-2 534, 681, 682-696
  Richardson letter to Senate Foreign Relations
    Committee on legality of wiretaps of **NSI4** 29,
    31, 193, 194-195, 199, 200-201
  SEC transfers ITT documents to **II 2** 1042-1043
  Watergate coverup and Nixon's contacts with
    SUMM I 87-101
  Watergate investigation **SI2** 2, 103, 122
  See also ITT, antitrust suits against

Department of Transportation
  impoundment of funds in 1973 and **SI12** 5

deRoulet, Vincent SIAPP4 12
  Kalmbach on campaign contribution and ambas-
    sadorship commitment to **TW 3** 631-632, 645-
    649

**Detroit, Michigan, as proposed site for Republican
National Convention SI5-1** 450

Detroit News, The **SI7-2** 1137-1138

Devine, Jim
  on inclusion of Erikson exhibits in record **SI5-2**
    934

DEWEY CANYON operation SI11 274

deYoung, Russell SIAPP2 257-262
  *See also U.S. v. Goodyear Tire and Rubber Com-
    pany and Russell deYoung*

Diamond International Corporation SIAPP2 253-256
  *See also U.S. v. Diamond International Corpora-
    tion and Ray Dubrowin*

Dibble, Robert L. SIAPP2 323
  *See also U.S. v. George Steinbrenner III, and the
    American Shipbuilding Company*

Dickstein, Sidney SIAPP2 12-17
  See also U.S. v. Ehrlichman, et al

Diem cables II 2 783; **RHJC** 36; **SUMM I** 37; **SI7-2**
    558-559, 1029-1030, 1031-1079
  Colson states he did not tell Silbert about **TW 3**
    469, 514-515

Hunt on **SI5-2** 781
Hunt's fabrication of **II 2** 1173-1174
material in Hunt's safe on **SI7-3** 1559
Mitchell on **TW 2** 192-193
in status report of House Judiciary Committee
  Impeachment Inquiry staff **II 3** 2227
withheld from FBI by Dean **SI2** 2, 43, 415, 419

Dillow, Konrad C. TW 3 45

Dirksen, Everett
  statements that he was briefed on MENU opera-
    tions **SI11** 61-62, 63, 315-316, 319-321

Dirty tricks SI7-2 526, 575, 576
  Colson on Nixon's comments on **TW 3** 268
  Ehrlichman on **SI4-1** 516-517
  Hunt on **SI7-3** 1482-1484
  Magruder gives Ehrlichman names of White
    House personnel involved in **SI4-2** 818-819
  newspaper disclosures on **SI7-4** 1617, 1657, 1658-
    1675
  Nixon-Ehrlichman-Haldeman discussion on **SI4-2**
    795-796
  in status report of House Judiciary Committee
    Impeachment Inquiry staff **II 3** 2227
  talking paper from Strachan to Mitchell on
    SIAPP4 42
  See also Segretti, Donald

Dita Beard matter II 2 1003, 1025, 1026-1027; **II 3**
    1757-1771, 1773; **NSI2** 122
  Colson and **TW 3** 454
  Colson on **TW 3** 250-253, 513-514
  Hunt states he was not aware of any role Liddy
    played in Beard's departure from Washington
    NSI2 13, 153, 154
  investigations of **NSI2** 16, 189, 190-202
  Liddy informs LaRue and Mardian about **SI3-1** 3,
    87, 88-95; **TW 1** 197; **II 2** 778
  McLaren on **NSI2** 126
  Mitchell on learning about from LaRue and
    Mardian **SI3-1** 102, 105
  See also ITT, antitrust suits against; ITT matter;
    St. Clair, James D., presentation of evidence in
    behalf of Nixon on ITT matter

Dixon, William P. SUMM I 1
  discussion on leaked memos by **II 2** 1325-1331
  memos obtained by press and **II 2** 1303

DNC v. *McCord* depositions
  Ehrlichman **SI4-1** 23, 445, 468-470
  Haldeman **SI4-1** 19, 374-382

Doar, John II 2 844-846; **SIAPP1** 70, 71, 75, 79-80;
    SUMM I 1
  on access of House Judiciary Committee Impeach-
    ment Inquiry to materials of legal staff **II 1** 62-
    64, 87-88
  on accuracy of White House logs **II 2** 874
  on Acree's role at IRS and general organization
    of IRS **II 2** 1274-1275
  on analogy between House Judiciary Committee
    Impeachment Inquiry and grand jury proceed-
    ing **II 1** 222, 242-243
  announces serving of subpoena to Nixon **II 2** 971
  on appeal from Sirica's ruling on turning Grand
    Jury materials over to House Judiciary Commit-
    tee Impeachment Inquiry **II 2** 225-226
  on Background Information to presentation of evi-
    dentiary material on Watergate coverup to

House Judiciary Committee Impeachment Inquiry II 1 554-560
on background and organization of House Judiciary Committee Impeachment Inquiry legal staff II 1 55-58
biography of II 3 2143
briefing on progress of Impeachment Inquiry II 1 205-207
on Byrne's qualifications for post of FBI Director II 2 1224
on calling witnesses before House Judiciary Committee Impeachment Inquiry II 3 1633, 1634, 1646-1647
on classified information on IRS information passed to Dean II 2 1301-1302
on completion date for House Judiciary Committee Impeachment Inquiry II 1 13-14
on confidentiality of evidentiary material presented to House Judiciary Committee Impeachment Inquiry II 1 581, 582, 637
on constitutional vs. statutory crime SUMM I 11
on conversations with St. Clair II 1 189
correspondence with St. Clair on materials requested by House Judiciary Committee Impeachment Inquiry II 1 170-190
on coverup of Fielding break-in II 2 711-717
on crime of conspiracy and Watergate coverup II 3 1932-1934
on crimes committed by Nixon SUMM I 14
on dealings with St. Clair II 1 236
on Dennis' motion for House Judiciary Committee Impeachment Inquiry filing amici curiae briefs for Nixon's materials II 2 933
Dennis's criticism of his letter to St. Clair requesting materials for House Judiciary Committee Impeachment Inquiry II 1 210-211
and discussion on legal questions involved in White House staff members obtaining IRS information II 2 1271-1275
and discussion on procedures for House Judiciary Committee Impeachment Inquiry II 1 255-278, 281-304
discussion with Hogan on Minority of House Judiciary Committee Impeachment Inquiry representation during interviews with witnesses II 1 96-97
discussion with House Judiciary Committee Impeachment Inquiry on invitation by Sirica to attend proceeding on sealed material from Watergate Grand Jury II 1 134-148
discussions with St. Clair on materials requested by House Judiciary Committee Impeachment Inquiry II 1 205-208
on Dorothy Hunt's death II 3 2000
on dropping investigation of some grounds for impeachment of Nixon II 1 266
on efforts to cover up Hunt's link to White House II 1 593-597, 600-605
on efforts to obtain materials from Jaworski II 1 106-115
on Ehrlichman's taping of conversations II 2 747
on elimination of investigation of tax fraud from House Judiciary Committee Impeachment Inquiry II 1 362-363
on erasure on Nixon tape of first Haldeman-Nix-

on discussion after Watergate SUMM I 8-9
on erasure on Nixon tape of June 20, 1972 meeting II 1 607
on FBI activities overseas II 2 1112
on FBI files on Sullivan's wiretapping of Kraft II 2 1112
on FBI Watergate investigation II 1 594-596, 680-695
on handling of classified material on domestic surveillance II 2 1089-1090
on House Judiciary Committee Impeachment Inquiry access to information of Joint Committee on Taxation II 1 68
on House Judiciary Committee Impeachment Inquiry approach to evidence II 3 1976-1977
and House Judiciary Committee Impeachment Inquiry discussion on Nixon's noncompliance with subpoena II 1 409-440
on House Judiciary Committee Impeachment Inquiry procedures for taking depositions II 1 229-230, 233-234
on House Judiciary Committee Impeachment Inquiry receiving two versions of Ehrlichman's handwritten notes II 3 1884-1885, 1917
on Hunt's actions after Watergate arrests in presentation to House Judiciary Committee Impeachment Inquiry II 1 587
on impeachment and tax evasion II 3 1458-1459
on including St. Clair's oral presentation in House Judiciary Committee Impeachment Inquiry record II 3 1915-1916
on indictment of Colson and Ehrlichman II 2 1426-1427
on interview with Byrne II 2 1208-1209, 1219-1221, 1222-1223, 1241
on interview with Kleindienst II 2 1413-1416
introduces staff members to House Judiciary Committee Impeachment Inquiry II 1 552, 586-587
on investigation of bombing of Cambodia in House Judiciary Committee Impeachment Inquiry II 1 368-373
on investigation of illegal campaign contributions and activities in House Judiciary Committee Impeachment Inquiry II 1 367
on investigation of milk fund contributions in House Judiciary Committee Impeachment Inquiry II 1 375-376
on IRS audit of Rebozo II 2 1300
on IRS Code pertaining to deductions for gift of papers II 3 1470-1471, 1508-1509
on IRS policy of delaying sensitive inquiries until after elections II 2 1287-1290
on issuing subpoenas to Nixon II 1 297-298, 312, 326, 333, 644-648, 650, 651-652, 655, 659, 660, 663-664, 665-666; II 2 1150
on Jaworski's material II 1 67
on Jaworski's staff examining White House files II 1 211-212
on judicial review of impeachment articles II 1 69
on justification memorandum on subpoenas for additional Nixon tapes and materials II 2 945-946, 947
on lack of required material from White House II 2 843-844

presentation of summary of evidentiary material to House Judiciary Committee Impeachment Inquiry **II 3** 1925-1936, 1958-1973

presentation to House Judiciary Committee Impeachment Inquiry of draft articles on impeachment of Nixon **SUMM I** 2-14

on procedures for House Judiciary Committee Impeachment Inquiry **II 1** 5-6, 7

on procedures for interviews, depositions, and interrogatories **II 1** 98-99

on procedures for legal definition of grounds for impeachment **II 1** 72-73

on procedures for taking depositions **II 1** 241

on projected date for completion of House Judiciary Committee Impeachment Inquiry **II 1** 151-152

on purpose of presentation on IRS **II 2** 1259

on relationship with Joint Committee on Internal Revenue Taxation **II 1** 95-96

on relevance of line of questioning of Mitchell **TW 2** 145

report on his appearance with Jenner before Sirica **II 1** 161-168

and report to House Judiciary Committee Impeachment Inquiry on meeting with St. Clair **II 1** 79-84, 99-100

on reported difficulty of locating tapes in White House **II 1** 217-218

on retaining Folsom as expert on taxation **II 3** 1495, 1499, 1518-1519

on right of judicial review in Impeachment Inquiry **II 1** 12-13

on right of Minority of House Judiciary Committee Impeachment Inquiry to subpoena witnesses **II 1** 27-28

on rules for Impeachment Inquiry staff **II 1** 129-130

on rules of evidentiary procedures for House Judiciary Committee Impeachment Inquiry **II 1** 476-477, 484, 527, 528

on safeguarding documents in White House **II 1** 295-296

on schedule for presentation of evidence to House Judiciary Committee Impeachment Inquiry **II 2** 771-778, 894, 1148-1152, 1198

on security and control of documents subpoenaed by House Judiciary Committee Impeachment Inquiry **II 1** 85-91

on Senate Select Committee turning over files to House Judiciary Committee Impeachment Inquiry **II 1** 94-95

on source of Ehrlichman's note of approval of Fielding break-in **II 2** 1169-1171

on source of Krogh memo with Ehrlichman's note of approval of Fielding break-in **II 2** 1187

on St. Clair's inquiry to House Judiciary Committee Impeachment Inquiry on procedures for taking depositions **II 1** 208-210

on St. Clair's opinion on impeachable offenses **II 1** 93-94

on St. Clair's participation in House Judiciary Committee Impeachment Inquiry **II 1** 293-295

on St. Clair's presentation in behalf of Nixon **II 3** 1927-1931

on St. Clair's responses to House Judiciary Committee Impeachment Inquiry's requests for materials **II 1** 215

on St. Clair's responses to House Judiciary Committee Impeachment Inquiry's requests for materials from White House **II 1** 244-246

on staff interviews with witnesses on Nixon's gift of Presidential papers **II 3** 1458

statement on scope of Butterfield's testimony **TW 1** 7-8

on status of Ehrlichman's trial for Fielding break-in **II 2** 1178

status report on House Judiciary Committee Impeachment Inquiry **II 1** 105-106, 359-360

on Strachan's destruction of Political Matters Memoranda **II 1** 611-613

on subpoena powers of House Judiciary Committee **II 1** 33, 44-45

on Supreme Court consideration of Nixon's claim of Executive privilege **II 2** 1354

on television reports on White House refusal of materials **II 1** 100

on timing for calling witnesses **II 2** 989

on unreliability of White House transcripts of Nixon tapes **II 2** 844-846

on using subpoena powers of House Judiciary Committee **II 1** 188

on Watergate coverup and CIA **II 1** 619-631

on Watergate coverup and materials in Hunt's safe **II 1** 600-605

on White House decision-making structure **II 2** 1021-1022

on wiretapping by prior administrations **II 2** 1090

See also House Judiciary Committee Impeachment Inquiry, business meetings; House Judiciary Committee Impeachment Inquiry, executive sessions

Doar, John, questioning by
Bittman **TW 2** 2-29
Butterfield **TW 1** 6-62
Colson **TW 3** 184-224, 230-231, 233-241
Dean **TW 2** 220-257
LaRue **TW 1** 225-232, 242-243
Mitchell **TW 2** 124-136, 137-143
O'Brien **TW 1** 124-129, 131-133, 135, 142
Petersen **TW 3** 2-4, 73-87, 95-105

Dobrovir, William A. SI6-1 462

Dobrovir, William A., questioning by
Chotiner **NSI3** 168-170, 172-173; **SI6-1** 415-421, 423; **SI6-2** 751-753
Hillings **NSI3** 97-106
Kalmbach **NSI3** 176-178, 180-191; **SI6-1** 92, 222-224
Nelson **NSI3** 43-50; **SI6-2** 699, 700

Dogole, S. Harrison
on enemies list **SI8** 75, 109

Dole, Robert SIAPP1 19; **SIAPP4** 50, 52, 60, 79, 91; **SI1** 88; **SI2** 2, 304; **SI5-1** 455, 466; **SI5-2** 586
in "LH" note to Timmons **SI5-1** 477
meeting with Nixon, Haldeman, and Timmons on site of Republican National Convention **SI5-2** 576-577
memo from Good, on San Diego as site of Republican National Convention **SI5-2** 486, 561, 578-581

Dole, Robert *(Continued)*
    and milk producers' contributions **SI6-1** 302, 303; **SI6-2** 497, 498
    on public reaction to Watergate **SI9-1** 136
    and San Diego as possible site for Republican National Convention **SI5-2** 575

Domenici, Pete SI1 80, 85

Domestic Council SIAPP4 31; **SI1** 83
    Ehrlichman memo to members on antitrust policy **SI5-1** 23, 393, 396-397
    wiretapping of White House aide on staff of **SI7-1** 12, 259, 260-278

Domestic intelligence
    interagency coordination of, in Huston memo to Haldeman **SI7-1** 442
    Nixon appoints ad hoc committee to study **SI7-1** 22, 275, 376-382
    White House responsibility for, transferred from Huston to Dean **SI7-1** 28, 487, 488-496

Domestic Intelligence Division
    wiretapping of White House staff and **SI7-1** 269-270

Dominican Republic
    Donald Nixon's visit to, decision to wiretap and **SI7-1** 509-513

Dominick, Peter SIAPP1 19; **SI6-2** 955

Donley, Owen SI2 2, 303

Donohue, Harold D. SUMM I 1
    on attorney-client privilege and Bittman's answers to St. Clair **TW 2** 30-31
    on calling witnesses before House Judiciary Committee Impeachment Inquiry **II 3** 1639
    on campaign contributions by predecessors of AMPI **II 2** 1085-1086
    as chairman of House Judiciary Committee Impeachment Inquiry executive session **TW 2** 79-98; **TW 3** 693-744
    on confidentiality of evidentiary material presented to House Judiciary Committee Impeachment Inquiry **II 1** 545
    on derivation of rules for procedures for handling Impeachment Inquiry materials **II 1** 116-117
    on issuing subpoenas to Nixon **II 1** 650
    motion limiting debate on discussion on issuing subpoenas to Nixon **II 1** 308
    motion to subpoena Nixon for materials requested by House Judiciary Committee Impeachment Inquiry **II 1** 306-307
    on nature of House Judiciary Committee Impeachment Inquiry and St. Clair's participation in **II 1** 222
    on Nixon tapes monitored by Haldeman **II 2** 1332
    on Nixon's income tax **II 3** 1529-1530
    on Nixon's noncompliance with House Judiciary Committee Impeachment Inquiry subpoenas **II 1** 437-438
    on Nixon's request for extension of time on answering House Judiciary Committee Impeachment Inquiry subpoena **II 1** 344-345
    on release of House Judiciary Committee Impeachment Inquiry evidentiary material to public **II 3** 1611-1612

resolution on Articles of Impeachment of Nixon **II 3** 2255-2258
    resolution on investigatory powers of House Judiciary Committee Impeachment Inquiry **II 1** 1-2
    on Sirica's invitation to Doar and Jenner **II 1** 145

Donohue, Harold D., questioning by
    Bittman **TW 2** 111
    Butterfield **TW 1** 92-93
    Colson **TW 3** 509-511
    Kalmbach **TW 3** 739-740
    LaRue **TW 1** 272-273
    Mitchell **TW 2** 166-168, 192-193

Doolin, Dennis
    statement on clearance by government before bombing sorties in Cambodia or Laos **SI11** 24, 183

Dore, Ann SIAPP4 66, 76-77; **SI1** 49

Dorne, Bernadette SI5-1 324

Dorsen, David M.
    interview with Chotiner **SI6-2** 677, 744-750

Dorsen, David M., questioning by
    Helms **SI2** 2, 382-384
    Kleindienst **SI2** 2, 104, 570-571, 579-580, 1120-1122; **SI3-1** 592-594; **SI4-1** 405; **SI4-2** 866-867, 925, 999; **SI7-4** 1869-1871, 1984-1985
    Petersen **SI7-4** 1979-1980
    Porter **SI3-1** 160-161, 164, 292-293, 504-506
    Strachan **SI7-2** 658-659; **SI7-3** 1365-1367

Dorsen, Norman SI7-2 594

Dougherty, John SIAPP1 65

Douglas, William O.
    attempted impeachment of **II 1** 261, 262, 445-446
    statement in *New York Times Co.* v. *U.S.* **SI7-2** 595

Downing, C.F.
    memo to Conrad on Mitchell's signatures on documents authorizing wiretaps on government officials and newsmen **SI7-1** 4, 157, 168

Drinan, Robert F. SUMM I 1
    on calling witnesses before House Judiciary Committee Impeachment Inquiry **II 3** 1649, 1652
    on Caulfield memo on Walters **II 2** 1264
    on criteria for excising material from Nixon tapes **II 2** 844-846
    dissenting views supporting proposed Article of Impeachment on secret bombing of Cambodia **RHJC** 323-328
    on Doar-Jenner interview with Byrne **II 2** 1241
    on effects of impoundment of funds **II 2** 1319-1320
    on House Judiciary Committee Impeachment Inquiry issuing subpoenas to Nixon **II 3** 1537, 1549
    on impoundment of funds by Nixon Administration **II 2** 1310-1311
    on investigation of bombing of Cambodia in House Judiciary Committee Impeachment Inquiry **II 1** 368-369
    on IRS policy of delaying sensitive inquiries until after elections **II 2** 1285-1286, 1287-1290
    on issuing subpoenas to Nixon **II 1** 318, 644, 658-659

on legal aspects of impoundment of funds **II 2** 1316-1317

on legal challenges to impoundment of funds by Nixon Administration **II 2** 1305-1306

on mail on impeachment **II 1** 76

motion for subpoena for items not delivered by St. Clair **II 1** 183, 184-185

on Nixon-Petersen relationship **II 3** 2028-2029, 2030

on Nixon's alleged approval of Fielding break-in **II 2** 1165

on Nixon's discussion on Executive privilege with Richardson **II 2** 1337

on Nixon's income tax **II 3** 1515-1516

on Nixon's noncompliance with House Judiciary Committee Impeachment Inquiry subpoenas **II 2** 914-915

objection to conclusions in St. Clair's presentation of evidence in behalf of Nixon **II 3** 1736

on obtaining materials from Jaworski **II 1** 111-112

on procedures for House Judiciary Committee Impeachment Inquiry **II 1** 382-383, 389-390, 391, 392-393, 397, 398

on release of House Judiciary Committee Impeachment Inquiry evidentiary material to public **II 3** 1588

on rules of evidentiary procedures for House Judiciary Committee Impeachment Inquiry **II 1** 487-488

on Sirica's invitation to Doar and Jenner **II 1** 143-144

on St. Clair's opinion on impeachable offenses **II 1** 93-94

on St. Clair's participation in House Judiciary Committee Impeachment Inquiry **II 1** 238-239

on subpoena powers of House Judiciary Committee **II 1** 36-37

supplemental views on proposed Article of Impeachment on secret bombing of Cambodia **RHJC** 307-312

on transcripts of Nixon tapes used by St. Clair in his presentation of evidence in behalf of Nixon **II 3** 1747-1748

on Waldie's motion on hearing testimony of witnesses in executive session **II 3** 1874-1875

on Wiggins' amendment to subpoena to Nixon **II 2** 952-953

withdraws motion to subpoena White House materials **II 1** 190

Drinan, Robert F., questioning by
Bittman **TW 2** 94-95
Butterfield **TW 1** 108-110
Colson **TW 3** 481-482, 488
Dean **TW 2** 334-335
Kalmbach **TW 3** 727-728, 738-739
LaRue **TW 1** 260
Mitchell **TW 2** 196-197, 198-199
O'Brien **TW 1** 163-164
Petersen **TW 3** 132-134

Drumm, Hugo
letter to Gemmill on report on study of subdivision of Nixon's San Clemente property **SI10** 538-552

letters to Blech on subdivision of Nixon's San Clemente property **SI10** 523-537

qualifications of **SI10** 549-552

Dubrowin, Ray SIAPP2 253-256
See also U.S. v. *Diamond International Corporation and Ray Dubrowin*

Dudman, Dick SI7-2 711

Dugan, Patrick SIAPP4 5, 11

Dulles, Allen
Nixon on **SIAPP3** 79-80

"Dump Nixon" drive SI8 74, 108, 119

Duncan, Miss NSI1 74-75

Dunigan, Elizabeth II 2 1088

Dwinell, Lane SIAPP4 1, 18, 40

Dyson, Charles
on enemies list **SI8** 73, 107, 119

Dzu, Nho SI7-2 1036

Eagleton, Thomas F. SIAPP4 127, 128

East, Sherrod E.
and conflicts on date of Newman's visit to National Archives **SI10** 5-6, 91-94

memo of May 27, 1969 noting that most of Nixon's papers delivered to National Archives are not yet deeded to U.S. **SI10** 8, 170-173

Eastland, James O.
efforts to obtain ITT documents from Casey **II 2** 1041-1042

informed by Jaworski that Nixon will not cooperate further with Watergate investigation **SI9-2** 560, 935, 936-945

letter from Casey refusing request for ITT documents **SI5-2** 514, 864, 866

letter from Geneen on his discussions with government officials **SI5-1** 135-136

letter from Hoover on FBI locating Beard in Denver hospital **SI5-2** 498, 719, 725

letter from Jaworski on Nixon challenging his right to bring action against him **SI9-2** 575, 1019, 1020-1025

letter from Jaworski summarizing his understanding regarding his independence as Watergate Special Prosecutor **SI9-2** 557, 923, 924-925

letter from Kennedy, Bayh, Hart, Burdick and Tunney requesting ITT files from SEC **SI5-2** 514, 864, 865

and Senate Committee on the Judiciary requests for ITT documents in possession of SEC **SI5-2** 513-514, 863-864, 865-899

St. Clair's statement on Jaworski's letter to **SI9-2** 561, 947, 948-949

Eastland, James O., questioning by
Dean **SI5-2** 769
Gray **SI7-3** 1549
Kleindienst **SI5-2** 678

Eastwood, Clint SIAPP4 121

Eckert, Erhard E. SIAPP2 323
See also U.S. v. *George Steinbrenner III, and the American Shipbuilding Company*

Eckhardt, Bob SI7-2 594

Economic Opportunity Act of 1964
court litigation on impoundment of funds for **SI12** 25-26

Economic Stabilization Act of 1970, and Presidential power to impound funds SI12 38-39, 72-73

Edmisten, Rufus, questioning by
Stans SI3-1 170-171, 254-255; SI1 92, 182; SI2 2, 366-368, 407

Education programs
impoundment of funds for SI12A 23-25

Education of the Handicapped Act
impoundment of funds for sections of SI12 24-25

Edwards, Don SUMM I 1
additional views on Nixon's tax evasion as impeachable offense RHJC 343-347
on calling witnesses before House Judiciary Committee Impeachment Inquiry II 3 1624-1625, 1649, 1652, 1663
dissenting views supporting proposed Article of Impeachment on secret bombing of Cambodia RHJC 323-328
on Ehrlichman meeting with Byrne II 2 1221-1222
on FBI report to Justice Department on wiretapping of Ellsberg II 2 1134-1135
on House Judiciary Committee Impeachment Inquiry receiving two versions of Ehrlichman's handwritten notes II 3 1887
on IRS audits of politically active people in entertainment industry II 2 1280-1281
on IRS policy of postponing sensitive inquiries until after elections II 2 1289
on ITT's campaign contribution to Nixon re-election campaign II 2 1002
on leaked Dixon memos II 2 1326-1327
on legality of wiretapping II 2 1090
on Nixon's income tax II 3 1512
on Nixon's noncompliance with House Judiciary Committee Impeachment Inquiry subpoenas II 1 444-445; II 2 904-905, 908, 927
on Nixon's request for extension of time on answering House Judiciary Committee Impeachment Inquiry subpoena II 1 351-352
on opening evidentiary presentations of House Judiciary Committee Impeachment Inquiry II 2 966-967
on procedural rules for handling Impeachment Inquiry material II 1 124
questions authorization of lack of records of Halperin wiretaps at Justice Department II 2 1192
on release of House Judiciary Committee Impeachment Inquiry evidentiary material to public II 3 1583, 1593-1594, 1604-1605
on rules of evidentiary procedures for House Judiciary Committee Impeachment Inquiry II 1 492-493
on Sirica's invitation to Doar and Jenner and hoax telephone call to Ervin II 1 149
on St. Clair asking that House Judiciary Committee Impeachment Inquiry evidence be made public II 3 1456
on St. Clair's participation in House Judiciary Committee Impeachment Inquiry II 1 234, 302, 338-339
statement of additional views on Report of House Judiciary Committee Impeachment Inquiry RHJC 283-286

supplemental views on Report of House Judiciary Committee Impeachment Inquiry RHJC 287-288
on Waldie's motion on hearing testimony of witnesses in executive session II 3 1872
on Woods' list of contributors II 2 1084-1085

Edwards, Don, questioning by
Bittman TW 2 69-70
Colson TW 3 453-454, 511-512
Dean TW 2 296-297
Kalmbach TW 3 703-705
Petersen TW 3 126-128

Edwards, Ed SI1 86

Edwards, Lee SIAPP4 7

Efron, Edith SI7-2 711

Ehrlichman, John D. II 2 1115-1119; SIAPP2 7-28; SIAPP3 39; SI3-2 713, 997, 1135, 1145; SI4-1 3, 107, 108-211; SI4-3 1341; SI5-1 23, 314, 393, 401
and administration's antitrust policy SI5-1 23, 393-401
affidavit on Ellsberg investigation and Fielding break-in SI7-2 555, 981, 999-1001
affidavit on Nixon's role in restraint of publication of Pentagon Papers SI7-2 527, 591, 596-598
affidavit on Pentagon Papers and establishment of Plumbers unit with Young and Krogh as co-chairmen SI7-2 543, 795, 802-811
affidavit on reasons for establishing Plumbers unit NSI4 4, 43, 56-65
affidavit on White House reaction to publication of Pentagon Papers SI7-2 529, 619, 620-623
and Alexander's letter to Jaworski referring IRS investigation of Nixon's tax returns to Grand Jury SI10 403-404
allegedly assigned by Nixon to investigate Watergate II 2 849-850, 851-854
and antitrust suits against ITT SI5-1 164-165; SI5-2 957
appeal by his attorney on Sirica's ruling on turning Grand Jury materials over to House Judiciary Committee Impeachment Inquiry II 1 202
and approval of Fielding break-in II 2 1179-1180, 1182-1183
approves Dean contacting Kalmbach to raise funds for Watergate defendants SI3-1 9, 143, 144-155
asks CIA for assistance for Hunt SUMM I 91
asks Colson to raise money for "Special Project" TW 3 234-235
asks Cushman for assistance for Hunt from CIA SI7-2 538, 727, 728-738
asks Kalmbach to make "plant" on Lawrence O'-Brien II 2 1290-1292
assigned by Nixon to "investigation" of Watergate SUMM I 74-78
assigns Chotiner to milk people SI6-2 683-684
assigns Dean to contact Kalmbach on fundraising for Watergate defendants II 2 727-728
assigns Dean to monitor FBI Watergate investigation for White House SUMM I 37, 44
assigns Krogh to "special" national security project for White House NSI4 9, 85, 86-95
assigns Krogh and Young as co-chairman of Plumbers unit SI7-2 543, 795, 796-814; II 2

1139-1140

assigns Morgan and Krogh to look into desirability of Nixon contributing pre-Presidential papers **SI10** 40

assures Krogh that Hunt is "stable" **II 2** 825-826

attitude toward Ellsberg case **SUMM I** 129-130

authority concerning decisions regarding work and expenditures on Nixons' property at Nixon's San Clemente property **SI12** 99-100

briefing from Dent on North Carolina **SI1** 33

and Byrne's dismissal of charges against Ellsberg **SUMM I** 136

Byrne's statement on meetings with **SI7-4** 1651, 2041, 2042-2043

campaign assignments **SI1** 35

and cancellation of Brookings Institution plan **II 2** 1132

in Casey letter to Colson **SI5-2** 663, 664, 699, 700

and Caulfield **SI1** 41, 42

and Chapin's report on White House involvement with Segretti **SI7-4** 1619, 1681, 1692-1696

Chotiner and **SI6-1** 416, 417

and Chotiner's list of McGovern campaign staff members **II 2** 1269

and Chotiner's relationship with dairy industry representatives **SI6-2** 744-745

and CIA aid to Hunt **SI2** 2, 460, 461-462, 463, 464-465, 653-654

CIA employee affidavit on taped telephone conversation between Cushman and **SI2** 2, 47, 450, 468-470

and CIA psychological profile of Ellsberg **II 2** 1145-1146, 1174; **SI7-2** 550, 897, 898-909

Colson on his belief that he was keeping information away from him **TW 3** 502-503

Colson on instructions from on setting up of Plumbers unit **SI7-2** 824-825

in Colson memo to Haldeman on Kleindienst confirmation hearings **SI5-2** 807

Colson report on White House policy on Watergate investigation to **SI4-3** 1308

Colson reports on his meeting with Bittman to Dean and **TW 3** 313-314

Colson tells Ziegler he should resign **TW 3** 354-355

and Colson's assignment of Hunt to Pentagon Papers investigation for White House **NSI4** 6, 71, 72-74

and Colson's reports on information obtained by Plumbers unit **SI7-2** 546, 829, 830-841

and Colson's and Shapiro's recommendations on handling of Watergate matter **TW 3** 441-442, 444-445

complains to Walters about his "foot-dragging tactics" **II 2** 1285, 1287

and concealment of wiretapping of government officials and newsmen **SUMM I** 134-135

contacts with Geneen **II 2** 1004

contacts with Morgan **SI10** 4, 67-71

conversation with Dean on McCord's letter to Sirica **II 2** 835

conversation with Dean on using Dean as test for Executive privilege **SI3-2** 751

conversation with Gray on events at confirmation hearings **II 2** 782-783

conversation with Kalmbach on amount of money raised for Watergate defendants **SI3-1** 22, 281, 288-289

conversation with Nixon on June 20, 1972 Nixon tape **SI9-2** 529, 619, 620-648

copies of notes obtained from Nixon compared with copies obtained from Special Watergate Prosecutor **SUMM I** 108

copy of Walsh letter to Kleindienst delivered by Merriam to **SI5-1** 15, 283, 305

Cox requests records of items inserted into White House files after April 30, 1973 by **SI9-1** 26, 371, 372-373

criminal liability of discussed by Nixon and Moore **SI7-4** 1644, 1967, 1968-1974

Cushman asks him to restrain Hunt's requests for CIA assistance **II 2** 1179

and Cushman's identification of person requesting CIA assistance for Hunt **SI7-4** 1622, 1719, 1720-1730

and dairy industry contributions **II 2** 1077-1078

Dean denies instruction to conduct Watergate investigation from **SI2** 2, 61, 587, 590-592

Dean discusses Hunt's demands with **TW 2** 246-247, 296-297, 323-324

Dean informs about meetings on Liddy plan **SI2** 2, 168

Dean informs of theory of CIA involvement in Watergate break-in **NSI1** 15, 121, 123

Dean persuades him to call off Brookings Institution burglary **SI7-2** 747

Dean plays recording of Colson-Hunt conversation for **II 2** 752

and Dean Report **SUMM I** 73-74

Dean reports on meeting with Segretti to **SI3-1** 33, 391, 392-403

and Dean-Segretti meeting **II 2** 751-752

Dean on Watergate coverup and **NSI1** 43

and Dean's claim that he discussed Hunt's demands for money with Mitchell **II 2** 796-797

and Dean's efforts to obtain CIA funds for Watergate defendants **SI2** 2, 44, 427, 428-441; **SI3-1** 8, 129, 130-142

and Dean's efforts to retrieve documents connecting Hunt and Liddy to Fielding break-in from Justice Department **SI7-4** 1732

and Dean's instructions to Liddy to tell Hunt to leave country **SI2** 2, 20, 203, 209-210

and Dean's investigation of Watergate break-in **SI2** 2, 14, 143, 146, 153

and Dean's request for IRS audits of McGovern campaign staff members and contributors **SI8** 25, 237, 238-271

and delay of FBI interview of Chenow **SI7-3** 1205, 1569, 1570-1574

denies he investigated Watergate **SUMM I** 77

denies knowledge about Magruder's planned testimony before Watergate Grand Jury **II 2** 749

deposition in *DNC* v. *McCord* **SI4-2** 561, 717, 719-721

deposition in *DNC* v. *McCord*, on discussion with Strachan on political intelligence-gathering **SI4-2** 571, 881, 882-890

directs Dean to tell Ziegler to deny wiretapping of White House staff members and newsmen **SI7-4** 1625, 1741, 1742-1748

Ehrlichman, John D. *(Continued)*

directs Fielding to report on Dean's dismissal by law firm **SI4-1** 25, 471, 472 474

discusses Colson's forthcoming testimony with Nixon **SUMM I** 85

discusses Executive clemency with Nixon **SUMM I** 46

discusses his forthcoming testimony with Nixon **SUMM I** 84-85

discussion with Haldeman on Hunt's demands for money **SI3-2** 1124-1127

discussion with Nixon on blaming Mitchell for Watergate **SUMM I** 74-77

discussion with Nixon on Executive clemency for Hunt **SI3-2** 892-893

discussion with Nixon on Executive clemency for Watergate burglars **II 2** 732-737

discussion with Young on Fielding break-in and possibility of Hunt's disclosure of **SI7-4** 1633, 1841, 1842-1858

discussions with Byrne on possible appointment as FBI director **SI7-4** 1636, 1879, 1880-1889

discussions with Colson on Fielding break-in **TW 3** 236-237

discussions with Ervin on ground rules for testimony of White House staff members **SIAPP1** 12

discussions with Krogh on Hunt's demands for money **II 2** 1202-1204, 1205

in document from Plumbers unit file on Congressional investigation of Pentagon Papers **SI7-2** 834

does not recall signing of deed of Nixon's pre-Presidential papers in April of 1969 **SI10** 112

and efforts to cover up Hunt's link to White House **II 1** 593-594

and efforts to determine Hunt's status at White House after Watergate break-in **TW 3** 256-258, 260-261

and efforts to prevent granting of immunity to Dean **II 2** 857, 884-885, 886

electronic surveillance of member of his staff **SUMM I** 125

and Ellsberg case **SI4-3** 1107, 1501, 1503

and Ellsberg case, Nixon-Moore discussion on **SI4-3** 1107, 1501, 1503

and evidence of existence of taped conversations with Nixon **II 1** 412

and Executive clemency offers to Hunt **SUMM I** 63-65, 66

fair trial for, and release of House Judiciary Committee Impeachment Inquiry evidentiary material to public **II 3** 1592

false statements to Grand Jury on Fielding break-in **SIAPP2** 12-17

false statements on Pentagon Papers investigation to FBI **SIAPP2** 11-12

and FBI delivery of files and logs of wiretaps on Kraft to White House **SI7-2** 945, 947

and FBI interview of Chenow **SI2** 2, 51

FBI interview on FBI delivery of files and logs of wiretaps of Kraft to White House **SI7-2** 552, 925, 939-944

in FBI interview with Haldeman on wiretaps on White House staff members **SI7-1** 276, 278

FBI interviews on Fielding break-in **SI7-4** 1648, 2015, 2016-2018; **II 2** 1234-1236

and FBI reports on wiretapping **II 2** 1114

and FBI summaries of letters reporting on surveillance of three members of White House staff **SI7-1** 280

and FBI tapes of wiretaps on members of White House staff **SI7-1** 283

and FBI Watergate investigation **SUMM I** 40-41

and Fielding break-in **SI3-2** 941-943; **SI7-2** 555, 981, 982-1003

and Fielding's trip to London to get Chenow **SI2** 2, 518

first meeting with Nixon after Watergate arrests **SUMM I** 37-38

Geneen and **SI5-1** 132

Halperin wiretaps in safe of **II 2** 1192-1193

handwritten notes of certain meetings with Nixon **SIAPP3** 89-263

Higby informs Strachan that Watergate will by handled by **SI2** 2, 12, 131, 132

and hiring of Hunt **TW 3** 206-207; **SI7-2** 679

and hiring of Ulasewicz **SI7-1** 349; **II 2** 1111

House Judiciary Committee Impeachment Inquiry discussion on receiving two versions of handwritten notes of **II 3** 1884-1887, 1917

House Judiciary Committee Impeachment Inquiry discussion on subpoenaing **II 2** 981-992

House Judiciary Committee Impeachment Inquiry subpoenas for specified materials related to conversations between Nixon and **SI9-2** 568, 577, 977, 978-982, 1031, 1032-1036

House Judiciary Committee transcript of meeting with Nixon, Dean, and Haldeman on March 21, 1973 **TPC** 131-146

House Judiciary Committee transcript of meeting with Nixon, Dean, Haldeman, and Mitchell on March 22, 1973 **TPC** 147-186

Hunt denies saying he did "seamy things" for **SI3-2** 910-911

and Hunt-Liddy recommendation of break-in at Fielding's home **II 2** 1182

and Hunt-Liddy report on Fielding break-in **SI7-3** 1186, 1301, 1302-1332

and Hunt memo on Boudin **II 2** 1175

and Hunt's assignment to investigate publication of Pentagon Papers **SI7-2** 533, 675, 676-679

and Hunt's blackmail attempts **SI7-4** 1630, 1821, 1822-1828

and Hunt's connection with White House at time of Watergate arrests **SUMM I** 36

and Hunt's letter to Colson **SI3-1** 38-39, 455-456, 457-474

and Hunt's plan on "Neutralization of Ellsberg" **SI7-2** 913

Hunt's threats against **SI3-2** 1020-1021

and hush money **II 2** 795-796; **SIAPP1** 49; **SUMM I** 52

and Huston plan, *see* House Judiciary Committee Impeachment inquiry, presentation of evidence on Huston plan

identified by Colby as person arranging for Hunt to get assistance from CIA **II 2** 712-716

and improvements to Nixon's Key Biscayne and San Clemente properties **SI12** 106-107, 110-113, 115-116, 134, 137, 140-141, 151, 152, 172;

Ehrlichman, John D. *(Continued)*

143, 147-152, 153-162

memos to Mitchell on antitrust suits against ITT **SI5-2** 508-509, 525, 526, 803-804, 828, 829

memos to Morgan with questions on Nixon's 1969 tax without mention of gift of pre-Presidential papers **SI10** 8-9, 177-183

memos to Nixon on antitrust policy **SI5-2** 508-509, 803-804, 830-833

Merriam and **SI5-2** 814

and Mexican checks **SI2** 2, 97

Mitchell cancels meeting with Nixon after talking to on April 14, 1973 **TW 2** 141-142, 187

Mitchell on discussion of Watergate break-in with **TW 2** 217

nature of papers he instructs Young to put into Nixon's file **II 2** 1339-1342

New York Times on Dean's testimony on his involvement in Watergate coverup **SI9-1** 18, 313, 316

and newspaper stories on Segretti's activities **SI7-4** 1617, 1657, 1658-1675

Nixon announces resignation of **SIAPP1** 13, 15-16; **SI9-1** 5, 131, 132-137

Nixon assigns to Watergate investigation to replace Dean **SI4-1** 21, 23-24, 427, 429, 445-446, 448

Nixon-Dean discussion on indictability of **SI3-2** 1054-1057

Nixon-Dean discussion of possible resignation of **SI4-3** 73-77, 1294-1295

Nixon directs Haldeman to meet with on White House concern over possible disclosure of covert CIA or Plumbers activities **SI7-3** 1202, 1533, 1534-1540

Nixon on guilt or innocence of **SIAPP1** 65-66

Nixon informs him about discussions with Petersen **II 2** 883

Nixon instructs him to tell Magruder and Mitchell to go before Grand Jury **NSI1** 32, 207, 208-210

Nixon meeting with attorney for **SI4-3** 1108, 1511, 1515-1530

in Nixon-Moore discussion on Ellsberg case **II 2** 1232

Nixon-Petersen discussion of effects of Magruder's indictment on **SUMM I** 95

Nixon-Petersen discussion of evidence against **SI4-3** 1089, 1223, 1224-1249; **NSI** 1, 33, 211, 213-216

Nixon-Petersen discussion of possible resignation of **SI4-3** 1128-1129, 1402; **TW3** 110-112, 123-124

Nixon re-election campaign responsibilities of **SUMM I** 27

Nixon on relationship with Gray during FBI Watergate investigation **SIAPP1** 9

Nixon reports on meetings with Petersen to **SUMM I** 92, 96

Nixon on resignation of **SI3-2** 1242; **SI4-3** 1521-1523, 1527, 1535-1537

Nixon-Rogers discussion of possible resignation of **II 2** 886

Nixon on role played in Watergate investigation **SIAPP1** 45

Nixon tells him to urge Dean to go to Grand Jury **NSI1** 30, 199, 200-201

Nixon on testimony of **SIAPP1** 74

Nixon wants meeting between Dean, Haldeman, Mitchell and **NSI1** 24, 165, 166-167

and Nixon's assurances of leniency to Magruder and Mitchell **SUMM I** 66-67

and Nixon's efforts to cover up meaning of conversation with Dean on March 21, 1973 on hush money **SUMM I** 60-62

and Nixon's efforts to prevent Dean from getting immunity **SUMM I** 96-99

Nixon's false statements on Watergate investigation of, in Article of Impeachment I **RHJC** 84-88

and Nixon's gift of Presidential papers **SUMM I** 173-174

and Nixon's instructions to Mardian on FBI files and logs of 1969-71 wiretaps **SI7-2** 541, 775, 776-788

Nixon's opinion of **SIAPP1** 49

and Nixon's order for new Watergate investigation on March 21, 1973 **SIAPP1** 51-52

and Nixon's possible lack of knowledge of Watergate coverup, in Minority of House Judiciary Committee Impeachment Inquiry views on Articles of Impeachment **RHJC** 391

Nixon's television announcement of resignation of **SI4-3** 1119, 1657, 1658-1659

note of approval on Young's memo on plan for Fielding break-in **II 2** 1169-1173

notes of April 15, 1973 **SI4-2** 571, 871, 981-984

notes on April 14, 1973 meeting with Magruder on his disclosures to U.S. Attorneys **SI4-2** 564, 799, 803-809

notes on conversations with Krogh **SIAPP3** 250-260

notes on Fielding break-in in file of **SIAPP3** 239-242

notes on meeting with Colson and Shapiro on April 13, 1973 **SI4-2** 556, 599, 603-606

notes on meeting with Kalmbach on hush money **SI4-1** 34, 531, 536

notes on meeting with Paul O'Brien **SI4-1** 33, 508, 519-528

O'Brien informs him about payments to Hunt **TW 1** 145-146, 153-154, 159-160, 174

O'Brien's reasons for telling him about Hunt's demands for money **TW 1** 161-162

obstruction of Ellsberg trial by **RHJC** 172

and offer of position of FBI Director to Byrne **SUMM I** 138-140

and opening of Hunt's safe **TW 2** 235-236

opinion of Ellsberg **II 2** 1122

orders Hunt's safe drilled open **SUMM I** 37; **SI2** 2, 19, 189, 190-191, 192

on organizational chart from files of Special Investigations Unit **SI7-2** 814

partial transcript of taped telephone conversation with Cushman on CIA aid to Hunt **SI2** 2, 47, 450, 467

and Pentagon Papers matter **II 2** 1121

Petersen on involvement in Watergate of **SI4-2** 980-981

Petersen and Kleindienst inform Nixon of his involvement in Watergate **II 2** 878-879 and Petersen meeting with Geneen and Merriam on antitrust matters **SI5-1** 14, 277, 279, 281

Petersen reports on meeting with ITT officials to **SI5-1** 269

Petersen tells Nixon he might be indictable **SIAPP1** 45

Petersen's memo on evidence against **SUMM I** 91

Petersen's notes on Watergate coverup involvement of **SI4-2** 577, 974, 1001; **SI4-3** 1225,

in Petersen's report to Nixon on Watergate Grand Jury testimony **SI4-3** 1299, 1300-1301

and platform for 1972 Republican Convention **SIAPP4** 1-2, 134

Plumbers unit and **SIAPP1** 23; **SI1** 40

and Plumbers unit projects related to discrediting of Ellsberg **TW 3** 213-223

and political intelligence-gathering on Democratic party candidates **TW 3** 255-256

and political use of wiretapping information received from FBI **II 2** 1113-1114; **SI7-1** 20, 359, 360-368

and preparations for Fielding break-in **SI7-2** 1170

in Presidential party on Nixon's trip to Europe in 1969 **SI10** 4, 74, 75-76

and prevention of Stans' scheduled Watergate Grand Jury appearance **SUMM I** 45

prior association with Nixon **RHJC** 12

and proposal of Byrne as FBI director **SI7-4** 1635, 1867, 1868-1877

in questions for Nixon from Joint Committee on Internal Revenue Taxation on Nixon's 1969 income tax return **SI10** 417

and reaffirmation of AMPI $2 million pledge **SI6-2** 476, 727, 729-734

receives FBI wiretap reports on government employees and newsmen **SI7-1** 372-373

recommendations for Convention appointments **SIAPP4** 13

recommendations to McLaren on Antitrust Law and Enforcement Policy paper **SI5-1** 23, 393, 398-400

refuses to discuss payments to Liddy with Sloan **SI3-1** 6, 115, 116-120

and release of Hunt memo on Boudin **SI7-2** 563, 1125, 1126-1149

and removal of files on Kissinger tapes from FBI to White House **II 2** 1132-1139

and report from Young on plan for Pentagon Papers project **SI7-3** 1181, 1213

and reports from Intelligence Evaluation Committee **SI7-1** 500

reports to Nixon on Higby-Magruder conversation on Magruder's testimony before Watergate Grand Jury **II 2** 865

reports to Nixon on his meeting with Magruder and his attorneys **II 2** 867-868; **SI4-2** 565, 811, 812-828

reports to Nixon on his meeting with Mitchell **II 2** 867

reports to Nixon on Magruder's interview with Watergate Prosecutor **SUMM I** 89

reports to Nixon on Watergate **SI4-1** 475

requests meeting with Dean on April 15, 1973 **SI4-2** 579-580, 1021-1022, 1023-1024, 1027, 1031

resignation of **II 2** 893-894, 1333; **SI4-3** 1117, 1647, 1648-1650

and restraints on Hunt's requests for further aid from CIA **SI7-3** 1182, 1225, 1226-1238

role in Nixon Administration **RHJC** 15-16; **SUMM I** 25

role on White House staff **II 1** 557

second meeting with Byrne in Santa Monica park **SI7-4** 1637, 1891, 1892-1895

and Semer-Dent meeting **SI6-1** 110-111

and Sloan's payments to Liddy **II 2** 722-723

sources of handwritten notes of **SIAPP3** 1-2

and Stans' avoidance of testimony before Watergate Grand Jury **II 1** 695-697

and Stans being excused from Watergate Grand Jury testimony **SI2** 2, 564, 565, 568-569, 570-571

statement on Nixon authorizing any dealings with CIA **II 2** 1130, 1131

statement on Nixon saying Krogh could do whatever was necessary on Ellsberg investigation **II 2** 1161-1169

states that Krogh reported to Nixon **II 2** 1151

subpoenaed notes of, in Article of Impeachment I **RHJC** 131-132

and supervision of Plumbers unit **SI7-2** 651

in taped Cushman-Hunt conversation **SI7-2** 851

in taped Higby-Magruder telephone conversation **SI4-2** 622-623

taped telephone conversation with Colson **TW 3** 344-353

taped telephone conversation with Dean **SI3-2** 696, 777, 778-782

taped telephone conversation with Gray on Gray confirmation hearings and Watergate investigation **SI3-2** 696, 767, 768-776

taped telephone conversation with Kalmbach on fundraising for Watergate defendants **SI3-1** 21, 265, 277-279

taped telephone conversations of **II 2** 747-748, 783-784

taped telephone conversations with Clawson and Colson **II 1** 605-606; **SI2** 2, 20, 203, 212-213

and tapes of Dean-Segretti conversation **SI7-4** 1620, 1697, 1698-1707

tapes telephone conversation with Kalmbach prior to his testimony before Watergate Grand Jury **II 2** 889

telephone call to Cushman for aid to Hunt **II 2** 1128-1131

telephone call to Kleindienst on Nixon's questions about White House staff involvement in Watergate **SI4-1** 20, 399, 400-425

telephone call from Dean to inform him about McCord's letter to Sirica **SI4-1** 6, 235, 236-237

telephone conversation with Casey on SEC subpoenas for ITT documents **SI5-2** 744, 745-746; **II 2** 848-849

telephone conversation with Clawson on Dean's allegations **SI4-3** 1095, 1317, 1320-1324

telephone conversation with Colson on Colson's forthcoming Watergate Grand Jury testimony **SI4-3** 1103, 1443, 1447-1448

telephone conversation with Haldeman after Watergate arrests **SI2** 2, 11, 129, 130

Ehrlichman, John D. *(Continued)*

telephone conversation with Haldeman on problems posed by Watergate break-in for White House **SUMM I** 36

telephone conversation with Kalmbach on hush money **SI4-3** 1110, 1547, 1548-1552

telephone conversation with Kalmbach on Kalmbach's forthcoming Watergate Grand Jury testimony **SI4-3** 1103, 1443, 1444-1446

telephone conversation with Kleindienst on Magruder's information to U.S. Attorneys **SI4-2** 566, 829, 830-842

telephone conversation with Kleindienst on Magruder's Watergate Grand Jury testimony **II 2** 868

telephone conversation with Krogh on Hunt's demands **SI3-2** 708, 951, 960-962; **SI7-4** 1632, 1837, 1838-1839

telephone conversation with Magruder on plan to make full disclosure on Watergate **SI4-3** 1318-1319

telephone conversation with Nixon on Dean's, Magruder's, and Mitchell's forthcoming testimony to Watergate Grand Jury **SI4-1** 36, 543, 544-545

telephone conversation with Nixon on Dean's resignation **SI4-3** 1084, 1131, 1132-1133, 1134

telephone conversation with Nixon on immunity for top White House staff members **SI4-3** 1098, 1387, 1392-1393

telephone conversation with Nixon on Magruder's information to U.S. Attorneys **SI4-2** 468, 851, 852-861

telephone conversation with Nixon on preventing Dean from implicating Haldeman and Ehrlichman **SUMM I** 67

telephone conversation with Richardson on Krogh's information **SI4-3** 1652

telephone conversations with Gray on Hunt's safe **II 2** 881; **SI4-2** 583, 1059, 1060-1080

tells Colson it is okay to meet with Bittman about Hunt **TW 3** 301-302

tells Colson that Nixon told Petersen that Ellsberg matter is classified **TW 3** 237

tells Nixon on March 27, 1973 that no one at White House had prior knowledge of Watergate break-in **NSI1** 29, 195, 196-198

and threatened exposure of Kissinger tapes by *Time* magazine **II 2** 1201

transcript of taped meeting with Nixon and Krogh on SALT talks leak **SI7-2** 548, 863, 867-885

two versions of notes received by House Judiciary Committee Impeachment Inquiry **II 3** 1996-1999

and use of TAPE contribution for Fielding break-in **SI6-2** 832-836

and *Vesco* case **SI3-2** 1037-1038

Washington Star article on his meeting with Byrne **II 2** 1237

Watergate coverup and, in Article of Impeachment I **RHJC** 95-96

Watergate investigation of, in Cates' presentation of summary of evidence to House Judiciary Committee Impeachment Inquiry **II 3** 2018-2019

Watergate investigation of, in Doar's presentation of summary of evidence to House Judiciary Committee Impeachment Inquiry **II 3** 1969, 1970-1971

and White House efforts to obtain CIA money for Watergate defendants **II 2** 723-725

White House meeting on investigation of Ellsberg matter **NSI4** 16, 121, 122-123

and White House task force on Kleindienst hearings **SI5-2** 503, 759, 765

and wiretapping of Donald Nixon **SI7-1** 509-513

and wiretapping of government officials and newsmen in 1969 **SI7-1** 161

and wiretapping and surveillance of Kraft **SUMM I** 125-126; **II 2** 1110-1112, 1113; **SI7-1** 16, 313, 314-324, 356

wiretapping of White House staff and **SI7-1** 269-270

Young informs Malloy that Ellsberg psychological profile was requested by **SI7-2** 560, 1081, 1083

Young memo on meeting with on April 30, 1973 **SI7-4** 1650, 2027, 2037-2038

Young testifies that he gave advance approval to Fielding break-in **II 2** 1369; **SI9-1** 46, 503, 512-516

Young turns over documents from Plumber's file to **II 2** 1206

in Young's discussion with Colson of "California operation" **TW 3** 230-231

See also Nixon tapes; *U.S.* v. *John Ehrlichman, et al*; *U.S.* v. *John N. Mitchell, et al.*

Ehrlichman, John D., cited testimony of SI2 2, 19, 189, 190-191; **SI3-2** 713, 1135, 1138-1141; **SI4-3** 1117, 1647, 1649-16150

on approval of covert operation to examine Fielding's files on Ellsberg **SI7-2** 557, 1007, 1020-1021

on assigning Krogh to "special" national security project **NSI4** 9, 85, 94-95

on assignment of Liddy and Hunt to Plumbers unit **SI7-2** 544, 815, 819-820

on authorizing Liddy to conduct wiretaps in 1971 **SI7-2** 545, 827, 828

claims he does not recall Dean playing tape recorded Hunt-Colson conversation **SI3-1** 34-35, 405-406, 420

on dealings with IRS on O'Brien investigation **SI8** 23, 217, 223-225

on Dean's dismissal by law firm **SI4-1** 25, 471, 474

on Dean's efforts to obtain CIA funds for Watergate defendants **SI3-1** 8, 129, 130-131

on Dean's investigation of Watergate break-in **SI2** 2, 14, 143, 150-153

on Dean's report on Segretti **SI3-1** 33, 391, 398-399

denies approving Fielding break-in during telephone conversation with Krogh and Young **SI7-3** 1183, 1239, 1245

denies Dean informed him of Porter's and Magruder's false stories to Watergate Grand Jury on purpose of CRP payments to Liddy **SI3-1** 24, 297, 308-309

denies he or Nixon had prior knowledge of Watergate break-in **NSI1** 7, 53, 55 denies instructing Dean to tell Hunt to leave country **SI2** 2, 20, 203-210

denies Nixon ever authorized Plumbers unit to use illegal methods **NSI4** 13, 109, 112

denies receiving Dean's memo on "Dealing with Our Political Enemies" **SI8** 9, 95, 101-102

denies recollection of financing of Fielding break-in **SI7-3** 1184, 1247, 1254-1255

denies recollection of telephone call to Cushman requesting CIA aid for Hunt**SI7-2** 538, 727, 733, 734-737

denies seeing Dean memo on *Nader* v. *Butz* **SI6-2** 485, 877, 893-894

on discussion with Haldeman after Watergate arrests **SI2** 2, 11, 129, 130

on discussion with Nixon on possibility of Executive clemency for Watergate defendants **SI3-1** 13, 181, 182-191

on discussions with Byrne **SI7-4** 1636, 1879, 1881-1883

on discussions with Kalmbach on AMPI contribution **SI6-1** 6, 99, 106-108

on dissolution of Plumbers unit **SI7-3** 1193, 1421, 1422

on FBI files and logs of wiretaps on Kraft **SI7-2** 552, 925, 948-949

on FBI files and logs of 1969-71 wiretaps requested by White House **SI7-2** 541, 775, 781-782

on Fielding break-in **SI7-2** 564, 1151, 1166

on hiring of Ulasewicz as investigator for Nixon campaign **SI7-1** 18, 335, 336-342

House Judiciary Committee summary of **SI7-2** 538, 727,738

on Hunt's blackmail attempts **SI7-4** 1630, 1821, 1827-1828

on Hunt's hiring and assignment to study Pentagon Papers **SI7-2** 537, 713, 723-725

on Hunt's letter to Colson **SI3-1** 38-39, 455-456, 462-464

on Hunt's safe and Hunt's status at White House after Watergate arrests **SI2** 2, 18, 166, 173

on Huston plan **SI7-1** 22, 375, 381

on introducing Krogh and Young to Cabinet members and Agency heads **SI7-2** 553, 951, 956

on IRS audit of Lawrence O'Brien **II** 2 1286-1287

on Kalmbach's assignment to raise funds for Watergate defendants **SI3-1** 9, 143, 145-148

on learning about Fielding break-in **NSI4** 20, 137, 138

on learning about Hunt's connection to Watergate break-in **SI2** 2, 8, 117, 118

on MacGregor's telephone conversation with Nixon **SI2** 2, 56, 520

on materials from Hunt's safe **SI2** 2, 52, 501, 504-506

on meeting with Colson and Shapiro for their recommendations on Watergate matter **SI4-2** 555-556, 587-588, 596-597, 598-602

on meeting with Dean and Gray to turn over additional material from Hunt's safe **SI7-3** 1206, 1575, 1579-1581

on meeting with Dean and Haldeman on Dean's forthcoming Watergate Grand Jury testimony **SI4-1** 541-542

on meeting with Dean on contents of Hunt's safe **SI2** 2, 32, 317, 320-325

on meeting with Dean on Hunt's demands **SI3-2** 708, 951, 952-956

on meeting with Haldeman and Kleindienst on Byrne nomination for FBI director **SI7-4** 1635, 1867, 1874-1875

on meeting with Haldeman, Mitchell, and Dean on March 22, 1973 **SI3-2** 718, 1251, 1260-1266, 1268-1269

on meeting with Haldeman and Nixon to report on meeting with Magruder and his attorneys **SI4-2** 565, 811, 812-813

on meeting with Haldeman, Walters, and Helms **SI2** 2, 39, 376, 392-394

on meeting with Kalmbach on hush money **SI4-1** 34, 531, 533-535

on meeting with Kalmbach on legal propriety of fundraising for Watergate defendants **SI3-1** 21, 265, 271-274

on meeting with Krogh on Hunt's forthcoming testimony **SI3-2** 720, 1277, 1280-1281

on meeting with Magruder on his disclosures to U.S. Attorneys **SI4-2** 801-802

on meeting with Mitchell on April 14, 1973 **SI4-2** 561, 717, 724

on meeting with Nixon on forthcoming conference on Watergate break-in **SI2** 2, 61, 587, 588

on meeting with Paul O'Brien on White House involvement in Watergate **SI4-1** 33, 508, 510-518

on meeting with Strachan on April 12, 1973 on Strachan's Watergate Grand Jury testimony **SI4-1** 38, 549, 551

on meetings after Watergate break-in **SI2** 2, 23, 235, 242

on meetings with Haldeman, Dean, and Moore to discuss strategy for Ervin Committee hearings **SI3-1** 48, 535, 545-548

on meetings with Krogh, Young, and Nixon after Fielding break-in **SI7-3** 1187, 1333, 1334

on memo to Colson on "game plan" for Pentagon Papers investigation **SI7-3** 1181, 1213, 1214

on Nixon assigning Dean to Watergate **SI3-1** 52, 597, 612-613

on Nixon instructing him to tell Kleindienst to report all Watergate evidence to President **SI4-1** 18, 347, 350-351

on Nixon wanting Dean to go before Grand Jury **NSI1** 30, 199, 200

on Nixon's approval of Fielding break-in **II** 2 1176-1177

on Nixon's assigning him to Watergate investigation **SI4-1** 23, 445, 464-467, 468-470

on Nixon's requests for information on Watergate and Segretti matter **SI7-4** 1620, 1697, 1702-1703

on Nixon's suspicions about Dean's involvement in Watergate **SI4-1** 23, 445, 469-470

on original reasons for establishing Plumbers unit **NSI4** 4, 43, 44-46

on plan to burglarize Brookings Institution **SI7-2** 539, 739, 748-749

on Plumbers unit **SI7-2** 530, 649, 654

on Plumbers unit investigation of Ellsberg **SI7-2** 555, 981, 989-998

on Plumbers unit investigation of SALT leaks **SI7-2** 549, 887, 890

on Plumbers unit's efforts to encourage Congress to hold hearings on Pentagon Papers matter

duration of wiretapping of National Security Council staff members **SI7-1** 8, 201, 202-221

Ehrlichman on wiretaps conducted by Liddy in 1971 **SI7-2** 545, 827, 828

in Ehrlichman-Krogh discussions **SIAPP3** 260

of Ellsberg, FBI memos to and from Assistant Attorney General on **SI7-2** 542, 789, 790-794

of Ellsberg, memos to Byrne on **SI7-4** 1652, 2045, 2046-2055

of F. Donald Nixon **SUMM I** 127, 128

FBI files and logs of wiretaps on Kraft delivered to White House **SI7-2** 552, 925, 926-949

FBI files and logs of wiretaps ordered by White House **SI7-2** 540, 755, 756-773

files on Kissinger tapes transferred from FBI to White House **II 2** 1132-1139, 1157-1158, 1192-1193

Fulbright's request for House Judiciary Committee Impeachment Inquiry materials on Kissinger's role in 1969-1971 wiretaps **II 2** 1323-1324; **II 3** 1532

government affidavits denying Ellsberg coverage by **SI7-3** 1199, 1503, 1504-1511

of government employees, leaks on bombing of Cambodia and **SI7-1** 14, 291, 292-300

of government employees, results of **SI7-1** 15, 301, 302-312

government files affidavit stating there had been no electronic surveillance of Ellsberg **II 2** 1190-1192

of government officials and newsmen in 1969, concealment of records of **SUMM I** 134-136

of government officials and newsmen in 1969, Haig and **SI7-1** 189, 190

of government officials and newsmen in 1969, illegality of **SUMM I** 124-125

of government officials and newsmen in 1969, Mitchell and **SI7-1** 4, 5, 157, 158-172, 173-180

of government officials and newsmen in 1969, procedures for filing and copies **SI7-1** 6, 181, 182-190

Gray's denial that FBI wiretapped newsmen and White House officials **SI7-4** 1627, 1755, 1756-1773

and *Halperin* v. *Kissinger* **SI7-1** 17, 325, 326-333

House Judiciary Committee Impeachment Inquiry presentation of evidence on domestic surveillance **II 2** 1088-1114

Huston memo to Haldeman on recommendations on **SI7-1** 438-439

impeachment theories and **MMFL** 100-116

and intelligence collection against communist intelligence and, in Huston plan **SI7-1** 405

and intelligence collection against revolutionary groups, in Huston plan **SI7-1** 410

by Johnson and Kennedy administrations **II 2** 1090

Justice Department asks FBI for records on Ellsberg **II 2** 1126

of Kraft **SUMM I** 125-126, 128; **SI7-1** 16, 313, 314-324

of Kraft, Cox's request for White House records on **SI9-1** 47, 517, 518-521

of Kraft, Nixon-Dean discussion of **SI7-4** 1641, 1941, 1942-1945

of Laird's assistant **SI7-1** 299-300, 327

legal authority for wiretaps by government **NSI4** 30, 31, 197, 199, 200-201

in Liddy plan **SI1** 9, 53, 56-57, 59-60, 65, 67, 72, 132-133

in Magruder's disclosures to U.S. Attorneys **SI4-2** 564, 799, 800-809

in Magruder's Watergate Grand Jury testimony **SI4-2** 818

Mardian discloses delivery of 1969-71 wiretap records to White House **SI7-4** 1653, 2057, 2058-2073

meeting between Nixon, Mardian, and Ehrlichman on Sullivan's concerns over FBI files and logs of 1969-71 wiretaps ordered by White House **SI7-2** 541, 775, 776-788

in Minority of House Judiciary Committee Impeachment Inquiry views on Articles of Impeachment **RHJC** 443-450

Mitchell on 1969-1971 wiretaps of newsmen and government employees **TW 2** 196, 198-199, 205-206

of National Security Council members **SI7-1** 7, 191, 192-199

of National Security Council members, reports to Nixon, Kissinger, and Haldeman on **SI7-1** 9, 223, 224-238

of newsmen **SI7-1** 10, 11, 239, 240-248, 249, 250-257

in Nixon-Dean discussion of February 28, 1973 **SI3-1** 651-663

in Nixon-Dean discussion on CRP political intelligence-gathering operation **NSI1** 80

of Nixon in 1968 **SI3-2** 740

of Nixon in 1968, in Haldeman memo to Dean **SI3-1** 47, 527, 528-533, 541

Nixon on use of by other administrations **SIAPP1** 48

Nixon on wiretaps in 1969 **SIAPP1** 22

Nixon's approval of Huston plan on **SI7-1** 454

Nixon's approval of political-intelligence plan including **SUMM I** 29-32

Nixon's approval of and responsibility for Watergate **SUMM I** 12

Nixon's attitude toward **SUMM I** 29

Nixon's complaints about Cox's letters to IRS and Secret Service seeking information on guidelines for **SI9-1** 33, 403, 404-406

Nixon's opinion of **SI7-4** 1754

Nixon's refusal to comply with subpoenas related to **SUMM I** 158-159

Nixon's responsibility for **SUMM I** 12, 13

Nixon's responsibility for Watergate break-in and **II 3** 1934

and Omnibus Crime Act **SI1** 213

ordered by Nixon against government officials and newsmen **SI7-1** 3, 141, 142-155

Petersen on laws on **TW 3** 126-128

of Radford **SI7-3** 1439-1440

recipients of FBI summaries of "top secret" wiretap material **SI7-1** 21, 369, 370-373

recommendations in Huston plan **SI7-1** 414-416

reports from FBI to Justice Department on tapped conversations between Halperin and Ellsberg **SI7-2** 534, 681, 682-696

to leak at Rand Corporation and failed to act **NSI4** 10, 97, 98

See also Fielding break-in; House Judiciary Committee Impeachment Inquiry, presentation of evidence on Pentagon Papers matter; Pentagon Papers; *U.S. v. Colson*

Ellsberg case II 3 1815-1842; **SI9-2** 580, 1053, 1057-1058; **SI3-2** 714, 1147, 1168-1169; **SI7-3** 1199, 1503, 1504-1511

Byrne statement on meetings with Ehrlichman **SI7-4** 1651, 2041, 2042-2043

Byrne statement and Order of Dismissal **SI7-4** 1654, 2075, 2076-2083

Byrne's actions on material on Fielding break-in **SI7-4** 1647, 1995, 1996-2013

and CIA giving materials on Fielding break-in to Department of Justice **II 2** 711

and Colson's guilty plea **SI9-2** 580, 1053, 1057-1058

and Dean's information to Silbert on Fielding break-in **SI7-4** 1640, 1929, 1930-1939

effect of exposure of Fielding break-in on, presentation of evidence to House Judiciary Committee Impeachment Inquiry on **II 2** 1218-1265

and Ehrlichman's discussions with Byrne **SI7-4** 1636, 1879, 1880-1889, 1894-1895; **SIAPP1** 46-47

FBI informs Department of Justice that no Ellsberg conversations were monitored **II 2** 1134-1139

and FBI's unsuccessful attempts to interview Fielding **NSI4** 11, 99, 100-101

Kleindienst-Nixon meeting on **SI9-2** 554, 883, 887-890

memo to Ehrlichman from Krogh and Young on **NSI4** 17, 125, 126-127

Nixon on **SIAPP1** 23

Nixon admits telling Petersen to steer away from during Watergate investigation **SIAPP1** 65

Nixon discusses with Moore **SI4-3** 1107, 1501, 1502-1503

Petersen on **TW 3** 73-74, 144-145

Petersen's role in **II 2** 1231-1232

reports to Ehrlichman from Plumbers unit on **II 2** 1185

transcript of proceedings **SI7-4** 1647, 1995, 1998-2013

transcript of proceedings on Byrne's disclosures on meetings with Ehrlichman**SI7-4** 1649, 2019, 2020-2025

wiretaps on White House staff members and **SI7-1** 286

See also Ellsberg trial; St. Clair, James D., presentation of evidence in behalf of Nixon on electronic surveillance and Plumbers unit activities; *U.S. v. Russo*

Ellsberg trial

Ehrlichman letter to Mitchell suggesting voluntary nonsuit of **II 2** 1190

Ehrlichman reports to Nixon on impact of Fielding break-in exposure on **II 2** 1204

and Ehrlichman's meetings with Byrne **II 2** 1206-1209

and FBI investigation to locate Kissinger tapes **II** 2 1158

obstruction of, in Article of Impeachment II **RHJC** 172

obstruction of, Minority of House Judiciary Committee Impeachment Inquiry views on Articles of Impeachment and **RHJC** 467-468

Ellsberg v. Mitchell

Kissinger affidavit on leak on Nixon's decision to begin troop withdrawals from Vietnam **NSI4** 22, 153, 158-159

Kissinger affidavit on leak on Nixon's determination to remove nuclear weapons from Okinawa **NSI4** 26, 179, 182

Kissinger affidavit on leak on Nixon's directive on study of solutions to Vietnam War **NSI4** 21, 139, 143-151

Kissinger affidavit on leak on secret bombing of Cambodia **NSI4** 23, 161, 164-165

Kissinger affidavit on leak on secret official estimates for first strike capabilities of Soviet Union **NSI4** 25, 173, 176-178

Kissinger affidavit on resignation of Halperin from National Security Council **NSI4** 27, 183, 188-190

Kissinger affidavit on SALT leaks **NSI4** 24, 167, 168-172

Ellsworth, Robert SIAPP4 137

Emberton, Thomas SIAPP4 8, 244

Emergency Community Facilities Act of 1970

Nixon's statement on refusing to sign **SI12** 31

Emerson, Thomas I. SI7-2 594

Employment Act of 1946

and impoundment of funds by President **SI12** 70-72

Enemies list SI8 101-102

circulation to White House staff members **SI8** 7, 65, 66-77

Colson on **TW 3** 453, 471-472

Colson memo to Dean checking top priority names on **SI8** 10, 103, 104-109

Colson's letter to Thompson and Dash explaining use of **SI8** 7, 65, 76-77

Dean on White House use of IRS and **TW 2** 300-303, 311, 331-332, 350-351

Haldeman and **SI8** 11-12, 111-112, 113-129

House Judiciary Committee Impeachment Inquiry discussion on relevancy to Impeachment Inquiry **II 2** 1269-1271

and IRS audit of Greene **II 2** 1281

memo from Bell with **SI8** 7, 65, 72-75

and Nixon Administration's use of IRS **SUMM I** 141-142

and Nixon Administration's use of IRS, in Jenner's presentation of summary of evidence to House Judiciary Committee Impeachment Inquiry **II 3** 1980, 1983-1990

in Nixon-Dean-Haldeman discussion **SI8** 335-336

and White House use of IRS, in presentation of evidence to House Judiciary Committee Impeachment Inquiry **II 2** 1259-1263, 1268-1295

See also "Dealing with Our Political Enemies" memo; Internal Revenue Service; Political enemies project

English, George W.
impeachment case against **II 3** 2210-2212

English law
impeachment cases involving failure to spend appropriations as directed by Parliament **SI12** 41-42

Ennis, Bruce J. **SI7-2** 594

Entertainment industry
IRS audits of politically active people in **II 2** 1279-1281
IRS information sent from Caulfield to Dean on **SI8** 15, 155, 156-163
Nixon campaign use of **SIAPP4** 121

Environmental Impact Statement
for Cross-Florida Barge Canal, impoundment of funds for **SI12** 27

Environmental Protection Agency
impoundment of funds of **SI12** 9-11

Erikson, Ralph E.
correspondence with Staggers on House Interstate and Foreign Commerce Committee access to ITT materials **SI5-2** 518, 949, 950-953
letter from Casey on ITT documents **SI5-2** 517, 906, 924-925
and transfer of ITT files from SEC **SI5-2** 516-517, 905-906, 916-917, 926-929

Erikson, Ralph E., cited testimony of
on transfer of ITT documents from SEC to Justice Department **SI5-2** 517, 906, 930-953

Ervin, Sam J., Jr.
discussions with Garment **SI4-3** 1418
discussions on ground rules for Select Committee with Ehrlichman and Garment **SIAPP1** 12
on Gray's offer to turn over FBI files **SI3-2** 993
letter from Hoover on FBI investigation of Schorr **SI7-2** 1118-1119
letter to Nixon on his refusal of White House materials **II 2** 1358
letter to Nixon on White House materials and resolution authorizing him to meet with Nixon **SI9-1** 27, 375, 376-378
letters from Nixon declining to testify and stating he will not allow access to Presidential papers **SI9-1** 23, 34, 337, 338-346, 407, 411-412; **II 2** 1353, 1359; **SIAPP1** 26-27
letters from Nixon refusing to comply with request for Presidential tapes **SIAPP1** 29
letters from Nixon refusing to obey subpoenas for Presidential tapes and papers **SIAPP1** 30, 68
Nixon on **SI3-2** 846
on Shultz telephone call hoax **SI2** 2, 287-288
and Stennis Plan **SIAPP1** 53-54

Ervin, Sam J., Jr., questioning by
Baldwin **SI1** 226-227
Dean **SI3-1** 544; **SI7-1** 489, 491; **SI8** 202
Ehrlichman **SI3-1** 119, 273-274; **SI2** 2, 566-567
Gray **SI3-2** 725-727; **SI7-3** 1550
Haldeman **SI9-1** 439; **SI1** 162-163
Hunt **SI5-2** 782-783
Kalmbach **SI3-1** 275-276; **SI4-3** 1551-1552
Kleindienst **SI4-2** 869, 926-927
McCord **SI3-1** 493-494
McLaren **NSI2** 23, 114

Mitchell **SI3-1** 422; **SI5-1** 180-181
Petersen **SI4-3** 1634
Porter **SI3-1** 162, 294
Reisner **SI1** 239-240; **SI4-1** 491-493
Segretti **SI3-1** 397; **SI7-4** 1661-1662
Sloan **SI2** 2, 98-99, 370-371

Ervin Committee
See Senate Select Committee on Presidential Campaign Activities

Essaye, Anthony F. **SI7-2** 594

Evans, Bill **SI5-1** 438

Evans, L.J. (Bud), Jr. **SIAPP4** 86
and Older Voters project **SI1** 83

Evans, Thomas W. **SIAPP4** 4, 5, 31, 46, 50, 60, 75, 127, 137; **SI1** 32, 47; **SI5-1** 452
and AMPI contribution **SI6-1** 145
at AMPI meeting with Kalmbach **SI6-1** 14, 217, 218-233
and campaign finances **SIAPP4** 57
meeting with Magruder on role of RNC in campaign **SI1** 35
memo from Dean with draft charter for political committee for milk producers' contributions **SI6-2** 465, 493, 500-509
in Political Matters Memoranda **SIAPP4** 10
replacement of **SIAPP4** 36-37
role in Nixon re-election campaign **SI1** 86-87

Evans & Novak
items sent from CRP to **NSI1** 74
on political sides at White House **SI1** 85
on Viguerie **SIAPP4** 7

Evening Star, The
article on Nixon's decision to begin troop withdrawals from Vietnam **NSI4** 22, 153, 156-157
articles linking Magruder to Segretti **SI7-4** 1678

Everett, Chad **SIAPP4** 121

Executive clemency
in Article of Impeachment I **RHJC** 75-81
Bittman denies discussing in relation to Hunt **TW 2** 68
in Colson-Haldeman telephone conversation on Colson's dealings with Hunt **TW 3** 336-340
Dean on discussions of **TW 2** 322-323, 334-335, 337
discussed by Magruder and Mitchell **SI4-1** 341, 345
discussed by Nixon and Dean **SI3-2** 1051-1053, 1059-1060, 1079-1082; **SI4-3** 1182-1183, 1193-1195
discussed by Nixon and Ehrlichman **II 2** 732-734
discussed by Nixon, Ehrlichman, and Haldeman **SI4-1** 369-370
discussion on March 21 tape **SIAPP1** 74-75
discussion of, in Minority of House Judiciary Committee Impeachment Inquiry views on Articles of Impeachment **RHJC** 402-407
in Doar's presentation of summary of evidence to House Judiciary Committee Impeachment Inquiry **II 3** 1962
for former assistants of Nixon **SIAPP1** 72-73
for Hunt **SI3-2** 715, 892-893, 1153-1154, 1187, 1198-1203
for Hunt, in Colson-Haldeman discussion **II 2** 757-758

for Hunt, discussed by Nixon, Ehrlichman, and Haldeman **SI4-2** 668-670

for Hunt, Nixon's false statement to Petersen on **SUMM I** 101

for Watergate defendants, discussed by Nixon and Dean **SUMM I** 67-68

McCord's reasons for refusing **SI1** 230

Mitchell's and Magruder's scheduled talks with Watergate Prosecutors and **SUMM I** 67

Nixon asks Haldeman to inquire if Colson offered Hunt **SI4-1** 8, 249, 251-252

Nixon-Colson discussion on lack of offers of **TW** 3 359

Nixon-Dean discussion of **SI3-1** 671-673

Nixon denies offering to Watergate burglars **SIAPP1** 42, 64, 76; **SI1** 39

Nixon does not ask Petersen about legal aspects of offers of **SUMM I** 69

Nixon-Ehrlichman discussion on **SUMM I** 46; **SI4-2** 790

Nixon-Ehrlichman meeting on Watergate defendants and possibility of **SI3-1** 13, 181, 182-197

Nixon-Haig discussion on **SI9-1** 178-179

Nixon and offers of **SUMM I** 63-69

Nixon's fears that Hunt will tell Watergate Prosecutor about offers of **SUMM I** 81

Nixon's untrue public statements on **SUMM I** 69

O'Brien-Parkinson discussion on **TW 1** 168-169

offers to Hunt, in Article of Impeachment I **RHJC** 114-115

offers to McCord **II 2** 759; **SI3-1** 42, 487, 488-498

Executive mess privileges SI1 79-80

Executive Office Building
Plumbers unit set up in **SI7-2** 544, 815, 816-825

Executive privilege SI2 2, 24, 236, 257-258
Baker on **SI7-4** 1872

Buzhardt submits list of subpoenaed materials to Sirica particularizing claims of **SI9-2** 553, 875, 876-882

claimed for redated memo from Whitaker to Nixon on milk price supports **SI6-2** 484, 863, 867-868, 873-875

Colson-Shapiro recommendations to Ehrlichman on **TW 3** 343, 444-445

Cox's knowledge or lack of knowledge of Richardson-Nixon discussion on **II 2** 1395-1397

and Dean **SI3-1** 52, 597, 598-614; **SI3-2** 694, 746, 747, 749-751

Dean on White House discussions on **TW 2** 270-273, 276-277, 324-325, 341

and Dean's refusal to testify at Gray confirmation hearings **SI3-2** 702, 703, 802, 881, 892-896, 897, 898-900

discussed at Dean, Haldeman, Ehrlichman and Mitchell meeting **SI3-2** 1267, 1268, 1271, 1272-1274, 1275

discussed in Nixon-Dean meeting **SI3-1** 617-624, 634-636, 645-646; **SI3-2** 695, 753, 761

discussed by Nixon and Ehrlichman **SI4-1** 369-370

document freeing Colson from **TW 3** 445-449, 524

and Flanigan's refusal to testify at Kleindienst confirmation hearings **NSI2** 201-202

House Judiciary Committee Impeachment Inquiry subpoenas to Nixon and **RHJC** 206-212;

MMFL 148-153

in memo from Dean to Colson on documents related to *Nader* v. *Butz* **SI6-2** 892

Nixon claims he waived it on all individuals within Administration **SIAPP1** 58

Nixon claims with respect to Watergate Grand Jury subpoena for correspondence with Stans on selections and nominations for government offices **SI9-2** 579, 1045, 1046-1052

Nixon's discussions with Dean on **SI3-2** 698, 783, 791, 797, 820-821

Nixon on reasons for waiving for White House staff **SIAPP1** 74

Nixon-Richardson discussion on **II 2** 1335-1338, 1452-1454

Nixon statement on **SI3-2** 699, 741, 795, 796-797

Nixon states he would object to Dean testifying at Gray nomination hearings based on **SIAPP1** 5

Nixon states White House staff will refuse to testify at Select Committee hearings based on **SIAPP1** 10

in Nixon-Petersen discussion **SI4-3** 1243

Nixon's formal claim of in *U.S.* v. *Mitchell* **SI9-2** 572, 1005, 1007

and Nixon's noncompliance with House Judiciary Committee Impeachment Inquiry subpoenas **II 3** 2041-2043; **II 2** 1154; **SUMM1** 167-169

and Nixon's refusal to allow Dean to testify at Gray confirmation hearings **SIAPP1** 8-9, 10

Nixon's statements and letters of March 12, 1973 on **SIAPP1** 6-7

possible waiver by Nixon discussed in Nixon-Dean meeting **SI4-3** 1169, 1175

Supreme Court consideration of **II 2** 1354

and Supreme Court decision in *U.S.* v. *Nixon* **SIAPP2** 159-192

Watergate investigation and Nixon's waiver of **SI9-1** 8, 151, 152-159

and White House personnel appearing before Senate Select Committee **SI4-3** 1101, 1419, 1420

See also Nixon tapes

Executives' Club of Chicago
question-and-answer session with Nixon at meeting of **SIAPP1** 76-77

F.T.C. v. *Consolidated Foods Corporation* **SI5-1** 125

"Face the Nation"
Haig interview on **SI9-1** 14, 257, 266, 267, 276

McLaren's remarks on ITT antitrust cases on **NSI2** 11, 104, 126

Failer, Edward D. SIAPP4 141, 149

Falk, Richard SI7-2 1023

Fall, Albert SI3-2 1158

Farkas, Dr. Ruth
Kalmbach on campaign contribution and ambassadorship commitment to **TW 3** 649-651, 673-674

Farm vote
in memo from Strachan to Haldeman **SI1** 87

Farmers Home Administration
impoundment of funds for programs of **SI12** 16-17

Fat Jack **SI1** 110

See also Buckley, John R. (alias of)

Fay, Al **SIAPP3** 28

FBI **II 2** 1099, 1100, 1202; **SI4-3** 1614-1616; **SI7-1** 153, 161-162

attitude toward covert mail coverage, in Huston plan **SI7-1** 419

attitude toward increased electronic surveillance, in Huston plan **SI7-1** 416

attitude toward interagency coordination of intelligence, in Huston plan **SI7-1** 431

attitude toward restrictions on intelligence activities on campuses, in Huston plan **SI7-1** 424

attitude toward surreptitious entry, in Huston plan **SI7-1** 421

attitude toward use of military undercover agents to develop domestic intelligence, in Huston plan **SI7-1** 427

and CIA aid to Hunt **SI2** 2, 465-466; **SI7-3** 1237-1238

Colson discusses contacts with Hunt with **TW 3** 253

concealment of records of 1969-1971 wiretaps, in Article of Impeachment II **RHJC** 152-156

concern about CIA involvement in Watergate break-in **II 3** 1736, 1739-1740

Dean expects attack by Sullivan on **SI3-2** 824-834, 873, 877-878

and disclosure of Segretti's activities **SI7-4** 1659

efforts to interview Ellsberg's psychiatrist **SI7-2** 554, 967, 968-980

Ehrlichman compares Ulasewicz's role with role of **SI7-1** 341

Ehrlichman indicted for making false statements to **SI9-2** 564, 963, 964

false statements by Ehrlichman on Pentagon Papers investigation of **SIAPP2** 11-12

files and logs of wiretaps ordered by White House, Sullivan and Mardian and **SI7-2** 540, 755, 756-773

findings on Magruder-Strachan memos **SI1** 38

Gray denies wiretapping of newsmen and White House officials by **SI7-4** 1627, 1755, 1756-1773

Gray-MacGregor conversation on White House staff use of **SUMM I** 45

Gray's nomination as director withdrawn **SI4-1** 31, 503, 504-506

and Hunt's safe **TW 2** 34; **SI4-3** 1517-1518

informants in antiwar movement **SI7-1** 394

informs Department of Justice that no Ellsberg conversations were monitored **II 2** 1134-1139

interagency coordination and, in Huston plan **SI7-1** 430-431

interview arranged with Segretti, Dean-Segretti meeting prior to **SI7-3** 1203, 1541, 1542-1555

interviews Ehrlichman on Fielding break-in **SI7-4** 1648, 2015, 2016-2018; **II 2** 1234-1236

interviews Haldeman on wiretaps on White House staff members **SI7-1** 275-278

interviews Mardian on delivery of 1969-71 wiretap records to White House **SI7-4** 1653, 2057, 2058-2071

inventory of contents of Hunt's safe **SI2** 2, 43, 415, 422,-423; **SI7-3** 1204, 1557, 1564-1565

investigation to locate Kissinger tapes **II 2** 1157-1158

investigation of publication of Pentagon Papers **SI7-2** 609-611

investigation of SALT leaks **SI7-2** 549, 887, 891-894

investigation of Schorr **II 2** 1174, 1176; **TW 3** 238-241; **SI7-2** 562, 1111, 1112-1124

Justice Department requests electronic surveillance records for Ellsberg from **II 2** 1126

in Krogh-Young memo to Ehrlichman on national security leaks **NSI4** 134

and legal basis for domestic surveillance **II 2** 1093-1094

material sent to Plumbers unit by **SI7-2** 553, 951, 952-966

materials from Hunt's safe delivered to **SI7-3** 1204, 1557, 1558-1568

memo from Bolz to Bates on investigation of Segretti **SI7-3** 1203, 1541, 1551-1552

memos to and from Assistant Attorney General on electronic surveillance of Ellsberg and Halperin **SI7-2** 542, 789, 790-794

and Mexican checks, in Article of Impeachment I **RHJC** 48-50, 53-54

Mitchell denies transmission to CRP of reports from **SI1** 58

and need for Plumbers unit **NSI4** 95

Nixon-Colson discussion on Gray's nomination as Director of **TW 3** 320-321

Nixon-Dean discussion on possible directors of **SI7-4** 1629, 1813, 1814-1820

Nixon on lessened powers of in 1970 **SIAPP1** 22

Nixon on role in Hiss case **SIAPP1** 8-9, 10

Nixon tells Rogers he is considering Byrne for directorship of **SI7-4** 1642, 1947, 1948

Nixon withdraws Gray's nomination as Director of **SIAPP1** 11

in Nixon-Ziegler conversation **SI9-1** 185-195

Nixon's decision to announce new nominee for director of **SI7-4** 1634, 1859, 1860-1862

Nixon's misuse of, in Article of Impeachment II **RHJC** 177, 178

Nixon's remarks to Petersen on directorship of **SI4-3** 1546

ordered by Haig not to maintain records of 1969-1971 wiretaps of government officials and newsmen **SUMM I** 134

Petersen on use of wiretapping by **TW 3** 126-128

Plumbers unit and **SI1** 219

proposal of Byrne as director of **SI7-4** 1635, 1867, 1868-1877

reasons for Plumbers operations and **SI5-2** 781-782

recipients of summaries of "top secret" wiretap material from **SI7-1** 21, 369, 370-373

reports to Intelligence Evaluation Committee **SI7-1** 500

reports to Justice Department on wiretaps involving Ellsberg **SI7-2** 534, 681, 682-696

and results of wiretapping of government employees **SI7-1** 15, 301, 302-312

as source of theory of CIA involvement in Watergate break-in **NSI1** 15, 121, 122-123

Stanton tells Colson they had case connecting Ellsberg to leak at Rand Corporation and failed to act **NSI4** 10, 97, 98

summaries of information on wiretaps of government employees and newsmen **SI7-2** 568-569

summaries of letters reporting on surveillance of three White House staff members **SI7-1** 280-282, 302-304

summary of file on Kraft wiretap **SI7-1** 16, 19, 313, 324, 355, 356-357

summary of letters reporting on surveillance of four newsmen **SI7-1** 11, 249, 253-256

summary of letters reporting on wiretaps on National Security Council employees **SI7-1** 9, 223, 224-230

and surveillance of Kraft **SUMM I** 126

termination of wiretaps on government employees and newsmen **II 2** 1119-1120; **SI7-2** 525, 567, 568-574

in *Time* magazine article on White House wiretaps **SI7-4** 1747-1748

unsuccessful attempts to interview Fielding in 1971 **NSI4** 11, 99, 100-101

White House dissatisfaction with, establishment of Plumbers unit and **NSI4** 48

and wiretapping of government officials and newsmen in 1969 **SUMM I** 124-125

wiretaps associated with leaks on U.S. position on India-Pakistan War **SI7-3** 1193, 1421, 1422-1440

See also FBI Watergate investigation; Gray, Louis Patrick; Hoover, John Edgar; House Judiciary Committee Impeachment Inquiry, presentation of evidence on domestic surveillance; Huston plan

FBI Watergate investigation SI2 2, 31, 40, 51, 57, 311, 312-314, 397, 398, 399, 400, 401, 402, 483, 484-500, 555, 556-560, 649; **SI3-2** 727-728

in Article of Impeachment I **RHJC** 45

and Chenow **SI2** 2, 54, 518, 519

and Dean **SI2** 2, 31, 311, 312-315

Dean called to testify to Gray confirmation hearings on contacts with FBI during **SI3-2** 700, 799, 800-802

Dean on Kleindienst's report on **TW 2** 333-334

Dean obtains raw data from Gray on **TW 2** 226-227, 333

Dean on White House interference with **TW 2** 351-352

Dean's efforts to get CIA to stop Mexican check portion of **SI2** 2, 44, 427, 430, 434-435, 437, 440

Dean's presence at FBI White House interviews **SI3-2** 692, 729, 737-741, 764-765

Dean's role in containment of Watergate and **SUMM I** 44

in Doar's presentation of evidentiary material to House Judiciary Committee Impeachment Inquiry **II 1** 594-596, 680-695

Ehrlichman on **SI2** 2, 547-548

and false statements by Magruder on purpose of funds paid to Liddy **SI3-1** 19, 245, 246-251

Gray's offer to turn files over to senators **SI3-2** 993

Haldeman on **SI2** 2, 348-350

Haldeman-Helms-Walters meeting on **SI2** 2, 36, 38-39, 355-357, 361, 375-395

Haldeman's knowledge of White House interference with **SUMM I** 41

information provided by CIA for **SI2** 2, 530-532

and interview of Colson and inquiries about Hunt's office in EOB **SI2** 2, 33, 329, 330-336

and interview with Liddy **SI2** 2, 50, 477, 478, 479-481

Kleindienst asks Gray for briefing on **SI2** 2, 13, 135, 136-142

Magruder asks Porter to corroborate his story on reasons for CRP payments to Liddy **SI3-1** 10, 157, 158-164

memo from Bates to Bolz on **SI2** 2, 34, 337, 342-345

memo from Helms to Walters on **SI2** 2, 48, 471

and Mitchell's denial of knowledge about Watergate break-in **SI3-1** 15, 203, 204-206; **II 2** 735-736

Nixon on **SIAPP1** 3, 4, 34, 41-42; **SI2** 2, 35, 351, 352-353, 550, 551-553

Nixon discusses with Dean **SI3-2** 817-820

Nixon explains concern over CIA covert operations being exposed by **SIAPP1** 24

and Nixon-Gray telephone conversation of March 23, 1973 **SI4-1** 7, 241, 242, 243, 244-248

Nixon on Gray's behavior during **SIAPP1** 9

Nixon-Haldeman discussion on **SIAPP3** 40-44, 77-79

Nixon instructs Gray on **NSI1** 17, 129, 135

Nixon's efforts to ensure it does not expose CIA operation **NSI1** 16, 17, 125, 126-127, 129, 130-135

Nixon's knowledge of White House interference with **SUMM I** 47

Nixon's orders to Haldeman on **SI2** 2, 36, 355, 356-362

Petersen on documents received from CIA on questions asked during **TW 3** 3-4, 5-46

Porter tells FBI agents that money paid to Liddy was for lawful political activities **SI3-1** 18, 235, 236-244

and Porter's and Magruder's false statements on money paid to Liddy **II 2** 738

relationship to Department of Justice investigation **SI2** 2, 103

Walters-Gray meeting on, *see* Walters, Vernon A.

and Watergate coverup **SUMM I** 39-40

and Watergate coverup, in Doar's presentation of evidentiary material to House Judiciary Committee Impeachment Inquiry **II 1** 617-622

White House interference with **II 2** 778-786; **SUMM I** 46-47; **SI2** 2, 55-56, 519-520, 521-553

White House interference with, in Doar's presentation of summary of evidence to House Judiciary Committee Impeachment Inquiry **II 3** 1958-1961

See also Gray, Louis Patrick

Federal-Aid Highway Act of 1956

litigation on impoundment of funds for **SI12** 11-12

Federal Communications Commission (FCC)

and network television programming **SI5-1** 156-157

Ehrlichman tells Nixon effects on Ellsberg trial of II 2 1204

Ehrlichman-Young meeting on handling of questions on SI7-4 1650, 2027, 2028-2039

Ehrlichman's approval of II 2 1179-1180, 1182-1183, 1187; SI7-2 555, 557, 981, 982-1003, 1007-1028

Ehrlichman's conversation with Colson on SUMM I 36

events leading to SI7-2 554, 967, 968-980

FBI interview of Ehrlichman on SI7-4 1648, 2015, 2016-2018

and FBI's unsuccessful attempts to interview Fielding NSI4 11, 99, 100-101

financing of SI7-3 1184, 1247, 1248-1274

Hunt on SI1 209; SI3-2 923

Hunt and Liddy prepare for SI7-2 564, 1151, 1152-1177

and Hunt's efforts to extend to Fielding's home SI7-3 1186, 1301, 1302-1332

Hunt's recruitment of Barker, DeDiego, and Martinez for SI7-2 561, 1095, 1096-1110

Hunt's testimony to Watergate Grand Jury on TW 2 73-74, 100

and Hunt's threats against Ehrlichman SI3-2 1020-1021

indictments for conspiracy to violate civil rights of citizens in SI9-2 564, 963, 964

indictments related to II 2 1427

Kleindienst-Nixon meeting on SI9-2 554, 883, 887-890

Kleindienst and Petersen agree to disclose information on to Byrne SI7-4 1645, 1975, 1976-1982; II 2 1232

Kleindienst tells Nixon that Byrne should be informed of SUMM I 138

Krogh and Young claim Ehrlichman approved of SI7-3 1183, 1239, 1240-1246

Krogh pleads guilty to and states he received no instruction or authority regarding it from Nixon SI9-2 556, 901, 902-921

Krogh states he approved NSI4 13, 109, 114

Krogh's perjured testimony before Watergate Grand Jury on Hunt's and Liddy's participation in SI3-1 25, 311, 312-325

LaRue and Mardian report to Mitchell on SI7-3 1201, 1523, 1524-1531

Liddy informs LaRue and Mardian about II 2 178, 1194; SI2 2, 27, 277, 280, 281-282, 292; SI3-1 3, 87, 88-95; TW 1 197

and material from Hunt's safe SI2 2, 512

materials requested by Jaworski and refused by Nixon related to investigation of SI9-2 1052

memo from Martin to Maroney on SIAPP3 242

memo from Silbert to Petersen informing him of SIAPP3 239-241; SI4-2 578, 1013, 1016

Mitchell claims lack of knowledge about TW 2 193

Nixon on SIAPP1 23, 42; TW 3 268; SI3-2 1247-1248

Nixon authorizes Kleindienst to turn over material to Byrne on SI7-4 1646, 1983, 1984-1993

Nixon-Dean discussion of possible discovery of Hunt's and Liddy's involvement in SI4-3 90-91

in Nixon-Dean discussion on Hunt's demands for money NSI1 155

Nixon denies prior knowledge of SI1 39; SI4-1 359

Nixon, Ehrlichman, and Haldeman discuss defense of SI4-1 360-361

Nixon-Petersen discussion on Watergate prosecutors learning about SI7-4 1643, 1949, 1950-1966

Nixon tells Petersen Justice Department should not investigate II 2 1228-1229, 1231, 1232; TW 3 85-86, 97-100, 119-120, 124-126, 162-164; SI4-3 1645

Nixon's abuse of Presidential powers and SUMM I 132-133

Nixon's attitute toward SI2 2, 150

and Nixon's concealment of Plumbers unit activities SUMM I 136-138

Nixon's knowledge or lack of knowledge of II 2 1147, 1151, 1161-1169, 1176-1177, 1182-1183

Nixon's memo on learning about SUMM I 7

Nixon's notes on SUMM I 86

and offer of position of FBI Director to Byrne SUMM I 138-140

papers from criminal cases related to SIAPP2 3-50

Petersen on TW 3 73-74, 144-145

Petersen informs Nixon of II 2 1228-1229, 1231, 1232

Petersen shows Dean photographs of SI2 2, 66, 671, 672

photographs of Fielding's office sent to Justice Department by CIA TW 3 71-72

possible disclosure by Hunt discussed by Nixon, Ehrlichman, Haldeman, and Dean SI7-4 1631, 1829, 1830-1836

preparations for and carrying out of II 2 1141-1148, 1158, 1161-1173, 1178-1181

relationship to Watergate break-in II 2 1190

Richardson on SI4-3 1652

Watergate coverup and concealment of SUMM I 134

Young-Ehrlichman-Colson memos on plans for SI7-3 1181, 1213

Young-Ehrlichman discussion on possibility of Hunt disclosure on SI7-4 1633, 1841, 1842-1858

Young testifies that Ehrlichman gave advance approval to SI9-1 46, 503, 512-516

Young's discussion with Colson on TW 3 230-231

See also St. Clair, James D., presentation of evidence in behalf of Nixon on electronic surveillance and Plumbers unit activities

Fifth Amendment

applicability to House Judiciary Committee Impeachment Inquiry II 1 234

Hundley on not instructing Mitchell to take TW 2 118, 119, 122, 145

Nixon and Dean discuss use of SI3-2 1092

and parties subpoenaed in Ellsberg case SI7-2 1023

Finance Committee to Re-Elect the President (FCRP) SIAPP2 203-206

AMPI contribution and SI6-2 489, 965, 966-984

Ashland Oil voluntarily acknowledges illegal contribution to SI9-1 31, 397, 398

contributions to Republican Congressional campaign committees SI6-2 486, 945, 946-949

dairy organizations on list of pre-April 7, 1972 contributions SI6-2 486, 945, 946-949

Nixon-Dean discussion on Kalmbach's bank records **SI8** 429-432

Nixon-Dean discussion of Kalmbach's use of 1968 surplus funds **SI3-2** 1032-1036

Nixon on funding of Segretti **SI7-4** 1921

Nixon-Haldeman discussion on debt ceiling and other monetary matters **SIAPP3** 48-50

Nixon-Haldeman discussion on transfer of cash from White House to CRP **SI4-3** 1217-1221

Nixon tells Petersen that Haldeman had no authority over campaign funds **SUMM I** 92

Nixon's approval of Huston plan on **SI7-1** 455

obstruction of inquiries into campaign financing practices and use of campaign funds, in Article of Impeachment II **RHJC** 173-174

payment to Barker, Martinez, and DeDiego for Fielding break-in **SI7-3** 1307

payment to Timmons and Capen for investigation of San Diego **SI5-1** 428

photograph of check from Sheraton Harbor Island Corp. **SI5-2** 489, 603, 604

Porter tells FBI agents that money paid to Liddy was for lawful political activities **SI3-1** 18, 235, 236-244

Porter testifies falsely before Watergate Grand Jury on purposes of money paid to Liddy **SI3-1** 23, 291, 292-296

Porter's false testimony to FBI on money paid to Liddy **II 2** 729-730

proposed budget for Operation Sandwedge **SI7-3** 1118, 1339, 1345-1347

salaries at CRP in talking paper from Strachan to Mitchell **SIAPP4** 44-45

and San Diego City Council Resolution authorizing San Diego as site of Republican National Convention of 1972 **SI5-2** 563-567

Sheraton Harbor Island Corporation check delivered to San Diego convention and tourist bureau **II 2** 1024

source of payments to Ulasewicz **SI7-1** 342, 346

steps in federal funding processes **SI12** 3-4

Strachan informs Ehrlichman he gave mistaken testimony on amount of money delivered to La-Rue **SI4-1** 38, 549, 550-551

Strachan memo to Dean on "fat cats" attending fundraising meeting for Muskie **SI8** 120

in talking paper from Strachan to Mitchell **SIAPP4** 35

transfer of $350,000 discussed by Nixon, Wilson, and Strickler **SI4-3** 1515-1516, 1518-1519, 1526-1527

White House pay records for Hunt **SI7-2** 537, 713, 714-716

White House subsidiary account in memo from Strachan to Haldeman **SI1** 47

See also Campaign contributions; Campaign financing; Illegal campaign practices and contributions, papers from criminal cases related to; Impoundment of funds; Nixon's income tax; Report on government expenditures on Nixon's private properties

Finch, Robert **SIAPP4** 2, 4, 20, 50, 120, 135; **SI5-1** 432

Firestone, Leonard **SIAPP4** 4, 12, 118, 120; **SI1** 85

First Amendment
and Pentagon Papers matter **NSI4** 78-79

First Oceanic Corporation SIAPP2 221-226
See also U.S. v. Dwayne Andreas and First Interoceanic Corporation

Fish, Hamilton, Jr. SUMM I 1
on antitrust suits against ITT **II 2** 1010, 1028-1029

on calling witnesses before House Judiciary Committee Impeachment Inquiry **II 3** 1683, 1688

concurrence with McClory's additional views on Article of Impeachment III **RHJC** 349-354

concurring views with Report of House Judiciary Committee Impeachment Inquiry **RHJC** 355-358

on confidentiality of evidentiary material presented to House Judiciary Committee Impeachment Inquiry **II 1** 582

on Doar-St. Clair correspondence **II 1** 186-187

on House Judiciary Committee Impeachment Inquiry's rules of confidentiality **II 1** 221

on investigation of bombing of Cambodia in House Judiciary Committee Impeachment Inquiry **II 1** 371

on issuing subpoenas to Nixon **II 1** 315, 321, 326-327

on justification for discussion of Liddy's and Caulfield's efforts to obtain IRS posts **II 2** 1258

on leaks from House Judiciary Committee Impeachment Inquiry **II 2** 1265

on methods of obtaining materials **II 1** 113

on Nixon's gift of Presidential papers **II 3** 1467

on Nixon's income tax **II 3** 2015-2016

on Nixon's noncompliance with House Judiciary Committee Impeachment Inquiry subpoenas **II 1** 452; **II 2** 906-907, 925, 945

on obtaining testimony of witnesses to corroborate tapes **II 2** 860

on possibility of complete presentation by Doar without materials requested from White House **II 1** 269-270

on release of House Judiciary Committee Impeachment Inquiry evidentiary material to public **II 3** 1606

on rules of evidentiary procedures for House Judiciary Committee Impeachment Inquiry **II 1** 521, 522, 538

on setting completion date for House Judiciary Committee Impeachment Inquiry **II 1** 20

statement of concurring views with Report of House Judiciary Committee Impeachment Inquiry **RHJC** 281

on subpoena powers of House Judiciary Committee **II 1** 43

Fish, Hamilton, Jr., questioning by
Bittman **TW 2** 79-80
Butterfield **TW 1** 98
Colson **TW 3** 468-469
Dean **TW 2** 311-312
LaRue **TW 1** 254-255
Mitchell **TW 2** 188
O'Brien **TW 1** 151-152

Fish, Hamilton, Jr., questioning by *(Continued)*
Petersen **TW 3** 145-146

Fish, Ody **SI5-2** 585

Fisher, Max **SIAPP4** 5, 6, 51, 147

Fitchett, James C. **TW 3** 42-43

Flaherty, Tom **II 2** 1088

Flanagan, James L. **SI9-2** 552, 578, 867, 869-874, 1037, 1038-1044

Flanigan, Bob **SI5-2** 584

Flanigan, Dent **SIAPP4** 18
in Dean's memo on "Dealing with Our Political Enemies" **SI8** 99

Flanigan, Peter **SIAPP4** 49, 57, 118; **SI1** 32; **SI5-1** 133, 452
in Ehrlichman memo to Nixon on antitrust policy **SI5-1** 394
Kalmbach informs about AMPI contribution **SI6-1** 6, 99, 102
and Kalmbach's discussions on ambassadorships **TW 3** 617-629
Kleindienst and **SI5-2** 758
Kleindienst confirmation hearings and **NSI2** 16, 189, 201-202
in Kleindienst's statement on ITT matter **NSI2** 191
memo from Chapin advising him that no appointment has been set up between Nixon and Geneen **NSI2** 5, 25, 44
memo from Chapin on proposed appointment with Nixon for Geneen **SI5-1** 5, 131, 138
memo from Cohen on proposed Tax Reform Act of 1969 eliminating charitable deductions for gifts of private papers **SI10** 10, 243-252
memo from Ehrlichman on antitrust policy review **SI5-1** 23, 393, 401

Flemming, Arthur **SIAPP4** 78, 86; **SI1** 87, 95
Evans on **SIAPP4** 78
role in Nixon re-election campaign **SI1** 83

Flemming, Harry S. **SIAPP4** 6, 14, 19, 21, 31, 96; **SI1** 36; **SI5-1** 451; **SI5-2** 587, 789, 793; **SI6-2** 813
campaign activities **SIAPP4** 30
excused from Key Biscayne meeting during discussion on electronic surveillance **TW 1** 182
and Key Biscayne meeting on Liddy plan **TW 1** 181-182; **SI1** 132, 134
McWhorter report on Midwest Regional Republican Conference to **SIAPP4** 25-26
money given by Kalmbach to **SI6-1** 307
in New Hampshire **SIAPP4** 1
recommendations on meetings for Nixon **SIAPP4** 42-43
and Republican National Convention arrangements **SI5-2** 585
role in Nixon campaign **SI1** 32-33
in talking paper from Strachan to Mitchell **SIAPP4** 46

Fletcher, Miss **II 1** 63

Flint, Jonathan **II 2** 1331

Flom, Joseph H. **SI5-2** 646-649, 682-685

Florida **SIAPP4** 58
campaign in **SIAPP4** 50
laws on homosexuals in **SIAPP3** 55

primary elections in Political Matters Memoranda **SIAPP4** 80

Flowers, Walter **II 1** 77; **SUMM I** 1
on calling witnesses before House Judiciary Committee Impeachment Inquiry **II 3** 1625, 1641, 1642, 1643, 1676-1677, 1683, 1708, 1709
concurrence with Minority of House Judiciary Committee Impeachment Inquiry views on Article of Impeachment III **RHJC** 493
on criteria for excising material from Nixon tapes **II 2** 832
on Ehrlichman's meeting with Byrne **II 2** 1208
on House Judiciary Committee Impeachment Inquiry issuing subpoenas to Nixon **II 3** 1548-1549, 1558
on impact of leak on IRS investigation of Gerald Wallace on George Wallace's campaign **II 2** 1252
on leaks as reason for domestic surveillance **II 2** 1092
motion on commencing general debate on Articles of Impeachment **II 3** 2105-2129
on Nixon-Dean meeting of March 17 **II 2** 1360
on Nixon's attitude toward House Judiciary Committee Impeachment Inquiry **II 1** 216-217
on Nixon's gift of Presidential papers **II 3** 1464, 1468, 2003, 2005, 2006
on Nixon's noncompliance with House Judiciary Committee Impeachment Inquiry subpoenas **II 1** 421-422, 453-454; **II 2** 901-903, 906, 908
on Nixon's request for extension of time on answering House Judiciary Committee Impeachment Inquiry subpoena **II 1** 346-347
on presentation procedures for House Judiciary Committee Impeachment Inquiry **II 1** 264, 265
question on meaning of illegal mail covers **II 2** 1117
on release of House Judiciary Committee Impeachment Inquiry evidentiary material to public **II 3** 1595, 1603, 1604
on selection of impeachable offenses for House Judiciary Committee Impeachment Inquiry **II 1** 369
on separate Minority of House Judiciary Committee Impeachment Inquiry brief on impeachable offenses **II 1** 155
on setting completion date for House Judiciary Committee Impeachment Inquiry **II 1** 19-20
on St. Clair's participation in House Judiciary Committee Impeachment Inquiry **II 1** 340
on status of indictment of Colson **II 2** 1427
on Wallace campaign **II 2** 1253

Flowers, Walter, questioning by
Bittman **TW 2** 81-82
Colson **TW 3** 466-468
Dean **TW 2** 317-318
Kalmbach **TW 3** 715-716
LaRue **TW 1** 252-253
Mitchell **TW 2** 189-190

Folsom, Fred G. **II 3** 1457, 1495-1496, 2013
on auditing of Nixon's tax returns **II 3** 1496, 1498, 1521
on IRS Code related to audit of Nixon's income tax **II 3** 1509-1512, 1518-1519, 1523-1524, 1527, 1528, 1529

Fong, questioning by
Kleindienst **SI5-2** 852
Mitchell **SI5-1** 181
Reinecke **SIAPP2** 376-378

Fontainebleau Hotel, Miami, Florida **SI1** 10, 13, 115
See Democratic National Convention (1972)

Food Stamp Program
impoundment of funds for **SI12** 17

Ford, Benson **SI8** 83

Ford, Edwin H. **SI8** 83

Ford, Gerald **SIAPP4** 25; **SI2** 2, 621-622, 632; **SI5-2** 586
confirmation hearings **II 1** 244
in Dent's recommendations for campaign **SIAPP4** 13
in discussion on Patman Committee hearings **TW 2** 329-331, 352-353
on impeachment procedures **II 1** 261
Nixon-Dean-Haldeman discussion on **SI8** 315-317
and Nixon's efforts to prevent Patman Committee hearings **SUMM I** 49-51
speech attacking Jenner **II 1** 476
testimony denying he was contacted to block House Banking and Currency Committee hearings **SUMM I** 116-117
on use of subpoenas during Douglas investigation **II 1** 445

Ford, Henry II **SI8** 83

Ford, Wendell **SIAPP4** 24

Ford Foundation
Brookings Institution and **SI8** 85-86
in memo from Dean to Krogh **SI8** 82-84

Fore, Rich **SIAPP4** 122

Foreign Assistance Act of 1971
bombing of Cambodia and **SI11** 400-402
provisions linking expenditures to release of impounded funds for certain domestic programs **SI12** 37-38

Foreign intelligence
black extremist groups and **SI7-1** 399-400

Foreign Intelligence Advisory Board
memo on meeting of sub-committee on Pentagon Papers **SI7-2** 529, 619, 635-637

Foreign policy
Brookings Institution program for studies of **SI7-2** 539, 739, 741-745
Nixon on effects of Pentagon Papers publication on **SI1** 40

Foreign relations
impact of Watergate hearings on **SI1** 163

Forrester, David **II 2** 1267

Fortune **SI5-2** 957

Fortune 500 list **SI5-1** 121, 125

Forzberg, Miss (Mrs. Mitchell's secretary) **SI1** 118

Foster, Dr. John F. **SI11** 4, 133

Founding Fathers
Jenner on **SUMM I** 15-16, 18

Fourth International
Trotskyist groups in U.S. and **SI7-1** 408

Foust, Jon **SIAPP4** 110

Fraekel, Osmond K. **SI7-2** 594

Frampton, George T., Jr., questioning by
Bittman **SI3-2** 1229-1230
Dean **SI1** 69-75
Hunt **SI3-2** 1233-1235
Millican **SI3-2** 1198-1203
O'Brien, Paul L. **SI3-2** 946
Unger **SI3-2** 1204-1210

Frankel, Max **SI7-1** 364
article on Nixon's directive on study of solutions to Vietnam War **NSI4** 21, 139, 140-142

Frankfurter, Felix **II 1** 404

Fredericks, Laura **II 2** 815, 816
at LaRue's home with Millican and Unger **SI3-2** 1189, 1199, 1205
House Judiciary Committee Impeachment Inquiry discussion on subpoenaing **II 2** 981-992

Free, Lloyd **SIAPP4** 95

FREEDOM DEAL bombings SI11 8
Moorer on **SI11** 281-282

Freeman, Neal **SI1** 49

Freidheim, Jerry
blames Clements and Moorer for false documentary submission to Congress on Cambodian bombings in press briefing **SI11** 75, 372-373
denies Defense Department knowingly submitted false data on Cambodian bombings to Senate Armed Services Committee **SI11** 64, 323-324
on reasons for false documentary submission to Congress on Cambodian bombings **SI11** 75, 369-371
on Richardson's role in submission of false data on Cambodian bombings by Defense Department to Senate Armed Services Committee **SI11** 65, 326-327
statement at press briefing on extent of secret bombings of Cambodia **SI11** 76, 77, 375-377, 382-383
statement at press briefing on MENU dual reporting system **SI11** 70-71, 72-73, 343-346, 355-359
statement at press briefing on Nixon's authorization of secret bombings of Cambodia **SI11** 71-72, 349-354
statement at press briefings on Members of Congress being informed of secret bombings of Cambodia **SI11** 73-74, 360-367

Friedman, Daniel M. **SI7-2** 594
memo from Randolph on appeal from adverse decision in ITT antitrust case **NSI2** 6, 45, 60-61
memo to Griswold recommending appeal from adverse decision in ITT antitrust case **NSI2** 6, 45, 55-59

Friends of the FBI SIAPP4 7

Friends of Richard Nixon Seminar SIAPP4 54

Froehlich, Harold V. **SUMM I** 1
additional views on Article of Impeachment III **RHJC** 503-505, 519-524
on calling witnesses before House Judiciary Committee Impeachment Inquiry **II 3** 1683-1684, 1686, 1700
concurrence with Minority of House Judiciary Committee Impeachment Inquiry views on Article of Impeachment III **RHJC** 493

Froehlich, Harold V. *(Continued)*
on House Judiciary Committee Impeachment Inquiry issuing subpoenas to Nixon **II 3** 1551-
1552, 1553-1554, 1555
on leaked Dixon memos **II 2** 1330-1331
on Nixon's noncompliance with House Judiciary
Committee Impeachment Inquiry subpoenas **II
2** 927-929
statement of concurring views with Report of
House Judiciary Committee Impeachment inquiry **RHJC** 281
on subpoenaing Sirica for Nixon tapes he has in
his possession **II 2** 990-991

Froehlich, Harold V., questioning by
Butterfield **TW 1** 110-111
Colson **TW 3** 496-497
Mitchell **TW 2** 201-203

Fugitives
Weatherman leaders **SI7-1** 393

Fulbright, James William SI7-2 568
request to House Judiciary Committee Impeachment Inquiry for material on Kissinger's role in
1969-1971 wiretaps **II 3** 1532
Richardson letter on legality of Justice Department wiretaps **NSI4** 29, 31, 193, 194-195, 199,
200-201
Rogers replies to accusation that he has misled
him in regard to Cambodia **SI11** 35-36, 225-226

Gable, Robert SI1 85

Gadbois, Robert SI5-1 444

Gaffney, James J. SI7-2 682, 683

Gallup polls SIAPP3 33, 81
Independents and **SIAPP4** 41

Galuardi, John
advised not to question GSA expenditures on Nixon's San Clemente property **SI12** 120
and boundary survey at Nixon's San Clemente
property **SI12** 128, 130
on GSA paying for housekeeping services at Nixon's San Clemente property **SI12** 155
and GSA payment for sewer system installation at
Nixon's San Clemente property **SI12** 112-113
and installation of den windows at Nixon's San
Clemente property **SI12** 123-125
and installation of new heating system at Nixon's
San Clemente property **SI12** 107
and Mrs. Nixon's approval of restoration of
"point" gazebo at Nixon's San Clemente property **SI12** 138-139
requests from Ehrlichman for landscaping at Nixon's San Clemente property **SI12** 115-116

Gammon, Sam NSI4 14, 115, 116-118

Garbarino, Ernest
objects to GSA billings for work at Nixon's San
Clemente property **SI12** 102-103
responds to letter of complaint on landscape up-
keep at Nixon's San Clemente property **SI12**
119
and restoration of "point" gazebo at Nixon's San
Clemente property **SI12** 138

Garcia, Brigido
employed as gardener at Nixon's San Clemente
property **SI12** 117, 185

Gardner, James F. SI1 33

Gardner, John SIAPP4 118

Garff, Ken SI5-2 584

Garland, Dr. David SI5-2 788, 789, 793

Garment, Leonard SI5-1 461
affidavit claiming Executive privilege for redated
memo from Whitaker to Nixon on milk price
supports **SI6-2** 484, 863, 873-875
attitude toward Mitchell running campaign from
space at Mudge, Rose, Guthrie, and Alexander
SIAPP4 47
discussions with Ervin **SIAPP1** 12; **SI4-3** 1418
in Ehrlichman-Krogh discussions **SIAPP3** 250
Haldeman informs Nixon of advice of **SI4-3** 1217-
1219, 1221
meeting with Haig and Kissinger **SI4-3** 1219-1220
meeting with Richardson, Haig, Buzhardt, and
Wright on Cox's rejection of Stennis Plan **SI9-2**
540, 787, 788-796
Nixon on **SI4-3** 1308, 1521
Nixon announces that he will take on Dean's duties as counsel **SIAPP1** 13
Nixon-Ziegler discussion on advice of **SI4-3** 1263
in Nixon's plan for blaming Watergate on Mitchell **SUMM I** 76
and Nixon's promises to Urban League **SI1** 80, 85

Garrison, Samuel, III II 2 1046; **SUMM I** 1
biography of **II 3** 2144
on bipartisanship of House Judiciary Committee
Impeachment Inquiry staff **II 3** 2036-2038
discussion on scheduling presentation to House
Judiciary Committee Impeachment Inquiry of
II 3 1945-1946
on issuing subpoenas to Nixon **II 1** 297, 313, 327
Jenner on **SUMM I** 14, 15
on legislation to increase milk price supports introduced into Congress **II 2** 1063-1064, 1065
on Nixon's noncompliance with House Judiciary
Committee Impeachment Inquiry subpoenas **II
1** 436-437, 439; **II 3** 2041-2043
presentation schedule **II 3** 1923-1924
presentation of summary of evidence to House
Judiciary Committee Impeachment Inquiry on
Articles of Impeachment **II 3** 2035-2051, 2081-
2093; **MMFL** 1-29
on procedures for House Judiciary Committee Impeachment Inquiry **II 1** 393, 399
request to present memorandum to House Judiciary Committee Impeachment Inquiry **SUMM I**
1-2
on role of politics in impeachment process **II 3**
2038-2041, 2050
on separate Minority of House Judiciary Committee Impeachment Inquiry brief on impeachable
offenses **II 1** 155
on St. Clair's participation in House Judiciary
Committee Impeachment Inquiry **II 1** 296-297

Gaston, David D. SI10 403

Gatalucci, Al SIAPP4 121

Gaunt, Loie
and selection of pre-Presidential papers for Nixon's gift to National Archives **SI10** 2-3, 59, 60-
61

Geneen, Harold S., cited testimony of *(Continued)*
 on use of Sheraton Harbor Island Hotel as
 Republican National Convention center **SI5-2**
 487, 562, 590-591
General Services Administration (GSA) SI12 93-94,
 101-102, 112-113
 and Chattel Deeds for Nixon's gifts of pre-Presidential papers **SI10** 2, 48-54
 expenditures in connection with Key Biscayne
 SI12 156-157
 expenditures in connection with San Clemente
 since 1969 **SI12** 100
 expenditures on Nixon's private properties, *see*
 Report on government expenditures on Nixon's
 private properties
 report on Classified Documents in Custody of,
 1946-1963 **SIAPP3** 184-185
 representative countersigns deed of Nixon's gift of
 pre-Presidential papers to National Archives as
 "accepted" **SI10** 2-3, 59, 60-61
 Rhoads' letter to Administrator that "second installment" of Nixon's gift of papers was not given in 1969 **SI10** 11, 282-287
 statutory authority to make expenditures to enable
 Secret Service to protect the President **SI12** 93-94
 See also Galuardi, John; Key Biscayne, Fla.; government expenditures on Nixon's property at;
 Kunzig, Robert L.; Rice, Robert; San Clemente,
 government expenditures on Nixon's property
 at; Wilson, James.
"Generation of Peace, A" SIAPP4 27
Geneva Accords of 1954
 and Cambodian-U.S. relations **SI11** 3
 in Nixon's speech on terms of proposed settlement
 of Vietnam War **SI11** 29, 199-200
Gephart, Cleo TW 3 49-50, 70
Gerrity, Edward "Ned" II 2 1000-1001; **SI5-2** 620,
 647-648, 683-684
 Beard and **SI5-2** 787, 791
 Beard on meeting on Anderson memo with **SI5-2**
 720-721
 cited testimony of, on meeting with Beard on
 Anderson memo **SI5-2** 498, 719, 722
 letter to Agnew on antitrust suits against ITT
 SI5-1 7, 143, 163-165; **SI5-2** 508-509, 513-514,
 674-676, 710-712, 803-804, 813-815, 863-864,
 897-899, 937-938
 memo to Ryan on antitrust policy **SI5-2** 513-514,
 863-864, 894
 memo to Ryan on antitrust suits against ITT **SI5-1** 7-8, 143-144, 185; **SI5-2** 936-937
 memo to Ryan on contacts with Nixon Administration officials **SI5-2** 671, 707
 See also ITT matter
Gerstenberg, Richard SI5-1 381; **SI5-2** 654, 690
Gesell, Gerhard A. II 2 965-966, 1057, 1123, 1329;
 SIAPP2 12-17; **SIAPP3** 1
 letter from Nixon on Plumbers unit **SI7-2** 530,
 649, 652-653
 provision of material from Fielding break-in grand
 jury to House Judiciary Committee Impeachment Inquiry **II 2** 1159-1161
 See also U.S. v. *Ehrlichman, et al*

Gibbons, Harold J.
 Caulfield memo to Dean requesting IRS audit of
 II 2 1284; **SI8** 22, 213, 214-216
Gibson, D. Jack SI5-1 467, 469
Gifford, K. Dunn SI7-2 1023
Gifford, William
 memo to Shultz on milk price-support issue **SI6-1**
 22-23, 329-330, 348, 349
Gill, Richard H. II 1 587; **II 2** 874, 1249, 874;
 SUMM I 1
 biography of **II 3** 2145
 at Doar-Jenner interview with Byrne **II 2** 1220
 on illegal, covert, and legal mail covers **II 2** 1117-1118
 on Nixon-Petersen relationship **II 3** 2031
 presentation of evidence on activities of Plumbers
 unit to House Judiciary Committee Impeachment Inquiry **II 2** 1123-1147
 presentation of evidence on domestic surveillance
 to House Judiciary Committee Impeachment Inquiry **II 2** 1088-1114
 presentation of evidence on Fielding break-in to
 House Judiciary Committee Impeachment Inquiry **II 2** 1141-1148, 1158, 1161-1173, 1178-1181, 1218-1265
 presentation of evidence on Huston plan to House
 Judiciary Committee Impeachment Inquiry **II 2**
 1115-1119
 presentation of evidence on Pentagon Papers matter to House Judiciary Committee Impeachment
 Inquiry **II 2** 1120-1123
 presentation of evidence on Sandwedge plan and
 Segretti activities to House Judiciary Committee
 Impeachment Inquiry **II 2** 1184-1186
Gilleas, Ben
 recommended by Colson for investigation of Pentagon Papers publication **SI7-2** 678
Gillenwaters, Edgar SI5-1 444, 455; **SI5-2** 715
 meeting with Haldeman and Reinecke **SI5-1** 429
Ginn, Opal SI5-2 792, 793
Gipson, Fred A. SIAPP2 308-309
 See also U.S. v. *David Parr*
Girard, Thomas SIAPP4 76
Glanzer, Seymour
 learns about Fielding break-in from Dean **II 2**
 1226-1228
 and rumors implicating Nixon in Watergate coverup **SI4-3** 1635-1636
 Wilson reports to Nixon on meeting with **SI4-3**
 1519-1521
Glanzer, Seymour, questioning by
 LaRue **SI1** 132-135
Glaser, Edward SIAPP4 12
Gleason, Jack A. II 2 1048; **SIAPP4** 93; **TW 3** 506;
 SI1 79; **SI2** 2, 44, 427, 428-441; **SI5-2** 809
 and AMPI contribution to special White House
 project on Congressional campaigns **SI6-1** 8,
 127, 130-152
 in Dean memo to Ehrlichman on *Nader* v. *Butz*
 SI6-2 889
 letter to Payson on political contributions to 1970
 Senatorial campaigns **SI6-1** 8, 141-144
 letter to Semer requesting names of people in Associated Dairymen's group **SI6-1** 6, 99, 118

memo from Colson with article on AMPI contribution to unopposed Democratic Congressional candidates **SI6-1** 13, 213, 215-216

memo to Colson on handling of responsibilities re milk producers **SI6-1** 7, 8, 119, 120-125, 127, 128-129

memo to Dent on White House Special Project expenses **SI6-1** 8, 127, 147-152

milk money and **SIAPP4** 85

refers Semer to Kalmbach on AMPI contribution **SI6-1** 60, 63

request to speak to reporters in memo from Strachan to Haldeman **SI1** 82

role in fundraising **SI6-1** 307

and Semer-Dent meeting **SI6-1** 109-110

telephone call to Kalmbach on contribution solicitation assignment **SI6-1** 8, 127, 130, 131

and White House Special Project on Congressional candidates **SI6-1** 140

See also House Judiciary Committee Impeachment Inquiry, presentation of evidence on dairy industry campaign contributions; ITT matter

Glendon, William R. SI7-2 594

Globe Security Systems SI8 75, 109

Godofsky, Stanley SI7-2 594

Goldberg, Lawrence Yale SIAPP4 6, 51

Caulfield investigation of income tax returns of **II 2** 1271; **SI8** 13, 131, 132-144

Goldbloom, Stanley, questioning by

Chotiner **NSI3** 170-172; **SI6-1** 421-423

Harrison **NSI3** 196-197; **SI6-1** 461-462

Kalmbach **NSI3** 178-180

Nelson **NSI3** 51, 192-193; **SI6-1** 457

Parr **NSI3** 194-195; **SI6-1** 459-460

Goldman, Henry, questioning by

Gray **SI4-2** 1072-1074, 1075, 1077

Ziegler **SI4-1** 321

Goldwater, Barry

Baroody gets speech on Watergate prepared for **SI3-2** 811-812

on electronic surveillance **II 3** 1993-1994

on Nixon's responsibility for secrecy on bombings of Cambodia **SI11** 325

role in Nixon re-election campaign **SIAPP4** 19, 54

Gompers, Elliot SI3-2 813

Gonzalez, Virgilio SIAPP2 67-70

guilty plea of **SI3-1** 41, 483, 485

See also U.S. v. G. Gordon Liddy, et al

Gonzalez, Virgilio, cited testimony of SI1 22, 201, 202-213

on first unsuccessful break-in attempts **SI1** 22, 201, 206-208

See also U.S. v. G. Gordon Liddy, et al; Watergate burglars

Good, Jo SI5-1 451

memo to Dole on San Diego as site of Republican National Convention **SI5-2** 486, 561, 578-581

Good, Terry SI10 79

Goode, Mark SIAPP4 27

Goodell, Charles SI7-2 1137

Goodman, Robert SIAPP4 27

Goodrich, Bernie SI5-2 619

Goodyear Tire and Rubber Company SIAPP2 257-262

See also U.S. v. Goodyear Tire and Rubber Company and Russell deYoung

GOP Moderates

in Political Matters Memoranda **SIAPP4** 18

Gordon, Kermet SI8 83, 88

Gorman, Patrick SIAPP4 7

Government Accounting Office (GAO)

Nixon on Watergate investigation of **SIAPP1** 3

Government employees

and antiwar movement **SI7-1** 391

FBI termination of wiretaps on **SI7-2** 525, 567, 568-574

Krogh arranges polygraph tests for **SI7-2** 895

polygraph tests for, discussed at Nixon-Ehrlichman-Krogh meeting **SI7-2** 868-885

results of wiretapping of **SI7-1** 15, 301, 302-312

wiretaps on after leaks on bombing of Cambodia **SI7-1** 14, 291, 292-300

Governors' Conference, Houston, Texas SIAPP4 121

Graham, Billy NSI2 128-129; **SIAPP4** 8-9; **SI5-1** 432, 451

calls for special prosecutor to investigate Watergate **SI9-1** 136

IRS audit of **II 2** 1279

IRS information sent to Dean on **SI8** 14, 145, 146-154

IRS investigation of **II 2** 1275

Grantsmanship

and Urban League **SI1** 80, 85

Gray, Elbert SI5-1 196

Gray, Louis Patrick II 1 617-622; **SIAPP1** 5; **SI2** 2, 36, 48, 355, 357, 359, 362, 471

asks Nixon to drop his nomination as FBI Director **II 2** 855

assured by Helms that CIA was not involved in Watergate **SI2** 2, 38, 375, 382-384

containment of Watergate from July 1 until elections and **SUMM I** 44

and contents of Hunt's safe **II 1** 684-685; **SI4-2** 1014-1015, 1018-1019; **SI4-3** 1517-1518

conversation with Helms on FBI Watergate investigation **NSI1** 16, 125, 127

Dean's information to Petersen on giving material from Hunt's safe to **TW 3** 75-78, 122, 130-131, 140-141, 145-146

and Dean's request to hold up Ogarrio and Dahlberg interviews **SI2** 2, 49, 473, 474-475

delays FBI interview of Chenow **SI7-3** 1205, 1569, 1570-1574

denial that FBI wiretapped newsmen and White House officials **SI7-4** 1627, 1755, 1756-1773

denies Dean gave him documents **SI4-3** 1238

denies FBI has records on Kissinger tapes **II 2** 1202

denies he received Hunt's material **SI4-3** 1255-1257

and destruction of files from Hunt's safe **SI4-3** 1113, 1613, 1614-1624

and FBI Watergate investigation **II 1** 594-596; **SUMM I** 40-41

Gray, Louis Patrick *(Continued)*

given material from Hunt's safe by Ehrlichman and Dean **SI2** 2, 52, 501, 502-510

gives FBI raw data to Dean **TW 2** 226-227, 333; **SI2** 2, 57, 555, 556-559

informed by Ehrlichman that Dean will handle Watergate inquiry for White House **SI2** 2, 31, 311, 312-314

informs Dean that FBI has theory that CIA was involved in Watergate break-in **NSI1** 15, 121, 122-123

Kleindienst on **SI4-3** 1655; **SI7-4** 1871, 1873

list of meetings and conversations with Nixon **SI4-1** 7, 241, 242

log for March 23, 1973 **SI4-1** 7, 241, 243

log for April 17, 1973 **SI4-3** 1096, 1331, 1332-1333

log for April 27, 1973 **SI4-3** 1115, 1627, 1631-1632

log for June 20, 1972 **SI2** 2, 34, 337, 338

log for June 22, 1972 **SI2** 2, 31, 311, 312-313

log for June 23, 1972 **SI2** 2, 40, 397, 398-399

log for July 5, 1972 **SI2** 2, 56, 520, 521

log for July 6, 1972 **SI2** 2, 56, 520, 524-525

logs of meetings and telephone conversations with Nixon turned over to Jaworski **SI9-2** 554, 883, 884-890

MacGregor denies he was asked to call Nixon **SI2** 2, 533-537

and material from Hunt's safe **II 3** 1741

meeting with Dean on FBI Watergate investigation **SI2** 2, 31, 311, 315

meeting with Dean on Mexican checks **SI2** 2, 34, 337, 338, 339, 340-341

meeting with Petersen on Hunt's files **SI4-3** 1328-1329

meeting with Walters on White House staff's interference with Watergate investigation **SUMM I** 45

meets with Ehrlichman and Dean to recieve rest of material from Hunt's safe **SI7-3** 1206, 1575, 1576-1587

memo for record by Walters on meeting with **SI2** 2, 56, 520, 528-529

memo from Walters on aliases provided by CIA to Hunt **SI2** 4, 79, 86

memo from Walters on information provided by CIA to FBI on Watergate incident **SI2** 2, 56, 520, 530-532

Mitchell denies meeting with on June 17, 1972 **TW 2** 173

Nixon-Colson discussion on his nomination as Director of FBI **TW 3** 320-321

Nixon on comment that he was being mortally wounded **SIAPP1** 44

in Nixon-Dean discussion on possible directors of FBI **SI7-4** 1629, 1813, 1814-1820

in Nixon-Dean-Haldeman discussion **SI8** 300

Nixon-Dean-Haldeman discussion on confirmation hearings on **SI8** 392-398

Nixon-Haldeman discussion on FBI Watergate investigation and **SIAPP3** 40-44, 77-79

in Nixon-Haldeman discussion on Watergate **SI4-3** 1310

Nixon on his giving information to Dean and Ehrlichman on FBI Watergate investigation

SIAPP1 9

Nixon on his lack of knowledge of new Watergate investigation ordered on March 21, 1973 **SIAPP1** 51-52

in Nixon-Petersen discussion **SI4-3** 1401

Nixon withdraws nomination as Director of FBI **SIAPP1** 11

Nixon withholds Dean's information from **SUMM I** 7

in Nixon-Ziegler conversation **SI9-1** 185-195

Nixon's lack of awareness of his destruction of documents from Hunt's safe **NSI1** 18, 137, 138-139

nomination as director of FBI withdrawn **SI4-1** 31, 503, 504-506

obstruction of Ellsberg trial by **RHJC** 172

offer of access to FBI files to U.S. Senate **SI4-3** 1624

and origin of theory of CIA involvement in Watergate break-in **II 3** 1736

perjured testimony before Watergate Grand Jury **SUMM I** 91

and release of information on his burning files from Hunt's safe **II 2** 892-893

resignation as acting director of FBI **SI4-3** 1115, 1627, 1629-1632; **II 2** 892-893

role in Nixon Administration **RHJC** 16-17

says Dean probably lied to FBI on Hunt's status at White House **SI2** 2, 333; **SI4-1** 6, 109-111, 113-114, 235, 236, 238

taped telephone conversation with Ehrlichman on Gray confirmation hearings and Watergate investigation **SI3-2** 696, 767, 768-776

telegram from FBI Washington Field Office on Mexican checks **SI2** 2, 34, 337, 346-347

telephone call from Ehrlichman on Dean telling Watergate Prosecutors about Hunt's safe **II 2** 881

telephone call from Kleindienst on Watergate break-in investigation **SI2** 2, 13, 135, 136-142

telephone call from Nixon to **II 2** 836; **SUMM I** 87

telephone call to Helms on possible CIA involvement in Watergate **SI2** 2, 107-108, 109

telephone call to MacGregor on concern over White House staff use of FBI and CIA **SUMM I** 45

telephone conversation with Dean on FBI Watergate investigation **SI2** 2, 46, 449, 451, 453, 550, 551-553; **SI4-1** 7, 241, 242, 243, 244-248

telephone conversation with Nixon on White House use of FBI and CIA **SUMM I** 45-46

telephone conversations with Ehrlichman on Hunt's safe **SI4-2** 583, 1059, 1060-1080

in *Time* magazine article on White House wiretaps **SI7-4** 1747-1748

warning to Nixon, in Article of Impeachment I **RHJC** 58-59

and Watergate coverup **II 1** 689-691; **SUMM I** 39

Weicker and **SI4-1** 365, 371

withdrawal from nomination for FBI Director **II 2** 1206; **SI4-1** 354-355; **SI7-4** 1634, 1859, 1860-1862;

See also FBI Watergate investigation; Gray confirmation hearings; Walters, Vernon A.

Gray, Louis Patrick, cited testimony of SI2 2, 51, 57, 483, 487-488, 555, 556-557; SI3-2 691, 723, 727-728

on accessibility of FBI Watergate files SI3-2 725-726

claims no knowledge of FBI wiretapping of newsmen and White House officials SI7-4 1627, 1755, 1756-1760

on conversations with Nixon on withdrawal of his nomination as director of FBI SI4-1 31, 503, 504-505

on conversations with Walters re Watergate investigation and CIA SI2 2, 56, 520, 522-523

on Dean and FBI Watergate investigation SI2 2, 474-475

on Dean probably lying about Hunt's office at White House SI4-1 238

on destruction of files from Hunt's safe SI4-3 1113, 1613, 1614-1616; SI7-2 558-559, 1029-1030, 1076-1079

on discussions with MacGregor and Nixon on FBI Watergate investigation SI2 2, 56, 520, 551-553

on FBI interview with Chenow SI7-3 1205, 1569, 1573-1574

on FBI investigation of Segretti SI7-3 1203, 1541, 1547-1550

on FBI material given to Dean SI2 2, 57, 555, 556-557

on informing Dean of theories of Watergate break-in NSI1 15, 121, 122

on Liddy SI2 2, 51, 483, 496

on meeting with Dean on FBI Watergate investigation SI2 2, 314

on meeting with Dean on Mexican checks SI2 2, 34, 337, 339

on meeting with Petersen on Hunt's files SI4-3 1096, 1331, 1334

on meeting with Walters on FBI Watergate investigation SI2 2, 40, 397, 400-401

on Mexican checks and CIA involvement in Watergate SI2 4, 79, 95

on Nixon instructing him to conduct an aggressive and thorough investigation of Watergate NSI1 17, 129, 135

on Nixon's statement of April 30, 1973 on Watergate investigation SI4-1 7, 241, 244-248

on receiving additional material from Hunt's safe from Ehrlichman and Dean SI7-3 1206, 1575, 1577-1578

on receiving material from Hunt's safe from Ehrlichman and Dean SI2 2, 52, 501, 503

on resignation as director of FBI SI4-3 1115-1116, 1614-1616, 1627-1628, 1629-1630

on taped telephone conversation with Ehrlichman SI3-2 696, 767, 772-776

on telephone conversations with Ehrlichman on Hunt's safe SI4-2 583, 1059, 1072-1077, 1078

Gray confirmation hearings

Dean refuses to testify at SI3-2 702, 881, 882-886, 895-896

discussed at Nixon-Dean-Haldeman meeting SI4-1 109-113

discussed at Nixon-Dean meeting SI3-2 695, 740-741, 753, 761, 764-765, 991-993

Executive privilege for Dean and SI3-2 694, 746, 747, 749-751

Gray's testimony during SI2 2, 33, 51, 329, 335-337, 423, 483, 496; SI3-2 691, 723, 724-728; II 2 835

Nixon's refusal to allow Dean to testify at SIAPP1 5, 8-9, 10

Nixon's response to questions on revelations on Segretti matter at SIAPP1 9-10

Sullivan's expected testimony at SI3-2 824-834, 873, 877-878, 879

White House interference with FBI Watergate investigation and II 2 778-786

Grayson, Mel SIAPP4 28

Green, David SIAPP4 96

Green, Marshall

speech before Far East America Council on January 19, 1971 denying presence of ground troops in Cambodia SI11 47-48, 263-265

statement on U.S. air support in Cambodia in November 1970 SI11 18, 164

Green, Timothy NSI2 85; SI5-1 405

Greene, Robert W.

IRS audit of II 2 1281

New York State tax audit of SI8 16, 165, 174

White House efforts to obtain IRS audit of SI8 16, 165, 166-174

Greenspun, Herman II 2 1290-1292; SI2 2, 556-557

proposed break-in at office of SI1 65, 67

as target of Liddy plan SI1 10, 61

See also Greenspun matter

Greenspun matter

Colson on TW 3 344

Kalmbach on TW 3 615-617

Greenwood, Stephen Carter TW 3 53-54, 57, 58, 70

Gregg, Don

at meeting between Nixon and dairy industry leaders on March 23, 1971 SI6-2 613-614

Grider, Sam SI12 153

Griffin, Robert SIAPP4 25

Griffin, William E.

at meeting between Nixon and dairy industry leaders on March 23, 1971 SI6-2 589-591, 602

Grinnell Corporation SI5-1 4, 101, 104-105

McLaren memo to Mitchell on acquisition by ITT SI5-1 4, 101, 120-129

See also ITT, antitrust suits against

Griswold, Dean II 2 965-966

and Nixon's instructions to Petersen on Fielding break-in TW 3 99, 147-148

See also House Judiciary Committee Impeachment Inquiry, presentation of evidence on ITT matter; ITT matter

Griswold, Erwin N. II 3 1757-1771, 1773; SI5-1 265; SI5-2 534, 535, 802, 957

application for Further Extension of Time for ITT-Grinnell case SI5-1 16, 349, 350-358, 360-361, 364; SI5-2 863

authorization of appeal to Supreme Court from adverse decision in ITT antitrust case NSI2 6, 45, 46-64

and Kleindienst's request for extension of time on ITT-Grinnell appeal NSI2 7, 65, 66-72

Griswold, Erwin N. *(Continued)*
in Merriam letter to Peterson **SI5-2** 812
See also St. Clair, James D., presentation of evidence in behalf of Nixon on ITT matter
Griswold, Erwin N., cited testimony of
on *ITT-Grinnell* appeal **SI5-1** 16, 349, 354-357
on Kleindienst's request for extension of time on ITT-Grinnell appeal **NSI2** 7, 65, 66-67
Grose, Peter
article on secret official estimates for first strike capabilities of Soviet Union **NSI4** 25, 173, 174-175
Guest, Raymond SIAPP4 49
Guilfoile, Arne SI7-2 1023
Gulf Oil Corporation SIAPP2 263-266
See also U.S. v. *Gulf Oil Corporation and Claude C. Wild, Jr.*
Gull, George SIAPP1 63
Gunderson, T.L. SI7-3 1433
Gunn, Dr. Edward M. TW 3 44
Gurney, Edward J. SIAPP4 17
on Kleindienst's testimony **SI5-2** 731
on purpose of Select Committee hearing **SI1** 163
Gurney, Edward J., questioning by
Anderson **SI5-2** 618
Barker **SI1** 205; **SI7-2** 1109-1110; **SI7-3** 1276
Dean **NSI1** 42, 194; **SI2** 2, 507-510, 559; **SI4-1** 386-387; **SI7-3** 1582-1585; **SI8** 67
Ehrlichman **NSI1** 200; **SI3-1** 189, 462-464, 548, 612-613; **SI2** 2, 173, 320-322; **SI3-2** 1138-1141, 1268; **SI4-1** 350-351, 401-404, 464-467, 518, 533, 541-542; **SI4-2** 724, 812-813, 830-831, 1063; **SI4-3** 1132-1133, 1649-1650; **SI7-3** 1581
Haldeman **SI9-1** 438; **SI2** 2, 166-167, 276
Hume **SI5-2** 622
Hunt **SI1** 199-200
Kalmbach **SI3-1** 230-232
Kleindienst **SI4-2** 928, 1000
McCord **SI3-1** 492; **SI1** 188-189
Petersen **SI4-2** 1056; **SI4-3** 1124
Sloan **SI3-1** 560-561
Stans **SI2** 2, 265, 573
Strachan **SI1** 95-96
Ulasewicz **SI3-1** 216-217
Guthman, Ed
on enemies list **SI8** 73, 107, 119
Hahn, Walter SI5-1 437, 444
Haig, Alexander M., Jr. II 2 1090; **SIAPP3** 40; **SIAPP4** 141-142; **SI7-1** 327, 365
agreement with Jaworski **II 2** 1432
and arrangements for Buzhardt to report to Nixon on contents of taped Nixon-Dean telephone conversation **SI9-1** 17, 289, 290-312
in Butterfield memo to Magruder on Hoover's letter to Nixon re Clifford **SI7-1** 20, 359, 362-363
complains to Richardson about Cox's activities **SI9-1** 33, 158-159, 403, 404-406
complains to Richardson about Cox's investigation of San Clemente property expenditures **II 2** 1352
and Cox's firing as Special Watergate Prosecutor **SUMM I** 104
and Cox's rejection of Stennis Plan **SI9-2** 538, 773, 774-781

dealings with Richardson on Cox's alleged investigation of Nixon's expenditures on his San Clemente property **SI9-1** 21, 329, 330-332
and delivery of FBI files and logs of wiretaps on Kraft to White House **SI7-2** 927-929, 947
discussion with Colson on Watergate **TW 3** 361-362
discussion with Jaworski on conditions for accepting job as Watergate Special Prosecutor **SI9-2** 548, 837, 838-843
and domestic surveillance **II 2** 1096-1097, 1103-1104
and FBI wiretap material **SI7-1** 370
and firing of Cox and abolition of Watergate Special Prosecution Task Force **SI9-2** 544, 815, 816-825
Hoover's memo to Mitchell on wiretaps on White House staff member requested by **SI7-1** 267
informs Buzhardt that dictabelt of Nixon's recollections of April 15, 1973 conversation with Dean could not be located **SI9-2** 550, 849, 850-860
instructs FBI not to enter records of wiretaps of government officials and newsmen in indices **SUMM I** 124, 134
interview on "Face the Nation" on Cox's requests for Nixon's logs of meetings and telephone conversations with fifteen named individuals **SI9-1** 14, 257, 266, 267, 276
and lack of records of Halperin wiretaps at Justice Department **II 2** 1192, 1193
and leaks on U.S. position on India-Pakistan War **SI7-3** 1423
in letter from Jaworski to Eastland summarizing agreement made on independence of Watergate Special Prosecutor **SI9-2** 557, 575, 923, 924-925, 1019, 1020-1025
and Mardian's delivery of 1969-71 wiretap records to White House **SI7-4** 2061-2063
meeting with Garment and Kissinger **SI4-3** 1219-1220
meeting with Richardson, Garment, Buzhardt, and Wright on Cox's rejection of Stennis Plan **SI9-2** 540, 787, 788-796
meeting with Richardson and other Presidential aides on tapes litigation **SI9-2** 536, 755, 756-763
memo to Ehrlichman on delaying Ellsberg trial **SI7-3** 1478, 1479
memo to Heads of all U.S. Departments and Agencies requesting security clearance review **NSI4** 5, 67, 68-69
and missing Nixon tape of April 15 **II 2** 1405-1406
news conference of October 23, 1973 on meeting with Richardson, Garment, Buzhardt and Wright on Cox's rejection of Stennis Plan **SI9-2** 540, 787, 789-790
news conference of October 23, 1973 on Nixon authorizing Wright to inform Sirica that subpoenaed tapes will be turned over to him **SI9-2** 545, 827, 828-830
news conference of October 23, 1973 on Richardson and Ruckelshaus resignations and firing of Cox **SI9-2** 544, 815, 818-820
news conference of October 23, 1973 on tapes litigation **SI9-2** 536, 755, 757758

Nixon discusses tape of March 21, 1973 with
SUMM I 105
in Nixon-Ehrlichman-Krogh discussion on SALT
talk leaks SI7-2 870-872, 877
note to Woods on confusion over June 20, 1972
subpoenaed tape SI9-2 529, 619, 637
orders wiretapping of government employees after
leaks on bombing of Cambodia SI7-1 14, 291,
292-300
and Plumbers unit SI7-2 1006
in Political Matters Memoranda on programming
conservative leaders through White House
SIAPP4 3
and preparations for Nixon's review of subpoenaed tapes SI9-2 529, 619, 620-648
and removal of wiretaps on government employees and newsmen SI7-2 572
request on FBI filing procedures for domestic surveillance II 2 1095
role in wiretapping of government employees and
newsmen SI7-2 682
and selection of Jaworski as Special Watergate
Prosecutor II 2 1402-1404
Shultz tells Alexander he will inform him of decision to reopen audit of Nixons' 1969 tax return
SI10 17
and Soviet Embassy obtaining Pentagon Papers
TW 3 489-490, 512, 516-517
tape recording of June 4, 1973 conversation with
Nixon SI9-1 11, 169, 177-183
telephone call to Richardson complaining about
Cox's investigation II 2 1363
testimony at Ellsberg trial II 2 1099
and transfer of FBI files on Kissinger tapes to
White House II 2 1157-1158
and wiretapping of government officials and newsmen SI7-1 189, 190
and wiretapping of Halperin SI7-1 219
and wiretapping of National Security Council
members SI7-1 7, 191, 192-199, 202-203
and wiretapping of newsmen SI7-1 10, 149, 239,
240-242
and wiretapping of White House staff members
unrelated to national security SI7-1 264
See also Halperin v. *Haig*; House Judiciary Committee Impeachment Inquiry, presentation of
evidence on domestic surveillance
Haig, Alexander M., Jr., cited testimony of
on arranging for Buzhardt to hear tape of Nixon-
Dean telephone conversation SI9-1 17, 289,
300-301
on missing dictabelt of Nixon's recollections of
April 15, 1973 Nixon-Dean conversation SI9-2
550, 849, 853-858
on preparations for Nixon's review of subpoenaed
tapes SI9-2 528, 529, 607, 608-610, 619, 620-
623
on transfer of Nixon tapes from Secret Service to
White House SI9-1 28, 379, 385-387
Haiman, Robert SIAPP1 65-66
Hainsworth, Brad SIAPP4 107, 144
Haldeman, Harry Robins II 2 1090, 1115-1119; II 3
1626-1627; **SIAPP2 101-192; SI9-2 526, 591, 592-
593; SI3-2 701, 713, 803, 804-880, 1004-1005, 1135,
1145; SI4-1 3, 107, 108-211; SI4-3 1341; SI7-1 331;**

SI8 31, 359, 360-435
and access to Nixon TW 2 189-190
agenda for meeting with Nixon with item on Magruder's efforts to obtain government post SI3-1
49-50, 557-558, 574
agrees with Dean that he should discuss Hunt's
demands with Nixon TW 2 250, 297
alleged telephone call to Mitchell on Hunt's demands for money II 2 806-807, 809-810
and AMPI's initiation of political contribution
through Kalmbach SI6-1 3-4, 57-58, 81-82
appeal by his attorney on Sirica's ruling on turning Grand Jury materials over to House Judiciary Committee Impeachment Inquiry II 1 202
and approval of Dean contacting Kalmbach on
fundraising for Watergate defendants II 2 727-
728
and approval of Liddy plan NSI1 82
approves transfer of campaign contributions for
payment to Watergate defendants SI3-1 33-34,
425-426, 427-454
approves transfer of "political expenses" for
White House to CRP SI1 47
arranges for meeting with Mitchell NSI1 25, 169,
170-176
asks Dean to return from Camp David to meet
with Mitchell and Magruder II 2 840
asks Dean to write report on Watergate NSI1 28,
193, 194
asks Mitchell to come to Washington to see Nixon TW 2 126-128
attitude toward hush money NSI1 23, 161, 162
authorized by Nixon to listen to several tapes of
Nixon-Haldeman-Dean conversations SI9-1 25,
351, 352-370
authorizes Kalmbach to pay Segretti II 2 1120
blames Mollenhoff for leaked IRS information on
Wallace administration SI8 39
Butterfield on his relationship with CRP TW 1
52-53, 111
Butterfield on his role on White House staff TW
1 9, 37, 66-67, 99-101, 102-103, 112, 113, 115,
120
calendar for March 30, 1972 SI5-2 508-509, 803-
804, 837
calendar for April 4, 1972 SI1 16, 156, 161
calendar for June 20, 1972 SI2 2, 23, 235, 237
calendar for February 14 and 23, 1973 and March
2, 1973 SI3-1 49-50, 557-558, 579-581
calendar for February 22, 1973 SI3-1 51, 583, 590
calendar for March 21, 1973 SI3-2 713, 1135,
1137
calendar for March 22, 1973 SI3-2 718, 1251,
1253
calendar for March 26, 1973 SI4-1 12-13, 311-
312, 316
calendar for April 25-26, 1973 SI4-3 1112, 1557,
1608-1611
Chapin's false declarations to Watergate Grand
Jury and SI7-4 1910, 1914
cited meetings with Nixon SI5-2 508-509, 510,
803-804, 841, 845
and Colson memo of June 25, 1971 on *New York
Times* and Pentagon Papers article TW 3 187-
198

Haldeman, Harry Robins *(Continued)*

Colson states he believed he was keeping information away from him **TW 3** 502-503

Colson tells Ziegler he should resign **TW 3** 354-355

Colson on $350,000 fund of **TW 3** 510-511

and Colson's assignment of Hunt to Pentagon Papers investigation for White House **NSI4** 6, 71, 72-74

Colson's opinion of **TW 3** 478, 491-492

and construction of block wall at Nixon's San Clemente property **SI12** 152

conversation with Nixon on Fielding break-in **SUMM I** 136-138

conversation with Nixon on June 20, 1972 Nixon tape **SI9-2** 529, 531, 619, 620-648, 687, 688-719

copy of Colson-Hunt taped telephone conversation on Pentagon Papers matter sent to **SI7-2** 535, 697, 698-702

and dairy industry contributions **II 2** 1061

Dean on his insistence on Camp David trip **TW 2** 279

Dean on his knowledge of payments to Watergate defendants **SI3-1** 150-151, 152

Dean on his role at White House **TW 2** 334, 344, 346, 349-350

Dean informs about Liddy plan **SI1** 60, 66; **SI3-2** 1000-1001

Dean informs him that his lawyers have met privately with Watergate prosecutors **SI4-1** 30, 501, 502

Dean informs him of theory of CIA involvement in Watergate break-in **NSI1** 15, 121, 123

Dean plays recording of Colson-Hunt conversation for **II 2** 752

and Dean Report **SUMM I** 73-74

Dean reports on meeting with Gray to **SI2** 2, 34, 337, 349-350

Dean reports on meeting with Segretti to **SI3-1** 33, 391, 392-403

Dean reports on second meeting on Liddy plan to **NSI1** 9, 63, 64-65; **SI1** 10, 61

and Dean-Segretti meeting **II 2** 751-752

Dean tells Nixon he had no prior knowledge of Watergate break-in **NSI1** 51

Dean tells Nixon he received reports on wiretapping of Democratic National Committee headquarters **SUMM I** 33-34

Dean on Watergate coverup and **NSI1** 43

and Dean's briefing paper for meeting between Nixon and Kleindienst **SI3-1** 51, 583, 584-595

and Dean's "investigation" of Watergate **SUMM I** 71

decision-making and **II 2** 1021-1022

and delivery of FBI files and logs of wiretaps on Kraft to White House **SI7-2** 929

denies discussion of political intelligence with Mitchell or Nixon **SI1** 15, 155, 162-163, 167

denies giving Strachan instructions to destroy materials **SI1** 15, 155, 167

directs Magruder to return to Washington to meet with Dean, Strachan, and Sloan on Watergate arrests **SUMM I** 36

discusses Colson's forthcoming testimony with Nixon **SUMM I** 85

discusses hush money with Nixon and Dean on March 21, 1973 **SUMM I** 59-60

discusses possible resignation with Ehrlichman and Nixon **SI7-4** 1923

discusses Segretti matter with Nixon **II 2** 1199

discussion with Colson on Mitchell's possible responsibility for Watergate break-in **TW 3** 318-319

discussion with Colson on payments to Hunt **TW 3** 315-317

discussion with Dean on his testifying before Watergate Grand Jury without immunity **II 2** 840-841

discussion with Dean on use of dairy industry contribution **SI6-2** 480, 784, 808-812

discussion with Nixon and Dean on Dean working through IRS **II 2** 1293-1295, 1298

discussion with Nixon and Dean on September 15, 1972 of indictment against Watergate defendants **SI3-1** 30, 369, 370-371

discussion with Nixon and Ehrlichman on blaming Mitchell for Watergate in Ehrlichman Report **SUMM I** 75-77

discussions with Nixon on his forthcoming testimony **SUMM I** 83-84

Doar on Nixon assigning him to hear tapes **II 3** 1929-1930, 1972

and efforts to determine Hunt's status at White House after Watergate break-in **TW 3** 258-259

Ehrlichman-Kalmbach discussion on **SI4-3** 1550

and Ehrlichman's false testimony under oath **SUMM I** 84-85

and enemies list **SI8** 11-12, 111-112, 113-129; **II 2** 1269

and evidence of existence of taped conversations with Nixon **II 1** 412

and false testimony by Porter and Magruder on purpose of funds given Liddy **SI3-1** 44, 501, 502-516

and FBI investigation of Schorr **II 2** 1174; **SI7-2** 562, 1111, 1112-1124

and FBI reports on wiretapping **II 2** 1114; **SI7-2** 694

first meeting with Nixon after Watergate arrests **SUMM I** 8-9

handling of Political Matters Memoranda by **SI1** 37-38

hears Colson's report on his conversation with Bittman **II 2** 757-758

hears Dean's report on Liddy plan but does not order its termination **SUMM I** 30-31

and Hillings' letter to Nixon on dairy import quotas **NSI3** 8, 75, 76-110

and hiring of Butterfield **TW 1** 8-9

and hiring of Hunt **II 2** 1126-1128; **TW 3** 198-200; **SI7-2** 679

and hiring of Segretti **SI7-2** 577, 583, 586-587

Hoover's memo to Mitchell on wiretaps on White House staff member requested by **SI7-1** 268

House Judiciary Committee Impeachment Inquiry discussion on subpoenaing **II 2** 981-992

House Judiciary Committee Impeachment Inquiry subpoenas for specified materials related to conversations between Nixon and **SI9-2** 568, 573, 577, 977, 978-982, 1009, 1010-1013, 1031, 1032-1036

House Judiciary Committee transcript of meeting with Nixon, Dean, and Ehrlichman on March 21, 1973 **TPC** 131-146

House Judiciary Committee transcript of meeting with Nixon, Dean, Ehrlichman, and Mitchell on March 22, 1973 **TPC** 147-186

House Judiciary Committee transcripts of meetings with Nixon and Dean **TPC** 1-18, 47-78, 79-130

and Hunt-Liddy meeting with Segretti **II 2** 1190

and Hunt's assignment to investigate publication of Pentagon Papers **SI7-2** 533, 675, 676-679

and Hunt's termination from White House staff **SIAPP3** 265-266

and hush money **II 2** 734-735, 755-757; **SUMM I** 52; **TW 1** 259; **SI3-2** 1016-1017; **SI4-3** 1515-1516, 1526-1527

and Huston plan **SUMM I** 126

Huston plan and Huston memo sent to **SI7-1** 23, 24, 383, 437, 438-444, 443

implementation of Nixon's policies by **SUMM I** 29

indictment of **II 2** 1425; **SUMM I** 84

informed by Dean of CRP fundraising for Watergate defendants **SI3-1** 14, 199, 200-202

informed by Kalmbach of AMPI contribution **SI6-1** 6, 99, 100-101

informed by Strachan that documents were destroyed **SI2** 2, 26, 269, 272-273, 276

informed by Strachan that Sandwedge plan is scrapped and Liddy will head up political intelligence at CRP **SUMM I** 30

informs Huston that Dean is taking over his duties on internal security matters **SI7-1** 488

informs Nixon about Hunt's Grand Jury appearance **SI4-4** 1634, 1859, 1860-1862

instructed by Nixon to ask Colson if he offered Executive clemency to Hunt **SI4-1** 8, 249, 251-252

instructed by Nixon to give Strachan report of Magruder's testimony **SI4-2** 565, 811, 820

instructed by Nixon to meet with CIA officials on FBI Watergate investigation **NSI1** 16, 125, 126-127

instructions to Haynes on recipients of FBI "top secret" wiretap material at White House **SI7-1** 21, 369, 370

instructions to Kalmbach on form of political contributions **SI6-1** 65

instructions to Kalmbach on funds left over from 1968 campaign **II 2** 1046

instructs Strachan, Buchanan, Chapin, and Walker to develop recommendations for "political intelligence and covert activities" **SUMM I** 29

instructs Strachan to telephone Segretti **SI1** 166

and interference with Senate Select Committee **II 2** 760-767

interviewed by FBI on wiretaps on White House staff members **SI7-1** 275-278

and investigation of Schorr **SUMM I** 127

involvement with hush money **SUMM I** 93

involvement with Strachan's Watergate Grand Jury testimony **SUMM I** 83

involvement with Watergate coverup **SUMM I** 41-42

and IRS audit of Greene **II 2** 1281; **SI8** 16, 165, 166-174

and IRS investigation of George and Gerald Wallace **II 3** 1983-1984; **SUMM I** 141

and IRS investigations of Nixon's friends **II 2** 1275-1281

and ITT matter **SUMM I** 145-148; **SI5-2** 614

Kalmbach informs about $100,000 contribution from Semer **II 2** 1048

in Kalmbach letter to Silbert **SI6-1** 306, 307

and Kalmbach's handling of milk producers' contributions **SI6-1** 19, 299, 300-315

and Kalmbach's instructions to GSA to cancel landscape maintenance contract for Nixon's San Clemente property **SI12** 117

Kehrli and **SIAPP3** 265

and knowledge about Magruder's planned testimony before Watergate Grand Jury **II 2** 749

LaRue on contacts with **TW 1** 178

LaRue's first knowledge of his $350,000 account **TW 1** 242-243

and leak of IRS investigation of George and Gerald Wallace **II 2** 1250-1255

leave of absence requested by **SI4-3** 1270

letter from Hoover on publication of Pentagon Papers **SI7-2** 527, 529, 609-611

letter from Kalmbach on pledges and contributions to Congressional candidates **SI6-1** 8, 127, 140

Liddy plan and **II 1** 574-575

list of meetings and conversations with Haldeman **SI4-1** 12-13, 311-312, 315

list of meetings and conversations with Nixon **SI4-1** 8, 18, 249, 250, 347, 348

listens to Nixon tapes after his resignation **II 2** 1331-1332, 1355-1356

listens to Nixon tapes of February, March, and April 1973 and meets with Nixon on **SI9-1** 3, 107, 108-126

listens to tapes of Nixon-Dean meeting of March 21, 1973 **II 2** 890, 892

log for April 14, 1973 **SI4-2** 560, 707, 708

log of meeting with Nixon on June 20, 1972 **SI2** 2, 23, 235, 245

log of meetings and conversations with Nixon **SI1** 15, 155, 157-158

Magruder asks Mitchell for meeting with **II 2** 842-843

Magruder-Colson disputes and **SI1** 89

Magruder tells LaRue he notified him of Watergate break-in **TW 1** 190, 194

and Magruder's appointment to government job after perjured testimony **SUMM I** 80-81

and Magruder's efforts to obtain government post after Watergate **SI3-1** 49-50, 557-558, 559-581

and Magruder's forthcoming talks with Watergate Prosecutor **SUMM I** 81-83

and Magruder's and Porter's perjury before Grand Jury **NSI1** 20, 145, 146-148

and Mardian's instructions from Nixon on FBI files and logs of 1969-71 wiretaps **SI7-2** 778

meeting with Colson and MacGregor on continuation of support or withdrawal of Kleindienst nomination **SI5-2** 508-509, 803-804, 805

meeting with Dean after he meets with Watergate Prosecutors **II 2** 842-843

Haldeman, Harry Robins *(Continued)*

meeting with Dean and Ehrlichman on Dean's Watergate Grand Jury testimony **SI4-1** 35, 537, 538-542

meeting with Dean and Ehrlichman on expected indictments of White House staff members **SI4-2** 559, 698-706

meeting with Dean and Ehrlichman on March 21, 1973 on Mitchell's role in Watergate **SI3-2** 713, 1135, 1136-1144

meeting with Dean and Nixon on March 13, 1973 **SI3-2** 701, 803, 804-880

meeting with Dean and Nixon on March 21, 1973, Nixon's summary of tape on **SIAPP1** 93-96

meeting with Dean on uses for milk fund **II 2** 1078-1079

at meeting to discuss Hunt's White House status **SI2** 2, 17-18, 165-166

meeting with Ehrlichman, Helms, and Walters on FBI Watergate investigation **SI2** 2, 38-39, 375-376, 377-395

meeting with Ehrlichman, Mitchell, and Dean on March 22, 1973 **SI3-2** 718-719, 1251-1252, 1253-1275

meeting with Ehrlichman and Mitchell on Watergate arrests **SUMM I** 37

meeting with Mitchell and Magruder on Magruder's false testimony on approval of Liddy plan **II 2** 847-848

meeting with Mitchell and Magruder on March 28, 1973 **SI4-1** 341, 343, 345

meeting with Mitchell, Magruder, and Strachan on Sandwedge plan **SUMM I** 29-30

meeting with Mollenhoff, Ehrlichman, and Ziegler on leaked IRS information **SI8** 39

meeting with Morgan **SI10** 71

meeting with Nixon on April 15, 1973 after he is briefed by Kleindienst **II 2** 870

meeting with Nixon on April 16, 1973 on Haldeman's involvement in transfer of cash from White House to CRP **SI4-3** 1211

meeting with Nixon and Dean on IRS investigation of O'Brien **SI8** 28-29, 331-332, 333-349

meeting with Nixon and Dean on September 15, 1973 on Watergate matter **SI2** 2, 62, 593, 594-656

meeting with Nixon on Dean's working through IRS **SI8** 27, 287, 288-330

meeting with Nixon and Ehrlichman on April 16, 1973 **SI4-3** 1084, 1131, 1137-1139, 1203, 1204-1211

meeting with Nixon, Ehrlichman and Dean on Hunt's blackmail threats **SI7-4** 1631, 1829, 1830-1836

meeting with Nixon and Ehrlichman on March 27, 1973 on Kleindienst **SI4-1** 18, 347, 350-351, 353, 354-371

meeting with Nixon, Ehrlichman, Mitchell, and Dean on Nixon's new plan on Watergate **SUMM I** 86-87

meeting with Nixon on June 20, 1972 **SI2** 2, 23-24, 235-236, 243-260

meeting with Nixon on June 23, 1972 **SI7-3** 1202, 1533, 1534-1540

meeting with Nixon on LaRue's testimony to Watergate Grand Jury and Dean's efforts to get immunity **SI4-3** 1094, 1307, 1308-1311

meeting with Nixon on March 23, 1973 **SI4-1** 8, 249, 250, 251-252

meeting with Nixon and Mitchell on April 4, 1972 **NSI2** 15, 157, 158-188

meeting with Nixon and Mitchell on Kleindienst confirmation hearings **II 2** 1038-1040; **SI5-2** 510, 841, 842-847

meeting with Nixon and Mitchell on Watergate break-in **SI2** 2, 53, 513, 514-516

meeting with Nixon and Timmons on site of Republican National Convention **SI5-2** 576-577

meetings and conversations with Nixon **SI4-3** 1112, 1557, 1558; **SI5-2** 500, 735, 739-740

meetings and conversations with Nixon on April 25-26, 1973 **SI9-1** 3, 107, 126

meetings and conversations with Nixon between April 30-June 3, 1973 **SI9-1** 11, 169, 239-241

meetings with Ehrlichman, Dean, and Moore to discuss strategy for Ervin Committee hearings **SI3-1** 48, 535, 536-556

meetings with Magruder, Mitchell, and Dean on Magruder's testimony on Liddy plan **SI4-1** 19, 373, 374-397

meetings with Nixon on April 16, 1973 after Nixon-Dean meeting on Dean's discussions with Watergate Prosecutors **II 2** 882

meets with Nixon and Mitchell after discussing CRP's political-intelligence gathering systems **SUMM I** 31

meets with Nixon and Mitchell to discuss Mitchell's resignation **SUMM I** 41, 42

on memo from Dean to Krogh on Brookings Institution **II 2** 1263-1265

and Mexican checks **SI2** 2, 97

Mitchell on advice on Huston plan to **SI7-1** 477

Mitchell on arrangements for LaRue's use of for payments to Hunt **TW 2** 128-132, 133-134, 161-164, 167-168, 171, 195

Mitchell arranges meeting between O'Brien and **TW 2** 139-140

Mitchell denies informing on Liddy plan **SI1** 123

Mitchell discusses disapproval of Huston plan with **SI7-1** 465

Mitchell on his role in Nixon's re-election campaign **TW 2** 202-203

Mitchell on his role at White House **TW 2** 209-210

and money transferred from Stans to Kalmbach **II 2** 738-739

name eliminated from Chapin's report to Ehrlichman on White House involvement with Segretti **SI7-4** 1619, 1681, 1692-1696

New York Times on Dean's testimony on his involvement in Watergate coverup **SI9-1** 18, 313, 316

and newspaper stories on Segretti's activities **SI7-4** 1617, 1657, 1658-1675

and Nixon Administration misuse of IRS **II 2** 1264

Nixon announces resignation of **SIAPP1** 13, 15-16; **SI9-1** 5, 131, 132-137

Nixon asks him to listen to tapes despite information from Petersen that he may be criminally liable **SUMM I** 7-8

and Nixon assigning Dean to Watergate **SI3-1** 52, 597, 614

in Nixon-Dean discussion on CRP political intelligence-gathering operation **NSI1** 80

Nixon-Dean discussion of possible resignation of **SI4-3** 73-77, 1294-1295

Nixon-Dean discussion on potential indictability of **SI3-2** 1054-1055

Nixon-Dean discussion on Watergate hearings and **SI3-2** 862-863; **SI8** 416-422

at Nixon-Dean meeting on March 21, 1973 **SI3-2** 1062-1116

Nixon discusses tapes of Nixon-Dean meetings with **SI9-1** 11, 169, 170-241

Nixon-Ehrlichman discussion on possible resignation of **SI4-2** 857-858

Nixon-Ehrlichman telephone conversation on preventing Dean from implicating **SUMM I** 67

Nixon gives reasons for allowing him to hear March 21, 1973 tape **SIAPP1** 59

Nixon gives reasons for allowing him to hear September 15 tape **SIAPP1** 45

Nixon-Kleindienst discussion of Watergate involvement of **SI4-2** 949-950

Nixon on guilt or innocence of **SIAPP1** 65-66

Nixon learns that Magruder may implicate in Watergate **SUMM I** 6-7

Nixon meeting with attorney for **SI4-3** 1108, 1511, 1515-1530

Nixon on perjury charges against **SIAPP1** 72

Nixon-Petersen discussion of effects of Magruder's indictment on **SUMM I** 95

Nixon-Petersen discussion of evidence against **SI4-3** 1089, 1223, 1224-1249

Nixon-Petersen discussion of possible resignation of **TW3** 110-112, 123-124; **SI4-3** 1128-1129

in Nixon-Petersen discussion of Strachan **II 2** 889

Nixon reports on Peterson's information on Watergate Grand Jury to **SUMM I** 96

Nixon on resignation of **SI3-2** 1242; **SI4-3** 1521-1523, 1527, 1535-1537

Nixon-Rogers discussion on possible resignation of **II 2** 886; **SI9-1** 44, 495, 496-497

Nixon tapes on problems with his involvement with Segretti **SI7-4** 1639, 1915, 1916-1927

Nixon tells him to urge Dean to go to Grand Jury **NSI1** 30, 199, 200-201

Nixon tells Petersen he had no authority over use of campaign funds for Liddy plan **SUMM I** 92

Nixon on testimony of **SIAPP1** 74

Nixon wants meeting between Dean, Ehrlichman, Mitchell and **NSI1** 24, 165, 166-167

and Nixon's assurances of leniency to Magruder and Mitchell **SUMM I** 66-67

and Nixon's contacts with dairy industry leaders **II 2** 1062

Nixon's decision-making method and **RHJC** 20-21

and Nixon's directives on FBI Watergate investigation **SI2** 2, 36, 355, 356-362

and Nixon's efforts to cover up meaning of conversation with Dean on March 21, 1973 on hush money **SUMM I** 60-62

and Nixon's efforts to prevent Dean from getting immunity **SUMM I** 96-99

Nixon's knowledge of his involvement in Watergate, in Article of Impeachment I **RHJC** 113-114

Nixon's opinion of **SIAPP1** 49

and Nixon's possible lack of knowledge of Watergate coverup, in Minority of House Judiciary Committee Impeachment Inquiry views on Articles of Impeachment **RHJC** 390-391

and Nixon's recall of decision memo approving recommendations of Huston plan**SI7-1** 27, 469, 470-485

Nixon's re-election campaign and **RHJC** 21-24

note on Dean memo on IRS investigation of Graham **SI8** 146

note on meeting of March 22, 1973 with Nixon, Haldeman, Ehrlichman, Mitchell, and Dean **SI4-1** 3, 107, 212

note on memo from Dean to Krogh on "turning off" Brookings Institution government contracts **SI8** 92

notes of meeting with Nixon on June 20, 1972

notes on erased Nixon tape **II 2** 1392-1393, 1411-1412

notes on meeting with Dean and Nixon on September 15, 1972 **II 2** 709-710; **NSI4** 34, 223, 224-225; **SI2** 2, 24, 236, 246-248

notes on Nixon-Dean taped conversation of March 21, 1973 **SI9-1** 443-473; **SI4-3** 1112, 1557, 1575-1605

notes released by White House **SI2** 2, 258

notes of September 15, 1973 meeting with Dean and Nixon **SI2** 2, 61, 62, 587, 593, 637-646

O'Brien's efforts to meet with **TW 1** 129, 132, 134, 135

and Operation Sandwedge proposal **SI7-3** 1188-1189, 1339-1340,1372-1376

orders political intelligence switched from Muskie to McGovern **SI3-2** 1005

on organizational chart from files of Special Investigations Unit **SI7-2** 814

and payments to Hunt from his $350,000 fund **TW 1** 146

Petersen informs Nixon of his receipt of wiretap reports from Strachan **SUMM I** 90

Petersen on involvement in Watergate of **SI4-2** 981

Petersen and Kleindienst inform Nixon of his involvement in watergate **II 2** 878-879

Petersen recommends that Nixon dismiss **SUMM I** 99-100

Petersen tells Nixon he might be indictable **SIAPP1** 45

Petersen's memo on evidence against **SUMM I** 91

Petersen's notes on Watergate coverup involvement of **SI4-3** 1225-1226

Petersen's notes on Watergate involvement of **SI4-2** 577, 974, 1001-1002

in Petersen's report to Nixon on Watergate Grand Jury testimony **SI4-3** 1299

places $350,000 in campaign funds under his control **SI1** 11, 77, 78, 90-91, 92, 93-94, 95-98, 99-100

Plumbers unit and **SIAPP1** 23

and political intelligence-gathering on Democratic party candidates **TW 3** 255-256

Haldeman, Harry Robins *(Continued)*
Political Matters Memoranda from Strachan, *see*
Political Matters Memoranda
and political use of wiretapping information received from FBI **II 2** 1113-1114; **SI7-1** 20, 359, 360-368
present during Nixon's instructions to Ziegler to announce his confidence in Dean **SI4-1** 14, 319, 321
prior association with Nixon **RHJC** 12
and proposal of Byrne as FBI director **SI7-4** 1635, 1867, 1868-1877
proposes surveillance of Kennedy **II 2** 1123
questions Colson about telephone conversation with Magruder **SI4-1** 9, 261, 263-264
receives FBI reports on surveillance of State Department employee **SI7-1** 302
receives FBI wiretap reports **II 2** 1099, 1100, 1202; **SI7-2** 684
receives FBI wiretap reports on government employees and newsmen **SI7-1** 372-373
receives FBI wiretap reports on White House staff members **SI7-1** 281, 282
receives reports on surveillance of Democratic National Committee headquarters **SUMM I** 33
relationship with Liddy's intelligence plan discussed by Dean and Nixon **SI3-2** 701, 803, 865-867
report from Huston on IRS investigation of political activities of tax-exempt organizations **II 2** 1255
and reports from Intelligence Evaluation Committee **SI7-1** 500
reports from Strachan on CRP's political intelligence-gathering activities **NSI1** 10, 67, 68-69
reports to Nixon on Dean-Gray meeting **SI2** 2, 34, 337, 349, 350
reports to Nixon on Higby's taped telephone conversation with Magruder prior to his talking to Watergate Prosecutor **SUMM I** 82-83
request for wiretapping of National Security Council staff member by **SI7-1** 7, 191, 198-199, 207
and requests for IRS audits **SI8** 17, 175, 176-182
requests 24-hour-a-day surveillance of Edward Kennedy **SI7-2** 531, 655, 656-661
resignation of **II 2** 893-894, 1333
responsibilities for Nixon's re-election campaign **SUMM I** 26-28
role in containment of Watergate from July 1 until elections **SUMM I** 43-44
role in Nixon Administration **SUMM I** 25-26, 28
role in Nixon re-election campaign **SI1** 90-9L
role in political intelligence-gathering **II 3** 1941-1945
role in San Clemente improvements **SI12** 172
role on White House staff **II 1** 554-555
and Segretti and CRP activities during Democratic primary campaigns **SI7-3** 1190, 1377, 1378-1390
and Segretti matter **SI3-2** 1038-1039
and Segretti's activities **II 2** 1184; **SI7-3** 1197, 1481, 1482-1494
and selection of San Diego as site of Republican National Convention of 1972 **II 2** 1020-1021, 1023-1024

Strachan tells Dean about cleaning out files of **SI2** 2, 168
and Strachan's destruction of documents **II 1** 611-613; **SI2** 2, 25, 261, 262-267; **SI7-3** 1486
Strachan's perjury and **SUMM I** 78-79
suggests Dean tape telephone conversation with Magruder **SI4-1** 332
in Sullivan memo to Tolson on wiretap on White House staff member **SI7-1** 274
and summary of FBI letters reporting on wiretaps on National Security Council staff members **SI7-1** 229, 230
in taped Higby-Magruder telephone conversation **SI4-2** 616
taped telephone conversation with Magruder **II 2** 865; **SI4-2** 560, 562, 707, 708-715, 769, 773-776
and tapes of Dean-Segretti conversation **SI7-4** 1620, 1697, 1698-1707
telephone call from Ehrlichman on problems posed by Watergate break-in for White House **SUMM I** 36
telephone call to Colson on his commitments to Hunt **II 2** 836-838
telephone call to Magruder after Watergate break-in **SI2** 2, 10, 125, 126, 127
telephone conversation with Colson on his dealings with Hunt **TW 3** 336-340
telephone conversation with Dean on his report on Watergate **II 2** 839
telephone conversation with Ehrlichman after Watergate arrests **SI2** 2, 11, 129, 130
telephone conversation with Higby with message from Dean to Nixon **SI4-2** 579-580, 1021-1022, 1031
telephone conversation with Nixon on conflicts betweeen recollections of Magruder and Strachan on Watergate **SI4-2** 575, 961, 968-971
telephone conversation with Nixon on Magruder's information to U.S. Attorneys **SI4-2** 567, 843-849
telephone log for March 21, 1973 **NSI1** 25, 169, 170-171; **SI3-2** 712, 1117, 1118-1119
telephone log for March 28, 1973 **SI4-1** 19, 373, 388
tells Nixon he should have told Dean blackmail was wrong **SUMM I** 60
tells Nixon his receiving wiretapping reports does not have to be made public **SUMM I** 34
tells Nixon on March 27, 1973 that no one at White House had prior knowledge of Watergate break-in **NSI1** 29, 195, 196-198
and transfer of FBI files on Kissinger tapes to White House **II 2** 1157-1158
and transfer of Liddy's "capabilities" from Muskie campaign **SI1** 20, 191, 192-195
transfer of $350,000 cash fund to and from Butterfield **TW 1** 53-55, 83-84, 96, 104, 108-110
and Ulasewicz's surveillance of Kennedy **SI7-1** 351-352
and Walters-Gray meeting **SI2** 2, 36, 355, 357, 359, 362
Watergate coverup and, in Article of Impeachment I **RHJC** 94-95
White House edited transcript of meeting with Nixon and Mitchell of April 4, 1972 **SIAPP3** 3-34

White House edited transcript of meeting with Nixon of June 23, 1972 **SIAPP3** 39-87
White House edited transcript of meeting with Nixon of March 22, 1973 **SIAPP3** 35-38
White House employees and other agents of Nixon reporting to **RHJC** 13-15
and wiretapping of government officials and newsmen in 1969 **SUMM I** 124-125
and wiretapping of White House staff members unrelated to national security **SI7-1** 263-264
See also Haldeman memos; *Halperin* v. *Kissinger*, House Judiciary Committee Impeachment Inquiry, discussion on calling witnesses; House Judiciary Committee Impeachment Inquiry, presentation of evidence on domestic surveillance; Nixon tapes; *U.S.* v. *John N. Mitchell, et al.*

Haldeman, Harry Robins, cited testimony of
on actions after Watergate arrests **SI2** 2, 10, 125, 127
on antitrust suits against ITT and Kleindienst confirmation hearings **SI5-2** 508-509, 803-803, 834-836
on assignment of Krogh and Young to Plumbers unit **SI7-2** 543, 795, 813
on contents of Nixon tape of Dean-Nixon meeting of March 21, 1973 on hush money **SI9-1** 39, 433, 434-473
on Dean informing him of CRP fundraising for Watergate defendants **SI3-1** 14, 199, 200-201
on Dean retaining attorneys and attorneys meeting with U.S. Attorneys **SI4-1** 27, 483, 485
denies AMPI contribution in 1969 **SI6-1** 3, 57, 78, 98
denies he or Nixon had prior knowledge of Watergate break-in **NSI1** 7, 53, 54
denies he recalls being informed by Magruder that Magruder and Porter would perjure themselves on purpose of payments to Liddy **SI3-1** 44, 501, 516
denies recalling briefing memo from Dean on increasing political responsiveness of IRS or conversation with Secretary of the Treasury **SI8** 203-204
on discussions of political intelligence with Nixon and Mitchell **SI1** 16, 156, 162-163, 167
on discussions with Connally on milk producers' contribution **SI6-2** 465, 493, 510-511
on discussions with Nixon on newspaper stories linking Segretti with Kalmbach **SI7-4** 1618, 1677, 1678-1680
on FBI Watergate investigation **SI2** 2, 34, 337, 348-349, 350
on FBI Watergate investigation and CIA **SI2** 2, 36, 355, 360-362
on hiring of Segretti and Segretti's actions **SI7-2** 526, 575, 578
on his memo to Dean on dealing with Ervin Committee **SI3-1** 47, 527, 529-531
on his role and staff **SI2** 2, 12, 131, 133
on Hoover's objections to Huston plan **SI7-1** 23, 383, 434
on Huston plan **SI7-1** 22, 375, 379-380
on Huston plan and memo from Huston **SI7-1** 23, 383, 444
on June 20, 1972 meeting with Ehrlichman,

Mitchell, Kleindienst and Dean to discuss Watergate break-in **SI2** 2, 23-24, 235-236, 237, 238, 239, 240-241, 242
on lack of discussion of political intelligence at April 4, 1972 meeting with Mitchell and Nixon **NSI1** 13, 85, 86
on learning that Dean's lawyers have met with U.S. Attorneys **SI4-1** 30, 501, 502
on listening to Nixon tapes **II 2** 1364-1366; **SI9-1** 3, 25, 107, 109-122, 351, 354-365
on Magruder's efforts to obtain government post after Watergate **SI3-1** 49-50, 557-558, 566-569
on meeting with Ehrlichman and Dean on Mitchell's role in Watergate **SI3-2** 713, 1135, 1145
on meeting with Ehrlichman, Helms, and Walters **SI2** 2, 39, 376, 385-391
on meeting with Ehrlichman, Mitchell, and Dean on March 22, 1973 **SI3-2** 718, 1251, 1257-1258, 1267
on meeting with Nixon and Dean on March 21, 1973 and telephone call to Mitchell **SI3-2** 712, 1117, 1120-1132
on meeting with Nixon and Dean on September 15, 1972 **SI8** 28-29, 331-332, 333
on meeting with Nixon on June 23, 1972 **SI7-3** 1202, 1533, 1534-1535, 1538-1540
on meeting between Nixon, Kleindienst, and Petersen on information received from Dean and Magruder **SI4-2** 576-577, 973-974, 999-1000
on meeting with Nixon and Mitchell on April 4, 1972 and discussion of ITT-Kleindienst confirmation hearings situation **SI5-2** 510, 841, 846-847
on meetings after Watergate break-in **SI2** 2, 23, 235, 240-241
on meetings with Ehrlichman, Dean, and Moore to discuss strategy for Ervin Committee hearings **SI3-1** 48, 535, 549-550
on Nixon's approval of Huston plan recommendations **SI7-1** 25, 445, 446
on Nixon's concern over Executive clemency offers to Hunt **SI4-1** 8, 251-251
on Nixon's instructions on FBI investigation **SI2** 2, 36, 355, 356-357
on obtaining tape of Nixon-Dean meeting of March 21, 1973 **SI4-3** 1112, 1557, 1561-1562, 1568-1574
on reasons for meeting with CIA officials on FBI Watergate investigation **NSI1** 16, 125, 126
on reasons for ordering FBI investigation of Schorr **SI7-2** 562, 1111, 1120-1121
on reporting on contents of tape of Nixon-Dean meeting of March 21, 1973 **SI4-3** 1112, 1557, 1562-1563, 1573-1574
on rescinding approval of Huston plan **SI7-1** 27, 469, 478-479
on stay in San Clemente with Nixon and Ehrlichman from April 1-8, 1973 **SI4-1** 475
on Strachan's destruction of documents **SI2** 2, 25, 26, 261, 262-267, 269, 270-273
on Strachan's instructions to Liddy to transfer "capabilities" from Muskie to McGovern **SI1** 20, 191, 195
on Strachan's loyalty **SI1** 195

Hardin, Clifford M. *(Continued)*
position on milk price supports **SI6-1** 367
proposal for meeting between Nixon and dairy industry leaders **SI6-1** 21, 319, 320-331, 322, 323
reaction to March 12, 1971 announcement on not raising milk price supports **NSI3** 12, 127, 128-120
in redated Whitaker memo to Nixon on milk price supports **SI6-2** 864, 865, 866
and Tariff Commission Report on dairy import quotas **NSI3** 6, 59, 60-68
Whitaker reports to Ehrlichman that he believes Congress will raise milk price supports **NSI3** 14, 137, 138
See also House Judiciary Committee Impeachment Inquiry, presentation of evidence on dairy industry campaign contributions; Milk price-support issue
Hardin, Helen SI7-3 1384
Harkins, Paul SI5-2 780
Harlan, John M. SI5-1 264, 265
U.S. v. *ITT* order extending time for *ITT-Grinnell* appeal **SI5-1** 16, 349, 350-358, 360-361, 364
Harless, Raymond F.
and audit of Nixons' 1969 tax return **SI10** 18
Harlow, Bryce N. NSI2 44; **SIAPP4** 50, 91; **SI1** 88; **SI5-1** 138; **SI8** 313
memo from Campbell recommending that Nixon address AMPI convention **NSI3** 3, 29, 30-31
memo from Hardin on dairy import quotas **NSI3** 7, 69, 74
Nixon re-election campaign responsibilities of **SUMM I** 27
and political intelligence-gathering on Democratic party candidates **TW 3** 255-256
role in Nixon campaign **SIAPP4** 36
Harmony, Sally J.
subpoenaed by Senate Select Committee on Presidential Campaign Activities **SI4-1** 488-489
Harmony, Sally J., cited testimony of
on logs of DNC telephone conversations and Gemstone stationery **SI1** 25, 233, 243-244
Harper, Dr. Edward SIAPP4 7, 50
Harper, John SI5-1 381; **SI5-2** 654, 690
Harriman, Averell SI11 201
and Diem coup **SI7-2** 1058
Harrington, William SI5-1 444
Harris, Jack A. TW 3 45
Harris, Lou SI7-2 717
and credibility of government **SI7-2** 669
and effect of Pentagon Papers on Nixon campaign **SI7-2** 672
See also Harris polls
Harris, Patricia SI8 327
Harris polls SIAPP3 32; **SIAPP4** 54
Lindsay and **SIAPP4** 1
Harrison, Marion Edwyn II 2 1056, 1057-1058
and AMPI relationship with Wagner & Baroody **SI6-1** 18, 273, 282-290
at AMPI meeting with Kalmbach **SI6-1** 14, 217, 218-233
at meeting between Nixon and dairy industry leaders on March 23, 1971 **SI6-2** 582-583

Colson memo to Chotiner complaining about **SI6-1** 16, 259, 260, 261
and Hillings' letter **SI6-2** 683
introduces Chotiner to Parr and Nelson **SI6-2** 677
letter to Hanman with list of political committees for AMPI contributions **SI6-2** 479, 783, 785-786
letter to Nelson on TAPE contributions and *Washington Post* article on unopposed Democratic congressional candidates **SI6-1** 14, 217, 228-233
letter to Nelson with list of committees for AMPI contributions **SI6-2** 479, 783, 787-793
letters to Colson on results of March 12 milk price-support decision **SI6-1** 27, 401, 403-404, 405-406
memo from Colson to Chotiner on AMPI contribution to unopposed Democratic Congressional candidates and **SI6-1** 13, 213, 214
memo on Tariff Commission recommendations on dairy imports attached to Hillings letter to Nixon **SI6-1** 240-255
memo to Whitaker urging change in March 12 decision on milk price supports **SI6-1** 27, 401, 403-404, 405-406
relationship with Colson **SI6-2** 742, 743
and TAPE contributions **SI6-1** 293
See also House Judiciary Committee Impeachment Inquiry, presentation of evidence on dairy industry campaign contributions
Harrison, Marion Edwyn, cited testimony of
on AMPI contribution to People United for Good Government **SI6-2** 481, 821, 822-824
on dairy trust contributions to Nixon campaign **SI6-1** 298
denies quid pro quo between milk price-support increase and campaign contributions **NSI3** 25, 175, 196-197; **SI6-1** 28, 402, 461-462
on meeting with Kalmbach **SI6-1** 214, 217, 225-227
on TAPE contribution and Colson **SI7-3** 1184, 1247, 1272-1274
Hart, Philip A. SI5-1 163; **SI5-2** 674, 710, 813, 865
Hart, Philip A., questioning by
Bork **SI9-2** 865-866
Hume **SI5-2** 619-620
McLaren **NSI2** 112
Mitchell **SI5-1** 182
Richardson **SI9-1** 275; **SI9-2** 598
Rohatyn **NSI2** 122
Silbert **SI3-1** 111-114
Richardson **SI9-2** 598
Hart, Tom
memo to Nesbitt on Nixon's meeting with Kleindienst on April 15, 1973 **SI4-2** 571, 572, 574, 575, 871, 901-903, 905, 909-911, 924, 933-935, 961, 965-967
Hart Committee
in Nixon-Mitchell discussion **SI5-1** 374-375
Harter, M. Earl TW 3 44
Hartford Fire Insurance Company SI5-1 4, 101, 104-105
McLaren memo to Mitchell on acquisition by ITT **SI5-1** 4, 101, 106-119, 121
retention by ITT during negotiation of ITT antitrust cases **NSI2** 9, 81, 82-101

and settlement of antitrust suits against ITT **SI5-2** 485, 549, 550-556
See also ITT, antitrust suits against

Harutunian, Al NSI2 128-129; **SI5-1** 432, 438, 451

Harvey, Annette SI6-2 759

Hatfield, Mark SIAPP1 66; **SIAPP4** 26

Hathaway, Richard
and construction of block wall at Nixon's San Clemente property **SI12** 152
and GSA payment for boundary survey at Nixon's San Clemente property **SI12** 130
and GSA payment for den windows at Nixon's San Clemente property **SI12** 123, 125
and GSA payment for handrails at Nixon's San Clemente property **SI12** 143-144
and GSA payment for housekeeping services at Nixon's San Clemente property **SI12** 153-155
and GSA payment for structural investigations at Nixon's San Clemente property **SI12** 133
and installation of den windows at Nixon's San Clemente property **SI12** 124
interviewed on meeting on Key Biscayne improvements at Kalmbach's office **SI12** 99
and paving at Nixon's San Clemente property **SI12** 135

Hauser, Rita SIAPP4 106-107; **SI6-2** 813
differences with Mitchell **SIAPP4** 29
in Political Matters Memoranda **SIAPP4** 4
role in Nixon re-election campaign **SIAPP4** 6

Hawaii SIAPP4 89

Hayes, Helen
FBI investigation of **SI7-2** 1121

Haynes, Richard H.
and delivery of FBI wiretapping reports to White House **SI7-2** 684
memo to Sullivan on recipients of FBI wiretap material at White House **SI7-1** 21, 369, 370
in Sullivan memo to Tolson on wiretap on White House staff member **SI7-1** 274

Hays, Brooks II 1 299

Haywood Ranch, Texas
government expenditures during Johnson Administration on **SI12** 175-179, 181

Health programs
impoundment of funds for **SI12** 19-20

Healy, Paul F. SIAPP1 73

Heard, Alexander SI8 83

Hearing, George A. SIAPP2 320-321
See also U.S. v. *Donald Segretti*

Hearsay evidence
Dennis on **TW 1** 193-194
Hogan on **II 2** 821
Minority of House Judiciary Committee Impeachment Inquiry views on Articles of Impeachment on House Judiciary Committee Impeachment Inquiry reliance on **RHJC** 372-374
Waldie on **II 2** 850
Wiggins' objections to **II 2** 807-808

Hebert, F. Edward II 2 1178
and Defense Department response to special House Resolution requesting information on bombings in Laos and Cambodia from 1969 to April 1970 **SI11** 57, 63, 295-297, 319-321

Hecht, Bill II 2 1142
and Plumbers unit's efforts to get Senate to hold hearings on Pentagon Papers matter **SI7-2** 835-836

Hegarty, William E. SI7-2 594

Heininger, Erwin C. SIAPP2 219-220
See also U.S. v. *Associated Milk Producers, Inc.*

Heinz, John, III SIAPP4 24

Helms, Richard M. SI7-1 23, 383, 384-431
appointed to ad hoc committee to study domestic intelligence **SI7-1** 22, 375, 377, 381, 382
and CIA aid to Hunt **SI2** 2, 465-466, 657
and CIA psychological profile of Ellsberg **SI7-2** 550, 897, 898-909; **II 2** 1145-1146
conversation with Young on CIA involvement with Pentagon Papers **NSI4** 12, 103, 104-107
and documents sent by CIA to Justice Department on questions asked by FBI during Watergate investigation **TW 3** 3-4, 5-46
Ehrlichman introduces to Krogh and Young **SI7-2** 956
Ehrlichman's memo to Nixon on meeting of October 8, 1971 with **SIAPP3** 204-205
and FBI Watergate investigation **SUMM I** 40-41
and Harriman's role in Diem coup **SI7-2** 1058
and Hunt's requests for additional aid from CIA **SI7-3** 1226-1227, 1237-1238
and Huston plan **II 2** 1116
Krogh-Young memo to Ehrlichman on meeting with **SI7-2** 553, 951, 963-966
letter to Young on secrecy of CIA preparation of psychological profile of Ellsberg **II 2** 1185; **SI7-3** 1192, 1399, 1412-1413
in McCord's letter to Caulfield **SI3-1** 476
meeting with Ehrlichman, Colby, and Dean **SI2** 2, 64, 651, 652-658
meeting with Haldeman, Ehrlichman, and Walters on FBI Watergate investigation **SI2** 2, 38-39, 375-376, 377-395
meeting with Mitchell on Huston plan **SI7-1** 472
meeting with Walters and Nixon **II 3** 1961
memo on conversation with Gray on Watergate **NSI1** 16, 125, 127
memo on FBI Watergate investigation **SI2** 2, 46, 449, 459
memo from Huston on Nixon's approval of Huston plan recommendations **SI7-1** 25, 445, 454-461
memo for the record on discussion with Mitchell on Nixon's approval of Huston plan recommendations **SI7-1** 26, 463, 468
memo returning Nixon's decision memo approving Huston plan recommendations **SI7-1** 27, 469, 474
memo to Walters on Watergate investigation and Mexican checks **SI2** 2, 48, 471
Nixon directs Haldeman to meet with on White House concern over possible disclosure of covert CIA or Plumbers activities **SI7-3** 1202, 1533, 1534-1540
in Nixon-Haldeman discussion on Watergate **SIAPP3** 43, 75, 79
role in Nixon Administration **RHJC** 16-17

Hiss, Alger **SI7-2** 1132
Hiss case **SI3-2** 740, 741, 899-900; **SI3-2** 1158
    Hunt compares with Ellsberg case **II 2** 1127
    Nixon on **NSI1** 218; **SIAPP1** 4, 8-9, 10
History of U.S. Decision-Making Process on Viet Nam Policy see Pentagon Papers
Hoffa, James
    Bittman and prosecution of **TW 2** 3
Hofgren, Daniel **SIAPP4** 75, 87; **SI1** 85; **SI4-2** 657
Hogan, Lawrence J. **SUMM I** 1
    additional views on proposed Article of Impeachment on secret bombing of Cambodia **RHJC** 301-302
    on attorney-client privilege and O'Brien's testimony on Mitchell **TW 1** 130-131
    on calling witnesses before House Judiciary Committee Impeachment Inquiry **II 3** 1647-1648, 1680
    on confidentiality of evidentiary material presented to House Judiciary Committee Impeachment Inquiry **II 1** 580, 636, 637
    on deletion of expletives from Nixon tape transcripts **II 1** 434
    on discrepancies between transcripts and tapes **II 3** 1973-1975
    discussion with Doar on Minority of House Judiciary Committee Impeachment Inquiry representation during interviews with witnesses **II 1** 96-97
    on dismantling of Office of Economic Opportunity and hiring of Tetzlaff **II 1** 148-149
    on Doar-St. Clair correspondence **II 1** 173
    on efforts to determine person who leaked information on IRS investigation of Gerald and George Wallace **II 2** 1254
    on Ehrlichman's meeting with Byrne **II 2** 1209
    on FBI report to Justice Department on wiretapping of Ellsberg **II 2** 1135-1136, 1138
    on FBI reports on wiretapping of National Security Council employees **II 2** 1001
    on Hillings letter to Nixon **II 2** 1057
    on House Judiciary Committee Impeachment Inquiry access to St. Clair's brief **II 1** 83-84, 297, 316
    on House Judiciary Committee Impeachment Inquiry interviewing Sullivan and DeLoach **II 2** 1092
    on House Judiciary Committee Impeachment Inquiry issuing subpoenas to Nixon **II 3** 1551, 1555, 1560, 1561
    on identification of voices on Nixon tapes **II 2** 1074
    on interpretation of evidence **II 2** 747-748
    on Jenner's presentation of summary of evidence to House Judiciary Committee Impeachment Inquiry **II 3** 1992-1993
    on legal aspects of impoundment of funds **II 2** 1309
    on Minority report on presentation procedures for House Judiciary Committee Impeachment Inquiry **II 1** 296
    on Nixon's approval of Goldwater quote on electronic surveillance **II 3** 1993-1994
    on Nixon's gift of Presidential papers **II 3** 1471

    on Nixon's noncompliance with House Judiciary Committee Impeachment Inquiry subpoenas **II 2** 905, 925
    on Nixon's offer to verify tapes **II 2** 853
    objection to hearsay testimony **II 2** 821
    objections to Doar's citations of direct evidence **II 3** 1935
    on Petersen-Nixon relationship and Nixon's abuse of power **II 3** 2025-2026
    on procedural rules for handling Impeachment Inquiry material **II 1** 128
    on purpose of AMPI 1970 contribution **II 2** 1053
    on questions during presentation of evidentiary material to House Judiciary Committee Impeachment Inquiry **II 1** 679
    on release of House Judiciary Committee Impeachment Inquiry evidentiary material to public **II 3** 1607
    requests citations by Doar for direct evidence of Nixon's responsibility for electronic surveillance plan **SUMM I** 13
    on rules of evidentiary procedures for House Judiciary Committee Impeachment Inquiry **II 1** 475-476, 480, 482-483, 484-486, 489, 517-518, 541
    on security arrangements for House Judiciary Committee Impeachment Inquiry **II 1** 638
    on separate Minority of House Judiciary Committee Impeachment Inquiry brief on impeachable offenses **II 1** 156
    on setting completion date for House Judiciary Committee Impeachment Inquiry **II 1** 20-21
    on St. Clair's right to be present at House Judiciary Committee Impeachment Inquiry **II 1** 83
    statement of concurring views with Report of House Judiciary Committee Impeachment Inquiry **RHJC** 281
    on subpoena powers of House Judiciary Committee **II 1** 85,
    on using subpoena powers of House Judiciary Committee **II 1** 188
    on Waldie's motion on hearing testimony of witnesses in executive session **II 3** 1876-1877
    on Wiggins' amendment to subpoena to Nixon **II 2** 953
Hogan, Lawrence J., questioning by
    Bittman **TW 2** 83-84
    Butterfield **TW 1** 99-101
    Colson **TW 3** 477-479
    Dean **TW 2** 324-326
    Kalmbach **TW 3** 720-721, 723
    LaRue **TW 1** 258
    O'Brien **TW 1** 155-157
Hogan, Thomas
    letter to Nixon recommending Petersen for FBI director **TW 3** 150
    retained by Dean **SI4-1** 27, 483, 484, 485
Hogan & Hartson
    and Bittman's dealings with Hunt **TW 2** 43-44, 60-63, 81-82, 84
Holm, Holly **TW 3** 324, 326, 329
Holshouser, James **SI1** 33, 86

Holton (Governor of Virginia) SIAPP4 50, 58; SI1 33

Holtzman, Elizabeth SI11 408-416; SUMM I 1
additional views on Nixon's tax evasion as impeachable offense RHJC 343-347
additional views on Report of House Judiciary Committee Impeachment Inquiry RHJC 321-322
on AMPI's decision to discontinue contributions II 2 1086
asks about Operation Sandwedge II 1 59-60
on calling witnesses before House Judiciary Committee Impeachment Inquiry II 3 1642-1644, 1651, 1673, 1674, 1675, 1688, 1709-1710
on closing House Judiciary Committee Impeachment Inquiry sessions on evidentiary material II 1 546
on confidentiality of evidentiary material presented to House Judiciary Committee Impeachment Inquiry II 1 579
on contents of erased Nixon tape II 2 1392
on Diem cables II 2 1173
on discrepancies between transcripts and tapes II 2 848-849
on discrepancies between White House logs and tapes II 2 877
dissenting views supporting proposed Article of Impeachment on secret bombing of Cambodia RHJC 323-328
on Doar-St. Clair correspondence II 1 172
on Doar's meeting with St. Clair on material required by House Judiciary Committee Impeachment Inquiry II 2 973
on extent of 1969-1971 wiretaps II 2 1139
on gap in Nixon tape of June 20 II 1 634-635
on House Judiciary Committee Impeachment Inquiry issuing subpoenas to Nixon II 1 320, 331, 335, 650-651; II 3 1552, 1557, 1716
on impoundment of funds by previous administrations II 2 1308
on initiators of IRS investigation of Gerald and George Wallace II 2 1252, 1253
on investigation of bombing of Cambodia in House Judiciary Committee Impeachment Inquiry II 1 372-373
on investigation of Nixon's income taxes in House Judiciary Committee Impeachment Inquiry II 1 361
on IRS Code on assigning proceeds of writings to charitable organizations II 3 1471
on Kleindienst's testimony before Ervin Committee II 2 1041
on legal aspects of impoundment of funds II 2 1315-1316
on legal questions involved in White House staff members obtaining IRS information II 2 1274
on Mardian's involvement in removal of files of Kissinger tapes to White House II 2 1193-1194
motion on insertion of staff notes of interview with Kleindienst and memo from Davis on questions and answers to Kleindienst II 3 2131-2132
on Nixon-Petersen relationship II 3 2030
on Nixon tape of April 15 II 2 1357

on Nixon tapes taken to Camp David II 2 1374
on Nixon's alleged approval of Fielding break-in II 2 1166
on Nixon's contacts with Geneen II 2 1001
on Nixon's gift of Presidential papers II 3 1487, 2014
on Nixon's income tax II 3 1513, 1528-1529
on Nixon's noncompliance with House Judiciary Committee Impeachment Inquiry subpoenas II 1 434-435
on Nixon's refusal to give additional White House materials to House Judiciary Committee Impeachment Inquiry II 1 244-246
on Nixon's request for extension of time on answering House Judiciary Committee Impeachment Inquiry subpoena II 1 350-351
Nussbaum and II 3 1459-1460
objection to conclusions in St. Clair's presentation of evidence in behalf of Nixon II 3 1865
objection to St. Clair's use of complete transcripts during questioning of witnesses TW 3 442-444
objections to conclusions in Nixon's Statement of Information NSI1 20, 22, 145, 157
objects to St. Clair's line of questioning of witness TW 1 83
on obtaining information on IRS treatment of White House friends II 2 1299
on obtaining materials from Jaworski II 1 107
on papers put into Nixon's file by Young II 2 1340
on pocket veto II 1 198
on procedural rules for handling Impeachment Inquiry material II 1 122, 126-127
on procedures for taking of depositions and interrogatories by House Judiciary Committee II 1 11-12
on purpose of AMPI 1970 contribution II 2 1054
question on *Newsday* articles on Rebozo II 2 1281
on release of House Judiciary Committee Impeachment Inquiry evidentiary material to public II 3 1607-1608, 1610
requests briefing session on House Judiciary Committee Impeachment Inquiry requests to White House for materials II 1 195
on right of Minority of House Judiciary Committee Impeachment Inquiry to subpoena witnesses II 1 27-28
on rules of evidentiary procedures for House Judiciary Committee Impeachment Inquiry II 1 477-478, 513-516, 521, 525
on safekeeping of White House materials II 1 114-115, 295-296
on Sirica's invitation to Doar and Jenner II 1 145-146, 151
on St. Clair's participation in House Judiciary Committee Impeachment Inquiry II 1 296
statement of additional views on Report of House Judiciary Committee Impeachment Inquiry RHJC 283-286
on subpoena powers of House Judiciary Committee II 1 37
on tax liability vs. tax fraud II 3 2006
on television coverage of House Judiciary Committee Impeachment Inquiry II 1 103
on transcripts of Nixon tapes used by St. Clair in his presentation of evidence in behalf of Nixon

House Resolution 803 SI1 3

House Subcommittee on Appropriations
Hoover's scheduled apperance before, termination of wiretaps on government employees and newsmen prior to SI7-2 525, 567, 569-570

House Un-American Activities Committee
Truman letter to Velde declining to comply with subpoena from cited by NixonSIAPP1 26-27, 45

Houser, Tom SIAPP3 26-27

Housing discrimination
Nixon-Ehrlichman discussion on SI5-1 326-327

Housing programs SI12 12-16
litigation on impoundment of funds for SI12 12-16
See also Rent supplement programs; Urban renewal

Houston, Lawrence
and CIA aid to Hunt SI2 2, 657
letter from Hunt on change in CIA annuity survivorship benefits SI2 2, 18, 166, 185

Houston, Texas
as proposed site for Republican National Convention SI5-1 449, 472

Houthakker, Hendrik S.
and dairy import quotas NSI3 115
memo from Seevers on milk price supports SI6-1 24-25, 359-360, 361-362, 363-364
memo to Paarlberg on dairy import quotas NSI3 73

Howard, Malcolm J.
St. Clair introduces to House Judiciary Committee Impeachment Inquiry II 3 1720

Howard, W. Richard SI2 2, 169, 170
Cox's efforts to obtain memo to Kehrli from SI9-1 35, 37, 42, 413, 414-417, 425, 426-427, 485, 486-4
and efforts to determine Hunt's status at White House after Watergate break-in TW 3 257
finds memo to Kehrli on taking Hunt off payroll TW 3 261-263
and Hunt's status at White House SI2 2, 187-188
memo from Kehrli on Hunt's annuity rights if he leaves White House staff SIAPP3 269-270
memo to Kehrli on Hunt's employment status at White House II 2 1366-1368; SIAPP3 271; SI2 2, 18, 166, 171, 181-183, 184
in Nixon-Ehrlichman discussion SI4-3 1256
Nixon gives Select Committee memo to Kehrli from SIAPP1 31
and termination of Hunt's employment on White House staff SI2 2, 176

Howard Johnson motel, Washington, D.C.
in McCord's financial accounts SI1 190
and monitoring of tapped DNC telephones SI1 175, 181

Howell's State Trials SI12 41-42

Hruska, Jan SI4-2 832, 837-838
in Colson memo to Haldeman on Kleindienst confirmation hearings SI5-2 805
in memo from Ehrlichman to Kalmbach on Nixon's income tax returns SI10 428

Hruska, Jan, questioning by
Colson SI7-2 677, 705
Ehrlichman SI7-2 724, 736
Griswold SI5-1 354
Jaworski SI9-2 841
McLaren NSI2 116
Mitchell SI5-2 773

HUD. *See* Department of Housing and Urban Development (HUD)

Hughes (senator)
obtains report from Richardson on bombing of Cambodia SI11 22

Hughes (senator), questioning by
Abrams SI11 51, 272, 290, 300, 301, 304
Clements SI11 315
Moorer SI11 273, 274, 281-282, 305, 315
Wheeler SI11 286, 288, 289, 299

Hughes, Howard
Rebozo and TW 3 735-739

Hughes, James D. SI12 155
memo to Ehrlichman on conversation with Beard about antitrust suits against ITT SI5-1 6, 141, 142

Hughes, Michael II 2 1267

Hughes Tool Company
IRS investigation of O'Brien and SI8 23, 217, 223-225

Hullin, Todd SI7-2 1066; SI7-4 1699
and Dean's report to Ehrlichman and Haldeman on his meeting with Segretti II 2 751-752
memo from Mclaren for Ehrlichman on ITT SI5-1 7, 143, 147-152, 153-162
memo to Dean asking for information on legal aspects of leaks of secret government information to newspapers NSI4 3, 37, 39
memo to Ehrlichman on points of discussion in forthcoming meeting with Geneen SI5-1 7, 143, 145-146
memo to McLaren on Ehrlichman-Geneen meeting SI5-1 7, 143, 168; SI5-2 508-509, 803-804, 827
memo to Mitchell with memos and correspondence on antitrust suits against ITT SI5-1 7-8, 143-144, 178
note from Dean with memo on statutes relating to disclosure of intelligence information to newspapers NSI4 40-42

Hume, Brit SI5-2 557, 790-791
contacts Rohatyn on Beard memo to Merriam SI5-2 491, 613, 626-627
Mitchell contradicts testimony of SI5-2 773

Hume, Brit, cited testimony of
on investigation of Beard memo to Merriam SI5-2 491, 613, 619-625

Hummell, Robert NSI2 85, 86; SI5-1 405; SI5-2 553, 555, 596

Humphrey, Hubert H. SIAPP2 320-321
Haldeman on letters defaming SI7-2 578
reaction to March 12 milk price-support decision SI6-1 409-413
Segretti slanders against SI7-3 1384, 1390
sponsors bill raising milk price-support levels NSI3 13, 131, 135

Humphrey, Hubert H. *(Continued)*
See also U.S. v. Donald Segretti

Humphrey campaign
Colson on Andreas obtaining information on **TW 3** 255-256
and Dogole's name on enemies list **SI8** 75, 109
and illegal campaign contributions **SIAPP2** 221-226
Sedan Chair II activity and **NSI1** 10, 67, 68-75; **SI1** 148-149
Sedan Chair II report on **SI1** 14, 147, 148, 149
Segretti's activities against **SI7-3** 1190, 1377, 1378-1390

Humphreys, West H.
impeachment case against **II 3** 2204-2205

Hundley, William G. TW 2 113-124
on discrepancies between transcripts of Nixon tapes **TW 2** 184-185
House Judiciary Committee Impeachment Inquiry discussion on his statement on Mitchell's appearance jeopardizing his right to fair trial **TW 2** 113-124
O'Donnell's letter to **TW 1** 129-130
objections to line of questioning of Mitchell **TW 2** 143-146, 152, 154-155, 155-159, 160, 168
See also Mitchell, John N., testimony before House Judiciary Committee Impeachment Inquiry

Hungate, William L. SUMM I 1
additional separate views on proposed Article of Impeachment on secret bombing of Cambodia **RHJC** 329
on calling witnesses before House Judiciary Committee Impeachment Inquiry **II 3** 1636-1637, 1640, 1706-1707, 1708
on confidentiality of evidentiary material presented to House Judiciary Committee Impeachment Inquiry **II 1** 636, 637-638
on Constitution and presentation procedures of House Judiciary Committee Impeachment Inquiry **II 1** 298-299
dissenting views supporting proposed Article of Impeachment on secret bombing of Cambodia **RHJC** 323-328
on dropping some grounds for impeachment of Nixon **II 1** 268
on enemies list **II 2** 1262-1263
on FBI report to Justice Department on wiretapping of Ellsberg **II 2** 1138, 1139
on Fulbright's request for House Judiciary Committee Impeachment Inquiry material on Kissinger **II 2** 1324
on House Judiciary Committee Impeachment Inquiry issuing subpoena to Clerk of House of Representatives for records of dairy industry campaign contributions **II 3** 1577, 1578-1579
on House Judiciary Committee Impeachment Inquiry issuing subpoenas to Nixon **II 1** 642, 652, 658; **II 3** 1560
on House Judiciary Committee Impeachment Inquiry subpoenas for additional witnesses **II 2** 984
on immunity for witnesses called by House Judiciary Committee Impeachment Inquiry **II 2** 987-988

on leaks from House Judiciary Committee Impeachment Inquiry **II 2** 706
on legal remedies for impoundment of funds **II 2** 1320
on Nixon-Petersen relationship **II 3** 2032
on Nixon's approval of wiretapping **II 3** 1993
on Nixon's gift of Presidential papers **II 3** 2011
on Nixon's income tax **II 3** 1500-1501
on Nixon's noncompliance with House Judiciary Committee Impeachment Inquiry subpoenas **II 1** 423-424, 447-448; **II 2** 919-920
on papers put into Nixon's file by Young **II 2** 1340
on procedures of House Judiciary Committee Impeachment Inquiry **II 1** 12
on questions during presentation of evidence **II 2** 808
questions on AMPI contributions to Nixon campaign **II 2** 1050
on release of House Judiciary Committee Impeachment Inquiry evidentiary material to public **II 2** 978; **II 3** 1585, 1586, 1606-1607, 1612
on relevancy of evidence on enemies list **II 2** 1271
on report of Joint Committee on Internal Revenue Taxation **II 1** 267-268
on right of Minority of House Judiciary Committee Impeachment Inquiry to subpoena witnesses **II 1** 28-29
on rules of evidentiary procedures for House Judiciary Committee Impeachment Inquiry **II 1** 496-497, 500, 512-513, 519, 526-527, 528
on rules on cross-examination of witnesses **TW 1** 91-92
on schedule for House Judiciary Committee Impeachment Inquiry **II 2** 1217
on separate Minority of House Judiciary Committee Impeachment Inquiry brief on impeachable offenses **II 1** 157-158
on setting completion date for House Judiciary Committee Impeachment Inquiry **II 1** 19
on setting date for final report from House Judiciary Committee Impeachment Inquiry **II 1** 48
on Sirica's invitation to Doar and Jenner **II 1** 137-138
on submission of written interrogatories to Nixon **II 3** 1616, 1617
on terms under which Jaworski accepted post as Special Watergate Prosecutor **II 2** 1403
on witnesses called by House Judiciary Committee Impeachment Inquiry **II 2** 988, 992

Hungate, William L., questioning by
Butterfield **TW 1** 96-97
Dean **TW 2** 298-299
Kalmbach **TW 3** 707-708
Mitchell **TW 2** 171-173
Petersen **TW 3** 128-130

Hunt, Dorothy (Mrs. E. Howard Hunt) TW 2 5
Bittman informs Colson of death of **TW 2** 13, 20
Bittman on her use in conspiracy to obstruct justice **TW 2** 95-96
Colson on communication with Hunt after death of **TW 3** 300
Colson on not attending funeral of **TW 3** 459-460
Colson tells Dean about her telephone call **TW 3** 454-455

conversation with O'Brien **TW 1** 144

Dean-Nixon discussion on death of **SUMM I** 64, 65; **SI3-2** 1023-1024

death of **II 2** 879, 881; **TW 1** 126; **TW 2** 23, 37, 87; **SI4-1** 248; **SI4-2** 668-669

death of, and Hunt's letter to Colson **SI3-1** 38-39, 455-456, 457-474

and distribution of money for Watergate defendants **II 2** 736-737, 748, 750-751

effect of death on Hunt **SI3-2** 905-906

estate of **TW 2** 45, 86

and final deliveries of funds for Watergate defendants **SI3-1** 31, 373, 374-377

insurance taken out prior to fatal flight of **TW 2** 44, 86, 95

letter from Hunt to Colson after death of **TW 3** 296, 297-300

memos to Bittman on amounts received and distributed **SI3-1** 17, 22, 31, 221, 233, 281, 290, 378, 383; **TW 2** 16-19, 46-47, 63-66, 68-69

method of receiving money from Ulasewicz **SI3-1** 17, 221, 222-233

Rangel gives House Judiciary Committee Impeachment Inquiry information on death of **II 3** 2000

telephone conversation with Hall **TW 3** 283-284, 286-287

and trip to Chicago **SI3-2** 1016

Ulasewicz's payments to **SI3-1** 22, 281, 282-290

See also Bittman, William O., testimony before House Judiciary Committee Impeachment Inquiry

Hunt, E. Howard II 2 1123-1147; **RHJC** 66-74; **SIAPP2** 67-70; **TW 1** 172-173; **TW 2** 5; **SI7-2** 651

actions after Watergate arrests **II 1** 587; **SUMM I** 35; **SI2** 2, 3, 71

advised to leave country **SI2** 2, 20, 203, 204-221

Amato and **TW 3** 33-34

arrest, indictment, and guilty plea of **SI1** 27, 255, 256

assigned to Plumbers unit **SI7-2** 544, 815, 816-825

assignment to Pentagon Papers investigation for White House **II 2** 1141; **NSI4** 6, 71, 72-74; **TW 3** 207, 209

believes Colson has abandoned him **SI3-2** 1030-1031

Bittman arranges meeting between Shapiro and **TW 3** 322-323

Bittman on commutation of sentence of **TW 2** 90, 93-94, 105

Bittman denies discussion of Executive clemency with anyone **TW 2** 68

Bittman denies knowledge of threats made by **TW 2** 70-71, 89-90, 93-94

Bittman on discussion of legal fees with **TW 2** 30, 31, 38-39, 83-84, 95, 99, 112

Bittman on first knowledge about commitments to **TW 2** 49-50, 76, 103-105

Bittman on his deliveries of envelopes to **TW 2** 28-29, 45-46, 69-70, 71-72, 74-75, 88

Bittman on his financial status **TW 2** 95

Bittman on his testimony before Ervin Committee **TW 2** 53-54

Bittman on his testimony before Watergate Grand Jury **TW 2** 53-55, 59-60, 66-67, 73-74, 98-99, 100, 106-107

Bittman on meeting with **TW 1** 173-174

Bittman on meeting between O'Brien and **TW 2** 25-27, 47-49, 50-52, 70, 79-80

Bittman on reasons for accepting legal fees in unorthodox fashion from **TW 2** 109

Bittman on relationship with **TW 2** 39-40, 50

Bittman on terminating legal relationship with **TW 2** 80-81, 106-107

Bittman's opinion of **TW 2** 87

blackmail attempts **SI7-4** 1630, 1821, 1822-1828

and break-in at DNC headquarters and wiretapping of Lawrence O'Brien's and Oliver's telephones **SI1** 23, 215, 216-222

Butterfield on lack of White House employment records on **TW 1** 55-57, 98, 107-108, 110

Chapin denies knowing **SI7-4** 1675

and Chenow **SI2** 2, 495

CIA aid to **II 1** 631

in CIA documents sent to FBI **TW 3** 7-14, 16-18, 19, 22-46

CIA employee affidavit on aid given to **SI2** 2, 47, 450, 460-466

CIA memos to FBI on aid given to **TW 3** 9-10, 39-40

CIA memos to Justice Department on **TW 3** 49-58, 62-65, 68-70, 178-179

Colby on CIA aid to **SI2** 2, 64, 651, 653-656

Colson-Bittman meetings on **TW 3** 302-315

Colson denies Executive clemency offers to **TW 3** 472-474

Colson on efforts to determine date of Bittman receiving last payment for **TW 3** 356-359, 362-363

Colson on efforts to determine his status at White House after Watergate break-in **TW 3** 256-264

Colson-Haldeman discussions on payments to **TW 3** 315-317

Colson-Haldeman telephone conversation on Colson's dealings with **TW 3** 336-340

Colson on his relationship with **TW 3** 416-417

Colson informs Ehrlichman of expected testimony of **SI4-2** 555, 587, 597

Colson memo on **SI1** 12, 101, 104-109

Colson plays tape for Dean of his conversation with **TW 2** 232-233

Colson tells Ehrlichman he opposed second Watergate break-in **SI4-2** 555, 587, 597

Colson tells Nixon he was not White House employee at time of Watergate break-in **SUMM I** 37

in Colson's memos to file on dealings with Bittman **SI3-1** 38-39, 455-456, 465-474

Colson's reasons for consulting with Dean on **TW 3** 477-478, 495

communication with Colson after Watergate break-in **TW 3** 271-298

concealment of Fielding break-in and payments to **SUMM I** 134

conflict over his employment at White House **TW 2** 21, 33-37

connection with White House discovered during Watergate arrests **SUMM I** 36

contacts with Segretti **II 2** 1196

Cox obtains memo from Howard to Kehrli on **SI9-1** 42, 485, 486-487

Cushman asks Ehrlichman to restrain his demands for further CIA assistance **II 2** 1179

Hunt, E. Howard *(Continued)*

Cushman memo to Ehrlichman identifying White House person requesting aid for II 2 1200

Cushman's identification of person requesting aid from CIA to SI7-4 1622, 1719, 1720-1730

date of last payment to TW 3 451-452, 497-498

date of last payment to, in St. Clair's presentation of evidence in behalf of Nixon II 3 1754-1757

date of meeting with Paul O'Brien TW 1 156

Dean-Colson conversation on his being ordered out of country TW 3 266

Dean on demands for money made by SI3-1 202

Dean instructed to get him out of country SI2 2, 146

Dean instructs Liddy to get him out of country SI4-3 1310

Dean meeting with Paul O'Brien on demands for hush money of SI3-2 707, 945, 946-949

Dean-Nixon discussion on Sirica's attitude toward SI3-2 855-856

Dean-Petersen meeting on documents from CIA connecting him to Fielding break-in SI7-4 1623-1731, 1732

Dean plays his recorded conversation with Colson for Mitchell TW 2 134-135

Dean tells Colson he should meet with Bittman about TW 3 300-302

Dean's efforts to retrieve materials sent from CIA to Justice Department linking him to Fielding break-in SI2 2, 67, 673, 674-680; SI7-4 1624, 1733, 1734-1739

Dean's testimony on O'Brien's contacts with TW 1 169-170

delivery of $75,000 to Bittman for SI3-2 715, 1187, 1188-1237

and demands for money SI4-3 1574

demands for money discussed by Dean, Haldeman, Ehrlichman, and Mitchell SI3-2 1256, 1257-1259, 1260-1266, 1269

demands for money discussed by Ehrlichman and Dean SI3-2 708, 951, 952-956, 957

demands for money discussed by Ehrlichman and Krogh SI3-2 708, 951, 960-962

demands for money discussed by Nixon and Dean SI3-2 1030-1032, 1095-1096

demands for money, Haldeman on SI3-2 1123-1128

demands for money, Moore states he believes Nixon had no knowledge of NSI1 8, 57, 59-61

demands for money, O'Brien's concerns over TW 1 166-169

Dennis' proposal to call him as witness TW 3 744-746

and Diem cables SI7-2 558-559, 1029-1030, 1031-1079

discussed by Nixon, Ehrlichman, and Haldeman SI4-2 668-670

discussions of clemency for, in Article of Impeachment I RHJC 75-78

efforts of Impeachment Inquiry staff to interview II 3 1970

efforts to cover up link to White House II 1 593-597, 600-605, 611-612, 615, 679-680

efforts to find out if he was on White House payroll TW 3 505-506, 509-510

efforts to raise money for SI3-2 704, 901, 902-927

Ehrlichman denies requesting CIA aid for SI2 2, 457

Ehrlichman-Krogh meeting on forthcoming testimony of SI3-2 720, 1277, 1278-1281

Ehrlichman-Krogh telephone conversation on blackmail threats of SI7-4 1632, 1837, 1838-1839

Ehrlichman learns about connection to Watergate break-in SI2 2, 8, 117-120

Ehrlichman learns of White House status of II 1 592

Ehrlichman and Nixon discuss perjury by SI4-2 913-914

Ehrlichman requests CIA aid for SUMM I 91; SI7-2 538, 727, 728-738

Ehrlichman tells Nixon he will testify and Magruder and Mitchell will be indicted SUMM I 74

employment at Mullen & Co. TW 2 21, 35-37, 100; TW 3 11-12

evidence tying Watergate break-in to SUMM I 32

Executive clemency discussed at March 21, 1973 meeting of Nixon, Haldeman, Ehrlichman and Dean SI3-2 715, 1187, 1198-1203

Executive clemency offers to SUMM I 63-66

and fabrication of Diem cables II 2 1173-1174

false documents given by CIA to SI2 4, 79, 86

FBI agents question Dean about EOB office for SI2 2, 33, 329, 332-334, 336

in FBI interview of Colson SI2 2, 334

and FBI reports on wiretapping of government employees and newsmen SI7-2 690

Fielding break-in and SI2 2, 66, 671, 672; SIAPP1 23

granted immunity II 2 1206

Gray says Dean lied about White House status of SI4-1 6, 109-111, 113-114, 235, 236, 238

guilty plea of SI3-1 41, 483, 484; TW 2 24, 41-42, 56-58, 82

Haldeman-Colson telephone conversation on Executive clemency offers to SI4-1 255-256, 257-259

Haldeman informs Nixon of impending Grand Jury appearance of SI7-4 1634, 1859, 1860-1862

Haldeman reports to Nixon on Grand Jury testimony of SI4-1 357-358

Hall's notes for Colson on conversation with TW 3 275, 276, 278-285

hired as White House consultant and introduced to Ehrlichman SI7-2 537, 713, 714-726

hiring of II 2 1125-1128

House Judiciary Committee Impeachment Inquiry discussion on subpoenaing II 2 981-982

Howard memo to Kehrli on dropping him from White House staff II 2 1366-1368; SIAPP3 271; TW 3 261-263

identified by Baldwin as one of Watergate burglars SUMM I 45

indictment of SI3-1 29, 357, 358-367

informed by Liddy that DNC headquarters will be target of electronic surveillance SI1 21, 197, 198-200

intelligence activities prior to Democratic National Convention SI1 26, 245, 246-253 interview with Beard **II 2** 1035-1036; **SI5-2** 505, 777, 778-794

involvement in Fielding break-in **SI4-2** 1016

involvement in Watergate discussed by Ehrlichman and Haldeman **SI2** 2, 11, 129, 130

Kehrli memo to Howard on his annuity rights if he leaves White House staff **SIAPP3** 269-270

Kehrli's affidavit on termination of his employment at White House **SIAPP3** 265-268

Krogh indicted for perjury about activities for White House of **SI9-2** 534, 741, 742-746

Krogh's perjured testimony before Watergate Grand Jury on his participation in Fielding break-in **SI3-1** 25, 311, 312-325; **SI7-3** 1209, 1603, 1604-1613

Lambert and **TW 3** 287-288

LaRue's delivery of funds to Bittman for legal fees for **SI3-1** 32, 385, 386-389

LaRue's payment to, in St. Clair's presentation of evidence in behalf of Nixon **II 3** 1754

letter to Colson **SI3-1** 38-39, 455-456, 457-474; **TW 3** 272-275

letter to Houston on change in CIA annuity survivorship benefits **SI2** 2, 18, 166, 185

Liddy informs LaRue and Mardian of his role in Watergate break-in and other Plumbers unit operations **SI2** 2, 27, 277, 279-281, 285-287, 289-290; **SI3-1** 3, 87, 88-95

Liddy tells Dean he was not involved in Watergate break-in **NSI1** 40

meeting with Colson and Liddy on Liddy plan **SUMM I** 31; **TW 3** 244-249; **SI1** 12, 101, 102-103, 105, 110-111, 112, 113-114

meeting to discuss White House status of **SI2** 2, 17-18, 165-166

meeting between Nixon, Haldeman, Ehrlichman, and Dean on blackmail threats of **SI7-4** 1631, 1829, 1830-1836

meeting with Segretti **SI7-3** 1197, 1481, 1482-1494; **II 2** 1190

meeting with Shapiro **SUMM I** 53-54; **TW 2** 52-53, 89; **TW 3** 323-331, 333; **SI3-2** 925-926

meeting with Young, Liddy, and Malloy on Ellsberg psychological profile **SI7-2** 560, 1081, 1082-1093

memo from Colson to Dean on his status at White House **SI2** 2, 18, 166, 170-172

memo from Howard to Kehrli on his status at White House **SI2** 2, 18, 166, 181-184

memo from Silbert to Petersen on role in Fielding break-in **SIAPP3** 239-241

and memo on Boudin **II 2** 1175

memo on Boudin released by Colson **SI7-2** 563, 1125, 1126-1149

memo on meetings with Beard **SI5-2** 505, 777, 787-794

memo to Colson on "Neutralization of Ellsberg" **TW 3** 208-209; **SI7-2** 551, 911, 914

memo to Colson requesting aid in obtaining survivorship benefits from CIA **SI2** 2, 18, 166, 178-179

memos to Colson on Diem coup **SI7-2** 558-559, 1029-1030, 1057-1062

Mitchell denies knowledge of relationship between Liddy and **SI1** 122

money from Liddy given to Watergate burglars after arrests by **SUMM I** 52

name appearing in material belonging to Watergate burglars **SI2** 4, 79, 84, 94

name deleted from White House telephone list **SI2** 2, 28, 297, 298-299

names of experienced CIA retirees given to in CIA memo to FBI **TW 3** 41

Nixon asks Haldeman to inquire if Colson offered Executive clemency to **SI4-1** 8, 249, 251-252

Nixon-Colson discussion on **TW 3** 318

Nixon-Dean discussion on delaying sentencing of **NSI1** 166, 22, 157, 158-160

Nixon-Dean discussion on Executive clemency for **SI3-2** 892-893

Nixon-Dean discussion on Fielding break-in and **SI4-3** 90-91

Nixon-Dean discussions on demands for money by **NSI1** 21, 22, 149, 150-155, 157, 158-160

Nixon-Dean-Haldeman discussion on Sirica's probable sentence for **SI8** 410, 411

Nixon-Dean meeting on Exeuctive clemency offers to **SUMM I** 67-68

Nixon on demands of **SI3-2** 1246-1247

Nixon-Ehrlichman discussion on forthcoming testimony of **SI4-2** 665-666

Nixon-Haldeman discussion on money demands of **SIAPP3** 35-36

in Nixon-Haldeman discussion on Watergate **SIAPP3** 44, 75, 77

Nixon memo on possibility of blackmail by **SUMM I** 6

in Nixon memo on Watergate **SUMM I** 7

and Nixon's involvement with hush money **SUMM I** 52-62

in Nixon's recollections of March 21 **II 3** 1929

Nixon's television announcement of resignation of **SI4-3** 1119, 1657, 1658-1659

O'Brien informs Dean of his discussion with **TW 1** 127-128, 138-141, 151, 155-157

O'Brien informs Ehrlichman of his meeting with **TW 1** 135-136, 143

O'Brien on knowledge of actual payments made to **TW 1** 171-172

O'Brien-LaRue discussion on payments to **TW 1** 133, 134

O'Brien on meeting with **TW 1** 125-127, 137-138

O'Brien on others possibly informing Dean on his demands for money **TW 1** 163-164

O'Brien tells Ehrlichman about payments to **TW 1** 145-146, 153-154, 159-160, 174

O'Brien's concerns over meeting with **TW 1** 149-151, 152-154, 155

O'Brien's reasons for not telling Mitchell or LaRue but telling Ehrlichman about his demands for money **TW 1** 161-162

obtains Conein's telephone number and address **SI7-2** 558-559, 1029-1030, 1040-1041

offers of Executive clemency to, in Article of Impeachment I **RHJC** 114-115

pardon or clemency for discussed by Nixon, Haldeman, Ehrlichman and Dean **SI3-2** 1153-1154

participation in Fielding break-in **SI7-3** 1185, 1275, 1276-1299

on obtaining materials from CIA for disguise for De Motte interview **SI7-2** 547, 843, 853

on preparations for Fielding break-in **SI7-2** 561, 564, 1095, 1102-1107, 1151, 1152-1155

on receiving first payment from Bittman **SI3-1** 16, 207, 218-219

on release of memo on Boudin to terHorst **SI7-2** 563, 1125, 1126

on resignation **SI4-3** 1117, 1647, 1648

on reviewing contents of his safe **SI2** 2, 16, 161, 162-163

states he was unaware of Liddy's role in Beard's disappearance from Washington **NSI2** 13, 153, 154

on tape recorded conversation with Colson on need for more funds for Watergate defendants **SI3-1** 34-35, 405-406, 411-412

on taped telephone conversation with Colson on Pentagon Papers matter **SI7-2** 535, 697, 698

on Watergate break-ins **SI7-3** 1198, 1495, 1499-1500

Hunt-Liddy Special Project. *see* Fielding break-in

Hunt's safe

Bittman's efforts to obtain information on **TW 2** 6-7, 21-22, 32-33

and Bittman's motion to suppress **II 3** 1966-1967; **TW 2** 33, 34-35, 76-77

Colson on **SI2** 2, 177

contents of **II 2** 1195; **SUMM I** 37 ·

Dean on **TW 2** 234-236, 287-288

Dean-Colson conversation on **TW 3** 264-266

Dean discloses his destruction of documents from **NSI1** 19, 141, 142-143; **TW 2** 236-237, 292-293, 307-308, 309-310, 337

Dean-Ehrlichman meeting on contents of **SI2** 2, 32, 317, 318-327

Dean and Fielding deliver material to FBI agents from **SI2** 2, 43, 415, 416-426

Dean-Haldeman discussion on Dean's delay in turning over evidence on **II 2** 841

Dean's interview with Petersen on **SI4-2** 578, 1013, 1014-1015

in discussion among Nixon, Wilson, and Strickler **SI4-3** 1516-1518

in Doar's presentation of evidentiary material to House Judiciary Committee Impeachment Inquiry **II 1** 600-605, 684-685

Ehrlichman on **SI4-3** 1447-1448

in Ehrlichman-Clawson telephone conversation **SI4-3** 1321-1323

Ehrlichman and Dean give Gray material from **SI2** 2, 52, 501, 502-510; **SI7-3** 1206, 1575, 1576-1587

Ehrlichman on Dean's testimony on **SI2** 2, 173

Ehrlichman orders it drilled open **SUMM I** 37

Ehrlichman's instructions to Dean on contents of **SI4-2** 1001

Ehrlichman's telephone conversations with Gray on **SI4-2** 583, 1059, 1060-1080

FBI inventory of contents of **SI2** 2, 43, 415, 422,-423

Gray confirmation hearings and **II 2** 783

Gray on contents of **SI4-1** 248

Gray on destruction of files from **SI7-2** 558-559, 1029-1030, 1076-1079

Gray on FBI receiving contents of **SI3-2** 773

Gray tells Petersen he destroyed files from **SI4-3** 1096, 1331, 1332-1339

Gray's destruction of files from **SI4-3** 1113, 1613, 1614-1624

Hunt removes money from after Watergate arrests **SUMM I** 35

Hunt reviews contents of and informs Colson of **SI2** 2, 16, 161, 162-163

Hunt's motion for return of **SUMM I** 63

information on Gray burning files from released to press **II 2** 892-893

materials delivered to FBI and materials kept from **SI7-3** 1204, 1557, 1558-1568

Nixon and Ehrlichman discuss Gray's receiving material from **SI4-3** 1255-1257

Nixon on Gray's destruction of documents from **II 3** 1741

Nixon requests Ehrlichman to discuss documents from with Gray **SUMM I** 90

Nixon's lack of awareness that Gray destroyed documents from **NSI1** 18, 137, 138-139

opening of **SI2** 2, 19, 189, 190-201

Petersen on Dean's destruction of material from **TW 3** 151-152, 157-158, 179

Petersen on Dean's information on material from **TW 3** 75-78, 122, 130-131, 140-141, 145-146

taped telephone conversation between Ehrlichman and Clawson on **SI2** 2, 20, 203, 212-213

White House interference with FBI Watergate investigation and **II 3** 1961

White House reaction to Dean telling Watergate Prosecutors about **II 2** 879, 881

Huntley, Chet, on enemies list SI8 66, 113, 114-116, 117, 121-122

Hush money TW 1 147; **TW 2** 5, 7-19, 30, 38-39, 40-41, 42-44; **TW 3** 534-558, 559-578, 680-685, 704-710, 712-714, 732-7

in Article of Impeachment I **RHJC** 51, 66-74

campaign contributions used for **SI3-1** 22, 281, 282-290

Colson on **TW 3** 454-455

Colson denies discussing payments to Hunt with Nixon **TW 3** 418-419

Colson-Haldeman discussions on payments to Hunt **TW 3** 315-317

Colson-Hunt taped telephone conversation on **II 2** 752-759

Dean and **II 2** 795-798, 841

Dean believes he is criminally liable on **SUMM I** 86

Dean, Haldeman, Ehrlichman, and Mitchell's involvement in **SI3-2** 1016-1017

Dean on his involvement with **TW 2** 238-239, 245-251, 258-270, 290-297

Dean's awareness of Haldeman's $350,000 fund and payments to Watergate defendants from **TW 2** 229-234

Dean's meeting with Paul O'Brien on Hunt's demands for **SI3-2** 707, 945, 946-949

delivered to Bittman for Hunt **SI3-2** 715, 1187, 1188-1237

O'Brien denies Hunt used term in conversation with him **TW 1** 138, 170

O'Brien on uselessness of paying **TW 1** 147-148

and O'Brien's meeting with Hunt **II 2** 786-792

Petersen discussion with Nixon on **SI4-2** 1007-1008

Petersen informs Nixon of Watergate Grand Jury discussions on **SUMM I** 93

in St. Clair's presentation of evidence in behalf of Nixon **II 3** 1899-1901

scheme for distribution of **II 2** 736-739, 748

and Stans' delivery of $75,000 to Kalmbach **SI3-1** 11, 165, 166-173

Stans' involvement with **SI3-1** 20, 253, 254-263

transfer of campaign contributions from White House to CRP for payments to Watergate defendants **SI3-1** 33-34, 425-426, 427-454

transferred from Stans to Kalmbach **II 2** 738-739

Ulasewicz's method of delivery **SI3-1** 17, 221, 222-233

Watergate coverup and **SUMM I** 40-41

White House efforts to obtain from CIA **II 2** 723-727

See also Bittman, William O., testimony before House Judiciary Committee Impeachment Inquiry; Kalmbach, Herbert Warren, testimony before House Judiciary Committee Impeachment Inquiry, on his involvement with hush money; O'Brien, Paul L., testimony before House Judiciary Committee Impeachment Inquiry

Hushen, John SI7-4 1757

Huston, Tom Charles SI7-1 521-522

Dean on attitude toward formation of Intelligence Evaluation Committee **SI7-1** 501-502

in discussion between Nixon, Wilson, and Strickler **SI4-3** 1529

efforts to obtain Haldeman's assistance in overriding Hoover's objections to Huston plan **SI7-1** 434

memo from Haldeman on Nixon's approval of Huston plan recommendations **SI7-1** 25, 445, 446

memo to Haldeman with report on IRS investigation of political activities of tax-exempted organizations **II 2** 1255

memo to Haldeman with status report of IRS Special Service Group **SI8** 4, 43, 44-51

memo to Helms on Nixon's approval of Huston plan recommendations **SI7-1** 25, 445, 454-461

memo to Haldeman seeking aid for approval of Huston plan **SI7-1** 27, 469, 478, 480-484, 485

Nixon appoints as White House liaison to ad hoc committee to study domestic intelligence **SI7-1** 22, 275, 376-382

and Nixon's recall of decision memo approving recommendations of Huston plan **SI7-1** 27, 469, 470-485

sends Huston plan and memo entitled "Operational" Restraints on Intelligence Collection" to Haldeman **SI7-1** 24, 437, 438-444

White House responsibility for domestic intelligence transferred to Dean from **SI7-1** 28, 487, 488-496

See also Huston plan

Huston, Tom Charles, cited testimony of

on Hoover's objections to Huston plan placed in footnote **SI7-1** 23, 383, 432-433

on memo from Haldeman on Nixon's approval of Huston plan recommendations **SI7-1** 25, 445, 449-450

on need for improvement of domestic intelligence **SI7-1** 22, 375, 378, 382

on Nixon's recall of decision memo approving recommendations of Huston plan **SI7-1** 27, 469, 470-473

on reasons for Dean assuming his responsibilities **SI7-1** 28, 487, 496

on sending Huston plan and memo on recommendations to Haldeman **SI7-1** 23, 383, 443

on transfer of responsibilities to Dean **SI7-1** 28, 487, 488

Huston plan SI7-1 23, 383, 384-436

on antiwar movement **SI7-1** 391-392

in Article of Impeachment II **RHJC** 151-152

on assessment of current intelligence procedures against black extremist groups **SI7-1** 400-401

on assessment of current intelligence procedures against communist intelligence **SI7-1** 405

on assessment of current internal security threat of Communist Party **SI7-1** 408

on assessment of current internal security threat of Socialist Workers Party and other Trotskyist groups **SI7-1** 408

on black extremist movement **SI7-1** 397-401

on budget and manpower restrictions **SI7-1** 428-429

contents of **SI7-1** 23, 383, 384-431

Ehrlichman on **SI7-1** 22, 375, 381

evaluation of interagency coordination in **SI7-1** 430-431

Fielding break-in and **II 2** 1168

Haldeman on **SI7-1** 22, 375, 379-380, 444

Haldeman on Hoover's objections to **SI7-1** 23, 383, 434

Helms memo for the record on discussion with Mitchell on **SI7-1** 26, 463, 468

Hoover and Mitchell oppose Nixon's approval of recommendations of **SI7-1** 26, 463, 464-468

Hoover's objections to **SI7-1** 23, 383, 432-433

House Judiciary Committee Impeachment Inquiry presentation of evidence on **II 2** 1115-1119; **II 3** 1978

on intelligence services of communist countries **SI7-1** 402-407

Kissinger denies involvement with **SI7-1** 150

memo from Helms returning Nixon's decision memo on **SI7-1** 27, 469, 474

memos from Huston to Haldeman on **SI7-1** 27, 469, 478, 480-484, 485

on militant New Left groups **SI7-1** 389-396

in Minority of House Judiciary Committee Impeachment Inquiry views on Articles of Impeachment **RHJC** 452-456

Mitchell-Helms meeting on **SI7-1** 472

Mitchell on opposition to **SI7-1** 27, 469, 475-477

Nixon on **SIAPP1** 21, 22; **SI7-1** 23, 383, 435-436

U.S. v. *Diamond International Corporation and Ray Dubrowin* **SIAPP2** 253-256

U.S. v. *Donald Segretti* **SIAPP2** 315-322

U.S. v. *Dwayne Andreas and First Interoceanic Corporation* **SIAPP2** 221-226

U.S. v. *Dwight Chapin* **SIAPP2** 243-252

U.S. v. *Francis Carroll* **SIAPP2** 239-242

U.S. v. *George Steinbrenner III, and the American Shipbuilding Company* **SIAPP2** 323-346

U.S. v. *Goodyear Tire and Rubber Company and Russell deYoung* **SIAPP2** 257-262

U.S. v. *Gulf Oil Corporation and Claude C. Wild, Jr.* **SIAPP2** 263-266

U.S. v. *Harold Nelson* **SIAPP2** 285-296

U.S. v. *Herbert Kalmbach* **SIAPP2** 267-272

U.S. v. *James Allen* **SIAPP2** 197-200

U.S. v. *John H. Melcher, Jr.* **SIAPP2** 277-280

U.S. v. *Lehigh Valley Cooperative Farmers* **SIAPP2** 273-276

U.S. v. *Minnesota and Mining and Manufacturing Company, and Harry Heltzer* **SIAPP2** 281-284

U.S. v. *Northrop Corporation and Thomas Jones* **SIAPP2** 297-300

U.S. v. *Phillips Petroleum Company and William W. Keeler* **SIAPP2** 311-314

U.S. v. *Richard Allison* **SIAPP2** 201-202

Illinois

Nixon campaign in **SIAPP4** 149

Immunity

Dean on efforts to obtain **TW 2** 277-279, 323

Ehrlichman does not want for White House aides **SI4-1** 37, 547, 548

for Dean **SUMM I** 92-93, 96-99; **SI4-3** 1524-1525, 1537-1538

    Colson discussion with Ehrlichman on **TW 3** 352-353

    in Garrison's presentation of summary of evidence to House Judiciary Committee Impeachment Inquiry **II 3** 2088-2089

    in St. Clair's presentation of evidence in behalf of Nixon **II 3** 1753

    Nixon-Petersen discussions on **II 3** 2026-2027; **TW** 96-97, 113-114

    Petersen on **TW 3** 116-117, 176-177

granted to Hunt **II 2** 1206

types of **SI4-3** 1525

White House efforts to prevent Dean from getting **II 2** 857, 884-885, 886

for White House personnel, discussed by Dean, Haldeman and Ehrlichman **SI3-2** 1139-1140, 1149-1150, 1158

for witnesses called by House Judiciary Committee Impeachment Inquiry **II 2** 987-988

Impeachment II 1 1-51

"abuse of power" and, in Minority of House Judiciary Committee Impeachment Inquiry views on Articles of Impeachment **RHJC** 431-433

cases in U.S. **II 3** 2175-2179, 2199-2215

criminality issue and, in House Judiciary Committee Impeachment Inquiry staff report **II 3** 2180-2183, 2216-2218

Danielson's views on grounds for **RHJC** 303

Doar on awesomeness of task of House Judiciary Committee Impeachment Inquiry **II 3** 1926-1927

Garrison on role of politics in **II 3** 2038-2041, 2050

historical origins of, in House Judiciary Committee Impeachment Inquiry staff report **II 3** 2162-2179

House Judiciary Committee Impeachment Inquiry staff on Constitutional grounds for **II 3** 2159-2185

House of Representatives powers during inquiry on **SUMM I** 164-165

impoundment of funds as grounds for **II 2** 1304, 1319; **SI12** 7-8, 41-92

legal definition of **TW 1** 2-3

Nixon on **SIAPP1** 70, 81-82, 85

Nixon's noncompliance with House Judiciary Committee subpoenas as grounds for **SUMM I** 170

political judgement and **MMFL** 44-45

in Proceedings of Constitutional Convention of 1787 **II 3** 2187-2198

tax evasion and **II 3** 1458-1459

See also House Judiciary Committee Impeachment Inquiry

Impeachment Inquiry staff MMFL 32-37

biographies of **II 3** 2143-2155

breakdown of and biographies of counsel **II 3** 2141-2155

Garrison on bipartisanship of **II 3** 2036-2038

list of **II 3** 2142

notes on interview with Kleindienst inserted into House Judiciary Committee Impeachment Inquiry record **II 3** 2131-2132

organization of **II 3** 2137-2140

procedures for handling Impeachment Inquiry material **II 3** 2221

Report on American impeachment cases **II 3** 2199-2215

Report on Constitutional Grounds for Presidential Impeachment **II 3** 2159-2185

Report on work of **II 3** 2137-2140

rules for **II 3** 2222

Special staff and biography of counsel **II 3** 2234-2236

status of work as of April 24, 1974 **II 3** 2239-2248

status of work as of March 1, 1974 **II 3** 2225-2233

See also Minority Impeachment Inquiry staff, Memorandum on Facts and Law

Impoundment of funds II 2 1304; **SI12** 2-3, 41-88

actions of Nixon Administration **SI12** 4-27

arguments presented on behalf of executive justifying **SI12** 55-88

budgetary reserves in reports filed by OMB since enactment of Federal Impoundment and Information Act **SI12** 6

Congressional actions dealing with during Nixon Administration **SI12** 34-40

and Congressional declination to enact expenditure ceilings **SI12** 39

Congressional removal of claimed statutory authority for **SI12** 38-39

and Constitutional grant of "executive power" to

Impoundment of funds (*Continued*)
President **SI12** 76-80
control legislation **SI12** 39-40
determination by courts to take jurisdiction of cases involving **SI12** 7-8
and discretion conferred by other statutes and President's duty under "take care" clause **SI12** 67-75
factual background **SI12** 2-40
historical precedent for **SI12** 81-88
and laws linking expenditures to release of **SI12** 37-38
laws specifically limiting **SI12** 36-37
legal opinions prepared for government on **SI12** 85-88
and mandatory spending language in appropriations measures **SI12** 37
methods used for **SI12** 2-3
Nixon's role in **SI12** 28-33
Nixon's statement during news conference on his Constitutional right **SI12** 33
and passage of different programs **SI12** 50
"sense of Congress" provisions and **SI12** 38
statements by Nixon and other executive officers on Nixon's role in **SI12** 28-33
and statutory construction of spending statutes **SI12** 57-66
in status report of House Judiciary Committee Impeachment Inquiry staff **II 3** 2232, 2248
and statutes with expenditure ceilings **SI12** 75
steps in federal funding processes and **SI12** 3-4
See also Budgetary reserve, establishment from appropriated funds; Contract authority, failure to allot; Court cases on Presidential impoundment of funds; House Judiciary Committee Impeachment Inquiry, presentation of evidence on impoundment of funds by Nixon Administration; Impeachment, impoundment of funds as grounds for

In re Grand Jury
motion and Sirica's decision on Nixon tape of September 15, 1972 **SI8** 28-29, 331, 332, 340-349

In re Grand Jury, cited testimony from
Buzhardt **SI2** 2, 24, 236, 249-250

Income taxes. *See* Nixon's income tax

Independent Bancorporation SIAPP2 222-226
See also U.S. v. *Dwayne Andreas and First Interoceanic Corporation*

India-Pakistan War
disclosures on U.S. position on, wiretapping activities and **II 2** 1185; **SI7-3** 1193, 1421, 1422-1440

Indian Education Act
impoundment of funds for **SI12** 24-25

Inflation
as campaign issue **SIAPP4** 9-10
as Presidential motive to impound funds **SI12** 69, 70-72, 84

Informants
in black extremist groups, Huston plan on **SI7-1** 401
FBI, in antiwar movement **SI7-1** 394

in Miami **SI1** 246
Inouye, Daniel K., questioning by SI4-1 247-248
Dean **NSI1** 46, 163; **SI4-1** 387; **SI7-1** 490; **SI8** 117, 336
Ehrlichman **SI3-1** 399; **SI4-1** 510-517; **SI4-2** 598-602, 1064; **SI7-4** 1703, 1874-1875, 1881-1883, 1892-1893
Haldeman **SI9-1** 439; **SI1** 163
Hunt **NSI2** 154; **SI7-2** 1050; **SI7-3** 1482-1484
Kleindienst **SI7-4** 1872-1873
Laird **SI11** 157-158, 161
Mitchell **SI7-1** 466-467, 477
Petersen **SI2** 2, 583
Segretti **SI3-1** 396; **SI7-4** 1699
Sloan **SI3-1** 562
Stans **SI1** 183
Strachan **NSI1** 84

Insurance industry SI5-1 108-110, 124-125
See also Hartford Fire Insurance Company

Intelligence activities SI7-1 402-407
against black extremist groups, in Huston plan **SI7-1** 400-401
against New Left, Huston plan assessment of **SI7-1** 393-395
of communist countries, Huston plan on **SI7-1** 402-407

Intelligence agencies SI1 39-40
Nixon on **SI1** 39-40
See also CIA; FBI; Huston plan

Intelligence Evaluation Committee SUMM I 126
creation of **SI7-1** 29, 497, 498-505
establishment of **SI7-1** 489-491
Mitchell on reasons for formation of **SI7-1** 505
Nixon on reasons for creation of **SIAPP1** 22; **SI1** 40
Nixon's approval of Huston plan on **SI7-1** 456-457
on organizational chart from files of Special Investigations Unit **SI7-2** 814
report on demonstrations planned for Republican National Convention **SI1** 82

Internal Revenue Service (IRS) RHJC 139-183; **SI10** 17; **SI8** 32, 437, 438-440
audit of DeAntonio proposed by Caulfield **SI8** 18, 183, 184-194
and audit of Lawrence O'Brien **II 2** 1284-1287, 1296-1297; **SUMM I** 142
audit of Rebozo **II 2** 1300
audit report arguing for re-auditing of Nixons' income tax returns for 1970-1972 **SI10** 412-415
audits of several politically active people in entertainment industry **II 2** 1279-1281
and Brookings Institution's tax returns information at White House **SI8** 8, 79, 80-94
Browne's memo on civil fraud penalties related to Nixon's 1969 federal income tax return **SI10** 387-394
and *Center on Corporate Responsibility* v. *Shultz* **II 2** 1298, 1299, 1302
Colson on relationship to enemies list **TW 3** 472
and confidentiality of information on Nixon's income tax **II 3** 1457
Dean and Caulfield preparation of briefing paper for Haldeman on increasing political responsiveness of **SI8** 19, 195, 196-204

Dean memo to Haldeman and others suggesting audit of "enemy" journalist **SI8** 21, 211, 212

Dean on White House use of **TW 2** 300-303, 311, 331-332, 350-351

and Dean's efforts to obtain information on McGovern campaign staff members **II 2** 1293, 1297-1298; **SI8** 25, 26, 30, 237, 238-271, 273, 274-279, 351, 352-353

discussed by Nixon, Dean and Haldeman **SI3-2** 813

Doar on organizational structure of **II 2** 1274-1275

and enemies list **II 2** 1259-1263, 1268-1295; **SUMM I** 141-142; **SI8** 116, 117

House Judiciary Committee Impeachment Inquiry discussion on obtaining Nixon's tax returns and audits from **II 2** 1242

Huston memo to Haldeman with status report of Special Service Group investigations of tax-exempt organizations **SI8** 4, 43, 44-51

and improvements on Nixon's San Clemente and Key Biscayne properties **SI12** 94-95

Income Tax Audit Changes form for Nixons' 1969-1972 federal income taxes **SI10** 410-411

information on Goldberg given to Caulfield by **II 2** 1271; **SI8** 13, 131, 132-144

information on Graham sent to Dean **SI8** 14, 145, 146-154

information on investigations of George and Gerald Wallace sent to White House by **SI8** 3, 35, 36-42

informs Ehrlichman of termination of O'Brien investigation **SI8** 24, 227, 228-235

Intelligence Division investigates DeMarco, Newman, and Morgan on gift of Nixon's papers and recommends Grand Jury proceeding **SI10** 18-19, 376-386

investigation of George and Gerald Wallace by **II 2** 1250-1255; **SUMM I** 141

investigation of Nixon's tax returns **SUMM I** 171-176

investigation of O'Brien by **SI8** 23, 217, 218-225

investigation of political activities of tax-exempt organizations **II 2** 1255

investigations of Nixon's friends **II 2** 1275-1281

in Jenner's presentation of summary of evidence to House Judiciary Committee Impeachment Inquiry on Nixon's abuse of power **II 3** 1980, 1983-1990

Joint Committee on Internal Revenue Taxation report on use of IRS for political purposes **SI8** 26, 273, 280-285

legal questions involved in White House staff members obtaining information from **II 2** 1271-1275

and Liddy's and Caulfield's efforts to obtain position of Director of Alcohol, Tobacco, and Firearms Division of **II 2** 1257-1258

memo for record on re-audit of Nixon's income tax returns for 1969-1972 **SI10** 373-374, 423-434

memos on political responsiveness of **II 2** 1283

Nixon-Haldeman-Dean discussion on Dean working through **II 2** 1293-1295, 1298; **SI8** 27, 287, 288-330

Nixon-Haldeman-Dean taped discussion of O'Brien investigation by, court litigation on **SI8** 28-29, 331-332, 333-349

Nixon and Thrower's resignation as Commissioner of **SI8** 6, 59, 60-64

Nixon's abuse of Presidential power and misuse of **SUMM I** 141-143; **MMFL** 121-125

Nixon's complaints about Cox's letters to **SI9-1** 33, 403, 404-406

notifies Nixons of adjustment of tax liability for 1969-1972 and receives payment from Nixons for 1970-1972 **SI10** 19-20

and opinion in *Center on Corporate Responsibility* v. *Shultz* **SI8** 32, 437, 438-440

policy of delaying sensitive inquiries until after elections **II 2** 1285-1286, 1287-1290

in Political Matters Memoranda **SIAPP4** 3

practices of previous administrations related to **II 2** 1264-1265

presentation of evidence to House Judiciary Committee Impeachment Inquiry on Nixon Administration misuse of **II 2** 1249-1265, 1275-1302

Referral Reports to Intelligence Division on DeMarco, Morgan, and Newman **SI10** 378-386

report of Intelligence Division on investigation of DeMarco, Newman, and Morgan related to Nixon's 1969 income tax return **SI10** 395-402

section of audit report on Nixons on possibility of fraud in gift of Nixon's papers **SI10** 376-377

special service group of **II 2** 1256

transmittal of tax audit information on Wayne and other enterainers to Caulfield **SI8** 15, 155, 156-163

used by White House for political enemies project **SI8** 21, 22, 211, 212, 213, 214-216

Walters gives Dean's list of McGovern supporters to Joint Committee on Internal Revenue Taxation **SI8** 26, 273, 274-279

Waters letter to Nixons notifying them of re-auditing of 1971 and 1972 federal income tax returns **SI10** 374-375

White House efforts to obtain audit of Greene **SI8** 16, 165, 166-174

White House efforts to place Caulfield in **SI8** 5, 53, 54-58

White House requests for audits from, conflicting testimony on **SI8** 17, 175, 176-182

See also Alexander, Donald C.; Article of Impeachment II; *Center on Corporate Responsibility* v. *Shultz*; Nixon's income tax

Internal security SI7-1 397-400
See also National security

International Telephone and Telegraph Corporation.
See ITT, antitrust suits against; ITT matter

"Investigation into Certain Charges of the Use of the Internal Revenue Service for Political Purposes"
SI8 16, 26, 165, 174, 273, 280-285

Iredell, James SUMM I 147

Ireland, C.T., Jr.
memo to Geneen on ITT acquisition of Hartford **SI5-2** 934-935

143-144, 145-188

and meeting between Kleindienst, McLaren, Rohatyn and other representatives **SI5-1** 24, 403, 404-422

and memo from Colson to Ehrlichman on Casey letter **SI5-1** 7, 143, 177

and memo from Colson to Ehrlichman with McLaren's speech on antitrust policy**SI5-1** 9, 189, 193-211

memo from Hughes to Ehrlichman on conversation with Board on **SI5-1** 6, 141, 142

memo from Hullin to Mitchell on **SI5-1** 7, 143, 178

memo from McLaren to Kleindienst on filing ITT-Canteen complaint **SI5-1** 88

memos from Ehrlichman to Mitchell on **SI5-2** 508-509, 803-804, 828, 829

memos from McLaren for Ehrlichman on **SI5-1** 7, 143, 147-152, 153-162

mergers and acquisitions since January 1, 1960 **SI5-1** 107

and Merriam, Casey, and Petersen meeting **SI5-1** 13, 267, 268-276

and Merriam letter to Connally **SI5-2** 508-509, 658-659, 694-695, 803-804, 810-811

and Merriam letter to Peterson **SI5-2** 508-509, 513-514, 803-804, 812, 855, 863-864, 883-884

Mitchell on **SI5-1** 3, 69, 92-93

Mitchell denies discussing with Nixon **SI5-2** 493, 494, 503, 631-632, 639-643, 759, 772-775

Nixon-Ehrlichman-Shultz meeting on **SI5-1** 16, 311, 312-345

Nixon-Kleindienst telephone conversation on dropping Justice Department appeal on *ITT-Grinnell* **SI5-1** 16, 311, 315-326, 346-348

Nixon-Mitchell-Haldeman conversation on **SI5-2** 510, 841, 846-847

Nixon-Mitchell meeting on *ITT-Grinnell* appeal **SI5-1** 21, 371, 372-376

Nixon's abuse of Presidential power and **SUMM I** 144-148

Nixon's news conference on McLaren's role in **SI5-2** 507, 799, 802

and Nixon's refusal to meet with Geneen **NSI2** 5, 35, 36-44

Notice of Docketing of Appeal in *ITT-Grinnell* **SI5-2** 483, 533, 534-535

and Petersen memo to Nixon on meeting with Geneen **SI5-1** 14, 277, 281

Poole memo on conference between McLaren and defendant's counsel **SI5-1** 7, 143, 166-167

press coverage of Kleindienst confirmation hearings and **SI5-2** 512, 855, 856-860

press release on Geneen's meetings with government officials **SI5-1** 133

and Ramsden Report on ITT divestiture of Hartford **SI5-2** 534, 535

Ryan memo to Merriam on **SI5-2** 672, 708

SEC subpoenas for documents from **SI5-2** 495, 497, 500, 645, 646-676, 681-712, 735, 743-748

settlement of **SI5-2** 485, 488, 549, 550-559, 595, 596-602

settlement negotiations and retention of Hartford Fire Insurance Co. **NSI2** 9, 81, 82-101

and Stigler Report **NSI2** 4, 25, 26-30

transfer of documents obtained by SEC from **SI5-2** 516-517, 905-906, 907-948

trial and judgement in **SI5-1** 10, 213, 214-253

U.S. v. *International Telephone & Telegraph Corporation and Grinnell Corporation* docket **SI5-1** 4, 9, 101, 102-103, 189, 190-191

U.S. v. *International Telephone & Telegraph Corporation and Hartford Fire Insurance Company* docket **SI5-1** 4, 101, 104-105

U.S. v. *ITT (Canteen)* docket **SI5-1** 3, 69, 89-90

and *U.S.* v. *Ling-Temco-Vought* **SI5-2** 666-670, 702-706

and Walsh's efforts to deal*y ITT-Grinnell* appeal **SI5-1** 15, 283, 284-305

Washington Post on connection between ITT-Sheraton pledge and **SI5-2** 493, 633, 634-637

and White House concern with Kleindienst confirmation hearings **SI5-2** 508-509, 803-804, 805-839

and White House task force on Kleindienst hearings **SI5-2** 503, 759, 760-769

and White House White Paper on "The ITT Anti-Trust Decision" **SI5-1** 5, 131, 139-140; **SI5-2** 519, 955, 956-963; **NSI2** 4, 25, 31-32

and Wilson's role in obtaining contribution pledge from ITT **NSI2** 14, 155, 156

See also Dita Beard matter; ITT matter; Geneen, Harold S.; House Judiciary Committee Impeachment Inquiry, presentation of evidence on ITT matter; Kleindienst confirmation hearings; St. Clair, James D., presentation of evidence in behalf of Nixon on ITT matter

ITT Anti-Trust Decision, The (White House "White Paper") **SI5-2** 519, 955, 956-963

ITT matter II 2 987-988; **NSI2** 16, 189, 194-197; **SIAPP2** 368-369; **TW 3** 381-398

and abuse of powers charge against Nixon **MMFL** 126-135

and Beard memo allegations **NSI2** 16, 189, 190-202

and choice of Sheraton hotels for Republican National Convention **SI5-2** 585

Colson on **TW 3** 400-402, 465-466, 482-488, 506-507

Cox requests and receives Fielding's file on **II 2** 1346-1351, 1360-1364, 1366-1367; **SI9-1** 15, 269, 170-176

Dean's telephone call to Schlesinger on **SI2 2**, 674-675

IRS and **II 2** 1300

Kleindienst's testimony on **NSI2** 191, 192-193

letter from St. Clair to Doar on House Judiciary Committee Impeachment Inquiry requests for materials on **II 2** 804-805

memo from Colson to Dean on **NSI2** 16, 189, 194-197

in Minority of House Judiciary Committee Impeachment Inquiry views on Articles of Impeachment **RHJC** 470-476

Nixon on **SIAPP3** 6, 12, 17

in Nixon-Mitchell conversation **SIAPP3** 3

Nixon's overseas trips and **NSI2** 17, 203, 204-208

Nixon's refusal to comply with subpoenas for materials related to **SUMM I** 158-159

ITT matter *(Continued)*
    in St. Clair's presentation of evidence in behalf of Nixon **II 3** 1757-1771, 1773, 1891-1892
    and selection of San Diego as site for Republican National Convention of 1972 **NSI2** 12, 127, 128-151
    See also Beard, Dita; Colson, Charles, testimony before House Judiciary Committee Impeachment Inquiry, on ITT-Kleindienst hearings matter; House Judiciary Committee Impeachment Inquiry, presentation of evidence on ITT matter; ITT, antitrust suits against; *U.S.* v. *Howard Edwin Reinecke*; *U.S.* v. *Richard Kleindienst*

Jablonski, Lee SIAPP4 23; **SI1** 172, 178

Jackson, Henry M. SIAPP2 320-321
    Segretti slanders against **SI7-3** 1384, 1390
    See also Jackson campaign; *U.S.* v. *Donald Segretti*

Jackson, Henry M., questioning by
    Laird **SI11** 134

Jackson, Morton Barrows TW 2 87
    in CIA memo to Justice Department **TW 3** 68-69

Jackson, William N.
    and report of IRS Intelligence Division on investigation of Nixons' 1969 income tax return **SI10** 18-19, 395-402

Jackson campaign
    and Munro on enemies list **SI8** 74, 108
    in Political Matters Memoranda **SIAPP4** 6, 20
    talking paper from Strachan to Mitchell on **SIAPP4** 42

Jackson State University
    in Presidential statement on 1970 intelligence plan **SIAPP1** 22; **SI7-1** 377

Jacobs, Ephraim
    and settlement of ITT antitrust cases **NSI2** 84

Jacobsen, Jake SIAPP2 294-295
    and AMPI contribution **SI6-1** 80
    meeting with Connally **II 2** 1068; **SI6-2** 467, 519, 520
    meeting with Kalmbach and Mehren **SI6-2** 914-915, 923-937
    in memo to Haldeman **SI1** 79
    Nelson on meetings between Connally and **SI6-1** 448-450
    telephone conversation with Connally **SI6-2** 474, 673, 698
    See also U.S. v. *David Parr; U.S.* v. *Harold Nelson; U.S.* v. *Jake Jacobsen; U.S.* v. *John Connally, and Jake Jacobsen*

Jacobsen, Jake, cited testimony of
    on AMPI campaign contributions and antitrust suit against AMPI **SI6-2** 486, 895, 939-941
    on discussions with Connally on behalf of AMPI's efforts to obtain increase in milk price supports **SI6-1** 27-28, 401-402, 424-426

Jacobson, O.T.
    memo to Walters on Halperin-Ellsberg contacts **SI7-2** 534, 681, 682-684

James, Howard, telegram to San Diego County Convention and Tourist Bureau on use of Sheraton Harbor Island Hotel as Republican National Convention center SI5-2 487, 562, 588-589

Japan
    leak on Nixon's determination to remove nuclear weapons from Okinawa and negotiations with **NSI4** 26, 179, 180-182

Jarriel, Tom SIAPP1 45, 51, 70

Javits, Jacob
    on Kissinger's background **SI11** 312

Jaworski, Leon SIAPP2 34-37; **SI7-2** 918-920, 1139-1141; **SI7-3** 1611
    and amendment filed by Bork to Watergate Special Prosecutor's charter **SI9-2** 551, 861, 862-866
    appointed Watergate Special Prosecutor by Bork **SI9-2** 549, 845, 846-848
    Buzhardt sends logs of meetings and telephone conversations between Nixon and six individuals to **SI9-2** 554, 883, 884-890
    Colson's negotiated guilty plea and **SI9-2** 580, 1053, 1054-1058
    cooperation with House Judiciary Committee Impeachment Inquiry **II 1** 18, 59, 60-61
    efforts to obtain White House materials **II 2** 1418-1434
    files indictment against Chapin for testifying falsely before Watergate Grand Jury on Segretti's activities **SI9-2** 555, 891, 892-900
    House Judiciary Committee Impeachment Inquiry discussion of obtaining materials from **II 1** 106-115
    informs Eastland that Nixon will not cooperate further with Watergate investigation **SI9-2** 560, 935, 936-945
    and investigation of IRS audit of Lawrence O'Brien and Watergate break-in **II 2** 1296-1297
    and Krogh's guilty plea and statement **SI9-2** 556, 901, 902-921
    Latta on television statement on credibility of witness by **II 1** 91
    letter from Alexander referring IRS investigation of Nixon's 1969 income tax returns to Grand Jury **SI10** 403-404
    letter from St. Clair on release of information to House Judiciary Committee Impeachment Inquiry **II 1** 106
    letter to Doar with list of materials Nixon has refused to provide **SI9-2** 560, 579, 935, 941-945, 1045, 1048-1052
    letter to Eastland **SI9-2** 557, 575, 923, 924-925, 1019, 1020-1025; **II 2** 1423, 1424-1425
    letter to Miller, on Kleindienst's plea **SI5-2** 520, 965, 969-970
    letter to O'Connor on acceptance of Kalmbach's guilty plea **SI9-2** 562, 951, 957-958
    letter to Percy **II 2** 1428-1429; **SI9-2** 589, 983, 984-985
    letter to St. Clair informing him that he will seek subpoena for materials for Mitchell's trial **SI9-2** 567, 973, 974-975
    letter to St. Clair requesting access to taped conversations and related documents for Government preparation of Mitchell's trial **SI9-2** 565, 965, 966-967
    letter to Shapiro on Colson's guilty plea **SI9-2** 580, 1053, 1057-1058

letter to Shulman on Krogh's guilty plea **SI9-2** 556, 901, 908-909

letters to Pickle on ITT investigation **SI5-2** 897-980

list of materials obtained from White House given to House Judiciary Committee Impeachment Inquiry by **II 1** 105, 206-207

meeting with Haig on conditions for accepting job as Watergate Special Prosecutor **SI9-2** 548, 837, 838-843

motion for reconsideration and affidavit on Nixon tape of September 15, 1972 **SI8** 28-29, 331-332, 340-346

motion for trial subpoena in *U.S.* v. *Mitchell* directing Nixon to produce certain tapes and documents **SI9-2** 570, 987, 988-990

and negotiations with Nixon's attorneys for further materials **SIAPP1** 71

New York Times article on his telling Wilson that no legal action was being planned against him **NSI2** 14, 155, 156

Nixon on **SIAPP1** 65

Nixon states he has provided everything needed to conclude his investigation **SI9-2** 559, 931, 932-933

Nixon's motion to quash subpoena issued on April 18, 1974 by **SI9-2** 572, 1005, 1006-1007

on Nixon's refusal to cooperate **RHJC** 125

Nixon's refusal to cooperate with, in Article of Impeachment I **RHJC** 125

and Nixon's refusal to testify before Watergate Grand Jury **SIAPP1** 70

relationship with House Judiciary Committee Impeachment Inquiry **II 1** 89, 92

release of documents to House Judiciary Committee Impeachment Inquiry discussed between Doar, Jenner, and St. Clair **II 1** 81

St. Clair statement that Nixon believes he furnished sufficient evidence to **SI9-2** 561, 947, 948-949

selection as new Special Watergate Prosecutor **II 2** 1402-1404

Sirica denies Nixon's motion to quash his subpoena and orders Nixon to produce material **SI9-2** 574, 1015, 1016-1017

Sirica's order granting his motion on Nixon tape of September 15, 1972 **SI8** 28-29, 331-332, 347-349

and subpoena powers of House Judiciary Committee **II 1** 66

subpoenas White House for materials involving neither Watergate coverup nor Fielding break-in **SI9-2** 566, 969, 970-972

and *U.S.* v. *Kleindienst* information **SI5-2** 520, 965, 966-967

See also Fielding break-in, papers from criminal cases; Illegal campaign practices and contributions; Nixon Administration, attempts to improperly influence; Watergate break-in, papers from criminal cases

Jaworski, Leon, cited testimony of

on acceptance of job as Watergate Special Prosecutor **SI9-2** 548, 837, 838-843

Jefferson, Thomas SIAPP1 66-67

impoundment of funds for gunboats in 1803 **SI12** 81, 82

Jefferson rule **SIAPP1** 66-67

Jenner, Albert E., Jr. SUMM I 1, 3

on agreement with Doar's presentation of summary of evidentiary material **II 3** 1937, 1940

asks Mitchell for his campaign schedule records **TW 2** 165-166

on awesomeness of impeachment proceedings **SUMM I** 15-16, 18

biography of **II 3** 2143

birthday greetings to **II 3** 1455

Brady case and **II 2** 1429-1430E

on Buzhardt attending Jenner-Doar-St. Clair meetings on materials requested by House Judiciary Committee Impeachment Inquiry **II 1** 208

on calling witnesses before House Judiciary Committee Impeachment Inquiry **II 3** 1626-1627, 1647

comments on task of House Judiciary Committee Impeachment Inquiry **II 3** 1936-1941

on comparison between Warren Commission and Impeachment Inquiry **SUMM I** 17-18

on completion date for House Judiciary Committee Impeachment Inquiry **II 1** 13-14

on confidentiality of material from Fielding break-in grand jury **II 2** 1159-1161, 1177-1178

on Dean's relationship to Watergate investigation **II 2** 724-725

on Dennis' motion for House Judiciary Committee Impeachment Inquiry filing amici curiae briefs for Nixon's materials **II 2** 933-934

discussion with House Judiciary Committee Impeachment Inquiry on invitation by Sirica to attend proceeding on sealed material from Watergate Grand Jury **II 1** 134-148

discussions with St. Clair on materials requested by House Judiciary Committee Impeachment Inquiry **II 1** 205-208

on distinction between White House papers and Presidential papers **II 2** 1339-1340

on Ehrlichman implicating Nixon in his call to CIA for aid to Hunt **II 2** 1131

on enemies list **II 2** 1262

on enforcement of subpoenas **II 1** 114

on evidence of Nixon's connection with IRS audit of Lawrence O'Brien **II 2** 1290

on existence or nonexistence of Nixon tape of April 15, 1973 Nixon-Dean meeting **II 2** 880

Ford's speech on **II 1** 476

on hiring of Tetzlaff **II 1** 148-149

on House Judiciary Committee Impeachment Inquiry issuing subpoenas to Nixon **II 1** 648, 649, 651, 653-654, 655, 656-657, 664; **II 3** 1534-1537, 1550, 1551, 1554-1556

on Hunt's employment at White House **II 1** 679-680

on immunity for witnesses called by House Judiciary Committee Impeachment Inquiry **II 2** 988

on indictment of Colson **II 2** 1427

interview with Byrne **II 2** 1219-1221, 1222-1223, 1241

on interview with Johnnie M. Walters **II 2** 1284-

Jenner, Albert E., Jr. *(Continued)*
1286
on interview with Kalmbach II 2 1290-1292
on investigation of bombing of Cambodia in House Judiciary Committee Impeachment Inquiry II 1 370
on IRS policy of delaying sensitive inquiries until after elections II 2 1285-1286, 1287-1290
on justification for additional House Judiciary Committee Impeachment Inquiry subpoenas to Nixon II 2 946
on leaked Dixon memos II 2 1327
on leaks from House Judiciary Committee Impeachment Inquiry II 2 1329; II 3 1837
on legalities involved in overhearing Ellsberg on Halperin wiretap II 2 1191
on materials given to House Judiciary Committee Impeachment Inquiry by Sirica II 1 607-608
on materials held by Sirica II 1 165
on meeting with St. Clair II 1 99
on need for additional materials requested from White House before beginning Impeachment Inquiry II 1 219
on Nixon's discussion on Executive privilege with Richardson II 2 1336-1337, 1354
on Nixon's noncompliance with House Judiciary Committee Impeachment Inquiry subpoenas II 2 920-921
and preparation of Minority report on presentation procedures for House Judiciary Committee Impeachment Inquiry II 1 286-288
on presentation of evidentiary material to House Judiciary Committee Impeachment Inquiry II 1 577
presentation of ITT matter to House Judiciary Committee Impeachment Inquiry II 2 994-1043
presentation of summary of evidence before House Judiciary Committee Impeachment Inquiry MMFL 32-37
presentation of summary of evidence to House Judiciary Committee Impeachment Inquiry on Articles of Impeachment II 3 2096-2101
presentation of summary of evidence to House Judiciary Committee Impeachment Inquiry on Nixon's abuse of powers II 3 1977-1990
on presentation procedures for House Judiciary Committee Impeachment Inquiry II 1 257-258
presentation to House Judiciary Committee Impeachment Inquiry on draft Articles of Impeachment SUMM I 14-19
on problems obtaining information from Jaworski II 1 89
on procedures for taking of depositions and interrogatories by House Judiciary Committee II 1 9
on release of House Judiciary Committee Impeachment Inquiry evidentiary material to public II 3 1600, 1601
on relevance of line of questioning of Mitchell TW 2 144-145
on relevancy of discussion on Operation Sandwedge II 2 1185
report on his appearance with Doar before Sirica II 1 161-168
and report to House Judiciary Committee Impeachment Inquiry on meeting with St. Clair II 1 79-84, 99-100

on Reum II 2 1267-1268
on right of judicial review in Impeachment Inquiry II 1 13
on role as Minority counsel in House Judiciary Committee Impeachment Inquiry II 1 237, 238
on rules of evidence SUMM I 16-17
on rules of evidentiary procedures for House Judiciary Committee Impeachment Inquiry II 1 503-504, 505, 506-513, 534
on Sirica's decision on release of Nixon tape with IRS abuse material II 2 1295-1296
on Sirica's ruling on turning Grand Jury materials over to House Judiciary Committee Impeachment Inquiry II 1 203
on Sloan's payments to Liddy II 2 721
on subpoena powers of House Judiciary Committee II 1 33-34
on television reports on White House refusal of materials II 1 100

Jenner, Albert E., Jr., questioning by
Bittman TW 2 55-66
Butterfield RHJC 21; SUMM I 26; TW 1 62-70
Colson TW 3 241-397, 454, 524-526
Dean TW 2 354-355
Kalmbach TW 3 528-669
LaRue TW 1 175-191, 194-207, 209-225, 241-242
Mitchell TW 2 147-154, 155, 159, 217
Petersen TW 3 105-107

Jentes, William SI5-1 166-167
and settlement of ITT antitrust cases NSI2 82-93

Jerry Rubin Fund SI8 44

Jewish organizations
Caulfield memo to Dean with Goldberg's tax returns showing contributions to SI8 13, 131, 133-137, 143-144

Jewish vote SIAPP4 51, 147
in Political Matters Memoranda SIAPP4 6

Jews
Nixon on SIAPP3 24, 67

Joanou, Phil SIAPP4 111, 138; SI1 95

Johansen, Robin II 2 1046, 1249

Johnson, Andrew SIAPP1 82
and alleged immunity of Presidents from criminal prosecution RHJC 304
impeachment case against II 1 238; II 3 2205-2207; SUMM I 164-165
length of time of impeachment investigation of II 1 19

Johnson, Bill SI1 212-213
See also Baldwin, Alfred (alias of)

Johnson, Bos SIAPP1 78

Johnson, Donald E. SI1 80, 85

Johnson, Lyndon Baines
advises Nixon to look into contributing pre-Presidential papers to National Archives for tax deduction SI10 1, 31, 33, 36
impoundment of funds by SI12 84
and milk price supports SI6-2 710
Nixon on SIAPP3 83
and public reaction to publication of Pentagon Papers SI7-2 666

Johnson, Roger

Hillings delivers letter to Nixon to **NSI3** 103

and Hillings' letter to Nixon on dairy import quotas **NSI3** 8, 75, 76-110

memo to Haldeman on Hillings letter to Nixon **SI6-1** 237

Johnson, Wallace H. II 2 994-1043; **SI4-1** 165-166, 208

affidavit on ITT and Kleindienst hearings **SI5-2** 503, 759, 763-766

affidavit on receiving ITT documents **SI5-2** 497, 681, 713-716

in Colson memo to Haldeman on Kleindienst confirmation hearings **SI5-2** 805, 806

and decision that Hunt should interview Beard **SI5-2** 505, 777, 778-794

and delivery of ITT documents to Mitchell **SI5-2** 497, 681, 682-717

and Hunt's interview of Beard **SI5-2** 783

at meeting with Hunt on Beard interview **TW 3** 250

and White House task force on Kleindienst hearings **SI5-2** 503, 709, 765

See also ITT matter

Johnson Administration

government expenditures on Presidential properties during **SI12** 175-179, 181

impoundment of funds by **II 2** 1308

Nixon on ITT and **SI5-2** 802

taping of Presidential conversations during **SIAPP1** 44

Joint Chiefs of Staff

Command organizational structure and officials **SI11** 83

and leaks on U.S. position on India-Pakistan War **SI7-3** 1193, 1421, 1422-1440

Joint Committee on Internal Revenue Taxation SI10 436-552

examination of Nixon's tax returns by **II 3** 1858-1859

filing of report by **II 1** 267-268

on improvements on Nixon's San Clemente and Key Biscayne properties **SI12** 94-95

"Investigation into Certain Charges of the Use of the Internal Revenue Service for Political Purposes" **SI8** 16, 26, 165, 174, 273, 280-285

letter to Gemmill and Rose with questions for Nixon on his 1969 income tax deduction for gift of pre-Presidential papers **SI10** 416-422

memo from Gemmill and Rose on bases sustaining Nixon's 1969 charitable contributions deductions **SI10** 447-505

memo from Gemmill and Rose supporting non-recognition of gain on sale of Nixons' New York City residence in 1969 **SI10** 506-522

Walters gives Dean's list of McGovern supporters to **SI8** 26, 273, 274-279

See also Joint Committee on Internal Revenue Taxation Report; Nixon's income tax

Joint Committee on Internal Revenue Taxation Report

on alleged discussion between Morgan and Demarco of gift of Nixon's pre-Presidential papers in early April 1969 **SI10** 107-108

authenticity of supposed signing in 1969 of deed dated March 27, 1969 for second gift of Nixon's papers **SI10** 328

copy of attachment to Nixon's 1969 tax return on charitable contribution claimed **SI10** 317

on correspondence between Newman and Livingston on Nixon's 1969 gift of papers **SI10** 304-305

on dates of DeMarco's contacts with Newman **SI10** 95-97

on delivery of Nixon's pre-Presidential papers to representative of National Archives **SI10** 59

on DeMarco's alleged conversation with Blech in May 1969 on future deductions for Nixon's gift of pre-Presidential papers **SI10** 140-141

on discussion between White House Staff and National Archives personnel on March 11, 1969 on transfer of Nixon's papers **SI10** 77-78

on drafts of Chattel Deeds for Nixon's gifts of pre-Presidential papers in 1968 **SI10** 57

events surrounding preparation of final appraisal document for second gift of Nixon's papers, March-April 1970 **SI10** 292-297

on impressions of National Archives staff and personnel on status of Nixon's papers in early 1970 **SI10** 174-176

memo from DeMarco on 1969 gift of Nixon's pre-Presidential papers **SI10** 103-105

on Morgan's trip to California in April 1969 and 1969 deed for contribution of Nixon's pre-Presidential papers **SI10** 109-112, 125-128

on moving of Nixon's papers from EOB to National Archives **SI10** 81-82

on Newman's April 1969 visit to National Archives **SI10** 91-94

on Newman's impressions of Nixon's gift of pre-Presidential papers as of end of 1969 **SI10** 277

on Newman's work on Nixon's undeeded pre-Presidential papers in November and December of 1969 **SI10** 199-204

on Nixon's treatment of gift of pre-Presidential papers on tax returns **SI10** 62, 63

on people assigned to work on Nixon's gift of pre-Presidential papers **SI10** 40

on preparation and signing of second deed of gift of Nixon's papers in April 1970 **SI10** 309-310, 318-319

on receipt of 1968 deed for pre-Presidential papers by DeMarco **SI10** 131-132

Joint Resolution Continuing Appropriations for Fiscal Year 1974

bombing of Cambodia and **SI11** 406

Jones, Charles R., Jr. SI1 86

Jones, Courtland

note on surveillance of "Washington correspondent" **SI7-1** 10, 239, 248

Jones, Jerry

memo to Higby and Dean on job options for Magruder **SI3-1** 49-50, 557-558, 577-578

Jones, Jim

memo to Krogh with names for handling of Nixon's contribution of pre-Presidential papers to National Archives **SI10** 39

Jones, Nubby TW 2 61
See also Hogan & Hartson
Jones, Paul R. SIAPP4 123
Jones, Thomas V. SIAPP2 297-300
campaign contribution used for payments to Watergate defendants SI3-1 22, 281, 282-290
interview on campaign contribution given to Kalmbach SI3-1 22, 281, 286-287
money given to Kalmbach by II 2 748
See also U.S. v. Northrop Corporation and Thomas Jones
Jordan, Barbara SUMM I 1
on confidentiality of evidentiary material presented to House Judiciary Committee Impeachment Inquiry II 1 581
on issuing subpoenas to Nixon II 1 657
on leaks from House Judiciary Committee Impeachment Inquiry II 1 90-91
on letter from Doar to St. Clair II 1 253
on Nixon's knowledge of wiretapping of Kraft II 2 1111
on Nixon's request for extension of time on answering House Judiciary Committee Impeachment Inquiry subpoena II 1 348-349
on obtaining Nixon's tax returns and audits from IRS II 2 1244
on presentation procedures for House Judiciary Committee Impeachment Inquiry not including recommendation on St. Clair's participation II 1 277
on procedures for House Judiciary Committee Impeachment Inquiry II 1 40-41
on procedures for taking of depositions by House Judiciary Committee Impeachment Inquiry II 1 240, 241
on release of House Judiciary Committee Impeachment Inquiry evidentiary material to public II 3 1582, 1605-1606, 1714
on right of members of House Judiciary Committee to examine materials of legal staff II 1 174
on rules of evidentiary procedures for House Judiciary Committee Impeachment Inquiry II 1 476, 529
on scheduling St. Clair's presentation of evidence II 3 1566-1567
statement of additional views on Report of House Judiciary Committee Impeachment Inquiry RHJC 283-286
on Waldie's motion on Nixon's noncompliance with House Judiciary Committee Impeachment Inquiry subpoenas II 2 941
Jordan, Barbara, questioning by
Bittman TW 2 98-99
Colson TW 3 494-496
Kalmbach TW 3 733
LaRue TW 1 264-265, 271
Mitchell TW 2 203-205
Petersen TW 3 159-160
Jordan, Peter SIAPP4 13
Justice Department
Dean-Petersen meeting on documents sent from CIA to SI7-4 1623, 1731, 1732

Kalb, Bernard SI11 260-262
Kalb, Marvin SI11 260-262
Kalmbach, Herbert Warren II 2 1046; II 3 1626-1627; SIAPP2 244-252; SIAPP4 81-83
affidavit on serving as Nixon's representative at his San Clemente property with handwritten memo from Ehrlichman on installations to be made SI12 182-184
and Alexander's letter to Jaworski referring IRS investigation of Nixon's tax returns to Grand Jury SI10 403-404
and ambassadorships SIAPP4 12, 57; SI1 32
and AMPI contribution offer SI6-1 3-4, 57-58, 59-87
and AMPI contribution to special White House project on Congressional campaigns SI6-1 8, 127, 130-152
assigned by Dean to raise funds for Watergate defendants SI3-1 9, 143, 144-155
assignment to handle milk producers' contributions SI6-1 19, 299, 300-315
attitude toward campaign spending legislation SIAPP4 81
authorization for collection of money for Watergate defendants SI4-3 1299
and boundary surveys at Nixon's San Clemente property SI12 126-132
calendar for July 26, 1972 SI3-1 21, 265, 266
calendar showing meetings with Semer in 1969 SI6-1 3, 57, 70-77
and campaign finances SI1 78
in Chapin's memo to Ehrlichman on White House involvement with Segretti SI7-4 1686
checks issued to Segretti by SI7-2 526, 575, 588-590
Chotiner on meeting with dairy leaders and SI6-2 679, 684-685
and dairy industry campaign contributions II 2 1061-1062; SI1 84-85
and dairy industry campaign pledge SI6-2 809, 814-815
Dean's awareness of role in fundraising for Watergate defendants TW 2 231-232
decision to assign him as fundraiser for Watergate defendants II 2 727-729
decision to bill GSA for work at Nixon's San Clemente property SI12 102, 105
and discrepancy over date of 1969 deed for contribution of Nixon's pre-Presidential papers SI10 6-7, 101-135
Ehrlichman and Haldeman agree to use as fundraiser for Watergate defendants SUMM I 40-41
Ehrlichman's discussion of Watergate with SI4-2 598, 599
Ehrlichman's taped telephone conversation with II 2 889
entry in diary on meeting with Ehrlichman and Nixon and Nixon's comments on work done at San Clemente SI12 171
final delivery of funds for Watergate defendants and meeting with LaRue and Dean to resign from assignment SI3-1 31, 373, 374-383
fundraising activities SIAPP4 49, 57, 69-70

in Gleason letter to Payson on Senatorial campaign contributions **SI6-1** 141

and Gleason memo to Dent on operating expenses of White House Special Project **SI6-1** 152

and GSA payment for housekeeping services at Nixon's San Clemente property **SI12** 153-155

guilty plea **SI9-2** 562, 951, 952-958

and Haldeman's knowledge of fundraising for Watergate defendants **SUMM I** 41

in Hillings' letter to Nixon **SI6-1** 145

and hiring of Segretti **SI7-2** 526, 575, 576, 577, 578

and hush money **SUMM I** 52; **SI3-2** 1016, 1084; **SI4-3** 1102, 1421

and hush money, in Article of Impeachment I **RHJC** 51

and implication of Ehrlichman in hush money payments **SI4-3** 1355-1356

informs Jenner of Ehrlichman's request for "plant" on Lawrence O'Brien **II 2** 1290-1292

and installation of beach cabana and railroad crossing at Nixon's San Clemente property **SI12** 140-141

and installation of new heating system at Nixon's San Clemente property **SI12** 106-107

instructions from Ehrlichman on expenditures on Nixons' San Clemente property **SI12** 99-100

instructs GSA to cancel landscape maintenance contract for Nixon's San Clemente property in 1970 **SI12V** 117

intelligence gathering and **SIAPP4** 35-36

involvement with hush money **SI3-1** 20, 253, 254-263

and IRS audit of Lawrence O'Brien **SUMM I** 142

itinary for March 24-27, 1971 **SI6-2** 757, 760, 765-766

and landscaping at Nixon's San Clemente property **SI12** 115

LaRue on hush money and **TW 1** 198-206, 211-212, 214-232, 236-241, 265-275

in LaRue's guilty plea **SI9-1** 324

letter from Correa on GSA payment for installation of chimney exhaust fan at Nixon's San Clemente property **SI12** 102-103

letter to Haldeman on pledges and contributions to Congressional candidates **SI6-1** 8, 127, 140

letter to Silbert on involvement with campaign finances **SI6-1** 19, 299, 304-315

meeting with AMPI and Nixon campaign representatives **SI6-1** 14, 217, 218-233

meeting with Ehrlichman on hush money **SI4-1** 34, 531, 532-536; **II 2** 741-743, 745-749, 856-857; **SI3-1** 21, 265, 266-279

meeting with Jacobsen and Mehren **SI6-2** 914-915, 923-937

meeting with LaRue on methods of getting funds to Watergate defendants **SI3-1** 12, 175, 176-180

meeting with Nelson and Chotiner **SI6-2** 476, 727, 735-740

meetings with Semer on objectives of dairy industry **II 2** 1046-1047

meets with Chotiner and Nelson in his hotel room **II 2** 1077-1078

meets with Morgan and Bath on October 8, 1969 to arrange for appraisal of Nixon's pre-Presidential papers **SI10** 185-187

memo from Dean with draft charter for political committee for milk producers' contributions **SI6-2** 465, 493, 500-509

memo from Ehrlichman on Nixon's income tax returns **SI10** 428

memo on 1970 Senatorial campaign pledges **SI6-1** 8, 127, 132-135

memo to 1970 contributions file on telephone call from Gleason on contribution solicitation assignments **SI6-1** 8, 127, 130-152

Mitchell on learning about his role in fundraising for Watergate defendants **TW 2** 188

money given by Stans to **II 2** 730-731, 738-739

and Nader milk suit **SIAPP4** 82; **SI1** 79

and Nixon campaign finances **SI1** 82, 84-85

Nixon-Dean discussion on Caulfield and **SI3-2** 876-877

in Nixon-Dean discussion on Chappaquiddick investigation **SI7-4** 1782, 1789-1792

Nixon-Dean discussion of his forthcoming testimony **SI3-1** 677-681

Nixon-Dean discussion of surplus funds from 1968 campaign handled by **SI3-2** 1032-1036

in Nixon-Dean-Haldeman discussion on Sloan's testimony **SI8** 405-408

Nixon expresses concern to Dean on exposure of his San Clemente records **SI12** 172-173

Nixon-Haldeman discussion on **SI4-3** 1310, 1441-1442

Nixon-Haldeman discussions on newspaper stories linking Segretti to **SI7-4** 1618, 1677, 1678-1680

Nixon tells Haldeman to inform him that LaRue has talked **SUMM I** 94

Nixon, Wilson, and Strickler discuss **SI4-3** 1519

notes on campaign pledges **SI6-1** 8, 127, 132-139

obtains $75,000 from Stans and delivers to Ulasewicz **SI3-1** 11, 165, 166-173

and paving at Nixon's San Clemente property **SI12** 134

and payment for sewer system installation at Nixon's San Clemente property **SI12** 110-112

and payment from Jones **II 2** 748

and payments to Segretti **II 2** 1120; **SI7-3** 1591

payments to Ulasewicz **II 2** 1111

in Political Matters Memoranda **SIAPP4** 5

possible testimony of, discussed by Nixon and Dean **SI3-2** 701, 803, 851-853

and purchase of lanterns for Nixon's San Clemente property **SI12** 149-150

receives campaign contribution from Jones and delivers to Ulasewicz **SI3-1** 22, 281, 282-290

receives $100,000 from Semer **II 2** 1048

replaced by Nunn for milk fund responsibilities **SI6-2** 957

resignation from Finance Committee **SI6-1** 310

resigns from fundraising assignment and burns records **II 2** 750-751; **SUMM I** 52

and restoration of "point" gazebo at Nixon's San Clemente property **SI12** 137

role in containment of Watergate from July 1 until elections **SUMM I** 43, 44

role in deliveries of money for Watergate defendants **SI3-1** 17, 221, 222-233

role in milk producers' contributions **SI6-2** 497

Kalmbach, Herbert Warren *(Continued)*

role in Nixon Administration **RHJC** 15

role in Watergate coverup, in Doar's presentation of summary of evidence to House Judiciary Committee Impeachment Inquiry **II 3** 1961

and Sandwedge plan **SIAPP4** 11

Segretti and **SIAPP1** 9-10; **SI3-2** 813-814

and Segretti's Grand Jury testimony **SI7-3** 1598-1599

Semer delivery of $100,000 cash contribution from AMPI to **SI6-1** 5, 89, 90-98

serves as primary on-site representative of Nixon, supervising work performed at San Clemente **SI12** 98-99

and Stans' list of 1968 campaign commitments **SIAPP4** 11

Strachan memo to Haldeman on telephone conversation on dairy industry contribution with **SI6-2** 813-815

and structural investigation of Cotton home and Nixon's residence at San Clemente property **SI12** 132-134

taped telephone conversation with Ehrlichman on fundraising for Watergate defendants **SI3-1** 21, 265, 277-279; **SI4-3** 1110, 1547, 1548-1552

telephone conversation with Ehrlichman on his forthcoming Watergate Grand Jury testimony **SI4-3** 1103, 1443, 1444-1446

Ulasewicz and, in Nixon-Dean discussion of Watergate hearings **SI8** 429-432

and Ulasewicz's first delivery of money for Watergate defendants to Bittman **SI3-1** 16, 207, 208-219

See also House Judiciary Committee Impeachment Inquiry, discussion on calling witnesses; House Judiciary Committee Impeachment Inquiry, presentation of evidence on dairy industry campaign contributions; Political Matters Memoranda, on campaign finances; *U.S.* v. *Dwight Chapin*; *U.S.* v. *Herbert Kalmbach*

Kalmbach, Herbert Warren, cited testimony of SI4-3 1110, 1547, 1551-1552

on AMPI's objectives in relationship to contribution **SI6-1** 5, 89, 94-95

on arranging for Semer-Dent meeting **SI6-1** 6, 99, 103-105

on contacts with Semer for AMPI contribution **SI6-1** 3, 57, 62-69

on dealings with milk producers after filing of *Nader* v. *Butz* suit **SI6-2** 486, 895, 914-922

denies any knowledge of relationship between campaign contributions and governmental actions affecting dairy industry **NSI3** 25, 175, 176-191

denies knowledge of amounts of ADEPT, TAPE and SPACE contributions **SI6-1** 4, 58, 87

on final deliveries of funds for Watergate defendants and resignation as fundraiser **SI3-1** 31, 373, 378-379

on Haldeman's involvement in AMPI contribution **SI6-1** 4, 58, 81-82

on Haldeman's $350,000 fund **SI1** 11, 77, 99-100

on hiring of and payments to Segretti **SI7-2** 526, 575, 579-581

on informing Haldeman of AMPI contribution **SI6-1** 6, 99, 100-101

on meeting with Ehrlichman on legal propriety of fundraising for Watergate defendants **SI3-1** 21, 265, 268-270, 275-276

on meeting with LaRue on methods for collecting and distributing money for Watergate defendants **SI3-1** 12, 175, 178-180

on meeting with Nelson and Chotiner on March 24, 1971 **SI6-2** 763-764

on meetings with AMPI representatives **SI6-1** 14, 217, 218-224

on Mehren's request for contact with White House on anti-trust suit against AMPI **SI6-2** 486, 895, 942-943

on money given to Nunn campaign **TW 3** 666-667, 668, 715-716

on Nixon's decision-making methods **SUMM I** 28

on Nixon's interest in grounds of his San Clemente property **SI12** 171-172

on persons informed of AMPI contribution **SI6-1** 6, 99, 102-103

on pledges to Finance Committee **SI1** 32

on reaffirmation of AMPI $2 million pledge to Nixon campaign **SI6-2** 476, 477, 727-734, 757-764

on reasons for accepting assignment from Dean to raise funds for Watergate defendants **SI3-1** 9, 143, 153-155

on receiving $75,000 from Stans and giving it to Ulasewicz **SI3-1** 11, 165, 166-169

on receiving campaign contribution from Jones and delivering it to Ulasewicz **SI3-1** 22, 281, 282-283

on relationship with Ulasewicz **SI7-1** 18, 335, 343

on responsibilities and activities on Nixon's behalf **SI6-1** 3, 57, 61

on system for collecting and distributing money for Watergate defendants **SI3-1** 17, 221, 229-232

on transfer of campaign contributions for payments to Watergate defendants **SI3-1** 20, 253, 259-261

on Ulasewicz's first delivery of money for Watergate defendants to Bittman **SI3-1** 16, 207, 208-209

on uses of AMPI contribution **SI6-1** 6, 99, 101-102

Kalmbach, Herbert Warren, deposition of

on assignment to fundraising role for Nixon's 1972 campaign **SI6-1** 19, 299, 300

denies quid pro quo on dairy contributions and milk price-support increase **SI6-2** 477, 728, 755-756

on hiring of and payments to Segretti **SI7-2** 526, 575, 582-585

on surplus funds from 1968 campaign **SI6-2** 477, 720, 756

on uses of AMPI contribution **SI6-1** 5, 89, 92-93

Kalmbach, Herbert Warren, testimony before House Judiciary Committee Impeachment Inquiry TW 3 527-744

on becoming personal counsel to Nixon **TW 3** 530-531

on campaign contributions and ambassadorial appointments **TW 3** 617-631, 649-651, 673-680, 707-708, 718-719, 721-727

on campaign funds for Brewer campaign **TW 3**
664-666, 669-670
on charging Nixon for expenses **TW 3** 614-615
on disbursements to Nixon's family and friends
from campaign funds **TW 3** 693-695, 696-697
on discussions with Nixon **TW 3** 729-730
exhibits related to **TW 3** 571, 581-593, 599, 621-
627, 633-644, 648, 653-655, 696-698, 743
on frequency of meetings with Nixon **TW 3** 703-
704
on Government expenditures on Nixon's property
at San Clemente, Ca. **TW 3** 651-660, 693-694
on Greenspun matter **TW 3** 615-617
on handling of campaign finances **TW 3** 671-673,
694-703, 731-732, 734-735, 740
on his background **TW 3** 528-529
on his hypothesis that Mitchell may have initiated
Watergate break-in **TW 3** 728
on his involvement with hush money **TW 3** 534-
558, 559-578, 680-685, 704-710, 712-714, 715,
725-726, 730-731, 732-737, 740-742
on his motivations for actions **TW 3** 725-726
on his political relationship with Nixon **TW 3**
529-532
on his relationship with Dean **TW 3** 533-534
on his relationship with Mitchell **TW 3** 532-533
on his relationship with Rebozo **TW 3** 534
on indictment against him **TW 3** 617
on milk fund **TW 3** 580-611, 612, 685-692, 710,
714-715, 717-718, 723
on Nixon's income tax deduction for gift of Presidential papers **TW 3** 662-664, 670, 712, 727,
729
on Nixon's thank-you call after election campaign
TW 3 727-728
on Rebozo-Hughes matter **TW 3** 735-739
states that he never discussed his activities with
Nixon **TW 3** 711-712
on suspicions of illegality **TW 3** 720-722
swearing in **TW 3** 528
on telephone calls made on his Republican National Finance Committee credit card **TW 3**
613-614
on Town House operation **TW 3** 660-661, 664,
671, 733, 735
Kammeyer, Kenneth
and landscape construction and maintenance at
Nixon's San Clemente property **SI12** 115, 117,
119
selected as landscape architect for work on Nixon's San Clemente property **SI12** 99
Karalekas, Steve SI7-2 678
Karpatkin, Marvin M. SI7-2 594
Kastenmeier, Robert W. SUMM I 1
additional views on Nixon's tax evasion as impeachable offense **RHJC** 343-347
on composition of panel of experts examining gap
on Nixon tape **II 2** 1408-1409
on confidentiality of evidentiary material presented to House Judiciary Committee Impeachment
Inquiry **II 1** 581-582
and discussion on procedures for House Judiciary
Committee Impeachment Inquiry **II 1** 377-341
and discussion on rules of evidentiary procedures
for House Judiciary Committee Impeachment

Inquiry **II 1** 467-542
dissenting views supporting proposed Article of
Impeachment on secret bombing of Cambodia
RHJC 323-328
on Doar's expectations on St. Clair's response to
request for White House materials **II 1** 291-292
on dropping some grounds for impeachment of
Nixon **II 1** 270
on FBI reports to White House on wiretapping of
National Security Council employees **II 2** 1001
on forthcoming report on rules of procedures for
House Judiciary Committee Impeachment Inquiry **II 1** 403-409
on investigation of Nixon's income taxes in House
Judiciary Committee Impeachment Inquiry **II 1**
361-362
on issuing subpoenas to Nixon **II 1** 312-313
on leaked Dixon memos **II 2** 1329-1330
on legal staff and question of definition of impeachable offense **II 1** 92-93
on Nixon's gift of Presidential papers **II 3** 1465
on Nixon's noncompliance with House Judiciary
Committee Impeachment Inquiry subpoenas **II
2** 929
on patent for Daughters of the American Revolution **II 3** 1714-1716
on procedural rules for handling Impeachment Inquiry material **II 1** 125
on projected date for completion of House Judiciary Committee Impeachment Inquiry **II 1** 151-152
on reasons for keeping House Judiciary Committee Impeachment Inquiry closed **II 2** 777
on release of House Judiciary Committee Impeachment Inquiry evidentiary material to public **II 2** 980-981; **II 3** 1584, 1588-1589
on rules on cross-examination of witnesses **TW 1**
87
on scheduling St. Clair's presentation of evidence
II 3 1565
on Sirica's invitation to Doar and Jenner **II 1** 135,
136
statement of additional views on Report of House
Judiciary Committee Impeachment Inquiry
RHJC 283-286
on submission of written interrogatories to Nixon
II 3 1619
on subpoena powers of House Judiciary Committee **II 1** 44-45
Kastenmeier, Robert W., questioning by
Bittman **TW 2** 68-69
Butterfield **TW 1** 120, 121
Colson **TW 3** 449-451
Kalmbach **TW 3** 701-703
O'Brien **TW 1** 144-145
Petersen **TW 3** 123-124
Katzenbach Report
and restraints on intelligence activity on campuses
and with student-related groups, in Huston plan
SI7-1 422
Kaupinen, Allan G. SIAPP4 149
denied White House mess privileges **SIAPP4** 19
letter to Magnuson on Nixon's gifts of papers to
National Archives **SI10** 437-438

Keaton, Darius **SIAPP4** 113
Keeler, William W. **SIAPP2** 311-314
See also U.S. v. Phillips Petroleum Company and William W. Keeler
Keene, David **SIAPP4** 7, 19, 51
Kehrli, Bruce Arnold SIAPP4 94; **SI2** 2, 150
affidavit on termination of Hunt's employment at White House **SIAPP3** 265-268
Butterfield asks him about Hunt's employment at White House **TW 1** 56-57
Cox's efforts to obtain memo from Howard to **SI9-1** 35, 37, 42, 413, 414-417, 425, 426-427, 485, 486-4
deposition of, on opening of Hunt's safe **SI2** 2, 19, 189, 193-196
excused from Watergate Grand Jury testimony **SI2** 2, 564, 569
and Fielding's trip to London to get Chenow **SI2** 2, 518
at meeting to discuss Hunt's White House status **SI2** 2, 17-18, 165-166
memo from Howard on dropping Hunt from White House staff **SIAPP3** 271
memo from Howard on Hunt's employment status at White House **SI2** 2, 18, 166, 171, 181-183
memo from Howard on Hunt's request **SI2** 2, 170, 171, 182-183, 184
memo to Howard on Hunt's annuity rights if he leaves White House staff **SIAPP3** 269-270
memos from Howard on Hunt **II 2** 1366-1368; **TW 3** 261-263
Nixon gives Select Committee memo from Howard to **SIAPP1** 31
and opening of Hunt's safe **TW 2** 235-236; **SI2** 2, 19, 189, 190, 193-196, 198, 199
questioned by Ehrlichman and Colson on Hunt's status at White House **SI2** 2, 169
role in Nixon Administration **SUMM I** 25N
Keith case **II 2** 1093-1094, 1108; **SI7-3** 1439
government wiretaps and **NSI4** 194
Keller, Vicki **SIAPP4** 86; **SI1** 83
Kelly, Douglas **SI7-3** 1485
Kempster, Norman **SIAPP1** 73; **SI2** 2, 119
Kendall, Don **SI3-2** 740; **SI5-1** 452
in Haldeman memo to Dean on dealing with Ervin Committee **SI3-1** 47, 527, 528-533, 541
Kennahan, John Edward **II 2** 1088
biography of **II 3** 2149
Kennedy, Edward M.
Dean on Ulasewicz's investigation of **SI7-1** 18, 335, 350-352
and Dellums **SI8** 75, 109
Haldeman proposes surveillance of **II 2** 1123; **SI7-2** 531, 655, 656-661
on Kleindienst nomination as Attorney General **SI5-2** 612
Lasky on **SI8** 124
letter to Eastland requesting ITT files from SEC **SI5-2** 514, 864, 865
letter to Staggers on transfer of ITT files from SEC to Justice Department **SI5-2** 514, 864, 867-868
Magruder, Haldeman, Mitchell and Strachan discuss surveillance of **SUMM I** 30

in Nixon-Dean discussion **SI3-2** 873-877
Nixon-Mitchell-Haldeman discussion of likelihood of candidacy in 1972 of **SIAPP3** 19-20
in Political Matters Memoranda **SIAPP4** 9
surveillance of in talking paper from Strachan to Mitchell **SIAPP4** 46
Ulasewicz's investigation of **SI7-1** 18, 335, 354
Kennedy, Edward M., questioning by
Geneen **SI5-1** 132-135; **SI5-2** 588-589
Gray **SI2** 2, 556-557; **SI7-3** 1547-1548; **SI7-4** 1756-1760
Griswold **NSI2** 66-67; **SI5-1** 355-357
Hume **SI5-2** 621-622, 625
Kleindienst **II 2** 1031-1032; **NSI2** 70-72, 95, 117; **SI5-2** 733-734, 757-758, 851
McLaren **NSI2** 68-69, 111, 112, 115, 124
Merriam **SI5-1** 258
Mitchell **SI5-1** 183-184
Richardson **SI9-2** 761
Walsh **SI5-1** 285-286, 308
Kennedy, John F.
and Bay of Pigs invasion, in Colson memo to Haldeman **SI7-2** 699, 701-702
and Diem cables **SI2** 2, 162
impoundment of funds by **SI12** 81, 83
Jenner on Warren Commission investigation of assassination of **II 3** 1940-1941
Nixon on **SIAPP3** 80, 83
Kennedy, Robert F.
Colson on possible role in preparation of Pentagon Papers **SI7-2** 671
Ford Foundation awards to former aides of **SI8** 84
Kennedy Administration
government expenditures on Presidential properties during **SI12** 179-181
and Hunt's fabrication of Diem cables **II 2** 1173-1174
income tax information submitted by Ehrlichman on **SI4-2** 600
Nixon on ITT and **SI5-2** 802
taping of Presidential conversations during **SIAPP1** 44
Kennedy campaign
in Political Matters Memoranda **SIAPP4** 20
talking paper from Strachan to Mitchell on **SIAPP4** 41-42
Kennedy family, and Hunt's interview of DeMotte SI7-2 853
Kennedy-Johnson papers SI7-2 667
See also Pentagon Papers
Kent, Natasha SI7-2 1133
Kent, Rockwell SI7-2 1133
Kent State University
deaths of students at **SI7-1** 389
in Presidential statement on 1970 intelligence plan **SIAPP1** 22; **SI7-1** 377
Kentucky
elections for governor in **SIAPP4** 8
Keogh, James
memo to Magruder on Nixon's remarks on Vietnam and Thieu **SI7-1** 20, 359, 364

Kissinger, Henry *(Continued)*
  1973 **SI11** 77, 380-381
  statement on reasons for MENU double reporting procedures **SI11** 60-61, 311-313
  and summary of FBI letters reporting on wiretaps on National Security Council staff members **SI7-1** 227, 229, 230
  in taped Cushman-Hunt conversation **SI7-2** 852
  and transfer of FBI files on Kissinger tapes to White House **II 2** 1157-1158
  Wheeler assumes he briefed Members of Congress on MENU operations **SI11** 61, 314
  and wiretapping of government officials and newsmen **SI7-1** 152-153, 160
  and wiretapping of Halperin **II 2** 1099; **SI7-1** 218-219, 220
  and wiretapping of Laird's assistant **SI7-1** 299-300, 327
  and wiretapping of National Security Council members **SI7-1** 202-203, 205
  and wiretapping of White House staff members unrelated to national security **SI7-1** 260
  Young informs Malloy that Ellsberg psychological profile was requested by **SI7-2** 560, 1081, 1083
  See also Halperin v. *Kissinger*; House Judiciary Committee Impeachment Inquiry, presentation of evidence on domestic surveillance
Kissinger, Henry, cited testimony of
  on authorizations for wiretaps on newsmen **SI7-1** 10, 239, 247
  on leaks on U.S. position on India-Pakistan War **SI7-3** 1193, 1421, 1423-1424
  on motives for wiretaps on government employees and newsmen **SI7-2** 525, 567, 569,571
  on receipt of FBI "top secret" wiretap material **SI7-1** 21, 369, 371
  on role in wiretaps of National Security Council members **SI7-1** 9, 223, 231
  submits Richardson letter on legality of government wiretaps **NSI4** 29, 31, 193, 194-195, 199, 200-201
  on wiretapping of government employees after leaks on bombing of Cambodia **SI7-1** 305; **SI7-2** 570
  on wiretapping of government officials and newsmen **SI7-1** 3, 141, 148-150
  on wiretapping of National Security Council members **SI7-1** 8, 201, 214-217
  on wiretapping of White House staff members unrelated to national security **SI7-1** 12, 259, 261-266
Klein, Herbert G. SIAPP4 4, 50
  memo from Haldeman assigning Colson to Special Project **SI6-1** 12, 197, 198
  memo from Magruder on Colson's Special Project and campaign advertising **SI6-1** 12, 197, 199-202
  memo to Haldeman on Republican National Convention site **SI5-2** 486, 510, 561, 568-573, 841, 842-847
  memo to Nixon on San Diego as site for Republican National Convention **SI5-2** 486, 561, 575
  Nixon on **SIAPP3** 56-57, 70

as recipient of political enemies project memos **SI8** 21, 211, 212
and replacement for Shumway **SI1** 48, 49
role in Nixon Administration **RHJC** 14
statement on Agnew running on 1973 ticket **SIAPP4** 47
Kleindienst, Richard G. II 3 1757-1771, 1773; **SIAPP2** 372-381; **SIAPP3** 7; **SIAPP4** 6; **SI2** 2, 27, 277, 280-281, 282, 289-290, 291-296; **SI7-2** 953
  and Anderson articles on ITT-Sheraton pledge **SI5-2** 493, 633-636
  approves settlement of ITT antitrust cases **NSI2** 8, 73, 74-79
  arranges meeting with Nixon after briefing by U.S. Attorneys **SI4-2** 570, 873, 874-879
  briefed by U.S. Attorneys on evidence implicating White House and CRP officials in Watergate break-in and coverup **II 2** 869; **SI4-2** 569, 863, 866-871
  Brown letter to on Stans' testimony **TW 3** 165-169
  Colson on Nixon's withdrawal of nomination of **TW 3** 525
  Dean's efforts to obtain FBI Watergate investigation reports from **SI2** 2, 57, 555, 560
  and Dean's indictable list **SI4-2** 701, 702
  Dean's memo to Nixon recommending his retention as Attorney General **SI3-1** 51, 583, 584-595
  decision to inform Nixon that Byrne should be told of Fielding break-in **II 2** 1232
  denies discussing ITT cases with White House **SI5-2** 496, 499, 677-680, 729, 730-734
  denies interference by White House in ITT cases **SI5-2** 502, 765, 756-758
  directed by Nixon to report anything in Watergate area to him **II 2** 847
  directs Griswold to apply for another extension of time on *ITT-Grinnell* Appeal **SI5-1** 16, 349, 350-358
  discussed by Nixon and Ehrlichman **SI4-2** 786
  discussed by Nixon, Ehrlichman, and Haldeman **SI4-2** 821-822
  Doar's interview with **II 2** 1413-1416
  and documents received from CIA on questions asked by FBI during Watergate investigation **TW 3** 3-4, 5-46, 47-70
  documents to Petersen on CIA aid to Hunt **SI2** 2, 657-658
  draft complaint against ITT-Canteen merger **SI5-1** 3, 69, 76-87
  and Ehrlichman meeting with Byrne **II 2** 1223, 1224
  Ehrlichman on relations with **SI4-2** 732
  and Ehrlichman's efforts to prevent Stans' scheduled Watergate Grand Jury appearance **SUMM I** 45
  establishment of White House task force to monitor confirmation hearings **SI5-2** 503, 759, 760-769
  on final settlement of ITT antitrust cases **NSI2** 10, 103, 117-121
  Gray on meeting with on destruction of Hunt's files **SI4-3** 1113, 1613, 1614-1616
  guilty plea of **II 2** 1033

Haldeman on confirmation hearings and antitrust suits against ITT **SI5-2** 508-509, 803-804, 834-836

House Judiciary Committee Impeachment Inquiry interview with **II 2** 1425-1426

House Judiciary Committee Impeachment Inquiry subpoena for specified tapes of conversations between Nixon and **SI9-2** 568, 977, 978-982

information filed in U.S. District Court by Watergate Special Prosecution Force **SI5-2** 520, 965, 966-967

informed by Petersen of Dean's information on Watergate coverup **TW 3** 79-80

informs Petersen that Ehrlichman does not want any White House aides to be granted immunity **II 2** 857

insertion of Impeachment Inquiry staff notes on into record of House Judiciary Committee Impeachment Inquiry **II 3** 2131-2132

instructions to Petersen on treatment of Watergate burglars **SI2** 7, 105, 112

interviews McLaren for position with Antitrust Division, Department of Justice **NSI2** 3, 21-24

and ITT-Grinnell case appeal delay **SI5-2** 658, 694

and ITT matter **II 2** 1009-1010, 1013-1014, 1023

ITT situation and nomination of **SI5-2** 508-509, 803-804, 805-839

in Johnson affidavit **SI5-2** 715

letter from Brown on Patman Committee hearings **SUMM I** 51

letter from Jaworski to Miller on guilty plea of **SI5-2** 520, 965, 969-970

letter from Walsh urging delay of *ITT-Grinnell* appeal **SI5-1** 15, 283, 284-305

log furnished to Watergate Special Prosecutor without entry on April 25, 1973 meeting with Nixon **SI9-2** 554, 883, 884-890

logs of **II 2** 1413-1416

meeting with Ehrlichman on consideration of Byrne for FBI Director **II 2** 1206-1209

at meeting on June 20, 1972 with Haldeman, Ehrlichman, Mitchell, and Dean to discuss Watergate break-in **SI2** 2, 23-24, 235-236, 237, 238, 239, 240-241, 242

meeting with Liddy after Watergate arrests **SI2** 7, 105, 110-112; **SI3-2** 1015

meeting with McLaren, Rohatyn, and other ITT and Antitrust Division staff members **SI5-1** 24, 403, 404-422

meeting with Nixon on April 15, 1973 on continuation of Watergate investigation **NSI1** 33, 211, 212

meeting with Nixon on evidence against White House personnel **SI4-2** 573-574, 923-924, 925-959

meeting with Nixon and Petersen on April 15, 1973 on information held by Watergate Grand Jury **II 2** 878-879; **SUMM I** 90

meeting with Nixon and Petersen on information received from Dean and Magruder **SI4-2** 576-577, 973-974, 975-1011

meeting with Powell Moore and Liddy **SI2** 2, 104, 110-112

meeting with Rohatyn on ITT and Hartford Fire Insurance Company **SI5-1** 20, 367, 368-370

meetings and conversations with Nixon **SI4-1** 4, 213, 215; **SI4-3** 1113, 1613, 1622

meetings with Nixon on April 15, 1973, in Article of Impeachment I **RHJC** 104-106

meetings with Nixon on Watergate Grand Jury information **SUMM I** 89-90

meetings and telephone conversations with Nixon on February 23, 1973 **SI3-1** 51, 583, 591

meets with McLaren and Griswold to request extension of time on ITT-Grinnell appeal **NSI2** 7, 65, 66-72

meets with Nixon after briefing by Watergate Prosecutors **II 2** 869-870

memo from McLaren on filing ITT-Canteen complaint **SI5-1** 88

memo from McLaren on *ITT-Grinnell* appeal **SI5-1** 307, 309-310

memo from McLaren on proposed procedure in ITT antitrust cases **SI5-2** 485, 549, 550-552, 554-555

memo on settlement of ITT merger cases from McLaren **SI5-2** 597-598

memo to Ehrlichman on ITT-Canteen merger **SI5-1** 3, 69, 70-75

and memo to Ehrlichman from McLaren on ITT-Canteen merger suit proposal **SI5-2** 503-504, 803-804, 821-826

memo to Petersen on disclosing information on Fielding break-in to Byrne **SI7-4** 1645, 1647, 1975, 1981-1982, 1995-1997

Mitchell denies discussing ITT litigation with **SI5-1** 180

at negotiations for settlement of ITT antitrust cases with McLaren **NSI2** 85

Nixon on **SI7-4** 1818

Nixon announces resignation of **SIAPP1** 13; **SI9-1** 5, 131, 132-137

in Nixon-Dean discussion on possible delay of sentencing of Watergate defendants **SI3-2** 1110-1111

Nixon-Dean discussion on relationship between Senate Select Committee on Presidential Campaign Activities and **SI4-1** 163-167, 207

Nixon-Dean discussion of withdrawal of **SI4-3** 1156-1157

Nixon directs Ehrlichman to instruct him to report directly to President on all Watergate matters **SI4-1** 18, 347, 350-371; **SUMM I** 87-88

Nixon-Ehrlichman discussion on interview with **SI4-3** 1211

Nixon-Ehrlichman discussion on *ITT-Grinnell* appeal and **SI5-1** 312-313

Nixon-Ehrlichman discussion on possible resignation of **SI4-2** 859

Nixon, Ehrlichman, and Haldeman discuss Executive privilege and **SI4-2** 681

Nixon on his lack of knowledge of new Watergate investigation ordered on March 21, 1973 **SIAPP1** 51-52

Nixon on resignation of **SIAPP1** 15

Nixon on role played in Watergate investigation **SIAPP1** 45

Nixon orders him to drop Grinnell appeal **NSI2** 7, 65, 66-72

and Nixon's instructions to Petersen on Fielding break-in **TW 3** 99, 147-148

Kleindienst, Richard G. *(Continued)*

Nixon's news conference of March 24, 1972 on **SI5-2** 507, 799, 801

in Nixon's plan for blaming Watergate on Mitchell **SUMM I** 76

Nixon's remarks on at swearing-in ceremonies for **SI5-2** 515, 901, 904

Nixon's telephone call on handling Baker **SUMM I** 87

Nixon's television announcement of resignation of **SI4-3** 1119, 1657, 1658-1659

nomination for post of Attorney General **SI5-2** 490, 605, 606-612

notes of April 29, 1971 meeting on antitrust suits against ITT **SI5-1** 24, 403, 410-418

obtains Nixon's authorization to turn over material on Fielding break-in to Byrne **SI7-4** 1646, 1983, 1984-1993; **II 2** 1233

Petersen delivers material on Fielding break-in to **SI7-4** 1645, 1975, 1976-1982

Petersen mentions Byrne as possible candidate for head of FBI to **TW 3** 107-108, 125-126, 128, 153

Petersen on reporting to on Watergate break-in and coverup **TW 3** 2-3

pleads guilty to refusing or failing fully to respond to Senate Committee on the Judiciary questions **SI5-2** 520, 965, 966-969

possible resignation discussed by Nixon and Ehrlichman **SI4-2** 917

and proposal of Byrne as FBI director **SI7-4** 1635, 1867, 1868-1877

recommends to Nixon that Byrne be informed of Fielding break-in **SUMM I** 138

refuses to discuss Watergate arrests with Liddy **SUMM I** 35

and release of information on Gray's burning files from Hunt's safe **II 2** 892-893

reports to Dean, Mitchell, Ehrlichman and Haldeman on FBI Watergate investigation **TW 2** 333-334

reports to Nixon on evidence against White House and CRP staff members **II 2** 874-875

and request for extension of time to appeal *ITT-Grinnell* case **SI5-2** 501, 751, 752-754

requests reopening of Senate Judiciary Committee confirmation hearings **SI5-2** 493, 633, 637

resignation as Attorney General **II 2** 1333; **SI2** 2, 110; **SI4-3** 1118, 1651, 1652-1655

and resumed confirmation hearings **SI5-2** 496, 677, 678-680

Rohatyn and **SI5-2** 810

role in Nixon Administration **RHJC** 16-17

Senate confirmation of nomination as Attorney General **SI5-2** 901, 902-904

and Senate Select Committee on Presidential Campaign Activities **SI4-1** 116-122, 177, 188, 365-366

and settlement of ITT antitrust cases **NSI2** 10-11, 103-104, 105-126; **SI5-2** 485, 549, 550-559, 601

Sirica and **NSI1** 159, 166

and Stans being excused from Watergate Grand Jury testimony **SI2** 2, 564, 569

statement on ITT matter **NSI2** 16, 189, 191

and Sullivan's possible testimony on FBI **SI3-2** 842

telephone call from Ehrlichman on Nixon's questions about White House staff involvement in Watergate **SI4-1** 20, 399, 400-425

telephone call from Nixon re contacting Baker re Senate Select Committee on Presidential Campaign Activities hearings **SI4-1** 4, 123-127, 213, 214, 215,

telephone call from Petersen informing him of Watergate arrests **SI2** 6, 101, 102-104

telephone call to Gray on Watergate break-in **SI2** 2, 13, 135, 136

telephone call to Petersen on immunity for White House aides **SI4-1** 37, 547, 548

telephone conversation with Ehrlichman on Magruder's information to U.S. Attorneys **SI4-2** 566, 829, 830-842

telephone conversation with Ehrlichman on Magruder's Watergate Grand Jury testimony **II 2** 868

telephone conversation with Ehrlichman with questions on Watergate investigation **II 2** 848-849

telephone conversation with Nixon on April 15, 1973 **II 2** 876-877

telephone conversation with Nixon on dropping *ITT-Grinnell* appeal **SI5-1** 16, 311, 315-326, 346-348

telephone conversation with Nixon on Petersen joining their up-coming meeting **SI4-2** 575, 961, 972

telephone conversation with Walsh on *ITT-Grinnell* appeal delay **SI5-1** 16, 307, 308

telephone conversations with Petersen on Watergate break-in **SI2** 2, 9, 121, 122-123

tells Dean about meeting with Liddy and Powell Moore **SI2** 2, 168

and transfer of ITT material from SEC to Justice Department **SI5-2** 914, 915

and White House interference with Gray confirmation hearings **II 2** 782

and White House interference with Senate Select Committee on Presidential Campaign Activities **II 2** 764, 834

at White House meeting on investigation of Ellsberg matter **NSI4** 16, 121, 122-123

See also Kleindienst confirmation hearings; St. Clair, James D., presentation of evidence in behalf of Nixon on ITT matter; *U.S.* v. *Howard Edwin Reinecke*; *U.S.* v. *Richard Kleindienst*

Kleindienst, Richard G., cited testimony of

on antitrust suits against ITT **SI5-1** 3, 69, 91

on Application for Extension of Time for *ITT-Grinnell* appeal **SI5-1** 16, 349, 350

on approving of settlement of ITT antitrust cases after McLaren's recommendation **NSI2** 78-79

on attitude toward Ehrlichman taping their telephone conversation **SI4-1** 405

denies discussing ITT antitrust suits with White House **SI5-2** 496, 499, 511, 677, 678-680, 729, 731-732, 849, 850-852, 853

denies recollection of reasons for filing for delay of appeal in *ITT-Grinnell* case **SI5-2** 499, 729, 733-734 denies White House interference in ITT antitrust cases **SI5-2** 502, 765, 756-758

in Doar's presentation of evidentiary material to House Judiciary Committee Impeachment Inquiry **II 1** 591-592

on Fielding break-in and Ellsberg case **SI7-4** 1645, 1975, 1979-1980

on Gray's resignation **SI4-3** 1113, 1613, 1623-1624

on interviewing McLaren for position with Antitrust Division, Department of Justice **NSI2** 3, 21, 24

on ITT matter **NSI2** 16, 189, 192-193

on learning about Watergate arrests **SI2** 6, 101, 102-103

on meeting with Dean and Ehrlichman on Magruder's possible involvement in Watergate **SI2** 2 60, 575, 579-580

on meeting with Ehrlichman and Haldeman on Byrne nomination for FBI director **SI7-4** 1635, 1867, 1869-1873

on meeting with Liddy and Powell Moore after Watergate arrests **SI2** 7, 105, 110-112

on meeting with McLaren and Griswold to request extension of time on ITT-Grinnell appeal **NSI2** 7, 65, 70-72

on meeting with McLaren, Rohatyn, and other ITT Antitrust Division staff members **SI5-1** 24, 403, 404

on meeting with Nixon and Petersen on information received from Dean and Magruder **SI4-2** 999-1000

on meeting with Nixon on April 25, 1973 **SI9-2** 554, 883, 886

on meeting with Nixon to brief him on evidence against White House personnel **SI4-2** 573-574, 923-924, 925-928

on meeting with Petersen and Silbert on Dean and Magruder's disclosures **SI4-2** 569, 863, 866-871

on meeting with Rohatyn on *ITT-Hartford Fire Insurance* case **SI5-1** 20, 367, 368-369

on Nixon's request that he stay on as Attorney General and act as liaison to minority members of Ervin Committee **SI3-1** 51, 583, 592-594

on obtaining Nixon's authorization to turn over material on Fielding break-in to Byrne **SI7-4** 1646, 1983, 1984-1986

on Petersen's comments on Magruder's Watergate Grand Jury testimony **SI2** 2, 580

on request for extension of time to appeal *ITT-Grinnell* **SI5-2** 501, 751, 752-754

on resignation as Attorney General **SI4-3** 1118, 1651, 1654-1655

on setting up meeting with Nixon on information from U.S Attorneys **SI4-2** 570, 873, 877-879

on settlement of ITT antitrust cases **NSI2** 9, 81, 95, 101; **SI5-2** 485, 488, 549, 558-559, 595, 602

on Stans being excused from Watergate Grand Jury testimony **SI2** 2, 58-59, 561-562, 570-571

on telephone call from Ehrlichman on Nixon's questions about White House Staff involvement in Watergate **SI4-1** 20, 399, 405

on telephone call and letter from Walsh on *ITT-Grinnell* appeal **SI5-1** 15, 283, 284

on telephone conversation with Ehrlichman on his investigation of Watergate **SI4-2** 566, 829, 832-833, 837-839

Kleindienst confirmation hearings NSI2 7, 65, 66-72; **SI3-1** 3, 87, 88-95; **TW 3** 381-398

and abuse of powers charge against Nixon **MMFL** 126-135

denial by Kleindienst of discussions with White House on antitrust suits against ITT **SI5-2** 511, 849, 850-853

discussed at Haldeman-Mitchell-Nixon meeting **SI1** 15, 155

and Dita Beard matter **SI2** 2, 27, 277, 280-281, 282, 289-290, 291-296

House Judiciary Committee Impeachment Inquiry presentation of evidence on ITT matter and **II 2** 1025-1043

in Jenner's presentation of summary of evidence to House Judiciary Committee Impeachment Inquiry on Nixon's abuse of power **II 3** 1980

Kleindienst's cited testimony in **SI5-1** 3, 69, 91

in Minority of House Judiciary Committee Impeachment Inquiry views on Articles of Impeachment **RHJC** 470-476

Mitchell's cited testimony in **SI5-1** 3, 69, 92-93

Nixon and, in Article of Impeachment II **RHJC** 174-176

Nixon-Mitchell-Haldeman discussion of **SI5-2** 510, 841, 842-847

Nixon's abuse of Presidential power and **SUMM I** 144-148

press coverage on **SI5-2** 512, 855, 856-860

See also Colson, Charles, testimony before House Judiciary Committee Impeachment Inquiry, on ITT-Kleindienst hearings matter; Dita Beard matter; ITT, antitrust suits against

Kleppe, Thomas SI5-1 331

Kloock, Dean, letter from Hanman on ADEPT program and milk price-support increases SI6-2 480, 784, 819, 820

Knight, Hal, statement on MENU dual reporting system existing to "...deceive Congress..." SI11 57, 298

Knott, Lawson

in memo from Johnson staff member to Krogh **SI10** 39

and National Archives acceptance of Nixon's gift of pre-Presidential papers **SI10** 59

Knowles, Bob SI5-2 584, 585

Kolstad, Jim SIAPP4 121

Kopechne, Mary Jo

Rodino on reports that House Judiciary Committee Impeachment Inquiry is investigating death of **II 1** 611

Kovach, William SI7-2 610

Kraft, Joseph, wiretapping and surveillance of II 2 1110-1112, 1113; **RHJC** 36; **SUMM I** 125-126, 128; **SI7-1** 16, 313, 314-324; **SI7-2** 828

in Article of Impeachment II **RHJC** 150

Cox's efforts to obtain records on **II 2** 1372

Cox's request for White House records on **SI9-1** 47, 517, 518-521

FBI files on **II 2** 1112

Kraft, Joseph, wiretapping and surveillance of *(Continued)*

FBI files and logs of wiretaps delivered to White House **SI7-2** 552, 925, 926-949; **II 2** 1157-1158

in Jenner's presentation of summary of evidence to House Judiciary Committee Impeachment Inquiry **II 3** 1978

in Minority of House Judiciary Committee Impeachment Inquiry views on Articles of Impeachment **RHJC** 451-452

Nixon-Dean discussion on **SI7-4** 1641, 1941, 1942-1945; **II 2** 1228

summary of FBI file on **SI7-1** 19, 355, 356-357

Krogh, Egil SIAPP2 38-39; **SI1** 7, 31, 34, 199

affidavit on arrangements for Fielding break-in **SI7-2** 561, 1095, 1096-1101

affidavit on assignment with Young as co-chairmen of Plumbers unit **SI7-2** 543, 795, 796-801

affidavit on Ehrlichman assigning him to "special" national security project **NSI4** 9, 85, 86-93

assigned by Ehrlichman as co-chairman of Plumbers unit **SI7-2** 543, 795, 796-814; **II 2** 1139-1140

assigned by Ehrlichman to look into desirability of Nixon contribution of pre-Presidential papers **SI10** 40

assigned by Ehrlichman to "special" national security project for White House **NSI4** 9, 85, 86-95

assured by Ehrlichman that Hunt is "stable" **II 2** 825-826

and Chenow interview **SI2** 2, 51

claims Ehrlichman approved of Fielding break-in **SI7-3** 1183, 1239, 1240-1246

Colson on Hunt assigned to work under **TW 3** 207, 209

Colson suggests to Ehrlichman that he could conduct study of leaks appearing in *New York Times* **NSI4** 15, 119, 120

Cox files indictment against **SI9-2** 534, 741, 742-746

Dean informs Nixon about perjury in grand jury testimony of **SI3-2** 1029-1030

discussion with Dean on their legal problems **TW 2** 247-248

and discussions with Ehrlichman on Hunt's demands for money **II 2** 795-796, 797

dropped from Plumbers unit **II 2** 1185

in Ehrlichman memo to Nixon on antitrust policy **SI5-1** 395

Ehrlichman states he reported to Nixon **II 2** 1151

Ehrlichman's notes on conversations with **SIAPP3** 250-260

Ehrlichman's suggestion to Richardson that he meet with **SI4-3** 1652

and establishment of Plumbers unit **NSI4** 46

false testimony before Watergate Grand Jury **II 2** 1196-1197; **SUMM I** 44; **SI7-3** 1209, 1603, 1604-1613

and financial arrangements for Fielding break-in **SI7-3** 1184, 1247, 1248-1274

guilty plea of **II 2** 1175, 1416; **SI9-2** 556, 901, 902-921

and Hunt **SI1** 106

and Hunt memo to Colson on "Neutralization of Ellsberg" **SI7-2** 551, 911, 916, 917

and Hunt's blackmail attempts **SI7-4** 1630, 1631, 1821, 1822-1828, 1829, 1830-1836

and Hunt's demands for money **II 2** 1202-1204, 1205

and Hunt's memo to Colson on creation of Ellsberg file **SI7-2** 551, 911, 912-923

and Hunt's preparations for Fielding break-in **SI7-2** 564, 1151, 1152-1177

and Hunt's recommendation of break-in at Fielding's home **SI7-3** 1186, 1301, 1302-1332

at interview with Stewart on FBI investigation of SALT leaks **SI7-2** 891-894

and ITT matter **II 2** 1016-1017

knowledge of Hunt's demands for money **SUMM I** 54

letter of resignation on illegal acts being his own responsibility **NSI4** 13, 109, 113

letter from Ritzel on Nixon's future gifts of pre-Presidential and Presidential papers **SI10** 4, 72-73

logs of meetings and telephone conversations with Nixon turned over to Jaworski **SI9-2** 554, 883, 884-890

McClory on testimony of **II 2** 1131

meeting with Ehrlichman on Fielding break-in **SI7-4** 1845-1846

meeting with Ehrlichman on Hunt's forthcoming testimony **SI3-2** 720, 1277, 1278-1281

meeting with Ehrlichman on inability to gain access to Fielding's files on Ellsberg **SI7-2** 555, 981, 982-1003

meeting with Nixon and Ehrlichman after SALT leak **II 2** 1143-1144; **NSI4** 13, 109, 110-114

meetings with Ehrlichman and Young after Fielding break-in **SI7-3** 1187, 1333, 1334-1337

memo for Ehrlichman on CIA preparation of psychological profile of Ellsberg **SI7-2** 550, 897, 905-908

memo from Colson with Hunt memo on Diem coup **SI7-2** 558-559, 1029-1030, 1057-1058

memo from Dean on Brookings Institution **II 2** 1263-1265

memo from Jones with names for handling of Nixon's contribution of pre-Presidential papers to National Archives **SI10** 39

memo from Peterson with attached letters from Merriam to Petersen on delay of *ITT-Grinnell* appeal **SI5-1** 22, 377, 388-392

memo to Ehrlichman with agenda item for meeting on Diem coup **SI7-2** 558-559, 1029-1030, 1063-1065

memo to Ehrlichman on article in *New York Times* endangering life of clandestine CIA operative **NSI4** 19, 133, 134-136

memo to Ehrlichman on difficulty of prosecuting Ellsberg **SI7-3** 1191, 1391, 1392-1397

memo to Ehrlichman on investigations by Plumbers unit **SI7-2** 563, 1125, 1127

memo to Ehrlichman on meeting with Helms and Osborn **SI7-2** 553, 951, 963-966

memo to Ehrlichman on meeting with Laird and Buzhardt **SI7-2** 553, 951, 961-962

memo to Ehrlichman on Pentagon Papers project **SI7-2** 557, 1007, 1022-1028

memo to Ehrlichman on status of Ellsberg inquiry **NSI4** 17, 125, 126-127; **SI7-2** 553, 951, 957-960
memo to Macomber requesting copies of State Department cable files covering Vietnam during 1963 **SI7-2** 558-559, 1029-1030, 1031-1034
memo to McLaren on Ehrlichman's request for clarifications and additions on antitrust policy paper **SI5-1** 23, 393, 398-400
memos from Dean on Brookings Institution as recipient of government contracts **SI8** 8, 79, 80-90
Nixon assigns to investigate Ellsberg **SI1** 40
Nixon on role of **SIAPP1** 23
Nixon's memo on **SUMM I** 7
on organizational chart from files of Special Investigations Unit **SI7-2** 814
perjured testimony before Watergate Grand Jury on Hunt's and Liddy's participation in Fielding break-in **SI3-1** 25, 311, 312-325
and Plumbers **SI1** 40
recommends Liddy to Dean **SI3-2** 997
and release of Hunt memo on Boudin **SI7-2** 563, 1125, 1126-1149
removed from Plumbers unit after refusal to authorize wiretaps **SI7-3** 1193, 1421, 1432
role in Nixon Administration **RHJC** 15
role on White House staff **II 1** 557
and salary increase for Liddy **SI7-3** 1446
statement on approving Fielding break-in **NSI4** 13, 109, 114; **SI9-2** 556, 901, 910-921
takes two versions of deed of gift of pre-Presidential papers and memo from Ritzel to Nixon **SI10** 1-2, 44-57
telephone conversation with Ehrlichman on Hunt's blackmail threats **SI7-4** 1632, 1837, 1838-1839
transcript of taped meeting with Nixon and Ehrlichman on SALT talks leak **SI7-2** 548, 863, 867-885
and use of TAPE contribution for Fielding break-in **SI6-2** 832-836
at White House meeting on investigation of Ellsberg matter **NSI4** 16, 121, 122-123
See also U.S. v. Egil Krogh, Jr.
Krogh, Egil, cited testimony of
on advising Ehrlichman of feasibility of Fielding break-in **SI7-3** 1183, 1239, 1240-1241
on assigning of Liddy and Hunt to Plumbers unit and setting up offices **SI7-2** 544, 815, 816-818
on discussion of possibility of Fielding break-in **SI7-2** 554, 967, 968-971
on events after Fielding break-in **SI7-3** 1186, 1301, 1310-1317
on financial arrangements for Fielding break-in **SI7-3** 1184, 1247, 1256-1259
on formation of Plumbers unit **SI3-1** 25, 311, 324-325
on meeting with Ehrlichman on Fielding break-in **SI7-2** 555, 981, 982-984
on meeting with Ehrlichman on Hunt's blackmail threats **SI7-4** 1631, 1829, 1833-1836
on meeting with Ehrlichman on Hunt's forthcoming testimony **SI3-2** 720, 1277, 1278-1279
on meetings with Dean and Ehrlichman on Hunt's blackmail attempts **SI7-4** 1630, 1821, 1822-1826

on preparations for Fielding break-in **SI7-2** 564, 1151, 1167-1169
on telephone conversation with Ehrlichman on Hunt's blackmail threats **SI7-4** 1838-1839
on telephone conversation with Ehrlichman on Hunt's demands **SI3-2** 708, 951, 960-962
Kueny, LaRonna
and retyping of 1969 deed of gift of Nixon's papers in 1970 **SI10** 13-14, 309-314
Kunzig, Robert L.
fact sheet from Galuardi on restoration of "point" gazebo at Nixon's San Clemente property **SI12** 139
and GSA payment for part of landscaping work at Nixon's San Clemente property **SI12** 116
and GSA payment for sewer system installation at Nixon's San Clemente property **SI12** 112-113
and Kalmbach's request for GSA payment for housekeeping services at Nixon's San Clemente property **SI12** 155
Kuykendall, Dan SIAPP4 25
Labor
and antiwar movement **SI7-1** 391
New Left and, in Huston plan **SI7-1** 390
Trotskyist groups and, in Huston plan **SI7-1** 408
Labor-HEW appropriations legislation
for fiscal year 1973, Nixon's message to Congress on **SI12** 31
for fiscal year 1974, provision limiting impoundment of funds **SI12** 36-37
impoundment of funds under **SI12** 19-20
pocket veto and funding of **SI12** 32
Labovitz, John R. II 2 1304, 874
biography of **II 3** 2150
Lackritz, Marc, questioning by
Caulfield **SI7-1** 317-320, 321-322, 353-354, 508-511, 518-520; **SI7-2** 656-657, 750-753; **SI7-3** 1352-1353; **SI8** 93-94, 138-144, 148-151, 161-163, 168-170, 179-180, 192-194
Ehrlichman **SI8** 223
Lacovara, Philip A., affidavit on serving subpoena duces tecum to Nixon SI9-1 417
Laird, Barbara SIAPP4 9
Laird, Melvin R.
Abrams on his role in decision to bomb Cambodia **SI11** 51, 272
and admission of bombings of Cambodia in May 1970 **SI11** 15-17, 149-151, 152-155, 156-161
authorizes tactical air strikes into northeastern Cambodia in April 1970 **SI11** 7-8
and Beard's lobbying on antitrust suits against ITT **SI5-1** 142
and decision to withdraw substantial U.S. forces from South Vietnam in 1969 **SI11** 52, 273-274
denies knowledge of request from Joint Chiefs to attack Viet Cong or North Vietnamese bases in Cambodia **SI11** 29, 198
draft letter from Ehrlichman on difficulties of prosecuting Ellsberg **SI7-3** 1394, 1397
Krogh-Young memo to Ehrlichman on meeting with **SI7-2** 553, 951, 961-962
and leaks on U.S. position on India-Pakistan War **SI7-3** 1424
news conference of January 20, 1971 on continued

Laird, Melvin R. *(Continued)*
  use of air power in Cambodia **SI11** 48, 266
  news conference of January 29, 1974 on wiretapping of Pursley **SI7-1** 299-300
  and origin of MENU reporting procedures **SI11** 345-346
  statement on Cambodia's role in Vietnam War in March 1969 **SI11** 10-11, 139-142
  statement on policy in Cambodia in 1969 and 1970 **SI11** 14, 15-17, 19-20
  statement on possibility of ground troops and air support in Cambodia after July 1970 **SI11** 17, 161
  statement on status of air war in Cambodia in December 1970 compared to earlier in year **SI11** 19, 166-169
  statement on U.S. policy in Cambodia on May 12, 1970 **SI11** 4, 133-136
  statement on use of ground forces in Cambodia **SI11** 159-160
  Wheeler assumes he briefed Members of Congress on MENU operations **SI11** 61, 314
Lake, Anthony SI7-4 1754
Lambert, Ross Ward TW 3 43, 46
Lambert, Samuel M., on enemies list SI8 75, 109
Lambert, William SI7-2 1068; **SI7-3** 1559
  and Diem cables **SI2** 2, 162
  Hunt and **TW 3** 287-288
  interviewed on Diem cable **SI7-2** 558-559, 1029-1030, 1070-1075
Lamprey, Stewart SIAPP4 1
Land, Lestor SI5-1 444
Landauer, Jerry SI6-2 848, 849-851
Landon, Alf, calls for special prosecutor to investigate Watergate SI9-1 136
Lanigan, Charles SIAPP4 18
Laos SI11 188
  Defense Department answer to House Resolution requesting information on pre-May 1970 bombings of **SI11** 57, 63, 295-297, 319-321
  DEWEY CANYON operation in **SI11** 274
  map of **SI11** 80
  See also Bombing of Laos; Laos Accords of 1962
Laos Accords of 1962
  in Nixon's speech on terms of proposed settlement of Vietnam War **SI11** 29, 199-200
Larkin, Leo P., Jr. SI7-2 594
Larsen, Roy E. SI8 83
LaRue, Frederick C. II 3 1626-1627; **SIAPP2** 61-66; **SIAPP4** 6
  Bittman on deliveries of money from **TW 2** 14-16, 79, 88
  briefs Mitchell on meeting with Liddy **II 2** 1194
  conflict with Malek **SIAPP4** 116
  date of payment to Hunt, in St. Clair's presentation of evidence in behalf of Nixon **II 3** 1754-1757
  Dean on discussing Hunt's demands for money with **TW 2** 260, 261-262
  Dean suggests he consult with Mitchell on Hunt's request for money **NSI1** 26, 177, 178-185
  and deliveries of funds for Watergate defendants to Bittman **SI3-1** 33-34, 425-426, 427-454; **SUMM I** 52; **SI3-2** 715, 1187, 1188-1237; **SI3-1**

32, 385, 386-389
  and final deliveries of funds for Watergate defendants **SI3-1** 31, 373, 374-377
  guilty plea of **II 2** 1351-1352
  House Judiciary Committee Impeachment Inquiry discussion on subpoenaing as witness **II 2** 981-992
  and Hunt's demands for money **SI3-2** 959
  informed of Fielding break-in after Watergate break-in **SI7-3** 1200, 1513, 1514-1521
  informed by Magruder of Watergate arrests **SI2** 2, 107
  informs Kalmbach on his Watergate Grand Jury testimony **SI4-3** 1444
  and involvement with hush money **II 2** 736, 755-756, 760; **SI3-1** 16, 17, 20, 207, 208-219, 221, 222-233, 253, 254-263; **SUMM I** 52, 93; **SI4-2** 785; **SI4-3** 1643
  Kalmbach's collection of hush money and **SUMM I** 44
  and Kalmbach's resignation from assignment as fundraiser for Watergate defendants **II 2** 750-751; **SI3-1** 31, 373, 374-383
  learns about Plumbers unit activities from Liddy **II 2** 718-719; **II 2** 1194; **II 1** 613-614
  Magruder informs of Watergate arrests **SUMM I** 35
  meeting with Dahlberg, Stans, and Mardian **SI2** 2, 41, 405, 407
  meeting with Dean on Watergate Grand Jury testimony **SI4-2** 607
  meeting with Kalmbach on methods of getting funds to Watergate defendants **SI3-1** 12, 175, 176-180
  at meeting in Key Biscayne, Florida with Mitchell and Magruder on Liddy plan **SI1** 13, 115, 116-140
  meeting with Mardian and Liddy on White House Plumbers operations **SI2** 2, 27, 277, 278-296
  meeting with Mardian and Mitchell to inform Mitchell about meeting with Liddy **SI3-1** 4, 97, 98-106
  meeting with Mitchell after Watergate break-in **TW 2** 152-153, 203
  meeting with Mitchell, Mardian, and Dean to discuss CIA aid for Watergate defendants **SI3-1** 7, 121, 122-127
  meeting with Mitchell, Mardian, LaRue, and Dean on Watergate arrests **SUMM I** 37
  at meetings with Mitchell, Dean, Magruder, and Mardian to discuss Watergate break-in **SI2** 2, 7, 21, 105, 108, 223, 224-229
  Mitchell and arrangements for his use of Haldeman's $350,000 fund for payments to Hunt **TW 2** 128-132, 133-134, 161-164, 167-168, 171, 195
  Mitchell on meeting with Mardian and on June 22, 1973 **TW 2** 176-177
  and Mitchell's first knowledge of payments to Watergate defendants **TW 2** 185-187, 192, 213
  named by Magruder as participant in wiretapping plans against Democrats **SI4-2** 564, 799, 800-809
  Nixon tells Haldeman he has talked to Watergate Prosecutor **SUMM I** 94
  on Nixon's decision-making methods **SUMM I** 28

Paul O'Brien denies discussing payment to Hunt with **TW 1** 147

payment to Hunt, in St. Clair's presentation of evidence in behalf of Nixon **II 3** 1754

and payment to Liddy's attorney **SI3-1** 43, 499, 500

and payments to Bittman from White House campaign contributions **SI3-1** 45, 517, 518-519

Petersen reports to Nixon on Watergate Grand Jury testimony of **SI4-3** 1298-1299, 1407

Petersen tells Nixon he has confessed to participating in crime of obstruction of justice **SUMM I** 93, 95

pleads guilty of conspiracy to obstruct justice and agrees to testify as government witness **SI9-1** 20, 321, 322-328

and problems between Magruder and Liddy **SI2** 2, 187

reports to Mitchell on his meeting with Liddy **SI7-3** 1201, 1523, 1524-1531; **II 2** 719-720

role in Nixon Administration **RHJC** 14-15

role in Nixon re-election campaign **SIAPP4** 84, 150; **SI1** 81

at second meeting on Liddy plan **SUMM I** 31

and solicitation of hush money **SI3-2** 1027, 1085-1086

Strachan informs Ehrlichman he gave mistaken testimony **SI4-1** 38, 549, 550-551

See also House Judiciary Committee Impeachment Inquiry, discussion on calling witnesses; *U.S. v. Fred LaRue*

LaRue, Frederick C., cited testimony of

on approval of Liddy plan **SI1** 13, 115, 130-135

on delivery of $75,000 for Hunt to Bittman **SI3-2** 715, 1187, 1188-1197

on delivery of funds to Bittman for Hunt's legal fees **SI3-1** 32, 385, 386-387

in Doar's presentation of evidentiary material to House Judiciary Committee Impeachment Inquiry **II 1** 590-591

on first knowledge of Watergate arrests **SI2** 7, 105, 107-108

on informing Mitchell of meeting with Liddy **SI7-3** 1201, 1523, 1524

on Kalmbach's resignation as fundraiser for Watergate defendants and burning of his records **SI3-1** 31, 373, 380-381

on Liddy debriefing **SI2** 2, 27, 277, 278-283

on Magruder's telephone call from Colson on Liddy plan **SI1** 12, 101, 112

on meeting of June 19, 1972 with Mitchell, Dean, Magruder, and Mardian to discuss Watergate break-in **SI2** 2, 21, 223, 228-229

on meeting with LaRue on methods for collecting and distributing money for Watergate defendants **SI3-1** 12, 175, 176-177

on meeting with LaRue and Mitchell to inform Mitchell about meeting with Liddy **SI3-1** 4, 97, 98

on meeting with Liddy and Mardian after Watergate arrests **SI3-1** 3, 87, 88-92

on meeting with Liddy and Mardian on Plumbers unit activities and bail money for Watergate burglars **SI7-3** 1200, 1513, 1514-1518

on Mitchell's approval of Liddy plan **SI1** 13, 115, 118-121

on payment to Liddy's attorney **SI3-1** 43, 499

on payments to Bittman **SI3-1** 45, 517, 518-519

on telephone conversation with Dean on Hunt's requests for money **NSI1** 26, 177, 179-182

on transfer of campaign contributions from White House to CRP for payments to Watergate defendants **SI3-1** 20, 33-34, 253, 257-258, 425-426, 436-438

LaRue, Frederick C., testimony before House Judiciary Committee Impeachment Inquiry TW 1 175-275

on authorizations for payments of money to Watergate defendants **TW 1** 247-249

on awareness of illegality of his actions **TW 1** 250-251, 258, 264

background **TW 1** 175-177

on being informed of Watergate break-in while in Los Angeles **TW 1** 183-185, 233-234

on briefing Mitchell on meeting with Liddy **TW 1** 197-198, 261

conversation with O'Brien on payments to Hunt **TW 1** 133, 134

on delivery of money to Bittman **TW 1** 251-255

denies knowledge of Hunt's threat to "tell all" **TW 1** 246-247

denies knowledge of Nixon's involvement with Watergate break-in **TW 1** 243-246

denies prior knowledge of Watergate break-in **TW 1** 232-233

on destruction of documents **TW 1** 259-260

on first knowledge of Haldeman's $350,000 account **TW 1** 242-243

on informing Mitchell of Watergate break-in **TW 1** 186, 233-234

on involvement with hush money **TW 1** 197, 198-206, 211-212, 214-232, 236-241, 265-275

on Kalmbach's role in fundraising for Watergate defendants **TW 1** 255

on knowing that Watergate break-in was CRP project **TW 1** 187-189, 234-235

on last delivery of money to Bittman **TW 1** 259-260

on learning about activities of Plumbers unit from Liddy **TW 1** 197, 235-236, 261

on meeting in Key Biscayne on Liddy plan **TW 1** 180-183

on meeting with Mitchell, Magruder, and Mardian on Watergate break-in **TW 1** 186-188

on meetings on Watergate break-in after return from California to Washington **TW 1** 195-197, 210

on Mitchell's statement after Watergate break-in **TW 1** 188-190, 212-214, 241-242, 261, 261

on purpose of payments to Watergate defendants **TW 1** 232, 263-264

on returning leftover money to Finance Committee **TW 1** 256-257

on role at White House and relationship with other staff members **TW 1** 176-178

swearing in **TW 1** 174-175

on transfer from White House to CRP **TW 1** 178-180

on upcoming testimony and sentencing **TW 1** 255-256

Lasky, Bernard SIAPP4 31

Lasky, Victor SI8 124

Latta, Delbert L. RHJC 359-493; SUMM I 1
addition to House Judiciary Committee Impeachment Inquiry **II 1** 79
additional views on Article of Impeachment III **RHJC** 503-505
additional views on Articles of Impeachment **RHJC** 525
on amendment on issuing subpoenas to Nixon **II 1** 332-338
on attorney-client privilege and O'Brien's testimony on Mitchell **TW 1** 130
on calling witnesses before House Judiciary Committee Impeachment Inquiry **II 3** 1625-1626, 1659-1660, 1661
on Cox's jurisdiction over Fielding break-in matter **II 2** 1370-1371
on dairy industry during Kennedy and Johnson administrations **II 2** 1047
on Doar-Jenner interview with Byrne **II 2** 1220-1221
on Ehrlichman's alleged authorization of Fielding break-in **II 2** 1236
on Ehrlichman's opinion of Ellsberg **II 2** 1122
on House Judiciary Committee Impeachment Inquiry issuing subpoenas to Nixon **II 1** 321, 322; **II 3** 1540
on House Judiciary Committee Impeachment Inquiry receiving two versions of Ehrlichman's handwritten notes **II 3** 1887
on IRS audits of Wayne **II 2** 1280
on Jaworski's statement on television on credibility of one of his witnesses **II 1** 91
on leaked Dixon memos **II 2** 1303, 1327
on members studying St. Clair's brief prior to official presentation of **II 2** 1216-1217
on methods of receiving dairy industry campaign contributions **II 2** 1049
on Mollenhoff and leak on IRS investigation of Gerald and George Wallace **II 2** 1255
on Nixon Administration antitrust policies **II 2** 1004
on Nixon's income tax **II 3** 1525-1526
on Nixon's noncompliance with House Judiciary Committee Impeachment Inquiry subpoenas **II 1** 430-431; **II 2** 907, 941
on Nixon's request for extension of time on answering House Judiciary Committee Impeachment Inquiry subpoena **II 1** 350
objects to Doar's criticism of St. Clair's defense of Nixon **SUMM I** 5
on partisanship of House Judiciary Committee Impeachment Inquiry **II 1** 299-301
on pocket veto **II 1** 199
on practices of other election campaigns **II 2** 774
on questions during presentation of evidentiary material to House Judiciary Committee Impeachment Inquiry **II 1** 678, 679
questions relevancy of evidence on enemies list **II 2** 1269-1270
requests biographical sketch of Nussbaum **II 3** 1459-1460
requests citations by Doar for direct evidence **SUMM I** 12

on results of domestic surveillance **II 2** 1110
on Richardson-Nixon discussion on Executive privilege **II 2** 1395-1396
on rules on cross-examination of witnesses **TW 1** 90
on rules of evidentiary procedures for House Judiciary Committee Impeachment Inquiry **II 1** 478
on St. Clair's participation in House Judiciary Committee Impeachment Inquiry **II 1** 243
on Sirica's invitation to Doar and Jenner **II 1** 150
on transcripts of Nixon tapes used by St. Clair in his presentation of evidence in behalf of Nixon **II 3** 1747
See also Minority of House Judiciary Committee Impeachment Inquiry views on Articles of Impeachment

Latta, Delbert L., questioning by
Bittman **TW 2** 105
Butterfield **TW 1** 113-114
Colson **TW 3** 500-502
Dean **TW 2** 344-346
Kalmbach **TW 3** 731-732
LaRue **TW 1** 268-269
O'Brien **TW 1** 169-170

LaVelle, John D. SI11 26

Law SI12 42
Anti-Deficiency Act of 1905 as statutory basis for impoundment of funds **SI12** 4, 70, 81
enacted in response to impoundment of funds by Nixon Administration **SI12** 35-40
on expenditures for protection of President **SI12** 93-94
involved in White House staff members obtaining IRS information **II 2** 1271-1275
legal opinions on impoundment of funds **SI12** 85-88
Nixon comments on mishandling of campaign finances as technical violations of **SIAPP1** 3
statutory, relating to bombing of Cambodia **SI11** 393-406
statutory construction of spending statutes and impoundment of funds **SI12** 57-66
See also English law

Lawford, Peter **II 2** 1279
tax information on **SI8** 157

Lawrence, Ernest SI5-1 205

Lawrence, Harding L. SIAPP2 231-234
See also U.S. v. *Braniff Airways, Inc. and Harding Lawrence*

LBJ Ranch, Texas
government expenditures during Johnson Administration on **SI12** 175-179, 181

Leaks **II 2** 1088-1089; NSI4 13, 109, 110-114; SI7-1 9, 223, 224-238; SI7-2 625, 627
and antitrust policy proposals **SI5-1** 394
on bombing of Cambodia, wiretaps on government employees and **SI7-1** 14, 291, 292-300
Cohen on **II 1** 168-169
Colson memo to Ehrlichman recommending study of those appearing in *New York Times* **NSI4** 15, 119, 120
Colson on Plumbers unit and **TW 3** 511-512

discussed by Nixon and Ehrlichman **SI4-3** 1137-1138

Ehrlichman memo to Dean on legal aspects of **NSI4** 3, 37, 38-42

establishment of Plumbers unit for dealing with **NSI4** 4, 43, 44-66

as excuse for wiretaps of government officials and newsmen **SUMM I** 124-125; **SI7-2** 571

in FBI, Dean on **SI3-2** 814

in FBI, Ehrlichman on **SI2** 2, 456

of FBI information on Segretti's activities **SI7-4** 1672

and FBI Watergate investigation **SI2** 2, 526-527

from House Judiciary Committee Impeachment Inquiry **II 2** 703-709, 739-740, 777-778, 1115, 1160, 1214-1215, 1242, 1325-1331, 1451; **II 3** 1855-1856

from Kleindienst confirmation hearings **SI5-2** 853

from Senate Select Committee on Presidential Campaign Activities **II 2** 855; **SI4-1** 29, 497, 498-500

from Watergate Grand Jury **SI3-2** 1102-1103

from Watergate Grand Jury, in discussion between Nixon, Wilson and Strickler **SI4-3** 1520-1521

on GOP Moderates meeting **SIAPP4** 18

on House Judiciary Committee Impeachment Inquiry requests for White House materials **II 1** 191-193

on India-Pakistan War **II 2** 1185

on IRS investigation of George and Gerald Wallace **SI8** 3, 35, 36-42; **II 2** 1250-1255

as justification for warrantless wiretaps, in Minority of House Judiciary Committee Impeachment Inquiry views on Articles of Impeachment **RHJC** 443-450

on Kalmbach's role as director of campaign finance **SIAPP4** 5

Kraft wiretapping and **SI7-4** 1944

Krogh and Young memo to Ehrlichman on article in *New York Times* endangering life of CIA operative **NSI4** 19, 133, 134-136

and memos prepared by House Judiciary Committee Impeachment Inquiry legal staff **II 2** 1303

Nixon on 1969 wiretaps and **SIAPP1** 22

and Nixon's authorization of wiretaps against government officials and newsmen **SI7-1** 3, 141, 142-155

on Nixon's decision to begin troop withdrawals from Vietnam **NSI4** 22, 153, 154-159

on Nixon's determination to remove nuclear weapons from Okinawa **NSI4** 26, 179, 180-182

on Nixon's directive on study of solutions to Vietnam War **NSI4** 21, 139, 140-151

and resignation of Halperin as chief of National Security Council planning group **NSI4** 27, 183, 184-190

Rodino on **II 1** 89-90, 203-204

in St. Clair's presentation of evidence in behalf of Nixon on electronic surveillance and Plumbers unit **II 3** 1815-1842

on SALT talks, Nixon meeting with Ehrlichman and Krogh on **SI7-2** 548, 863, 864-885

on SALT talks, Plumbers unit and **SI7-2** 549, 887, 888-895

on secret bombing of Cambodia **NSI4** 23, 161, 162-165

Stanton tells Colson FBI had case connecting Ellsberg to leak at Rand Corporation and failed to act **NSI4** 10, 97, 98

on U.S. position on India-Pakistan War **SI7-3** 1193, 1421, 1422-1440

and Waldie's motion on hearing testimony of witnesses in executive session **II 3** 1869-1879

and wiretapping of Radford **II 2** 1185

on wiretaps of White House staff members and newsmen, Nixon-Dean discussion on **SI7-4** 1752

Young memo for record on meeting at CIA headquarters to discuss problem of **NSI4** 18, 129, 130-131

See also Electronic surveillance; House Judiciary Committee Impeachment Inquiry, presentation of evidence on domestic surveillance; Pentagon Papers; SALT leaks

Leeper, Paul W., cited testimony of
on arrests of Watergate burglars **SI2** 2, 3, 4, 71, 72-74, 79, 81-85

Lehigh Valley Cooperative Farmers SIAPP2 239-242
See also U.S. v. Francis Carroll; U.S. v. Lehigh Valley Cooperative Farmers; U.S. v. Richard Allison

Lenzner, Terry F., questioning by
Caulfield **SI7-1** 316, 320-321, 512-513, 514-518; **SI7-3** 1351-1352, 1353; **SI8** 151-152, 181-182
Hunt **SI7-2** 832
Moore **NSI1** 61; **SI4-2** 703; **SI5-2** 761-762; **SI7-4** 1664, 1794-1795, 1972-1974
Reisner **SI1** 128-129, 237-238; **SI4-1** 490
Ulasewicz **SI3-1** 172-173, 210-215, 222-228, 284, 374-376; **SI7-1** 344

Leonard, Frank SIAPP4 64-65

Leonard, Jerris
memo to Timmons on San Diego as site of Republican National Convention of 1972 **NSI2** 12, 127, 145

Lepkowski, Stanley J. SIAPP2 323
See also U.S. v. George Steinbrenner III, and the American Shipbuilding Company

Levy, Gus SI1 85

Lewis, Jerry, tax information on SI8 157

Library Services and Construction Act of 1956
impoundment of funds for **SI12** 23

Liddy, G. Gordon SIAPP2 67-86; **SIAPP4** 75; **SUMM I** 33; **SI1** 9, 53, 54, 55, 56-57, 58-60, 99; **SI7-2** 651
actions immediately after Watergate arrests **SI2** 2, 3, 71
advises Hunt to leave country **SI2** 2, 20, 203, 204-221
agrees not to use CRP employees for Liddy plan **SUMM I** 31-32
arrest, indictment, and plea of **SI1** 27, 255, 256-259, 263-266
asked by Dean to tell Hunt to leave country **SI4-3** 1323-1324, 1328
asks Kleindienst to get his men out of jail **SI3-2** 1015
assigned to Plumbers unit **II 2** 1141; **SI7-2** 544, 815, 816-825

Liddy, G. Gordon *(Continued)*

assigned to political intelligence **SIAPP4** 59; **SI7-3** 1374

assignment to CRP and political enemies project with Dean **SI8** 20, 205, 206-209

authorized by Ehrlichman to conduct wiretaps in 1971 **SI7-2** 545, 827, 828

Baldwin delivers logs and summaries of tapped telephones at DNC to **SI1** 24, 223, 229

and Beard's departure from Washington **II 2** 1030

becomes General Counsel to CRP **SIAPP4** 67

becomes General Counsel to CRP, in memo from Strachan to Haldeman **SI1** 7, 31, 34

Bittman's knowledge of Hunt's employment by **TW 2** 8, 35

and break-in at DNC headquarters and wiretapping of Lawrence O'Brien's and Oliver's telephones **SI1** 23, 215, 216-222

in Chapin's memo to Ehrlichman on White House involvement with Segretti **SI7-4** 1687-1688

CIA memo on his relationship with CIA **TW 3** 59

court order compelling Watergate Grand Jury testimony of **SI4-1** 16, 335, 336

criminal docket against **SI1** 263-266

Dean on hiring of **TW 2** 222-223

Dean informs Ehrlichman of involvement in Watergate of **SI2** 2, 14, 143, 146, 153

Dean informs Nixon of reasons for hiring of **SI3-2** 997-998

Dean-Nixon discussion on jail sentence of **SI3-2** 855, 856, 857

Dean-Petersen meeting on documents from CIA connecting him to Fielding break-in **SI7-4** 1623, 1731, 1732

Dean's efforts to retrieve materials sent from CIA to Justice Department linking him to Fielding break-in **SI7-4** 1624, 1733, 1734-1739

Dean's knowledge of Watergate involvement of **SI4-3** 1402

declination of FBI interview and firing of **II 1** 682-683

and Democratic National Convention of 1972 **SIAPP4** 116

directed to meet Kleindienst to discuss Watergate arrests **SUMM I** 35

discussed by Ehrlichman and Strachan **SI4-2** 885

discussed by Nixon and Petersen **SI4-3** 1241

dismissed from Finance Committee **SI2** 2, 50, 477, 478-482

Doar on Nixon's delay in firing **II 3** 1931; **SUMM I** 9

efforts to obtain position of Director of IRS Alcohol, Tobacco, and Firearms Division **II 2** 1257-1258

in Ehrlichman memo to Colson on "Special Project" **TW 3** 232-234

Ehrlichman's instructions to **SI4-3** 1257-1258

employed by Plumbers unit **SI7-2** 797

false statements by Magruder to FBI agents on purpose of funds paid to **SI3-1** 19, 245, 246-251

false testimony by Porter and Magruder during trial of **SI3-1** 44, 501, 502-516

and FBI reports on wiretapping of government employees and newsmen **SI7-2** 690

and financial arrangements for Fielding break-in **SI7-3** 1184, 1247, 1248-1274

gives McCord instructions from Mitchell for wiretapping DNC **SI7-3** 1498

gives money to Hunt prior to Watergate burglars **SUMM I** 52

Gray on **SI2** 2, 51, 496

Haldeman on **SIAPP3** 44, 75, 77

in Higby-Magruder taped telephone conversation **SI4-2** 621, 625-627, 631M 636

Hunt states he was unaware of his role in Beard's disappearance from Washington **NSI2** 13, 153, 154

and Hunt's requests for aid from CIA **SI7-3** 1226-1227

indictment against **SI3-1** 29, 357, 358-367; **SI9-2** 564, 963, 964

informs Dean Watergate break-in was CRP operation **SUMM I** 37

informs Hunt that DNC headquarters will be target of electronic surveillance **SI1** 21, 197, 198-200

informs LaRue and Mardian of Fielding break-in and and discusses bail money for Watergate burglars **SI7-3** 1200, 1513, 1514-1521

informs Magruder of Watergate arrests **SUMM I** 35; **SI2** 7, 105, 106, 107-108

informs Mardian and LaRue about Plumbers unit activities **II 2** 718-719

intelligence activities prior to Democratic National Convention **SI1** 26, 246-253

involvement in Fielding break-in **SI4-2** 1016

Krogh indicted for perjury about activities for White House of **SI9-2** 534, 741, 742-746

Krogh's perjured testimony before Watergate Grand Jury on his participation in Fielding break-in **SI3-1** 25, 311, 312-325; **SI7-3** 1209, 1603, 1604-1613

LaRue and Mardian inform Mitchell of meeting with **SI7-3** 1201, 1523, 1524-1531

LaRue and Mardian meeting with Mitchell to discuss his report **SI3-1** 4, 97, 98-106

LaRue on meeting for first time **TW 1** 180

LaRue's payment to his attorney **SI3-1** 43, 499, 500

leaves White House for CRP post **II 2** 1185; **SI7-3** 1194, 1441, 1442-1448

Magruder advises Sloan to perjure himself on amount of money he gave to **SI3-1** 5, 7, 108-114

Magruder asks Porter to lie to FBI on reasons for CRP payments to **II 2** 729-730; **SI3-1** 10, 157, 158-164

Magruder authorizes Sloan to disburse cash to **SI1** 17, 171, 172-175

Magruder tells LaRue he has received unusual telephone call from **TW 1** 184-185

Magruder's preparations for false testimony before Watergate Grand Jury on purpose of money paid to **SI3-1** 24, 297, 298-309

Mardian and LaRue brief Mitchell on their meeting with **TW 1** 197-198, 261

McCord names as source of information that Mitchell, Colson, Dean, and Magruder had prior knowledge of Watergate bugging **SI4-1** 22, 431, 432-433

meeting with Colson and Hunt on Liddy plan
SUMM I 31; TW 3 244-249
meeting with Dean after Watergate break-in NSI1
3, 39, 40
meeting with Kleindienst and Powell Moore on
Watergate arrests SI2 7, 105, 110-112
meeting with LaRue and Mardian on hush money
and Plumbers unit activities TW 1 197, 235-236,
261; SI2 2, 27, 277, 278-296
meeting with LaRue and Mardian after Watergate
arrests SI3-1 3, 87, 88-92
meeting with Magruder after Watergate arrests
SI2 2, 126
meeting with Powell Moore and Kleindienst SI2
2, 104, 110-112
meeting with Segretti II 2 1190; SI7-3 1197, 1481,
1482-1494
meeting with Young, Hunt, and Malloy on Ellsberg psychological profile SI7-2 560, 1081,
1082-1093
memo from Silbert to Petersen on role in Fielding
break-in SIAPP3 239-241
method of receiving money from Ulasewicz SI3-1
17, 221, 222-233
and Mexican checks SI2 2, 4, 37, 79, 96-97, 99,
363, 364, 369, 371
Mitchell confirms Magruder's authorization of
payments to SI1 18, 177, 178-186
Mitchell on CRP hiring of TW 2 125-126
Mitchell denies knowledge of Watergate break-in
during FBI interview despite knowledge of his
role SI3-1 15, 203, 204-206
Mitchell on meeting with Mardian and LaRue on
activities of TW 2 176-177
money to McCord from SI1 19, 187, 188-189
in Nixon-Dean discussion SI3-2 869
in Nixon-Dean discussion on CRP political intelligence-gathering operation NSI1 79
Nixon-Dean discussion on Fielding break-in and
SI4-3 90-91
Nixon-Dean discussion on stopping Watergate
investigation on SI3-2 1075-1076
in Nixon-Dean discussion of Watergate hearings
SI8 422-424
in Nixon-Dean-Haldeman discussion on Mexican
checks SI8 403
Nixon-Dean-Haldeman discussion on Sirica's
probable sentence for SIAPP3 35; SI8 410, 411
Nixon-Ehrlichman-Haldeman discussion on silence of SI4-2 666
Nixon and Haldeman discuss probable immunity
given by Sirica to SI4-1 358
Nixon instructs Petersen to tell him to cooperate
with Watergate investigation NSI1 33, 211, 213-
216
in Nixon memo on Watergate SUMM I 7
Nixon tells Dean he is glad indictments for Watergate stopped at NSI1 47
participation in Fielding break-in SI7-3 1185,
1275, 1276-1299
Petersen tells Nixon to encourage him to give information to U.S. Attorneys SI4-2 1033, 1034
in Petersen's report to Nixon on Watergate Grand
Jury testimony SI4-3 1299, 1301-1302
photographed at Fielding break-in SI3-2 943-944

and Plumbers SI1 40
Porter tells FBI agents that money paid to him
was used for lawful political activities SI3-1 18,
235, 236-244
Porter testifies falsely before Watergate Grand
Jury on purposes of money paid to SI3-1 23,
291, 292-296
Porter's and Magruder's false statements on
money paid to II 2 738
and preparations for Fielding break-in SI7-2 564,
1151, 1152-1177
recommends break-in at Fielding's home II 2
1181-1182; SI7-3 1186, 1301, 1302-1332
remains as general counsel to FCRP despite
White House knowledge of his directing Watergate break-in SUMM I 37
remains silent and makes no money demands
SUMM I 52
reports to Mardian and LaRue on Plumbers unit
activities II 1 613-614
and requests for money for Watergate burglars
SUMM I 52
role in Nixon Administration RHJC 15-16
role on White House staff and at CRP II 1 557-
558
sentencing of SI4-1 219
shreds money used for Watergate break-in
SUMM I 39
Sloan discusses his payments to with Ehrlichman
and Chapin SI3-1 6, 115, 116-120
Sloan's payments to II 2 720-723
telephone call from Reisner with approval of
political intelligence plan SI1 13, 115, 116, 128-
129, 139, 140-146
and transfer of "capabilities" from Muskie campaign to McGovern campaign SI1 20, 191, 192-
195
transfer to CRP II 1 563-564
transfer from White House to CRP, in memo
from Strachan to Haldeman SI1 8, 45, 46-51
transfer from White House to CRP, for political-
intelligence assignment SUMM I 30
use of McCord for Watergate break-in SUMM I
32
White House efforts to appoint to IRS SI8 55-56
See also Liddy plan; Plumbers unit; U.S. v. G.
Gordon Liddy, U.S. v. G. Gordon Liddy, et al;
U.S. v. John Ehrlichman, et al

Liddy charts
Dean tells Liddy to destroy SI1 66
description SI1 56, 59, 64

Liddy plan
in Article of Impeachment I RHJC 37-41
Colson on his efforts to get approval for TW 3
504-505
controversy over Mitchell's alleged approval of
SI1 13, 115, 116-117, 119, 120, 121, 122-125
Dean and Haldeman agree it should be dropped
after second meeting on NSI1 9, 63, 64-65
Dean-Haldeman discussion on Dean's involvement
in II 2 841
Dean informs Nixon about first meeting on SI3-2
998-1000
designed to be untraceable to CRP or White
House SUMM I 31-32

Liddy plan *(Continued)*

in Doar's presentation of evidentiary material to House Judiciary Committee Impeachment Inquiry **II 1** 564-574

Ehrlichman-Nixon discussion on Mitchell's role in **SI4-2** 783, 784

Ehrlichman-O'Brien meeting on information obtained from Magruder on **II 2** 856

first meeting on **SUMM I** 30; **SI1** 9, 53, 54, 55, 56-57, 58-60

as forerunner of Watergate, in summary of evidence to House Judiciary Committee Impeachment Inquiry **II 3** 1943-1945

in Haldeman-Dean discussion **SI4-1** 317

Haldeman does not order its termination **SUMM I** 30-31

Haldeman tells Nixon he believes Mitchell approved **SI4-1** 355-357

Haldeman's knowledge of **SUMM I** 41

Hunt and Liddy talk to Colson about approval for **TW 3** 244-249

implementation of **SUMM I** 33-34

LaRue on first meeting on **TW 1** 180-183

LaRue on his knowledge that Watergate break-in was part of **TW 1** 187-189, 234-235

Magruder and his attorneys discuss with Ehrlichman **II 2** 867

Magruder-Mitchell-Haldeman meeting on Magruder's false testimony on approval of **II 2** 847-848

and Magruder's information to U.S. Attorneys **SI4-2** 848

Magruder's and Mitchell's approval of **NSI1** 82

Magruder's and Porter's perjury and **SUMM I** 79-81

in Magruder's Watergate Grand Jury testimony **SI4-2** 817-818

meeting in Key Biscayne, Florida of Mitchell, Magruder, and LaRue on **SI1** 13, 115, 116-140; **SUMM I** 31

meeting with Magruder, Mitchell, Haldeman, and Dean on March 28, 1973 on Magruder's testimony on **SI4-1** 19, 373, 374-397

and Mitchell **SI4-1** 533-534

Mitchell denies discussing with Nixon **TW 2** 160-161, 170

Mitchell on presentation at Key Biscayne meeting of **TW2** 188

Mitchell's and Haldeman's knowledge of discussed by Dean and Nixon **SI3-2** 701, 803, 865-867

Nixon, Haldeman, and Ehrlichman discuss Mitchell's supposed approval of **SI4-1** 359

Nixon tells Petersen Haldeman had no authority over funds for **SUMM I** 92

and Operation Sandwedge **II 2** 1184-1185

participants in third meeting on **SI4-3** 1298

Petersen informs Nixon of Mitchell's approval of **SUMM I** 90

in Petersen's notes **SI4-2** 1001-1002

and Reisner **SI4-1** 493

replaces Sandwedge plan **SUMM I** 30-31

second meeting on **SI1** 10, 53, 62, 63, 64-65, 66, 67-68, 69-75

in St. Clair's presentation of evidence in behalf of Nixon **II 3** 1727-1730

Strachan's perjury and **SUMM I** 78-79

in Strachan's Political Matters memoranda **SI2 2**, 25, 261, 262-267

telephone call from Colson to Magruder for approval for **SI2 2**, 107

telephone call from Colson to Magruder for approval of **SI1** 12, 101, 102-103, 105, 110-111, 112, 113-114

telephone call from Reisner to Liddy approving of **SI1** 13, 115, 116, 128-129, 139, 140-146

White House and coverup of **II 2** 749-750

Liebengood, Howard S.

memo to Thompson on interview with Stewart on FBI investigation of SALT leaks **SI7-2** 891-894

Liebengood, Howard S., questioning by

Gonzalez **SI1** 206-208

Hunt **SI1** 209-211

MacGregor **SI2 2**, 533

Life magazine **SIAPP4** 26, 122; **SI1** 82; **SI7-1** 360

and Colson's memo to Ehrlichman on "rekindling Pentagon Papers issue" **SI7-2** 1068-1069

Lilly, Leonard W.

and transfer of Haldeman's reserve fund **TW 1** 54-55

Lilly, Robert A. SIAPP2 294-295; **SI2 2**, 495

alleged meeting with Connally **II 2** 1067

at Louisville airport meeting with Alagia **SI6-2** 704-711

See also U.S. v. *David Parr, U.S.* v. *Harold Nelson*

Lilly, Robert A., cited testimony of

on AMPI contributions to Republican Congressional and Senatorial campaign committees **SI6-2** 487, 489, 951, 962-963, 965, 979-984

on duties with AMPI **SI6-1** 436-437

on Isham's position with AMPI until 1972 **SI6-1** 11, 191, 195-196

on meeting between Connally and dairy leaders at Page Airways **SI6-1** 28, 402, 438-440

on milk producers' attitudes toward contributions after March 12 milk price-support decision **SI6-2** 468, 523, 530-531

Lincoln, Abraham SUMM I 16, 18

Nixon on **SIAPP1** 51

Lindholm, Dick SI12 127

Lindsay, John V. SI7-2 560, 1081, 1090-1091

in Strachan memo to Dean on Miller **SI8** 123-125

See also Lindsay campaign

Lindsay campaign

and enemies list **SI8** 74, 108

in Political Matters Memoranda **SIAPP4** 1

Lisagor, Peter SIAPP1 57, 58, 75

Liszka, Dr. SI5-2 620, 757

Lithuanian defector matter NSI1 42; **SI2 2**, 149

Livermore, Put SIAPP4 2, 115

Livingston, Mary Walton

letter from Newman of March 27, 1970, on general description of Nixon's papers designated as gift in 1969 **SI10** 12, 298-301

letter to Newman describing Nixon's papers listed in Newman letter of March 27, 1970, with delivery date to National Archives **SI10** 13, 306-307

on Newman's work on Nixon's undeeded pre-Presidential papers in November and December

of 1969 **SI10** 200-202, 204
telephone conversations with Newman on Nixon's gift of 1969 papers **SI10** 11-12, 13, 292-300, 304-308

Lodge, Henry Cabot
informs Plenary Session of Paris Peace Conference in July 1969 that U.S. respects independence and territory of Cambodia **SI11** 3
joint press conference with Nixon of May 15, 1969 on Vietnam War and Abrams' orders **SI11** 30, 201

Loeb, William SIAPP4 52
in Dean and Caulfield briefing memo on IRS **SI8** 197

Lofton, John SIAPP4 90; **SI1** 87

Lombard, Thomas SI3-2 980-981

Lon Nol, General
continued secrecy over Cambodian bombings after takeover of **SI11** 281-282
heads Cambodian government after Sihanouk overthrow **SI11** 4
and U.S. bombing of Cambodia **SI11** 158

London Times
"leak" on bombing of Cambodia and **SI7-1** 300

Los Angeles Times **SIAPP4** 26; **SI4-3** 1303, 1308
Colson tells Nixon about Shapiro's conversation with reporter from **TW 3** 353-354
on Dean's Watergate Grand Jury testimony **SI4-3** 1326
on Ehrlichman's involvement in Middle East **SI4-3** 1649
on McCord's testimony that Dean and Magruder had prior knowledge of Watergate **SI4-1** 12-13, 311-312, 313-314
on Nixon expressing total confidence in Dean **SI4-1** 14, 319, 324

Lott, Trent RHJC 359-493; **SUMM I** 1
on calling witnesses before House Judiciary Committee Impeachment Inquiry **II 3** 1631, 1640-1641, 1642, 1695
on deletions from Nixon tapes **II 2** 1012-1013
discussion on amendment on procedures for House Judiciary Committee Impeachment Inquiry **II 1** 41-45
discussion on dairy industry contributions **II 2** 1084
on House Judiciary Committee Impeachment Inquiry issuing subpoenas to Nixon **II 1** 318-319, 652-653; **II 3** 1535
on Nixon's noncompliance with House Judiciary Committee Impeachment Inquiry subpoenas **II 1** 446-447; **II 2** 949-950
on obtaining Nixon's tax returns and audits from IRS **II 2** 1245
on release of House Judiciary Committee Impeachment Inquiry evidentiary material to public **II 3** 1585, 1586, 1593
on St. Clair's participation in House Judiciary Committee Impeachment Inquiry **II 1** 235
on St. Clair's responses to House Judiciary Committee Impeachment Inquiry requests for White House materials **II 1** 235-236
on scheduling St. Clair's presentation of evidence **II 3** 1565

on witnesses called by House Judiciary Committee Impeachment Inquiry **II 2** 988, 990
See also Minority of House Judiciary Committee Impeachment Inquiry views on Articles of Impeachment

Lott, Trent, questioning by
Bittman **TW 2** 93
Butterfield **TW 1** 106-108
Dean **TW 2** 335-337
Kalmbach **TW 3** 728-729

Louderback, Harold
impeachment case against **II 3** 2212-2213

Loudon, John H. SI8 83

Louisville, Kentucky, as possible site for Republican National Convention SI5-1 449-450, 473

Lowenstein, Allard, on enemies list SI8 74, 108, 119

Lucchino, Lawrence II 2 803
biography of **II 3** 2235

Luce, Gordon SIAPP4 18; **SI5-1** 438, 444; **SI5-2** 586

Lugar, Richard SIAPP4 24

Lyles, C.W. SI7-3 1433

Lynch, Harold
and bills for boundary survey at Nixon's San Clemente property **SI12** 129-130
bills GSA for den furnishings at Nixon's San Clemente property **SI12** 148
and construction of block wall at Nixon's San Clemente property **SI12** 152
and construction of redwood vs. chain link fence at Nixon's San Clemente property **SI12** 145, 146, 147
discussions with Nixon on design of swimming pool at San Clemente property **SI12** 170
and installation of beach cabana and railroad crossing at Nixon's San Clemente property **SI12** 141
and installation of den windows at Nixon's San Clemente property **SI12** 123
and installation of new heating system at Nixon's San Clemente property **SI12** 106, 107
Kalmbach selects as Nixon's personal architectural consultant on San Clemente improvements **SI12** 98-99
and landscaping at Nixon's San Clemente property **SI12** 115
and paving at Nixon's San Clemente property **SI12** 134
in Political Matters Memoranda **SIAPP4** 12
and purchase of lanterns for Nixon's San Clemente property **SI12** 149-150
recommends sewer work at Nixon's San Clemente property **SI12** 110-113
and reinforcement of handrails at Nixon's San Clemente property **SI12** 144

MacGregor, Clark II 2 1063; **NSI1** 135; **SIAPP4** 24, 27, 84; **SI1** 81; **SI8** 333
Cox requests copies of records of telephone conversations and meetings between Nixon and **SI9-1** 26, 371, 372-373
in Dean memo on action against tax-exempt foundations **SI8** 88
denies Gray asked him to call Nixon **SI2** 2, 56, 520, 533-537

MacGregor, Clark *(Continued)*
in discussion between Nixon, Dean, and Haldeman **SI2** 2, 598
Ehrlichman on telephone conversation between Nixon and **SI2** 2, 547-548
Gray informs him that both he and Walters are concerned about White House staff using FBI and CIA **SUMM I** 45
Gray tells Nixon about discussion with **SI2** 2, 553
instructions from Nixon on role at CRP **SUMM I** 46, 47
and ITT matter **II 2** 1017
meeting with Colson and Haldeman on Kleindienst confirmation hearings and ITT case **SI5-2** 508-509, 803-804, 805
at meeting with Hunt on Beard interview **TW 3** 250
memo to Ehrlichman and Shultz on milk price-support issue **SI6-1** 22-23, 329-330, 344-347
memo to Ehrlichman and Shultz on Mills' appeals for increased milk price supports **NSI3** 11, 123, 124
memo to Ehrlichman and Shultz on Rice's memo **SI6-1** 24-25, 359-360, 370
Nixon on investigations conducted by **SIAPP1** 45
Nixon re-election campaign responsibilities of **SUMM I** 27
Nixon states that he is investigating Watergate **SIAPP1** 3
and Plumbers unit's efforts to get Senate to hold hearings on Pentagon Papers matter **SI7-2** 841
and political intelligence-gathering on Democratic party candidates **TW 3** 255-256
in Political Matters Memoranda **SIAPP4** 131-132, 136, 146-147
role at CRP **II 1** 558
telephone conversation with Ehrlichman on April 17, 1973 on plan to make full disclosure on Watergate **SI4-3** 1318-1319
and Watergate coverup **II 1** 689-691
MacIver, John SI1 87
MacLaine, Shirley SIAPP4 121
MacLaury, Bruce NSI2 85; **SI5-1** 405
Maclean, Donald SI7-1 402
MacMurry, Fred
tax information on **SI8** 157
Macomber, William B., Jr.
and Congressional investigation of Pentagon Papers affair **SI7-3** 1215, 1219
memo from Young and Krogh requesting State Department papers for Pentagon Papers project **SI7-2** 558-559, 1029-1030, 1031-1034
Mad Dog SI7-1 393
Magnuson (senator), letter from Weinberger on impoundment of funds for HEW SI12 20
Magruder, Jeb Stuart SIAPP2 91-100; **SIAPP4** 13; **SI2** 2, 12, 131
advice to Sloan on perjuring himself on amount of money he gave to Liddy **SI3-1** 5, 7, 108-114
allegation discussed by Strachan and Ehrlichman **SI4-2** 571, 881, 885-887, 896
and appointment of Julie Nixon Eisenhower to youth registration drive **SIAPP4** 63
appointment to government job after perjured testimony of **SUMM I** 80-81

and approval of Liddy plan **SI4-1** 356-357
asks Porter to lie to FBI on reasons for CRP payments to Liddy **SI3-1** 10, 157, 158-164; **II 2** 729-730
asks Reisner to go with him to U.S. Attorneys **SI4-1** 491
assistance from Dean and Mitchell in preparation of his testimony before Watergate Grand Jury **II 2** 748-749
attitude toward Segretti's activities **SI7-3** 1197, 1481, 1482-1494
authorization to Sloan for disbursal of cash to Liddy **SI1** 17, 171, 172-175
Butterfield's memo to on Hoover's letter to Nixon on Cliffords **TW 1** 57-62, 85-86, 113-114
calendar for September 13, 1972 **SI3-1** 27, 341, 349
and campaign approach to youth **SIAPP4** 26-27
campaign assignments **SI1** 35-36
Chisholm candidacy and **SIAPP4** 46
Colson calls on Hunt's and Liddy's intelligence plan **TW 3** 504-505
Colson calls to urge approval of Liddy plan **SI3-2** 1001-1002; **SUMM I** 31
Colson-Haldeman discussion on his possible responsibility for Watergate break-in **TW 3** 318-319
in Colson memo to Haldeman on Kleindienst confirmation hearings **SI5-2** 808
Colson's forthcoming testimony and **SUMM I** 85
conflict with Malek **SIAPP4** 116
and Convention site decision paper **SI5-1** 25-26, 423-424, 465-477
CRP political intelligence-gathering activities and **NSI1** 10, 67, 68-75
Dean on his requests for backing up his story **TW 2** 279-280
Democratic party primaries and **SIAPP4** 20, 21
directed to destroy documents related to political surveillance after Watergate arrests **SUMM I** 37
discussed in Nixon-Dean meeting **NSI1** 51; **SI3-2** 1100-1101, 809-810, 1074-1075, 1078-1079
discusses Liddy plan with Colson **II 2** 838-839
discussions of clemency for, in Article of Impeachment I **RHJC** 78-80
disputes with Colson **SIAPP4** 92; **SI1** 89
efforts to obtain government post after Watergate **SI3-1** 49-50, 557-558, 559-581
Ehrlichman discusses reasons for testimony implicating White House **SI4-1** 366-368
Ehrlichman informs Mitchell that he intends to talk with U.S. Attorneys **SI4-2** 787-788
Ehrlichman informs Nixon that Hunt's testimony will lead to indictment of **SUMM I** 74
Ehrlichman-Kleindienst telephone conversation on information given to U.S. Attorneys **SI4-2** 566, 829, 830-842
Ehrlichman-Mitchell discussion on **SI4-2** 722
Ehrlichman questions Strachan on allegation to U.S. Attorneys by **SI4-2** 896
Ehrlichman reports to Nixon on meeting with **SI4-2** 565, 811, 812-828
Ehrlichman reports to Nixon on Mitchell's comments on Watergate Grand Jury testimony **SI4-**

Magruder, Jeb Stuart *(Continued)*

Nixon-Ehrlichman telephone conversation on information given to U.S. Attorneys by **SI4-2** 468, 851, 855-861

Nixon-Haldeman discussion on **SI4-2** 773-776; **SI4-3** 1311

Nixon-Haldeman discussion on hush money and **SIAPP3** 37

Nixon, Haldeman, and Ehrlichman discuss possible perjury of **SI4-1** 363

Nixon-Haldeman telephone conversation on information given to U.S. Attorneys by **SI4-2** 567, 843, 844-849

Nixon instructs Ehrlichman to tell him to go before Grand Jury **NSI1** 32, 207, 208-210

Nixon-Petersen discussion of effects of indictment on Haldeman and Ehrlichman **SUMM I** 95

Nixon-Petersen discussion of guilty plea for **SI4-3** 1129-1130, 1232, 1234, 1235-1236

Nixon on possible effects of testimony of **SI7-4** 1917-1918

Nixon on reasons for his remaining in White House **SIAPP1** 45

and Nixon's assurances of leniency prior to his talks with Watergate Prosecutors **SUMM I** 66-67

Nixon's attitude toward perjury before Grand Jury by **NSI1** 20, 145, 146-148

Nixon's discussion with Haldeman and Ehrlichman on forthcoming testimony of **SUMM I** 81-83

Nixon's knowledge of perjury by **SUMM I** 79-81

Nixon's memo on Dean's information that he might admit perjury and implicate Mitchell, Strachan, and Haldeman **SUMM I** 6-7

Nixon's opinion of **SUMM I** 6; **SI3-2** 1246-1247

Nixon's reaction to his meeting with Watergate Prosecutor **SUMM I** 74

in Nixon's recollections of March 21 **II 3** 1928

O'Brien on investigations of **TW 1** 158-159

and Operation Sandwedge proposal **SI7-3** 1188-1189, 1339-1340, 1372-1376

perjured testimony before Watergate Grand Jury **SUMM I** 91

perjury by, in Article of Impeachment I **RHJC** 89-90

Petersen meeting with Nixon and Kleindienst to report on information received from **SI4-2** 576-577, 973-974, 975-1011

Petersen on impact of his talking to Watergate Prosecutors **TW 3** 117-119

in Petersen's notes **SI4-2** 1002

and plan to bug Lawrence O'Brien's convention suite **SI3-2** 1008

and political intelligence in 1973 Presidential campaign **SIAPP4** 2

in Political Matters Memoranda on programming conservative leaders through White House **SIAPP4** 3

press policy at CRP and **SIAPP4** 13

reaction to not receiving news summary from Haldeman **SIAPP4** 79

receives reports on surveillance of Democratic National Committee headquarters **SUMM I** 33

and Reisner's subpoena by Senate Select Committee on Presidential Campaign Activities **II 2**

842-843

and Republican National Convention of 1972 **SIAPP4** 8

resignation as Director of Policy Development for Department of Commerce **SI4-3** 1114, 1625, 1626

role in Nixon Administration **RHJC** 14

role in Nixon re-election campaign **SI1** 83, 87-89

role in Watergate discussed by Dean and Nixon **SI3-2** 701, 803, 863-864

role on White House staff **II 1** 556-557

at second meeting on Liddy plan **SUMM I** 31

and Sloan's payments to Liddy **II 2** 720-723

Strachan on approval of Liddy plan by **NSI1** 82

in Strachan memo to Haldeman on CRP political intelligence-gathering system **SI1** 14, 147, 148-150, 153-154

taped telephone conversation with Dean **II 2** 842

taped telephone conversation with Haldeman **SI4-2** 560, 562, 707, 708-715, 769, 773-776

taped telephone conversation with Higby **II 2** 865; **SUMM I** 82-83; **SI4-2** 557, 609, 610-659, 667

telephone call from Colson on Hunt and Liddy plans **SI1** 12, 101, 102-103, 105, 110-111, 112, 113-114

and telephone call from Reisner to Liddy approving intelligence plan **SI1** 13, 115, 116, 128-129, 139, 140-146

telephone call to Dean on Watergate arrests **SI2** 2, 144

telephone conversation with Colson on Watergate **SI4-1** 9, 255-256, 257-259, 261, 262-264

telephone conversations with Haldeman after Watergate break-in **SI2** 2, 10, 125, 126-127

tells Haldeman he will make full disclosure to Watergate Grand Jury **II 2** 865

tells LaRue he notified Haldeman of Watergate break-in **TW 1** 190, 194

transcript of taped telephone conversation with Dean **SI4-1** 15, 331, 333-334

and transcripts of conversations on tapped telephones at DNC headquarters **SI1** 25, 233, 234-244

Watergate coverup and, in Article of Impeachment I **RHJC** 91-96

Watergate Grand Jury testimony of **SI4-3** 1529

White House interest in Watergate Grand Jury testimony of **II 2** 865-869; **SI2** 2, 60, 575, 576-586

See also Political Matters Memoranda, on Magruder's projects; *U.S. v. Jeb Stuart Magruder*

Magruder, Jeb Stuart, cited testimony of SI4-2 557, 609, 610

on actions after Watergate arrests **SI2** 2, 10, 125, 126

on approval of Liddy plan **SI1** 13, 115, 136-139

on asking Porter to lie to FBI on reasons for CRP payments to Liddy **SI3-1** 10, 157, 158-159

on attitude toward CRP's political intelligence-gathering activities and Sedan Chair II project **NSI1** 10, 67, 70-71

on cooperating with U.S. Attorneys **SI4-1** 393, 397; **NSI1** 31, 203, 205

on false statements he made to FBI on purpose of funds paid to Liddy **SI3-1** 19, 245, 246-247 on first knowledge of Watergate arrests **SI2** 7, 105, 106

on first meeting on Liddy plan **SI1** 9, 13, 53, 56-57, 115, 116-140

on Gemstone files **SI1** 25, 233, 234-236

on his efforts to obtain government post after Watergate **SI3-1** 49-50, 557-558, 564-565

on Hunt's status at White House **SI2** 2, 18, 166, 187-188

on meeting with Ehrlichman to inform him of disclosures to U.S. Attorneys **SI4-2** 564, 799, 800-809

on meeting with Haldeman, Mitchell, and Dean on his testimony **SI4-1** 19, 373, 392-397

on meeting of June 19, 1972 with Mitchell, Dean, Mardian, and LaRue to discuss Watergate break-in **SI2** 2, 21, 223, 225-226

on meeting with Mitchell and Dean to plan his Watergate Grand Jury testimony **SI3-1** 27, 341, 342-344

on meetings with Mitchell and Haldeman **SI4-1** 17, 339, 340-341, 342, 343

on Mitchell's approval of Liddy plan **SI1** 13, 115, 116-117

on preparations for and testimony to Watergate Grand Jury on purpose of CRP payments to Liddy **SI3-1** 24, 297, 298-301

on reasons for perjuring himself on purpose of payments to Liddy **SI3-1** 44, 501, 513-515

on Reisner's testimony and reasons for retaining attorney **SI4-1** 28, 487, 494-496

on relationship with Liddy **SI2** 2, 186

on second meeting on Liddy plan **SI1** 10, 53, 64-65

on Sloan's payments to Liddy **SI1** 17, 18, 171, 177, 174-175, 180-181

on taped conversation with Higby **SI4-2** 557, 609, 611

on telephone call from Colson on Liddy plan **SI1** 12, 101, 113-114

on telling Sloan he might have to commit perjury on amount of money he gave to Liddy **SI3-1** 5, 107, 108-109

Mahaffie, Charles NSI2 85, 86; **SI5-1** 405; **SI5-2** 555

Mahen, Daniel SI2 2, 495

Mahon (senator)
Clements and Moorer claim he was briefed on MENU operations **SI11** 61-62, 315-316

Mahon (senator), questioning by
Laird **SI11** 149-151, 154-155
Wheeler **SI11** 149-151

Mahoney, Harry T. TW 3 43-44

Mail covers
Huston memo to Haldeman on recommendations on **SI7-1** 439
illegal, covert, and legal **II 2** 1117-1118
Nixon's approval of Huston plan on **SI7-1** 454
use of legal and covert, in Huston plan **SI7-1** 417-419

Malek, Frederick V. SIAPP4 78, 91, 93, 94, 110, 116; **SI1** 33, 88
in Ehrlichman-MacGregor telephone conversation **SI4-3** 1318
Evans on **SIAPP4** 145

and FBI investigation of Schorr **SI7-2** 1114, 1115-1116

role at White House **SI1** 49

role in Nixon re-election campaign **SI1** 87

role on Budget Committee **SI1** 85

Mallory, Charles King, cited testimony of
on delivery of ITT documents to Justice Department **SI5-2** 517, 906, 926-929

Malloy, Bernard Mathis SI7-2 1023
affidavit on meeting with Young, Hunt, and Liddy on Ellsberg psychological profile **SI7-2** 560, 1081, 1082-1089
affidavit on preparation of expanded psychological profile of Ellsberg **SI7-3** 1192, 1399, 1400-1407
cited testimony of, on meeting with Young, Hunt and Liddy on Ellsberg psychological profile **SI7-2** 560, 1081, 1090-1091
and expanded psychological profile of Ellsberg **SI7-3** 1192, 1399, 1400-1420

Mann, James R. SUMM I 1
additional views on proposed Article of Impeachment on secret bombing of Cambodia **RHJC** 301-302
on calling witnesses before House Judiciary Committee Impeachment Inquiry **II 3** 1696-1696, 1698
on House Judiciary Committee Impeachment Inquiry issuing subpoenas to Nixon **II 1** 316, 338
on Nixon's noncompliance with House Judiciary Committee Impeachment Inquiry subpoenas **II 1** 449
on rules of evidentiary procedures for House Judiciary Committee Impeachment Inquiry **II 1** 537
on rules on cross-examination of witnesses **TW 1** 89
on scheduling St. Clair's presentation of evidence **II 3** 1563, 1564, 1565

Mann, James R., questioning by
Butterfield **TW 1** 99
Colson **TW 3** 469-471
Dean **TW 2** 319
Kalmbach **TW 3** 718-720
Mitchell **TW 2** 190-191
O'Brien **TW 1** 154-155
Petersen **TW 3** 144-145

Manning, Gordon SI7-2 1114

Mansfield, Mike SI3-2 837-838
letter from Nixon warning of hazards of ending U.S. bombing of Cambodia **SI11** 69, 340
Nixon-Haldeman discussion on **SIAPP3** 47-48

Manson, Charles II 1 298

Manson case
Nixon on error made in discussing **SIAPP1** 4

Mao Tse-tung, Black Panther ideology and, in Huston plan SI7-1 398

Maps
of bombing of Cambodia **SI11** 389-392
of Cambodia **SI11** 80, 388-392
of Cambodia, Laos, South Vietnam and North Vietnam **SI11** 80

and records of White House wiretaps on staff members and newsmen **SI7-4** 1742
reports to Mitchell on his meeting with Liddy **II 2** 719-720; **SI7-3** 1201, 1523, 1524-1531
returns to Washington after Watergate arrests **SUMM I** 35
role in Nixon Administration **RHJC** 16-17
and Sullivan's recommendation that FBI records of wiretaps on White House staff members be moved to White House **SI7-1** 285
summary of FBI interview with **SI7-2** 541, 554, 775, 783-788, 967, 968-980
and transfer of files on Kissinger tapes from FBI to White House **II 2** 1132-1139, 1157-1158, 1192-1193
and White House task force on Kleindienst hearings **SI5-2** 503, 767
See also U.S. v. John N. Mitchell, et al.

Mardian, Robert C., cited testimony of
on actions after Watergate arrests **SI2** 7, 105, 114-115
on approval of Liddy plan **SI1** 13, 115, 126-127
on FBI delivery of files and logs of wiretaps on Kraft to White House **SI7-2** 552, 925, 945-947
on informing Mitchell of meeting with Liddy **SI7-3** 1201, 1523, 1515
on Liddy debriefing **SI2** 2, 27, 277, 284-290
on meeting of June 19, 1972 with Mitchell, Dean, Magruder, and LaRue to discuss Watergate break-in **SI2** 2, 21, 223, 227
on meeting with LaRue and Liddy after Watergate arrests **SI3-1** 3, 87, 93-95
on meeting with LaRue and Mitchell to inform Mitchell about meeting with Liddy **SI3-1** 4, 97, 99-100; **SI7-3** 1200, 1513, 1519-1521
on meeting with Mitchell, LaRue, and Dean on possibility of CIA aid for Watergate defendants **SI3-1** 7, 121, 124
on meetings with Nixon re Sullivan's concerns over FBI files and logs of 1969-71 wiretaps requested by White House **SI7-2** 541, 775, 776-780
on role with White House task force on Kleindienst hearings **SI5-2** 505, 777, 787-794
on trip to see Nixon on FBI files and logs on wiretaps requested by White House **SI7-2** 540, 755, 766-770

Marijuana use, in wiretaps of Halperin SI7-2 683, 696
Marik, Dr. Robert SIAPP4 18, 29, 91, 111; **SI1** 95
role in Nixon re-election campaign **SI1** 88
Maroney, Kevin T.
informs Petersen that there is no evidence in Ellsberg case emanating from Fielding break-in **II 2** 1227
memo from Martin denying information in Ellsberg case came from Fielding break-in **SI7-4** 1640, 1929, 1932; **SIAPP3** 242
memo to Petersen on information from Fielding break-in not affecting Ellsberg case **SI7-4** 1640, 1929, 1933
Petersen consults with on Nixon's instructions on Fielding break-in **TW 3** 99, 147-148

Maroulis, Peter
LaRue's payment to **SI3-1** 43, 499, 500
Mitchell telephone call to **SI4-2** 723
Marro, Anthony SI8 171-172
Marsh, John, Jr.
letter to Symington of December 11, 1973 with report on bombings in Indochina **SI11** 88-89
Marshall, Chief Justice SIAPP1 66-67
on balance of power **SI12** 57
Martin, John L. SIAPP4 78
informs Petersen that there is no evidence in Ellsberg case emanating from Fielding break-in **II 2** 1227
memo to Maroney on Fielding break-in **SIAPP3** 242
memo to on Fielding break-in **SI7-4** 1640, 1929, 1932
Martinez, Eugenio SIAPP2 7-28; **SI1** 22, 201, 202-213
CIA memos to FBI on **TW 3** 15
guilty plea of **SI3-1** 41, 483, 485
indictment of **SI9-2** 564, 963, 964
payment for Fielding break-in **SI7-3** 1307
recruited by Hunt for Fielding break-in **II 2** 1174; **SI7-2** 561, 1095, 1096-1110
role in Fielding break-in **SI7-3** 1185, 1275, 1276-1299
telephone directory of **SI2** 2, 51, 483, 493-494
See also U.S. v. John Ehrlichman, et al; Watergate burglars
Martinez, Eugenio, cited testimony of
on Fielding break-in **SI7-3** 1185, 1275, 1292
on Watergate break-ins **SI7-3** 1198, 1495, 1501-1502
Marx, Mrs. Louis SI7-2 1023
Marx, Spencer SI7-2 1023
Marxism
Black Panther ideology and, in Huston plan **SI7-1** 398
Huston plan on identification of "New Left" groups with **SI7-1** 389
Massachusetts
in Nixon-Mitchell-Haldeman discussion on Presidential election of 1972 **SIAPP3** 31
Mathias, Charles
letter from Richardson on proposing Stennis Plan to Cox **SI9-2** 537, 765, 768-770
Mathias, Charles, questioning by
Mitchell **SI5-2** 774
Richardson **SI9-2** 793-794
Maxie, David SIAPP4 122
Mayne, Wiley II 1 271; **RHJC** 359-493; **SUMM I** 1
additional and separate views of **RHJC** 509-510
additional views on Article of Impeachment III **RHJC** 503-505
on calling witnesses before House Judiciary Committee Impeachment Inquiry **II 3** 1708
concurrence with Minority of House Judiciary Committee Impeachment Inquiry views on Articles of Impeachment I and II **RHJC** 493
on confidentiality of evidence on wiretapping **II 2** 1005
on confidentiality of material from Fielding break-in grand jury **II 2** 1160

Mayne, Wiley *(Continued)*
on congressional actions on milk price-support issue **II 2** 1070-1071
on dairy industry contributions to Congressmen and Senators **II 2** 1071-1072
on dropping some grounds for impeachment of Nixon **II 1** 271-273
on Haldeman listening to Nixon tapes **II 2** 1356
on hearsay evidence **II 2** 851
on House Judiciary Committee Impeachment Inquiry issuing subpoena to Clerk of House of Representatives for records of dairy industry campaign contributions **II 3** 1571-1572, 1573, 1575-1576, 1577, 1578
on House Judiciary Committee impeachment Inquiry issuingsubpoenas to Nixon **II 1** 315-316, 668
on investigation of milk fund contributions in House Judiciary Committee Impeachment Inquiry **II 1** 373-376
on leaks from House Judiciary Committee Impeachment Inquiry **II 1** 90; **II 2** 705-706, 1451
on legislation to increase milk price supports introduced into Congress **II 2** 1064
on materials held by Sirica **II 1** 168
on Nixon's alleged approval of Fielding break-in **II 2** 1162
on Nixon's income tax **II 3** 1521-1522
on Nixon's knowledge or lack of knowledge of Fielding break-in **II 2** 1229, 1238
on Nixon's noncompliance with House Judiciary Committee Impeachment Inquiry subpoenas **II 2** 925
on procedural rules for handling Impeachment Inquiry material **II 1** 128
on reliability of transcripts of Nixon tapes **II 2** 853-854
on respect for St. Clair **II 1** 237, 238
on rules of evidentiary procedures for House Judiciary Committee Impeachment Inquiry **II 1** 537-538, 541
on separate Minority of House Judiciary Committee Impeachment Inquiry brief on impeachable offenses **II 1** 154-155
on setting completion date for House Judiciary Committee Impeachment Inquiry **II 1** 20
on Sirica's invitation to Doar and Jenner **II 1** 139-140
on transcripts of Nixon tapes used by St. Clair in his presentation of evidence in behalf of Nixon **II 3** 1745, 1746
See also Minority of House Judiciary Committee Impeachment Inquiry views on Articles of Impeachment

Mayne, Wiley, questioning by
Bittman **TW 2** 82
Butterfield **TW 1** 98-99
Dean **TW 2** 318-319
Kalmbach **TW 3** 717-718, 723-724
LaRue **TW 1** 255-256

Mays, John SI6-2 711

McAuliffe, Daniel J., affidavit in *U.S.* v. *Russo* denying electronic surveillance of Ellsberg **SI7-3** 1199, 1503, 1504-1506

McBee, Susanna, article on Richardson proposing Stennis Plan to Cox SI9-2 537, 765, 771-772

McCahill, James A. II 1 552
and presentation of evidence in behalf of Nixon **II 3** 1720-1771, 1773-1866

McCall, Robert SIAPP4 26; **SI5-2** 790

McCandless, Robert C. SIAPP4 120; **SI8** 67

McCarthy, Eugene
Colson on impact of Pentagon Papers publication on **SI7-2** 666
Mitchell authorizes direct mail fund raising for **SI1** 50

McCarthy campaign
supporters on enemies list **SI8** 74, 75, 108, 109

McCausland, Mrs. M.J., report on Beard's illness on United Air Lines flight SI5-2 498, 719, 724

McClellan, George B., questioning by SI2 2, 389-391
Cushman **SI7-2** 860-861
Ehrlichman **SI7-2** 654; **SI7-3** 1231
Haldeman **SI2** 2, 348-349
Jaworski **SI9-2** 839-840
Malloy **SI7-2** 1090-1091

McClory, Robert SUMM I 1
on access of House Judiciary Committee Impeachment Inquiry to materials of legal staff **II 1** 87, 88
on additional subpoenas to Nixon **II 2** 895
additional views on Article of Impeachment III **RHJC** 349-354
on adverse effects of pressure on IRS **II 2** 1301
on alleged delivery of Pentagon Papers to Soviet Embassy **II 2** 1141
announcement of Hutchinson's hospitalization **II 2** 863-864
on brief delivered by St. Clair **II 2** 1189
on calling witnesses before House Judiciary Committee Impeachment Inquiry **II 2** 1155-1156; **II 3** 1622-1623, 1636, 1639-1640, 1655, 1661, 1663-1665, 1669, 1670, 1695, 1703, 1713, 1714
and Caulfield's testimony on stopping IRS audits on Nixon's friends **II 2** 1276
on closing House Judiciary Committee Impeachment Inquiry sessions on evidentiary material **II 1** 546
on confidentiality of discussion on Ehrlichman's note of approval of Fielding break-in **II 2** 1172
on confidentiality of evidence on wiretapping **II 2** 1105-1106
on considering other legislation during House Judiciary Committee Impeachment Inquiry **II 3** 1716-1717
on criteria for excising material from Nixon tapes **II 2** 832
on discrepancies between transcripts of Nixon tapes **II 2** 812-814
and discussion on his amendment on completion date for House Judiciary Committee Impeachment Inquiry **II 1** 14-23
on Doar-St. Clair correspondence **II 1** 171, 175, 183
on Doar's and Jenner's appearance before Sirica **II 1** 164, 166
on domestic surveillance **II 2** 1001

on Ehrlichman implicating Nixon in his call to CIA for aid to Hunt **II 2** 1131

on Fulbright's request for House Judiciary Committee Impeachment Inquiry material on Kissinger's role in 1969-1971 wiretaps **II 3** 1532

on Garrison's statement that Impeachment Inquiry staff is bipartisan **II 3** 2038

on government affidavit stating there had been no electronic surveillance of Ellsberg **II 2** 1191-1192

on hard work of legal staff **II 1** 93

on House Judiciary Committee Impeachment Inquiry issuing subpoenas to Nixon **II 1** 311-312, 323-324, 335-336, 643-645, 647, 657, 663, 664; **II 3** 1533, 1538, 1539, 1549-1550. 1552, 1557-1558, 1561

on House Judiciary Committee Impeachment Inquiry obtaining names of wiretapped White House staff members **II 2** 1004-1005

on House Judiciary Committee Impeachment Inquiry procedures for taking depositions **II 1** 230-231

on House Judiciary Committee Impeachment Inquiry receiving two versions of Ehrlichman's handwritten notes **II 3** 1885-1886

on House Judiciary Committee Impeachment Inquiry using same language used by White House staff members **II 2** 1268

on Hunt's CIA background **II 2** 1125-1126

on impoundment of funds as grounds for impeachment **II 2** 1319

on IRS policy of postponing sensitive inquiries until after elections **II 2** 1288-1290

on IRS practices in previous administrations **II 2** 1286

on Jenner's role as Minority counsel **II 1** 238

on justification for domestic surveillance **II 2** 1109

on leaked Dixon memos **II 2** 1325, 1330

on leaks from House Judiciary Committee Impeachment Inquiry **II 1** 222; **II 2** 705, 1214-1215

on legal aspects of impoundment of funds **II 2** 1309-1310

on legal aspects of SALT leaks **II 2** 1143-1144

on legal questions involved in White House staff members obtaining IRS information **II 2** 1272

on legality or illegality of Hardin's decision to increase milk price supports **II 2** 1080-1081

on legality of IRS investigation of political activities of tax-exempt organizations **II 2** 1256-1257

on making O'Brien and LaRue testimony public **TW 1** 206-207

on materials requested from White House **II 1** 193

on members studying St. Clair's brief prior to official presentation of **II 2** 1215-1216

memo entitled "Dealing With Our Political Enemies" **II 2** 1268

on motivation for domestic surveillance **II 2** 1097

on need for speedy adoption of rules of procedures for House Judiciary Committee Impeachment Inquiry **II 1** 406

on need to verify Nixon tapes **II 2** 853

on Nixon's discussion on Executive privilege with Richardson **II 2** 1341, 1353-1354

on Nixon's income tax **II 3** 1495, 1499, 1518-1519

on Nixon's noncompliance with House Judiciary Committee Impeachment Inquiry subpoenas **II 1** 414-416, 438; **II 2** 903-904, 905, 906, 913, 915, 941, 946-947; **II 3** 1999-2000

on Nussbaum **II 3** 1459-1460

on obtaining materials from Jaworski **II 1** 107-109

on obtaining Nixon's tax returns and audits from IRS **II 2** 1242-1243

on organization and bipartisan nature of House Judiciary Committee Impeachment Inquiry legal staff **II 1** 84

on Pentagon Papers matter **II 2** 1121

on political activities of House Judicary Committee Impeachment Inquiry legal staff members **II 1** 56-57

on power of House Judiciary Committee Impeachment Inquiry **II 1** 85

on presentation procedures for House Judiciary Committee Impeachment Inquiry**II 1** 258-259, 264, 265, 283-286

on procedural rules for handling Impeachment Inquiry material **II 1** 127

on procedure for House Judiciary Committee Impeachment Inquiry interrogation of witnesses **II 3** 1879-1880

on procedures for House Judiciary Committee Impeachment Inquiry **II 1** 2-3, 7

on purpose of Plumbers unit **II 3** 1979

question on efforts made to corroborate Thrower's statement on efforts to meet with Nixon **II 2** 1258-1259

questions connection between IRS audit of Lawrence O'Brien and Watergate break-in **II 2** 1296-1297

questions relevancy of evidence on enemies list **II 2** 1260-1261, 1271

on release of House Judiciary Committee Impeachment Inquiry evidentiary material to public **II 2** 974-975; **II 3** 1583, 1584, 1586, 1587, 1597, 1603

on rules on cross-examination of witnesses **TW 1** 89

on rules of evidentiary procedures for House Judiciary Committee Impeachment Inquiry **II 1** 470-471, 479, 481-482, 514, 516-517, 521, 525, 530, 533-534

and St. Clair's participation in House Judiciary Committee Impeachment Inquiry **II 1** 291, 340-341

on scheduling of presentation of evidence **II 2** 775

on scheduling St. Clair's presentation of evidence **II 3** 1563, 1564, 1565

on separate Minority of House Judiciary Committee Impeachment Inquiry brief on impeachable offenses **II 1** 157

on Sirica's invitation to Doar and Jenner **II 1** 135, 137

on television coverage of House Judiciary Committee Impeachment Inquiry **II 1** 104-105; **II 2** 859-860

on transcripts of Nixon tapes used by St. Clair in his presentation of evidence in behalf of Nixon **II 3** 1723, 1724, 1731

on Waldie's motion on hearing testimony of witnesses in executive session **II 3** 1868-1869, 1875,

McClory, Robert *(Continued)*
1877
on Wiggins' amendment to subpoena Nixon **II 1**
358; **II 2** 951
on wiretapping by prior administrations **II 2** 1090
on witnesses called by House Judiciary Committee
Impeachment Inquiry **II 2** 989, 991-992

McClory, Robert, questioning by
Bittman **TW 2** 66-68, 100
Butterfield **TW 1** 93-94, 118, 119, 120, 121
Colson **TW 3** 451-452
Dean **TW 2** 293-296
Kalmbach **TW 3** 698-701
LaRue **TW 1** 243-244
Mitchell **TW 2** 168-170
O'Brien **TW 1** 142-144
Petersen **TW 3** 124-126

McCloskey, Pete **SI5-1** 431

McCloskey, Robert
daily news conference of May 14, 1970 on Rogers'
admission of air activity over Cambodia prior to
May 1970 **SI11** 37-38, 233-235
declares U.S. recognition and respect for neutrality of Cambodia at daily news conference of
April 16, 1970 **SI11** 31-32, 211-214
denies change in orders in regard to bombing in
Cambodia at daily news conference of March
26, 1970 **SI11** 31, 209-210

McCloskey campaign **SIAPP4** 30, 78
activities in New Hampshire **SIAPP4** 51-52, 57-58
in Political Matters Memoranda **SIAPP4** 2, 6
in talking paper from Strachan to Mitchell
SIAPP4 40, 47

McClure, Harold, Jr. **SIAPP4** 5

McClure, James **SIAPP4** 13

McCman, John D.
requests that Dean retrieve material from Department of Justice **SI2** 2, 66, 671, 672

McCone, John **SI5-1** 381; **SI5-2** 654, 690

McConnell, John P.
statement on need to bomb Cambodia in April
1969 **SI11** 11-14

McCord, James W., Jr. **SIAPP2** 67-70; **TW 3** 259
accounting of expenditure of $76,000 **SI1** 19, 187,
190
Alch and **SI4-1** 517
arrest of **SUMM I** 35; **SI2** 2, 3, 71, 72-74
assigns alias to Baldwin **SI1** 212
Baldwin delivers logs and summaries of tapped
telephones at DNC to **SI1** 23, 223, 224-231
break-in at DNC and wiretapping of Lawrence
O'Brien's and Oliver's telephones by **SI1** 23,
215, 216-222
Caulfield gives Dean letter from **II 2** 758-759
CIA memos on relationship between Hunt and
TW 3 16-18
in CIA memos to Justice Department **TW 3** 61
Colson denies knowing **SI4-1** 155
Executive clemency offers to **II 2** 759; **SI3-1** 42,
487, 488-498; **TW 2** 337
expenditures on Liddy plan **SUMM I** 33
Haldeman's knowledge of link to Watergate
break-in **SUMM I** 41
Hunt and **SI4-1** 357-358

Hunt places his briefcase in safe after Watergate
arrests **SI2** 2, 3, 71
and hush money **SI3-2** 1018
impact of Grand Jury testimony on Hunt **SI7-4**
1862
intelligence activities prior to Democratic National Convention **SI1** 26, 245, 246-253
involvement in Watergate discussed by Haldeman
and Ehrlichman **SI2** 2, 11, 129, 130
LaRue on relationship with **TW 1** 180
letter to Caulfield on danger of blaming CIA for
Watergate **SI3-1** 40, 475, 476-482
letter to Rugaber **SI4-1** 220-221
letter to Sirica **II 2** 834-835; **SIAPP2** 82-86;
SUMM I 81; **SI4-1** 5, 6, 8, 217, 218, 220-225,
235, 236-237, 249, 250, 251-252, 391, 395
letter to Sirica, in Article of Impeachment I
RHJC 102-103
Liddy tells Dean he was involved in Watergate
break-in **NSI1** 40
Liddy uses for Watergate break-in despite agreement not to use CRP employees **SUMM I** 32
Los Angeles Times article on testimony that Dean
and Magruder had prior knowledge of Watergate **SI4-1** 12-13, 311-312, 313-314
money from Liddy for purchasing electronic
equipment **SI1** 19, 187, 188-190
names of CIA employees given to in CIA memo
to FBI **TW 3** 41-46
O'Brien's contacts with his attorney **TW 1** 168
tells Watergate Prosecutors that Dean and Magruder had prior knowledge of Watergate break-
in **II 2** 840
Washington Post on testimony of **SI4-1** 488-489
See also U.S. v. G. Gordon Liddy, et al

McCord, James W., Jr., cited testimony of
on break-in at DNC headquarters and wiretapping
of Lawrence O'Brien's and Oliver's telephones
SI1 23, 215, 216-218
on Caulfield's offers of Executive clemency **SI3-1**
42, 487, 492-496
on conversations with Liddy re prior knowledge
of Mitchell, Colson, Dean, and Magruder of
Watergate bugging operation **SI4-1** 22, 431,
434-443
on duties at CRP **SI2** 2, 75
on his letter to Caulfield on pressures to blame
CIA for Watergate **SI3-1** 40, 475, 478-480
on intelligence activities in preparation for Democratic National Convention **SI1** 26, 245, 250-251
on logs and summaries of monitored telephone
conversations at DNC headquarters **SI1** 24,
223, 229-231
on money from Liddy for purchase of electronic
equipment **SI1** 19, 187, 188-189
on money received from Liddy **SI1** 188-189
on Watergate break-ins **SI7-3** 1198, 1495, 1496-
1498

McCracken, Paul W.
at meeting with President on economy **SI6-1** 384-
385, 386-387
memo from Ehrlichman on antitrust policy review
SI5-1 23, 393, 401
memo from Paarlberg with attachments on dairy
import quotas **NSI3** 7, 69, 70-72

memo from Seevers on milk price supports **SI6-1** 24-25, 359-360, 361-362, 363-364

McDonald, James D.
and construction of block wall at Nixon's San Clemente property **SI12** 152-153
and restoration of "point" gazebo at Nixon's San Clemente property **SI12** 138

McDonald Construction Company SI12 125, 152
and restoration of "point" gazebo at Nixon's San Clemente property **SI12** 139

McGinn, John B. TW 3 44

McGonigle, Paul SIAPP1 79

McGovern, George
Colson on impact of Pentagon Papers publication on **SI7-2** 666
Dean on White House efforts to embarrass **SI7-1** 351-352
Nixon on defeat of **SIAPP3** 86
Nixon-Mitchell-Haldeman discussion of role in Democratic party primaries **SIAPP3** 20
room at Democratic National Convention **SI1** 135

McGovern, George, questioning by Kissinger SI11 279, 317

McGovern campaign
advertising against **SIAPP4** 136
Dean receives list of staff members of **II 2** 1269
Dean's efforts to get IRS action against supporters of **II 2** 1293, 1297-1298; **SI8** 25, 26, 30, 237, 238-271, 273, 274-279, 351, 352-353
and enemies list **SUMM I** 141-142
Haldeman's knowledge of political intelligence-gathering in **SUMM I** 41
instructions to Liddy to transfer "capabilities" from Muskie campaign to **SI1** 20, 191, 192-195
IRS investigation of supporters of, in Article of Impeachment II **RHJC** 143-145
IRS investigation of supporters of, in Minority of House Judiciary Committee Impeachment Inquiry views on Articles of Impeachment **RHJC** 440-441
list of staff members and contributors given by Dean to Walters for IRS audit **SI8** 25, 237, 244-271
in Nixon-Dean discussion on CRP political intelligence-gathering operation **NSI1** 80
Nixon-Dean discussion on wiretapping of **SUMM I** 34
Nixon-Haldeman-Dean discussion on **SI8** 305-307
Nixon-Haldeman discussion on Dean's working through IRS and **SI8** 27, 287, 288-290
Nixon suggests IRS investigation of **SUMM I** 142-143
Plumbers unit activities and **SUMM I** 129
in Political Matters Memoranda **SIAPP4** 128
Segretti's activities against **SI7-3** 1190, 1377, 1378-1390
staff members on enemies list **SI8** 66, 113, 116
supporters on political enemies list, in Jenner's presentation of summary of evidence to House Judiciary Committee Impeachment Inquiry on Nixon's abuse of powers **II 3** 1984-1985
unsuccessful break-in attempts at headquarters of **SI1** 22, 201, 202, 204, 205, 212-213
use of celebrities in **SIAPP4** 121

Woods memo to Haldeman on **SIAPP4** 126

McGraw, Robert II 2 1331

McGrory, Mary
on enemies list **SI8** 75, 109, 119

McHugh, Mrs. Keith SI5-1 467, 469

McIntyre (senator), questioning by
Knight **SI11** 298
Laird **SI11** 159

McKay, Lawrence J. SI7-2 594

McKeithen, R. L. Smith II 2 1249; **II 3** 1457
biography of **II 3** 2150
on Nixon's failure to report certain royalty income **II 3** 1513-1514
on Nixon's gift of Presidential papers **II 3** 1466, 1467, 1470, 1487, 1498, 1501, 1529-1530
on Nixon's gift of Presidential papers and tax legislation **II 3** 2010

McKnight, John G. SI9-2 552, 578, 867, 869-874, 1037, 1038-1044

McLane, Jamie SIAPP4 78

McLaren, Richard W.
and Casey letter to Colson **SI5-2** 664-665, 700-701
Colson memo to Ehrlichman on antitrust policies of **SI5-1** 7, 143, 177
draft complaint against ITT-Canteen merger **SI5-1** 3, 69, 76-87
Ehrlichman memo to Mitchell requesting meeting on ITT antitrust cases with **SI5-1** 192; **SI5-2** 481, 525, 526, 828-829
in Gerrity letter to Agnew **SI5-2** 674, 710, 813, 814-815
in Gerrity memo to Ryan **SI5-2** 671, 707
interviewed by Mitchell and Kleindienst for position with Antitrust Division, Department of Justice **NSI2** 3, 21-24
involvement in antitrust suits against ITT **SI5-1** 91
and Kleindienst application to Supreme Court for extension of time on *ITT-Grinnell* appeal **SI5-1** 16, 349, 350-358
Kleindienst arranges meeting between Rohatyn and **SI5-1** 369
and Kleindienst's knowledge of Flanigan's role in *ITT-Grinnell* case **SI5-2** 758
and Kleindienst's request for extension of time on ITT-Grinnell appeal **NSI2** 7, 65, 66-72
letter from Gerrity to Agnew on antitrust suits against ITT and **SI5-1** 7, 143, 163-165
letter from Rohatyn on settlement of ITT antitrust cases and impact of divestiture of Hartford **SI5-1** 24, 403, 419-422; **NSI2** 9, 81, 96-99
and letter from Walsh on *ITT-Grinnell* appeal **SI5-1** 284, 285
letter to Hullin with memo for Ehrlichman on ITT **SI5-1** 7, 143, 147-152
letter to Stuckey on antitrust policy **SI5-2** 978-980
meeting with ITT counsel **SI5-1** 169-170
meeting with Kleindienst, Rohatyn, and other ITT and Antitrust Division staff members **SI5-1** 24, 403, 404-422
memo concerning negotiations for settlement of ITT antitrust cases **NSI2** 9, 81, 84-87
memo from Hullin on Ehrlichman-Geneen meeting **SI5-1** 7, 143, 168; **SI5-2** 508-509, 803-804, 827

statement of additional views on Report of House Judiciary Committee Impeachment Inquiry **RHJC** 283-286

on transcripts of Nixon tapes used by St. Clair in his presentation of evidence in behalf of Nixon **II 3** 1730, 1732, 1733

on witnesses called by House Judiciary Committee Impeachment Inquiry **II 2** 989-990

Mezvinsky, Edward, questioning by
Bittman **TW 2** 107-109
Butterfield **TW 1** 115
Colson **TW 3** 507-508
Dean **TW 2** 350-352
Kalmbach **TW 3** 736-738
LaRue **TW 1** 270-271
Mitchell **TW 2** 206-208
O'Brien **TW 1** 172-173
Petersen **TW 3** 165-167

Miami, Florida
as proposed site for Republican National Convention **SIAPP3** 11-14, 16, 55-58; **SI5-1** 449, 471

Michel, Robert SIAPP1 19

Michigan
Nixon campaign in **SIAPP4** 25
Nixon-Mitchell-Haldeman discussion on Republican apparatus in **SIAPP3** 29-30

Middle America
Magruder's memo to Attorney General on **SI1** 36

Middlesex, Lord Treasurer SI12 42

Mideast
Nixon on his policies in **SIAPP1** 57

Midwest Regional Republican Conference
McWhorter report on **SIAPP4** 25-26

Military
antiwar activity in, in Huston plan **SI7-1** 392
Black Panther propaganda appeals to black servicemen, Huston plan on **SI7-1** 398
counterintelligence agencies of, and interagency coordination in Huston plan **SI7-1** 430-431
Trotskyist groups and, in Huston plan **SI7-1** 408
use of undercover agents for domestic intelligence, in Huston plan and memo **SI7-1** 425-427, 441, 455

Military Assistance Command in Vietnam (MACV)
Command organizational structure and officials **SI11** 83

Milk fund SI1 100
See also Dairy industry campaign contributions; Milk price-support issue

Milk price-support issue II 2 1046; **II 3** 1744-1814; **NSI3** 4, 35, 36-52; **TW 3** 364-381
Agricultural Act of 1949 on advance announcement of reduction of **SI6-1** 26, 389, 390-391
bills introduced in Congress after Hardin's March 12, 1971 announcement on not raising supports **NSI3** 13, 131, 132-135
Campbell's telephone call to Nelson on conditions for Administration raising milk price supports **NSI3** 23, 163, 164-166
Chotiner denies discussing in connection with campaign contributions of dairy industry **NSI3** 24, 167, 168-173
congressional pressure on Nixon administration for increased supports **NSI3** 11, 123, 124-125

dairy industry lobbying efforts on **II 2** 1063-1065, 1069-1070; **NSI3** 10, 117, 118-121; **SI6-1** 22-23, 329-330, 330-357
decision of March 25, 1971 to raise price supports **II 2** 1078
denials by dairy leaders of quid pro quo between milk price-support increase and campaign contributions **NSI3** 25, 175, 192-197
Department of Agriculture recommendation on **SI6-1** 24-25, 359-360, 361-387
and filing of *Nader* v. *Butz* suit **SI6-2** 485, 877, 878-894
Hardin affidavit on reasons for changing decision on supports **NSI3** 26, 199, 200-217
Hardin's March 12 decision on **SI6-1** 26, 389, 390-399
increase in price supports on March 25, 1971 **SI6-2** 478, 767, 768-781
increase in price supports and reaffirmation of AMPI $2 million pledge to Nixon campaign **SI6-2** 476-477, 727-728, 729-766
and initiation of AMPI contribution **SI6-1** 3-4, 57-58, 67
Jacobsen-Connally meetings on **SI6-1** 424-426, 427-435
letter from Cox to Richardson requesting access to files relating to possible relationship between milk fund and increase in **SI9-1** 41, 481, 482-484
and March 12, 1971 decision by Department of Agriculture **II 2** 1065-1073
and meeting between Alagia and AMPI officials **SI6-2** 710
and meeting between Nixon and dairy representatives on March 23, 1971 **SI6-2** 471, 473, 565, 566-620, 627, 628-671; **II 2** 1073-1075
meeting of White House aides with Campbell and Hardin on March 19, 1971 on **SI6-2** 466, 513, 514-518
meetings and telephone calls between Administration officials and AMPI representatives prior to March 24, 1971 decision **SI6-2** 474, 673, 674-701
memo from Schultz to Ehrlichman on telephone call from Mills on **SI6-1** 22-23, 329-330, 341
Nelson denies discussing campaign contributions with government officials in connection with **NSI3** 51
newspaper articles on connection between AMPI contributions and increase in **SI6-2** 483, 847, 848-861
and Nixon-Connally telephone conversation of March 23, 1971 **SI6-2** 470, 555, 556-563; **NSI3** 15, 139, 140-142
Nixon's abuse of Presidential power and **SUMM I** 149-150
and Nixon's meeting with dairy leaders on March 23, 1970 **NSI3** 17, 151, 152
Nixon's meeting with Hardin, Connally, Ehrlichman, Shultz, Whitaker, Campbell, and Rice on March 23, 1971 on **NSI3** 18-22, 153-161
Nixon's refusal to comply with subpoenas for materials related to **SUMM I** 158-159
pressures on Administration to increase milk price supports after March 12 decision **SI6-1** 27-28, 401-402, 403-462

on factual allegations of Article of Impeachment II **RHJC** 434-477

on historical context of Article of Impeachment II **RHJC** 431-433

on hush money **RHJC** 407-414

on Huston plan **RHJC** 452-456

individual views of Hutchinson in support of **RHJC** 495-502

on Kleindienst confirmation hearings **RHJC** 470-476

on legal considerations in Article of Impeachment II **RHJC** 427-433

on "missing" or incomplete tapes **RHJC** 424-426

on Nixon's relationship with office of the Watergate Special Prosecutor **RHJC** 414-424

on Nixon's violation of "take care" duty **RHJC** 462-467

preliminary statement on legal standards for impeachment **RHJC** 359-381

relationship to Watergate break-in **RHJC** 383-388

on reliance on adverse inferences **RHJC** 374-377

on reliance on hearsay evidence **RHJC** 372-374

signers of partial concurrences with **RHJC** 492-493

on standard of proof for conviction by Senate and impeachment by House **RHJC** 377-381

on subpoena power of House of Representatives in an Impeachment Inquiry **RHJC** 483-491

summary on Article of Impeachment I **RHJC** 360

on tragedy of Nixon's presidency **RHJC** 361

on Watergate break-in and Nixon's policies **RHJC** 383-388

Minority Impeachment Inquiry staff Memorandum on Facts and Law MMFL 121-125

citations **MMFL** 163

on exercise of political judgement in impeachment decision **MMFL** 44-45

on government expenditures on Nixon's property **MMFL** 137-141

on Huston plan and abuse of powers charge against Nixon **MMFL** 117-120

on inferential nature of case against Nixon **MMFL** 41-44

on Kleindienst hearings and abuse of powers charge against Nixon **MMFL** 126-135

on Nixon's gift of Presidential papers **MMFL** 155-161

on Nixon's noncompliance with House Judiciary Committee subpoenas **MMFL** 143-153

on Watergate coverup **MMFL** 47-52

on wiretapping as grounds for impeachment **MMFL** 53-116

Minot, North Dakota News

on March 12 milk price-supports decision **SI6-1** 408

Mississippi v. *Johnson* **RHJC** 304

Mitchell, John N. II 1 298; **II 2** 1089-1090; **II 3** 1626-1627; **SIAPP2** 372-381; **SIAPP4** 77; **SI9-2** 567, 973, 974-975; **SI4-1** 3, 107, 108-211; **SI5-1** 455; **SI7-1** 331

affidavit on documents subpoenaed by SEC with attachments **SI5-2** 495, 645, 646-676, 681, 682-712

alleged telephone call from Haldeman on Hunt's demands for money **II 2** 806-807, 809-810

and Americans for Agnew **SI1** 51

and AMPI contribution **SI6-1** 60, 100, 102

Anderson articles on ITT settlement and **SI5-2** 493, 628, 633-637

and antitrust policy **SI5-2** 660, 696

and antitrust suits against ITT **SUMM I** 145-148; **SI5-1** 91, 140

and appointment of Julie Nixon Eisenhower to youth registration drive **SIAPP4** 63

and approval of LaRue's arrangements for delivery of cash to Hunt **II 2** 815-821; **SI3-2** 715, 1187, 1193-1196, 1235, 1236-1237

and approval of Watergate break-in **SI1** 216, 218

approves revised Liddy plan **SI3-2** 1004

approves wiretapping of government employees **SI7-1** 295-297; **SI7-2** 692

articles linking Segretti to **SI7-4** 1617, 1657, 1658-1659, 1678

attitude toward Executive privilege **TW 2** 276-277

authorization of LaRue's payment to Hunt, in St. Clair's presentation of evidence in behalf of Nixon **II 3** 1754

and authorization of wiretaps on government officials and newsmen in 1969 **SI7-1** 4, 157, 158-172; **SI7-2** 571, 572

authorizes direct mail fund raising for McCarthy **SI1** 50

Beard and **II 2** 1025, 1030

Bittman tells Dean he is aware of his involvement in pre-Watergate electronic surveillance activities **SUMM I** 63

briefed by Mardian and LaRue on their meeting with Liddy **TW 1** 197-198, 261; **SI7-3** 1201, 1523, 1524-1531

Butterfield on meetings between Nixon and **TW 1** 78-80

in Casey letter to Colson **SI5-2** 663, 699

Colson advises Hunt and Liddy to talk to on approval of their plans **TW 3** 249

Colson-Haldeman discussion on his possible responsibility for Watergate break-in **TW 3** 318-319

Colson on his press release after Watergate break-in **TW 3** 506

in Colson-Shapiro recommendations to Ehrlichman **TW 3** 343

in Colson's recommendations on Watergate **SI4-2** 607-608

committments made as condition to Wilson's campaign pledge **SI5-2** 486-487, 561-562, 574

confirms Magruder's authorization of payments to Liddy **SI1** 18, 177, 178-186

Dean discusses Huston plan with **SI7-1** 489, 491

Dean on discussing Hunt's demands with **TW 2** 248, 354-355

Dean on discussions with Ehrlichman and Haldeman on his taking the blame for Watergate **TW 2** 251, 267-268

Dean on Grand Jury appearance of **SI3-2** 1012

Dean on his knowledge of payments to Watergate defendants **SI3-1** 150-151, 152

Dean plays recording of Colson-Hunt conversation for **SI3-1** 34-35, 405-406, 418-419; **II 2** 752; **TW 2** 233

Dean suggests LaRue consult with on Hunt's requests for money **NSI1** 26, 177, 178-185

Mitchell, John N. *(Continued)*

Dean on Watergate coverup and **NSI1** 43

Dean's claim that he discussed Hunt's demands for money with **II 2** 796-797

and Dean's hiring of Liddy **SI3-2** 998

on Dean's indictable list **SI4-2** 704

and Dean's Watergate Grand Jury testimony **SI4-1** 35, 537, 541-542

and delivery of ITT documents by Johnson **SI5-2** 497, 681

denies discussing ITT antitrust cases with Nixon **SI5-2** 493, 494, 503, 631-632, 639-643, 759, 772-775

denies knowledge of Liddy's role in Watergate break-in to FBI **II 2** 735-736

denies Nixon had prior knowledge of Watergate break-in **II 3** 1726

denies reviewing wiretaps on government officials and newsmen **SI7-1** 5, 173, 174-180

denies telling Hoover that FBI records of wiretaps on White House staff members were destroyed **SI7-1** 285

Dent and **SIAPP4** 16-17

in Dent's recommendations for campaign **SIAPP4** 14

in Department of Justice press release on ITT antitrust cases **SI5-2** 492, 631, 632

directs Liddy to meet with Kleindienst after Watergate arrests **SUMM I** 35

discussed by Nixon and Ehrlichman **SI4-2** 913

discusses Dean Report with Nixon, Haldeman, and Ehrlichman **SUMM I** 73-74

discussion with Colson on Hunt's involvement in Watergate **TW 3** 270-271

discussion with Dean on development of political intelligence capability **II 2** 1119; **SI1** 7, 31, 34

in discussion with Haldeman, Ehrlichman, Dean, and Moore on strategy for Ervin Committee hearings **SI3-1** 48, 535, 536-556

in discussion with Nixon, Wilson, and Strickler **SI4-3** 1519-1520, 1521

discussion with O'Brien on arrangements for him to meet with Haldeman **TW 1** 129, 132, 134, 135

discussion with Schorr **SI4-2** 921

discussions of clemency for, in Article of Impeachment I **RHJC** 78-80

discussions with Haldeman on San Diego as possible Republican National Convention site **SI5-1** 427, 428

Ehrlichman informs Kleindienst of his involvement in Watergate **SI4-2** 834

Ehrlichman informs Nixon that Hunt's testimony will lead to indictment of **SUMM I** 74

Ehrlichman reports to Nixon on meeting with **SI4-2** 562, 769, 781-788

Ehrlichman tells Krogh he spoke with on Hunt's blackmail threats **SI7-4** 1632, 1837, 1838-1839

Ehrlichman's discussion of Watergate with **SI4-2** 598, 599, 601-602

and establishment of Plumbers unit **SI7-1** 341-342

evidence for approval of Liddy plan by **SUMM I** 31

FBI interviews on wiretaps on government officials and newsmen in 1969 **SI7-1** 4, 157, 160-165

and FBI reports given to Dean **SI2** 2, 558

and FBI summaries of letters reporting on surveillance of three members of White House staff **SI7-1** 280

and first meeting on Liddy plan **SUMM I** 30; **SI1** 9, 13, 53, 54, 55, 56-57, 58-60, 115, 116-140; **SI3-2** 999

first weekly report of campaign activities submitted to **SIAPP4** 51

and Gemstone files **SI1** 25, 233, 235, 237-238

Geneen and **SI5-1** 133

Haldeman arranges for meeting with **NSI1** 25, 169, 170-176

Haldeman denies discussing fund raising for Watergate defendants with **SI3-2** 712, 1117, 1120-1132

Haldeman denies discussing political intelligence with **SI1** 15, 155

in Haldeman memo to Dean on dealing with Ervin Committee **SI3-1** 47, 527, 528-533, 541

Haldeman tells Nixon he approved Liddy plan **SI4-1** 355-357

Hauser and **SIAPP4** 29

Helms' memo for the record on discussion on Huston plan with **SI7-1** 26, 463, 468

and Honorary Executive Mess Privileges **SIAPP4** 94

House Judiciary Committee Impeachment Inquiry discussion on subpoenaing **II 2** 981-982

House Judiciary Committee transcript of meeting with Nixon, Dean, Ehrlichman, and Haldeman on March 22, 1973 **TPC** 147-186

and Hunt-Liddy meeting with Segretti and Magruder **II 2** 1190

and Hunt's demands for money **SUMM I** 52; **SI3-2** 961

and hush money **II 2** 754-755, 795; **SIAPP1** 49; **SI3-2** 1015-1016; **SI4-3** 1643

and implementation of Liddy plan **SUMM I** 33-34

implication of Haldeman in Segretti matter and **SI7-4** 1916

indictment of **II 2** 1425; **SI9-2** 563, 959, 960-961; **SI2** 2, 20, 203, 214-216; **SI4-3** 1103, 1443, 1450-1452

informed by Dean that he will testify before Grand Jury and will not support Magruder's prior testimony **NSI1** 31, 203, 204

and interference with Senate Select Committee on Presidential Campaign Activities **II 2** 760-767

interviews McLaren for position with Antitrust Division, Department of Justice **NSI2** 3, 21-24

involvement in Watergate coverup **SUMM I** 13

involvement in Watergate discussed by Nixon, Haldeman, and Ehrlichman **SI4-2** 659, 661, 665-696, 825

involvement in Watergate discussed by Nixon, Rogers, Ehrlichman and Haldeman **SI4-3** 1429

involvement in Watergate discussed at Paul O'Brien-Ehrlichman meeting **SI4-1** 32-33, 507-508, 509-729

and ITT matter **II 2** 997-998, 1004-1006, 1015-1017, 1018, 1022, 1026; **SI5-2** 614

in Johnson affidavit **SI5-2** 713, 714, 715

Kalmbach on his relationship with **TW 3** 532-533
in Kalmbach letter to Silbert **SI6-2** 309
Kalmbach on possibility that he initiated Watergate break-in **TW 3** 728
and Kalmbach's handling of milk fund **SI1** 79
and Kalmbach's role in raising money for Watergate defendants **SI4-3** 1444
Kleindienst on **SI4-1** 407, 418
and Kleindienst confirmation hearings **SI5-2** 805, 807, 808-809
Kleindienst informs Nixon the he is indictable **SI4-2** 942
Kleindienst nominated as his successor as Attorney General **SI5-2** 490, 605, 606-612
and Kraft wiretapping **II 2** 1113
LaRue on contacts with **TW 1** 178
LaRue discusses use of Haldeman's $350,000 account for Watergate defendants with **TW 1** 243
LaRue on first meeting on Liddy plan with **TW 1** 180-183
LaRue on his statement after Watergate break-in **TW 1** 188-190, 212-214, 241-242, 261, 261
LaRue informs about Watergate break-in **SUMM I** 35; **TW 1** 186, 233-234
and LaRue's deliveries of hush money to Bittman **TW 1** 229-231, 236-241, 265-275
and LaRue's testimony before Watergate Grand Jury **SUMM I** 93, 95
and LaRue's transfer from White House to CRP **TW 1** 178-180
and Lawrence O'Brien matter **II 2** 1290-1292
letter from Ehrlichman suggesting voluntary nonsuit of Ellsberg prosecution **II 2** 1190
letter from Jaworski to St. Clair requesting taped conversations and documents required for trial of **SI9-2** 565, 965, 966-967
letter from Ruckelshaus on his authorization of wiretaps on government officials and newsmen **SI7-1** 4, 157, 169-170, 171-172, 173, 177-180
letter to Ruckelshaus denying authorization of wiretaps on government officials and newsmen **SI7-1** 4, 157, 166, 167
Liddy plan and **SI4-1** 533-534; **II 1** 564-574
Liddy tells Hunt he ordered Watergate break-in **SI4-2** 597
Liddy tells Kleindienst he is following instructions of **SI2** 2, 112
log for September 17, 1970 **SI7-1** 28, 487, 492
log for November 4 and 24, 1971 **SI7-3** 1118-1119, 1339-1340, 1369-1371
log for March 2, 1972 **SI5-2** 497, 681, 717
log for March 14, 1972 **SI5-2** 503, 759, 775
log for March 18, 1972 **SI5-2** 506, 795, 797
log for March 21-April 4, 1972 **SI5-2** 510, 841, 842-844
log for June 20, 1972 **SI2** 2, 23, 235, 239
log for June 23, 1972 **SI2** 2, 37, 363, 373
log for August 17, 1972 **SI3-1** 24, 297, 306
log for September 13, 1972 **SI3-1** 27, 341, 348
log for November 15, 1972 **SI3-1** 423
logs **SI1** 9, 10, 16, 53, 54, 55, 62-63, 156, 159-160
Magruder says he protected **SI4-2** 624
Magruder's perjury before Watergate Grand Jury and **SUMM I** 44-45
and Magruder's recommendation of Julie Nixon Eisenhower for Honorary Chairman of "Regis-

tration '72" **SI1** 2, 42, 409, 412, 414
Mardian discusses Sullivan's concerns over FBI files and logs of 1969-71 wiretaps with **SI7-2** 784
Mardian on Kleindienst hearings and **SI5-2** 767
Mardian and LaRue brief him on their meeting with Liddy **II 2** 719-720, 1194; **SI2** 2, 27, 277, 280-281, 282, 289-290, 291-296
McCord on instructions for wiretapping of DNC from **SI7-3** 1498
McCord testimony on prior knowledge of Watergate of **SI4-1** 22, 431, 432-443
and meeting between LaRue, Mardian, and Liddy after Watergate break-in **SI7-3** 1200, 1513, 1514-1521
meeting on covering up Liddy plan **II 2** 719-720
meeting with Dean, Magruder, Mardian and LaRue to discuss Watergate break-in **SI2** 2, 21, 223, 224-229
meeting with Dean and Magruder to outline Magruder's false story for Watergate Grand Jury on purpose of money paid to Liddy **SI3-1** 24, 297, 298-309
meeting with Ehrlichman on April 14, 1873 **SI4-2** 561, 717, 718-768
meeting with Geneen **SI5-1** 169
meeting with Haldeman, Ehrlichman, Mitchell, Dean, and Kleindienst to discuss Watergate break-in **SI2** 2, 23-24, 235-236, 237, 238, 239, 240-241, 242
meeting with Haldeman on campaign **SIAPP4** 21
meeting with Haldeman, Ehrlichman, and Dean on March 22, 1973 **SI3-2** 718-719, 1251-1252, 1253-1275
meeting with Haldeman and Ehrlichman on Watergate arrests **SUMM I** 37
meeting with Haldeman and Magruder on Magruder's false testimony on approval of Liddy plan **II 2** 847-848
meeting with Haldeman, Magruder and Strachan on Sandwedge plan **SUMM I** 29-30
and meeting with Haldeman on Sandwedge plan **SUMM I** 29-30
meeting with Helms on Huston plan **SI7-1** 472
meeting with LaRue and Mardian to hear report on their meeting with Liddy **SI3-1** 4, 97, 98-106
meeting with Magruder and Dean to plan Magruder's Watergate Grand Jury testimony **SI3-1** 27, 341, 342-352
meeting with Magruder and LaRue on Watergate arrests **SI2** 7, 105, 108
meeting with Magruder, Mardian, and LaRue after Watergate break-in **TW 1** 186-188
meeting with Magruder, Mardian, LaRue, and Dean on Watergate arrests **SUMM I** 37
meeting with Mardian, LaRue, and Dean on CIA assistance for Watergate defendants **SI3-1** 7, 121, 122-127
meeting with Miller on campaign **SI1** 32-33
meeting with Nixon and Haldeman on April 4, 1972 **NSI1** 13, 85, 86-118; **NSI2** 15, 157, 158-188
meeting with Nixon and Haldeman on Kleindienst confirmation hearings **II 2** 1037, 1038-1040; **SI5-2** 510, 841, 842-847

Mitchell, John N. *(Continued)*

meeting with Nixon and Haldeman on Watergate break-in **SI2** 2, 53, 513, 514-516

meeting with Nixon on *ITT-Grinnell* appeal **SI5-1** 21, 371, 372-376

meetings with Magruder, Haldeman, and Dean on March 28, 1973, on Magruder's testimony on Liddy plan **SI4-1** 19, 373, 374-397

meets with Ehrlichman on Magruder's pending disclosures to Watergate Grand Jury **II 2** 866-867

meets with Magruder on possibility of perjury charges against him **II 2** 842-843

meets with Nixon after Watergate break-in **SUMM I** 7

meets with Nixon and Haldeman to discuss his resignation **SUMM I** 41, 42

meets with Nixon, Haldeman, Ehrlichman, and Dean on Nixon's new plan on Watergate **SUMM I** 86-87

in memo from Colson to Haldeman **SI5-2** 836

memo from Dean on creation of interagency domestic intelligence unit **SI7-1** 28, 487, 493-495

memo from Ehrlichman on antitrust policy review **SI5-1** 23, 393, 401

memo from Ehrlichman on consideration of voluntary non-suit of Ellsberg prosecution **SI7-3** 1196, 1477, 1478-1479

memo from Ehrlichman on *ITT-Grinnell* litigation **SI5-1** 9, 189, 192

memo from Ehrlichman requesting meeting with McLaren about ITT antitrust cases **SI5-2** 481, 525, 526, 828-829

memo from FBI Director on results of surveillance of newsmen **SI7-1** 11, 249, 257

memo from Hoover on Haig's requests for wiretaps **SI7-1** 7, 10, 191, 192-197, 239, 240-242, 267, 292-293

memo from Hoover on Haldeman's request for wiretapping National Security Council staff member **SI7-1** 7, 191, 199

memo from Hoover on Haldeman's request for wiretaps on White House staff member **SI7-1** 268

memo from Hullin with memos and correspondence on antitrust suits against ITT **SI5-1** 7, 143, 178

memo from Magruder on Republican National Convention site and Republican National Committee Denver meeting **SI5-2** 486-487, 561-562, 582-587

memo from Magruder on Segretti **SI1** 166

memo from Magruder and Timmons on selection of San Diego as site for Republican National Convention **SI5-1** 25-26, 423-424, 466-475; **SI5-2** 486, 561, 568; **NSI** 12, 127, 136-144

memo from McLaren on ITT acquisition of Grinnell Corporation **SI5-1** 3, 4, 69, 94-101, 120-129

memo from McLaren on ITT acquisition of Hartford Fire Insurance Company **SI5-1** 4, 101, 106-119

memo from McLaren on preliminary injunction re ITT acquisition of Canteen Corporation **SI5-1** 3, 69, 94-100

in memo from Strachan to Haldeman **SI1** 32-33

memo to Ehrlichman advising against Nixon meeting Geneen and attaching Geneen's letter to Stans **NSI2** 5, 25, 43

memo to Haldeman and Mitchell on "Matter of potential embarrassment" **II 2** 1190

memos from Ehrlichman on antitrust suits against ITT **SI5-2** 508-509, 525, 526, 803-804, 828, 829

memos from Hoover on Haig's request for wiretapping of government employees after leaks on Cambodia bombing **SI7-1** 295-297

Moore on meetings with during Kleindienst hearings **SI5-2** 761-762

and Mudge, Rose, Guthrie, and Alexander **SI1** 36

name eliminated from Chapin's report to Ehrlichman on White House involvement with Segretti **SI7-4** 1619, 1681, 1692-1696

named by Magruder as participant in wiretapping plans against Democrats **SI4-2** 564, 799, 800-809

New York Times on Dean's testimony on his involvement in Watergate coverup **SI9-1** 18, 313, 316

Nixon on **SI4-3** 1529-1530

Nixon attempts to blame Executive clemency offers to Hunt on **SUMM I** 67-68

Nixon on attitude toward Watergate investigation of **SIAPP1** 45

Nixon-Colson discussion on his possible role in Watergate break-in **TW 3** 317-318, 320, 331

in Nixon-Dean discussion on CRP political intelligence-gathering operation **NSI1** 79

Nixon-Dean discussion of Executive clemency and **SI4-3** 1182-1183

Nixon-Dean discussion of his role in Watergate **SI3-1** 686-687

in Nixon-Dean discussion of Segretti matter **SI8** 421-422

Nixon-Dean discussion on role in raising money for Watergate defendants **SI3-2** 1026-1027, 1070-1071, 1083-1084

Nixon-Dean-Haldeman discussion on forthcoming testimony of **SI8** 405-408

in Nixon-Dean-Haldeman discussion of Patman Committee hearings **SI8** 323-324

Nixon discusses probable not guilty plea of **SI4-2** 971

Nixon discusses with Wilson and Strickler **SI4-3** 1515

Nixon-Ehrlichman discussion on blaming him for Watergate **SUMM I** 74-77

Nixon-Ehrlichman discussion of testimony of **SI4-1** 368

Nixon-Ehrlichman telephone conversation on forthcoming Watergate Grand Jury testimony of **SI4-1** 36, 543, 544-545

in Nixon-Haldeman discussion on Watergate **SIAPP3** 44-45

Nixon-Haldeman-Ehrlichman discussion of forthcoming Watergate Grand Jury testimony of **SI4-2** 674-680

Nixon on his silence on Watergate **SIAPP 1** 45

Nixon instructs Ehrlichman to tell him to go before Grand Jury **NSI1** 32, 207, 208-210

Nixon learns that Magruder may implicate in Watergate **SUMM I** 6-7

Nixon-Petersen discussion on Watergate involvement of **SI4-3** 1407

Nixon on reasons why he did not ask him about Watergate **SIAPP1** 67

Nixon says he will testify at Select Committee hearings **SIAPP1** 10

Nixon states he employed law firm to investigate Watergate **SIAPP1** 3

Nixon wants meeting between Dean, Haldeman, Ehrlichman and **NSI1** 24, 165, 166-167

and Nixon's approval of political-intelligence plan including electronic surveillance **SUMM I** 29-32

and Nixon's assurances of leniency prior to his talks with Watergate Prosecutors **SUMM I** 66-67

Nixon's involvement in misleading explanation for resignation of **SUMM I** 47

Nixon's letter accepting resignation as Attorney General **SI5-2** 490, 605, 608

and Nixon's possible lack of knowledge of Watergate coverup, in Minority of House Judiciary Committee Impeachment Inquiry views on Articles of Impeachment **RHJC** 392

in Nixon's press statement of June 22, 1972 **SI2** 2, 35, 351, 352-353

Nixon's questions for Kleindienst on possible involvement in Watergate of **SI4-1** 401

and Operation Sandwedge proposal **SI7-3** 1188-1189, 1339-1340,1372-1376

opposes Huston plan **SUMM I** 126; **SI7-1** 26, 463, 464-468

opposes use of Caulfield for infiltration plan **SI3-2** 997

and Pentagon Papers matter **II 2** 1120-1123

Petersen informs Nixon of approval of Liddy plan and Gemstone plan by **SUMM I** 90

Petersen report to Nixon on LaRue Watergate Grand Jury testimony on **SI4-3** 1298-1299

in Petersen's notes **SI4-2** 1001-1002

plan to resign as Attorney General and run campaign from office space at Mudge, Rose, Guthrie, and Alexander **SIAPP4** 31, 47-48

political intelligence and **SIAPP4** 18

and political intelligence-gathering on Democratic party candidates **TW 3** 255-256

in Political Matters Memoranda **SIAPP4** 4, 6

Political Matters Memoranda on meeting with Haldeman with "talking paper" for **SIAPP4** 23, 32-38

possible testimony of, discussed by Nixon and Dean **SI3-2** 701, 803, 853

and preparation of Magruder's testimony before Watergate Grand Jury **II 2** 748-749

in press coverage of ITT case **SI5-2** 847, 856-860

press policy at CRP **SIAPP4** 13

press statement denying CRP involvement in Watergate break-in **II 1** 615; **SI2** 2, 29, 301, 302-303; **SUMM I** 35

prior association with Nixon **RHJC** 12

quoted in *Washington Post* article on Watergate break-in **TW 1** 191-193

reaction to Watergate arrests **SI2** 7, 105, 109

and recall of Nixon's decision memo approving recommendations of Huston plan **SI7-1** 27, 469, 470-485

receives reports on surveillance of Democratic National Committee headquarters **SUMM I** 33

as recipient of political enemies project memos **SI8** 21, 211, 212

relationship with Liddy's intelligence plan discussed by Dean and Nixon **SI3-2** 701, 803, 865-867

relationship with Nixon **SUMM I** 29-30

and Republican National Convention of 1972 **SIAPP4** 13

request for FBI's views on type of surveillance to be used on Kraft **SI7-1** 19, 355, 356-357

requests for wiretaps **SI7-1** 10, 239, 243-244

resignation as Attorney General **SI5-2** 612

resignation as CRP director **SI2** 2, 515-516

resignation as CRP director, in Article of Impeachment I **RHJC** 50-54; **SUMM I** 27

role in campaign finances **SIAPP4** 16

role at CRP **II 1** 558

role in Nixon Administration **RHJC** 16-17

role in Nixon re-election campaign **SIAPP4** 20-21, 29-30

role in Watergate matter discussed by Haldeman, Ehrlichman and Dean **SI3-2** 1141, 1142, 1144, 1145

and Sandwedge plan **SIAPP4** 11; **SI1** 41, 42

at second meeting on Liddy plan **NSI1** 9, 63, 64-65; **SUMM I** 31; **SI1** 10, 53, 62, 63, 64-65, 66, 67-68, 69-75

Segretti's activities and **SI7-3** 1197, 1481, 1482-1494

and Semer's contact with Kalmbach **SI6-1** 63, 80

and settlement of ITT antitrust cases **NSI2** 10-11, 103-104, 105-126

and signing of authorizations for domestic surveillance **II 2** 1094-1095

as spokesperson for CRP on Watergate break-in **SIAPP1** 2

Strachan on approval of Liddy plan by **NSI1** 82

Strachan's talking paper for Haldeman's meeting with **SI1** 14, 147, 152, 153

subpoena to Nixon for specified materials related to conversations with **SI9-2** 573, 1009, 1010-1013

in taped Higby-Magruder telephone conversation **SI4-2** 617-618, 629-630, 641-642

telephone conversation with Dean on Hunt's demands **SI3-2** 957-959

telephone conversation with DeLoach on White House staff wiretapping **SI7-1** 269-270

telephone conversation with Nixon on June 20, 1972 **SIAPP1** 63; **SI9-2** 547, 835, 836

telephone conversation with Nixon on Watergate break-in **SI2** 2, 30, 305, 306-310

telephones Nixon on meeting with Magruder **SI4-1** 365

tells Dean, Ehrlichman, and Haldeman that Hunt is no longer a problem **II 2** 824-825

tells FBI he has no knowledge about Watergate break-in **SI3-1** 15, 203, 204-206

testifies before Watergate Grand Jury that he had no prior knowledge of CRP's or Liddy's illegal intelligence operations **SI3-1** 26, 353, 354-356; **II 2** 750

and Thrower's efforts to discuss resignation as Commissioner of Internal Revenue with Nixon

Mitchell, John N. *(Continued)*
SI8 63-64
and transfer of ITT files from SEC SI5-2 914, 917-918
and *Vesco* case SI3-2 976; SI4-2 683-684; SI4-3 1649
White House edited transcript of meeting with Nixon and Haldeman of April 4, 1972 SIAPP3 3-34
at White House meeting on investigation of Ellsberg matter NSI4 16, 121, 122-123
and White House subsidiary account SI1 47
and wiretapping of government officials and newsmen in 1969 SUMM I 124; SI7-1 153
and wiretapping of Kraft SI7-1 324
and wiretapping of White House staff members unrelated to national security SI7-1 261, 272-273
and wiretaps of White House staff members and newsmen SI7-1 271; SI7-4 1751
See also Halperin v. *Kissinger*; House Judiciary Committee Impeachment Inquiry, discussion on calling witnesses; House Judiciary Committee Impeachment Inquiry, presentation of evidence on domestic surveillance; Nixon tapes; Political Matters Memoranda; *U.S.* v. *Howard Edwin Reinecke*; *U.S.* v. *John N. Mitchell, et al.*; *U.S.* v. *Mitchell*

Mitchell, John N., cited testimony of SI2 2, 7, 27, 105, 113, 277, 291-296
on antitrust suits against ITT SI5-1 3, 69, 92-93
on approval of Liddy plan SI1 13, 115, 122-125
on contacts with ITT representatives SI5-1 7-8, 143-144, 179-184
on Dean playing tape recorded Colson-Hunt conversation for him SI3-1 34-35, 405-406, 421-422
denies discussing ITT litigation with Nixon SI5-2 503, 759, 772-774
on discussion with LaRue on Hunt's requests for money NSI1 26, 177, 183-184
in Doar's presentation of evidentiary material to House Judiciary Committee Impeachment Inquiry II 1 592
on final settlement of ITT antitrust cases NSI2 10, 103, 123
on first meeting on Liddy plan SI1 9, 53, 58
on Haldeman's political relationship with Nixon SUMM I 26
on hearing Liddy's report from Mardian and La-Rue SI7-3 1201, 1523, 1526-1531
on his opposition to Huston plan SI7-1 26, 27, 463, 464-467, 469, 475-477
on meeting of June 19, 1972 with Dean, Magruder, Mardian, and LaRue to discuss Watergate break-in SI2 2, 21, 223, 224
on meeting with Ehrlichman on April 14, 1873 SI4-2 561, 717, 722-723
on meeting with Haldeman, Ehrlichman, and Dean on March 22, 1973 SI3-2 719, 1252, 1275
on meeting with LaRue and Mardian to hear report on their meeting with Liddy SI3-1 4, 97, 101-106
on meeting with LaRue, Mardian, and Dean on possibility of CIA aid for Watergate defendants SI3-1 7, 121, 125, 126-127

on meeting with Magruder and Dean on Magruder's forthcoming Watergate Grand Jury testimony SI3-1 24, 27, 297, 302-305, 341, 345
on meeting with Magruder, Haldeman, and Dean on Liddy plan approval SI4-1 19, 373, 389-391
on meeting with Magruder on March 27, 1973 SI4-1 17, 339, 344-345
on meeting with Moore on strategy for Ervin Committee hearings SI3-1 48, 535, 554-556
on Mexican checks SI2 2, 37, 363, 364
on money delivered to Bittman for Hunt SI3-2 715, 1187, 1236-1237
on Nixon's decision-making methods SUMM I 28
on Operation Sandwedge proposal SI7-3 1118-1119, 1339-1340, 1368
on reasons for denying knowledge of Watergate break-in during FBI interview after briefing by LaRue and Mardian SI3-1 15, 203, 204-206
on reasons for formation of Intelligence Evaluation Committee SI7-1 29, 497, 505
on second meeting on Liddy plan SI1 10, 53, 67-68
on Sloan's payments to Liddy SI1 18, 177, 184-186
states that he believes Nixon had no knowledge of Watergate break-in or Watergate coverup NSI1 8, 57, 58
on wiretaps on government officials and newsmen in 1969 SI7-1 5, 173, 174-175

Mitchell, John N., testimony before House Judiciary Committee Impeachment Inquiry TW 2 113-217
on access to Nixon TW 2 189-190
on actions after learning about Watergate break-in TW 2 146-154, 155, 159, 166-167, 171-172
on arrangements with LaRue for use of Haldeman's $350,000 fund for payments to Hunt TW 2 128-132, 133-134, 161-164, 167-168, 171, 195
on arranging meeting between O'Brien and Haldeman TW 2 139-140
campaign log submitted to House Judiciary Committee Impeachment Inquiry TW 2 181-184
on concern over Watergate break-in TW 2 159
on contacts with Nixon after his re-election in 1972 TW 2 126-128
on conversation with Nixon on June 20, 1972 TW 2 210-211
on CRP hiring Liddy TW 2 125-126
on Dean playing recorded Hunt-Colson conversation for TW 2 134-135
on decision not to have scheduled meeting with Nixon after meeting with Ehrlichman on April 14, 1973 TW 2 141-142, 187
denies discussing Liddy plan with Nixon TW 2 160-161, 170
denies informing Nixon of payments to Hunt TW 2 132, 180-181
denies Nixon had any knowledge of payments to Watergate defendants TW 2 208-209
denies pressures to plead guilty TW 2 203, 212-213
denies recollecting conversation with Dean of March 20, 1973 on money for Watergate defendants TW 2 177
denies recollection of calls made to White House on March 21, 1973 from New York TW 2 210-211

denies recommending withholding of information from investigative bodies **TW 2** 216-217
on discrepancies between transcripts of Nixon tapes **TW 2** 213-214
on discussing leaks with Kissinger **TW 2** 205
on discussion of Watergate break-in with Ehrlichman **TW 2** 217
on Fielding break-in **TW 2** 193
on first knowledge of provision of money to Watergate defendants **TW 2** 185-187, 192, 213
on Haldeman's role at White House **TW 2** 209-210
on Haldeman's role in Nixon's re-election campaign **TW 2** 202-203
on his professional background **TW 2** 124-125
on his reaction to Liddy plan **TW 2** 188
and House Judiciary Committee Impeachment Inquiry discussion on Hundley's statement on limitation of his testimony **TW 2** 113-124
Hundley's objections to line of questioning of **TW 2** 143-146, 152, 154-155, 155-159, 160, 168
on information kept from Nixon **TW 2** 190
on lack of acquaintainship with Hunt **TW 2** 192-193
on learning about Kalmbach's role in fundraising for Watergate defendants **TW 2** 188
on learning about Watergate break-in from Magruder **TW 2** 187, 194
on maintaining logs of telephone calls and records of appointments **TW 2** 126-127, 172-173, 176
on meeting between O'Brien and Ehrlichman **TW 2** 188-189
on meeting with Mardian and LaRue on June 22, 1973 **TW 2** 176-177
on meetings and telephone conversations of March 20 and 21, 1973 **TW 2** 138-140
on meetings with White House staff members during March and April 1973 **TW 2** 140-141, 142-143
on Moore's request that he help raise money for Watergate defendants **TW 2** 135
on Nixon tape of discussion of his resignation as director of CRP **TW 2** 136, 137-138, 168-170
on Nixon's attitude toward Dean **TW 2** 190
on Nixon's attitude toward his pleading guilty **TW 2** 200-201
on Nixon's role in decision making **TW 2** 191, 202
on possibilities of McGovern winning in 1972 **TW 2** 209
on press release after learning about Watergate break-in **TW 2** 149-152, 204-205
on purpose of $350,000 White House fund **TW 2** 214
on reasons for keeping information from Nixon **TW 2** 206-208, 215-216
on relationship with Nixon **TW 2** 189-190, 192
on resignation as director of CRP **TW 2** 135-136, 137-138, 173-175, 203
on taped conversations with Nixon and others on payments to Watergate defendants **TW 2** 177-181
on telephone conversation with Nixon on Watergate break-in **TW 2** 165
on White House horrors **TW 2** 132-133

on wiretaps in 1968-1971 **TW 2** 196, 198-199, 205-206
Mitchell, Martha (Mrs. John N. Mitchell) SIAPP4 6; **SI1** 118, 138; **SI4-2** 787; **SI5-1** 180
campaign activities **SIAPP4** 77
Dean on **TW 2** 355
at GOP fund raising appearance in South Carolina **SI1** 34
Kalmbach on incident involving Watergate break-in **SI6-1** 310
LaRue on decision not to disclose CRP involvement in Watergate break-in to **TW 1** 195, 210-211
Mitchell claims he resigned as director of CRP because of problems with **TW 2** 136, 137-138, 168-170
in Nixon-Haldeman-Mitchell discussion on Watergate **SI2** 2, 515-516
in Political Matters Memoranda **SIAPP4** 13
role in Nixon re-election campaign **SIAPP4** 18, 59
statements on White House putting blame on Mitchell **TW 2** 212
upset over meetings in Key Biscayne **SI1** 131
Mitchell, Michael
affidavit on SEC efforts to obtain ITT files **II 2** 1026-1028; **SI5-2** 514, 864, 869-899
Johnson on receiving ITT documents from **SI5-2** 497, 681, 713-716
Mittler, Austin TW 2 61
Bittman and **TW 2** 6, 43
See also Hogan & Hartson
Mollenhoff, Clark SIAPP1 73
accused of leaking information on IRS investigation of Gerald and George Wallace **II 2** 1254
affidavit on obtaining IRS reports on Wallace investigation for Haldeman **SI8** 3, 35, 38-39
and IRS investigation of George and Gerald Wallace **II 3** 1983-1984
Latta on **II 2** 1255
meeting with Haldeman, Ehrlichman, and Ziegler on leaked IRS information on Wallace administration **SI8** 39
memo to Haldeman transmitting IRS information on Gerald Wallace **II 2** 1251-1255; **SI8** 3, 35, 36
Nixon and Dean on **SI3-2** 844-845
in Nixon-Dean-Haldeman discussion **SI8** 399-400
Nixon informs that his statement on Executive privilege will be available shortly **SIAPP1** 5
obtains IRS investigation of George and Gerald Wallace **SUMM I** 141
at Richardson press conference **SI4-3** 1653
in Thrower affidavit on leaked IRS information on Wallace administration given to White House **SI8** 39
and White House obtaining IRS information **II 2** 1273
Montez (caretaker at Nixon's San Clemente property) SI12 116
Montoya, Joseph M., questioning by
Dean **SI3-2** 1144
Ehrlichman **NSI1** 7, 53, 55; **SI3-1** 398; **SI4-1** 534-535, 551; **SI4-2** 801-802, 895-897, 1068; **SI7-4** 1702; **SI8** 101-102

Montoya, Joseph M., questioning by *(Continued)*
Haldeman **SI9-1** 439; **SI7-2** 1120-1121; **SI7-4** 1678-1680; **SI8** 127-129
Harrison **SI6-1** 225
Hunt **SI1** 249
Kleindienst **SI4-3** 1624
LaRue **SI2** 2, 282-283
Magruder **NSI1** 71
McCord **SI1** 230, 250-251
Mitchell **SI1** 58
Reisner **SI1** 241
Mooney, Thomas E. **SUMM I** 1
Moore, Arch **SIAPP4** 89; **SI1** 86
Moore, Carruthers **SIAPP4** 128
Moore, John **SIAPP4** 118
Moore, Powell
Magruder and **SI2** 2, 126
meeting with Liddy and Kleindienst on Watergate arrests **SI2** 2, 7, 104, 105, 110-112
Moore, Richard Anthony **SUMM I** 91; **SI3-2** 1063; **SI4-3** 1258
advice to Dean **TW 2** 238, 246, 248-249
asks Mitchell to help raise money for Watergate defendants **TW 2** 135
conversation with Dean on Hunt's demands **SI3-2** 709, 965, 966-968
Dean and **SI3-2** 878
Dean consults with on Camp David report **SI4-1** 272-273, 279
denies Nixon had prior knowledge of Watergate break-in **II 3** 1726-1727
discussion with Dean on Sullivan's possible testimony on FBI **SI3-2** 841, 842, 843
discussion with Nixon on Ehrlichman's possible criminal liability in regard to Ellsberg case **SI7-4** 1644, 1967, 1968-1974; **II 2** 1232
draft memo on Segretti matter from Dean and **SI7-4** 1628, 1775, 1797-1810
and FBI reports given to Dean **SI2** 2, 558
knowledge of Hunt's demands for money **SUMM I** 54
meeting with Nixon and Dean on March 20, 1973 **SI3-2** 709, 965, 976
meetings with Haldeman, Ehrlichman, and Dean to discuss strategy for Ervin Committee hearings **SI3-1** 48, 535, 536-556
and newspaper stories on Segretti's activities **SI7-4** 1617, 1657, 1658-1675
Nixon informs Haldeman of his discussion with **SI4-2** 968
and White House task force on Kleindienst hearings **SI5-2** 503, 759, 761-762
Moore, Richard Anthony, cited testimony of **SI3-2** 709, 965, 966-967
on Dean's list of indictable White House personnel **SI4-2** 559, 697, 703-706
on discussion with Nixon on Ehrlichman's possible criminal liability **SI7-4** 2644, 2967, 2972-1974
on meeting with Dean and Nixon on March 14 on Executive privilege for Dean **SI3-2** 894
on meeting at White House after newspaper disclosures on Segretti's activities **SI7-4** 1617, 1657, 1664-1671

on meetings with Haldeman, Ehrlichman, and Dean to discuss strategy for Ervin Committee hearings **SI3-1** 48, 535, 551-553
on preparation of report for Nixon on Segretti matter **SI7-4** 1628, 1775, 1794-1796
on role as White House liaison for Kleindienst hearings **SI5-2** 503, 759, 761-762
states he believes Nixon had no knowledge of Watergate break-in or Watergate coverup **NSI1** 8, 57, 59-61
Moorer, Thomas H. **SI11** 4, 133; **SI7-3** 1424
Freidheim blames for false documentary submission to Congress on Cambodian bombings **SI11** 75, 372-373
speech of March 1, 1971 on U.S. "air, sea, and logistic support supplied by U.S. forces" to South Vietnamese in Cambodia **SI11** 49, 268
statement claiming Members of Congress were briefed on MENU operations **SI11** 61-62, 315-316
statement on decision to withdraw substantial U.S. forces from South Vietnam related to Cambodian bombings **SI11** 52, 273-274
statement on origins of MENU reporting procedures **SI11** 56, 293
statement on purpose of MENU dual reporting system **SI11** 59, 305
statement on reasons for bombing of Cambodia **SI11** 54,281-282
statement on reasons for "double reporting" system on bombings of Cambodia and Sihanouk's attitude toward bombings **SI11** 53-54, 277-278
supplies information on bombing of Cambodia indicating no air strikes prior to May 1970 **SI11** 23, 180-181
Moorhead, Carlos J. **RHJC** 359-493; **SUMM I** 1
additional views on Article of Impeachment III **RHJC** 503-505
on calling witnesses before House Judiciary Committee Impeachment Inquiry **II 3** 1654
on issuing subpoenas to Nixon **II 1** 320
on mail on impeachment **II 1** 76
on Nixon's noncompliance with House Judiciary Committee Impeachment Inquiry subpoenas **II 1** 434
on St. Clair's participation in House Judiciary Committee Impeachment Inquiry **II 1** 239
on Waldie's motion on hearing testimony of witnesses in executive session **II 3** 1872
See also Minority of House Judiciary Committee Impeachment Inquiry views on Articles of Impeachment
Moorhead, Carlos J., questioning by
Bittman **TW 2** 99
Butterfield **TW 1** 112
Colson **TW 3** 488-489, 490
LaRue **TW 1** 265-266
O'Brien **TW 1** 167
Petersen **TW 3** 157-159
Morehead (FBI agent) **SI7-2** 975
Morgan, Ben F., Jr. **SI6-2** 721
and loan from SPACE to ADEPT **SI6-2** 708-709, 710

Morgan, Edward L.
and Alexander's letter to Jaworski referring IRS
investigation of Nixon's tax returns to Grand
Jury **SI10** 403-404
assigned by Ehrlichman to look into desirability
of Nixon contribution of pre-Presidential papers
SI10 40
and discrepancy over date of 1969 deed for contribution of Nixon's pre-Presidential papers **SI10**
6-7, 101-135
and discussions with Nixon on future gifts of pre-
Presidential papers in 1969 **SI10** 4, 67-71
does not recollect signing deed of gift for Nixon's
papers on April 10, 1970 but admits signature is
his **SI10** 14, 325-326
does not remember conversation with DeMarco
about receipts for Nixon's pre-Presidential papers in April 1969 **SI10** 7, 136-137, 138, 139
Ehrlichman's questions on Nixon's 1969 income
tax sent to **SI10** 8-9, 177-183
investigated by Intelligence Division of IRS on
Nixon's 1969 income tax return **SI10** 18-19,
376-394
letter to Reed on organizing and inventorying of
Nixon's pre-Presidential papers **SI10** 80
meets with Stuart and Archives officials on Nixon's pre-Presidential and Presidential papers on
March 11, 1969 **SI10** 4-5, 77-78, 79-80
memo from Barth answering Ehrlichman's questions on Nixon's 1969 income tax **SI10** 9, 180-
183, 429-432
in memo from Ehrlichman to Kalmbach on Nixon's income tax returns **SI10** 428
memo from Ehrlichman on Nixon's 1969 income
taxes **SI10** 433-434
memo to Parker on execution of deed of gift of
Nixon's papers on April 21, 1969 without mention of re-execution **SI10** 15, 332-335
and Newman's appraisal of Nixon's pre-Presidential papers in November 1969 **SI10** 9, 184-196
and Nixon's gift of Presidential papers **SUMM I**
173, 175, 176
notified of relocation of Nixon's papers to National Archives and signs "limited right to access"
for Newman **SI10** 5, 87-90
in Presidential party on Nixon's trip to Europe in
1969 **SI10** 4, 74, 75-76
"re-executes" deed of gift of Nixon's papers for
1969 for DeMarco **SI10** 14, 319-322
role in Nixon Administration **RHJC** 16
role on White House staff **II 1** 558
and selection of pre-Presidential papers for Nixon's gift to National Archives **SI10** 2-3, 59, 60-
61
statement prepared for White House in August
1973 on gifts of Presidential papers **SI10** 14,
323-324
Morgan, Robert SI1 95
**Morris, Dwight, cited testimony on Parr's telephone
call from White House SI6-1** 27, 401, 414
Morton, Gary, tax information on SI8 157
Morton, Thurston SIAPP4 83; **SI1** 80, 85

Moscow
timing of ITT matter and Nixon's trip to **NSI2**
17, 203, 207-208
Moser, John SI6-2 721
Mosher for Congress Committee SIAPP2 332
Mote, Thomas SI4-3 1614
**Motion Picture Association, complaint on television
networks SI5-1** 157
Mott, Stewart Rawlings, on enemies list SI8 75, 109
Movie industry
Nixon re-election campaign and **SIAPP4** 53
Mudge, Rose, Guthrie, and Alexander SIAPP4 31;
SI10 37; **SI1** 36; **SI5-2** 918
Magruder's offices at **SIAPP4** 51
Nixon's and Mitchell's association with **II 2** 997
selection of pre-Presidential papers for Nixon's
gift to National Archives in offices of **SI10** 2-3,
59, 60-61
See also Tannian, Pat
Mueller, Jim SI6-2 711
Muggings
in Liddy plan **SI1** 57
Muhammed, Elijah, in Huston plan SI7-1 399
Mulcahy, John A. SIAPP4 118
and milk producers' contributions **SI6-1** 318
Mullen & Co.
Hunt's employment with **TW 2** 21, 35-37, 100
Munro, S. Sterling, Jr., on enemies list SI8 74, 108
Murfin, William SIAPP4 70, 76
Murphy, Michael II 2 806
Murphy, Robert Paul II 1 587
biography of **II 3** 2150
Murray, Hyde II 2 1066-1067; **SI6-1** 371
recommendations on maintaining status quo on
dairy price supports **SI6-1** 22-23, 329-330, 348,
349
Murray, John SI7-3 1384
Muskie, Edmund S. SIAPP3 265
Dean on White House efforts to embarrass **SI7-1**
351-352
and Greenspun break-in **SI1** 65
Haldeman on letters defaming **SI7-2** 578
Halperin and **SI7-1** 330
Nixon-Mitchell-Haldeman discussion of likelihood
of candidacy in 1972 of **SIAPP3** 20-21, 32
Segretti's activities against **SI7-3** 1485
on wiretapping of National Security Council
members **SI7-1** 8, 201, 202-211
See also Muskie campaign
Muskie, Edmund S., questioning by
Kissinger **SI7-1** 231, 305
Muskie, Mrs. Edmund
Segretti's activities against **SI7-3** 1483
Muskie campaign
CRP political intelligence-gathering and **NSI1** 74
fundraising by Semer for **II 2** 1052
illegal contributions to **SIAPP2** 253-256
instructions to Liddy to transfer "capabilities" to
McGovern campaign instead of **SI1** 20, 191,
192-195
letter drafted on stationery from **SI7-3** 1190,
1377, 1384

Muskie campaign *(Continued)*
    Magruder-Colson dispute over **SIAPP4** 92; **SI1** 89
    in Nixon-Dean discussion on CRP political intelligence-gathering operation **NSI1** 80
    Nixon-Dean discussion on plant in **SUMM I** 34
    plant in **SIAPP4** 28
    in Political Matters Memoranda **SIAPP4** 6, 9, 13, 20, 79
    Segretti's activities against **SI7-3** 1190, 1377, 1378-1390; **II 2** 1184
    Segretti's activities against in Chapin memo to Ehrlichman **SI7-4** 1688-1689
    Strachan memo to Dean on "fat cats" attending weekend in Kennebunkport for **SI8** 120
    talking paper from Strachan to Mitchell on **SIAPP4** 41-42
    trial heats against Nixon in Delaware **SIAPP4** 9-10
    wiretapping of, in Article of Impeachment II **RHJC** 147
Myers, Hank SIAPP3 11
Nader, Ralph SI6-2 915
    See also Nader v. *Butz*
Nader v. *Butz* **SI9-1** 40, 475, 476-480
    Chotiner deposition on discussions with dairy leaders **NSI3** 24, 167, 168-173
    depositions from dairy leaders denying quid pro quo between milk price-support increase and campaign contributions **NSI3** 25, 175, 192-197
    filing of **SI6-2** 485, 877, 878-894
    Hardin's affidavit on reasons for changing decision on milk price supports **NSI3** 26, 199, 200-217
    Hillings' deposition on letter to Nixon on dairy imports **NSI3** 8, 75, 96-106
    Kalmbach's deposition denying knowledge of any relationship between campaign contributions and governmental actions affecting dairy industry **NSI3** 25, 175, 176-191
    Nelson's deposition on first meeting with Nixon **NSI3** 4, 35, 47-52
    Nelson's deposition on Nixon's invitation to dairy leaders to meet with him **NSI3** 33-34
    Parr's deposition on first meeting with Nixon **NSI3** 4, 35, 43-46
    Parr's deposition on Nixon's meetings with dairy leaders **NSI3** 16, 143, 145-148
    and redated memo from Whitaker to Nixon on milk price supports **SI6-2** 484, 863, 867-875
    in Strachan memo to Haldeman **SI1** 79; **SI2** 2, 44, 427, 428-441
Nation of Islam (NOI)
    in Huston plan **SI7-1** 398-399
National Advisory Council on Indian Education
    court litigation on appointments to **SI12** 24-25
National Archives II 3 1471; **SI10** 1, 31, 33, 36
    acceptance of Nixon's gift of pre-Presidential papers **SI10** 59
    conflicts on date of Newman's visit to **SI10** 5-6, 91-94
    discrepancy over date of 1969 deed for contribution of Nixon's papers to **SI10** 6-7, 101-135
    Johnson advises Nixon to contribute his pre-Presidential papers to for tax deduction **SI10** 1, 31,

33, 36
    lacks knowledge or memoranda indicating gift of papers by Nixon in 1969 **SI10** 8, 174-176
    letter from Kaupinen to Magnuson on Nixon's gifts of papers to **SI10** 437-438
    memo from files of March 21, 1969 on meeting with White House staff on Nixon's pre-Presidential paper **SI10** 79
    memo of May 27, 1969 from East noting that most of Nixon's papers are not deeded to U.S. **SI10** 8, 170-173
    Morgan and Stuart meet with officials of on Nixon's pre-Presidential and Presidential papers on March 11, 1969 **SI10** 4-5, 77-78, 79-80
    Newman works with Nixon's pre-Presidential papers on November 17-20 and December 8, 1969 at **SI10** 10, 199-204
    Nixon's papers moved to for inventorying and organizing in March 1969 **SI10** 5, 81-82, 83, 84, 85-86
    See also House Judiciary Committee Impeachment Inquiry, presentation of evidence on Nixon's income tax; Nixon's income tax
National Association of Broadcasters
    question-and-answer session with Nixon at 1974 Convention of **SIAPP1** 78-82
National Council of Community Mental Health Centers, Inc. v. *Weinberger* **SI12** 7
National Defense Education Act
    impoundment of funds for sections of **SI12** 23
National Emergency Civil Liberties Committee SI7-2 594
National Institute of Mental Health
    and termination of Community Mental Health Centers Act **SI12** 21
National Journal **SIAPP4** 9
National Lawyers Guild SI7-2 1132
National Milk Producers Federation, and lobbying SI6-1 338
National Movement for the Student Vote
    Political Matters Memoranda on tax exempt status of **SIAPP4** 3
National Observer **SI8** 126
National security
    and appointment of ad hoc committee to study intelligence needs and restraints **SI7-1** 22, 275, 376-382
    assessment of black extremist threat to in Huston plan **SI7-1** 397-400
    as Caulfield's rationale for Operation Sandwedge **SI7-3** 1352-1353
    and creation of Plumbers unit **NSI4** 4, 43, 44-46; **SI7-2** 530, 649, 650-654
    and Dean's efforts to retrieve documents connecting Hunt and Liddy to Fielding break-in **SI7-4** 1732
    discussed in Nixon-Dean meeting as explanation for Watergate **SI3-2** 1072-1074
    Edwards on rights of Americans and **RHJC** 287-288
    and Ehrlichman's instructions to Young on handling of questions on Fielding break-in **SI7-4** 1650, 2027, 2028-2036

Ehrlichman's notes on classified documents and SIAPP3 180-186
and Eisenhower's relationship with press during World War II NSI4 83
as excuse for Fielding break-in SUMM I 136-138; SI7-3 1330
as excuse for wiretaps of government officials and newsmen SUMM I 124-125, 127-128
and Fielding break-in SI4-1 360-361; SI4-3 1475-1476, 1482-1483, 1488, 1489-1490
and House Judiciary Committee Impeachment Inquiry security and control of subpoenaed documents II 1 85-91
Kraft wiretapping and SUMM I 125
Krogh assigned by Ehrlichman to "special" project related to NSI4 9, 85, 86-95
Krogh on Fielding break-in and SIAPP2 49
and legal authority for warrantless wiretaps NSI4 30, 31, 197, 199, 200-201
and legality of Justice Department wiretaps NSI4 29, 31, 193, 194-195, 199, 200-201
and materials requested by House Judiciary Committee Impeachment Inquiry II 1 177
in Nixon-Dean discussion on Hunt's demands for money NSI1 155
in Nixon-Dean discussion on Kraft wiretapping SI7-4 1641, 1941, 1942-1945
in Nixon-Dean discussion on Watergate SI8 434
Nixon discussion with Ehrlichman and Krogh on leaks and SI7-2 872-876
Nixon on Watergate investigation and SIAPP1 21-25, 65; SI1 39-40
Nixon orders security clearance review by all U.S. Departments and Agencies NSI4 5, 67, 68-69
and Nixon tapes II 2 1369, 1409-1410; SIAPP1 44; SI9-1 45, 499, 500-501
as Nixon's reason for telling Petersen not to investigate Fielding break-in II 2 1228-1229, 1231, 1232; TW 3 85-86, 97-100, 119-120, 124-126, 162-164
and Nixon's refusal of Ervin's request for Presidential tapes SIAPP1 29
Rodino on real meaning of II 1 543-544
and security clearances for House Judiciary Committee Impeachment Inquiry legal staff II 1 94
Sparkman and Case report to Senate Foreign Relations Committee on FBI summary of wiretaps placed on individuals related to leaks in field of SI7-2 525, 567, 568-570
Wiggins' proposal for procedure for Nixon's potential refusal of materials to House Judiciary Committee Impeachment Inquiry on grounds of II 1 356-359
wiretapping and MMFL 56-61
National Security Agency SI7-1 438-439
interagency coordination and, in Huston plan SI7-1 430-431
See also Huston plan
National Security Council SI7-1 454
approval of Cambodian bombings SI11 313
Command organizational structure and officials SI11 81-82
and decision to bomb Cambodia SI11 4, 133

duration of wiretapping of staff members of SI7-1 8, 201, 202-221
Halperin's resignation from NSI4 27, 183, 184-190
and leaks on U.S. position on India-Pakistan War SI7-3 1193, 1421, 1422-1440
wiretapping of staff members of II 2 1097-1103, 1111; SUMM I 124-125; SI7-1 7, 17, 191, 192-199, 292-293, 325, 326-333
See also Huston plan
National Strike Information Center SI7-1 389-390
See also National Student Strike
National Student Strike (NSS), in Huston plan SI7-1 389-390
Naylor, Jack
and delivery of Nixon's gift of pre-Presidential papers to National Archives SI10 61
Neal, Edward B., questioning by
Gray SI2 2, 553
Neal Report
Geneen on NSI2 34
Nelson, Harold S. II 2 1048, 1053; SIAPP2 294-295
Chotiner and SI6-2 677
letter from Harrison with list of committees for AMPI contributions SI6-2 479, 783, 787-793
letter from Harrison on TAPE contributions and upcoming meeting with Administration representatives SI6-1 14, 217, 228-233
at Louisville airport meeting with Alagia SI6-2 704-711
meeting with Chotiner and Kalmbach in Kalmbach's hotel room II 2 1077-1078
and meeting with Dent SI6-1 110
meeting with Kalmbach and other AMPI representatives SI6-1 14, 217, 218-233
at meeting between Nixon and dairy industry leaders on March 23, 1971 SI6-2 575-578, 584-587, 602, 609-610, 616
meeting with Parr and Nixon SI6-1 169, 188-190
memo to Dent on invitation to Nixon to address annual meeting of Associated Dairymen, Inc. SI6-1 6, 99, 111, 117
in memo to Haldeman SI1 79; SI2 2, 44, 427, 428-441
"photo opportunity" meeting with Nixon II 2 1052-1053
and schedule proposal for Nixon's meetings with dairy industry leaders SI6-1 324
telephone call from Nixon to SI6-1 10, 161, 168
telephone conversation with Campbell on conditions for Administration raising milk price supports NSI3 23, 163, 164-166
telephone conversation with Campbell on milk price-support decision reversal SI6-2 474, 673, 693-697
visit with Nixon during Presidential "Open Hour" on September 9, 1970 NSI3 4, 35, 36-52
See also House Judiciary Committee Impeachment Inquiry, presentation of evidence on dairy industry campaign contributions; U.S. v. David Parr, U.S. v. Harold Nelson
Nelson, Harold S., cited testimony of
on amount pledged by dairy industry to Nixon re-election campaign NSI3 5, 53, 54-55

text of Kleindienst statement on ITT **SI5-2** 511, 849, 853

text of Krogh's letter of resignation in **NSI4** 13, 109, 113

text of Richardson's statement on appointment of Special Watergate Prosecutor **SI9-1** 6, 139, 140

on Wilson statement that Jaworski informed him no legal action was being considered in relation to ITT matter **NSI2** 14, 155, 156

See also Pentagon Papers

New York Times Co. v. *U.S.*

Supreme Court decision in **SI7-2** 527, 591, 594-595

New Yorker Films, Inc., Caulfield proposes IRS audit of SI8 186

Newman, Paul, on enemies list SI8 75, 109

Newman, Ralph II 3 1476, 1501-1502, 1504, 1520-1521

and Alexander's letter to Jaworski referring IRS investigation on Nixon's tax returns to Grand Jury **SI10** 403-404

alleged telephone calls from DeMarco after passage of Tax Reform Act of 1969 asking him to complete appraisal of Nixon's papers **SI10** 11, 289-291

and arrangements for appraisal of Nixon's pre-Presidential papers **SI10** 1, 37, 39

conflicts on date of visit to National Archives to verify volume of Nixon's pre-Presidential papers for 1969 deduction **SI10** 5-6, 91-94

date of first contact with DeMarco **SI10** 6, 95-97, 98-100

on discrepancy in his affidavit on dates of examining papers constituting Nixon's 1969 gift of pre-Presidential papers **SI10** 12-13, 303

discusses appraisal of pre-Presidential papers with Nixon on November 16, 1969 **SI10** 9, 197-198

and evaluation of Nixon's pre-Presidential papers **SI10** 4, 9, 73, 184-196

informed by DeMarco in March 1970 that Nixon had made bulk gift of papers in 1969 and provides further description **SI10** 11-12, 292-300

interview with **SI10** 37

investigated by Intelligence Division of IRS on Nixon's 1969 income tax return **SI10** 18-19, 376-394

letter to DeMarco asking for instructions with reference to Nixon's papers "in light of the Tax Reform Act of 1969" **SI10** 11, 288

letter to Livingston of March 27, 1970, on general description of Nixon's papers designated as gift in 1969 **SI10** 12, 298-301

McClory on affidavit of **II 3** 2012

in memo from Johnson staff member to Krogh **SI10** 39

obtains "limited right to access" to Nixon's 1969 gift papers from Morgan **SI10** 5, 87-90

and selection of pre-Presidential papers for Nixon's gift to National Archives **SI10** 2-3, 45, 59, 60-61

telephone conversation with DeMarco on deduction for gifts of papers being eliminated **SI10** 10-11, 277-281

telephone conversations with Livingston on Nixon's gift of 1969 papers **SI10** 13, 304-308

works at National Archives examining Nixon's pre-Presidential papers on November 17-20 and December 8, 1969 **SI10** 10, 199-204

See also House Judiciary Committee Impeachment Inquiry, presentation of evidence on Nixon's income tax

Newsday

articles on Rebozo, White House efforts to audit author of **SI8** 16, 165, 166-174; **II 2** 1281

Newsmen, wiretapping of SUMM I 134-135; **SI7-1** 11, 249, 250-257; **II 2** 1103-1104; **SUMM I** 124-125

in Article of Impeachment II **RHJC** 146-150

legal authority for **NSI4** 30, 31, 197, 199, 200-201

Mitchell's authorization of **SI7-1** 4, 157, 158-172

Nixon's authorization of **SI7-1** 3, 141, 142-155

responsibility for **SI7-1** 10, 239, 240-248

results of **SI7-1** 11, 249, 250-257

Richardson letter to Senate Foreign Relations Committee on legality of **NSI4** 29, 31, 193, 194-195, 199, 200-201

termination of **NSI4** 30, 199, 200-201; **SI7-2** 525, 567, 568-574

See also Electronic surveillance, of government officials and newsmen; Press

Newsweek **SIAPP4** 26

Nicholas, Anthony SIAPP2 294-295

See also U.S. v. *Harold Nelson*

Nissen, David R. SIAPP3 242; **SI7-4** 1981

actions on material on Fielding break-in **SI7-4** 1647, 1995, 1996-2013

affidavit in response to oral interogatories on indictment against Ellsberg **SI7-3** 1195, 1449, 1475-1476

deposition taken by House Judiciary Committee Impeachment Inquiry from **II 2** 1187

and information on Fielding break-in **II 2** 1233

signature on indictment of Ellsberg **SI7-3** 1474

Nixon, Edward C.

role in Nixon re-election campaign **SIAPP4** 149; **SI1** 79

Nixon, F. Donald

Kalmbach and **SI1** 84

Kalmbach on money given to **TW 3** 693-695, 696-697

Ulasewicz assigned to locate **SI7-1** 354

Ulasewicz's role in locating **SI7-1** 18, 335, 354

wiretapping and surveillance of **SUMM I** 127, 128; **SI7-1** 30, 507, 508-522

wiretapping and surveillance of, in Article of Impeachment II **RHJC** 151

wiretapping and surveillance of, in Jenner's presentation of summary of evidence to House Judiciary Committee Impeachment Inquiry **II 3** 1978

Nixon, Julie

demonstrations against **SIAPP3** 67

Nixon, Patricia R. (Mrs. Richard M. Nixon) SI10 18; **SI12** 98-99

memo from Stuart on restoration of "point" gazebo at Nixon's San Clemente property **SI12** 138-139

Nixon on attitude toward Miami Beach Convention **SIAPP3** 57-60

Nixon, Richard M. *(Continued)*

1509; **SI7-4** 1644, 1967, 1968-1971
for July 6, 1972 **SI2** 2, 56, 520, 544-546
for June 4, 1973 **SI9-1** 11, 169, 237-238
for June 20, 1972 **SI2** 2, 23, 30, 235, 243-244, 305, 306-307
for September 29, 1973 **SI9-2** 530, 649, 669
for October 1, 1973 **SI9-2** 531, 687, 708-710
dealings with Richardson on Cox's alleged investigation of his expenditures on San Clemente property **SI9-1** 21, 329, 330-332
Dean denies ever receiving assignment to conduct Watergate investigation for **TW 2** 226
Dean on his knowledge of White House use of IRS **TW 2** 300-303, 311, 331-332, 350-351
Dean on immunity and **SI4-3** 1494
Dean on reasons for not informing him earlier on Hunt's demands for money **TW 2** 258-270, 282-287, 293-297, 299-300, 345-346
Dean Report and **SUMM I** 72-74
Dean testimony on asking IRS to be "turned off" on friends of his **SI8** 14, 145, 153-154
and Dean's "investigations" of Watergate **SUMM I** 70-74
and Dean's refusal to testify at Gray confirmation hearings **II 2** 781-782, 785-786
Dean's testimony on Watergate coverup and **NSI1** 4, 41, 42-43
decides to review subpoenaed tapes with assistance of Woods and Bull **SI9-2** 528, 607, 608-618
decision on Chapin leaving White House **SI7-4** 1620, 1697, 1698-1707
decision on containment policy on Watergate from July 1 until elections **SUMM I** 43-51
decision to have new plan on handling Watergate after election **SUMM I** 86-87
decision-making methods of **II 2** 1021-1022; **TW 1** 69-78, 80-82, 98-101, 102-103, 105
decision to withdraw nomination of Gray as FBI Director **II 2** 1206
and decisions on his re-election campaign **RHJC** 21-24
DeLoach memo to Tolson on wiretapping of White House staff and **SI7-1** 269-270
denies necessity for apology to American people on secrecy of Cambodian bombings during news conference of August 22, 1973 **SI11** 76, 378-379
dictabelt of recollections of events of March 21, 1973 **SI3-2** 717, 1243, 1244-1249
Doar on **II 3** 1928-1929
played for House Judiciary Committee Impeachment Inquiry **II 2** 822-824
directs Connally to attack foundations and other tax-exempt organizations **SI8** 87
directs Ehrlichman to replace Dean on Watergate investigation **SI4-1** 23-24, 445-446, 448
directs Ehrlichman to tell Kleindienst to report information from Watergate Grand Jury to White House **SUMM I** 87-88
directs Kleindienst to report anything in Watergate area directly to him **II 2** 847
directs Mardian to transfer files on Kissinger tapes from FBI to Ehrlichman **II 2** 1132-1139
on discrediting of FBI **SI3-2** 834-835

discusses Agnew matter and discharging Cox with Richardson **SI9-2** 533, 737, 738-740
discusses Ellsberg case with Moore **II 2** 1232
discusses Executive privilege with Richardson **II 2** 1335-1338
discusses Segretti matter with Haldeman **II 2** 1199
discussion with Colson on his nomination of Gray as Director of FBI **TW 3** 320-321
discussion with Colson on Mitchell's possible responsibility for Watergate break-in **TW 3** 317-318, 320, 331
discussion with Colson on possible indictment of Magruder **TW 3** 285-286
discussion with Colson on Shapiro's recommendations on his strategy for Watergate **TW 3** 333-335
discussion with Dean on Sullivan's possible testimony on FBI at Gray confirmation hearings **SI3-2** 824-834, 841-842, 873, 877-878, 879
discussion with Ehrlichman on blaming Mitchell for Watergate **SUMM I** 74-77
discussion with Ehrlichman on Executive clemency for Watergate burglars **II 2** 732-734; **SUMM I** 46
discussion with Haldeman and Dean on Dean working through IRS **II 2** 1293-1295, 1298
discussion with Kleindienst on evidence against White House and CRP staff members **II 2** 874-875
discussion with Moore on Ehrlichman's possible criminal liability relating to Ellsberg case **SI7-4** 1644, 1967, 1968-1974
discussion with Petersen on immunity for Dean **NSI1** 35, 223, 224-225
discussion with Richardson on Executive privilege **II 2** 1353-1354, 1452-1454
discussions and actions on Segretti's relationship with Dean **SI7-4** 1628, 1775, 1776-1811
discussions with Colson after Watergate break-in **TW 3** 259
discussions with Colson on inquiries about FBI investigation of Schorr **TW 3** 238-241
discussions with Colson on never talking about Executive clemency **TW 3** 359
discussions with Dean on wiretapping of Democratic National Committee headquarters **SUMM I** 33-34
discussions with Haldeman on newspaper stories linking Segretti with Kalmbach **SI7-4** 1618, 1677, 1678-1680
discussions with Stans on Watergate **SI2** 2, 573
Doar announces serving of House Judiciary Committee Impeachment Inquiry subpoena on **II 2** 971
Doar on his April 30, 1973 statement on Watergate denying White House involvement **SUMM I** 9
Doar on his early knowledge of Watergate involvement of White House staff members **SUMM I** 6-7
Doar on his reaction to information from Petersen **II 3** 1929, 1930
Doar on Liddy remaining on White House staff after Watergate arrests **SUMM I** 9

Doar on reponsibility for Watergate coverup
SUMM I 12-13

Doar's presentation to House Judiciary Committee Impeachment Inquiry of draft Articles of Impeachment of SUMM I 2-14

does not meet with Haldeman, Ehrlichman, and Mitchell after Watergate arrests SUMM I 8, 37

Donohue resolution on Articles of Impeachment against II 3 2255-2258

draft letters from Dean to on resignation or leave of absence SI4-3 1085, 1141, 1148

drops plan for Dean to testify before Watergate Grand Jury II 2 841

and efforts to block House Banking and Currency Committee hearings SUMM I 115-117

efforts to change nature of March 21, 1973 conversation with Dean on hush money SUMM I 60-62

efforts to ensure that FBI Watergate investigation does not expose CIA operation NSI1 16, 17, 125, 126-127, 129, 130-135

efforts to prevent granting of immunity to Dean SUMM I 92-93, 96-99

efforts to prevent Patman Committee hearings SUMM I 49-51, 54

Ehrlichman discusses effects of Fielding break-in exposure on Ellsberg trialII 2 1204

Ehrlichman instructs Young to put Plumbers unit files in his file SI9-1 4, 127, 128-130

Ehrlichman reports on Watergate to SI4-1 475

in Ehrlichman request to Cushman for aid to Hunt SI2 2, 467

Ehrlichman statement on his authorization of any dealings with CIA II 2 1130, 1131

Ehrlichman states Krogh reported to II 2 1151

Ehrlichman on telephone conversation between MacGregor and SI2 2, 547-548

Ehrlichman telephones Kleindienst on instructions of SI4-1 20, 399, 400-425

Ehrlichman tells Colson that he says Ellsberg matter is classified TW 3 237

Ehrlichman on wiretaps authorized by SI7-2 948-949

and Ehrlichman's false testimony under oath SUMM I 84-85

Ehrlichman's handwritten notes of certain meetings with SIAPP3 89-263

and Ehrlichman's "investigation" of Watergate SUMM I 74-78

and Ehrlichman's knowledge of CRP and White House involvement in Watergate and of hush money payments SUMM I 46

and Ehrlichman's meeting with Byrne on FBI directorship II 2 1206-1209

on Ehrlichman's meeting with Strachan SI4-2 572, 905, 906-921

and Ehrlichman's meetings with Byrne II 2 1219

Ehrlichman's memo on meeting with Helms on Presidential access to CIA documents SIAPP3 204-205

Ehrlichman's motion for issuance of subpoena duces tecum to SIAPP2 19

and Ehrlichman's requests to CIA SI7-2 735, 738

Ehrlichman's statement on his saying Krogh could do whatever was necessary on Ellsberg investigation II 2 1161-1169

and Ehrlichman's suspicions about Dean's involvement in Watergate SI4-1 469-470

and Ehrlichman's telephone conversations with Gray on Hunt documents SI4-2 583, 1059, 1063-1080

on electronic surveillance in other campaigns SI2 2, 603-605

and Ellsberg investigation SI7-2 555, 981, 982-1003

and erased and missing tapes subpoenaed by Special Watergate Prosecutor SUMM I 105-107

and erasure on tape SI9-2 531, 687, 688-719

Ervin Committee Resolution authorizing Ervin to meet with SI9-1 27, 375, 377-378

establishes dairy import quotas different from Tariff Commission's recommendations NSI3 9, 111, 112-114

and establishment of Plumbers unit NSI4 47-55; SI7-2 530, 649, 650-654, 803

evidence presented after vote of House Judiciary Committee Impeachment Inquiry, Latta on RHJC 525

and Executive clemency offers SUMM I 63-69

explains refusal to turn over White House tapes to Cox and/or Ervin in Address to the Nation of August 15, 1973 SI9-1 43, 489, 490-494

explanation for domestic surveillance program in 1969 to 1971 II 2 1088-1089

false information to Petersen on Dean Report SUMM I 91-92

false and misleading statements by, in Minority of House Judiciary Committee Impeachment Inquiry views on Articles of Impeachment RHJC 397-401

false statement on hush money and Executive clemency to Petersen SUMM I 100-101

and FBI concern over CIA involvement in Watergate break-in II 3 1736, 1739-1740

and FBI files on Ellsberg and Pentagon Papers turned over to Plumbers unit SI7-2 553, 951, 952-966

and FBI investigation of Schorr II 2 1174, 1176; SI7-2 1113

and FBI Watergate investigation SI2 2, 36, 355, 356-362

Federal Rules of Evidence in Impeachment Inquiry against SUMM I 16-17

files claim of constitutional privilege with respect to Watergate Grand Jury subpoena for his correspondence with Stans on government positions SI9-2 579, 1045, 1046-1052

and firing of Cox and abolition of office of Watergate Special Prosecution Task Force SI9-2 544, 815, 816-825

first meeting with Ehrlichman after Watergate arrests SUMM I 37-38

first meeting with Haldeman after Watergate arrests SUMM I 8-9

Flemming's recommendations for meetings for SIAPP4 42-43

Flowers on his attitude toward House Judiciary Committee Impeachment InquiryII 1 216-217

foreign policy decisions during Watergate problem TW 3 410-412

Foreign Policy Report to Congress of February 25, 1971 on bombing of Cambodia SI11 20-21,

Nixon, Richard M. *(Continued)*
170-173
Foreign Policy Report to Congress of May 3, 1973 on Hanoi's attitude toward neutrality of Cambodia **SI11** 24, 182
Freidheim states he authorized secret bombings of Cambodia **SI11** 71-72, 349-354
and funding of black candidate fourth party project **SIAPP4** 17
in future history, Hutchinson on **RHJC** 502
Geneen's efforts to meet with **NSI2** 5, 35, 36-44; **SI5-1** 5, 131, 137-138
goes to Key Biscayne with Bull and Woods, taking Nixon tapes and tape recorder **SI9-2** 532, 721, 722-735
on Gray **SI3-2** 838-839
Gray asks him to drop his nomination as FBI Director **II 2** 855
Gray and Walters discuss informing of FBI Watergate investigation problems **SI2** 2, 523, 527
and Gray's destruction of documents from Hunt's safe **II 3** 1741
and Gray's withdrawal from nomination as FBI director **SI4-1** 31, 503, 504-506
Haig discusses Jaworski's conditions for accepting job as Watergate Special Prosecutor with **SI9-2** 548, 837, 838-843
Haig informs Buzhardt that he cannot locate dictabelt of April 15, 1973 Nixon-Dean conversation **SI9-2** 550, 849, 850-860
and Haig's order for wiretaps on government employees after leaks on bombing of Cambodia **SI7-1** 14, 291, 292-297
Haldeman denies discussing political intelligence with **SI1** 15, 155
and Haldeman and Ehrlichman meetings with Helms and Walters **SUMM I** 39-40
and Haldeman and Ehrlichman resignations **SI4-3** 1117, 1647, 1648-1650
Haldeman and Ehrlichman testify that they do not believe he had prior knowledge of Watergate break-in **NSI1** 7, 53, 54-55
Haldeman reports on Dean-Gray meeting to **SI2** 2, 34, 337, 349, 350,
Haldeman tells him he should have told Dean blackmail was wrong **SUMM I** 60
and Haldeman's false testimony under oath **SUMM I** 83-84
Haldeman's notes on June 20, 1972 meeting with **NSI4** 34, 223, 224-225; **SI2** 2, 24, 236, 246-248
Haldeman's political relationship with **SUMM I** 25-26, 28
Haldeman's work relationship with **SI2** 2, 133
Hardin advises Whitaker he should increase milk price supports since Congress will legislate increases **NSI3** 14, 137, 138
and Hardin's recommendations on dairy import quotas **NSI3** 7, 69, 70-74
Hillings' letter on dairy import quotas and AMPI's $2 million pledge to **NSI3** 8, 75, 76-110
Hoover and Mitchell oppose his approval of Huston plan recommendations **SI7-1** 26, 463, 464-468
House Judiciary Committee Impeachment Inquiry discussion on issuing subpoenas to **II 1** 307-341; **II 3** 1532-1563

House Judiciary Committee Impeachment Inquiry discussion on request for extension of time on answering subpoena **II 1** 344-356
House Judiciary Committee Impeachment Inquiry discussion on submission of written interrogatories to **II 3** 1616-1619
House Judiciary Committee Impeachment Inquiry discussions of his failure to comply with subpoenas **II 1** 409-465; **II 2** 901-957
House Judiciary Committee Impeachment Inquiry presentation of evidence on his interference with Cox's Watergate investigation **II 2** 1331-1387, 1389-1454
House Judiciary Committee Impeachment Inquiry subpoenas issued to **SI9-2** 568, 573, 577, 977, 978-982, 1009, 1010-1013, 1031, 1032-1036
and Hughes contribution **TW 3** 735-739
hush money and **II 3** 1741-1747
Huston plan and recommendations sent to **SI7-1** 444
on immunity for Dean **SI4-3** 1341
informed by Dean of Magruder's and Porter's perjury **SUMM I** 79-81
informed by Dean that Sedan Chair II is legal **NSI1** 11, 77, 78-80
informed by Dean of Strachan's perjury **SUMM I** 78-79
informed by Ehrlichman that Hunt's testimony will lead to indictment of Mitchell and Magruder **SUMM I** 74
informed by Haldeman that he believes Mitchell approved Liddy plan **SI4-1** 355-357
instructions to Petersen on Watergate prosecutors learning about Fielding break-in **SI7-4** 1643, 1949, 1950-1966
instructs Colson to publicize something on Pentagon Papers project **SI7-2** 563, 1125, 1126-1149
instructs Haldeman to call Colson on his commitments to Hunt **II 2** 836-838
instructs Haldeman to listen to White House tapes after his resignation **II 2** 1331-1332, 1355-1356
instructs Haldeman to listen to White House tapes after Petersen has recommended his dismissal **SUMM I** 100
instructs Krogh to investigate source of leaks **NSI4** 89
instructs Mardian on FBI files and logs of 1969-71 wiretaps **SI7-2** 541, 775, 776-788
instructs Ziegler to announce his confidence in Dean **II 2** 841-842; **SI4-1** 14, 319, 320-323
and investigation of leaks on U.S. position on India-Pakistan War **SI7-3** 1428
and investigation of Watergate break-in **NSI1** 17, 187, 188-191
invitation to address annual meeting of Associated Dairymen, Inc. **SI6-1** 6, 99, 117, 120, 128-129
invites AMPI leaders to meet with him after he is unable to address AMPI convention in 1970 **NSI3** 3, 29, 30-34
involvement in coverup at time of June 17, 1972 meeting with Dean **SUMM I** 47
involvement in deceptions and concealments on supposed investigations by Dean and Ehrlichman **SUMM I** 70-78

and involvement in decisions on FBI Watergate
investigation **II 1** 691-695
involvement in false statements under oath made
by White House staff members**SUMM I** 78-85
involvement with hush money **SUMM I** 52-62
involvement with re-election campaign **SUMM I**
27-28
involvement with Strachan's Watergate Grand
Jury testimony **SUMM I** 83
IRS audits of friends of **II 2** 1275-1281
and IRS investigation of George and Gerald Wallace **II 2** 1250-1255
Jaworski's list of materials he has refused to provide **SI9-2** 579, 1045, 1048-1052
Jaworski's right to prosecute **SI9-2** 839
Jenner's presentation to House Judiciary Committee Impeachment Inquiry on draft Articles of
Impeachment against **SUMM I** 14-19
Kalmbach on Government expenditures on his
property at San Clemente, Ca. **TW 3** 651-660,
693-694
Kalmbach on his political relationship with **TW 3**
529-532
Kalmbach's activities in behalf of **SI6-1** 61
key associates of **RHJC** 12
in Key Biscayne at time of Watergate arrests
SUMM I 35-36
Kissinger denies he had knowledge of MENU
double bookkeeping reporting procedure **SI11**
56-57, 294
Kleindienst denies discussing ITT antitrust suits
with **SI5-2** 496, 677, 678-680
and Kleindienst's resignation as Attorney General
and Richardson's nomination as Attorney General **SI4-3** 1118, 1651, 1652-1655
and knowledge of CRP involvement in Watergate
break-in **SI2** 2, 153
knowledge of Haldeman's reserve fund **TW 1** 53
knowledge of improvements on San Clemente and
Key Biscayne properties and their financing
SI12 170-174
knowledge or lack of knowledge of Fielding
break-in **II 2** 1147, 1151, 1161-1169, 1176-1177,
1182-1183
knowledge or lack of knowledge of payments to
Hunt **II 2** 1203-1204
on lack of discipline in government **SI5-1** 330-333
lack of knowledge that Gray destroyed documents
from Hunt's safe **NSI1** 18, 137, 138-139
lack of prior knowledge of Watergate break-in, in
St. Clair's presentation of evidence in behalf of
Nixon **II 3** 1726-1727, 1735
Laird on authority for sending troops into Cambodia **SI11** 155
LaRue denies he had any knowledge of Watergate
break-in **TW 1** 243-246
and leak on decision to begin troop withdrawals
from Vietnam **NSI4** 22, 153, 154-159
and leak on determination to remove nuclear
weapons from Okinawa **NSI4** 26, 179, 180-182
and leak on directive on study of solutions to Vietnam War **NSI4** 21, 139, 140-151
letter accepting Mitchell's resignation as Attorney
General **SI5-2** 490, 605, 608
letter drafted by Parr on dairy imports addressed
to **SI6-1** 7, 119, 122-125

letter from Berry attempting to set up Nixon-Ge-
neen meeting **NSI2** 5, 35, 36-42
in letter from Buzhardt to Cox expressing regret
for delays in responding to Cox's requests **SI9-1**
30, 399, 400-401
letter from Cox to Buzhardt requesting statement
on Dean's testimony before Ervin Committee
from **SI9-1** 19, 317, 318-320
letter from Ervin on his refusal of White House
materials **II 2** 1358
letter from Ervin on White House materials requested by Committee **SI9-1** 27, 375, 376-378
letter from Hardin requesting Tariff Commission
investigation on dairy import quotas **NSI3** 6,
59, 60-64
letter from Hillings on AMPI contribution **SI6-1**
8, 14, 127, 145-146, 170, 235-257; **II 2** 1056,
1057-1058; **II 3** 1783-1789
letter from Hoover on wiretapped information
SI7-1 20, 359, 360-361, 362-363
letter from Jaworski to Eastland summarizing arrangement made on independence of Watergate
Special Prosecutor **SI9-2** 557, 923, 924-925
letter from Lawrence O'Brien requesting special
prosecutor **SI2** 2, 97
letter from Richardson on dealings with Cox on
Stennis Plan **SI9-2** 543, 811, 812-813
letter to Ervin on refusal to testify before Senate
Select Committee **SI9-1** 23, 337, 338-346
letter to Ervin refusing to turn over Nixon tapes
SI9-1 34, 407, 411-412
letter to Gesell on Fielding break-in **SI7-2** 530,
649, 652-653
letter to Hoover requesting he give Krogh files on
Pentagon Papers matter **II 2** 1158
letter to Richardson on Cox's attempts to obtain
subpoenaed White House materials **SI9-2** 541,
797, 798
letter to Ruckelshaus on impoundment of funds
for Federal Water Pollution Control Act
Amendments of 1972 **SI12** 32
letter to Shultz directing that no Secret Service of-
ficer or agent testify before Senate Select Committee **SI9-1** 28, 379, 384; **II 2** 1358-1359
letter to Sihanouk in April 1969 on sovereignty
and neutrality of Cambodia **SI11** 3, 127-128
letter to Sirica agreeing to furnish Strachan's
Political Matters Memoranda file to Cox **SI9-2**
526, 591, 594-595
letter to Sirica declining to obey subpoena except
for Howard and Strachan memoranda **SI9-1** 37,
425, 426-427
letters to Albert and Mansfield of August 3, 1973
warning of hazards of ending bombings in Cambodia **SI11** 69, 340
letters to Ervin declining to testify and stating he
will not allow access to Presidential papers **II 2**
1353, 1359
letters to Rodino declining to comply with House
Judiciary Committee Impeachment Inquiry subpoenas **SI9-2** 576, 1027, 1028-1030; **II 2** 827,
1153-1154
and Liddy plan **II 3** 1729-1730
list of House Judiciary Committee Impeachment
Inquiry subpoenas issued to with justification
memoranda **RHJC** 233-278

Nixon, Richard M. *(Continued)*

list of meetings and conversations with Dean **SI4-1** 10, 265, 269

list of meetings and conversations with Ehrlichman **SI4-1** 18, 23, 33, 36, 347, 349, 445, 449-450, 508, 529, 543, 544

list of meetings and conversations with Gray **SI4-1** 7, 241, 242

list of meetings and conversations with Haldeman **SI4-1** 8, 12-13, 249, 250, 311-312, 315, 347, 348

list of presidential assistants and their staffs **SI2** 2, 18, 166, 180

listens to tapes and discusses them with Haig and Ziegler **II 2** 1342-1344

log of contacts with Connally on March 11-May 11, 1971 **NSI3** 15, 139, 142

log of meetings and conversations with Haldeman **SI1** 15, 155, 157-158; **SI2** 2, 23, 235, 245

Magruder says he protected **SI4-2** 624

and Magruder's appointment to government job after perjured testimony **SUMM I** 80-81

and Magruder's forthcoming talks with Watergate Prosecutor **SUMM I** 81-83

and Magruder's and Porter's perjury before Grand Jury **NSI1** 20, 145, 146-148

makes decision to increase milk price supports at March 23, 1971 meeting with Administration officials **NSI3** 20, 157

Mardian discloses he ordered files of Kissinger tapes delivered to Ehrlichman **II 2** 1239

Mardian on trip to see on FBI files and logs on wiretaps requested by White House **SI7-2** 540, 755, 766-770

and Mardian's disclosure of delivery of 1969-71 wiretap records to White House at direction of **SI7-4** 1653, 2057, 2058-2073

on media's coverage of Watergate **SIAPP1** 58

meeting with Administration officials to discuss milk price supports on March 23, 1971 **NSI3** 18-22, 153-161

meeting with Colson after Watergate arrests **SUMM I** 37; **TW 3** 267-270

meeting with Connally on March 23, 1971 **SI6-2** 474, 673, 674

meeting and conversations with Petersen in March and April 1973 **SI4-3** 1532-1534

meeting with dairy industry leaders on March 23, 1971 **II 2** 1073-1075; **SI6-2** 471, 565, 566-620; **NSI3** 17, 151, 152

meeting with Dean on April 15, 1973 after his discussions with U.S. Attorneys **II 2** 879-880; **SI4-2** 579-580, 1021-1022, 1024, 1025-1027

meeting with Dean and Haldeman on March 21, 1973, Nixon's summary of tape on **SIAPP1** 93-96

meeting with Dean and Haldeman on September 15, 1972 **II 2** 750

meeting with Ehrlichman on April 15, 1973 **SI4-2** 572, 575, 905, 906-921, 961, 963

meeting with Ehrlichman on Executive clemency for Watergate defendants **SI3-1** 13, 181, 182-197

meeting with Ehrlichman after Fielding break-in **SI7-3** 1187, 1333, 1334-1337

meeting with Ehrlichman on forthcoming public statements on Watergate break-in **SI2** 2, 61,

587, 588

meeting with Ehrlichman and Haldeman on Dean's information to U.S. Attorneys **SI4-3** 1084, 1131, 1137-1139

meeting with Ehrlichman and Krogh after SALT leaks **II 2** 1143-1144

meeting with Ehrlichman and Shultz on antitrust suits against ITT **SI6-2** 472, 621, 622-624

meeting with Haldeman after Watergate break-in **SI7-3** 1202, 1533, 1534-1540

meeting with Haldeman and Dean on September 15, 1973 on Watergate matter **SI2** 2, 62, 593, 594-656

meeting with Haldeman and Ehrlichman on April 15, 1973 on Gray and Hunt's safe **SI4-2** 583, 1059, 1060-1080

meeting with Haldeman and Ehrlichman on April 16, 1973 on Nixon's meeting with Dean **SI4-3** 1203, 1204-1211

meeting with Haldeman, Ehrlichman, and Dean on Hunt's blackmail threats **SI7-4** 1631, 1829, 1830-1836

meeting with Haldeman, Ehrlichman and Mitchell on new plan on Watergate **SUMM I** 86-87

meeting with Haldeman on June 20, 1972 **SI2** 2, 23-24, 235-236, 243-260

meeting with Haldeman on LaRue's testimony to Watergate Grand Jury and on Dean's efforts to get immunity **SI4-3** 1094, 1307, 1308-1311

meeting with Haldeman on March 23, 1973 **SI4-1** 8, 249, 250, 251-252

meeting with Haldeman and Mitchell on Kleindienst confirmation hearings **II 2** 1037, 1038-1040

meeting with Haldeman and Mitchell on Watergate break-in **SI2** 2, 53, 513, 514-516

meeting with Kleindienst on April 15, 1973 **SI4-2** 570, 571, 572, 573-574, 575, 577, 579-580, 581-582, 583, 871, 873, 874-876, 898-900, 901-903, 905, 906-908, 923-924, 925-959, 930-932, 961, 962-964, 974, 975-977, 1021-1022, 1035-1037, 1039-1040, 1049-1051, 1059, 1060-1062

meeting with Mitchell on antitrust suits against ITT **II 2** 1015-1016

meeting with Mitchell and Haldeman on Kleindienst confirmation hearings **SI5-2** 510, 841, 842-847

meeting with Moore **II 2** 887-888

meeting with Nelson and Parr **SI6-1** 169, 188-190

meeting with Petersen on adverse information on President **SI4-3** 1115-1116, 1627-1628, 1633-1645

meeting with Petersen on Haldeman, Ehrlichman, and Liddy involvement in Watergate **NSI1** 33, 211, 213-216

meeting with Petersen and Kleindienst on April 15, 1973 **II 2** 878-879; **SUMM I** 90; **SI4-2** 576-577, 973-974, 975-1011

meeting with Walters and Helms **II 3** 1961

meetings with Colson from June 14 through July 20, 1971 **SI7-2** 529, 619, 638-642

meetings and conversations with Colson **SI5-2** 500, 506, 735, 741, 795, 798

meetings and conversations with Dean on February 27, 1973 **SI3-1** 52, 597, 598-604 meetings and conversations with Ehrlichman **SI5-2** 500, 735, 737-738

meetings and conversations with Haldeman **SI4-3** 1112, 1557, 1558; **SI5-2** 500, 735, 739-740

meetings and conversations with Haldeman between April 30-June 3, 1973 **SI9-1** 11, 169, 239-241

meetings and conversations with Haldeman on April 25-26, 1973 **SI9-1** 3, 107, 126

meetings and conversations with Kleindienst **SI 4-1** 4, 213, 215; **SI4-3** 1113, 1613, 1622

meetings and conversations with Petersen **SI4-3** 1113, 1115-1116, 1613, 1618, 1627-1628, 1633

meetings and conversations with Petersen during March and April, 1973, discrepancies in listing sent to Cox **SI9-1** 16, 277, 278-287

meetings with Ehrlichman from June 14 through July 19, 1971 **SI7-2** 529, 619, 643-647

meetings with Haldeman on contents of Nixon tapes of February, March, and April 1973 **SI9-1** 3, 107, 108-126

meetings with Kleindienst on Watergate Grand Jury information **SUMM I** 89-90

meetings on Pentagon Papers matter **II 2** 1121

meetings and telephone conversations with Kleindienst on February 23, 1973 **SI3-1** 51, 583, 591

meetings and telephone conversations with Petersen to obtain information from Watergate Grand Jury **SUMM I** 91-92, 93, 94-96, 98-101

meetings with White House staff members on effects of publication of Pentagon Papers **SI7-2** 529, 619, 620-647

meets with attorneys for Haldeman and Ehrlichman **II 2** 887

meets with Ehrlichman and Krogh on July 24, 1971 on finding source of SALT leaks **NSI4** 13, 109, 110-114

meets with Haldeman and Mitchell to discuss Mitchell's resignation **SUMM I** 41, 42

memo from Colson on meeting with AMPI officers **SI6-1** 9, 10, 153, 154-156, 161, 181-183

memo from Ehrlichman on antitrust policy **SI5-1** 23, 314, 393-401

in memo from Huston to Haldeman on political use of IRS information **SI8** 44

memo from Klein on San Diego as site for Republican National Convention **SI5-2** 486, 561, 575

memo from Petersen on meeting with Geneen and Merriam **SI5-1** 14, 270, 277, 281

memo from Timmons on meeting on site of Republican National Convention **SI5-2** 486, 561, 576-577

memo from Whitaker on meeting with dairy industry leaders **SI6-1** 26, 389, 396-397; **SI6-2** 469, 545, 546-553

memorandum of substance of calls and meetings with Dean, February 27, 1973 **SI3-1** 52, 597, 605-607

memos from Ehrlichman on antitrust policy **SI5-2** 508-509, 803-804, 830-833

mention of new posts to Petersen **SI4-3** 1542-1544, 1546

and MENU reporting procedures **SI11** 72, 345

misleading public statements on investigation of Watergate **SUMM I** 46-47

and misuse of IRS **II 2** 1296

Mitchell on access to **TW 2** 189-190

Mitchell on advice on Huston plan to **SI7-1** 477

Mitchell cancels meeting on April 14, 1973 with **TW 2** 141-142, 187

Mitchell on contacts with after his re-election **TW 2** 126-128

Mitchell denies discussing ITT litigation with **II 2** 1026, 1034-1035; **SI5-2** 493, 494, 503, 631-632, 639-643, 759, 772-775

Mitchell denies discussing Liddy plan with **TW 2** 160-161, 170

Mitchell denies he had any knowledge of payments to Watergate defendants **TW 2** 208-209

Mitchell denies he informed him of payments to Hunt **TW 2** 132, 180-181

Mitchell denies informing about Mardian and LaRue's briefing on White House horrors **SI7-3** 1201, 1523, 1524-1531

Mitchell discusses disapproval of Huston plan with **SI7-1** 465

Mitchell on his being influenced by others in White House **TW 2** 200-201

Mitchell on his relationship with **TW 2** 189-190, 192

Mitchell on his role in decision-making **TW 2** 191, 202

Mitchell on information kept from **TW 2** 190

Mitchell and Moore testify that they believe he had no knowledge of Watergate break-in or Watergate coverup **NSI1** 8, 57, 58-61

Mitchell on reasons for keeping information from **TW 2** 206-208, 215-216

Mitchell on reasons for not informing about meeting with LaRue and Mardian **SI3-1** 103

Moore advises Dean to tell him about Hunt's demands **II 2** 797-798

Morgan and Ehrlichman on trip to Europe from February 23 to March 2, 1969 with **SI10** 4, 74, 75-76

named as unindicted coconsiprator in *U.S.* v. *John N. Mitchell, et al.* **MMFL** 47; **II 2** 1450-1452

Nelson's notes on meeting with Shultz and **SI6-2** 474, 673, 699-701

news conference after Watergate arrests **SUMM I** 38-39

news conference of August 22, 1973 on conversation with Dean on fundraising for Watergate defendants **SI9-1** 44, 495, 496-497

news conference of August 29, 1972 **SI2** 2, 61, 587, 589

news conference of February 17, 1971 on future use of air power in Cambodia **SI11** 48-49, 267

news conference of February 25, 1974 on tax deduction taken for donation of pre-Presidential papers **SI10** 36

news conference of January 30, 1970 on action if enemy takes "advantage of our troop withdrawal" in Vietnam **SI11** 30-31, 203-207

news conference of March 4, 1969 on options for response to enemy attacks in South Vietnam **SI11** 28, 194

news conference of March 14, 1969 on response to growing casualties in Vietnam **SI11** 28, 195-

Nixon, Richard M. *(Continued)*
196
news conference of March 21, 1970 on protection of Cambodia's neutrality **SI11** 31, 208
news conference of March 24, 1972 on Kleindienst confirmation hearings and McLaren's actions against ITT **SI5-2** 810-811; **II 2** 1036-1037
news conference of May 8, 1970 on Cambodian operation and plans for withdrawal from Cambodia **SI11** 36, 227-228
news conference of October 5, 1972 **SI2** 2, 63, 647, 648-649
news conference of October 26, 1973 on appointment of Jaworski and reasons for dismissing Cox **SI9-2** 546, 831, 832-834
news summaries received by **TW 1** 105, 117
and *Newsday* article on Rebozo **SI8** 171-172
nomination of Kleindienst for Attorney General post **SI5-2** 490, 605, 607
noncompliance with House Judiciary Committee Impeachment Inquiry subpoenas,
  in Garrison's presentation of summary of evidence to House Judiciary Committee Impeachment Inquiry as ground for impeachment of **SUMM I** 170; **II 3** 2041-2043, 2089-2093
  in Jenner's presentation of summary of evidence to House Judiciary Committee Impeachment Inquiry **II 3** 2096-2100
  Minority Impeachment Inquiry staff Memorandum on Facts and Law on **MMFL** 143-153
  Nussbaum's presentation of summary of evidence to House Judiciary Committee of summary of evidence to House Judiciary Committee Impeachment Inquiry on **II 3** 1994-2000
and noncompliance with Jaworski's requests for material from White House **II 2** 1418-1434
notes on meeting with Dean on April 15, 1973 on his discussions with U.S. Attorneys **SI4-2** 581-582, 1039-1040, 1047-1050
notes on meeting with Kleindienst of April 15, 1973 **SI4-2** 574, 924, 929
notes on meeting with Petersen and Kleindienst on April 15, 1973 **SI4-2** 576-577, 973-974, 1005
notes on recollections of March 21, 1973 **SUMM I** 86
opening statement for meeting with AMPI officials **SI6-2** 552
Order to Show Cause from Sirica on compliance with subpoena **SI9-1** 38, 429, 430-431
on ordering investigation of Ellsberg **SI1** 40
orders Kleindienst to drop Grinnell appeal **NSI2** 7, 65, 66-72
orders security clearance review by all U.S. Departments and Agencies on June 30, 1971 **NSI4** 5, 67, 68-69
orders Tariff Commission investigation of cheese imports **SI6-1** 26, 389, 392-395, 397
organization of White House staff by **SUMM I** 25-26
on organizational chart from files of Special Investigations Unit **SI7-2** 814
Patman on White House efforts to block House Banking and Currency Committee hearings

SUMM I 119
Pentagon Papers and **SI7-2** 527, 591, 596-598
Petersen on impropriety or propriety of his reporting to **TW 3** 134-144, 148-149, 152-153, 154-157
Petersen informs of Hunt and Liddy's involvement in Fielding break-in **SI7-4** 1938-1939
Petersen on legal aspects of his disclosing information to **TW 3** 103-105
Petersen on meeting with Kleindienst and on Dean's information on Watergate coverup **TW 3** 80-85, 105-108
Petersen on reasons for not believing he was implicated in Watergate coverup **TW 3** 133-134
Petersen on reporting to him on Justice Department Watergate investigation **TW 3** 86-105, 110-117, 128-130, 146-147
Petersen tells him Gray is innocent victim **SI4-3** 1619-1620
on Petersen's investigation of Watergate **SI3-2** 1013-1014
Petersen's notes on meetings with **TW 3** 88-94
"photo opportunity" meeting with Parr and Nelson **II 2** 1052-1053
places Ehrlichman in charge of Watergate **SUMM I** 37
pledges Administration cooperation with Richardson and Special Watergate Prosecutor **SI9-1** 6, 139, 141
pledges to bring those guilty of Watergate to justice **SUMM I** 102
on Plumbers **SI1** 40
and Plumbers unit **SI7-2** 654
and Political Matters Memoranda on political intelligence-gathering **NSI1** 12, 81, 82-84
on possibility of disclosure **SI3-2** 870
possible lack of knowledge of Watergate coverup, in Minority of House Judiciary Committee Impeachment Inquiry views on Articles of Impeachment **RHJC** 388-397
power of House Judiciary Committee Impeachment Inquiry to subpoena **II 1** 8-9, 12-13
preparations at Camp David for review of subpoenaed tapes by **SI9-2** 529, 619, 620-648
presidential statement of May 22, 1973,
  on approval of Huston plan recommendations **SI7-1** 25, 445. 451-453
  on assigning Plumbers unit to investigate SALT leaks **SI7-2** 549, 887, 888-889
  on creation of Plumbers unit **SI7-2** 530, 649, 650-651
  on formation of Intelligence Evaluation Committee **SI7-1** 29, 497, 498-499
  on Haldeman listening to tape of March 21, 1973 **SI9-1** 3, 107, 108
  on meeting with Haldeman on Plumbers unit activities **SI7-3** 1202, 1533, 1536-1537
  on 1970 intelligence plan **SI7-1** 22, 23, 275, 376-377, 383, 435-436
  on publication of Pentagon Papers by *New York Times* **SI7-2** 527, 591, 592-593
  on Watergate and 1969 wiretaps **SI7-1** 3, 141, 146-147
press briefing by Defense Department spokesman on August 10, 1970 on policy on air operations in Cambodia of **SI11** 47, 259

press conference of August 22, 1973
  on authorizing Kleindienst to turn over
    materials on Fielding break-in to Byrne **SI7-4** 1646, 1983, 1991-1993
  on contacts with Byrne **SI7-4** 1635, 1867, 1876-1877
  on discussion with Petersen on Fielding break-in **SI7-4** 1643, 1949, 1962-1963
  on Ehrlichman's discussions with Byrnes **SI7-4** 1636, 1879, 1884-1885
  on instructions to Kleindienst on Watergate evidence **SI4-1** 18, 347, 352-353
press conference of June 22, 1972 **SI2** 2, 35, 351, 352-353
in press coverage of ITT case and Kleindienst confirmation hearings **SI5-2** 856-86
press statement of May 22, 1972 **SI2** 2, 63, 578, 647, 648-649
procedures for memos to **TW 3** 241-244
proclamation on imports of dairy products **SI6-1** 17, 263, 264-266
and promises to Whitney Young **SI1** 80, 85
public opinion on possible impeachment of **II 1** 70-72, 74-77
public statements on Watergate **II 2** 710-711, 885
questions for Kleindienst posed by **II 2** 848-849
reaction to Colson's suggestion that Mitchell take responsibility for Watergate **TW 3** 498
reaction to Cox's rejection of Stennis Plan **SI9-2** 541, 797, 798-800
reaction to McCord's letter to Sirica **II 2** 835, 836-837
reaction to Watergate break-in **II 3** 1721-1722; **SI4-1** 359
recalls decision memo approving Huston plan recommendations **SI7-1** 27, 469, 470-485
receives reports on FBI wiretaps on White House staff members **SI7-1** 281, 302; **II 2** 1099, 1100, 1202
reception for people responsible for San Clemente improvements **SI12** 171
as recipient of FBI letters reporting on "top secret" wiretaps **SI7-1** 372-373
recollection of telephone conversation with Mitchell on CRP personnel involved with Watergate break-in **SI2** 2, 30, 305, 310
recommendations from Whitaker on milk price-support issue **II 2** 1069
redated memo from Whitaker on his meeting with dairy leaders **II 2** 1080-1082; **SI6-2** 484, 863, 864-875
refusal to comply with House Judiciary Committee subpoenas **SUMM I** 102-109, 155-170
refusal to comply with House Judiciary Committee subpoenas, power of House of Representatives in impeachment inquiry and **SUMM I** 164-165
refusal to confer with Thrower on resignation as Commissioner of Internal Revenue **SI8** 6, 59, 60-64
refusal to testify before Ervin Committee **SI9-1** 23, 337, 338-346
refuses to turn over Nixon tapes to Cox or Ervin **SI9-1** 12, 34, 243, 244-255, 407, 408-412
relationship with Mitchell **SUMM I** 29-30

relationship with office of the Watergate Special Prosecutor, in Minority of House Judiciary Committee Impeachment Inquiry views on Articles of Impeachment **RHJC** 414-424
relationship with Petersen, abuse of power and **II 3** 2024-2027, 2028-2032
and release of information on Gray's burning files from Hunt's safe **II 2** 892-893
releases White House transcripts of tapes **II 2** 1430
remarks before Associated Press Managing Editors Association **SI10** 33-34; **SI2** 2, 30, 305, 308-309
remarks to 74th National Convention of Veterans of Foreign Wars on secret bombings of Cambodia **SI11** 68-69, 74, 75, 337-339, 368, 374
remarks at swearing-in ceremonies for Kleindienst as Attorney General **SI5-2** 515, 901, 904
and removal of files of Kissinger tapes to White House **II 2** 1194
and reports from Intelligence Evaluation Committee **SI7-1** 500
reports given to House Judiciary Committee Impeachment Inquiry on **SI1** 4
requests legal action to prohibit further publication of Pentagon Papers material **SI7-2** 527, 591, 592-611
requests for wiretaps **SI7-1** 10, 239, 243-244, 271
resignation of, Holtzman on **RHJC** 321-322
and resignations of Haldeman, Ehrlichman, and Dean **II 2** 893-894
Resolution impeaching **RHJC** 1-4
response to question on House Judiciary Committee Impeachment Inquiry requests for material **II 1** 189-190
response to statutes on reporting federal impoundment of funds **SI12** 35-37
response to Watergate arrests **SUMM I** 35-42
response to Watergate arrests, in Article of Impeachment I **RHJC** 42-54
responsibility for secrecy on bombings of Cambodia **SI11** 325
and review of Nixon tapes at Camp David **II 2** 1373-1384
and Richardson's announcement on appointment of Special Watergate Prosecutor **SI9-1** 6, 139, 140-143
St. Clair statement that he believes he furnished sufficient evidence to Jaworski **SI9-2** 561, 947, 948-949
St. Clair's arguments in defense of **SUMM I** 5-6
St. Clair's presentation of evidence on behalf of, *See also* St. Clair, James D., presentation of evidence on behalf of Nixon
schedule of **II 1** 559-560
and selection of Republican National Convention site **SI5-1** 458
sends proposals for tax reform to Congress in April 1969 **SI10** 7-8, 146-148, 149-151
Shipley's statement on Segretti's comments on **SI7-4** 1699
on Sigma Delta Chi Convention statement on campaign issues **SI1** 35
signs proclamation lowering dairy import quotas **SI6-1** 17, 263, 264-272

Nixon, Richard M. *(Continued)*

on Sirica **SI3-2** 854-857

Sirica denies his motion to quash Jaworski's subpoena and orders him to produce material **SI9-2** 574, 1015, 1016-1017

Sneed on his role in impoundment of funds **SI12** 28

special appearance and motion to quash Watergate Special Prosecutor's April 18, 1974 subpoena **SI9-2** 572, 1005, 1006-1007

speech at AMPI 1971 convention **SI6-2** 482, 841, 842-845

speech to Associated Press Managing Editors Association on surveillance of Donald Nixon **SI7-1** 30, 507, 521-522

staff access to **TW 3** 411-412

and Stans' scheduled testimony before Watergate Grand Jury **SUMM I** 45

State of the Union Address of January 30, 1974 claiming Watergate Special Prosecutor has everything needed to conclude his investigations **SI9-2** 559, 931, 932-933

statement at news conference of August 22, 1973 on Haldeman listening to Nixon tapes **SI9-1** 25, 351, 352-353

statement at news conference of December 8, 1969 on people of U.S. having right to know everything with regard to U.S. involvement abroad **SI11** 30, 202

statement at news conference on his Constitutional right to impound funds **SI12** 33, 76

statement at news conference on March 21, 1970 on Cambodia's neutrality **SI11** 4, 132

statement of April 5, 1973 on Gray's withdrawal from nomination as FBI director **SI4-1** 31, 503, 506

statement of April 17, 1973 on immunity for White House officials **SI4-3** 1101, 1419, 1420

statement of April 17, 1973 on new inquiries into Watergate **SI3-2** 716, 1239, 1240

statement of April 30, 1973 on Watergate **II 3** 1931-1932; **SUMM I** 23-24

statement of April 30, 1973 on White House resignations **SI9-1** 5, 131, 132

statement of August 15, 1973 on assigning Ehrlichman to Watergate investigation **SI4-1** 23, 445, 447-448

statement of August 15, 1973 on Ehrlichman's telephone call to Kleindienst on White House involvement in Watergate **SI4-1** 20, 399, 422-423

Statement of August 29, 1973 in Article of Impeachment I **RHJC** 59-60

statement on discussion with Dean on hush money **II 2** 1368-1369

statement on Executive privilege **SI3-2** 699, 795, 796-797

statement on firing of Cox **II 2** 1401

statement of July 1, 1973 on continued air activities over Cambodia **SI11** 50, 270

statement of May 22, 1973

denying prior knowledge of Watergate break-in **NSI1** 6, 49, 50

on FBI Watergate investigation and uncovering of CIA operations **NSI1** 17, 129, 130-134

on meeting with Kleindienst on April 25, 1973 **SI9-2** 554, 883, 887-888

on waiver of Executive privilege during Cox investigation of Watergate **SI9-1** 8, 151, 152-153

on Watergate investigation **SI2** 2, 36, 355, 358-359

statement on milk price-supports decision at Associated Press Managing Editors Association convention **SI6-2** 26, 389, 398-399

statement of November 12, 1973

on listening to tapes of his conversations with Dean **SI9-1** 11, 169, 170

on missing dictabelt of recollections of April 15, 1973 discussion with Dean**SI9-2** 550, 849, 859-860

on requesting Haldeman to listen to tape of Nixon-Dean meeting of March 21, 1973 **SI4-3** 1112, 1557, 1567

on unrecorded meetings of April 15, 1973 **SI4-2** 574, 924, 936

statement of October 19, 1973 on Cox's rejection of Stennis Plan **SI9-2** 541, 797, 799-800

statement on Richardson's selection of Cox as Special Watergate Prosecutor **II 2** 1344

and statement on Schorr investigation **TW 3** 507

statement to Richardson on getting rid of Cox **II 2** 1384-1385

statements on authorizing Kleindienst to turn over materials on Fielding break-in to Byrne **SI7-4** 1646, 1983, 1987-1990

statements denying authorization of Plumbers unit use of illegal methods **NSI4** 13, 109, 110, 111

statements on discussions with Ehrlichman on possibility of Executive clemency for Watergate burglars **SI3-1** 13, 181, 192-197

statements on House Judiciary Committee Impeachment Inquiry's requests for materials **II 1** 214-215

statements on impoundment of funds **SI12** 29-33

statements on telling Petersen to stay away from Fielding break-in investigation **SI7-4** 1643, 1949, 1958-1961

statements on Watergate investigations **SUMM I** 70-71, 72

states Jaworski has sufficient evidence to complete his investigation **II 2** 1423, 1424-1425

and Stennis Proposal **SI9-2** 762-763

subpoena for handwritten notes of Ehrlichman of certain meetings with **SIAPP3** 1

and summary of FBI letters reporting on wiretaps on National Security Council staff members **SI7-1** 229

takes charge of Watergate investigation **II 2** 834

taped telephone conversation with Dean on March 20, 1973 **SI3-2** 710, 979, 980-987

Tariff Commission report on dairy import quotas to **SI6-1** 17, 263, 267-268

task of House Judiciary Committee Impeachment Inquiry in determining role in Watergate cover-up **SUMM I** 23

tax evasion by **SUMM I** 171-176

telephone call to Dean at Camp David **SI4-1** 10, 265, 269

telephone call to Dean instructing him to go to Camp David **SI4-1** 6, 235, 237, 239 telephone call to Dean wishing him a happy Easter **SI4-3** 1111, 1553, 1554-1555

telephone call to Gray on Watergate investigation on March 23, 1973 **SI4-1** 7, 241, 242, 243, 244-248

telephone call to Gray without telling him about Dean's information on Watergate **SUMM I** 87

telephone call to Kleindienst on contacting Baker re Senate Select Committee on Presidential Campaign Activities hearings **SI4-1** 4, 123-127, 213, 214, 215,; **SUMM I** 87

telephone call to Nelson at Chicago AMPI convention **SI6-1** 10, 161, 168

telephone conversation with Colson on Watergate break-in **SI2** 2, 15, 155, 156-160

telephone conversation with Connally on milk price-support issue **II 2** 1070, 1072-1073; **SI6-2** 470, 555, 556-563

telephone conversation with Ehrlichman on Dean's, Magruder's, and Mitchell's forthcoming Watergate Grand Jury testimony **SI4-1** 36, 543, 544-545

telephone conversation with Ehrlichman on Dean's resignation **SI4-3** 1084, 1131, 1132-1133, 1134

telephone conversation with Ehrlichman on immunity for top White House staff members **SI4-3** 1098, 1387, 1392-1393

telephone conversation with Ehrlichman on Magruder's information to U.S. Attorneys **SI4-2** 468, 851, 852-861

telephone conversation with Ehrlichman on preventing Dean from implicating Haldeman and Ehrlichman **SUMM I** 67

telephone conversation with Gray on White House use of FBI and CIA **SUMM I** 45-46

telephone conversation with Haldeman on conflicts between recollections of Magruder and Strachan on Watergate **SI4-2** 575, 961, 968-971

telephone conversation with Haldeman on Magruder's information to U.S. Attorneys **SI4-2** 567, 843, 844-849

telephone conversation with Kleindienst agreeing to have Petersen meet with them **SI4-2** 575, 961, 972

telephone conversation with Kleindienst on dropping *ITT-Grinnell* appeal **SI5-1** 16, 311, 315-326, 346-348

telephone conversation with Kleindienst on Gray resigning **SI4-3** 1623, 1624

telephone conversation with Mitchell on Watergate break-in **TW 2** 165; **SI2** 2, 30, 305, 306-310

telephone conversation with Petersen on April 15, 1973 on Dean's information to Watergate Prosecutor's **SI4-3** 1083, 1123, 1124-1130

telephone conversation with Petersen on April 16, 1973 **II 2** 883-884

telephone conversation with Petersen on Watergate **SI4-3** 1093, 1297, 1298-1303

telephone conversations with Connally on March 22, 1971 **SI6-2** 467, 519, 521

telephone conversations with Petersen on Dean's information to U.S. Attorneys **SI4-2** 579-580, 1021-1022, 1032-1034, 1055

televised address of April 20, 1970 on actions planned if Vietnamese increase military action **SI11** 32-33, 216-217

televised address of April 30, 1970 on planned attack on Communist sanctuaries in Cambodia **SI11** 33-35, 218-224

televised address of April 30, 1973 on resignations of Haldeman, Ehrlichman, Kleindienst and Dean and appointment of Richardson as Attorney General **SI4-3** 1119, 1657, 1658-1659

televised address on House Judiciary Committee Impeachment Inquiry **II 1** 498

televised address of June 3, 1970 on policy in Cambodia **SI11** 39-40, 237-240

televised address of June 30, 1970 on his report "The Cambodian Operation" **SI11** 41-45, 241-252

televised address of May 14, 1969 on terms of proposed settlement of Vietnam War **SI11** 29, 199-200

television interview of July 1, 1970 on withdrawal from Cambodia and possibility of future bombings **SI11** 46, 253-258

television interview of March 22, 1971 on use of air power in Southeast Asia **SI11** 49, 269

tells Colson about Petersen's reports and asks him about newspaper reports that he is about to tell everything **TW 3** 353-354

tells Dean and Haldeman to meet with Mitchell **NSI1** 24, 165, 166-167

tells Dean that Hunt's demands should be met **SUMM I** 57-59

tells Dean one million dollars is available to avoid disclosure of coverup **SUMM I** 56-57

tells Ehrlichman and Haldeman to instruct Kleindienst to report directly to him **SI4-1** 18, 347, 350-351, 352, 353, 354-371

tells Ehrlichman and Haldeman to urge Dean to go to Grand Jury **NSI1** 30, 199, 200-201

tells Ehrlichman to instruct Magruder and Mitchell to go before Grand Jury **NSI1** 32, 207, 208-210

tells Petersen Haldeman had no authority over campaign funds **SUMM I** 92

tells Petersen Justice Department should not investigate Fielding break-in **II 2** 1228-1229, 1231, 1232; **TW 3** 85-86, 97-100, 119-120, 124-126, 162-164

tells Rogers he is considering Byrne for post of FBI Director **II 2** 1228

tells Scott there will be no intervention in selection of Special Watergate Prosecutor or subsequent investigation **SI9-1** 6, 139, 142-143

testimony of White House staff members on his decision-making methods **SUMM I** 28

threats to Watergate coverup and **SUMM I** 81-85

and Thrower's efforts to meet with him on political influence in IRS **II 2** 1258

told by Ehrlichman and Haldeman that no one at White House had prior knowledge of Watergate break-in **NSI1** 29, 195, 196-198

tragedy of, in Minority of House Judiciary Committee Impeachment Inquiry views on Articles of Impeachment **RHJC** 361

transcript of taped meeting with Ehrlichman and Krogh on SALT talks leak **SI7-2** 548, 863, 867-

Nixon, Richard M. *(Continued)*
885
and transfer of FBI files on Kissinger tapes to White House **II 2** 1157-1158
trip to Russia and delay of House Judiciary Committee Impeachment Inquiry **II 1** 301-302
trips to Key Biscayne during construction work **SI12** 98
unaware of Magruder and Porter perjuring themselves before Watergate Grand Jury **II 3** 1741
untrue statements on Executive clemency offers **SUMM I** 69
usual work schedule in Washington **TW 1** 30-38, 39-45, 51-52, 65-66, 106-107
visited by Nelson and Parr on September 9, 1970 **NSI3** 4, 35, 36-52
Waldie on resignation of **RHJC** 298-299
and Watergate coverup **NSI1** 14, 119, 120
and Watergate coverup after Ehrlichman's and Haldeman's resignations **SUMM I** 102-109
Watergate Grand Jury subpoena requiring production of nine Nixon tapes and other White House materials **SI9-1** 35, 413, 414-417
Watergate Prosecutors decide to inform him of Dean's information on Watergate coverup **TW 3** 79
Wheeler on his knowledge of nature and extent of Cambodian bombings **SI11** 55-56, 289
Wheeler states decision to keep bombing of Cambodia secret was made by **SI11** 59
whereabouts during ITT antitrust negotiations **NSI2** 17, 203, 204-208
Whitaker memo for record on March 23, 1971 meeting between dairy industry leaders and **SI6-2** 470, 555, 562-563
White House meetings on Watergate break-in and **II 1** 606-611
White House record of contacts with Colson on March 23, 1971 **SI6-2** 472, 621, 625
White House record of contacts with Connally **SI6-2** 467, 470, 474, 519, 521, 555, 560, 673, 674
White House record of contacts with Whitaker **SI6-2** 473, 627, 672
and White House staff members testifying before Watergate Grand Jury, in St. Clair's presentation of evidence in behalf of Nixon **II 3** 1750-1755
and White House "White Paper" on "ITT Anti-Trust Decision" **SI5-1** 5, 131, 139-140; **SI5-2** 956-963; **II 2** 1043
and wiretapping of Kraft **SI7-1** 16, 313, 323
and wiretapping of White House staff members unrelated to national security **SI7-1** 261
withholds information from Gray and Petersen **SUMM I** 7
work habits of **TW 1** 63-64
Wright tells Sirica he stated that one of subpoenaed tapes contained highly sensitive national security material **SI9-1** 45, 499, 500-501
Young informs Malloy that Nixon was informed of Ellsberg study **II 2** 1174; **SI7-2** 560, 1081, 1083
See also Articles of Impeachment; House Judiciary Committee Impeachment Inquiry; Nixon-Dean meetings; Nixon tapes; *Nixon v. Sirica;*

Nixon's income tax; Nixon's statements and letters on Watergate; *U.S. v. Nixon*

Nixon, Tricia
Nixon-Haldeman discussion on demonstrations against **SIAPP3** 65-68
Nixon on role at Miami Beach Convention **SIAPP3** 57-60

Nixon Administration SIAPP2 348-381
congressional pressure for increased milk price supports **NSI3** 11, 123, 124-125
meeting between ITT officials and representatives of **II 2** 1002-1003
presentation of evidence by House Judiciary Committee Impeachment Inquiry on impoundment of funds by **II 2** 1304-1321
presentation of evidence to House Judiciary Committee Impeachment Inquiry on misuse of IRS by **II 2** 1249-1265, 1275-1302; **II 3** 1980, 1983-1990

Nixon Administration, attempts to improperly influence, papers from criminal cases related to SIAPP2 348-381
U.S. v. *Howard Edwin Reinecke* **SIAPP2** 371-381
U.S. v. *Jake Jacobsen* **SIAPP2** 361-364
U.S. v. *John Connally, and Jake Jacobsen* **SIAPP2** 347-360
U.S. v. *Richard Kleindienst* **SIAPP2** 365-370

Nixon-Dean meetings II 2 883-884; **TPC** 1-18; **SI4-3** 1554
of April 15, 1973, missing subpoenaed tape of **SI9-2** 530, 649, 672-679, 680-685
of April 16, 1973 **SI4-3** 1085, 1141, 1148-1202, 1091, 1265, 1271-1296
Buzhardt's list of **SI3-2** 709, 730-736, 754-760, 784-790, 882-888; **SI3-2** 929-935, 965, 969-975; **SI4-1** 6, 235, 239
on conversation of March 21, 1973 among Nixon, Dean and Haldeman **SI4-3** 1164-1168, 1171-1174
Cox requests April 15, 1973 tape of and is refused **SI9-1** 12, 243, 244-255
on damage to the Presidency **SI3-2** 1041, 1043-1045
Dean on **TW 2** 227-229, 237-245, 249-251, 253-257, 262-267, 270-273, 293-297, 311-312, 324-326, 340-342, 346-3
on Dean being called to testify at Gray confirmation hearings **SI3-2** 802
on Dean remaining as Nixon's counsel **SI4-3** 1185
on Dean submitting letter of resignation or request for leave of absence **SI4-3** 1148, 1155, 1158, 1159, 1198-1200
on Dean telling the truth **SI4-3** 1181-1182, 1191, 80
on Dean's discussions with U.S. Attorneys **SI4-2** 581-582, 1039-1040, 1041-1053
and Dean's knowledge of LaRue's arrangements for delivery of money to Hunt **II 2** 821-822
on Dean's presence at FBI White House interviews **SI3-2** 692, 729, 730-741
on Dean's proposed Watergate Grand Jury testimony on Haldeman's prior knowledge of Watergate break-in **SI4-3** 80-85
on Dean's refusal to testify at Gray confirmation hearings **SI3-2** 892-893

on Dean's resignation and testimony to Grand
Jury NSI1 34, 217, 218-222
on description of events after Watergate break-in
and after March 21, 1973 SI4-3 1169-1175,
1189-1190
discussion on IRS II 2 1250
discussion of surveillance of Kraft II 2 1228
on Ehrlichman's potential criminal liability SI3-2
1054-1055
on Ehrlichman's proposal for another grand jury
SI3-2 1090-1094, 1101-1110
on Executive clemency SI4-3 1182-1183, 1193-
1195
on Executive clemency for Hunt SUMM I 65-66
on Executive clemency for Watergate defendants
SI3-2 1051-1052
on Executive privilege and Gray confirmation
hearings SI3-2 695, 753, 754-765
of February 27, 1973 SI3-1 52, 597, 598-604
of February 28, 1973, on *Time* magazine story
about 1969-71 wiretaps SI7-4 1626, 1749, 1750-
1754
of February 28, 1973, transcript of SI3-1 53, 615,
616-687
Haig informs Buzhardt that Nixon's dictabelt of
recollections of April 15, 1973 conversation is
missing SI9-2 550, 849, 850-860
House Judiciary Committee Impeachment Inquiry
subpoena for specified tapes of SI9-2 568, 977,
978-982
on Hunt's demands for money SI3-2 1030-1032,
1095-1096
on Hunt's and Liddy's involvement in Fielding
break-in SI4-3 90-91
of June 17, 1972 SUMM I 47-51
on legal problems of White House aides SI4-3
1185-1189, 1192-1198
on Magruder's negotiations with U.S. Attorneys
SI4-3 78, 1286-1287
of March 8 and 10, 1973 SI3-2 698, 783, 784-792
of March 13, 1973 SI3-2 701, 803, 804-880
of March 13, 1973 on possible FBI directors and
Sullivan's information on 1969-71 wiretaps SI7-
4 1629, 1813, 1814-1820
of March 17, 1973 SI3-2 705-706, 927-928, 936,
939-940, 941-944; II 2 1360
of March 20, 1973 SI3-2 709, 965, 966-968
of March 21, 1973 SUMM I 54-62; SI3-2 713,
717, 981-982, 1135, 1136-1144, 1243, 1244-1249
of March 21, 1973, Haldeman's testimony on SI9-
1 39, 433, 434-473
Nixon discusses tapes of with Haig and Ziegler
SI9-1 11, 169, 177-236
Nixon listens to tapes for February and March
1973 of, and discusses with Haldeman SI9-1 11,
169, 170-241
on Nixon statement on Watergate SI4-3 1271-
1273, 1285, 1288, 1296
Nixon's description of tapes on SIAPP1 60-61
on obstruction of justice charges and Executive
clemency offers to Hunt SUMM I 67-68
on possibility of Dean having to go to jail SI3-2
1047-1050
on possibility of full disclosure SI3-2 1046-1050

on possible criminal offenses SI3-2 1030-1040
on possible involvement of White House personnel
in Watergate matter SI3-2 989, 995-1018
on possible resignation of Haldeman, Ehrlichman,
and Dean SI4-3 1294-1295
on possible waiver of Executive privilege by Nixon SI4-3 1169, 1175
on reasons for Magruder talking to U.S. Attorneys and Nixon's desire to take credit for SI4-3
1178-1181
on Segretti matter II 2 1202; SI3-2 1038-1041
on Senate Select Committee and failure of "containment policy" on Watergate SI4-3 92-94
Thompson affidavit on list of SI3-2 738-739, 762-
763, 793-794
Thompson memo on SI3-2 889
on Watergate defendants SI3-2 1024-1029, 1050-
1053, 1079
White House memo of SI4-2 581-582, 1039-1040,
1052
on wiretaps of newsmen and government employees II 2 1201-1202
See also Nixon tapes, House Judiciary Committee
transcripts of
**Nixon re-election campaign SIAPP2 196-345;
SIAPP4 70, 76**
approach to youth SIAPP4 26-27
Dent's recommendations, *See* Political Matters
Memoranda, on Dent's recommendations
first report submitted to Mitchell on SIAPP4 51
handling of surrogate candidates SIAPP4 6
issues in SIAPP4 91
Older Voters project SIAPP4 78
organizational set-up of SIAPP4 109-110
polling in SIAPP4 86
regular meetings and attendees SIAPP4 98-104
role of Cabinet in SIAPP4 37-38
use of celebrities in SIAPP4 53
volume of written material in SIAPP4 97
See also Committee to Re-Elect the President
(CRP); Illegal campaign practices and contributions, papers from criminal cases related to
Nixon Re-Elector SI1 88
proposal for in Political Matters Memoranda
SIAPP4 64-65
proposal for publication of SI1 47-48
**Nixon tapes II 1 411-412; SI9-2 540, 578, 581, 787,
788-796, 1037, 1038-1044, 1059, 1061-1069; TPC 1-
18; SI3-2 981-982**
altered and missing, in Article of Impeachment I
RHJC 126-132
analyses of technical report of gap on June 20,
1972 tape RHJC 227-231
of April 14, 1973 II 2 872-873; SI4-2 557, 558,
562, 565, 609, 656-659, 661, 662-696, 769, 773-
776, 777, 781-798, 811, 817-828
of April 15, 1973 II 2 872-873; SI4-2 571, 574,
871, 912-921, 924, 938-959
of April 16, 1973 SI4-3 1088-1090, 1213, 1217-
1221, 1223-1249, 1491-1492; SI5-1 1251, 1255-
1263
of April 17, 1973 SI4-3 1097, 1099, 1100, 1102,
1345, 1350-1386; SI5-1 1395, 1400-1404, 1411,
1416-1418, 1421, 1426-1442

of April 19, 1973 **SI4-3** 1108, 1511, 1515-1530

of April 27, 1973 **SI4-3** 1115-1116, 1627-1628, 1635-1637, 1538-1645

Butterfield on Nixon's speaking style on **TW 1** 103

Butterfield reveals existence of **SI9-1** 28, 379, 380-387

Buzhardt informs Sirica that June 20, 1972 tape contains erasure **SI9-2** 552, 867, 868-874

Buzhardt submits list of subpoenaed materials to Sirica particularizing claims of Exeuctive privilege **SI9-2** 553, 875, 876-882

cited in Minority of House Judiciary Committee Impeachment Inquiry views on Articles of Impeachment **RHJC** 385-389, 392-394, 396, 399, 400, 401, 403-407, 411

conflict over existence of tape of April 15, 1973 Nixon-Dean meeting **II 2** 880; **SUMM I** 106-107

conversations between Nixon and Haig and Nixon and Ziegler on June 4, 1973 **SI9-1** 11, 169, 177-236

Cox-Buzhardt correspondence on security of **SI9-1** 30, 393, 394-396

Cox letter to Buzhardt requesting **SI9-1** 29, 389, 390-392

Cox rejects Stennis Plan on **SI9-2** 538, 773, 774-781

Cox requests and is refused April 15, 1973 tape of Nixon-Dean conversation **SI9-1** 12, 243, 244-255

Cox's subpoenas for, in Minority of House Judiciary Committee Impeachment Inquiry views on Articles of Impeachment **RHJC** 414-424

custody transferred from Secret Service to White House **SI9-1** 28, 379, 380-387

on Dean Report **SI4-1** 3, 107, 129-130, 159-160, 164, 181-182

Dean tells Nixon on March 21, 1973 that no one at White House knew about plans for Watergate break-in **NSI1** 6, 49, 51

Dean tells Nixon that he has not spoken to Mitchell and LaRue about Hunt's demands for money **NSI1** 26, 177, 185

demonstration of type of machine used to transcribe **II 2** 1435-1450

denied to House Judiciary Committee Impeachment Inquiry by White House **II 2** 780

discrepancies between transcripts of **II 2** 792-795, 812-813, 852; **SUMM I** 107-108

discussion in House Judiciary Committee Impeachment Inquiry on criteria for excising material from **II 2** 828-832

discussion with Dean on his involvement with Segretti **SI7-4** 1628, 1775, 1779-1792

discussion on ITT matter at meeting between Nixon, Haldeman, and Mitchell on April 4, 1972 **NSI2** 15, 157, 158-188

discussion of March 21, 1973 on CRP political intelligence-gathering operation **NSI1** 11, 77, 78-80

discussion with Peterson on Gray's destruction of documents from Hunt's safe **NSI1** 18, 137, 138-139

discussions on Senate Select Committee on Presidential Campaign Activities in **RHJC** 117-118

Doar and Jenner discussions with St. Clair on House Judiciary Committee Impeachment Inquiry obtaining **II 1** 205-208

Doar and Jenner on erasures on **II 1** 607-608

Doar on importance of missing material **II 2** 843-844

Doar on unreliability of White House transcripts of **II 2** 844-846

in Doar's presentation of summary of evidence to House Judiciary Committee Impeachment Inquiry **II 3** 1962-1963, 1968

document accompanying transcripts of **SIAPP1** 92-102

document on Analysis, Index, and Particularized Claims of Executive privilege for Subpoenaed Materials **SI2** 2, 24, 236, 257-258

Ehrlichman informs Nixon on March 21, 1973 that no one in White House had involvement with Watergate break-in **NSI1** 7, 58, 56

Ehrlichman tells Nixon Dean will go before Grand Jury **NSI1** 30, 199, 201

erased **II 2** 1373-1384, 1410-1412; **SUMM I** 8-9, 37-38, 105-107

as evidence for Article of Impeachment I, Hutchinson on **RHJC** 497-499

of February, March, and April 1973, Haldeman listens to and meets with Nixon on **SI9-1** 3, 107, 108-126

in Garrison's presentation of summary of evidence to House Judiciary Committee Impeachment Inquiry **II 3** 2082, 2083, 2084

Haldeman and Ehrlichman tell Nixon that no one at White House had prior knowledge of Watergate break-in **NSI1** 29, 195, 196-198

Haldeman listens to after his resignation **II 2** 1331-1332, 1355-1356, 1364-1366

of Haldeman-Nixon conversation of June 20, 1972 **SI2** 2, 23-24, 235-236, 243-260

Haldeman on persons aware of **SI1** 163

Hogan on deletion of expletives from **II 1** 434

Hogan on discrepancies between transcripts of **II 3** 1973-1975

Holtzman on gaps in **II 1** 634-635

Holtzman on safekeeping of **II 1** 295-296

House Judiciary Committee Impeachment Inquiry discussion on release of **II 2** 974-981

House Judiciary Committee Impeachment Inquiry discussion on transcripts used by St. Clair in his presentation of evidence in behalf of Nixon **II 3** 1723-1726, 1730-1735

Hundley on discrepancies between transcripts of **TW 2** 184-185

Hungate on publicity on **II 1** 526-527, 528

on hush money **NSI1** 21, 22, 149, 150-155, 157, 158-160

inaccuracies in Presidential transcripts of, in Article of Impeachment I **RHJC** 128-131

installation and operation of recording system in White House **TW 1** 45-51, 78-79, 104

in Jenner's presentation of summary of evidence to House Judiciary Committee Impeachment Inquiry **II 3** 1989

lack of discussion on political intelligence at Nixon-Mitchell-Haldeman meeting of April 4, 1972

NSI1 13, 85, 87-118
LaRue on **TW 1** 246-247
list of equipment taken to Camp David for transcription of **SI9-2** 529, 619, 648
litigation over, in Article of Impeachment I **RHJC** 125-126
logs on **SI9-1** 11, 169, 171-176
on Magruder's and Porter's perjury before Grand Jury **NSI1** 20, 145, 146-148
of March 13, 1973 **SI3-2** 701, 803, 804-880
of March 17, 1973 **SI3-2** 941-944
of March 21, 1973 **SI3-2** 714, 1147, 1148-1186; **SI4-3** 1634, 1636
of March 21, 1973, Haldeman listening to and reporting on **SI4-3** 1112, 1557, 1558-1611
of March 21, 1973, Haldeman's testimony on **SI9-1** 39, 433, 434-473
of March 22, 1973 **SI4-1** 3, 107, 108-211
of March 27, 1973 **SI4-1** 18, 347, 453-371
McClory on damage done by public release of **II 2** 705
on means of delaying Hunt's sentencing **NSI1** 22, 157, 158-160
of meeting among Nixon, White House aides and dairy representatives on March 23, 1971 **SI6-2** 471, 473, 565, 566-616, 627, 628-671
of meeting of Nixon, Ehrlichman, and Ziegler on March 30, 1973 **SI4-1** 23, 445, 452-463
of meetings on April 14, 1973 between Nixon, Haldeman and Ehrlichman on Haldeman's involvement with Segretti **SI7-4** 1639, 1915, 1916-1927
method of recording **II 1** 555-556
methods of analyzing by House Judiciary Committee Impeachment Inquiry **SUMM I** 13-14
"missing" or incomplete, in Minority of House Judiciary Committee Impeachment Inquiry views on Articles of Impeachment **RHJC** 424-426
missing subpoenaed Nixon-Mitchell telephone conversation and April 15, 1973 Nixon-Dean meeting **SI9-2** 530, 649, 672-679, 680-685
Mitchell on **TW 2** 200-201
Mitchell on discrepancies between transcripts of **TW 2** 213-214
national security information on **II 2** 1369, 1409-1410
on need for meeting between Dean, Haldeman, Ehrlichman, and Mitchell **NSI1** 24, 165, 166-167
Nixon announces decision to furnish transcripts of relevant portions of those subpoenaed **SI9-2** 571, 991, 992-1004
Nixon arranges for Buzhardt to listen to Nixon-Dean telephone call of March 20, 1973 **SI9-1** 17, 289, 290-312
Nixon asserts they contain nothing reflecting unfavorably on his Watergate position **SIAPP1** 52
on Nixon assigning Dean to investigate Watergate **NSI1** 17, 187, 188-191
Nixon assigns Haldeman to listen to **SI9-1** 25, 351, 352-370; **SUMM I** 105
Nixon authorizes Wright to inform Sirica they will be turned over to court **SI9-2** 545, 827, 828-830

of Nixon-Colson discussion of June 20, 1972 **TW 3** 268-269
of Nixon-Dean discussion of April 16, 1973 on electronic surveillance of Kraft **SI7-4** 1641, 1941, 1942-1945
of Nixon-Dean-Haldeman meeting on September 15, 1972 in Article of Impeachment I **RHJC** 60-65
Nixon-Dean meeting of April 15, 1972 **II 2** 1405-1409
of Nixon-Dean meeting of April 16, 1973 **II 2** 881-882; **NSI1** 34, 217, 218-222; **RHJC** 80-81
of Nixon-Dean meeting of February 28, 1973 **SI3-1** 53, 615, 616-687
of Nixon-Dean meeting of March 20, 1973 **SI3-2** 710, 979, 980-987
of Nixon-Dean meeting of March 21, 1973, in Article of Impeachment I **RHJC** 69-73
of Nixon-Dean meeting of September 15, 1972 **II 2** 779
of Nixon-Dean meetings of February and March 1973, Nixon listens to and discusses with Haldeman **SI9-1** 11, 169, 170-241
Nixon-Ehrlichman on April 17, 1973 on immunity for top White House staff members **SI4-3** 1098, 1387, 1392-1393
of Nixon-Ehrlichman discussion of Dean's, Magruder's, and Mitchell's forthcoming Watergate Grand Jury testimony **SI4-1** 36, 543, 544-545
Nixon-Ehrlichman discussion on Magruder's information to U.S. Attorneys **SI4-2** 468, 851, 855-861
Nixon-Ehrlichman-Krogh meeting of July 24, 1971 on SALT talks leaks **SI7-2** 548, 863, 867-885
of Nixon-Ehrlichman-Shultz conversation of April 19, 1971 on antitrust suits against ITT **SI5-1** 16, 311, 312-345
Nixon on erasures on **SIAPP1** 85
Nixon explains reasons for refusing to turn over to Select Committee **SIAPP1** 35-36, 42-43
Nixon explains refusal to turn over to Cox and/or Ervin **SI9-1** 43, 489, 490-494
Nixon expresses concern to Dean on exposure of Kalmbach's San Clemente records **SI12** 172-173
of Nixon-Haldeman-Dean meeting of March 13, 1973 **SI8** 31, 359, 360-435
of Nixon-Haldeman-Dean meeting of September 15, 1973 **SI2** 2, 62, 593, 594-656; **SI3-1** 30, 369, 370-371; **RHJC** 441-443; **SI8** 27, 287, 291-349
Nixon-Haldeman discussion on April 15, 1973 on conflicts between recollections of Magruder and Strachan on Watergate **SI4-2** 575, 961, 968-971
Nixon-Haldeman discussion on Magruder's information to U.S. Attorneys **SI4-2** 567, 843, 847-849
of Nixon, Haldeman, Ehrlichman, Dean meeting of March 21, 1973 on Hunt's blackmail threats **SI7-4** 1631, 1829, 1830-1832
of Nixon-Haldeman-Ehrlichman discussion on March 27, 1973 on Magruder's forthcoming talks with Watergate Prosecutor **SUMM I** 81-83
of Nixon-Haldeman-Ehrlichman meeting of April 6, 1973 oninformation given by Dean to U.S. Attorneys **SI4-3** 1084, 1131, 1137-1139

St. Clair's presentation of evidence in behalf of Nixon on gap in tape of June 20, 1973 **II 3** 1843-1853

St. Clair's reference to transcript of March 22 conversation unavailable to House Judiciary Committee Impeachment Inquiry **II 3** 1906-1910

on Senate Select Committee on Presidential Campaign Activities **SI4-1** 3, 107, 114-126, 134-139, 142, 153-158, 165-168, 171-175

Sirica appoints panel of experts to examine gap on June 20, 1972 tape **II 2** 1405-1409, 1433-1434; **SI9-2** 552, 867, 868-874

Sirica denies Nixon's motion to quash Jaworski's subpoena for **SI9-2** 574, 1015, 1016-1017

in Sirica's possession, House Judiciary Committee Impeachment Inquiry discussion on issuing subpoena for **II 2** 990-991

Sirica's subpoena for and Nixon's petition for vacating of order **SI9-2** 525, 553, 585, 586-589, 878-882, 975

Stanford Research Institute, Dektor Counterintelligence and Security, Inc. and Home Services, Inc. on gap on Nixon tapes of June 20, 1972 **NSI4** 33, 207, 208-222

and Stennis Plan **II 2** 1385-1387

subpoenaed by House Judiciary Committee Impeachment Inquiry **II 2** 1345-1346; **SI9-2** 530, 568, 649, 667-668, 977, 978-982; **SI1** 6-7

summarization of White House transcripts of **SI4-1** 18, 347, 371-453; **II 2** 858-859

and Supreme Court decision in *U.S.* v. *Nixon* **SIAPP2** 159-192

taken to Camp David for review **II 2** 1373-1384

taken to Key Biscayne by Nixon, Bull and Woods on October 4, 1973 **SI9-2** 532, 721, 722-735

taping system at Camp David and **II 2** 890-892

trial subpoena in *U.S.* v. *Mitchell* for **SI9-2** 570, 987, 988-990

U.S. Court of Appeals procedure for **SIAPP1** 58

use of transcripts of by witnesses before House Judiciary Committee Impeachment Inquiry **TW 3** 122-123, 180

used by House Judiciary Committee Impeachment Inquiry **II 2** 717-718

on White House approach to disclosure **SI4-1** 3, 107, 177-181, 189, 193

on White House position on Executive privilege **SI4-1** 3, 107, 121, 126-128, 139-151, 169

on White House relationship to future Grand Jury investigations **SI4-1** 3, 107, 163-165

White House storage and retrieval system for **TW 1** 64-65, 67-69

on wiretapping of Democratic National Committee headquarters **SUMM I** 33-34

Woods' erasure on **SI9-2** 531, 687, 688-719

See also Advisory Panel on the White House Tapes; House Judiciary Committee Impeachment Inquiry, discussion on Nixon's noncompliance with subpoena of April 11, 1974; Nixon-Dean meetings; Nixon tapes, House Judiciary Committee transcripts of; Stennis Plan

Nixon tapes, House Judiciary Committee transcripts of

of Nixon-Dean-Ehrlichman-Haldeman meeting on March 21, 1973 **TPC** 131-146

of Nixon-Dean-Ehrlichman-Haldeman-Mitchell meeting on March 22, 1973 **TPC** 147-186

of Nixon-Dean-Haldeman meeting on March 13, 1973 **TPC** 47-78

of Nixon-Dean-Haldeman meeting on March 21, 1973 **TPC** 79-130

of Nixon-Dean-Haldeman meeting on September 15, 1972 **TPC** 1-18

of Nixon-Dean meeting on February 28, 1973 **TPC** 19-47

of Nixon-Dean meetings on April 16, 1973 **TPC** 187-218

Nixon v. *Sirica*

Judgement and Opinion, October 12, 1973 **SI9-2** 535, 747, 748-754

Petition for Writ of Mandamus, September 6, 1973 **SI9-2** 525, 585, 587-589

Richardson's meetings on October 15, 1973 on decision in **SI9-2** 536, 755, 756-763

Nixon's income tax II 3 1460-1505, 1507-1530; **SI10**; **SI12** 185-187

additional views of Mezvinsky, joined by others, on tax evasion by Nixon **RHJC** 343-347

approval of federal return for 1969 and issuing of refund check **SI10** 17, 365-366

Barth memo for Ehrlichman on **SI10** 429-432

and date of DeMarco's first contact with Newman **SI10** 6, 95-97, 98-100

DeMarco attaches Newman's appraisal of Nixon's 1969 gift of pre-Presidential papers to tax return **SI10** 14, 315-317

DeMarco-Blech telephone conversation in May 1969 on future deductions for gift of pre-Presidential papers **SI10** 7, 140-141, 142-143, 144-145

and discrepancy over date of 1969 deed for contribution of Nixon's pre-Presidential papers to National Archives **SI10** 6-7, 101-135

dissenting views on proposed Articles of Impeachment on emoluments and tax evasion **RHJC** 283-286, 305-306

in Doar's status report on House Judiciary Committee Impeachment Inquiry **II 1** 359-364

and effective date for elimination of charitable deduction for gifts of papers in Tax Reform Act of 1969 **SI10** 10, 205-257

Erlichman memo to Kalmbach on **SI10** 428

Ehrlichman memo on obtaining maximum charitable deductions on income taxes **SI10** 3, 64-65

Ehrlichman's questions to Morgan without mention of 1969 gift of pre-Presidential papers **SI10** 8-9, 177-183

and elimination of charitable deduction for gifts of personal papers **SI10** 8, 152-153

Federal income tax return for 1969 signed by Richard M. and Patricia R. Nixon **SI10** 336-363

for 1969-1972, materials submitted on behalf of Nixon **SI10** 436-552

Gemill-Rose memo on bases sustaining 1969 charitable deductions **SI10** 447-505

structions in light of Tax Reform Act of 1969 **SI10** 11, 288

meeting between Morgan, Stuart, and Archives officials on Nixon's pre-Presidential and Presidential papers on March 11, 1969 **SI10** 4-5, 77-78, 79-80

memo from Rose and Gemmill on bases sustaining 1969 charitable deduction for gift of **SI10** 447-505

Morgan memo to Parker on deed of gift of April 21, 1969 **SI10** 15, 332-335

Morgan "re-executes" deed of gift for 1969 papers for DeMarco **SI10** 14, 319-322

Morgan signs "limited right to access" allowing Newman to work with 1968 gift papers **SI10** 5, 87-90

Morgan signs re-executed deed of gift on April 10, 1970 for **SI10** 14, 325-326

Morgan's statement for White House in August 1973 on deed of gift of 1969 **SI10** 14, 323-324

moved from EOB to Archives for inventorying and organizing in March 1969 **SI10** 5, 81-82, 83, 84, 85-86

National Archives consultant's memo of May 27, 1969 noting that most of those delivered have not been deeded to U.S. **SI10** 8, 170-173

National Archives lacks knowledge or memoranda indicating 1969 gift of **SI10** 8, 174-176

Newman-Nixon discussion on November 16, 1969 of appraised worth of **SI10** 9, 197-198

Newman tells Livingston that his March 27, 1970 letter is only deed for Nixon's 1969 gift of **SI10** 13, 304-308

Newman's affidavit on dates of examining papers constituting 1969 gift **SI10** 12-13, 303

and Nixon's decision to execute restrictive deed in December 1968 for gift of **SI10** 2, 58

Rhoads' letter to Administrator of General Services that "second installment" was not given in 1969 **SI10** 11, 282-287

Ritzel asks Tannian to draft deed of gift of **SI10** 1, 43

treatment of gift of pre-Presidential papers on 1968 and 1969 tax returns **SI10** 3, 62, 63

See also House Judiciary Committee Impeachment Inquiry, presentation of evidence on Nixon's income tax; Nixon's income tax

Nixon's Quest for Peace (van der Linden) **SIAPP4** 126

Nixon's statements and letters on Watergate SIAPP1 1-110

Address to the Nation of April 29, 1973 on subpoena of Presidential tapes and materials by House Judiciary Committee Impeachment Inquiry **SIAPP1** 83-91

Address to the Nation of August 15, 1973 **SIAPP1** 32-39

on agreement reached with Select Committee on testimony of White House staff members **SIAPP1** 12

at Annual Convention of 1974 of National Association of Broadcasters **SIAPP1** 78-82

on appointment of new Special Prosecutor for Watergate matter **SIAPP1** 55-57

on attitude toward Watergate **SIAPP1** 80-81

on Buckley's call for his resignation **SIAPP1** 78-79

on causes and meaning of Watergate **SIAPP1** 37-39

comments on focus of press questions on Watergate rather than domestic and international issues **SIAPP1** 48

on Constitutional grounds for impeachment **SIAPP1** 70

on contradictory statements and letters on hush money **SIAPP1** 80

on creation of Plumbers Unit **SIAPP1** 23

on Dean's investigation **SIAPP1** 5

on decision to make transcripts of Presidential tapes public **SIAPP1** 83-103

denies giving Select Committee material they consider pertinent would speed up Watergate investigation **SIAPP1** 73

denies Haldeman and Ehrlichman's attorney is working with White House **SIAPP1** 75

denies prior knowledge of Watergate break-in on May 22, 1973 **SIAPP1** 24-25

denies prior knowledge of Watergate break-in on October 5, 1972 **SIAPP1** 4

denies prior knowledge of Watergate break-in or participation in coverup on August 15, 1973 **SIAPP1** 33, 40-41

denies prior knowledge of Watergate break-in, offers of clemency, or knowledge of hush money payments **SIAPP1** 64, 76

on discussions with Haldeman on hush money **SIAPP1** 72

document submitted to House Judiciary Committee Impeachment Inquiry in answer to subpoena for Presidential tapes and papers **SIAPP1** 92-102

on efforts to uncover facts **SIAPP1** 34-35, 41-42

on Executive clemency for former assistants **SIAPP1** 72-73

on Executive privilege **SIAPP1** 66

on Executive privilege for Dean **SIAPP1** 5

Executive privilege statement of March 12, 1973 **SIAPP1** 6-7

on exploitation of Watergate issue to keep him from doing his job **SIAPP1** 50

on FBI and CIA and Watergate investigations **SIAPP1** 44

on fundraising for Watergate defendants **SIAPP1** 49

on grounds for impeachment **SIAPP1** 73, 77

on guilt or innocence of Haldeman and Ehrlichman **SIAPP1** 65-66

on his intention to cooperate with Select Committee investigation **SIAPP1** 5

on House Judiciary Committee Impeachment Inquiry **SIAPP1** 81-82

on hush money payment on March 21 **SIAPP1** 75

on impact on American political system and his goals for second term as President **SIAPP1** 14-18

on impact of Watergate on off-year elections **SIAPP1** 73

on impact of Watergate on republic **SIAPP1** 62-63

on waiver of Executive privilege to end question of his involvement in Watergate **SIAPP1** 70

on waiving Executive privilege on all individuals within Administration **SIAPP1** 58

on Watergate and security operations initiated by his Administration **SIAPP1** 21-25

on whether he violated his oath of office **SIAPP1** 48

on wiretapping by other administrations **SIAPP1** 48

on wiretaps in 1969 **SIAPP1** 22

on withdrawing Gray's nomination as FBI Director at Gray's request **SIAPP1** 11

Nofziger, Lyn SIAPP4 18, 64-65, 79, 95, 96

Dean suggests as project coordinator for dealing with political enemies **SI8** 100

and Dole-Evans split **SI1** 35

and enemies list **SI8** 66, 113, 114-116, 121

Evans on **SIAPP4** 78

and monitoring of Democrats **SIAPP4** 9

role in Nixon re-election campaign **SIAPP4** 60

North Carolina

Republican campaigns in **SI1** 33

North Vietnam

map of **SI11** 80

Nixon on bombing of **SIAPP1** 17, 78-79

Northrop Corporation SIAPP2 197-200

See also U.S. v. Allen; U.S. v. Northrop Corporation and Thomas Jones

"Not for Women Only" (television show) SIAPP4 77

November Group SIAPP4 128

Nunn (senator), questioning by

Wheeler **SI11** 286-297, 332

Nunn, Lee SIAPP4 5, 11, 16, 49, 75, 81, 144; **SI1** 32, 80, 85; **SI6-2** 848

and AMPI's contributions to Republican Congressional campaign committees **SI6-2** 486, 945, 946-949, 487, 951, 952-963

assigned to Budget Committee **SI1** 85

and dairy industry campaign contributions **SI6-2** 808, 813, 814

Dent suggests replacing Evans with **SIAPP4** 37

role at CRP **SIAPP4** 13

Nunn, Lee, cited testimony of

on AMPI contributions to Republican Congressional campaign committees **SI6-2** 487, 951, 952-963

on transfer of money from Republican Congressional and Senatorial campaign committees to Republican National Finance Committee **SI6-2** 489, 965, 966-967

Nunn, Louis SI5-1 449-450

Kalmbach on money given to **TW 3** 666-667, 668, 715-716

Nurse Training Act of 1972

impoundment of funds for sections of **SI12** 22

Nussbaum, Bernard W. II 1 552; **SUMM I** 1

background of **II 3** 1459-1460

biography of **II 3** 2144

Doar on background of **II 1** 58-59

and presentation of evidence on Nixon's income tax **II 3** 1460-1505, 1507-1530

presentation of summary of evidence to House Judiciary Committee Impeachment Inquiry on

Nixon's income tax **II 3** 2001-2013

presentation of summary of evidence to House Judiciary Committee Impeachment Inquiry on Nixon's noncompliance with House Judiciary Committee Impeachment Inquiry subpoenas **II 3** 1994-2000

O'Brien, Lawrence F., Jr.

Baldwin monitors tapped telephone of **SI1** 23, 223, 224-231

and break-in and wiretapping of telephone at DNC headquarters **SI1** 23, 215, 216-222; **SI2** 2, 66, 671, 672

in Caulfield memos to Dean on *Millhouse: A White Comedy* **SI8** 184, 185

in Colson-Haig discussion **TW 3** 361-362

Colson tells Magruder information is needed about him **SUMM I** 31

court litigation on Nixon-Haldeman-Dean taped discussion of IRS investigation by **SI8** 28-29, 331-332, 333-349

Dean on White House efforts to embarrass **SI7-1** 351-352

Dean on White House interest in **SI1** 41

on DNC suit against CRP **SI2** 2, 302-303

Dyson and **SI8** 73, 107

Ehrlichman asks Kalmbach to make "plant" on **II 2** 1290-1292

Ehrlichman and IRS investigation of **SI8** 23, 217, 218-225

IRS audit of **II 2** 1284-1287

IRS audit of, Watergate break-in and **II 2** 1296-1297

IRS informs Ehrlichman of termination of investigation of **SI8** 24, 227, 228-235

IRS investigation of **SUMM I** 142

in Article of Impeachment II **RHJC** 142-143

in Jenner's presentation of summary of evidence to House Judiciary Committee Impeachment Inquiry on Nixon's abuse of powers **II 3** 1987-1989

in Minority of House Judiciary Committee Impeachment Inquiry views on Articles of Impeachment **RHJC** 440

letter to Nixon requesting special prosecutor **SI2** 2, 97

in Nixon-Haldeman-Dean discussion on Dean working through IRS **II 2** 1295-1296

Nixon's response to comment that Watergate burglars had direct link to White House **SIAPP1** 2

plan to wiretap convention suite of **SI3-2** 1007-1008

reason for electronic surveillance of **SI1** 65, 67, 72

as target of electronic surveillance **SI1** 71-72

as target of Liddy plan **SI1** 10, 61, 70, 71-72

O'Brien, Paul L. II 3 1626-1627

Bittman on meeting between Hunt and **TW 2** 25-27, 47-49, 50-52, 70, 79-80

Bittman on meetings with **TW 2** 5-6, 7-10, 32

Dean on conversation about Hunt's demands for money with **TW 2** 238-239, 245, 258-259

Haldeman tells Nixon he believes Mitchell approved Liddy plan **SI4-1** 355-357

House Judiciary Committee Impeachment Inquiry discussion on subpoenaing as witness **II 2** 981-982

O'Brien, Paul L. *(Continued)*
    and Hunt's demands for money **SI3-1** 202; **SI3-2** 1020; **SI4-3** 1643-1644
    informs Dean about McCord's letter to Sirica **SI4-1** 276-277
    informs Dean that McCord's letter to Sirica has been read in open court **SI4-1** 6, 235, 236-237
    meeting with Dean on Hunt's demands **II 2** 795; **SI3-2** 707, 945, 946-949
    meeting with Ehrlichman **TW 2** 140
    meeting with Ehrlichman on information obtained from Magruder on Liddy plan **II 2** 856
    meeting with Ehrlichman on Magruder's, Mitchell's and Dean's involvement in Watergate **SI4-1** 32-33, 507-508, 509-729
    meeting with Hunt on money for Watergate defendants **II 2** 786-792; **SI3-2** 704, 901, 902-923
    Mitchell arranges meeting between Haldeman and **TW 2** 139-140
    money for Hunt and **SI3-2** 1232, 1233
    reads FBI reports given to Dean **SI2** 2, 558
    Reisner asks him to represent him **SI4-1** 491-492
    U.S. Secret Service White House Appointment Record for **SI3-2** 707, 945, 949
    and Watergate coverup **SI4-1** 357
    See also House Judiciary Committee Impeachment Inquiry, discussion on calling witnesses
O'Brien, Paul L., cited testimony of
    on meeting with Dean on Hunt's demands **SI3-2** 707, 945
    on meeting with Hunt on financial commitments **SI3-2** 704, 901, 902-905
O'Brien, Paul L., testimony before House Judiciary Committee Impeachment Inquiry TW 1 124-174
    on access to EOB **TW 1** 141, 145, 148
    on background **TW 1** 124
    on being retained by CRP **TW 1** 124-125
    on concerns about meeting with Hunt **TW 1** 149-151, 152-154, 155
    on concerns over Hunt's demands for money **TW 1** 164-169
    on contact with McCord's attorney **TW 1** 168
    on contacts with Senate Select Committee staff **TW 1** 136, 141
    on conversation with LaRue on payments to Hunt **TW 1** 133, 134
    on conversation with Mrs. Hunt **TW 1** 144
    on date of meeting with Hunt **TW 1** 137, 171, 156
    on Dean's testimony on his meeting with Hunt **TW 1** 169-170
    denies discussing payments to Hunt with LaRue **TW 1** 147
    on discussion on Executive clemency with Parkinson **TW 1** 168-169
    on discussion with Mitchell to make arrangements for meeting with Haldeman **TW 1** 129, 132, 134, 135
    on his knowledge of source of funds to Hunt **TW 1** 145-146, 153-154, 159-160, 174
    on Hunt's attitudes during meeting with him **TW 1** 173-174
    on investigations into Magruder's activities **TW 1** 158-159
    on knowledge of payments made to Hunt **TW 1** 171-172
    on meeting with Dean on his discussion with Hunt **TW 1** 127-128, 138-141, 151, 155-157
    on meeting with Ehrlichman **TW 1** 135-136, 143, 148
    on meeting with Hunt **TW 1** 125-127, 137-138
    on others possibly informing Dean of Hunt's demands for money **TW 1** 163-164
    questioning by St. Clair **TW 1** 135-142
    on reasons for discussing Hunt's demands with Dean only **TW 1** 172-173
    on reasons for leaving CRP **TW 1** 167
    on reasons for not indicating suspicions to Dean on source of money for Hunt **TW 1** 146-147
    on reasons for not telling LaRue or Mitchell about Hunt's demands for money **TW 1** 161-162
    on reasons for recommending settling of Common Cause and Democratic party suits against CRP **TW 1** 162-163
    on reasons for telling Ehrlichman about Hunt's demands for money **TW 1** 161-162
    on reporting to Dean **TW 1** 160-161
    on telling Ehrlichman about payments to Hunt **TW 1** 145-146, 153-154, 159-160, 174
    on uselessness of paying Watergate defendants hush money **TW 1** 147-148
O'Connor, James H. SIAPP2 271-272; **TW 3** 527-744
    letter from Jaworski on acceptance of Kalmbach's guilty plea **SI9-2** 562, 951, 957-958
    See also Kalmbach, Herbert Warren, testimony before House Judiciary Committee Impeachment Inquiry; *U.S.* v. *Herbert Kalmbach*
O'Connor, James H., questioning by
    Kalmbach **NSI3** 178
O'Dell, Robert SIAPP4 85
O'Donnell, John Jude SI9-1 486; **TW 1** 124-174
    on attorney-client privilege and O'Brien's testimony on Mitchell **TW 1** 129
    letter to Mitchell's attorneys on O'Brien's testimony before House Judiciary Committee Impeachment Inquiry **TW 1** 129-130
    See also O'Brien, Paul L., testimony before House Judiciary Committee Impeachment Inquiry
O'Donnell, Peter SIAPP3 28-29
"O'Hara—The United States Treasury" (television series) SI5-1 320-331
O'Malley, Francis A. TW 3 41
O'Reilly, Richard SIAPP4 21
Ober, Richard NSI4 107
Oberdorfer, Don SI7-1 364
Obstruction of justice
    Bittman on being used in **TW 2** 95-96
    Colson pleads guilty to **SI9-2** 580, 1053, 1057-1058
    Dean pleads guilty to **SI9-2** 542, 801, 802-809
    in Ehrlichman's testimony on conversation with O'Brien **TW 1** 171-172
    indictment of Mitchell, Haldeman, Ehrlichman, and Strachan for **SI9-2** 563, 959, 960-961
    Magruder discusses probable charges against him of **SI4-2** 711

Cox requests tapes of Nixon's conversations with
II 2 1346-1351, 1360-1364, 1366-1367
Dean informs him of destruction of material from
Hunt's safe TW 2 309-310
and Dean's efforts to stop Patman Committee
hearings SUMM I 51
decision to disclose information on Fielding break-
in to Byrne SI7-4 1645, 1975, 1976-1982
discussed by Nixon, Dean, Haldeman, and Ehrlichman SI3-2 1180
discussed by Nixon and Dean as special prosecutor for new grand jury SI3-2 1093-1094, 1111-
1114
discusses Fielding break-in information with
Kleindienst II 2 1232
discusses Fielding break-in with Nixon SIAPP1
47
on discussion with Nixon on directorship of FBI
TW 3 108-109
discussion with Nixon on immunity for Dean
NSI1 35, 223, 224-225
Doar on Nixon's reaction to information from II
3 1929, 1930
in Ehrlichman-Krogh discussions SIAPP3 257-
259
House Judiciary Committee Impeachment Inquiry
subpoenas for specified materials related to conversations between Nixon and SI9-2 568, 577,
977, 978-982, 1031, 1032-1036
and immunity for Dean SI4-3 1355
informed by Ehrlichman that Nixon does not
want any White House aides to be granted immunity II 2 857
informs Kleindienst of White House link to Watergate break-in II 1 593
informs Nixon of Fielding break-in and is told
Justice Department should not investigate it II
2 1228-1229, 1231, 1232
informs Nixon that Gray has destroyed documents from Hunt's safe NSI1 18, 137, 138-139
informs Nixon that LaRue has confessed to participating to crime of obstruction of justice
SUMM I 93, 95
instructions from Kleindienst on Watergate burglars SI2 7, 105, 112
instructions to Silbert on questioning of Segretti
SI7-3 1208, 1595, 1596-1602
Kleindienst on SI2 2, 579
Kleindienst reports to Nixon on meeting with
SI4-2 938
letter to Patman TW 3 170-175
and materials on Fielding break-in from CIA II 2
711-712
meeting with Dean on documents from CIA connecting Hunt and Liddy to Fielding break-in
SI7-4 1623, 1731, 1732
meeting with Gray on Hunt's files SI4-3 1328-
1329
meeting with Nixon on adverse information on
President SI4-3 1115-1116, 1627-1628, 1633-
1645
meeting with Nixon on April 15, 1973 after he is
briefed by Kleindienst II 2 870
meeting of Nixon, Ehrlichman and Ziegler on information furnished by SI4-3 1090, 1251, 1255-
1263

meeting with Nixon on Gray's disclosures on
Hunt's files SI4-3 1096, 1331, 1340-1343
meeting with Nixon on Haldeman, Ehrlichman,
and Liddy involvement with Watergate NSI1
33, 211, 213-216
meeting with Nixon on immunity for high White
House officials SI4-3 1099, 1395, 1400-1409
meeting with Nixon and Kleindienst on April 15,
1973 on information held by Watergate Grand
Jury SUMM I 90
meeting with Nixon and Kleindienst on information received from Dean and Magruder SI4-2
576-577, 973-974, 975-1011
meeting with Nixon on U.S. Attorneys' evidence
implicating Haldeman and Ehrlichman SI4-3
1089, 1223, 1224-1249
meeting with Nixon on Watergate on March 21,
1973 SIAPP1 12
meetings and conversations with Nixon SI4-3
1113, 1115-1116, 1613, 1618, 1627-1628, 1633
meetings and conversations with Nixon during
March and April, 1973, discrepancies in listing
sent to Cox SI9-1 16, 277, 278-287
meetings with Nixon, in Article of Impeachment I
RHJC 104-106, 106-108, 109-111, 113-115
meetings and telephone conversations with Nixon
on investigation by Watergate Prosecutors II 2
878-879, 882, 883-884, 885, 886, 888-889, 893
meetings and telephone conversations with Nixon
on Watergate Grand Jury proceedings SUMM I
91-92, 93, 94-96, 98-101
meets with Kleindienst and U.S. Attorneys on evidence of involvement of White House and CRP
in Watergate break-in and coverup SI4-2 569,
863, 864-865, 866-871
memo from Kleindienst on disclosing information
on Fielding break-in to Byrne SI7-4 1645, 1647,
1975, 1981-1982, 1995-1997
memo from Maroney on information from Fielding break-in related to Ellsberg case SI7-4 1640,
1929, 1933
memo from Ruckelshaus on electronic surveillance of Ellsberg SI7-4 1652, 2045, 2046-2049
memo from Silbert on Fielding break-in SIAPP3
239-241; SI4-2 578, 1013, 1016; SI7-4 1640,
1929, 1930-1931
memo on Ehrlichman, Haldeman's and Strachan's
involvement in Watergate SI4-3 1089, 1223,
1225-1226
memo to Byrne on electronic surveillance of Ellsberg SI7-4 1652, 2045, 2050-2055
in message from Dean to Nixon SI4-2 1031
Nixon asks him whether there is evidence against
Colson SUMM I 69
Nixon briefs Rogers on meeting with SI4-3 1102,
1421, 1426-1430, 1432
Nixon-Dean discussion on investigation conducted
by SI3-2 1013-1014
Nixon discusses relationship with SI4-3 1260
Nixon discusses reports from SI4-3 1153, 1154-
1155, 1156-1157, 1162-1163
Nixon-Ehrlichman discussion on forthcoming
meeting on immunity for White House staff
with SI4-3 1098, 1387, 1392-1393
Nixon explains Dean Report to SUMM I 91-92

Petersen, Henry E. *(Continued)*

Nixon on his lack of knowledge of new Watergate investigation ordered on March 21, 1973 **SIAPP1** 51-52

Nixon and Kleindienst agree to his participation at their meeting **SI4-2** 575, 961, 972

Nixon on meeting with **SI3-2** 1240

Nixon reports to Ehrlichman and Haldeman on meeting with **SI4-3** 1100, 1411, 1416-1418

Nixon tells him Haldeman had no authority over use of campaign funds for Liddy plan **SUMM I** 92

Nixon withholds information from **SUMM I** 7, 8

Nixon, Wilson, and Strickler discuss **SI4-3** 1517-1518

and Nixon's efforts to conceal activities of Plumbers unit **SUMM I** 136-138

and Nixon's efforts to prevent immunity for Dean **SUMM I** 96-99

and Nixon's efforts to prevent immunity for Dean, in Article of Impeachment I **RHJC** 106-108, 109-111, 113-115

Nixon's false statement on hush money and Executive clemency to **SUMM I** 100-101

notes on Ehrlichman's, Haldeman's and Strachan's involvement in Watergate **SI4-2** 576-577, 973-974, 1001-1002

orders Justice Department investigation on information in Ellsberg trial emanating from Fielding break-in **II 2** 1226-1228

and photographs taken in front of Fielding's office **II 2** 1227-1228

and prevention of Stans' scheduled Watergate Grand Jury appearance **SUMM I** 45

provides White House with Watergate Grand Jury information **II 1** 697

questions Dean on documents taken from Hunt's safe **SUMM I** 63

refuses to give Dean FBI reports **SI2** 2, 560

relationship with Nixon, Nixon's abuse of power and **II 3** 2024-2027, 2028-2032

report to Byrne on Halperin wiretap **II 2** 1239

responsibilities in Ellsberg case **II 2** 1231-1232

role in Nixon Administration **RHJC** 16-17

St. Clair on his reports to Nixon on Watergate Grand Jury testimony **II 3** 1903-1905

shows Dean documents from CIA **SI2** 2, 66, 671, 672

Silbert gives Dean's Fielding break-in information to **II 2** 1226-1228

and Stans' avoidance of testimony before Watergate Grand Jury **II 1** 695-697

and Stans' Watergate Grand Jury testimony **SI2** 2, 564, 565

taped conversations with Nixon **SUMM I** 158

telephone call from Kleindienst informing him that Ehrlichman does not want immunity for White House aides **SI4-1** 37, 547, 548

telephone call to Silbert for information on Magruder's Watergate Grand Jury testimony **SI2** 2, 42, 409, 412, 414, 584-586

telephone conversation with Nixon on April 14, 1973 on Dean's discussions with U.S. Attorneys **SI4-3** 1083, 1123, 1124-1130

telephone conversation with Nixon on Dean's information to U.S. Attorneys **SI4-2** 579-580,

1021-1022, 1032-1034, 1055-1056

telephone conversation with Nixon on Watergate Grand Jury **SI4-3** 1093, 1297, 1298-1303

telephone conversation with Nixon on Watergate Prosecutors learning about Fielding break-in **SI7-4** 1643, 1949, 1950-1966

telephone conversations with Kleindienst on Watergate break-in **SI2** 2, 6, 9, 101, 102-104, 121, 122-123

tells Dean's attorneys that Dean should not meet with Ehrlichman on his discussions with U.S. Attorneys **SI4-2** 579-580, 1021-1022, 1023-1024

and transfer of ITT documents from SEC to Justice Department **SI5-2** 932

warns Nixon there might be enough evidence to indict Ehrlichman, Haldeman, and Dean **SIAPP1** 45

See also House Judiciary Committee Impeachment Inquiry, discussion on calling witnesses

Petersen, Henry E., cited testimony of

on conversations with Nixon on Haldeman and Ehrlichman's possible resignations **SI4-3** 1109, 1531, 1535-1537

on conversations with Nixon on hush money **SI4-3** 1109, 1531, 1538-1539

on conversations with Nixon on immunity for Dean **SI4-3** 1537-1538

on convincing Nixon to disclose Fielding break-in information to Byrne **SI7-4** 1645, 1975, 1976-1978

on discussion with Nixon on Fielding break-in **SI7-4** 1643, 1949, 1956-1957

on discussions with Nixon on Dean's information to U.S. Attorneys **NSI1** 33, 211, 213-215; **SI4-2** 579-580, 1021-1022, 1028-1029

on discussions with Nixon of press reports on Nixon's involvement in Watergate coverup **SI4-3** 1115-1116, 1627-1628, 1634

on documents from Kleindienst **SI2** 2, 64, 651, 657-658

on eliminating "dirty tricks" from Watergate Grand Jury questioning of Segretti **SI7-3** 1208, 1595, 1601-1602

on Gray's destruction of documents from Hunt's safe **SI4-2** 578, 1013, 1018-1019

on Gray's information on destruction of Hunt's files **SI4-3** 1096, 1331, 1335-1337, 1338-1339

on informing Nixon about Watergate Prosecutors' knowledge of Fielding break-in **SI7-4** 1640, 1929, 1934, 1936-1939, 1643, 1949, 1964-1966

on interview with Dean on materials from Hunt's safe **SI4-2** 578, 1013, 1014-1015

on learning about Watergate arrests **SI2** 6, 101, 102-103

on meeting with Gray on destruction of Hunt's files **SI4-3** 1113, 1613, 1619-1621

on meeting with Kleindienst on Watergate evidence **SI4-2** 569, 863, 864-865

on meeting with Nixon on April 16, 1973 on evidence against Haldeman and Ehrlichman **SI4-3** 1089, 1223, 1227-1228

on meeting with Nixon on Ehrlichman's Watergate investigation **SI4-2** 576-577, 973-974, 1006-1010

on meeting with Nixon and Kleindienst to report

on information received from Dean and Magruder
SI4-2 576-577, 973-974, 978-998
on memo on evidence against Ehrlichman, Haldeman, and Strachan **SI4-3** 1089, 1223, 1224
on Nixon's comments on his role as "adviser" to
President **SI4-3** 1109, 1531, 1542, 1544, 1546
on reporting to Dean on Magruder's Watergate
Grand Jury testimony **SI2** 2, 60, 575, 582, 583
on role of Department of Justice **SI4-3** 1544-1546
on Stans being excused from Watergate Grand
Jury testimony **SI2** 2, 58-59, 561-562, 568-569
on Strachan's Watergate Grand Jury testimony
SI4-3 1109, 1431, 1540-1541
on telephone conversation with Nixon on April
15, 1973 on Dean's discussions with U.S. Attorneys **SI4-3** 1083, 1123, 1124
on telephone conversations with Kleindienst after
Watergate break-in **SI2** 2, 9, 15, 121, 122-123,
155-160

**Petersen, Henry E., testimony before House Judici-
ary Committee Impeachment Inquiry TW 3** 1-181
on concessions made on Stans' testimony before
Watergate Grand Jury **TW 3** 132-133
on criminal indictments or complaints filed between April 10 and April 30, 1973 **TW 3** 159-
160
on Dean's destruction of material from Hunt's
safe **TW 3** 151-152, 157-158, 179
on Dean's information on material from Hunt's
safe **TW 3** 75-78, 122, 130-131, 140-141, 145-
146
on discussion with Nixon on Haldeman and Ehrlichman resigning **TW 3** 110-112, 123-124
on discussions with Dean **TW 3** 130-131, 153-154,
158-159
on discussions with Nixon on immunity for Dean
TW 3 113-114
on documents received from CIA on questions
asked by FBI during its Watergate investigation
TW 3 3-4, 5-46
exhibits included in **TW 3** 5-70, 72, 88-94, 168-
175
on expressing concern over Senate Select Committee holding public hearings on Watergate **TW 3**
121
on Fielding break-in and Ellsberg case **TW 3** 73-
74, 144-145
on Gray confirmation hearings **TW 3** 107-108,
125-126, 128, 153
on his professional background **TW 3** 2
on illegal and legal uses of wiretaps **TW 3** 126-
128
on immunity negotations with Dean **TW 3** 116-
117, 176-177
on impropriety or propriety of his reporting to
Nixon **TW 3** 134-144, 148-149, 152-153, 154-
157, 161-162, 180
on legality of his disclosing information to Nixon
TW 3 103-105
on Magruder talking to Watergate Prosecutors
TW 3 117-119
on meeting with Nixon and Kleindienst on Dean's
information on Watergate coverup **TW 3** 80-85,
105-108
on meeting with Watergate Prosecutors on Dean's

information on Watergate coverup **TW 3** 78-81
on nature of House Judiciary Committee Impeachment Inquiry **TW 3** 160-161
on Nixon telling him not to investigate Fielding
break-in **TW 3** 85-86, 97-100, 119-120, 124-126,
162-164
on Nixon's denials of involvement in Watergate
coverup **TW 3** 114-116, 132
notes on meetings with Nixon **TW 3** 88-94
questioning by Doar **TW 3** 2-4, 73-87, 95-105
questioning by House Judiciary Committee Impeachment Inquiry members **TW 3** 122-178
questioning by Jenner **TW 3** 105-107
questioning by St. Clair **TW 3** 107-122
on reasons for not believing Nixon was implicated
in Watergate coverup **TW 3** 133-134
on reporting to Kleindienst on Watergate break-in
and coverup **TW 3** 2-3
on reporting to Nixon on Justice Department Watergate investigation **TW 3** 86-105, 110-117,
128-130, 146-147, 156-158, 164-165, 180
and submission of Byrne's name to Kleindienst as
possible head of FBI **TW 3** 107-108, 125-126,
128, 153
swearing in **TW 3** 1-2
on White House interference with Patman Committee hearing **TW 3** 165-167

Peterson, John II 2 1249

Peterson, Peter G. SI8 80
affidavit on meeting with Merriam and Casey
SI5-1 13, 267, 268-270
affidavit on meeting with Merriam and Geneen
SI5-1 14, 277, 278-280
copy of Walsh letter to Kleindienst delivered by
Merriam to **SI5-1** 15, 283, 304
and dairy industry problems **SI6-1** 367
in Dean memo on Brookings Institution **SI8** 89
in Ehrlichman memo to Nixon on antitrust policy
SI5-1 394; **SI5-2** 830
and ITT matter **II 2** 1007-1009, 1016-1017
letter from Geneen with memo on antitrust policy
SI5-2 513, 652-657, 688-689, 863, 875-880
letters from Merriam on antitrust suits against
ITT **SI5-1** 13, 267, 271-276; **SI5-2** 508-509,
513-514, 803-804, 812, 855, 863-864, 883-884,
943
letters from Merriam on Nixon administration antitrust policy **SI5-2** 660-661, 662, 696-697, 698
meeting with Geneen and Merriam on antitrust
matters **SI5-1** 14, 277, 278-281
meeting with Merriam and Casey on antitrust
matters **SI5-1** 13, 267, 268-276
memo from Ehrlichman on antitrust policy review
SI5-1 23, 393, 401
memo from Geneen on antitrust policy **SI5-2** 940-
942
memo from Merriam with attached letter from
Geneen on *ITT-Grinnell* appeal **SI5-1** 22, 377,
378-385
memo to Ehrlichman and Krogh on delay of *ITT-
Grinnell* appeal **SI5-1** 22, 377, 388-392
memo to Nixon on meeting with Geneen and
Merriam **SI5-1** 14, 277, 281
in Merriam letter to Connally **SI5-2** 658-659, 694-
695, 810

Peterson, Rudolph **SI5-1** 381; **SI5-2** 654, 690

Peterson, Walter **SIAPP4** 42

Philadelphia, Pa., as proposed site for Republican National Convention SI5-1 450

Philby, H.A.R. (Kim) **SI7-1** 402

Phillips, Kevin **SIAPP4** 47, 58-59
  and Republican campaign **SI1** 56-57

Phillips Petroleum Company SIAPP2 311-314
  See also U.S. v. *Phillips Petroleum Company and William W. Keeler*

Phipps, Mrs. Ogden **SI1** 85

Photographs
  of DNC documents, in Magruder's Gemstone files **SI1** 25, 233, 234-244
  of documents relating to DNC contributors, during break-in at DNC headquarters **SI1** 23, 215, 218, 221-222
  of Liddy at Fielding break-in **SI3-2** 943-944
  taken at DNC headquarters **SI1** 175, 181, 221-222

Picker, Arnold M.
  on enemies list **SI8** 73, 107, 119

Picker, David **SI8** 73, 107

Picker, Ruth **SI8** 73, 107

Pickering, John
  impeachment case against **II 3** 2200-2201

Pickle, J.J.
  letter from Jaworski on ITT investigation **SI5-2** 978-980

Pickle, J.J., questioning by
  Casey **SI5-2** 915-916
  Colson **NSI2** 190; **SI5-2** 760, 784-786
  Dean **SI5-2** 769
  Mallory **SI5-2** 927

Pico, Reinaldo **SI4-1** 221

Pitchess, Pete **SIAPP3** 18

Plesser, Tully **SIAPP4** 1

Plumbers unit II 2 1141-1148, 1158, 1161-1173, 1178-1181
  activities of **II 2** 1123-1132
  activities of, in Article of Impeachment II **RHJC** 161-166
  and Brookings Institution plan **II 2** 1132
  Butterfield on **TW 1** 57, 108
  Buzhardt denies Cox's requests for inventory of files of **SI9-1** 13, 257, 258-261
  Chenow and **SI2** 2, 485-486
  and Chenow interview **SI2** 2, 51
  and CIA preparation of psychological profile of Ellsberg **II 2** 1145-1146
  and CIA psychological profile of Ellsberg **II 2** 1168-1169
  Colson on activities of **TW 3** 412-416, 457, 479-481, 511-512, 513-515
  Colson's responsibility for dissemination of information obtained by **SI7-2** 546, 829, 830-841
  concealment of activities of, in Article of Impeachment II **RHJC** 166-170
  creation of **SI7-1** 341-342; **SI7-2** 530-649, 650-654
  creation and purposes of, in Article of Impeachment II **RHJC** 157-159

discussed by Nixon and Ehrlichman **SI4-3** 1137
Doar on Jaworski's staff examining White House files of **II 1** 211-212
document entitled "Specific Projects as of August 10, 1971" from files of **SI7-2** 556, 1005, 1006
Ehrlichman assigns Krogh and Young as co-chairmen of **SI7-2** 543, 795, 796-814
Ehrlichman instructs Young to put files in Nixon's files **SI9-1** 4, 127, 128-130; **SUMM I** 102-103
Ehrlichman on reasons for establishment of **SI7-2** 602, 623
Elements of Project "Et Al." and Agency Responsibility document from files of **SI7-2** 526, 829, 834
and expanded CIA psychological profile of Ellsberg **SI7-3** 1192, 1399, 1400-1420
FBI Chenow interview and **SI7-3** 1205, 1569, 1570-1574
and Greenspun matter **II 2** 1292
House Judiciary Committee Impeachment Inquiry discussion on activities of **II 3** 2023-2024
Hunt on **SI5-2** 780-783
Huston plan and **MMFL** 117-120
investigation of SALT leaks **SI7-2** 549, 887, 888-895; **II 2** 1144
involvement in activities related to White House political intelligence plan **RHJC** 36
in Jenner's presentation of summary of evidence to House Judiciary Committee Impeachment Inquiry **II 3** 1979-1980
Kissinger denies involvement with **SI7-1** 150
Krogh assigned by Ehrlichman to "special" national security project for White House **NSI4** 9, 85, 86-95
Krogh dropped from **II 2** 1185
Krogh on formation of **SI3-1** 25, 311, 324-325
and leak on India-Pakistan War **II 2** 1185
Liddy and Hunt recruited to and office space made available for **SI7-2** 544, 815, 816-825
Liddy informs LaRue and Mardian about activities of **SI3-1** 3, 87, 88-95; **SI2** 2, 27, 277, 278-296; **SI7-3** 1200, 1513, 1514-1521; **TW 1** 197, 235-236, 261
Liddy leaves **SI7-3** 1194, 1441, 1442-1448
meetings with CIA officials on Pentagon Papers matter **II 2** 1158
memos of, in Hunt's safe **SI7-3** 1204, 1557, 1558-1568
in Minority of House Judiciary Committee Impeachment Inquiry views on Articles of Impeachment **RHJC** 456-462
Mitchell on activities of **TW 2** 132-133
Mitchell denies knowledge of **SI7-1** 476
Nixon authorizes creation of **II 2** 1122
Nixon-Colson discussions on activities of **TW 3** 161-162, 180
Nixon and concealment of activities of **SUMM I** 136-138
Nixon on creation of **SIAPP1** 23; **SI1** 40
and Nixon-Dean discussion on hush money **NSI1** 21, 149, 150-155
Nixon denies authorizing illegal activities of **SIAPP1** 42
Nixon expresses concern over possible disclosure of activities of **SI7-3** 1202, 1533, 1534-1540

Nixon's abuse of power and activities of **SUMM I**
129-133

and Nixon's directives on FBI Watergate investigation **SI2** 2, 36, 355, 357, 358, 359, 360-361

organization of **II 1** 557; **TW 3** 196-207

organizational chart from files of **SI7-2** 543, 795, 814

presentation of evidence to House Judiciary Committee Impeachment Inquiry on **II 2** 1123-1147

projects related to discrediting of Ellsberg **TW 3** 209-229

reasons for establishment of **NSI4** 4, 43, 44-66

removal of Krogh from **SI7-3** 1193, 1421, 1432

reports to Ehrlichman on Ellsberg case **II 2** 1185

reports to Ehrlichman on Pentagon Papers project and obtains approval for Fielding break-in **SI7-2** 557, 1007, 1008-1028

reports from FBI to **SI1** 219

in St. Clair's presentation of evidence in behalf of Nixon **II 3** 1895-1897

St. Clair's presentation of evidence in behalf of Nixon on **II 3** 1815-1842

sources of information used by **SI7-2** 553, 951, 952-966

staffing of, in Article of Impeachment II **RHJC** 159-161

Watergate coverup and **II 2** 1195-1197

White House meeting on investigation of Ellsberg matter **NSI4** 16, 121, 122-123

White House refuses review of files of two former staff members of **SI9-2** 560, 935, 936-945

wiretapping by in 1971 **SI7-2** 545, 827, 828

Young and Krogh assigned by Ehrlichman as co-chairmen of **II 2** 1139-1140

See also Fielding break-in

Poage, W. Robert, AMPI contribution to SI6-1 216

Pocket veto

House Judiciary Committee discussion on **II 1** 196-200

Pole, Michael de la SI12 41-42

Polish-American Union SI1 35

Political asylum

for black extremists in foreign countries, Huston plan on **SI7-1** 400

Political enemies project

Colson's memo to Dean requesting IRS audit of Gibbons **SI8** 22, 213, 214-216

and court litigation over Nixon-Haldeman-Dean meeting of September 15, 1972 **SI8** 28-29, 331-332, 333-349

Dean assigned to **SUMM I** 30

Dean memo to Haldeman and others on "enemy" journalist **SI8** 21, 211, 212

and Dean's efforts to get IRS action against McGovern supporters **SI8** 25, 26, 30, 237, 238-271, 273, 274-279, 351, 352-3

and Dean's list of McGovern supporters given to Joint Committee on Internal Revenue Taxation **SI8** 26, 273, 274-285

and IRS investigation of O'Brien **SI8** 23, 217, 218-225

Liddy and **SI7-3** 1374

in memo from Strachan to Haldeman **SI1** 7, 31, 34

and Nixon-Haldeman meeting on Dean's working through IRS **SI8** 27, 287, 288-290

and opinion in *Center on Corporate Responsibility v. Shultz* **SI8** 32, 437, 438-440

in Political Matters Memoranda **SIAPP4** 59

Strachan memo to Haldeman on Liddy assignment to work with Dean on **SI8** 20, 205, 206-209

and termination of IRS investigation of O'Brien **SI8** 24, 227, 228-235

Political intelligence-gathering II 2 1119; **SIAPP4** 13; **SUMM I** 33-34, 125-126, 128; **SI1** 21, 197, 198-200; **SI7-1** 411-427; **SI7-2** 678; **SI8** 4, 43, 44-51

in Article of Impeachment I **RHJC** 35-39

Caulfield submission of Operation Sandwedge proposal **SI7-3** 1188-1189, 1339-1340, 1372-1376

CRP and "Sedan Chair II" **NSI1** 10, 67, 68-75

Dean assigned to **II 2** 1119

Dean on his role in prior to Watergate break-in **TW 2** 347-348

Dean-Nixon discussions on Haldeman's knowledge about and legality of **NSI1** 11, 77, 78-80

Democratic party primaries and **SIAPP4** 20

discussed by Nixon, Dean, and Haldeman **SI3-2** 809-810

in Doar's status report on House Judiciary Committee Impeachment Inquiry **II 1** 359-360

Ehrlichman's discussions with Strachan on **SI4-2** 571, 881, 882-890

Haldeman states he and Mitchell did not discuss with Nixon on April 4, 1972 **NSI1** 13, 85, 86-118

Haldeman's instructions to transfer Liddy's "capabilities" from Muskie campaign to McGovern campaign **SI1** 20, 191, 192-195

illegal, Presidential abuse of power and **SUMM I** 124-128

by Liddy, Hunt, Barker, and McCord preparatory to Democratic National Convention **SI1** 26, 245, 246-253

McCloskey campaign and **SIAPP4** 6

and memo from Huston to Haldeman on IRS Special Service Group as source of **SI8** 4, 43, 44-51

memo from Strachan to Haldeman on CRP system for **SI1** 14, 147, 148-154

Mitchell testifies before Watergate Grand Jury that he had no prior knowledge of CRP's or Liddy's illegal intelligence operations **SI3-1** 26, 353, 354-356

Nixon-Colson meeting on **TW 3** 254-255

Nixon on Colson's role in **NSI1** 120

Nixon and concealment of evidence of **SUMM I** 134-140

Nixon-Dean discussion of **SI3-1** 675-677

Nixon denies knowledge of campaign activities involving **SI1** 40

and Nixon's approval of Huston plan recommendations **SI7-1** 25, 445, 446-461

Nixon's approval of plan including electronic surveillance for **SUMM I** 29-32

plant in Muskie headquarters in Political Matters Memoranda **SIAPP4** 6

in Political Matters Memoranda **SIAPP4** 9

Political intelligence-gathering *(Continued)*
    relationship to Watergate break-in, summary of
      evidence to House Judiciary Committee Im-
      peachment Inquiry on **II 3** 1941-1945
    in status report of House Judiciary Committee
      Impeachment Inquiry staff **II 3** 2227
    Strachan memo to Haldeman on Liddy assigned
      to work with Dean on political enemies project
      SI8 20, 205, 206-209
    Strachan on Nixon's lack of knowledge of Politi-
      cal Matters Memoranda on **NSI1** 12, 81, 82-84
    in talking paper from Strachan to Mitchell
      SIAPP4 35-36
    See also Electronic surveillance; House Judiciary
      Committee Impeachment Inquiry, presentation
      of evidence on Huston plan; Huston plan; Inter-
      nal Revenue Service; Liddy plan; Political ene-
      mies project; White House surveillance activities
Political Matters Memoranda **SIAPP4** 1-151
    on amount of AMPI pledge received **SI6-2** 480,
      784, 816, 817
    Brooks' motion on releasing to public **II 3** 2053-
      2068
    on Buchanan's activities **SIAPP4** 71
    on campaign finances **SIAPP4** 15-16, 23-24, 49,
      81-83, 87-88, 93, 105-106, 113-114, 118, 125,
      135-136, 143
    on Chotiner's activities **SIAPP4** 70-71, 108, 126,
      145
    cited **SI1** 7, 11, 31, 32-36, 77, 78-83, 84-89
    on Colson's activities **SIAPP4** 71
    on Connally's role in Nixon re-election campaign
      SIAPP4 138, 144-145
    on conversation with Kalmbach on use of dairy
      industry contribution **SI6-2** 480, 784, 813-815,
      816, 817
    Cox requests copies of **SI9-1** 26, 371, 372-373
    Cox's efforts to obtain **II 2** 1372
    on CRP activities **SIAPP4** 115-116, 121-123
    on CRP finances **SIAPP4** 69-70
    on CRP political intelligence-gathering system **SI1**
      7, 14, 32-36, 37, 147, 148-154
    on CRP press relations **SIAPP4** 65-67
    on Dean's activities **SIAPP4** 71
    on Dean's efforts to turn off fundraising dinner in
      Rhode Island **SIAPP4** 17
    on Dean's role in Nixon re-election campaign
      SIAPP4 109
    on Democratic party primaries **SIAPP4** 20, 21
    on Dent **SIAPP4** 8-9, 16-17, 24-25, 49-50, 58-59
    on Dent's recommendations **SIAPP4** 13-14, 70,
      76, 88-89 94-95, 114-115, 127, 137, 144
    on Dent's reports **SIAPP4** 83, 106-107
    on development of political intelligence capability
      SI1 7, 31, 32-36
    in Doar's presentation of evidentiary material to
      House Judiciary Committee Impeachment In-
      quiry **II 1** 560-564
    on documentary film for campaign **SIAPP4** 27
    on Evans **SIAPP4** 95, 145
    Evans recommendations in **SIAPP4** 89-90
    on Evans' reports **SIAPP4** 78
    file turned over to Cox **SI9-2** 526, 591, 592-593
    on Flemming **SIAPP4** 30, 96

    on forthcoming *Wall Street Journal* article on
      "milk money" **SI6-2** 483, 847, 848
    on Garment's activities **SIAPP4** 126, 136, 146
    on Gleason and milk money **SIAPP4** 85
    and Haldeman's authority over campaign funds
      SUMM I 92
    and Haldeman's link to CRP **SUMM I** 26-28
    on handling of surrogate candidates **SIAPP4** 6
    on intelligence operation, Ehrlichman discussion
      with Strachan on **II 2** 871-872
    on investigation of San Diego as possible Republi-
      can National Convention site **SI5-1** 25-26, 423-
      424, 427, 428, 430-447
    on issues in campaign in Delaware poll **SIAPP4**
      9-10
    on Julie Nixon Eisenhower and "Registration '72"
      SIAPP4 63
    on Kalmbach and Nader's milk suit **SIAPP4** 82
    on Liddy assignment to work with Dean on
      political enemies project **SI8** 20, 205, 206-209
    on Liddy's transfer from White House staff to
      CRP **SI1** 8, 45, 46-51; **SI7-3** 1194, 1441, 1442-
      1448
    on MacGregor **SIAPP4** 131-132, 136, 146-147
    on MacGregor's activities **SIAPP4** 140-141
    on Magruder reporting that CRP had "sophis-
      ticated political-intelligence gathering systems"
      SUMM I 31
    on Magruder's projects **SIAPP4** 6-7, 13, 18-19,
      26-30, 51-54, 60-61, 72-73, 78-80, 86, 90-92, 96-
      97, 110-111, 121-123, 127-132, 138-141, 146-149
    on Magruder's proposals to Mitchell for "political
      matters" cabinet meeting **SIAPP4** 29-30
    on Malek's projects **SIAPP4** 123-124, 132-133,
      141-142, 149-150
    on McWhorter's activities **SIAPP4** 25-26, 108,
      121
    on meeting between Mitchell and Haldeman with
      "talking paper" for **SIAPP4** 23, 32-38
    on milk fund **SI6-2** 483, 486, 847, 861, 895, 896-
      913
    on milk producers **SIAPP4** 16
    on Miller **SIAPP4** 30, 57-58
    on Miller's activities **SIAPP4** 76-77, 95
    on Miller's recommendations **SIAPP4** 84
    on Mitchell's resignation and running campaign
      from office space at Mudge Rose **SIAPP4** 31
    on money for intelligence plan **SI4-2** 880-890
    on monitoring of Democrats **SIAPP4** 9
    Nixon agrees to turn over to Select Committee
      SI9-1 37, 425, 426-427
    Nixon gives to Select Committee **SIAPP1** 31
    on Nixon's announcement that he will run for se-
      cond term **SIAPP4** 27-28
    on Nofziger's activities **SIAPP4** 95, 107, 115, 120-
      121
    on obtaining of opposition material **SIAPP4** 79
    on Operation Sandwedge proposal **SI7-3** 1118-
      1119, 1339-1340, 1354-1364, 1372-1376
    on organizational set-up of Nixon re-election cam-
      paign **SIAPP4** 109-110
    on Platform Hearings **SIAPP4** 133-134
    on policies toward Conservative movement
      SIAPP4 3
    on political intelligence and covert activities
      SIAPP4 2

on political responsiveness of IRS **II 2** 1283
portion on use of campaign funds for surveillance cut out from **SUMM I** 30
on Presidential election of 1972 **SIAPP4** 1-2
on regular meetings and attendees within campaign organization **SIAPP4** 98-104
on Republican National Committee budget **SIAPP4** 63
on Republican National Committee matters **SIAPP4** 31
on Republican National Convention of 1972 **SIAPP4** 4, 7-8, 12-13, 77-78, 85, 91
on San Diego as possible Republican National Convention site **SI5-1** 25-26, 423-424, 458-459
on Sears' activities **SIAPP4** 119
on Sedam's activities **SIAPP4** 148-149
on Sedam's responsibilities **SIAPP4** 130-131
on selection of Republican National Convention site **SI5-1** 25-26, 423, 424, 464, 465-477; **NSI2** 12, 127, 130-135
Strachan on **SI1** 37-38
Strachan on Nixon not initialing those with items on CRP political intelligence-gathering operations **NSI1** 12, 81, 82-84
Strachan on preparing Talking Papers for **NSI1** 83
Strachan's destruction of **II 1** 611-613
subpoenaed **SI9-1** 35, 413, 414-417
on terminating services of "Chapman's Friend" **SIAPP4** 17
on Timmons' activities **SIAPP4** 125-126
on transfer of campaign funds from White House to CRP **SI3-1** 33-34, 425-426, 443-454
on use of TAPE contribution **SI6-2** 481, 821, 837
Political Strategy Group
members of **SIAPP4** 50
talking paper from Strachan to Mitchell on **SIAPP4** 40-41
Polk, Franklin G. SUMM I 1
Polk, James K.
on impeachment power of House of Representatives **SUMM I** 165
Polls
Haldeman's interest in **SI1** 90
Political Matters Memoranda on **SIAPP4** 86
Stans on payment for **SI1** 78
Strachan on **SI1** 95-96
in Strachan memo to Haldeman **SI1** 83
on use of San Diego for Republican National Convention **SI5-2** 575
Polper, David SIAPP4 27
Polygraph tests
equipment obtained by Plumbers unit for **II 2** 1144
for government employees, discussed at Nixon-Ehrlichman-Krogh meeting **NSI4** 13, 109, 110-114; **SI7-2** 868-885
Osborn testimony on instructions from Krogh on provision of equipment and operators for **SI7-2** 895
by Plumbers unit **II 2** 1144, 1147
Poole, John W.
memo on meeting with Chaffetz, Jentes, Connell, and McLaren on settlement of ITT antitrust cases **SI5-1** 7, 143, 166-167; **NSI2** 9, 81, 82-83

Poorman, Paul SIAPP1 65
Popkin, Samuel SI7-2 1023
Porter, Bart SIAPP4 53, 129; **SI1** 182
Magruder's Watergate Grand Jury testimony on **SI4-2** 819
money from Sloan to **SI1** 92, 93-94
Nixon-Dean-Haldeman discussion of forthcoming testimony of **SI8** 408
Porter, Herbert Lloyd SIAPP2 193-194
agrees to lie to FBI on reasons for CRP payments to Liddy **SI3-1** 10, 157, 158-164
discussed by Ehrlichman and Nixon **SI4-2** 920
false testimony to FBI **II 2** 729-730, 738; **SUMM I** 44
false testimony in *U.S.* v. *Liddy* on purpose of funds given to Liddy **SI3-1** 44, 501, 502-516; **II 2** 759-760
FBI 302 interview with on money paid to Liddy **SI3-1** 18, 235, 236-241
Nixon, Haldeman, and Ehrlichman discuss possible perjury of **SUMM I** 79-81
Nixon's attitude toward perjury before Grand Jury by **NSI1** 20, 145, 146-148
perjury by, in Article of Impeachment I **RHJC** 89-90
role in Nixon Administration **RHJC** 14
role on White House staff **II 1** 557
tells FBI agents that money paid to Liddy was for lawful political activities **SI3-1** 18, 235, 236-244
testifies falsely before Watergate Grand Jury on purposes of money paid to Liddy **SI3-1** 23, 291, 292-296
See also *U.S.* v. *Herbert Porter*
Porter, Herbert Lloyd, cited testimony of
on legality of CRP political intelligence-gathering activities **NSI1** 10, 67, 74-75
on Magruder's request that he lie to FBI on reasons for CRP payments to Liddy **SI3-1** 10, 157, 160-164
on reasons for perjuring himself on purpose of payments to Liddy **SI3-1** 44, 501, 504-506
on testifying falsely before Watergate Grand Jury on purposes of money paid to Liddy **SI3-1** 23, 291, 292-294
Porter, Richard H. II 2 994
biography of **II 3** 2151
Portland, Oregon, campus situation in, in Huston memo to Haldeman SI7-1 485
Portnoy, Gerald G.
letter to Nixons reporting on IRS adjustment of tax liability for 1969-1972 and noting no legal obligation to pay 1969 deficiency **SI10** 19, 405-411
Post office, high level authorities in, possible reaction to illegal mail coverage in Huston plan SI7-1 418
Presidential election of 1972
Nixon on boycotting investigating committees until after **SIAPP3** 5-6
Nixon-Haldeman discussion on **SIAPP3** 85-87
Nixon-Mitchell-Haldeman discussion on strategies for **SIAPP3** 23-33
in Political Matters Memoranda **SIAPP4** 1-2

Presidential power, Nixon's abuse of

and concealment of evidence of intelligence-gathering activities **SUMM I** 134-140

and concealment of Plumbers unit activities **SUMM I** 136-138

and enemies list **SUMM I** 141-142

Huston plan and **SUMM I** 126

and illegal intelligence gathering **SUMM I** 124-128

and illegal wiretaps of government officials and newsmen **SUMM I** 124-125

and improvements to Nixon's Key Biscayne and San Clemente properties **SUMM I** 151-152

and investigation of Schorr **SUMM I** 127

and Kleindienst hearings and antitrust suits against ITT **SUMM I** 144-148

and milk price-support issue **SUMM I** 149-150

and misuse of IRS **SUMM I** 141-143

and offer of position of FBI Director to Byrne **SUMM I** 138-140

Plumbers unit and **SUMM I** 129-133

summation of evidence of **SUMM I,** 153-154

and wiretapping and surveillance of Donald Nixon **SUMM I** 127, 128

and wiretapping and surveillance of Kraft **SUMM I** 125-126, 128

Press SI4-1 12-13, 311-312, 313-314; **SI7-1** 11, 249, 250-257

accounts of House Judiciary Committee Impeachment Inquiry **II 1** 154

on Black Panther Party **SI7-1** 397

in Colson memo to Haldeman on impact of Pentagon Papers publication **SI7-2** 532, 663, 664-673

Colson's responsibility for releasing information obtained by Plumbers unit to **SI7-2** 832

coverage of Kleindienst confirmation hearings **II 2** 1040, 1041

coverage of Watergate, in Nixon-Dean-Haldeman discussion **SI8** 401

Dean memo to Haldeman and others on "enemy" journalist **SI8** 21, 211, 212

and disclosure of Segretti's activities **SI7-4** 1617, 1657, 1658-1675

and disclosures on milk fund **SI1** 79; **SI2** 2, 44, 427, 428-441

effort to question Dean on Gray's "probably lied" statement **SI4-1** 6, 235, 236

and Ehrlichman's request that Kalmbach make "plant" on Lawrence O'Brien **II 2** 1290-1292

and Gleason **SI1** 82

on Gray's resignation from FBI **SI4-3** 1630

on House Judiciary Committee Impeachment Inquiry requests for White House materials **II 1** 191-193

and leaks of so-called classified information from House Judiciary Committee Impeachment Inquiry **II 2** 703-709, 739-740, 1115

leftist, restrictions on intelligence activity against, in Huston plan **SI7-1** 422

Magruder tells Higby he did not talk to **SI4-2** 613-616, 622, 625, 634-636

on milk price-supports decisions and AMPI's campaign contributions **II 2** 1080; **SI6-1** 165-166; **SI6-2** 483, 847, 848-861

Mitchell's release to after learning about Watergate break-in **TW 2** 149-152, 204-205

Nixon-Ehrlichman-Ziegler discussion of handling of **SI4-1** 23, 445, 452-463

Nixon-Haldeman discussions on stories linking Kalmbach to Segretti **SI7-4** 1618, 1677, 1678-1680

Nofziger's information to **II 2** 1282-1283

and Pentagon Papers controversy, Buchanan on **SI7-2** 708-709

possible reaction to increased electronic surveillance, in Huston plan **SI7-1** 414

possible reaction to use of surreptitious entry, in Huston plan **SI7-1** 420

relations with Eisenhower during World War II **NSI4** 83

and release of Hunt memo on Boudin to terHorst **SI7-2** 563, 1125, 1126-1149

Rodino instructs Doar, Jenner, and Impeachment Inquiry staff to decline interview with **II 1** 203-204

on Sandman's absence from voting on issuing subpoenas to Nixon **II 1** 344

statements from Rodino on closed sessions of House Judiciary Committee Impeachment Inquiry to **II 2** 800-801

stories on Bittman being unindicted coconspirator in Watergate coverup **TW 2** 72. 109-110

Time magazine's plans to publish article on White House wiretapping of staff members and newsmen **SI7-4** 1625, 1741, 1742-1748

UPI and AP wires for March 22, 1973 on Nixon expressing total confidence in Dean **SI4-1** 14, 319, 325-329

Weicker discusses Gray's destruction of Hunt's files with **SI4-3** 1614

Ziegler's briefing on White House staff and Watergate Grand Jury testimony **SI4-1** 26, 477, 478-479

See also Los Angeles Times Media; *New York Times;* Newsmen; Underground press

Price, Ray SIAPP4 17, 28, 50, 93, 113

Colson's memo on points Nixon wanted included in Presidential statement on Pentagon Papers matter **NSI4** 8, 81, 82-84

Primary elections

in Political Matters Memoranda **SIAPP4** 80

See also Democratic party primaries

Professors for the Re-Election of the President SIAPP4 146

Prostitutes

in Liddy plan **SI1** 59

Public Citizen, Inc. SI6-2 915

See also Nader v. *Butz*

Public debt ceiling law

and Presidential power to impound funds **SI12** 73-75

Public Health Service Act

impoundment of funds for sections of **SI12** 21-22

Public housing programs SI12 12-16

See also Housing programs

Public opinion **SI5-2** 495, 497, 645, 646-676, 681-712
Colson memo to Haldeman on impact of Pentagon Papers publication on **SI7-2** 532, 663, 664-673
and mail to House Judiciary Committee **II 1** 70-72, 74-77
Nixon-Dean-Haldeman discussion on effects of Watergate on **SI8** 414-416
See also Polls
Puerto Rican nationalist extremist groups, in Huston plan SI7-1 409
Puerto Rico, bombings in, in Huston plan SI7-1 409
Pugh, Muriel II 2 1088
Pursley, Robert, Laird on wiretapping of SI7-1 299-300, 327
Quie, Al SI6-1 366, 370
and milk price-support issue **NSI3** 124
Quinn, John C. SIAPP1 62, 66
Rabinowitz, Victor SI7-2 594, 1132
Radford, Charles Edward II
and leak on U.S. position on India-Pakistan War **SI7-3** 1426-1429
Welander's statement on **SIAPP3** 215-216
wiretapping of **II 2** 1185; **SI7-3** 1439-1440
Rafferty, Joseph A., Jr. SI2 2, 304
Ragan, John SUMM I 125
and wiretapping of Kraft **SI7-1** 316-319
Railsback, Thomas F. SUMM I 1
additional views on Article of Impeachment III **RHJC** 503-505
on AMPI contributions to congressional candidates **II 2** 1051-1052
on brief delivered by St. Clair **II 2** 1189
on calling Dean as witness **II 3** 1754
on calling witnesses before House Judiciary Committee Impeachment Inquiry **II 3** 1625, 1635, 1636, 1648, 1650, 1651-1652, 1652-1653, 1675-1676, 1700
concurrence with Minority of House Judiciary Committee Impeachment Inquiry views on Article of Impeachment III **RHJC** 493
on confidentiality of evidentiary material presented to House Judiciary Committee Impeachment Inquiry **II 1** 578
on cooperation between Jaworski and House Judiciary Committee Impeachment Inquiry **II 1** 59, 60-61
on Dean-Walters meeting on CIA aid to Watergate defendants **II 2** 725
on Doar-St. Clair correspondence **II 1** 172-173
on Ehrlichman's meeting with Byrne **II 2** 1207
on Ehrlichman's note of approval of Fielding break-in **II 2** 1169-1171
on Ehrlichman's Watergate investigation **II 3** 1970
on enforcement of subpoenas to Nixon **II 2** 800-801
on forthcoming report on rules of procedures for House Judiciary Committee Impeachment Inquiry **II 1** 404
on front groups used for advertising in Nixon re-election campaign **II 2** 1055
on hearsay evidence **II 2** 850

on House Judiciary Committee Impeachment Inquiry issuing subpoenas to Nixon **II 1** 313, 319-320, 334-335, 668; **II 3** 1536, 1558
on House Judiciary Committee Impeachment Inquiry's rules of confidentiality **II 1** 221-222
on Hunt's role in CRP **II 1** 635
on identification of voices on Nixon tapes **II 2** 1073-1074
on investigation of bombing of Cambodia in House Judiciary Committee Impeachment Inquiry **II 1** 369
on leaked Dixon memos **II 2** 1326, 1327, 1328
on leaks from House Judiciary Committee Impeachment Inquiry **II 2** 703-704, 1215
on materials from Jaworski **II 1** 106-107
on Nixon-Petersen conversation of April 16 on Dean's testimony **II 2** 1369
on Nixon tape with erasure **II 2** 1390
on Nixon tapes subpoenaed by House Judiciary Committee Impeachment Inquiry **II 2** 1345-1346
on Nixon's income tax **II 3** 1498
on Nixon's knowledge or lack of knowledge of Fielding break-in **II 2** 1147
on Nixon's noncompliance with House Judiciary Committee Impeachment Inquiry subpoenas **II 1** 438-439; **II 2** 906, 917-919, 925-926
on Nixon's tapes related to ITT matter **II 2** 1011-1012
on presentation procedures for House Judiciary Committee Impeachment Inquiry **II 1** 261-262, 269, 290-291
on procedural rules for handling Impeachment Inquiry material **II 1** 120-121
on procedures for House Judiciary Committee Impeachment Inquiry **II 1** 8, 380-381, 387, 390, 393, 397-398, 399-400
question on Jenner's interview with Kalmbach **II 2** 1292
on release of House Judiciary Committee Impeachment Inquiry evidentiary material to public **II 2** 979; **II 3** 1588, 1600
on Rodino's statements to press **II 2** 800-801
on rules on cross-examination of witnesses **TW 1** 88
on rules of evidentiary procedures for House Judiciary Committee Impeachment Inquiry **II 1** 469-470, 486-487, 491-492, 504-505, 507
on St. Clair's participation in House Judiciary Committee Impeachment Inquiry **II 1** 213-214, 232, 293-295, 339
on St. Clair's right to be present at House Judiciary Committee Impeachment Inquiry **II 1** 83
on scheduling of St. Clair's presentation of evidence **II 2** 1156
on security problems **II 1** 90
on separate Minority of House Judiciary Committee Impeachment Inquiry brief on impeachable offenses **II 1** 158
on setting completion date for House Judiciary Committee Impeachment Inquiry **II 1** 18
statement of concurring views with Report of House Judiciary Committee Impeachment Inquiry **RHJC** 281
on subpoena powers of House Judiciary Committee Impeachment Inquiry **II 1** 33, 65-66, 293

Railsback, Thomas F. *(Continued)*
on summarization of key White House transcripts **II 2** 858
on testimony of witnesses **II 2** 899
on transcripts of Nixon tapes used by St. Clair in his presentation of evidence in behalf of Nixon **II 3** 1747
on using subpoena powers of House Judiciary Committee **II 1** 185
on Waldie's motion on hearing testimony of witnesses in executive session **II 3** 1869-1870
on Wiggins' amendment to subpoena Nixon **II 2** 953-954

Railsback, Thomas F., questioning by
Bittman **TW 2** 71-72
Colson **TW 3** 457-459
Dean **TW 2** 299-303
Kalmbach **TW 3** 573
LaRue **TW 1** 247-248
Mitchell **TW 2** 173-175
O'Brien **TW 1** 146-147
Petersen **TW 3** 134-136, 137-138

Ramsden, Richard SI5-2 534, 535
See also Ramsden Report

Ramsden Report SI5-1 406; **SI5-2** 534, 535, 596, 758

Rand Corporation
in indictment against Ellsberg **SI7-3** 1452-1453
and Pentagon Papers affair **SI7-3** 1216-1218
Stanton tells Colson FBI had not taken action on case connecting Ellsberg to leak at **NSI4** 10, 97, 98

Randolph, A. Raymond, Jr.
memo to Friedman on appeal from adverse decision in ITT antitrust case **NSI2** 6, 45, 60-61
memo to Griswold seeking appeal from adverse decision in ITT antitrust case **NSI2** 6, 45, 46-54

Rangel, Charles B. SUMM I 1
additional views on Nixon's tax evasion as impeachable offense **RHJC** 343-347
on availability of tape on Nixon-Kleindienst discussion on Fielding break-in **II 2** 1233
on calling witnesses before House Judiciary Committee Impeachment Inquiry **II 3** 1665, 1671, 1704
on checking materials received from White House **II 2** 1066
on confidentiality of evidentiary material presented to House Judiciary Committee Impeachment Inquiry **II 1** 547
on decisions on elimination of investigations from Impeachment Inquiry **II 1** 365
on discovery of Watergate break-in by Wills **RHJC** 314
dissenting views supporting proposed Article of Impeachment on secret bombing of Cambodia **RHJC** 323-328
on distinction between White House papers and Presidential papers **II 2** 1339
on Doar-St. Clair correspondence **II 1** 171-172, 183
on Dorothy Hunt's death **II 2** 737
on efforts to obtain materials from Jaworski **II 1** 107
on evidence on date of LaRue's last payment to Hunt **II 3** 1756

on giving House Judiciary Committee Impeachment Inquiry information on Dorothy Hunt's death **II 3** 2000
on House Judiciary Committee Impeachment Inquiry issuing subpoenas to Nixon **II 3** 1540, 1558-1559
on leaks from House Judiciary Committee Impeachment Inquiry **II 2** 1265, 1451-1452; **II 3** 1836-1837, 1856
on legal standing of St. Clair with House Judiciary Committee Impeachment Inquiry **II 1** 220
on legality of domestic surveillance **II 2** 1108-1109
on Nixon piercing rules of confidentiality of House Judiciary Committee **II 1** 194-195
on Nixon's income tax **II 3** 1499-1500, 1517-1518
on Nixon's noncompliance with House Judiciary Committee Impeachment Inquiry subpoenas **II 1** 430; **II 2** 945
on Nixon's request for extension of time on answering House Judiciary Committee Impeachment Inquiry subpoena **II 1** 347-348
on Nixon's responsibility for erasures on tapes **II 2** 1390
on Nixon's right to excise material from tapes **II 1** 276-277
on Nixon's trip to Russia delaying House Judiciary Committee Impeachment Inquiry **II 1** 301-302
objection to conclusions in St. Clair's presentation of evidence in behalf of Nixon **II 3** 1735-1736, 1740, 1864
on possibility that subpoenaed tapes were destroyed **II 2** 947
on procedural rules for handling Impeachment Inquiry material **II 1** 116-117
on procedures for House Judiciary Committee Impeachment Inquiry **II 1** 40-41
on proposed Article of Impeachment on emoluments and tax evasion by Nixon **RHJC** 317-319
on proposed Article of Impeachment on secret bombing of Cambodia **RHJC** 316-317
on release of House Judiciary Committee Impeachment Inquiry evidentiary material to public **II 2** 976-977; **II 3** 1601-1602
on rules on cross-examination of witnesses **TW 1** 90
on rules of evidentiary procedures for House Judiciary Committee Impeachment Inquiry **II 1** 476, 523-524
on St. Clair's lack of responsiveness to House Judiciary Committee Impeachment Inquiry's request for White House materials **II 1** 275-276
on St. Clair's statement in court after Nixon was named as unindicted coconspirator **II 2** 1450-1452
on schedule for House Judiciary Committee Impeachment Inquiry **II 2** 1059-1060
on scheduling of presentation of evidence **II 2** 776-777
separate and additional views on Report of House Judiciary Committee Impeachment Inquiry **RHJC** 313-320
on separate Minority of House Judiciary Committee Impeachment Inquiry brief on impeachable offenses **II 1** 153

statement of additional views on Report of House
Judiciary Committee Impeachment Inquiry
RHJC 283-286
on transcripts of Nixon tapes used by St. Clair in
his presentation of evidence in behalf of Nixon
II 3 1733, 1734, 1748
on using subpoena powers of House Judiciary
Committee **II 1** 185-186
on wiretaps performed by Liddy **II 2** 1147

Rangel, Charles B., questioning by
Bittman **TW 2** 95-98
Colson **TW 3** 490-492, 512, 513
Dean **TW 2** 337-338
Kalmbach **TW 3** 729-731
LaRue **TW 1** 262-264
Mitchell **TW 2** 200-201, 214
O'Brien **TW 1** 164-166
Petersen **TW 3** 155-157

Rankin, J. Lee SUMM I 54
Colson recommends to Nixon as possible special
counsel **TW 3** 333, 334

Rappeport, Michael SI8 124

Rarick, John SIAPP4 16

Raskin, Marcus SI7-2 1023

Rasmussan, Ethan SI6-2 819, 820

Rather, Dan SIAPP1 46-47, 48, 51, 57, 81; **SI7-4**
1885
interview with Haig on "Face the Nation" **SI9-1**
14, 257, 266, 267, 276

Rayborn, George G., Jr. II 2 1331
biography of **II 3** 2151
presentation of evidence on White House interference with Cox's Watergate investigation **II 2**
1323-1387

Re-Elector, The **SIAPP4** 91

Reagan, Ronald SIAPP4 77, 95; **SI1** 85, 118
meeting with Nixon scheduled **SIAPP4** 141-142
Nixon campaign in California and **SIAPP4** 107
in Nixon-Mitchell-Haldeman discussion on California as site for Republican National Convention of 1972 **SIAPP3** 17
in Political Matters Memoranda **SIAPP4** 19
role in Nixon campaign **SIAPP4** 120
tax information on **SI8** 157

Rebozo, Charles Gregory "Bebe" SIAPP3 11
articles in *Newsday* on **II 2** 1281
campaign contributions to **SIAPP4** 106
Colson on Hughes money and **TW 3** 507-508
and designs for fence and hedge screen at Nixon's
Key Biscayne property **SI12** 163
Hughes contribution and **II 3** 1990-1991, 1994;
TW 3 735-739
IRS audit of **II 2** 1300; **SI8** 153
Kalmbach claims attorney-client privilege on testimony on his dealings with **TW 3** 668, 735-736
Kalmbach on his relationship with **TW 3** 534
location of home at Key Biscayne, Fla. **SI12** 156
in Nixon-Mitchell conversation **SIAPP3** 3
purchases 23 acres of Nixons' San Clemente property **SI12** 96
and requests for improvements at Nixon's San
Clemente property **SI12** 101
White House efforts to obtain IRS audit of writer
of *Newsday* article on **SI8** 16, 165, 166-174

Reciprocity SI5-1 151
and antitrust suits against ITT **SI5-1** 170

Reed, Ben
and Kalmbach's request for GSA payment for
housekeeping services at Nixon's San Clemente
property **SI12** 153-155

Reed, Daniel J.
letter from Morgan on organizing and inventorying of Nixon's pre-Presidential papers **SI10** 80
letter to Morgan on receiving "limited right to access" allowing Newman to work on Nixon's
1968 gift papers **SI10** 5, 87
meets with Stuart and Morgan on Nixon's pre-
Presidential and Presidential papers on March
11, 1969 **SI10** 4-5, 77-78, 79-80
memo of January 11, 1974 and telephone call
notes of March 24, 1969 on transfer of Nixon's
papers to National Archives **SI10** 84-86
and moving of Nixon's papers to National Archives for inventorying and organizing **SI10** 5,
81-82, 83, 84, 85-86

Reese, Mary Virginia SI7-3 1384

Reeves and Harrison, and Wagner & Baroody SI6-1
12, 197, 207

Regal, Sally II 2 994

Regan, John SI5-1 470
and Republican National Convention of 1972 **SI5-
1** 431, 432

"Registration '72" SIAPP4 63; **SI1** 86

Rehnquist, William II 3 1580
on impoundment of funds **SI12** 87, 88

Reifel, Ben SIAPP4 95

Reinecke, Howard Edwin II 2 1019, 1020; **SIAPP2**
372-381; **SI5-2** 531, 635, 715
and ITT-Sheraton Convention pledge **SI5-2** 614
letter to Timmons on San Diego **SI5-1** 25-26, 423-
424, 455
meeting with Haldeman and Gillenwaters **SI5-1**
429
See also U.S. v. *Howard Edwin Reinecke*

Reisner, Robert A.
and destruction of Gemstone files **II 1** 576
and Gemstone files **SI1** 25, 233, 234-244
informed by Magruder of Watergate arrests **SI2** 2,
106
Magruder's reaction to subpoena by Senate Select
Committee on Presidential Campaign Activities
of **SI4-1** 28, 487, 494-496
removal of Magruder's files by **SI2** 2, 126
subpoenaed by Senate Select Committee on Presidential Campaign Activities **SI4-1** 28, 487, 488-
493; **II 2** 855
telephone call to Liddy with approval of political
intelligence plan **SI1** 13, 115, 116, 128-129, 139,
140-146

Reisner, Robert A., cited testimony of
on approval of Liddy plan **SI1** 13, 115, 128-129,
140-146
on employment at CRP **SI4-1** 490
on Gemstone files **SI1** 25, 233, 237-241
on Sedan Chair II project **NSI1** 10, 67, 72-73

memo from Campbell with draft press release announcing increase in milk price supports **SI6-2** 478, 767, 770-773

memo to Shultz and Ehrlichman on "decisions on dairy problems" **SI6-1** 24-25, 359-360, 365-369, 371-378

memo to Shultz on milk price supports **SI6-1** 24-25, 359-360, 371-378

and milk price-support issue **NSI3** 124

Whitaker memo agreeing with recommendations against raising milk price supports to **SI6-1** 379-381

See also House Judiciary Committee Impeachment Inquiry, presentation of evidence on dairy industry campaign contributions

Rice, Robert, statements before Senate subcommittees

on GSA partial payment for installation of sewer system at Nixon's San Clemente property **SI12** 113-114

on GSA payment for den furnishings at Nixon's San Clemente property **SI12** 149

on installation of den windows at Nixon's San Clemente property **SI12** 125

Rich, Spencer, article in *Washington Post* on public demand for Watergate investigation **SI9-1** 136

Richard A. Viguerie Company SIAPP4 7, 67; **SI1** 50

Richards, Dick SIAPP4 4

Richardson, Elliot L. SI11 323, 408-416; **SI7-2** 568

affidavit on conversation with Nixon on Executive privilege and Cox's Watergate investigation **SI9-1** 8, 151, 157-159

affidavit on dealings with Haig and Nixon on Cox's alleged investigation of Nixon's expenditures on his San Clemente property **SI9-1** 21, 329, 330-332

affidavit on discussion with Nixon on Agnew matter and discharging Cox **SI9-2** 533, 737, 738-740

affidavit on Haig's telephone calls on Nixon's complaints about Cox's activities **SI9-1** 33, 403, 404-406

affidavit on Nixon's comment on getting rid of Cox **II 2** 1384-1385

and Agnew's trial **II 1** 61

announcement that he will appoint Special Watergate Prosecutor if confirmed as Attorney General **II 2** 1333; **SI9-1** 6, 139, 140-143

appoints Cox as Special Watergate Prosecutor **SUMM I** 102

cited testimony at his confirmation hearings **SI4-3** 1118, 1651, 1652

confirmed as Attorney General **II 2** 1335

Cox tells him White House is attempting to place materials out of his reach **SI9-2** 527, 597, 598-606; **II 2** 1372-1373

and Cox's efforts to obtain file of documents on milk producers' campaign contributions **SI9-1** 40, 41, 475, 476-480, 481, 482-487

and Cox's jurisdiction over Fielding break-in material **II 2** 1370-1373

and Cox's rejection of Stennis Plan **SI9-2** 538, 773, 774-781

designates Cox as Special Watergate Prosecutor and provides guidelines for Watergate investiga-

tion **SI9-1** 7, 145, 146-150

designates Cox as Special Watergate Prosecutor and submits statement to Senate Judiciary Committee on duties and responsibilities of Special Watergate Prosecutor **II 2** 1333-1335

discussion with Nixon on Executive privilege **II 2** 1335-1338, 1353-1354, 1452-1454

in Ehrlichman-Krogh discussion **SIAPP3** 250, 251, 252, 253

and false data submitted by Defense Department to Senate Armed Services Committee **SI11** 65, 326-328

and firing of Cox **II 2** 1395-1401

guidelines for Special Watergate Prosecutor **II 2** 1338

Haig complains about Cox's activities to **II 2** 1352; **SI9-1** 33, 158-159, 403, 404-406

on legal basis for domestic surveillance **II 2** 1093-1094

letter from Nixon instructing him to direct Cox to make no further attempts to obtain subpoenaed White House materials **SI9-2** 541, 797, 798

letter to Mathias on proposing Stennis Plan to Cox **SI9-2** 537, 765, 768-770

letter to Nixon on dealings with Cox on Stennis Plan **SI9-2** 543, 811, 812-813

letter to Senate Foreign Relations Committee on legality of Justice Department wiretaps **NSI4** 29, 31, 193, 194-195, 199, 200-201

log for October 15, 1973 on meetings with Haig and Cox **SI9-2** 536, 755, 756

log for October 18, 1973 **SI9-2** 538, 773, 777

log for October 19, 1973 **SI9-2** 540, 787, 788

log for October 20, 1973 **SI9-2** 544, 815, 821

meeting with Haig, Garment, Buzhardt, and Wright on Cox's rejection of Stennis Plan **SI9-2** 540, 787, 788-796

meetings with Haig and Cox on tapes litigation **SI9-2** 536, 755, 756-763

memo to Buzhardt on Nixon's desire to refuse to turn over milk producers' campaign contributions file to Cox **SI9-1** 40, 41, 475, 479-480, 481, 483-484

news conference of October 23, 1973 on Cox's rejection of Stennis Plan **SI9-2** 538, 773, 778

Nixon announces nomination as Attorney General **SIAPP1** 13

Nixon on confidence in **SIAPP1** 17, 19

Nixon on selection of Cox as Special Prosecutor by **SIAPP1** 25

Nixon's television announcement of appointment as Attorney General **SI4-3** 1119, 1657, 1658-1659

and Nixon's waiver of Executive privilege for Watergate investigation **SI9-1** 8, 151, 152-159

nomination as Attorney General **II 2** 1333; **SI9-1** 5, 131, 132-135; **SI4-3** 1118, 1651, 1652-1655

prepares summary of reasons for resignation over possible order to fire Cox **SI9-2** 539, 783, 784-785

press conference on appointment of Special Prosecutor **SI4-3** 1118, 1651, 1653

press conference of October 23, 1973 on refusal to fire Cox and resignation **SI9-2** 544, 815, 816-817

Richardson, Elliot L. *(Continued)*
press interview of May 10, 1970 on invasion of Cambodia **SI11** 36-37, 229-230
refusal to fire Cox and resignation of **II 2** 1387; **SI9-2** 544, 815, 816-825
Senate confirmation as Attorney General **SI9-1** 8, 151, 156
Senate consideration of nomination for Attorney General **SI9-1** 8, 151, 154-155
and Stennis Plan **II 2** 1385-1387
submits statistical report on bombing of Cambodia indicating no air strikes from January 1965 to May 1970 **SI11** 22-23, 177-179
submits written proposal to Cox on third party verifier selected by Nixon preparing transcripts of subpoenaed tapes **SI9-2** 537, 765, 766-772
telephone call from Haig complaining about Cox's investigation **II 2** 1363
See also Holtzman v. *Richardson*

Richardson, Elliot L., cited testimony of
on authorization for wiretaps on newsmen **SI7-1** 10, 239, 245-246
on Buzhardt informing him that Cox would receive ITT file **SI9-1** 15, 269, 275
on Buzhardt's instructions on Cox's request for milk producers' campaign contributions file **SI9-1** 40, 475, 477-478
on Cox's complaint on removal of White House documents **SI9-2** 527, 597, 598
on Cox's rejection of Stennis Plan **SI9-2** 538, 773, 779-780
on FBI records of wiretaps on White House staff members and government employees **SI7-1** 283-284, 306-307
on meetings with Haig and Cox after Court of Appeals decision on tapes litigation **SI9-2** 536, 755, 759-761
on nomination as Attorney General **SI4-3** 1119, 1657, 1658-1659
on procedures for wiretapping **SI7-1** 4, 157, 158
on reactions to Cox's objections to Stennis Plan **SI9-2** 540, 787, 793-794
on results of wiretaps on National Security Council members **SI7-1** 9, 223, 233
on wiretapping of government officials and newsmen **SI7-1** 3, 141, 152-153
on wiretapping of White House staff members unrelated to national security **SI7-1** 12, 259, 260

Richey, Charles R. SI2 2, 607, 615; **SI8** 301-303, 328, 333

Rietz, Kenneth SIAPP4 7, 130; **SI1** 36
and campaign approach to youth **SIAPP4** 26-27
discussion with Porter on legality of CRP political intelligence-gathering activities **NSI1** 75
and political intelligence **SI3-2** 809
in Political Matters Memoranda **SIAPP4** 2-3
role in Nixon re-election campaign **SIAPP4** 18
youth vote and **SIAPP4** 41

Ring, Eleanor SI5-1 438

Ripon Society SIAPP3 14; **SIAPP4** 71
suit against Republican National Committee **SIAPP4** 53

Ritter, Halsted L.
impeachment case against **II 1** 499; **II 3** 2213-2215

Ritzel, Richard S. II 3 1459-1460
advises Nixon to contribute pre-Presidential papers **SI10** 1, 40, 41, 42
asks Tannian to draft Nixon's deed of gift of pre-Presidential papers **SI10** 1, 43
and discussions with Nixon on future gifts of pre-Presidential papers in 1969 **SI10** 4, 66
interview with **SI10** 38-39
letter to Krogh on Nixon's future gifts of pre-Presidential and Presidential papers **SI10** 4, 72-73
on memo to Krogh from Jones of President Johnson's staff on names for handling Nixon's contribution of pre-Presidential papers **SI10** 39
memo to Nixon with drafts of two versions of Nixon's deed of gift of pre-Presidential papers **SI10** 1-2, 44-57
and Nixon's decision to execute restrictive deed for gift of pre-Presidential papers in December 1968 **SI10** 2, 58
and selection of pre-Presidential papers for Nixon's gift to National Archives **SI10** 2-3, 59, 60-61
See also House Judiciary Committee Impeachment Inquiry, presentation of evidence on Nixon's income tax

Rivers (senator)
Defense Department states he was advised of Cambodian and Laotian bombings **SI11** 63, 317-318

Rivers, Mr. TW 2 6-7, 13-14, 20-22, 23-25, 90
See also Bittman, William O., testimony before House Judiciary Committee Impeachment Inquiry; Ulasewicz, Anthony T.

Rives, Lloyd M. SI11 126, 129, 131

Rizzo, Frank SIAPP4 121

Robert R. Mullen & Company
CIA memo to Justice Department on Hunt's role at **TW 3** 62-63
CIA memos to FBI on **TW 3** 11-12

Robertson, Walter
meets with Stuart and Morgan on Nixon's pre-Presidential and Presidential papers on March 11, 1969 **SI10** 4-5, 77-78, 79-80

Robinson, Ken SIAPP4 50

Robinson, William J.
and construction of chain link fence at Nixon's San Clemente property **SI12** 146, 147
letter to Steiner Electric Co. ordering new heating system at Nixon's San Clemente property **SI12** 108

Rockefeller, Jay SIAPP4 89

Rockefeller, Nelson SIAPP4 82, 95, 118; **SI7-4** 1751
in Nixon-Mitchell-Haldeman discussion **SIAPP3** 21

Rockefeller, Winthrop SIAPP4 7

Rodak, Michael, Jr. SI5-1 265, 364

Rodham, Hillary II 1 105; **II 2** 1331
biography of **II 3** 2152

Rodino, Peter W., Jr. II 2 773-774
on adoption by House Judiciary Committee Impeachment Inquiry of rules of procedures for House Judiciary Committee Impeachment Inquiry II 1 280-281
on Agnew case II 1 61
announces that Garrison will make presentation II 3 1923-1924
on answering of mail to House Judiciary Committee Impeachment Inquiry II 1 74
on appeal from Sirica's ruling on turning Grand Jury materials over to House Judiciary Committee Impeachment Inquiry II 1 202-203, 225-226
on attorney-client privilege and O'Brien's testimony on Mitchell TW 1 130-131, 134
on brief being prepared II 1 97-98
on brief delivered by St. Clair II 2 1188-1189, 1198-1199
on calling witnesses before House Judiciary Committee Impeachment Inquiry II 3 1631, 1636, 1639, 1644, 1660, 1671-1672
on change in seating arrangement during House Judiciary Committee Impeachment Inquiry II 1 201
on confidentiality of evidentiary material presented to House Judiciary Committee Impeachment Inquiry II 1 551-552, 577-578, 586
on Conyers' motion to cite Nixon for contempt of Congress for his noncompliance with House Judiciary Committee Impeachment Inquiry subpoenas II 1 462-463
on correspondence with Nixon on his cooperation with House Judiciary Committee Impeachment Inquiry II 1 169-170
correspondence with Nixon on House Judiciary Committee Impeachment Inquiry subpoena of May 30, 1974 SI9-2 581, 1059, 1061-1069
on counting of mail II 1 75
on delays in starting House Judiciary Committee Impeachment Inquiry II 1 196
on deletions from Nixon tapes II 2 1013
on discrepancies between transcripts of Nixon tapes II 2 814
and discussion of House Judiciary Committee Impeachment Inquiry issuing subpoenas to Nixon II 1 639-676
on discussions with White House on House Judiciary Committee Impeachment Inquiry requests for materials II 1 193
distributes letters from St. Clair and Nixon to House Judiciary Committee Impeachment Inquiry members II 2 827
on Doar, Jenner, and Impeachment Inquiry staff declining interviews with press II 1 203-204
on Doar-St. Clair correspondence II 1 186
on documents being made public SUMM I 1
on Drinan's motion for subpoena for undelivered White House material II 1 183-185
on evidentiary procedures and inclusion of St. Clair's participation in House Judiciary Committee Impeachment Inquiry II 1 305-306
foreword to Statement of Information SI1 3-4
on format for St. Clair's presentation of evidence in behalf of Nixon II 3 1719-1720
on forthcoming recommendations from Subcommittee on Civil liberties on rules of procedures

for House Judiciary Committee Impeachment Inquiry II 1 403
on Garrison's statement that Impeachment Inquiry staff is bipartisan rather than nonpartisan II 3 2037
on hard work of legal staff II 1 93
on House Judiciary Committee Impeachment Inquiry informing authorities of violations of the law it discovers II 2 1273
on House Judiciary Committee Impeachment Inquiry issuing subpoena to Clerk of House of Representatives for records of dairy industry campaign contributions II 3 1576-1577
on House Judiciary Committee Impeachment Inquiry obtaining materials on ITT and dairy industry contributions II 1 677-678
on House Judiciary Committee Impeachment Inquiry procedures for taking depositions II 1 230
on House Judiciary Committee Impeachment Inquiry receiving two versions of Ehrlichman's handwritten notes II 3 1886
on House Judiciary Committee Impeachment Inquiry rules of confidentiality II 1 221-222
on House Judiciary Committee Impeachment Inquiry rules on testimony and questioning of witnesses TW 1 5-6
instructed to write letter to Sirica requesting Watergate Grand Jury materials II 1 169
on invitation from Sirica to Doar and Jenner to attend proceeding on sealed material from Watergate Grand Jury II 1 134
on issuing subpoenas to Nixon II 1 282, 324-325, 327-328
on issuing subpoenas to Nixon and confidentiality II 1 334
on leaked Dixon memos II 2 1327-1328
on leaks from House Judiciary Committee Impeachment Inquiry II 1 89-90; II 2 703, 706-707, 739-740, 767-769, 777-778, 1087-1088, 1216
letter from Nixon declining to produce materials covered by House Judiciary Committee subpoena of May 15, 1974 SI9-2 576, 1027, 1028-1030
letter from Nixon refusing to comply with subpoena for Presidential tapes and papers in addition to transcripts provided SIAPP1 103
letter from Patman on efforts to block House Banking and Currency Committee Watergate investigation SUMM I 115-117
on letter from St. Clair to Doar II 1 132, 279-281
letter from St. Clair on Nixon's refusal to furnish material called for in House Judiciary Committee Impeachment Inquiry subpoena of May 30, 1974 SI9-2 581, 1059, 1060
on letter sent to Sirica requesting Watergate Grand Jury materials II 1 193
on mail on to House Judiciary Committee Impeachment Inquiry II 1 75-76
on Maraziti's proposed vote of confidence for Kissinger II 2 1214
and media coverage of House Judiciary Committee Impeachment Inquiry II 1 101-105, 129
on members studying St. Clair's brief prior to official presentation of II 2 1214-1217

Rodino, Peter W., Jr. *(Continued)*
on Nixon's letter declining to comply with subpoena **II 2** 1153-1154
on Nixon's noncompliance with House Judiciary Committee Impeachment Inquiry subpoenas **II 1** 449-450
on Nixon's request for extension of time on answering House Judiciary Committee Impeachment Inquiry subpoena **II 1** 344, 353-354
on notifying Senate Judiciary Committee of House Judiciary Committee Impeachment Inquiry discussion on Silbert's activities **II 2** 1230
on obtaining materials from Jaworski **II 1** 108-109, 112
on opening of House Judiciary Committee Impeachment Inquiry **II 2** 775
opening statement to House Judiciary Committee Impeachment Inquiry **TW 1** 1-2; **SI1** 2-4
on possibly forged letter from House Judiciary Committee Impeachment Inquiry **II 1** 70-72
on procedures for House Judiciary Committee Impeachment Inquiry **II 1** 3-4
on procedures for taking depositions **II 1** 240
on questions during presentation of evidentiary material to House Judiciary Committee Impeachment Inquiry **II 1** 678, 679
questions Jenner's line of questioning of Bittman **TW 2** 61-62
on record of House Judiciary Committee Impeachment Inquiry **II 1** 39-40
on relationship with Joint Committee on Internal Revenue Taxation **II 1** 95-96
on release of draft Articles of Impeachment **II 3** 1923-1924
on release of House Judiciary Committee Impeachment Inquiry evidentiary material to public **II 2** 977; **II 3** 1585-1586
on relevancy of evidence on enemies list **II 2** 1269-1270
remarks prior to presentation of evidentiary material to House Judiciary Committee Impeachment Inquiry **II 1** 543-544
report on other work of House Judiciary Committee **II 1** 54-55
on right of members of House Judiciary Committee to examine correspondence **II 1** 172
on right of Minority of House Judiciary Committee Impeachment Inquiry to subpoena witnesses **II 1** 25-26
Rodino on letter sent to for Watergate Grand Jury materials **II 1** 193
on rules for Impeachment Inquiry staff **II 1** 129-130
ruling on point of order on Dennis' motion for House Judiciary Committee Impeachment Inquiry subpoenas for additional witnesses **II 2** 986-987
ruling on St. Clair's right to object to line of questioning by House Judiciary Committee Impeachment Inquiry members **TW 2** 198
ruling on St. Clair's use of transcripts during questioning of witnesses **TW 3** 433-434
ruling on transcripts of Nixon tapes used by St. Clair in his presentation of evidence in behalf of Nixon **II 3** 1731-1732, 1732-1733

rulings on Hundley's objections to line of questioning of Mitchell **TW 2** 168, 198
on rumors that House Judiciary Committee Impeachment Inquiry is investigating death of Kopechne **II 1** 611
on St. Clair's lack of response to House Judiciary Committee Impeachment Inquiry's requests for White House materials **II 1** 249-251
on St. Clair's reference to transcript of March 22 Nixon tape refused to House Judiciary Committee Impeachment Inquiry **II 3** 1906-1910
on Sandman's absence from voting on issuing subpoenas to Nixon **II 1** 343
on schedule for Garrison's presentation **II 3** 2033
on schedule for House Judiciary Committee Impeachment Inquiry **II 1** 339; **II 2** 1059-1060
on scheduling of presentation of evidence **II 2** 773-774
on scheduling of St. Clair's presentation of evidence **II 2** 1156-1157; **II 3** 1531-1532
on security of House Judiciary Committee Impeachment Inquiry **II 1** 635
on selection of House Judicary Committee Impeachment Inquiry legal staff **II 1** 56
on separate Minority of House Judiciary Committee Impeachment Inquiry brief on impeachable offenses **II 1** 155-156
on setting completion date for House Judiciary Committee Impeachment Inquiry **II 1** 17, 18-19, 47, 48
on Sirica's invitation to Doar and Jenner **II 1** 147
on Sirica's ruling on turning Grand Jury materials over to House Judiciary Committee Impeachment Inquiry **II 1** 203
on statements in press on House Judiciary Committee Impeachment Inquiry requests for White House materials **II 1** 191-193
and timing of presentation on definition of impeachable offense **II 1** 92-93
on Waldie's motion on hearing testimony of witnesses in executive session **II 3** 1875, 1877
on *Washington Post* article on new information **II 3** 1977
on withdrawal of Wiggins' amendment to subpoena Nixon **II 1** 359
See also House Judiciary Committee Impeachment Inquiry

Rodino, Peter W., Jr., questioning by
Bittman **TW 2** 111-112
Butterfield **TW 1** 117-118, 119-120, 121
Colson **TW 3** 516-517
Dean **TW 2** 352-353
Kalmbach **TW 3** 741-742
Mitchell **TW 2** 214-215
O'Brien **TW 1** 173-174
Petersen **TW 3** 176-178

Rogers, James
in Nixon-Haldeman discussion **SI4-3** 1219, 1220; **SI4-2** 968, 970
in Nixon-Petersen discussion **SI4-3** 1248, 1402
Nixon's discussions on Watergate with **SI4-3** 1308
suggests Nixon appoints special counsel **SI4-3** 1401

Rogers, William P.
  admits air activity over Cambodia before change
    of government on May 13, 1970 SI11 37, 231-
    232, 233-235
  admits bombing of Cambodia in November 1970
    SI11 17, 162-163
  claims he neither approved nor knew about
    MENU dual reporting procedures in news con-
    ference of August 20, 1973 SI11 71, 347
  discusses Ehrlichman's forthcoming testimony
    with Nixon, Haldeman, and Ehrlichman
    SUMM I 84-85
  discussion with Nixon on Haldeman and Ehrlich-
    man's possible resignation SI4-3 1535
  meeting with Nixon on April 17, 1973 II 2 885-
    886
  meeting with Nixon, Haldeman, Ehrlichman SI4-
    3 1101, 1419, 1420
  Nixon discusses Byrne with SI7-4 1642, 1947,
    1948; II 2 1228
  speech at Cornell University on April 18, 1970
    reaffirming respect for neutrality of Cambodia
    SI11 32, 215
  statement on policy in Cambodia in 1969 and
    1970 SI11 14-15, 19-20, 145-146, 162-163
  television interview of January 15, 1971 on con-
    tinued air activity in Cambodia SI11 47, 260-
    262
  television interview of May 4, 1970 on Cambodian
    operation of May 1 SI11 35-36, 225-226
Rogovin, Mitchell, questioning by
  Webster SI6-2 829-831
Rohatyn, Felix G. SI5-1 132
  in Anderson column SI5-2 635
  discussions with Kleindienst SI5-2 679-680, 810
  and ITT matter II 2 1014, 1018
  letter to McLaren on consequences of ITT divesti-
    ture of Hartford SI5-1 24, 403, 419-422
  letter to McLaren on settlement of ITT antitrust
    cases and impact of divestiture of Hartford
    NSI2 9, 81, 96-99
  meeting with Kleindienst on ITT and Hartford
    Fire Insurance Company SI5-1 20, 367, 368-370
  meeting with Kleindienst, McLaren, and other
    ITT and Antitrust Division staff members SI5-1
    24, 403, 404-422
  in Merriam letter to Connally SI5-2 658, 694
  Mitchell and SI5-1 93
  Mitchell on contacts with SI5-1 179-180, 181
  and negotiations for settlement of ITT antitrust
    cases NSI2 84-85, 89-90
  and settlement of ITT antitrust cases SI5-2 555,
    558-559
  telephone call to Kleindienst NSI2 95
Rohatyn, Felix G., cited testimony of
  on Hume informing him about Beard's memo to
    Merriam SI5-2 491, 613, 626-627
  on meeting with Kleindienst and McLaren on
    ITT settlement SI5-1 407-409
  on meetings with Kleindienst and McLaren on
    ITT-Hartford Fire Insurance case SI5-1 20, 367,
    370
  on settlement of ITT antitrust cases NSI2 10,
    103, 122; SI5-2 485, 488, 549, 557, 595, 601

Rollins, John SIAPP4 17, 46, 127, 137, 144; SI1 85
Romney, George SI12 48, 49; SI5-1 327-328
  and impoundment of funds for federal housing
    programs SI12 12-16
Romney, Mrs. George SIAPP4 77
Roosevelt Administration
  impoundment of funds by SI12 81, 83
Roque, Vincent TW 2 61
  See also Hogan & Hartson
Rose, H. Chapman SI4-3 1258, 1261; SI8 80
  affidavit on Nixon's income taxes SI10 439-444;
    II 3 1857-1859
  letter from Joint Committee on Internal Revenue
    Taxation with questions for Nixon on 1969 in-
    come tax return SI10 416-422
  memo to Joint Committee on Internal Revenue
    Taxation on bases sustaining Nixon's 1969
    charitable contribution deductions SI10 447-505
  memo to Joint Committee on Internal Revenue
    Taxation supporting nonrecognition of gain on
    sale of Nixons' New York City residence in
    1969 SI10 506-522
Rosenfeld, Harry SI7-1 522
Rosenzweig, Harry SI5-2 584
Ross, George F. SI7-2 683
ROTC facilities, violence against, in Huston plan
  SI7-1 392
Rothblatt, Henry, in Nixon-Dean-Haldeman discus-
  sion on DNC suits SI8 326-327
Royal Inn at Wharf, San Diego, selection as Republi-
  can National Convention headquarters hotel SI5-2
  579
Rozamus, Michael Joseph SI7-2 682
Ruby I SI1 244
  See also Buckley, John
Ruby II SI1 244
  See also Gregory, Thomas
Ruckelshaus, William C.
  answers to interrogatories from Sullivan on han-
    dling of wiretaps on government officials and
    newsmen requested by White House SI7-1 6,
    181, 186-188; SI7-2 534, 540, 681, 688-694, 755,
    759-765
  and domestic surveillance II 2 1092, 1094-1095
  and exposure of wiretapping of Ellsberg SUMM I
    135-136
  on FBI termination of wiretaps on government
    employees and newsmen SI7-2 569-570
  and investigation to locate Kissinger tapes II 2
    1157-1158
  letter from Mitchell denying authorization of
    wiretaps on government officials and newsmen
    SI7-1 4, 157, 166, 167
  letter from Nixon on impoundment of funds for
    Federal Water Pollution Control Act Amend-
    ments of 1972 SI12 32
  letter to Mitchell on his signatures on documents
    authorizing wiretaps on government officials
    and newsmen SI7-1 4, 157, 169-170, 171-172,
    173, 177-180
  memo to Petersen on Ellsberg and wiretapping of
    Halperin SI7-4 1652, 2045, 2046-2049
  news conference of May 14, 1973 on wiretaps on
    government officials and newsmen in 1969 SI7-

Haig and Nixon complain to Richardson about
Cox's investigation of **II 2** 1352
on handrails **SI12** 143-144
haste of work on improvements at **SI12** 97-98
on housekeeping services **SI12** 153-155
on installation of beach cabana and railroad crossing **SI12** 140-142
on installation of fireplace exhaust fan in den
SI12 101-105
on installation of new heating system **SI12** 105-
109
on installation of sewer system at **SI12** 110-114
on landscape construction and maintenance **SI12**
115-123
on lanterns **SI12** 149-150
Minority Impeachment Inquiry staff Memorandum on Facts and Law on **MMFL** 137-141
Nixon's knowledge of **SI12** 170-173
overall expenditures made in connection with
SI12 100-101
on paving **SI12** 134-137
in Political Matters Memoranda **SIAPP4** 12
and Presidential representatives directing work
SI12 98-100
on restoration of "point" gazebo **SI12** 137-140
setting of property **SI12** 96-97
in status report of House Judiciary Committee
Impeachment Inquiry staff **II 3** 2239-2247
on structural investigation of Cotton home and
Nixon's residence **SI12** 132-134
San Diego, California **II 3** 1757-1771, 1773; **SIAPP2**
376-378
decision to use as Republican National Convention site **SI5-2** 486-487, 561-562, 563-594
in discussion of ITT matter by Nixon, Mitchell,
and Haldeman **NSI2** 163
Geneen-Wilson discussion on ITT financial support for Convention bid **SI5-2** 482, 527, 528-531
ITT contribution for Republican National Convention at, McLaren denies knowledge of **NSI2**
113, 126
map of **SI5-1** 446-447
in memo from Klein to Haldeman on Republican
National Convention site **SI5-2** 510, 841, 842-
847
memo from Timmons to Haldeman on locating
1972 Republican National Convention in **SI5-1**
423-424, 425
Nixon-Mitchell-Haldeman discussion as site for
Republican National Convention of 1972
SIAPP3 9-11, 15, 17-18, 33
reasons for selection as site for Republican National Convention of 1972 **NSI2** 12, 127, 128-
151
Republican National Committee Resolution select-
ing as site for Republican National Convention
of 1972 **SI5-2** 487, 562, 592-594
security survey of **SIAPP4** 77-78
Timmons' report on, as possible 1972 Republican
National Convention site **SI5-1** 433-447
White House task force on controversy over ITT
contribution **SI5-2** 760
White House White Paper on selection as Republican National Convention site **SI5-2** 962
See also St. Clair, James D., presentation of evidence in behalf of Nixon on ITT matter; *U.S.* v.

Howard Edwin Reinecke
San Diego City Council
memo from Klein to Haldeman on bid for Republican National Convention by **SI5-2** 486, 561,
569-573
memo from Magruder to Mitchell on bid for
Republican National Convention by **SI5-2** 486,
561, 568
resolution authorizing San Diego as site of Republican National Convention of 1972 **SI5-2** 486-
487, 563-567
San Diego County Convention and Tourist Bureau
photograph of check from Sheraton Harbor Island
Corp. to **SI5-2** 489, 603, 604
telegram from James on use of Sheraton Hotel as
Republican National Convention center **SI5-2**
487, 562, 588-589
San Diego International Sports Arena, photograph of
SI5-1 445
San Francisco, California, as proposed site for
Republican National Convention SI5-1 449, 475
Sanchez, Manuel SI4-2 901-902, 909-910
Sanders, Donald G.
and Chotiner interview **NSI3** 8, 75, 107-110; **SI6-**
2 677, 688, 741-743
memo to Thompson on interview with Stewart on
FBI investigation of SALT leaks **SI7-2** 891-894
Schmults memo on milk price-supports meeting to
SI6-2 466, 513, 516-517
Sanders, Donald G., questioning by
Kalmbach **SI6-1** 81-82; **SI6-2** 733-734
Parr **NSI3** 56-57; **SI6-1** 159-160
Sandman, Charles W., Jr. RHJC 359-493; **SUMM I**
1
additional views on Article of Impeachment III
RHJC 503-505
on calling witnesses before House Judiciary Committee Impeachment Inquiry **II 3** 1656, 1657,
1670, 1671, 1672, 1673, 1674
on delays caused by White House in House
Judiciary Committee Impeachment Inquiry **II 1**
196
on Doar-St. Clair correspondence **II 1** 178
on elimination of investigation of tax fraud from
House Judiciary Committee Impeachment Inquiry **II 1** 362-363
on his absence from voting on issuing subpoenas
to Nixon **II 1** 343-344
on House Judiciary Committee Impeachment Inquiry issuing subpoenas to Nixon **II 1** 313, 649-
650; **II 3** 1535-1536
on knowledge of existence of subpoenaed White
House materials **II 2** 947
on material included in House Judiciary Committee Impeachment Inquiry record **II 3** 1914
on Nixon's income tax **II 3** 1497-1498
on Nixon's noncompliance with House Judiciary
Committee Impeachment Inquiry subpoenas **II**
1 424-425; **II 2** 922
on presentation procedures for House Judiciary
Committee Impeachment Inquiry **II 1** 290
on procedural rules for handling Impeachment Inquiry material **II 1** 122
on reasons for presentation of evidence on domestic surveillance **II 2** 1109-1110

Sandman, Charles W., Jr. *(Continued)*
on release of House Judiciary Committee Impeachment Inquiry evidentiary material to public **II 3** 1596-1597
on rules of evidentiary procedures for House Judiciary Committee Impeachment Inquiry **II 1** 504-505, 507
on St. Clair's attitute toward House Judiciary Committee Impeachment Inquiry's request for materials **II 1** 217-218
on scheduling Garrison's presentation to House Judiciary Committee Impeachment Inquiry **II 3** 1945-1946
on Sirica's invitation to Doar and Jenner **II 1** 141
on subpoena powers of House Judiciary Committee **II 1** 34, 66-67
urges beginning House Judiciary Committee Impeachment Inquiry before additional White House materials are turned over **II 1** 218-219
on voting on rules of procedure for House Judiciary Committee Impeachment Inquiry **II 1** 288-289
on Waldie's motion on hearing testimony of witnesses in executive session **II 3** 1870-1871, 1877
See also Minority of House Judiciary Committee Impeachment Inquiry views on Articles of Impeachment

Sandman, Charles W., Jr., questioning by
Bittman **TW 2** 70-71
Colson **TW 3** 455-456
Dean **TW 2** 319-323
Petersen **TW 3** 130-132

Sandwedge plan II 1 59-60
in Article of Impeachment I **RHJC** 37
Caulfield submits **II 2** 1184-1185
development of **SUMM I** 29-30
as forerunner of Watergate, in summary of evidence to House Judiciary Committee Impeachment Inquiry **II 3** 1943-1944
Haldeman, Mitchell, Magruder, and Strachan meeting on **SUMM I** 29-30
Haldeman's knowledge of **SUMM I** 41
in memo from Strachan to Haldeman **SI1** 7, 31, 34
in Political Matters Memoranda **SIAPP4** 11, 21, 59
proposal for **SI7-3** 1118, 1118-1189, 1341-1344, 1339-1340,1372-1376
proposed budget for **SI7-3** 1118, 1339, 1345-1347
replaced by Liddy plan **SUMM I** 30-31
in talking paper from Strachan to Mitchell **SIAPP4** 35
termination of, in Strachan memo to Haldeman on political enemies project **SI8** 20, 205, 206-209

Sarbanes, Paul S. SUMM I 1
additional views on proposed Article of Impeachment on secret bombing of Cambodia **RHJC** 301-302
on calling witnesses before House Judiciary Committee Impeachment Inquiry **II 3** 1645, 1653, 1674, 1675
on FBI report to Justice Department on wiretapping of Ellsberg **II 2** 1136
on House Judiciary Committee Impeachment Inquiry issuing subpoenas to Nixon **II 1** 316-317,

325; **II 3** 1539
on House Judiciary Committee Impeachment Inquiry subpoenas for additional witnesses **II 2** 983
on leaked Dixon memos **II 2** 1326
on leaks from House Judiciary Committee Impeachment Inquiry **II 2** 740
on legal aspects of impoundment of funds **II 2** 1313-1314
on Nixon's alleged approval of Fielding break-in **II 2** 1163
on Nixon's gift of Presidential papers **II 3** 2004, 2005
on Nixon's income tax **II 3** 1523-1524, 2017
on Nixon's noncompliance with House Judiciary Committee Impeachment Inquiry subpoenas **II 1** 431-432, 432-433
on Petersen's role in Ellsberg case **II 2** 1231-1232
on possible Segretti-type activities to discredit House Judiciary Committee Impeachment Inquiry **II 1** 71
on possibly forged letter from House Judiciary Committee Impeachment Inquiry **II 1** 77
on presentation procedures for House Judiciary Committee Impeachment Inquiry **II 1** 273-275
on procedural rules for handling Impeachment Inquiry material **II 1** 120-121
on procedures of House Judiciary Committee Impeachment Inquiry **II 1** 98
on release of House Judiciary Committee Impeachment Inquiry evidentiary material to public **II 2** 981
on relevance of evidence on enemies list **II 2** 1260-1261, 1261
on right of Minority of House Judiciary Committee Impeachment Inquiry to subpoena witnesses **II 1** 28
on rules of evidentiary procedures for House Judiciary Committee Impeachment Inquiry **II 1** 516-517, 518-519, 525-526, 527-528
on St. Clair's participation in House Judiciary Committee Impeachment Inquiry **II 1** 236-237
on Sirica's invitation to Doar and Jenner **II 1** 151
on status report on nature of factual investigations for House Judiciary Committee Impeachment Inquiry **II 1** 374-375
on submission of written interrogatories to Nixon **II 3** 1618-1619
on subpoena powers of House Judiciary Committee **II 1** 66
on timing of House Judiciary Committee Impeachment Inquiry **II 1** 112
on timing of Nixon's letter to Shutlz prohibiting testimony by Secret Service agents or officers **II 2** 1358-1359
on transcripts of Nixon tapes used by St. Clair in his presentation of evidence in behalf of Nixon **II 3** 1725, 1733, 1734
on Wiggins' amendment to subpoena to Nixon **II 2** 949

Sarbanes, Paul S., questioning by
Bittman **TW 2** 84-85, 88
Butterfield **TW 1** 101-102
Colson **TW 3** 474-475

Dean **TW 2** 323-324
Petersen **TW 3** 146-148
Sargent, Francis W. SIAPP4 43
Saulnier, Dr. Raymond NSI2 84-85; **SI5-1** 405, 408
Saxbe, William SIAPP1 73-74
and Jaworski's letter to Eastland summarizing arrangement made on independence of Watergate Special Prosecutor **SI9-2** 557, 923, 924-925
Scali, John NSI4 120; **SIAPP4** 133
interview with Richardson on Cambodian invasion **SI11** 631-632
Scammon, Richard SIAPP4 26
Schell, Arden B. SUMM I 1
Schlesinger, Arthur
and CIA employee information on Hunt **SI2** 2, 298-299
Dean's efforts to retrieve CIA material on Hunt from Department of Justice **SI2** 2, 679-680
memo for record on telephone call from Dean on retrieval of CIA material from Department of Justice **SI2** 2, 67, 673, 674-675
Schlesinger, Arthur, cited testimony of
on Dean's efforts to retrieve CIA material on Hunt from Department of Justice **SI2** 2, 674
Schlesinger, James R. SI11 408-442
cited testimony of, on Dean's request for retrieval of CIA materials from Justice Department **SI7-4** 1624, 1733, 1736
and Dean's efforts to retrieve materials sent to Justice Department by CIA **SI7-4** 1624, 1733, 1734-1739
on full authorization for bombings of Cambodia **SI11** 330
letter to Symington admitting secret bombing of Cambodia prior to May 1970 **SI11** 26
letter to Symington on reasons for MENU reporting procedure **SI11** 308
memo for record on telephone call from Dean requesting CIA to retrieve materials from Justice Department **SI7-4** 1624, 1733, 1734-1735
statements following letter of July 16, 1973 acknowledging pre-incursion bombing of Cambodia **SI11** 51-77, 271-383
See also Holtzman v. Schlesinger
Schmidt, Robert SI5-1 185; **SI5-2** 934
Schmitz, John SI5-1 437
Schmults, Edward C.
memo to Hamilton and Sanders on milk price-supports issue **SI6-1** 22-23, 329-330, 342-343; **SI6-2** 466, 513, 516-517
Schochet, Barry, questioning by
Harrison **SI6-2** 822-823; **SI7-3** 1272-1273
Schorr, Alvin L. SI7-2 1113
Schorr, Daniel Louis SI4-2 921
cited testimony of, on White House-requested FBI investigation **SI7-2** 562, 1111, 1112-1119
Colson on Ziegler statement on **TW 3** 507
on enemies list **SI8** 75, 109, 119
FBI investigation of **II 2** 1174, 1176; **SI7-2** 1111, 1112-1124
in Article of Impeachment II **RHJC** 150-151
in Jenner's presentation of summary of evidence to House Judiciary Committee Impeachment Inquiry **II 3** 1979

illegal investigation of **SUMM I** 127
IRS investigation of **TW 2** 332
Nixon-Colson discussion on inquiries about reasons for FBI investigation of **TW 3** 238-241
Schrade, Jack SI5-1 437
Schram, Martin J. SIAPP1 73; **SI8** 171-172
Schreiber, Taft SIAPP4 53, 121, 137
Schroeder, Patricia, questioning by
Doolin **SI11** 188
Schwartz, Allen II 2 806, 1304
Schweiker, Richard S. SIAPP3 23
calls for "clean out" of White House staff after Watergate **SI9-1** 136
Scolaro, Richard SIAPP4 18
Scott, Hugh
on Kleindienst's testimony **SI5-2** 731
statement on Nixon pledging not to intervene in selection of Special Prosecutor or Watergate investigation **SI9-1** 6, 139, 142-143
Scott, Hugh, questioning by
Buzhardt **SI7-3** 1429
Kissinger **SI7-1** 262
Scribner, Fred C., Jr. SIAPP4 71; **SI5-1** 467, 469; **SI5-2** 587
Seamans, Robert C. SI11 11, 408-416
denies knowing about secret Cambodian bombings of 1969-1970 and explains chain of command for military operations **SI11** 65-66, 329
statistics submitted on Southeast Asia bombings by **SI11** 333, 335
submits classified report to Senate Armed Services Committee on Indochina bombing from 1965-1971 showing no bombing strikes in Cambodia prior to May 1, 1970 **SI11** 21, 174
See also Holtzman v. Richardson
Sears, Barnabas II 2 875-876, 877
Kleindienst on **SI4-2** 946, 947
Sears, John P. SIAPP4 119; **SI8** 93-94, 148-151
See also Caulfield, John J., cited testimony of
Sears, John P., questioning by
Caulfield **SI7-1** 320, 321, 322, 513-514
Seaver, E. Robert SI5-1 265, 364
Second Supplemental Appropriations Act of 1973
bombing of Cambodia and **SI11** 405
Secret Service SI12 93-94, 98-99, 123-125
access log for Key Biscayne safe, October 4-7, 1973 **SI9-2** 532, 721, 731-735
and boundary survey at Nixon's San Clemente property **SI12** 128, 131
and construction of block wall at Nixon's San Clemente property **SI12** 152
and construction of redwood fence at Nixon's San Clemente property **SI12** 145-148
and construction, replacement or reinforcement of handrails at Nixon's San Clemente property **SI12** 143-144
and den furnishings at Nixon's San Clemente property **SI12** 148-149
expenditures in connection with Key Biscayne **SI12** 156-157
expenditures in connection with San Clemente since 1969 **SI12** 100
and fence and hedge screen at Nixon's Key Biscayne property **SI12** 163-167

Senate

confirmation of Richardson as Attorney General **SI9-1** 8, 151, 156

consideration of Richardson's nomination for Attorney General **SI9-1** 8, 151, 154-155

resolution requesting Nixon to appoint special prosecutor on Watergate **SI9-1** 5, 131, 137

sources of information on bombing of Cambodia **SI11** 112-113

Senate Armed Services Committee

classified material on bombing of Cambodia from files of **SI11** 122-123

Defense Department report on aerial attacks in Cambodia submitted to **SI11** 88-104, 105-111

hearings on "Bombing in Vietnam" **SI11** 64-68, 85-87, 323-336

public statements on reasons for false documentary submission on Cambodian bombings to **SI11** 75, 369-374

unclassified correspondence on bombing of Cambodia from files of **SI11** 121

Senate Foreign Relations Committee, Sparkman and Case report on FBI summary of wiretaps related to leaks SI7-2 525, 567, 568-570

Senate Judiciary Committee

Executive Report recommending nomination of Kleindienst as Attorney General **SI5-2** 490, 605, 609-611, 612

and Jaworski's letter to Eastland on Nixon challenging his right to bring action against him to obtain evidence **SI9-2** 575, 1019, 1020-1025

and Jaworski's letter to Eastland summarizing arrangement made with Nixon on independence of Watergate Special Prosecutor **SI9-2** 557, 923, 924-925

and Jaworski's letter to Percy on failure of White House to produce needed evidence **SI9-2** 589, 983, 984-985

Senate Select Committee on Presidential Campaign Activities SIAPP1 31

Bittman on Hunt's testimony before **TW 2** 53-54

Colson's opening statement before **TW 3** 423-439, 439-441, 483-487, 524

Dean's testimony on Watergate coverup before **SI9-1** 18, 313, 314-316

discussed by Nixon, Haldeman, and Ehrlichman **SI4-2** 674-680, 826-827

Haldeman, Ehrlichman, Dean, and Moore meetings to discuss strategy for **SI3-1** 48, 535, 536-556

Haldeman's memo to Dean on dealing with **SI3-1** 47, 527, 528-533, 541

letter from Cox to Buzhardt requesting Nixon statement on Dean's testimony before **SI9-1** 19, 317, 318-320

letter from Nixon to Ervin refusing to testify or permit access to Presidential papers **SIAPP1** 26-27

letter from Nixon to Shultz on testimony of Secret Service agents before **SIAPP1** 28

materials given to House Judiciary Committee Impeachment Inquiry by **II 1** 105

McClory on use of political enemies list material by **II 2** 1271

Nixon on **SI3-2** 847; **SI4-3** 1527

Nixon asks Kleindienst to stay on as Attorney General and act as liaison to minority members of **SI3-1** 51, 583, 584-595

Nixon asserts his intention to cooperate with **SIAPP1** 5

Nixon on cooperation with and refusal to comment on work of **SIAPP1** 9-10

Nixon-Dean discussion on **SI3-1** 52, 597, 598-614, 673-687; **SI3-2** 858-865; **SI4-3** 92-94

Nixon-Dean-Haldeman discussion on **SI8** 366-391, 405-409, 413-414

Nixon and Ehrlichman discuss rules of **SI4-3** 1260-1261

Nixon-Ehrlichman-Haldeman discussion on **SI4-2** 794-795

Nixon and Haldeman discussion on **SI4-2** 971

Nixon-Petersen discussion on **SI4-3** 1233, 1401-1402

Nixon refuses to testify before **SI9-1** 23, 337, 338-346

Nixon refuses to turn White House tapes over to **SI9-1** 34, 407, 408-412

Nixon's interference with, in Article of Impeachment I **RHJC** 116-120

Nixon's letter to Sirica declining to obey subpoena **SI9-1** 37, 425, 426-427

Nixon's public announcement on appearance of White House personnel before **SI4-3** 1101, 1419, 1420

Petersen on relationship with Department of Justice and **SI4-3** 1544-1546

Resolution authorizing Ervin to meet with Nixon on materials sought by Committee **SI9-1** 27, 375, 377-378

resolution establishing **SI3-1** 46, 521, 522-525

subpoenas Reisner **II 2** 855

telephone call from Nixon to Kleindienst on contacting Baker on **SI4-1** 4, 123-127, 213, 214, 215,

votes to turn over files to House Judiciary Committee Impeachment Inquiry **II 1** 94-95

White House interference with **II 2** 760-767

White House meeting of March 22, 1973 on contacts with and activities of **SI4-1** 3, 107, 114-126, 134-139, 142, 153-158, 165-168, 171-175

Ziegler statement on leaks from **SI4-1** 29, 497, 498-500

See also Ervin, Sam J., Jr.

Sevareid, Eric SI11 253-255

Seventh Air Force officers SI11 84

Sexton, Ed SIAPP4 123

Sexual habits

in wiretapping reports on White House staff members **II 2** 1106-1107

Seymour, Sir Edward SI12 42

Shaffer, Charles Norman II 2 1399; **SIAPP2** 60; **TW 2** 220-355; **SI8** 67

and Dean's indictable list **SI4-2** 699

negotiations with Petersen on immunity for Dean **NSI1** 224-225

objections to line of questioning of Dean **TW 2** 268-269, 289, 304

retained by Dean **II 2** 854; **TW 2** 254, 322; **SI4-1** 27, 483, 484, 485

Sims, Louis, cited testimony of
on arranging for Buzhardt to hear tape of Nixon-Dean telephone conversation **SI9-1** 17, 289, 302-307
on new machine supplied to White House for transcription of Nixon tapes **SI9-2** 531, 687, 711-716

Sinatra, Frank
FBI investigation of **SI7-2** 1121
tax information on **SI8** 157

Sinay, Lynda SI7-3 1450

Sirica, John J. NSI1 142-143; **SI9-2** 535, 747, 748-754; **SI1** 40; **SI4-1** 8, 249, 250, 251-252
appeal from ruling on turning Grand Jury materials over to House Judiciary Committee Impeachment Inquiry **II 1** 202-203, 225-226
appoints panel of experts to examine gap on Nixon tape **SI9-2** 552, 867, 868-874; **II 2** 1405-1409, 1433-1434; **SUMM I** 110
and Bittman's motion to suppress **TW 2** 33, 34-35
Buzhardt submits list of subpoenaed materials with particularization of claims of Executive privilege to **SI9-2** 553, 875, 876-882
cooperation with House Judiciary Committee Impeachment Inquiry **II 3** 1985-1987
Dean on treatment of Sloan by **SI8** 405
and Dean's exposure of Huston plan **SIAPP1** 22
defers final sentencing of all Watergate defendants except Liddy **II 2** 834-835; **SI4-1** 5, 217, 226-233
denies Nixon's motion to quash Jaworski's subpoena and orders Nixon to produce material **SI9-2** 574, 1015, 1016-1017
and erasure on Nixon tape **II 2** 1393-1394
grants leave for Watergate defendants to testify under immunity before Watergate Grand Jury **II 2** 842
grants motion for subpoena directing Nixon to produce specified tapes and documents for *U.S. v. Mitchell* trial **SI9-2** 570, 987, 988-990
House Judiciary Committee Impeachment Inquiry discussion on invitation to Doar and Jenner to attend proceeding on sealed material from Watergate Grand Jury **II 1** 134-148
House Judiciary Committee Impeachment Inquiry discussion on subpoenaing for Nixon tapes he has in his possession **II 2** 990-991
and immunity for Liddy **SI4-1** 358
informed by Buzhardt that June 20, 1972 tape contains erasure **II 2** 1379; **SI9-2** 552, 867, 868-874
informed by Wright that one of subpoenaed tapes had highly sensitive national security material **II 2** 1369, 1409-1410; **SI9-1** 45, 499, 500-501
issues subpoena for White House tapes and documents **SUMM I** 104
Kleindienst and **NSI1** 159, 166
letter from McCord to **II 2** 834-835; **SIAPP2** 82-86; **SUMM I** 81
letter from McCord to, in Article of Impeachment **I RHJC** 102-103
letter from Nixon agreeing to furnish Strachan's Political Matters Memoranda file to Cox **SI9-2** 526, 591, 594-595

letter from Nixon declining to obey subpoena except for Howard and Strachan memoranda **SI9-1** 37, 425, 426-427
letter from Nixon refusing to comply with subpoenas for Presidential tapes **SIAPP1** 31
and Magruder's plea **SI4-3** 1130
and Magruder's sentencing **SI4-3** 1232
materials given to House Judiciary Committee Impeachment Inquiry by **II 1** 597-598, 607-608; **SIAPP1** 79-80
and missing subpoenaed tapes **SIAPP1** 63-64
Nixon on **SIAPP1** 16
Nixon authorizes Wright to inform him that subpoenaed tapes will be turned over to court **SI9-2** 545, 827, 828-830
Nixon-Dean discussion on probable sentencing of Watergate burglars by **SI3-2** 854-857
Nixon-Dean discussion of requesting delay of sentencing of Watergate defendants by **SI3-2** 1110-1111
Nixon-Dean discussion on sentences given to Watergate burglars by **SI3-2** 1060-1061, 1181-1184
in Nixon-Dean-Haldeman discussion on Watergate trial sentences **SI8** 410-412
Nixon-Petersen discussion on possible interrogation of Magruder by **SI4-3** 1300-1301
and Nixon tape with discussion on IRS **II 2** 1250
Nixon's statement on procedures for providing Watergate-related information to **SIAPP1** 59-61
and order compelling Hunt to testify before Watergate Grand Jury **SI4-1** 16, 335, 337
Order to Show Cause issued to Nixon on compliance with subpoena **SI9-1** 38, 429, 430-431
orders White House to turn over portion of Nixon tape of September 15, 1972 to Special Prosecutor **SI8** 28-29, 331-332, 347-349
reads McCord's letter in open court **SI4-1** 5, 217, 218, 220-225
and release of Nixon tape with IRS abuse material **II 2** 1295-1296
Report from Advisory Panel on the White House Tapes **SI9-2** 558, 925, 926-929; **SI2** 2, 24, 236, 251-256
report to House Judiciary Committee Impeachment Inquiry on Jenner's and Doar's appearance before **II 1** 161-168
Rogers on suspicions of Watergate coverup of **SI4-3** 1431
Senate resolution permitting him to establish and name independent Special Prosecutor on Watergate matter **SIAPP1** 57
and Senate Select Committee **SI4-3** 1233
sentences Liddy **SI4-1** 219
statement of October 31, 1973 on Buzhardt's informing him that certain subpoenaed tapes had never been made **SI9-2** 547, 835, 836
subpoenas Nixon tapes **SI9-2** 525, 553, 585, 586-589, 975, 878-882
and U.S. Court of Appeals procedure for Nixon tapes **SIAPP1** 58
See also McCord, James W., Jr., letter to Sirica; *Nixon* v. *Sirica*

Six Crises (Nixon) **II 3** 1993; **SIAPP2** 41; **SUMM I** 130

deductible contributions to charities of proceeds from sale of **SI10** 65

Nixon-Haldeman discussion on **SIAPP3** 61-63, 71, 72, 79-80

Sizoo, Joseph A. SI7-2 682

Skadden, Arps, Slate, Meagher & Flom SI5-2 646-647, 682-683, 869, 870

See also Mitchell, Michael, affidavit of

Slepica, Kent

and installation of den windows at Nixon's San Clemente property **SI12** 124, 125

Sloan, Debbie (Mrs. Hugh W. Sloan, Jr.) SI3-1 119

Sloan, Hugh W., Jr. SIAPP4 5, 11, 49, 125; **SI1** 32

and authorization of payments to Liddy **SUMM I** 33; **SI1** 17, 125, 171, 172-175

in Dean memo to Ehrlichman on *Nader* v. *Butz* **SI6-2** 889

discussions with Ehrlichman and Chapin on his cash disbursements to Liddy **SI3-1** 6, 115, 116-120

and false statements by Magruder to FBI agents on purpose of funds he paid to Liddy **SI3-1** 19, 245, 246-251

letter to Dean with list of political committees for AMPI contributions **SI6-2** 480, 784, 802-807

on Liddy agreeing not to use CRP employees for Liddy plan **SUMM I** 31-32

Magruder advises him to perjure himself on amount of money he gave to Liddy **SI3-1** 5, 7, 108-114

and Magruder's appointment to government job **SUMM I** 80

Magruder's authorization for payments to Liddy by **SI3-1** 99

and Magruder's efforts to obtain government post after Watergate **SI3-1** 49-50, 557-558, 559-581

memo to Ehrlichman with Geneen's letter to Stans **SI5-1** 5, 131, 137

and Mexican checks **SI2** 2, 4, 37, 79, 96-97, 363, 364, 366, 368-369, 370-371

Mitchell confirms Magruder's authorization of payments to Liddy by **SI1** 18, 177, 178-186

on money found at scene of Watergate break-in **SUMM I** 32

Nixon-Dean-Haldeman discuss forthcoming testimony of **SI8** 405-406

and payment of expenses to investigators of San Diego as possible Republican National Convention site **SI5-1** 427

possible testimony of, discussed by Nixon and Dean **SI3-2** 701, 803, 804-880

role on Budget Committee **SI1** 85

role in campaign finances **SIAPP4** 15-16

role at CRP **SIAPP4** 13

role in Nixon Administration **RHJC** 13-14

role on White House staff **II 1** 556

Sloan, Hugh W., Jr., cited testimony of

on discussions with Ehrlichman and Chapin on his cash disbursements to Liddy **SI3-1** 6, 115, 116-118

on Haldeman's $350,000 fund **SI1** 11, 77, 93-94

on Magruder telling him he might have to commit perjury on amount of money he gave to Liddy **SI3-1** 5, 7, 110

on Magruder's authorization of payments to Liddy **SI1** 17, 171, 172-173

on Magruder's efforts to obtain government post after Watergate **SI3-1** 49-50, 557-558

on Mexican checks **SI2** 2, 5, 37, 79, 98-99, 363, 370-371

on Mitchell's confirmation of Magruder's authorization of payments to Liddy **SI1** 18, 177, 178-186

on transfer of campaign contributions for payments to Watergate defendants **SI3-1** 20, 253, 256

Small, William SI7-2 1112-1113

Smathers, George A., *Newsday* article on Rebozo and **SI8** 171-172

Smith, C. Arnholt SI1 82; **SI5-1** 438, 470

Smith, Chesterfield, calls for special prosecutor to investigate Watergate SI9-1 136

Smith, Hedrick

article on Nixon's decision to begin troop withdrawals from Vietnam **NSI4** 22, 153, 154-155

article on Nixon's determination to remove nuclear weapons from Okinawa **NSI4** 26, 179, 180-181

Smith, Henry P., III RHJC 359-493; **SUMM I** 1

additional views on Article of Impeachment III **RHJC** 503-505

additional views on proposed Article of Impeachment on secret bombing of Cambodia **RHJC** 301-302

on calling witnesses before House Judiciary Committee Impeachment Inquiry **II 3** 1697-1698

on confidentiality of evidentiary material presented to House Judiciary Committee Impeachment Inquiry **II 1** 581

on Ehrlichman's note of approval of Fielding break-in **II 2** 1171-1172

on FBI report to Justice Department on wiretapping of Ellsberg **II 2** 1138-1139

on Mitchell's authorization of domestic surveillance **II 2** 1098

on Nixon's gift of Presidential papers **II 3** 1485-1486, 1514-1515

on Nixon's noncompliance with House Judiciary Committee Impeachment Inquiry subpoenas **II 1** 445; **II 2** 908, 927

on procedures for House Judiciary Committee Impeachment Inquiry **II 1** 388

question on Greenspun matter **II 2** 1292

retrieval of wiretapping records from White House **II 2** 1099, 1100, 1202

on Semer's statement on purpose of AMPI contribution in 1970 **II 2** 1052

See also Minority of House Judiciary Committee Impeachment Inquiry views on Articles of Impeachment

Smith, Henry P., III, questioning by

Bittman **TW 2** 69

Butterfield **TW 1** 95-96

Colson **TW 3** 454-455

Smith, Henry P., III, questioning by *(Continued)*
  Dean **TW 2** 296
  Kalmbach **TW 3** 708-710, 734
  LaRue **TW 1** 244, 270
  Mitchell **TW 2** 170-171
  O'Brien **TW 1** 145-146
Smith, Howard K.
  Colson briefs on Pentagon Papers case **SI7-2** 633
  and credibility of government **SI7-2** 669
Smith, J. T. SI7-2 568
Smith, Kent SIAPP4 5, 12
Smith, Robert SI5-1 444
Smith, T.J. SI7-3 1440
  memo to Miller on electronic surveillance of
    Kraft **SI7-2** 552, 925, 937-938
  memo to Miller on FBI receipt of records of wire-
    taps on White House staff members **SI7-1** 287-
    289, 310-312
  memo to Miller on recipients of "top secret" FBI
    wiretap material at White House **SI7-1** 21, 369,
    372-373
  memo to Miller on results of wiretaps on National
    Security Council members **SI7-1** 9, 11, 223,
    236-238, 249, 250-252
  memo to Miller on wiretaps of Ellsberg **SI7-2**
    534, 681, 695-696
  memo to Miller on wiretaps of National Security
    Council staff members **SI7-1** 8, 201, 202-211
Smyser, Richard SIAPP1 66
Sneed, Joseph T.
  discussed by Nixon and Kleindienst **SI4-2** 943,
    945, 955
  statements on impoundment of funds **SI12** 28, 87-
    88
Snyder, Dr. Joseph, medical report on Beard SI5-2
  498, 719, 726-728
Snyder, William, Jr. TW 2 5
Social Security
  Nixon-Haldeman discussion on **SIAPP3** 48
Socialist Workers Party (SWP)
  assessment of current internal security threat of,
    in Huston plan **SI7-1** 408
  and Student Mobilization Committee, in Huston
    plan **SI7-1** 391-392
Sokol, Nicholas SIAPP2 82-86; **SI4-1** 218
  See also U.S. v. *G. Gordon Liddy, et al*
Solicitor General NSI2 6, 45, 63-64
  See also Griswold, Erwin N.
South
  busing issue in **SIAPP4** 1
  Nixon campaign in **SIAPP4** 25
South Coast Engineering Service
  boundary survey at Nixon's San Clemente proper-
    ty **SI12** 126-132
  and structural investigations at Nixon's San Cle-
    mente property **SI12** 132-134
South Vietnam
  last contingent of American troops withdrawn in
    April 1973 **SI11** 9
  map of **SI11** 80
Southern GOP Conference
  Agnew's cancellation of appearance at **SI1** 34

**Soviet Committee for State Security (KGE), in Hus-
ton plan SI7-1** 402-403
Soviet Embassy
  alleged delivery of Pentagon Papers to **II 2** 1121,
    1122-1123, 1140-1141, 1144; **NSI4** 107; **SI7-2**
    633, 637
  Colson on alleged delivery of Pentagon Papers to
    TW 3 489-490, 512, 516-517
**Soviet intelligence, antiwar movement in U.S. and, in
Huston plan SI7-1** 392
Soviet Union NSI4 25, 173, 174-178
  article in *New York Times* on secret official esti-
    mates for first strike capabilities of **NSI4** 25,
    173, 174-178
  Nixon on U.S. relations with **SIAPP1** 20, 52, 91
  See also Soviet Embassy
SPACE SI6-1 87
  loan to ADEPT for campaign contributions **SI6-2**
    706-707, 712-714, 715-717
  report to Clerk of House of Representatives on re-
    ceipts and expenditures **SI6-2** 475, 703, 722-726
**Sparkman, John, report to Senate Foreign Relations
Committee on FBI summary of wiretaps related to
leaks SI7-2** 525, 567, 568-570
Special Foreign Assistance Act of 1971
  bombing of Cambodia and **SI11** 396
Special Investigations Unit. *See* Plumbers unit
**Special Report of Interagency Committee on Intelli-
gence.** *See* Huston plan
Special Watergate Prosecutor
  Jaworski selected as **II 2** 1402-1404
  public calls for **II 2** 1333
  Richardson designates Cox as and submits state-
    ment on his duties and responsibilities **II 2**
    1333-1335
  Richardson's guidelines for **II 2** 1338▪OWENS,
    WAYNE   •
Specter, Arlen
  in Nixon-Mitchell-Haldeman discussion on strate-
    gies for 1972 Presidential election **SIAPP3** 23-
    24
Sperling, Godfrey SI6-1 165-166
Spong (senator) SI1 33
Sporkin, Stanley SI5-2 646, 647, 682-683, 869, 919
Sprouse, Philip D. SI11 126, 129, 131
St. Clair, James D. II 1 471-472, 644; **SIAPP1** 70,
71, 75
  asks that House Judiciary Committee Impeach-
    ment Inquiry evidence be made public **II 3** 1456
  on confidentiality of evidentiary material present-
    ed to House Judiciary Committee Impeachment
    Inquiry **II 1** 552
  correspondence with Doar on materials requested
    by House Judiciary Committee Impeachment
    Inquiry **II 1** 170-190
  Danielson's views on expanded role in House
    Judiciary Committee Impeachment Inquiry for
    RHJC 303
  Dennis's criticism of Doar's letter requesting
    materials for House Judiciary Committee Im-
    peachment Inquiry to **II 1** 210-211
  discussion on his participation in House Judiciary
    Committee Impeachment Inquiry **II 1** 83, 338-
    339, 340-341

discussion on his requests for witnesses before House Judiciary Committee Impeachment Inquiry **II 3** 1629-1717

discussion on scheduling presentation by **II 2** 1156

discussions with Doar and Jenner on House Judiciary Committee Impeachment Inquiry's requests for **II 1** 205-208

Doar on his presentation in behalf of Nixon **II 3** 1927-1931; **SUMM I** 5-6

Doar's expectations on response to request for White House materials from House Judiciary Committee Impeachment Inquiry **II 1** 291-292

and efforts of House Judiciary Committee Impeachment Inquiry to obtain materials from Jaworski **II 1** 111-112

Holtzman objects to his use of complete transcripts during questioning of Colson **TW 3** 442-444

House Judiciary Committee Impeachment Inquiry discussion on brief delivered by **II 2** 1188-1189. 1198-1199

House Judiciary Committee Impeachment Inquiry discussion on cross-examination of witnesses by **TW 1** 87-92

House Judiciary Committee Impeachment Inquiry discussion on his presentation of evidence on behalf of Nixon **II 3** 1563-1569

House Judiciary Committee Impeachment Inquiry discussion on his request for participation in Impeachment Inquiry and deposition taking **II 1** 212-214, 216, 226-228, 231-244, 254-278

House Judiciary Committee Impeachment Inquiry discussion on members studying his brief prior to official presentation of **II 2** 1214-1217

informs Jaworski that Nixon will not comply with outstanding requests for White House materials **SI9-2** 560, 935, 936-945

and Jaworski's efforts to obtain White House materials **II 2** 1418-1434

Jenner report to House Judiciary Committee Impeachment Inquiry on meeting with **II 1** 79-84, 99-100

legal discussions with Colson **TW 3** 185-186

letter from Doar with further information on White House materials requested by House Judiciary Committee Impeachment Inquiry **II 1** 251-254

letter from Jaworski informing him that subpoena would be sought for material for Mitchell's trial **SI9-2** 567, 973, 974-975

letter from Jaworski requesting access to taped conversations and related documents for Government preparation of Mitchell's trial **SI9-2** 565, 965, 966-967

letter to Doar of April 9, 1974 on materials requested by House Judiciary Committee Impeachment Inquiry **II 1** 306-307

letter to Doar on House Judiciary Committee Impeachment Inquiry procedures for taking depositions **II 1** 208-210

letter to Doar on issuing subpoena by House Judiciary Committee Impeachment Inquiry for tape of Nixon-Haldeman conversation on June 23, 1972 **II 1** 640-641

letter to Doar promising to respond to House Judiciary Committee Impeachment Inquiry request for White House materials by April 8, 1974 **II 1** 279-281

letter to Jaworski on release of information to House Judiciary Committee Impeachment Inquiry **II 1** 106

letter to Rodino on leaks from House Judiciary Committee Impeachment Inquiry **II 2** 740, 744, 745, 768

letters to Doar **II 1** 132-134; **II 2** 804-805, 827

letters to Rodino declining to comply with House Judiciary Committee Impeachment Inquiry subpoenas **SI9-2** 581, 1059, 1060

Mayne on respect for **II 1** 237, 238

meeting with Doar on additional material required by House Judiciary Committee Impeachment Inquiry **II 2** 971-974

and Nixon's refusal to comply with House Judiciary Committee subpoenas **SUMM I** 155-170

objections to line of questioning of Mitchell **TW 2** 196-198

opinion on impeachable offenses **II 1** 93-94

Owens on participation in House Judiciary Committee Impeachment Inquiry by **RHJC** 331

participation in House Judiciary Committee Impeachment Inquiry **II 1** 632-633; **RHJC** 9

presence at House Judiciary Committee Impeachment Inquiry **SI1** 3-4

request for participation in House Judiciary Committee Impeachment Inquiry and nature of Impeachment Inquiry **II 1** 222

requests extension of time on Nixon answering subpoena from House Judiciary Committee Impeachment Inquiry **II 1** 344-356

and requests from House Judiciary Committee Impeachment Inquiry for materials on dairy industry and ITT matter **II 2** 799-800

Rodino on his lack of response to House Judiciary Committee Impeachment Inquiry's requests for White House materials **II 1** 249-251

Rodino on his participation in House Judiciary Committee Impeachment Inquiry **II 1** 305-306, 544

Sandman on his response to House Judiciary Committee Impeachment Inquiry's requests for materials **II 1** 217-218

schedule for presentation of evidence on behalf of Nixon **II 3** 1531-1532

and Sirica's decision on release of Nixon tape with IRS abuse material **II 2** 1295-1296

statement in court after Nixon was named as unindicted coconspirator **II 2** 1450-1452

statement of February 15, 1974 on Jaworski's letter to Eastland and Nixon's belief that he furnished sufficient evidence **SI9-2** 561, 947, 948-949

transmittal of Nixon's letter to Rodino declining to comply with subpoena **II 2** 1153-1154

on two versions of Ehrlichman's notes **II 3** 1996-1999

Waldie on his response to House Judiciary Committee Impeachment Inquiry's requests for materials **II 1** 214-215

St. Clair, James D., presentation of evidence in behalf of Nixon **II 3** 1720-1771, 1773-1866, 1889-1906
on affidavit from tax counsel **II 3** 1857-1859
on dairy industry campaign contributions **II 3** 1744-1814, 1892-1893
on electronic surveillance and Plumbers unit activities **II 3** 1895-1897
on gap in Nixon tape of June 20, 1973 **II 3** 1843-1853
House Judiciary Committee Impeachment Inquiry discussion on transcripts used in **II 3** 1723-1726, 1730-1735
on House Judiciary Committee Impeachment Inquiry receiving two versions of Ehrlichman's handwritten notes **II 3** 1886-1887
on ITT matter **II 3** 1757-1771, 1773, 1891-1892
on Nixon's income tax **II 3** 1893-1895
on not representing Nixon personally **II 3** 1853-1854
objections from House Judiciary Committee Impeachment Inquiry members to his reaching conclusions **II 3** 1735-1736, 1737-1739
on Plumbers unit **II 3** 1815-1842
Rodino on format for **II 3** 1719-1720
on Watergate break-in and Watergate coverup **II 3** 1721-1755
on Watergate coverup **II 3** 1898-1906

St. Clair, James D., questioning by
Bittman **TW 2** 29-55
Butterfield **TW 1** 70-87, 91
Colson **TW 3** 399-419, 439-442, 444-446, 517-518
Dean **TW 2** 257-288
Kalmbach **TW 3** 669-693
LaRue **TW 1** 232-241
Mitchell **TW 2** 160-165, 216-217
O'Brien **TW 1** 135-142
Petersen **TW 3** 107-122, 178, 179-181

Stacy, Mrs. Jack L. **SI5-1** 467, 469

Stafford, Gordon **SIAPP2** 323
See also U.S. v. *George Steinbrenner III, and the American Shipbuilding Company*

Staggers, Harley O. **SI5-2** 516-517, 905-905, 907, 909-911
correspondence with Erikson on House Interstate and Foreign Commerce Committee access to ITT materials **SI5-2** 518, 949, 950-953
efforts to obtain ITT documents from SEC **II 2** 1042
letter from Kennedy on transfer of ITT files from SEC to Justice Department **SI5-2** 514, 864, 867-868
letter to Casey requesting access to ITT material **SI5-2** 516-517, 905-905, 907, 909-911
letter to Geneen requesting ITT documents offered by Schmidt **SI5-2** 934
letters from Casey denying access to ITT material **SI5-2** 517, 906, 920-921, 922-923
statement on requests for access to ITT material **SI5-2** 516-517, 905-906, 908
See also House Interstate and Foreign Commerce Committee

Staggers, Harley O., questioning by
Casey **SI5-2** 912-914
Erikson **SI5-2** 930-934
Mallory **SI5-2** 928-929

Stamell, Jared **II 2** 994
biography of **II 3** 2153

Stanford Research Institute
report on Nixon tape of June 20, 1972 **II 2** 1435; **SUMM I** 114
review of technical report on gap on Nixon tape of June 20, 1972 **NSI4** 33, 207, 208-216

Stans, Maurice H. **II 1** 298; **SIAPP4** 11, 75, 87-88
and AMPI contributions to Republican Congressional campaign committees **SI6-2** 953-954
Ashland Oil admits illegal contribution to **SI9-1** 31, 397, 398
asks Kalmbach to return to Washington D.C. **SI1** 100
and assignment as Finance Chairman for 1972 **SIAPP4** 49
attitude toward campaign spending legislation **SIAPP4** 81
avoidance of Watergate Grand Jury subpoena by **SUMM I** 45
and Brown letter to Kleindienst **TW 3** 165-169
calendar for June 23, 1972 **SI2** 2, 37, 41, 363, 372, 405, 406
and campaign finances **SI1** 78
and campaign finances reports in Political Matters Memoranda **SIAPP4** 5
in Dean memo to Ehrlichman on *Nader* v. *Butz* **SI6-2** 889
Dean on money to LaRue from **TW 2** 231-232
on Dean's indictable list **SI4-2** 705
decision to handle campaign finances **SIAPP4** 15-16
delivers $75,000 to Kalmbach **SI3-1** 11, 165, 166-173
Dent recommends he resigns campaign post **SIAPP4** 144
dismisses Liddy as Counsel for Finance Committee **SUMM I** 37; **SI2** 2, 50, 477, 478-482
in Ehrlichman-Kalmbach discussion **SI4-3** 1548
evidence on Mitchell's approval of Liddy plan from **SUMM I** 31
excused from Watergate Grand Jury appearance **SI2** 2, 58-59, 561-562, 563-573; **SI4-3** 1634
as Financial Chairman **SIAPP4** 57
gives money to Kalmbach for fundraising assignment for Watergate defendants **SUMM I** 40-41
and ITT matter **II 2** 1002, 1006
Kalmbach informs about AMPI contribution **SI6-1** 6, 99, 102
in Kalmbach letter to Silbert **SI6-1** 304-305, 311
knowledge of Haldeman's reserve fund **TW 1** 53
letter from Geneen asking to see Nixon on ITT antitrust matters **NSI2** 5, 35, 37-42, 43
libel suit of **SI8** 301, 321-322
meeting with Dahlberg **SI2** 2, 41, 405, 406-408
meeting with Dahlberg, in Doar's presentation of summary of evidence to House Judiciary Committee Impeachment Inquiry **II 3** 1960
meeting with Mitchell on Mexican checks **SI2** 2, 37, 363, 364-473

and Mexican checks **SI2** 2, 96-97, 98, 99
and Mitchell's confirmation of Magruder's authorization for Sloan's disbursal of cash to Liddy
SI1 18, 178-186
money given to Kalmbach by **II 2** 730-731, 738-
739; **SI1** 99
moved to Nixon Finance Committee **SI1** 79
Nixon files claim of constitutional privilege with
respect to Watergate Grand Jury subpoena for
correspondence on government positions with
SI9-2 579, 1045, 1046-1052
Nixon-Haldeman discussion on Dahlberg and
SIAPP3 42-43
Nixon says he is conducting investigation of mishandling of campaign funds **SIAPP1** 3
offical move to Nixon Finance Committee
SIAPP4 82
one-million-dollar fund, in Political Matters
Memoranda **SIAPP4** 4
Petersen on concessions made on his testimony
before Watergate Grand Jury **TW 3** 132-133
possible testimony of, discussed by Nixon and
Dean **SI3-2** 701, 803, 852, 853
and post as Nixon Finance Chairman **SIAPP4** 11
proposed as financial chairman of Finance Committee **SI1** 32
refers to Gleason on AMPI contribution **SI6-1** 60
request for Executive mess privileges **SI1** 79-80
role as Nixon Finance Chairman in 1972 **SIAPP4**
35
role in Nixon Administration **RHJC** 17-18
role in Nixon re-election campaign **SI1** 82, 84-85
in Ryan memo to Merriam **SI5-2** 672, 708
subpoena to testify to Watergate Grand Jury **II 1**
695-697
telephone records for June 23, 1972 **SI2** 2, 37,
363, 374, 408
and transfer of campaign contributions for payments to Watergate defendants **SI3-1** 20, 33-34,
253, 254-263, 425-426, 427-454
Woods testimony on list of pre-April 7, 1972 contributions received from **SI6-2** 486, 945, 947-949
and Woods' list of contributors **II 2** 1085
See also Political Matters Memoranda, on campaign finances

Stans, Maurice H., cited testimony of
on approval of transfer of campaign funds to La-
Rue **SI3-1** 33-34, 425-426, 442
on delivering $75,000 to Kalmbach **SI3-1** 11, 165,
170-171
on discussions with Nixon on Watergate **SI2** 2,
58-59, 561-562, 573
on Haldeman's $350,000 fund **SI1** 11, 77, 92
on meetings with Dahlberg **SI2** 2, 41, 405, 406
on Mexican checks **SI2** 2, 37, 363, 365-369
on Sloan's payments to Liddy **SI1** 18, 177, 182-
183
on transfer of campaign contributions for payments to Watergate defendants **SI3-1** 20, 253,
254-255

Stanton, Frank
telephone conversation with Colson on FBI investigation of Schorr **TW 3** 238
tells Colson FBI had case connecting Ellsberg to
leak at Rand Corporation and failed to act
NSI4 10, 97, 98

Stanton, George T. TW 3 45
Starek, Roscoe B., III II 2 1046
biography of **II 3** 2153
State Department
polygraph tests for employees of discussed at Nixon-Ehrlichman-Krogh meeting**SI7-2** 868-885
results of wiretapping of employees of **SI7-1** 302,
304
as source of information on Ellsberg **SI7-2** 955
wiretapping of employees of after leaks on bomb-
ing of Cambodia **SI7-1** 292-293
Young memo for record on meeting on Pentagon
Papers at **NSI4** 14, 115, 116-118
Stavins, Ralph SI7-2 1023
Steadman, Richard SI7-2 1023
Steel Seizure Case SI12 47
See also Youngstown Sheet & Tube Co. v. *Sawyer*
Stein, Howard
on enemies list **SI8** 74, 108, 119
Stein, Jules SIAPP4 12
Steinbrenner, George M., III SIAPP2 323
See also U.S. v. *George Steinbrenner III, and the
American Shipbuilding Company; U.S.* v. *John
H. Melcher, Jr.*
Steiner Electric Co.
letter from GSA Construction Engineer on instal-
lation of new heating system at Nixon's San
Clemente property **SI12** 108
Stennis, John SI9-2 536, 755, 756-763; **SI3-2** 1060;
SI7-3 1427-1428
questions McConnell on need to bomb Cambodia
from military standpoint **SI11** 12-14
statements that he was briefed on MENU opera-
tions **SI11** 61-62, 63, 315-316, 319-321
See also Stennis Plan
Stennis Plan SIAPP1 53-54
Cox and **II 2** 1385-1387
Cox rejects **SI9-2** 538, 539, 773, 774-781, 783,
784-785
and firing of Cox **II 2** 1395-1401; **SUMM I** 104
meeting between Richardson, Haig, Garment,
Buzhardt, and Wright on Cox's rejection of
SI9-2 540, 787, 788-796
Nixon letter to Richardson and statement on
Cox's rejection of **SI9-2** 541, 797, 798-800
Nixon on rejection of **SIAPP1** 55-56
Nixon's orders to Richardson on Cox's rejection
of **SI9-2** 541, 797, 798
Richardson letter to Nixon on dealings with Cox
on **SI9-2** 543, 811, 812-813
Richardson proposes to Cox **SI9-2** 536, 537, 755,
756-763, 765, 766-772

Stevenson, John
speech on May 28, 1970 before New York City
Bar Association denying bombing of Cambodia
prior to May 1970 **SI11** 38, 236
**Stewart, Donald, interviewed on FBI investigation of
SALT leaks SI7-2** 549, 887, 891-894
Stewart, Potter NSI4 77-79
Stigler, George NSI2 4, 25, 26-34
See also Stigler Report; Task Force on Productivi-
ty and Competition

Stigler Report NSI2 4, 25, 26-30; SI5-1 289-290;
SI5-2 660-661, 696, 697, 957
  Geneen on NSI2 34
Stockham, Thomas G., Jr. SI9-2 552, 578, 867, 869-
874, 1037, 1038-1044
Stone, W. Clement SIAPP4 118
Strachan, Gordon C. SIAPP2 101-192; SI9-2 526,
591, 594-595; SI5-1 457; SI8 69, 115
  arranges meeting between Segretti and Dean prior
    to FBI interview of Segretti SI7-3 1203, 1541,
    1542-1555
  articles linking Segretti to SI7-4 1617, 1657, 1658-
    1659, 1678
  assigned responsibility for milk producers' file by
    Colson SI6-2 465, 493, 494-499
  in Chapin's memo to Ehrlichman on White House
    involvement with Segretti SI7-4 1686
  Dean places money in his safe for SI2 2, 169
  Dean tells Nixon he knew about Democratic Na-
    tional Committee headquarters wiretapping re-
    ports SUMM I 34
  on Dean's indictable list SI4-2 705
  destruction of Haldeman's files by SI1 195
  and destruction of Political Matters Memoranda
    SI1 15, 155, 164-166, 167
  destruction of Political Matters Memoranda in
    Doar's presentation of evidentiary material to
    House Judiciary Committee Impeachment In-
    quiry II 1 611-613
  discussed by Nixon, Haldeman, and Ehrlichman
    SI4-2 827
  Ehrlichman's discussion of Watergate with SI4-2
    598, 599
  and enemies list II 2 1269
  FBI interview of SI3-2 1014
  and Haldeman's instructions to transfer Liddy''s
    "capability" from Muskie campaign to McGov-
    ern campaign SI1 20, 191, 192-195
  and Haldeman's proposed surveillance of Kennedy
    II 2 1123
  and Haldeman's $350,000 White House fund SI1
    11, 77, 78, 90-91, 92, 93-94, 95-98, 99-100
  hires Segretti for disruption of Democratic cam-
    paigns for presidential nomination SI7-2 526,
    575, 576; II 2 1120
  and hush money II 2 755-756; TW 1 258, 265;
    SI3-2 1086; SI4-2 785-786
  hush money delivery to LaRue by TW 1 219,
    221-224
  indictment of II 2 1425; SI9-2 563, 959, 960-961
  information from wiretapping of DNC and SI3-2
    1004-1005
  informed by Higby that Ehrlichman was handling
    Watergate matter SI2 2, 12, 131
  informed of Kalmbach's desire to disengage him-
    self from dairy industry campagin contributions
    SI6-2 915
  informed by Magruder of Liddy plan SI1 64
  informs Chapin of Haldeman's approval of Segret-
    ti project SI7-2 586-587
  informs Ehrlichman that he gave mistaken tes-
    timony on amount of money delivered to LaRue
    SI4-1 38, 549, 550-551
  informs Haldeman that Mitchell has not yet ap-
    proved Sandwedge plan SUMM I 29

  informs Haldeman that Sandwedge plan is
    scrapped and Liddy will head up political intel-
    ligence at CRP SUMM I 30
  instructed by Haldeman to destroy all politically
    sensitive documents SUMM I 41; SI2 2, 25,
    261
  instructed by Haldeman to develop recommenda-
    tions for political-intelligence plan SUMM I 29
  instructions from Haldeman on Segretti's activties
    SI7-2 578
  LaRue on relationship with TW 1 180
  and Liddy's reasons for Watergate break-in SI3-2
    1006-1007
  logs of meetings and telephone conversations with
    Nixon turned over to Jaworski SI9-2 554, 883,
    884-890
  and Magruder's information to U.S. Attorneys
    SI4-2 849
  Magruder's Watergate Grand Jury testimony on
    SI4-2 818; SI7-4 1917-1918
  meeting with Ehrlichman on his contacts with
    Magruder and Haldeman relating to Watergate
    SI4-2 571, 881, 882-903
  meeting with Ehrlichman on Political Matters
    Memoranda on intelligence operation II 2 871-
    872
  meeting with Haldeman, Mitchell, and Magruder
    on Sandwedge plan SUMM I 29-30
  memo from Higby on discussion of San Diego as
    possible Republican National Convention site
    SI5-1 25-26, 423-424, 429
  memos to Dean with enemies list SI8 11-12, 111-
    112, 120-125
  Nixon discusses credibility of SI4-2 969
  Nixon and Ehrlichman discuss U.S. Attorneys
    questioning of SI4-3 1257
  Nixon-Ehrlichman discussion on immunity for
    SI4-3 1393
  Nixon-Haldeman discussion on SI4-2 773-776
  Nixon-Haldeman-Ehrlichman discussion on what
    he should be told on Magruder's information to
    Watergate Prosecutors II 2 867, 868, 869
  Nixon instructs Haldeman to give him report on
    Magruder's testimony SI4-2 565, 811, 820
  Nixon learns that Magruder may implicate in Wa-
    tergate SUMM I 6-7
  and Nixon-Mitchell-Haldeman conversation on
    antitrust suits against ITT and Kleindienst con-
    firmation hearings SI5-2 847
  Nixon-Petersen discussion on possibility of his be-
    coming a Watergate Grand Jury witness II 2
    889
  in Nixon-Petersen discussions SI4-3 1239, 1540-
    1541
  Nixon's discussion with Haldeman on forthcom-
    ing Watergate Grand Jury testimony of SUMM
    I 83
  Nixon's involvement with perjured testimony of
    SUMM I 89
  Nixon's knowledge of perjury by SUMM I 78-79
  Nixon's memo on his courage in transferring
    money from White House to CRP SUMM I 7
  Nixon's opinion of SI3-2 1248
  in Nixon's recollections of March 21 II 3 1929

and Operation Sandwedge **SI7-3** 1188-1189, 1339-1340,1372-1376

and payment to Segretti **SI7-3** 1591

perjury by, in Article of Impeachment **I**■#P90-91 **RHJC** 89-90

Petersen informs Nixon of his role in transmitting wiretap reports to Haldeman **SUMM I** 90

Petersen's memo on evidence against **SUMM I** 91

Petersen's notes on Watergate involvement of **SI4-2** 577, 974, 1002

in Petersen's report to Nixon on Watergate Grand Jury **SUMM I** 95

probability of going to jail discussed by Haldeman and Nixon **SI3-2** 1176-1177

role in Nixon Administration **RHJC** 13

role in Watergate discussed by Dean and Nixon **SI3-2** 701, 803, 862-863

Segretti and **SI7-3** 1543

and Segretti's Grand Jury testimony **SI7-3** 1598-1599

and selection of San Diego as site of Republican National Convention of 1972**II 2** 1020-1021

talking paper for Haldeman's meeting with Mitchell on CRP intelligence system **SI1** 14, 147, 152, 153

tells Dean he cleaned out Haldeman's files **SI2** 2, 168

tells Ehrlichman he gave mistaken testimony on money he gave to LaRue **II 2** 857-858

tells Magruder Haldeman wants Liddy plan approved **SI4-1** 356

testimony before Watergate Grand Jury **SUMM I** 91

and transfer of campaign contributions from White House to CRP for Watergate defendants **SI3-1** 33-34, 425-426, 427-454

and transfer of Haldeman's reserve fund **TW 1** 53-55

transmittal of enemies lists to Dean by **SI8** 11-12, 111-112, 113-129

and Ulasewicz's investigation of Kennedy **SI7-1** 351-352

Watergate coverup and, in Article of Impeachment I **RHJC** 93-94

and wiretapping plans against Democrats **SI4-2** 802

work relationship with Haldeman **SI1** 90-91, 95, 162

See also Political Matters Memoranda; *U.S.* v. *John N. Mitchell, et al.*

Strachan, Gordon C., cited testimony of SI1 7, 31, 37-38

on being informed that Ehrlichman was handling Watergate matter **SI2** 2, 12, 131, 132

on destroying memos on Segretti's activities **SI7-3** 1197, 1481, 1486-1487

on destruction of Haldeman's files **SI1** 165-166

on Haldeman and Liddy plan **II 1** 574-575

on Haldeman's instructions to transfer Liddy's "capabilities" from Muskie to McGovern **SI1** 20, 191, 192-194

on Haldeman's request for 24-hour-a-day surveillance of Edward Kennedy **SI7-2** 531, 655, 658-659

on Haldeman's $350,000 fund **SI1** 11, 77, 95-98

on hiring of Segretti **SI7-2** 526, 575, 577

on meeting with Chapin and Moore to prepare report to Nixon on Segretti matter **SI7-4** 1628, 1775, 1793

on memo to Haldeman on CRP political intelligence-gathering system **SI1** 14, 147, 148-152

on Nixon and Political Matters Memoranda on political intelligence-gatheringNSI1 12, 81, 82-84

on Operation Sandwedge proposal **SI7-3** 1118-1119, 1339-1340, 1365-1367

on reporting on Sedan Chair II and other political intelligence-gathering of CRP to Haldeman **NSI1** 10, 67, 68-69

on Segretti's activities **SI7-3** 1190, 1377, 1387-1388

on talking paper to Haldeman on political intelligence **SI1** 16, 156, 164-166

on transfer of campaign contributions from White House to CRP **SI3-1** 33-34, 425-426, 439

Strategic Air Command officers SI11 84

Strategic Arms Limitation talks. *See* SALT leaks; SALT talks

Stratton, Julius SI8 83

Stratton, Sam SI7-2 836

recommended by Colson for investigation of Pentagon Papers publication **SI7-2** 678

Strauss, Robert SIAPP4 123; **SI8** 126

and enemies list **SI8** 66, 113, 116

Strickler, Frank H. II 2 887; **SI5-2** 510, 841, 846-847

meeting with Nixon and Wilson **SI4-3** 1108, 1511, 1515-1530

Nixon's discussions with Petersen on meeting with **SI4-3** 1536-1537

See also Haldeman, Harry Robins, cited testimony of

Strickler, Frank H., questioning by

Ehrlichman **SI4-2** 720-721

Struve, Guy SI5-1 285, 286

Stuart, Charles

letter to Reed of March 14, 1969 on moving Nixon's papers to National Archives **SI10** 83

meets with Morgan and Archives officials on Nixon's pre-Presidential and Presidential papers on March 11, 1969 **SI10** 4-5, 77-78, 79-80

and moving of Nixon's papers to National Archives for inventorying and organizing **SI10** 5, 81-82, 83, 84, 85-86

Stuart, Constance

memo to Mrs. Nixon on restoration of "point" gazebo at Nixon's San Clemente property **SI12** 138-139

Stuckey, W.S., Jr.

letter from McLaren on antitrust policy **SI5-2** 978-980

Student demonstrations SI7-1 390

in Presidential statement on 1970 intelligence plan **SIAPP1** 22; **SI7-1** 377

strike of May, 1970, in Huston plan **SI7-1** 389

See also New Left groups

Student Mobilization Committee to End the War in Vietnam (SMC)

in Huston plan **SI7-1** 391-392

meeting between Nixon, Mardian, and Ehrlichman re his concerns over FBI files and logs of
1969-71 wiretaps **SI7-2** 541, 775, 776-788
memo from Haynes on recipients of FBI wiretap
material at White House **SI7-1** 21, 369, 370
memo from Hoover on Haldeman's request for
wiretapping of National Security Council staff
member **SI7-1** 7, 191, 198
memo from Hoover on leaks in government information **SI7-1** 3, 141, 142-145
memo on results of Kraft wiretap **SI7-1** 357
memo to DeLoach on Haig's request for wiretapping of government employees **SI7-1** 6, 181,
189, 294
memo to DeLoach on Nixon's request for wiretap
on White House staff member **SI7-1** 271
memo to Hoover on wiretapping of National
Security Council members **SI7-1** 17, 325, 326
memo to Tolson on wiretap of White House staff
member **SI7-1** 274
memo to Tolson on wiretaps requested by White
House **SI7-2** 525, 567, 572-574
in Nixon-Dean discussion on 1969-71 wiretaps
SI7-4 1629, 1813, 1814-1820, 1751
and surveillance of Kraft abroad **II 2** 1110-1112,
1113
and transfer of files on Kissinger tapes from FBI
to White House **II 2** 1132-1139, 1157-1158,
1192-1193
and wiretapping of government employees and
newsmen **RHJC** 35; **SUMM I** 124-125; **SI7-1**
153, 161-162; **SI7-2** 682-683
and wiretapping of Kraft abroad **SI7-1** 324, 356;
SI7-2 938

Summer Neighborhood Youth Corps Program
impoundment of funds for **SI12** 27

**Summer Olympics, 1972, and scheduling of Republi-
can National Convention SI5-1** 465, 466

**"Summer Work-Ins" of New Left, in Huston plan
SI7-1** 390

Summers, Dennis, interview with Chotiner SI6-2 677,
744-750

Supplemental Appropriations Act of 1969
Nixon's statement in connection with signing of
second **SI12** 30

Supreme Court
on antitrust litigation **SI5-1** 70-71
authorization of appeal from adverse decision in
U.S. v. *Grinnell* case **NSI2** 6, 45, 46-64
Bickel's argument on Pentagon Papers before
NSI4 7, 75, 76
consideration of Nixon's claim of Executive privilege **II 2** 1354
decision in Steel Seizure Case **SI12** 47
decision in *U.S.* v. *Nixon* **SIAPP2** 159-192
decision on legality of foreign policy warrantless
wiretaps **NSI4** 30, 199, 200-201
and doctrine of potential competition **SI5-1** 150
and impoundment of funds cases **SI12** 11, 15, 64
Nixon expresses confidence it would decide in his
favor on Presidential tapes **SIAPP1** 53
Nixon orders Kleindienst to drop Grinnell appeal
to **SI2** 7, 65, 66-72
Nixon on possible order for him to turn over
Presidential tapes to Select Committee **SIAPP1**

49-50, 51, 52
Notice of Docketing of Appeal in *ITT-Grinnell*
SI5-2 483, 533, 534-535
U.S. v. *ITT* Application for Extension of Time
and response to **SI5-1** 12, 259, 260-265

Surreptitious entry SI7-1 420-421, 521-522
Huston memo to Haldeman on recommendations
on **SI7-1** 439-440
Nixon's approval of Huston plan on **SI7-1** 454
See also Black bag jobs

Sutter, John Joseph SI7-1 344

Sutton, Gary William II 2 1249
biography of **II 3** 2153
presentation of evidence to House Judiciary Committee Impeachment Inquiry on Nixon Administration misuse of IRS **II 2** 1249-1265,
1268-1302

Swank, Emory Coblentz
Nixon's announcement on July 14, 1970 of inten-
tion to nominate as Ambassador to Cambodia
SI11 3-4, 126, 129, 131

Swank, Margaret Whiting SI11 126, 129, 131

Swayne, Charles
impeachment case against **II 3** 2208-2209

Symington, J. Fife, Jr. SIAPP2 271-272; **SIAPP4**
49-50
Kalmbach on campaign contribution and ambassadorship commitment to **TW 3** 617-629
See also U.S. v. *Herbert Kalmbach*

Symington, Stuart
on illegality of secret bombings of Cambodia **SI11**
330
on lack of knowledge in Pentagon of bombings of
Cambodia **SI11** 327
letter from Marsh of December 11, 1973 with report on bombings in Indochina **SI11** 88-89
letter from Schlesinger admitting secret bombings
of Cambodia prior to May 1970 **SI11** 26
letters from Schlesinger and Brown on reasons for
MENU reporting procedure **SI11** 308
obtains report from Moorer on bombing of Cambodia **SI11** 23, 180-181

Symington, Stuart, questioning by
Abrams **SI11** 271, 301-304, 330
Buzhardt **SI7-3** 1427-1428
Clements **SI11** 316
Freidheim **SI11** 323
Kissinger **SI11** 313, 318; **SI7-1** 262
Moorer **SI11** 277, 316
Richardson **SI7-1** 232-233, 283-284, 306-307
Ruckelshaus **SI7-1** 232-233, 283-284, 306-307
Ryan and Seamans **SI11** 174
Wheeler **SI11** 288-289, 292, 306-307, 314

Szukelewicz, Edward S.
biography of **II 3** 2154

Szulc, Tad NSI4 120, 135-136

Talbot, Daniel, Caulfield investigation of SI8 186-190

Talmadge, Herman E., questioning by
Barker **SI1** 204
Gray **SI4-3** 1616
Haldeman **SI2** 2, 266; **SI4-3** 1648; **SI8** 178, 203-
204
Hunt **SI1** 247-248; **SI5-2** 780-781; **SI7-2** 1047-
1049

Colson-Hunt on Ellsberg and Pentagon Papers matter **TW 3** 201-203

Colson-Magruder on Liddy plan **SI1** 12, 101, 102-103, 105, 110-111, 112, 113-114; **SI2** 2, 107; **SI3-2** 1001-1002

Colson tells Dean about Dorothy Hunt's telephone call **TW 3** 454-455

Connally-Jacobsen on March 23, 1971 **SI6-2** 474, 673, 698

Cox requests logs of Nixon's with fifteen named individuals **SI9-1** 14, 263, 264-267

Cushman-Ehrlichman on Hunt's demands for further CIA assistance **II 2** 1179; **SI7-3** 1227

Dean-Cushman on Dean's name appearing in list of possible persons requesting CIA assistance to Hunt **SI7-4** 1724

Dean-Ehrlichman on McCord's letter to Sirica **SI4-1** 6, 235, 236-237

Dean-Mitchell on Hunt's demands **SI3-2** 957-959

Dean-Schlesinger on retrieval of CIA material from Department of Justice **SI2** 2, 674-675

Dean's records of **TW 2** 314-316

DeMarco-Blech in May 1969 on Nixon's future deductions for gift of pre-Presidential papers **SI10** 7, 140-141, 142-143, 144-145

DeMarco-Newman after passage of Tax Reform Act of 1969 **SI10** 11, 289-291

DeMarco-Newman of October 31, 1969, asking Newman to appraise Nixon's pre-Presidential papers in National Archives **SI10** 9, 184-196

Ehrlichman-Casey on SEC and ITT documents **SI5-2** 744, 745-746

Ehrlichman-Dean on Dean's dismissal by law firm **II 2** 854

Ehrlichman-Gray on Hunt's safe **SI4-2** 583, 1059, 1063-1068, 1069-1071

Ehrlichman-Haldeman after Watergate arrests **SI2** 2, 11, 129, 130

Ehrlichman-Kleindienst **SI7-4** 1634, 1859, 1864-1866

Ehrlichman-Kleindienst on Nixon's questions about White House staff involvement in Watergate **SI4-1** 20, 399, 400-425

Ehrlichman-Krogh on forthcoming Hunt testimony **SI3-2** 1278-1279

Ehrlichman-Krogh on Hunt's blackmail threats **SI7-4** 1632, 1837, 1838-1839

Ehrlichman-Nixon on Dean going before Grand Jury **NSI1** 30, 199, 201

Ehrlichman-Ziegler and Colson on Hunt's connection with Watergate break-in **SI2** 2, 8, 117, 118-120

Ehrlichman's after Watergate arrests **SUMM I** 36

Gray-Helms on FBI Watergate investigation **NSI1** 16, 125, 127

Gray-MacGregor **SI2** 2, 533-537

Haig-Richardson on Cox's investigations **SI9-1** 33, 158-159, 403, 404-406

Haig-Richardson-Nixon on Cox's alleged investigation of Nixon's expenditures on San Clemente property **SI9-1** 21, 329, 330-332

Haldeman-Dean on Camp David report **SI4-1** 10, 12-13, 265, 266-269, 311-312, 317-318

Haldeman-Magruder after Watergate break-in **SI2** 2, 10, 125, 126, 127

Haldeman-Mitchell to arrange for meeting on Wa-

tergate **NSI1** 25, 169, 170-176

Haldeman-Mitchell on March 21, 1973 **SI3-2** 712, 1117, 1118, 1120-1132

Hall-Dorothy Hunt **TW 3** 283-284, 286-287

Higby-Dean asking Dean to attend meeting with Ehrlichman and Haldeman **SI4-1** 35, 537, 538-539

Higby-Magruder prior to Magruder talking to Watergate Prosecutor **SUMM I** 82-83

hoax call to Ervin from "Shultz" **SI2** 2, 287-288

Hunt-Cushman **II 2** 1142-1143

Hunt-Hall, notes for Colson on **TW 3** 275, 276, 278-285

Kleindienst-Ehrlichman on ITT-Canteen merger **SI5-1** 70

Kleindienst-Gray on Watergate investigation **SI2** 2, 13, 135, 136-142

Kleindienst-Petersen on Ehrlichman not wanting immunity for White House aides **SI4-1** 37, 547, 548

Kleindienst-Rohatyn **NSI2** 95

Kleindienst-Walsh on *ITT-Grinnell* appeal delay **SI5-1** 16, 284, 285, 286, 307, 308

Krogh-Young-Ehrlichman on Fielding break-in **SI7-3** 1183, 1239, 1240-1246

Magruder-Colson in February of 1972 **SI4-1** 9, 255-256, 261, 262-264

Magruder-Higby **II 2** 865

Mills-Shultz on milk price supports **NSI3** 11, 123, 125; **SI6-1** 341

Mitchell-Maroulis **SI4-2** 723

Newman-DeMarco on elimination of deduction for gifts of papers **SI10** 10-11, 277-281

Newman-Livingston on adding to list of Nixon's papers **SI10** 11-12, 292-300

Nixon-Colson on Watergate break-in **SI2** 2, 15, 155, 156-160

Nixon-Connally on March 22, 1971 **SI6-2** 467, 519, 521

Nixon-Connally on milk price supports **II 2** 1070, 1072-1073; **NSI3** 15, 139, 140-142

Nixon-Dean instructing Dean to go to Camp David **SI4-1** 6, 235, 237, 239

Nixon-Dean, listing of **SI3-2** 730-736

Nixon-Dean of March 20, 1973, Buzhardt listens to and reports to Nixon on **SI9-1** 17, 289, 290-312

Nixon-Ehrlichman on Dean resigning **SI4-3** 1084, 1131, 1132-1133, 1134

Nixon-Ehrlichman on preventing Dean from implicating Haldeman and Ehrlichman**SUMM I** 67

Nixon-Gray after Nixon gets information from Dean on CRP and White House complicity in Watergate **SUMM I** 87

Nixon-Gray on Watergate investigation **SI2** 2, 550, 551-553; **SI4-1** 7, 241, 242, 243, 244-248

Nixon-Kleindienst on April 15, 1973 **II 2** 876-877

Nixon-Kleindienst on contacting Baker re Senate Select Committee on Presidential Campaign Activities hearings **SI4-1** 4, 123-127, 213, 214, 215,; **SUMM I** 87

Nixon-Kleindienst on Gray resignation **SI4-3** 1623, 1624

Nixon-Mitchell of June 20, 1972, missing subpo-

on St. Clair's participation in House Judiciary Committee Impeachment Inquiry **II 1** 243-244

on security arrangements for House Judiciary Committee Impeachment Inquiry **II 1** 638

on security procedures within legal staff **II 1** 94

on Sirica's invitation to Doar and Jenner **II 1** 149

on television coverage of House Judiciary Committee Impeachment Inquiry **II 1** 104

Thornton, Ray, questioning by
Bittman **TW 2** 100
Butterfield **RHJC** 21
Colson **TW 3** 497-500
Dean **TW 2** 342-343
LaRue **TW 1** 265
Mitchell **SUMM I** 26; **TW 2** 210
Petersen **TW 3** 160-162

Thrower, Randolph W. II 2 1250-1255
affidavit on IRS investigation of Gerald Wallace **II 2** 1252-1254
affidavit on leak of IRS information on Wallace **SI8** 3, 35, 40-42
affidavit on resignation from IRS and efforts to confer with Nixon **SI8** 6, 59, 60-64
affidavit on White House efforts to place Caulfield in IRS **SI8** 5, 53, 54-58
and Caulfield's efforts to obtain position of Director of IRS Alcohol, Tobacco, and Firearms Division **II 2** 1257-1258
in Dean and Caulfield briefing memo on IRS **SI8** 197
efforts to meet with Nixon on political influence in IRS **II 2** 1258
and Ehrlichman's questions to Morgan on Nixon's 1969 income tax **SI10** 8-9, 177-183
and IRS investigation of George and Gerald Wallace **II 3** 1983-1984; **SUMM I** 141
and IRS sensitive reports sent to White House **SI8** 38
on meeting at White House with Ehrlichman, Haldeman, and Worthy on leak of IRS information on Wallace administration **SI8** 42
memo to Huston with status report on Special Service Group **SI8** 46
questions Mollenhoff on leaked IRS information **SI8** 39
See also House Judiciary Committee Impeachment Inquiry, presentation of evidence on misuse of IRS by Nixon Administration

Thurmond, Strom
letter from Um Sim, Ambassador under Lon Nol Government, on Sihanouk's attitude toward U.S. bombing of Cambodia **SI11** 53, 276
on military not being held responsible for carrying out orders of its civilian superiors **SI11** 325

Thurmond, Strom, questioning by
Buzhardt **SI7-3** 1426-1427
Clements **SI11** 331
Colby **SI12** 2, 656
Moorer **SI11** 278
Wheeler **SI11** 275, 291, 310

Tillotson-Ivy, Inc. SI12 161, 165

Timbers, Judge SI5-2 665, 701, 957

and ITT decision **SI5-1** 171, 217-253

Time magazine **SI7-1** 361
article on White House wiretapping of staff members and newsmen **SI3-2** 828; **SI7-4** 1625, 1741, 1747-1748
cover story on Nixon campaign **SIAPP4** 121
Dean's reactions to disclosures on 1969-71 wiretaps **SI7-4** 1815-1816
Gray denies knowledge of wiretaps revealed by **SI7-4** 1627, 1755, 1756-1773
Nixon-Dean meeting on article on 1969-71 wiretaps in **SI7-4** 1626, 1749, 1750-1754
plans to publish article on White House wiretapping of staff members and newsmen **SI7-4** 1625, 1741, 1742-1748
threatened exposure of Kissinger tapes by **II 2** 1201-1202
White House denial of disclosure of wiretappings by **SUMM I** 135

Timmons, William E. SIAPP4 4, 21, 24, 27, 30, 50, 52, 77-78, 111, 133; **SI1** 82; **SI5-1** 457, 458, 461; **SI5-2** 578; **SI8** 323
and Convention site decision paper **SI5-1** 25-26, 423-424, 465-477
and decision that Hunt should interview Beard **SI5-2** 505, 777, 778-794
and investigation of San Diego as possible Republican National Convention site **SI5-1** 427, 428
letter from Reinecke on San Diego **SI5-1** 25-26, 423-424, 455
in "LH" note to Dole **SI5-1** 477
at meeting with Hunt on Beard interview **TW 3** 250
memo from Department of Justice Law Enforcement Assistance Administration on San Diego as site for Republican National Convention of 1972 **NSI2** 12, 127, 145
memo from Odle attaching memo on selection of Convention site **SI5-1** 454
in memo from Odle to Magruder **SI5-2** 583
memo on Democratic National Convention **SIAPP4** 42
memo to Haldeman on Republican National Convention site for 1972 **SI5-1** 25-26, 423-424, 425, 463
memo to Haldeman on selection of San Diego as site for Republican National Convention of 1972 **NSI2** 12, 127, 128-129
memo to Haldeman with report on San Diego as possible Republican National Convention site **SI5-1** 25-26, 423-424, 431-447
memo to Magruder on Mitchell committing President's Convention campaign headquarters to San Diego Sheraton Hotel **SI5-2** 569
memo to Mitchell and Haldeman on selection of San Diego as site for Republican National Convention of 1972 **NSI2** 12, 127, 136-144
memo to Nixon on meeting on site of Republican National Convention **SI5-2** 486, 561, 576-577
in Political Matters Memoranda **SIAPP4** 1
and Republican National Convention of 1972 **SIAPP4** 7-8, 13
role in Nixon re-election campaign **SIAPP4** 125-126
and selection of San Diego as site for Republican

indictment and docket **SI7-4** 1638, 1897, 1898-1907

transcript **SI3-1** 26, 327, 328-340

U.S. v. *Egil Krogh, Jr.*
dates of major court proceedings **SIAPP2** 29
indictment **SIAPP2** 30-33
information **SIAPP2** 34-37
letter from Jaworski to Shulman accepting guilty plea to one-count charge **SIAPP2** 38-39
statement of defendant on the offense and his role **SIAPP2** 40-50

U.S. v. *Ehrlichman*
Colson's affidavit on reasons for establishing Plumbers unit **NSI4** 4, 43, 47-55
Ehrlichman's affidavit on reasons for establishing Plumbers unit **NSI4** 4, 43, 56-65
subpoena issued to Nixon for Ehrlichman's handwritten notes of certain meetings **SIAPP3** 1

U.S. v. *Ellsberg*
indictment **SI7-2** 528, 613, 616-617

U.S. v. *Francis Carroll* **SIAPP2** 239-242

U.S. v. *Fred LaRue* **SIAPP2** 61-66
dates of major court proceedings **SIAPP2** 61
information **SIAPP2** 62-65
letter from Cox to Vinson accepting guilty plea to one-count charge **SIAPP2** 66

U.S. v. *G. Gordon Liddy* **SIAPP2** 86-90
dates of major court proceedings **SIAPP2** 87
indictment **SIAPP2** 88-90

U.S. v. *G. Gordon Liddy, et al* **SIAPP2** 67-86
dates of major court proceedings **SIAPP2** 67-70
indictment **SIAPP2** 71-80
text of McCord letter to Sirica **SIAPP2** 82-86

U.S. v. *George Steinbrenner III, and the American Shipbuilding Company*
dates of major court proceedings **SIAPP2** 323
indictment **SIAPP2** 324-345

U.S. v. *Goodyear Tire and Rubber Company and Russell deYoung* **SIAPP2** 257-262

U.S. v. *Grinnell* **NSI2** 6, 45, 46-64
See ITT, antitrust suits against

U.S. v. *Gulf Oil Corporation and Claude C. Wild, Jr.* **SIAPP2** 263-266

U.S. v. *Harold Nelson*
dates of major court proceedings **SIAPP2** 285
indictment **SIAPP2** 286-293
letter from Ruth to Nicholas accepting guilty plea to one-count charge **SIAPP2** 294-295

U.S. v. *Herbert Kalmbach*
dates of court proceedings in **SIAPP2** 267
indictment **SIAPP2** 268-270
letter from Jaworski to O'Connor accepting guilty plea to one-count charge **SIAPP2** 271-272

U.S. v. *Herbert Porter* **SIAPP2** 193-194
dates of major court proceedings **SIAPP2** 193

U.S. v. *Howard Edwin Reinecke*
dates of major court proceedings **SIAPP2** 371
indictment **SIAPP2** 372-381

U.S. v. *Ingersoll Rand Co.,* **SI5-1** 71

U.S. v. *International Telephone & Telegraph Corporation and Canteen Corporation*
McLaren memo for Ehrlichman on **SI5-1** 148
Poole memo on conference between McLaren and

defendant's counsel **SI5-1** 7, 143, 166-167

U.S. v. *International Telephone & Telegraph Corporation and Grinnell Corporation* **SI5-1** 4, 9, 10, 101, 102-103, 189, 190-191, 213, 214-216
Application for Extension of Time **SI5-1** 12, 19, 259-265, 359, 360-364
McLaren memo for Ehrlichman on **SI5-1** 149-150
Notice of Docketing of Appeal, United States Supreme Court **SI5-2** 483, 533, 534-535
Supreme Court docket **SI5-1** 19, 359, 365
Supreme Court opinion in **SI5-1** 10, 213, 217-253

U.S. v. *International Telephone & Telegraph Corporation and Hartford Fire Insurance Co.* **SI5-1** 4, 101, 104-105, 148

U.S. v. *ITT*
civil docket **SI5-1** 3, 69, 89-90

U.S. v. *Jake Jacobsen* **SIAPP2** 361-364

U.S. v. *James Allen* **SIAPP2** 197-200

U.S. v. *Jeb Stuart Magruder* **SIAPP2** 91-100
dates of major court proceedings **SIAPP2** 91
information **SIAPP2** 92-99
letter from Cox to Sharp accepting guilty plea to one-count charge **SIAPP2** 100

U.S. v. *John Connally, and Jake Jacobsen*
dates of major court proceedings **SIAPP2** 349
indictment **SIAPP2** 350-360

U.S. v. *John Ehrlichman, et al*
dates of major court proceedings **SIAPP2** 5-7
indictment **SIAPP2** 7-28

U.S. v. *John H. Melcher, Jr.* **SIAPP2** 277-280

U.S. v. *John N. Mitchell, et al.* **SIAPP2** 101-192; **SI4-3** 1103, 1443, 1450-1459
dates of major court proceedings **SIAPP2** 101-102
Dennis' motion for House Judiciary Committee Impeachment Inquiry subpoenas to seek leave to file amici curiae briefs in **II 2** 932-939
indictment **NSI1** 36, 227, 228-242; **SIAPP2** 103-152
Nixon named as unindicted coconspirator in **MMFL** 47
subpoena issued to Nixon for tapes and documents needed for **SIAPP2** 153-158; **II 2** 1429-1430, 1432
and Supreme Court decision in *U.S.* v. *Nixon* **SIAPP2** 159-192

U.S. v. *John W. Dean, III* **SIAPP2** 53-60
dates of major court proceedings **SIAPP2** 53
information **SIAPP2** 54-59
letter from Cox to Shaffer accepting guilty plea to one-count charge **SIAPP2** 60

U.S. v. *Kalmbach*
information and docket **SI9-2** 562, 951, 952-956
letter from Jaworski to O'Connor on terms of Kalmbach's guilty plea **SI9-2** 562, 951, 957-958

U.S. v. *Krogh*
docket **SI3-1** 25, 311, 322-323
guilty plea in **NSI4** 13, 109, 114
indictment **SI3-1** 25, 311, 312-315
indictment, information and docket from **SI3-1** 25, 311, 316-319; **SI7-3** 1209, 1603, 1604-1613; **SI9-2** 534, 556, 741, 742-746, 901-907
Krogh's affidavit on Ehrlichman assigning him to "special" national security project **NSI4** 9, 85, 86-93

Vietnam War (*Continued*)
use of wiretapped information against opponents of Nixon's policy on **SI7-1** 20, 359, 360-368
and Watergate as national security issue **SI3-2** 1073-1074
See also Antiwar movement; Bombing of Cambodia; Pentagon Papers

Vinson, Fred M., Jr. SIAPP2 66; **TW 1** 175-275
on LaRue's guilty plea **TW 1** 250-253
letter from Cox accepting LaRue's guilty plea and agreement to cooperate with the Government **SI9-1** 328
See also LaRue, Frederick C., testimony before House Judiciary Committee Impeachment Inquiry; *U.S. v. Fred LaRue*

Violence, in Huston plan SI7-1 399
against ROTC facilities **SI7-1** 392
by antiwar movement **SI7-1** 391-392
of Black Panther Party **SI7-1** 397
of Puerto Rican nationalist groups **SI7-1** 409
threatened by New Left groups **SI7-1** 390
See also Black extremist groups; Terrorists

Virginia SIAPP4 58
Republican campaign in **SIAPP4** 50

Vocational Education Act of 1963
impoundment of funds for **SI12** 24

Volner, Jill W., questioning by SI4-2 996-998
Gray **SI4-2** 1074, 1075-1076
Hunt **SI3-2** 915-916, 922-923
Woods **SI9-2** 630-636, 640-642, 654-666, 690-707

Volpe, John A. SIAPP3 31; **SIAPP4** 38

von Kann, Curtis TW 2 61
See also Hogan & Hartson

Voter turnout survey SI1 86

Vu Van Thai SI7-3 1450, 1453

Wagner, Karl NSI1 16, 125, 127; **TW 3** 51; **SI2** 2, 474

Wagner & Baroody
and advertising by front groups in Nixon re-election campaign **II 2** 1055
AMPI campaign contributions and **II 2** 1059-1060
AMPI relationship with **SI6-1** 18, 273, 274-298
and AMPI special contribution to Colson **SI6-2** 838, 839
and Colson's Special Campaign Projects **SI6-1** 12, 197, 207-210
and dairy industry contributions **II 2** 1079
and money for Fielding break-in **II 2** 1181

Wagoner, James SIAPP3 242

Waldie, Jerome R. SUMM I 1
on access to materials by House Judiciary Committee members **II 1** 63-64
activities overseas **II 2** 1112
on additional subpoenas to Nixon **II 2** 896-897
on availability of materials for April 15, 1973 **II 2** 877-878
on brief delivered by St. Clair **II 2** 1189
on calling witnesses before House Judiciary Committee Impeachment Inquiry **II 3** 1623-1624, 1654-1655
on classified information on IRS information passed to Dean **II 2** 1301-1302
on Colson's comments on Harrison and Hillings

II 2 1057
on confidentiality of evidentiary material presented to House Judiciary Committee Impeachment Inquiry **II 1** 579-580, 586, 636
on Conyers' motion to cite Nixon for contempt of Congress for his noncompliance with House Judiciary Committee Impeachment Inquiry subpoenas **II 1** 462
on criteria for excising material from Nixon tapes **II 2** 831-832
on Dean going to Watergate Prosecutors **II 3** 2027
on discrepancies between transcripts of Nixon tapes **II 2** 812-813
dissenting views supporting proposed Article of Impeachment on secret bombing of Cambodia **RHJC** 323-328
on Doar-St. Clair correspondence **II 1** 176
on Doar's and Jenner's interview with Byrne **II 2** 1219-1220
on Ehrlichman's statement that Krogh reported to Nixon **II 2** 1151
on Ehrlichman's taping of his conversations **II 2** 747-748
on evidence of Nixon's connection with IRS audit of Lawrence O'Brien **II 2** 1290
on evidence on date of LaRue's last payment to Hunt **II 3** 1755
on Haldeman listening to Nixon tapes **II 2** 1357-1358
on hearsay evidence **II 2** 850
on House Judiciary Committee Impeachment Inquiry issuing subpoenas to Nixon **II 1** 315, 654; **II 3** 1553
on leaked Dixon memos **II 2** 1328
on leaks from House Judiciary Committee Impeachment Inquiry **II 2** 704-705, 739
legal aspects of his obtaining information from IRS **II 2** 1271-1272, 1273
on legal aspects of impoundment of funds **II 2** 1317-1318
on legal basis for domestic surveillance **II 2** 1092
on legal differences between electronic and physical surveillance **II 2** 1104
on legalities involved in IRS investigation of Gerald and George Wallace **II 2** 1254-1255
on materials held by Sirica **II 1** 164-166, 165
motion on hearing testimony of witnesses in executive sessions **II 3** 1867-1869
on Nixon-Petersen relationship **II 3** 2029
on Nixon tape with erasure **II 2** 1411
on Nixon's alleged approval of Fielding break-in **II 2** 1165-1166, 1167
on Nixon's discussion on Executive privilege with Richardson **II 2** 1337
on Nixon's explanation for Huston plan **II 2** 1118
on Nixon's gift of Presidential papers **II 3** 1476, 1501-1502, 1504, 1520-1521
on Nixon's justification for domestic surveillance **II 2** 1109
on Nixon's noncompliance with House Judiciary Committee Impeachment Inquiry subpoenas **II 1** 416-417, 439-440; **II 2** 906, 939-940, 941-942
on Nixon's prior knowledge of Fielding break-in **II 3** 1819
on Nixon's request for extension of time on an-

swering House Judiciary Committee Impeachment Inquiry subpoena **II 1** 345-346

on Nixon's and St. Clair's tactics in dealing with
House Judiciary Committee requests for materials **II 1** 214-215

objection to conclusions in St. Clair's presentation
of evidence in behalf of Nixon **II 3** 1737

on opening of House Judiciary Committee Impeachment Inquiry **II 2** 774-775

on possibly forged letter from House Judiciary
Committee Impeachment Inquiry**II 1** 78

on power of House Judiciary Committee to com-
pel Nixon's appearance under oath **II 1** 8-9

on purpose of discussion on Presidential logs **II 2**
874

question on results of surveillance of Kraft 326 **II
2** 1112

questions Caulfield's legal authority to obtain IRS
information **II 2** 1271-1272, 1273

on redated memo from Whitaker to Nixon on his
meeting with dairy leaders **II 2** 1081-1082

on release of House Judiciary Committee Impeachment Inquiry evidentiary material to public **II 2** 977-978; **II 3** 1582

on right of Minority of House Judiciary Committee Impeachment Inquiry to subpoena witnesses
II 1 26-27

on Rodino's press statements **II 2** 799

on rules of evidentiary procedures for House
Judiciary Committee Impeachment Inquiry **II 1**
497-498

on rules of procedure for House Judiciary Committee Impeachment Inquiry **II 1** 53-54

on St. Clair's intentions on materials requested by
House Judiciary Committee Impeachment Inquiry **II 1** 282-283

on St. Clair's participation in House Judiciary
Committee Impeachment Inquiry **II 1** 632-633

on scheduling St. Clair's presentation of evidence
II 3 1567-1568

separate comments on Report of House Judiciary
Committee Impeachment Inquiry**RHJC** 297-299

on Sirica's invitation to Doar and Jenner **II 1** 140,
148

on subpoena powers of House Judiciary Committee **II 1** 46, 64-65

on tapes needed by House Judiciary Committee
Impeachment Inquiry **II 2** 780

on taping system at Camp David **II 2** 891-892

on transcripts of Nixon tapes used by St. Clair in
his presentation of evidence in behalf of Nixon
II 3 1723, 1724, 1731

on two versions of Ehrlichman's notes **II 3** 1996-
1999

on veracity of date of Nixon's dictabelt of recollections of March 21, 1973 **II 2** 823-824

Waldie, Jerome R., questioning by
Bittman **TW 2** 77-79, 100-102
Butterfield **TW 1** 111-112
Colson **TW 3** 463-465, 513-515
Dean **TW 2** 309-311
Kalmbach **TW 3** 712-714
LaRue **TW 1** 248-250, 273-275
Mitchell **TW 2** 185-187, 215-216

O'Brien **TW 1** 149-151, 161-162
Petersen **TW 3** 141-142

Walker, Allan SIAPP4 18; **SI7-4** 1688

Walker, Charles
and Caulfield's efforts to obtain position of Director of IRS Alcohol, Tobacco, and Firearms
Division **II 2** 1257-1258
and White House efforts to appoint Caulfield to
IRS position **SI8** 5, 53, 54-58

Walker, Ronald H.
instructed by Haldeman to develop recommendation for political-intelligence plan **SUMM I** 29
role in Nixon re-election campaign **SIAPP4** 42

Walker, Roy F. SIAPP2 323
See also U.S. v. *George Steinbrenner III, and the
American Shipbulding Company*

Wall Street Journal SI8 85
article on dairy industry campaign contributions
to Nixon campaign and milk price-support increase **SI6-2** 483, 847, 849-851
memo from Strachan to Haldeman on forthcoming article on "milk money" in **SI6-2** 483, 847,
848

Wallace, Alan SI5-1 344

**Wallace, Carl, requests to discuss ITT antitrust suits
with Beard SI5-1** 142

Wallace, George C.
in Alabama election **SI1** 34
attempted assassination of **SI1** 104
Colson on attempted assassination of **TW 3** 457
and Democratic primary in Florida **SI1** 33
funding of Brewer's campaign against **SI6-1** 5, 89,
95, 109
information on IRS investigation sent to White
House **SI8** 3, 35, 36-42
IRS investigation of **II 2** 1250-1255; **SUMM I**
141
in Article of Impeachment II **RHJC** 141-145
in Jenner's presentation of summary of evidence to House Judiciary Committee Impeachment Inquiry on Nixon's abuse of
power **II 3** 1983-1984
in memo from Strachan to Haldeman **SI1** 86
in Nixon-Mitchell-Haldeman discussion on Presidential election of 1972 **SIAPP3** 32
Segretti's activities against **SI7-4** 1689

Wallace, Gerald, IRS investigation of II 2 1250-1255;
SUMM I 141
in Article of Impeachment II **RHJC** 141-145
information sent to White House **SI8** 3, 35, 36-42
in Jenner's presentation of summary of evidence
to House Judiciary Committee Impeachment Inquiry on Nixon's abuse of power **II 3** 1983-1984
Minority of House Judiciary Committee Impeachment Inquiry views on **RHJC** 439-440

Wallace campaign SIAPP4 50, 58, 59, 70, 71, 76, 89,
107
and IRS investigation of George and Gerald Wallace **SUMM I** 141
in Political Matters Memoranda **SIAPP4** 6
Political Matters Memoranda on payment for
withdrawing from election in California
SIAPP4 30
withdrawal in California **SIAPP4** 43

Wallis, Ben A., Jr. **II 2** 732
biography of **II 3** 2236
Wallrich, Burt **SI7-2** 1023
Walsh, Lawrence E. **TW 3** 333-334
contacts with Kleindienst on *ITT-Grinnell* appeal **SI5-1** 15, 283, 284-305
informed by Kleindienst of arrangements for extension of time on *ITT-Grinnell* appeal **SI5-1** 16, 349, 358
and ITT matter **II 2** 1009-1010
letter to Kleindienst urging delay of *ITT-Grinnell* appeal **SI5-1** 15, 283, 287-303, 355, 356
and request for extension of time to appeal *ITT-Grinnell* case **SI5-2** 753-754
telephone conversation with Kleindienst on *ITT-Grinnell* appeal delay **SI5-1** 16, 307, 308
Walsh, Lawrence E., cited testimony of
on Application for Extension of Time for *ITT-Grinnell* appeal **SI5-1** 16, 349, 358
on discussions with Kleindienst on *ITT-Grinnell* appeal **SI5-1** 15, 283, 285-286
Walsh, Paul **NSI4** 107
Walters, Barbara **SIAPP4** 77
Walters, Johnnie M. **II 3** 1984-1985; **SI3-2** 813; **SI8** 153
affidavit on Dean's request for IRS audits of McGovern campaign staff members and contributors **SI8** 25, 237, 238-241
affidavit on Ehrlichman's dealings with IRS on investigation of O'Brien **SI8** 23, 217, 218-222
affidavit on termination of IRS investigation of O'Brien and Ehrlichman's reaction to **SI8** 24, 227, 231-235
affidavits on Dean's efforts to get IRS action against McGovern supporters **SI8** 25, 30, 237, 238-241, 351, 352-355
in briefing memo prepared by Dean and Caulfield on increasing political responsiveness of IRS **SI8** 196, 197-198
in Dean memo on IRS action against Ford Foundation and Brookings Institution **SI8** 85-86
and Dean's efforts to get IRS action against McGovern supporters **SI8** 25, 26, 30, 237, 238-271, 273, 274-279, 351, 352-353
and Dean's requests for IRS audits **TW 2** 300-303, 311, 331-332, 350-351
Doar-Jenner interview with **II 2** 1284-1286
and Ehrlichman's dealings with IRS on investigation of O'Brien **SI8** 23, 217, 218-225
and enemies list **SUMM I** 141-142
handwritten notes on reaction to Dean's request for IRS audits of McGovern campaign staff members and contributors **SI8** 25, 30, 237, 242-243, 351, 356-357
and IRS audit of Lawrence O'Brien **II 2** 1284-1287; **SUMM I** 142
and termination of IRS investigation of O'Brien **SI8** 24, 227, 228-235
and White House efforts to make IRS "politically responsive" **II 2** 1283
See also Jenner, Albert E., Jr., presentation of summary of evidence to House Judiciary Committee Impeachment Inquiry on Nixon's abuse of powers

Walters, Robert J.
and Wallace campaign in California **SIAPP4** 30
Walters, Vernon A. **NSI1** 135
Caulfield memo on **II 2** 1264
conversations with Gray re Watergate investigation and CIA **SI2** 2, 56, 520, 522-523
and Dean's efforts to obtain CIA funds for Watergate defendants **SI3-1** 8, 129, 130-142; **SI2** 2, 44, 427, 428-441
and Dean's efforts to obtain information on McGovern campaign staff members **II 2** 1293, 1297-1298
and Dean's efforts to retrieve Fielding break-in photos from CIA **II 2** 715-716
and Dean's efforts to retrieve materials sent to Justice Department by CIA **SI7-4** 1624, 1733, 1734-1739
and FBI Watergate investigation **SUMM I** 40-41
informs Dean that CIA activities in Mexico cannot be jeopardized by FBI Watergate investigation **SI1** 2, 42, 409; **SI2** 2, 42, 409
meeting with Ehrlichman, Haldeman and Helms **II 1** 624-628
meeting with Gray on White House staff's interference with Watergate investigation **SUMM I** 45
meeting with Haldeman, Ehrlichman, and Helms on FBI Watergate investigation **SI2** 2, 36, 38-39, 355-357, 361, 375-395
meeting with Haldeman and Ehrlichman on Watergate investigation **SI2** 2, 36, 355, 356-362
meeting with Helms and Nixon **II 3** 1961
memo for Gray on information provided by CIA on Watergate incident **SI2** 2, 56, 520, 530-532
memo for record on CIA and FBI Watergate investigation **SI2** 2, 42, 409, 410-414
memo for record on meeting with Gray on FBI Watergate investigation **SI2** 2, 40, 397, 404
memo from Helms on Watergate investigation and Mexican checks **SI2** 2, 48, 471
memo from Jacobson on Halperin-Ellsberg contacts **SI7-2** 534, 681, 682-684
memo on conversation with Dean refusing to attempt to retrieve CIA material on Hunt from Department of Justice **SI2** 2, 67, 673, 674-680
memo on meeting with Gray on CIA and FBI Watergate investigation **SI2** 2, 56, 520, 528-529
memo on refusing Dean's request for retrieval of CIA material from Justice Department **SI7-4** 1624, 1733, 1737
memo to Gray on aliases provided by CIA to Hunt **SI2** 4, 79, 86
memos for record on Dean's efforts to obtain CIA funds for Watergate defendants **SI3-1** 8, 129, 140-142
Nixon directs Haldeman to meet with on White House concern over possible disclosure of covert CIA or Plumbers activities **SI7-3** 1202, 1533, 1534-1540
in Nixon-Haldeman discussion on FBI Watergate investigation **SIAPP3** 41, 78
Nixon's role in meeting with **SI2** 2, 36, 355, 357, 359, 362
in Nixon's taped conversation with Gray **SIAPP1** 44

refuses Dean's request to ask Justice Department to return Watergate investigation materials to White House **II 2** 1200

refuses to retrieve CIA material on Hunt from Department of Justice **SI2** 2, 680

role in Nixon Administration **RHJC** 16-17

and Watergate coverup **II 1** 689-691

and White House efforts to obtain money for Watergate defendants from CIA **II 2** 723-727

Walters, Vernon A., cited testimony of

on CIA and FBI Watergate investigation **SI2** 2, 40, 42, 397-404, 409, 410-413

on discussions with Gray on FBI investigation and White House interference **SI2** 2, 56, 520, 526-527

on meeting with Gray on FBI Watergate investigation **SI2** 2, 40, 397, 402-403

on meeting with Haldeman, Ehrlichman, and Helms **SI2** 2, 38, 375, 378-381, 395

Warnecke, John Carl SIAPP3 260

Warner, Bill SI5-2 584-585

Warner, John S., letter to Merrill on CIA aid to Hunt and Liddy SI7-2 564, 1151, 1162-1164

Warnke, Paul NSI4 106; **SI7-3** 1216-1218

Warren, Gerald L. SIAPP4 45; **SI8** 69, 115

announces Nixon's signing of Labor-HEW Appropriations Bill on December 18, 1973 **SI12** 20

memo from Bell with enemies list **SI8** 7, 65, 72-75

Warren, Robert, statement on ground rules for bombing of Cambodia SI11 18, 165

Warren Commission

and access to IRS returns **RHJC** 438-439

comparison between Impeachment Inquiry and **SUMM I** 17-18

Jenner on comparison between House Judiciary Committee Impeachment Inquiry and **II 3** 1940-1941

procedures used by **II 1** 8, 9

Washburn, C. Langhorne SIAPP4 5, 11

Washington, George

invocation of Executive privilege by **SIAPP1** 6

Washington, D.C., Police Department

Evidence Report on materials found after Watergate break-in **SI2** 2, 51, 483, 489, 492

Washington Monthly **SI8** 124

Washington Post **SIAPP4** 26; **SI5-2** 671, 707; **SI7-2** 527, 591, 596-598

on AMPI contribution to unopposed Democratic Congressional candidates **SI6-1** 216, 228-230

Anderson articles on U.S. position on India-Pakistan War **SI7-3** 1193, 1421, 1430-1431

article on IRS investigation of Wallace administration in Alabama **SI8** 3, 35, 37

article on Richardson proposing Stennis Plan to Cox **SI9-2** 537, 765, 771-772

articles linking Segretti to White House staff members **SI7-4** 1617, 1657, 1658-1659, 1678

on Dean's refusal to testify at Gray hearings **SI3-2** 895-896

on DNC suit and CRP denial of involvement in Watergate **SI2** 2, 29, 301, 302-303

in Higby-Magruder taped telephone conversation **SI4-2** 635-636

House Judiciary Committee Impeachment Inquiry discussion on memos leaked to **II 2** 1325-1331

on indictment of Ellsberg **SI7-2** 528, 613, 614-615

on ITT case and Kleindienst confirmation hearings **NSI2** 16, 189, 198-199; **SI5-2** 512, 855, 857, 859-861

on Magruder's resignation from Department of Commerce **SI4-3** 1114, 1625, 1626

on McCord's testimony linking Mitchell, Colson, Dean, and Magruder to Watergate break-in **SI4-1** 22, 431, 432-433

in Nixon-Dean-Haldeman discussion of Watergate **SI8** 320, 321-322

Nixon's threats against **TW 2** 289-290

photograph of Sheraton Harbor Island Corp. check **SI5-2** 489, 603, 604

on public demand for appointment of special prosecutor for Watergate investigation **SI9-1** 5, 131, 136

Rodino on article on Haldeman-Nixon conversation in **II 3** 1977

on Senate Judiciary Committee calling Dean to testify **SI3-2** 700, 799, 800-801

on subpoena for Reisner and McCord's testimony **SI4-1** 28, 487, 488-489

on Watergate break-in **SI2** 2, 22, 231, 232-234

White House reaction to stories on Segretti's activities **SI7-4** 1617, 1657, 1658-1675

on White House reasons for requesting FBI investigation of Schorr **SI7-2** 1119

Woodward and Bernstein article of June 19, 1972 on Watergate break-in **TW 1** 191-193

on Ziegler's statement on leaks from Senate Select Committee on Presidential Campaign Activities **SI4-1** 29, 497, 498, 499-500

See also Anderson, Jack; Pentagon Papers

Washington Star

article on Ehrlichman-Byrne meeting **II 2** 1237

leak on Stans' role as director of campaign finance **SIAPP4** 5

"milk money" stories in **SI** 82, 84-85

on Nixon's remarks abouth Thieu **SI7-1** 364

on White House connection to Watergate **SI2** 2, 160

Washington Star News

article on Byrne meeting with Nixon **SI7-4** 1649, 2019, 2026

Water Bank Program

termination of **SI12** 17

Water Pollution Control Act

litigation on impoundment of funds for **SI12** 9-11

Watergate arrests SI2 4, 79, 81-85

evidence of CRP involvement in at scene of break-in **SUMM I** 32

Liddy informs Magruder of **SI2** 7, 105, 106

Mitchell, Magruder, Mardian, LaRue, and Dean meet on **SUMM I** 37

Nixon's response to **SUMM I** 35-42

telephone call from Petersen to Kleindienst informing him of **SI2** 6, 101, 102-104

Watergate break-in SIAPP1 1-110; SIAPP2 51-194; SUMM I 51; SI2 2, 36, 38-39, 355-357, 361, 375-395; SI4-3 92-94

  Burch's remarks to Republican National Committee on April 26, 1974 on SIAPP1 105-110

  Butterfield denies hearing or seeing anything connecting Nixon to TW 1 97, 112

  Butterfield on learning about TW 1 112

  CIA documents sent to Justice Department on TW 3 47-70

  Colson on efforts to determine Hunt's status at White House after TW 3 256-264

  Colson-Haldeman discussion on Mitchell's possible responsibility for TW 3 318-319

  Colson hears about SI2 2, 174-175

  Colson's communications with Hunt after TW 3 271-298

  connection with IRS audit of Lawrence O'Brien II 2 1296-1297

  Dean investigation of SI2 2, 14, 143, 144-153

  Dean on learning about TW 2 223-227; SI3-2 1005-1006

  Dean on those knowing about SI3-2 1010-1011

  Dean tells Nixon on March 21, 1973 that no one on White House staff had prior knowledge of NSI1 6, 49, 51

  discussed at Paul O'Brien-Ehrlichman meeting SI4-1 32-33, 507-508, 509-729

  Doar on Nixon's responsibility for II 3 1934; SUMM I 12

  in Doar's presentation of evidentiary material to House Judiciary Committee Impeachment Inquiry II 1 576

  documents sent from CIA to Justice Department on TW 3 47-70

  Ehrlichman-Haldeman telephone conversation on problems posed for White House by SUMM I 36

  Ehrlichman learns about Hunt's connection to SI2 2, 8, 117-120

  Ehrlichman tells Nixon no one in White House was involved with NSI1 7, 58, 56

  Ehrlichman's telephone call to Kleindienst with Nixon's questions on SI4-1 20, 399, 400-425

  events following SI2 2, 3-67

  events prior to SI1 5-271

  executive sessions of House Judiciary Committee Impeachment Inquiry on II 1 551-583, 585-638

  Gray-MacGregor telephone conversation on SI2 2, 533-537

  Haldeman asks Dean to write report on SI4-1 10, 265, 266-268

  Haldeman and Ehrlichman testify that they do not believe Nixon had prior knowledge of NSI1 7, 53, 54-55

  Haldeman informs Magruder of SI2 2, 10, 125, 126-127

  and Haldeman's notes of his June 20, 1972 meeting with Nixon NSI4 34, 223, 224-225

  Hunt on SI7-3 1198, 1495, 1499-1500

  Hunt on approval of plan for SI1 198-199, 200

  impact on Presidency SI3-2 1115-1116

  and Impeachment Inquiry SI1 2

  indictment of Mitchell, Haldeman, Ehrlichman, Colson, Mardian, Parkinson, and Strachan for conspiracy related to SI9-2 563, 959, 960-961

LaRue admits knowing it was CRP project TW 1 187-189, 234-235

LaRue denies knowledge of any Nixon involvement with TW 1 243-246

LaRue denies prior knowledge of TW 1 232-233

LaRue on first knowledge of TW 1 183-185, 233-234

LaRue informs Mitchell about TW 1 186, 233-234

Lawrence O'Brien on SI2 2, 302-303

Liddy informs Dean on NSI1 3, 39, 40

Liddy meets with Mardian and LaRue on II 2 1194

Liddy's use of McCord for SUMM I 32

link to Nixon's approval of political-intelligence plan including electronic surveillance SUMM I 29

as logical outgrowth of Nixon's policies, Holtzman on RHJC 321-322

Magruder on impact on his life SI4-2 621

Magruder notifies Haldeman of TW 1 190, 194

Martinez on SI7-3 1198, 1495, 1501-1502

McCord on SI7-3 1198, 1495, 1496-1498

McCord testimony on Mitchell, Colson, Dean, and Magruder having prior knowledge of SI4-1 22, 431, 432-443

McCord's letter to Caulfield on danger of blaming CIA for SI3-1 40, 475, 476-482

meeting of June 19, of Mitchell, Dean, Magruder, Mardian, and LaRue to discuss SI2 2, 21, 223, 224-229

meeting on June 20, 1972 with Haldeman, Ehrlichman, Mitchell, Dean, and Kleindienst to discuss SI2 2, 23-24, 235-236, 237, 238, 239, 240-241, 242

meeting of Nixon, Mitchell, and Haldeman on SI2 2, 53, 513, 514-516

Metropolitan Police Department, Washington, D.C., Supplementary Evidence Report on SI2 4, 79, 92-94

Mitchell denies any knowledge of in FBI interview SI3-1 15, 203, 204-206

Mitchell on events after learning about TW 2 146-154, 155, 159, 166-167, 171-172

Mitchell-Nixon discussion of control over CRP people and SI2 2, 30, 305, 306-310

Mitchell's press statement on SI2 2, 29, 301, 302-303; TW 1 188-190, 212-214, 241-242, 261, 261

national security grounds for discussed in Nixon-Dean meeting SI3-2 1072-1074

in news summaries sent to Nixon TW 1 105

Nixon on SI3-2 1246-1247; SI4-3 1530

and Nixon Administration political-intelligence plan RHJC 35-39

Nixon announces nomination of Richardson as Attorney General with authority over decisions on SI9-1 5, 131, 132-137

Nixon-Colson discussion on Mitchell's possible role in TW 3 317-318, 320, 331

Nixon-Dean discussion of SI3-2 872, 1067-1068; SI8 291-304, 424-426

Nixon-Dean-Haldeman discussion on SI8 333

Nixon denies prior knowledge of NSI1 6, 49, 50; SI9-1 43, 489, 490-494; SI1 39

Nixon, Ehrlichman, and Haldeman discuss establishing special commission on SI4-1 361-361, 364, 370

Petersen on reasons for not believing Nixon was implicated in **TW 3** 133-134

and Petersen's reports to Nixon on Justice Department investigation of **TW 3** 86-105, 110-117, 128-130, 146-147

Rangel on implications of **RHJC** 313-320

in St. Clair's presentation of evidence in behalf of Nixon **II 3** 1721-1755, 1889-1890, 1898-1906

Sandman urges beginning House Judiciary Committee Impeachment Inquiry with **II 1** 218-219

and Sloan's payments to Liddy **II 2** 720-723

in status report of House Judiciary Committee Impeachment Inquiry staff **II 3** 2227-2231

task of House Judiciary Committee Impeachment Inquiry in determining Nixon's role in **SUMM I** 23

and White House dealings with FBI and CIA after Watergate break-in, in Doar's presentation of evidentiary material to House Judiciary Committee Impeachment Inquiry **II 1** 680-695

and White House interference with FBI Watergate investigation **II 2** 778-786

and White House interference with Senate Select Committee on Presidential Campaign Activities **II 2** 760-767

See also Article of Impeachment I

Watergate defendants SI2 2, 44, 427, 428-441

Dean assigns Kalmbach to raise funds for **SI3-1** 9, 143, 144-155; **II 2** 727-729

Dean informs Haldeman of CRP fundraising for **SI3-1** 14, 199, 200-202

Dean's efforts to obtain bail money from CIA for **SI3-1** 8, 129, 130-142

discussed by Nixon, Haldeman, Ehrlichman, and Dean **SI3-2** 1155-1158

granted leave by Sirica to testify under grant of immunity before Watergate Grand Jury **II 2** 842

guilty pleas of **SI3-1** 41, 483, 484-485

indictment of **SI3-1** 29, 357, 358-367

memo from Dorothy Hunt to Bittman on distribution of money to **TW 2** 16-19, 46-47, 63-66, 68-69

Mitchell, Mardian, LaRue, and Dean meet to discuss CIA assistance for **SI3-1** 7, 121, 122-127

Moore asks Mitchell to take over fundraising for **TW 2** 135

Nixon-Dean discussion of sentencing of **SI3-1** 665-667

Nixon-Dean-Haldeman discussion of indictment of **SI3-1** 30, 369, 370-371

Nixon-Ehrlichman discussion on possibility of Executive clemency for **SI3-1** 13, 181, 182-197

Nixon's statement on fundraising for **SI9-1** 44, 495, 496-497

sentencing of **SI3-2** 1181-1184

Sirica defers final sentencing of all except Liddy **II 2** 834-835; **SI4-1** 5, 217, 219, 226-233

See also Bail money for Watergate defendants; Hush money; Watergate burglars

Watergate Special Prosecution Task Force SIAPP2 34-37; **SI9-1** 30, 393, 394-396; **SI9-2** 559, 931, 932-933

Bork files amendment to charter of **SI9-2** 551,

861, 862-866

Buzhardt-Cox correspondence on security measures with respect to White House files **SI9-1** 9, 19, 161, 162-164, 165-168

Buzhardt denies Cox's requests for inventory of White House staff and Plumbers unit files **SI9-1** 13, 257, 258-261

and Cox's claim that White House documents are being placed among Presidential papers to avoid subpoenas **SI9-2** 527, 597, 598-606

Cox's requests for Fielding's file on ITT **SI9-1** 15, 269, 170-176

Cox's requests for logs of meetings and telephone conversations between Nixon and fifteen named individuals **SI9-1** 14, 263, 264-267

Dean pleads guilty to conspiracy to obstruct justice and agrees to cooperate with **SI9-2** 542, 801, 802-809

Dean's attorney's begin discussing with **II 2** 854

discrepancies in documents sent by Buzhardt to Cox listing Nixon-Petersen meetings **SI9-1** 16, 277, 278-287

Haig and Nixon contact Richardson on Cox's investigation of Nixon's expenditures on his San Clemente property **SI9-1** 21, 329, 330-332

letter from Cox to Buzhardt on lack of progress in obtaining access to papers in White House files **SI9-1** 24, 347, 348-350

letter from Cox to Buzhardt requesting certain Nixon tapes **SI9-1** 29, 389, 390-392

letter from Cox to Buzhardt requesting Nixon statement on Dean's testimony before Ervin Committee **SI9-1** 19, 317, 318-320

Memorandum in Response to Analysis, Index and Particularized Claims of Executive Privilege **SI9-2** 553, 875, 876-877

Nixon's firing of Cox and abolition of **SI9-2** 544, 815, 816-825

and Nixon's letter to Sirica declining to obey subpoena **SI9-1** 37, 425, 426-427

Order establishing **SI9-1** 7, 145, 150

press release on American Airlines Corp. voluntarily acknowledging illegal contributions to CRP **SI9-1** 22, 333, 324-325

press release on Ashland Oil voluntarily acknowledging illegal contribution to FCRP **SI9-1** 31, 397, 398

press release on indictments for consipiracy related to Watergate break-in **SI9-2** 563, 959, 960-961

press release on indictments for Fielding break-in **SI9-2** 564, 963, 964

refusal of Nixon tapes to Cox **SI9-1** 12, 243, 244-255

Silbert and Glanzer learn about Fielding break-in from Dean **II 2** 1226-1228

as source of Ehrlichman's handwritten notes **SIAPP3** 2

Strachan's Political Matters Memoranda file turned over to **SI9-2** 526, 591, 592-595

See also Cox, Archibald; Fielding break-in, papers from criminal cases; Illegal campaign practices and contributions; Jaworski, Leon; Nixon Administration, attempts to improperly influence

Wiggins, Charles E. **II 1** 2; **II 2** 1043; **RHJC** 359-493; **SUMM I** 1
amendment on nature of material to be subpoenaed **II 1** 32-39
amendment to subpoena to Nixon **II 2** 947-949
on attorney-client privilege and O'Brien's testimony on Mitchell **TW 1** 131, 133-134
on availability of written theories on possible impeachment **II 3** 1880
on *Brady* case **II 2** 1429-1430E
on calling witnesses before House Judiciary Committee Impeachment Inquiry **II 3** 1632, 1648, 1649-1650, 1672-1673, 1674, 1675, 1698-1699, 1704, 1713
on discrepancies between transcripts and tapes **II 2** 852
discussion on his amendment to procedural resolution on right of Minority of House Judiciary Committee Impeachment Inquiry to subpoena witnessses **II 1** 23-32
on Doar-St. Clair correspondence **II 1** 182-183
on Doar's and Jenner's appearance before Sirica **II 1** 163
on Ehrlichman's meeting with Byrne **II 2** 1208
on excising sections of Nixon tapes **II 2** 805
on FBI report to Justice Department on wiretapping of Ellsberg **II 2** 1137
on final payment to Hunt **II 2** 1203-1204
on Fulbright's request for House Judiciary Committee Impeachment Inquiry material on Kissinger **II 2** 1324
on House Judiciary Committee Impeachment Inquiry issuing subpoenas to Nixon **II 3** 1534, 1540, 1547-1548
on interviewing witnesses in view of missing Nixon tapes **II 2** 845-846
on IRS audits of politically active people in entertainment industry **II 2** 1280
on issuing subpoenas to Nixon **II 1** 651-652, 667
on Krogh's guilty plea **II 2** 1175
on leaks from House Judiciary Committee Impeachment Inquiry **II 2** 768-769; **II 3** 1856
on legal questions involved in White House staff members obtaining IRS information **II 2** 1273-1274
on legalities involved in overhearing Ellsberg on Halperin wiretap **II 2** 1191
on legality of domestic surveillance **II 2** 1107-1108
on material included in House Judiciary Committee Impeachment Inquiry record**II 3** 1916-1917
on Nixon's alleged approval of Fielding break-in **II 2** 1168
on Nixon's discussion on Executive privilege with Richardson **II 2** 1336, 1341
on Nixon's gift of Presidential papers **II 3** 1476, 1501-1502
on Nixon's income tax **II 3** 1516-1517
on Nixon's involvement or lack of involvement in stopping IRS audits of his friends **II 2** 1277-1278
on Nixon's noncompliance with House Judiciary Committee Impeachment Inquiry subpoenas **II 1** 411-412, 422-423, 432-433, 448-449, 450; **II 2** 907-908, 941

on Nixon's rights to excise material from tapes **II 1** 253-254
objections to hearsay evidence **II 2** 807-808
on obtaining Nixon's tax returns and audits from IRS **II 2** 1245-1246
on possibly forged letter from House Judiciary Committee Impeachment Inquiry**II 1** 70-72, 77
on presentation procedures for House Judiciary Committee Impeachment Inquiry**II 1** 265-266
on procedural rules for handling Impeachment Inquiry material **II 1** 119-120, 125-126
on procedures for House Judiciary Committee Impeachment Inquiry **II 1** 5, 6
on purpose of presentation on IRS **II 2** 1259
question on authority of Special Watergate Prosecutor **II 2** 1344
on relationship between House Judiciary Committee Impeachment Inquiry and legal staff **II 1** 62-64
on release of House Judiciary Committee Impeachment Inquiry evidentiary material to public **II 3** 1597-1598, 1599-1600, 1601, 1602
requests written statement with respect to scope of examination **II 3** 1879
resolution to establish procedure for dealing with national security grounds for Nixon refusing materials to House Judiciary Committee Impeachment Inquiry **II 1** 356-359
on right of Minority of House Judiciary Committee Impeachment Inquiry to subpoena witnesses **II 1** 28-29
on rules of evidentiary procedures for House Judiciary Committee Impeachment Inquiry **II 1** 510-511, 518, 526, 522-523, 524, 525, 527, 529-530, 537
on rules on cross-examination of witnesses **TW 1** 91
on St. Clair's letters to Doar on House Judiciary Committee Impeachment Inquiry requests for materials on dairy industry and ITT matter **II 2** 805
on St. Clair's participation in House Judiciary Committee Impeachment Inquiry **II 1** 215-216, 239-240, 633
on St. Clair's presentation **II 2** 1217
on scheduling St. Clair's presentation of evidence **II 3** 1568
on setting date for final report from House Judiciary Committee Impeachment Inquiry **II 1** 48
on Sirica's invitation to Doar and Jenner **II 1** 146-147
on submission of written interrogatories to Nixon **II 3** 1616-1617, 1618
on suit by Center on Corporate Responsibility **II 2** 1299
See also Minority of House Judiciary Committee Impeachment Inquiry views on Articles of Impeachment
Wiggins, Charles E., questioning by
Bittman **TW 2** 72-74
Butterfield **TW 1** 97
Colson **TW 3** 460-462
Dean **TW 2** 305-307, 312
Kalmbach **TW 3** 711-712

Wiggins, Charles E., questioning by *(Continued)*
LaRue **TW 1** 250-253
Mitchell **TW 2** 176-177
O'Brien **TW 1** 147-148
Petersen **TW 3** 139-141, 146, 159
Wild, Claude C., Jr. SIAPP2 263-266
See also U.S. v. Gulf Oil Corporation and Claude C. Wild, Jr.
Wiley, Sam SIAPP4 2, 121
Williams, C. Dickerman TW 2 5
Williams, Edward Bennett II 2 710; SI2 2, 605, 614-615
Nixon on SI8 308-310
Williams, Eleanor SIAPP4 85; SI1 82
Williams, Maurice S. SI6-2 852
Williams, William E.
informs House Judiciary Committee Impeachment Inquiry staff of status of payment of Nixon's 1969 tax deficiency **SI10** 19-20
Wills, Frank SI1 262
discovery of Watergate break-in by, Rangel on **RHJC** 314
Wilson, David, and Intelligence Evaluation Committee SI7-1 489, 500
Wilson, Denise II 2 1267
Wilson, James
and GSA payment for sewer system installation at Nixon's San Clemente property **SI12** 113
Wilson, Jerry SI3-2 835; SI7-4 1817
Nixon discusses as possible FBI director **SI7-4** 1819
Wilson, John J. II 2 886, 887
appeal from Sirica's ruling on turning Grand Jury materials over to House Judiciary Committee Impeachment Inquiry **II 1** 202
cited testimony of, on discussion with Geneen on ITT committment to San Diego Convention and Tourist Bureau **SI5-2** 482, 527, 530-531
discussion with Geneen on possibility of ITT financial support for San Diego as Republican National Convention site **SI5-2** 482, 527, 528-531
Haldeman and Ehrlichman report to Nixon on conversation with **SI4-3** 1002, 1421
meeting with Nixon and Strickler **SI4-3** 1108, 1511, 1515-1530
memo from Timmons to Magruder on Mitchell's committments to **SI5-2** 486-487, 561-562, 574
Nixon's discussions with Petersen on meeting with **SI4-3** 1536-1537
Wilson, Pete SI5-1 437
Wilson, Robert SIAPP1 19; SIAPP4 25; SI5-1 437, 438; SI6-2 955
article in *New York Times* on statement that no legal action was being taken against him **NSI2** 14, 155, 156
and ITT-Sheraton pledge **SI5-2** 614, 615
telegram from James on use of Sheraton Hotel as Republican National Convention center **SI5-2** 588-589
Winchester, Lucy SI8 69, 115
Winn, Willis J. NSI2 84-85; SI5-1 405, 408

Winslow, Walter G. SI5-2 787, 793-794
Wiretapping SI1 23, 215, 216-222; SI2 2, 66, 671, 672; SI7-1 4, 157, 158-172
See also Electronic surveillance
Wolper, David SIAPP4 128
Women
number on legal staff of House Judiciary Committee Impeachment Inquiry **II 1** 73
role in Republican campaign **SI1** 36
Women's GOP Federation, San Diego SI5-1 437
Women's liberation issue
Hauser and **SIAPP4** 29
Wong, Al
calls Butterfield after Watergate break-in and asks about Hunt's employment at White House **TW 1** 55-56, 107
and installation of den windows at Nixon's San Clemente property **SI12** 124
Woodcock, Leonard
on enemies list **SI8** 74, 108, 119
Woods, Joseph A., Jr. II 1 552
biography of **II 3** 2143
and discussion on procedures for House Judiciary Committee Impeachment Inquiry **II 1** 377-341
instructions from House Judiciary Committee Impeachment Inquiry on appeal on Sirica's ruling on turning Grand Jury materials over to House Judiciary Committee Impeachment Inquiry **II 1** 202, 203
on rules of evidentiary procedures for House Judiciary Committee Impeachment Inquiry **II 1** 511, 512
Woods, Rose Mary SIAPP3 39, 46; SIAPP4 81, 84, 107; SI4-2 1024, 1027
accompanies Nixon to Key Biscayne, taking Nixon tapes and tape recorder **SI9-2** 532, 721, 722-735
Caulfield and **SI7-1** 353-354
demonstration to House Judiciary Committee Impeachment Inquiry of equipment she used to transcribe Nixon tapes **II 2** 1435-1450
and erasures on June 20, 1972 Nixon tape **II 2** 1379; SI9-2 531, 687, 688-719; SUMM I 38, 110
list of contributors of **II 2** 1084-1085
memo to Haldeman on McGovern **SIAPP4** 126
Nixon decides to review subpoenaed tapes with assistance of **SI9-2** 528, 607, 608-618
Nixon on erasures on tapes and **SIAPP1** 85
Nixon on her opinion of Magruder **SUMM I** 6
and Nixon's dictabelts **TW 1** 63-64, 117
and Nixon's records **TW 1** 62-63
note from Haig on confusion over June 20, 1972 subpoenaed tape **SI9-2** 529, 619, 637
and preparations for Nixon's review of subpoenaed tapes **SI9-2** 529, 530, 619, 620-648, 649, 650-685
and Report of Technical Investigation on gap on Nixon tape of June 20, 1972 **NSI4** 32, 203, 204-205
role in Nixon Administration **RHJC** 16
and technical report on June 20, 1972 Nixon tape **II 2** 1435
Titus states she claimed Haldeman and Ehrlichman had erected shield in front of Nixon **TW 3**

Zeifman, Jerome M. SUMM I 1

Ziegler, Ronald L. SI1 48; SI2 2, 152; SI4-2 859; SI7-2 1113

announcement of intention to nominate Kleindienst SI5-2 606

announcement on Chapin leaving Nixon Administration II 2 1200

announces that Nixon has "absolute and total" confidence in Dean II 2 842

Colson tells him Ehrlichman and Haldeman should resign TW 3 354-355

confirms Chapin's leaving White House SI7-4 1713

and CRP press relations SIAPP4 65

on Dean's statement on not becoming scapegoat in Watergate case SI4-3 1495

and denial of White House wiretapping of staff members and newsmen SI7-4 1625, 1741, 1742-1748

denies any White House involvement in Watergate and announces members of White House staff may appear before Watergate Grand Jury SI4-1 26, 477, 478-481

denies *Time* magazine story on Kissinger tapes II 2 1201

discussed by Nixon and Dean SI4-1 141-142

discussion with Nixon on media SIAPP3 72-74

Ehrlichman informs him of Hunt's connection with Watergate break-in SUMM I 36; SI2 8, 117, 118

informed by Nixon of his discussions with Petersen II 2 882, 883

and inquiries about FBI investigation of Schorr TW 3 239

meeting with Mollenhoff, Haldeman, and Ehrlichman on leaked IRS information SI8 39

meeting with Nixon and Ehrlichman on information furnished by Petersen SI4-3 1090, 1251, 1255-1263

at meeting with Nixon, Haldeman, and Ehrlichman on April 17, 1973 SI4-3 1097, 1345, 1350-1386, 1408-1409

and newspaper stories on Segretti's activities SI7-4 1617, 1657, 1658-1675

Nixon-Dean-Haldeman discussion of role in Watergate hearings SI8 408-409

Nixon discusses role with Dean SI3-2 820, 821

Nixon discusses tape of March 21, 1973 with SUMM I 105

at Nixon-Ehrlichman discussion of April 16, 1973 SI4-3 1258, 1261, 1263

in Nixon-Haldeman-Ehrlichman discussion on Haldeman's involvement with Segretti SI7-4

1923-1924

at Nixon-Haldeman-Ehrlichman meeting of March 27, 1973 SI4-1 354

at Nixon-Petersen meeting of April 16, 1973 SI4-3 1089, 1223, 1240, 1242

at Nixon-Petersen meeting of April 27, 1973 SI4-3 1115-1116, 1627-1628, 1638-1640

Nixon reports on Petersen's information on Watergate Grand Jury to SUMM I 92, 96

Nixon states that he will not comment on Select Committee hearings SIAPP1 9-10

and Nixon's press conference of June 22, 1972 SI2 2, 35, 351, 352-353

planned statement on Watergate questions SI3-2 893

public statement on leaks from Senate Select Committee on Presidential Campaign Activities II 2 855; SI4-1 29, 497, 498-500

as recipient of political enemies project memos SI8 21, 211, 212

refuses comment during press briefing on requests from military commanders for bombings in Cambodia SI11 29

remarks on firing of Cox and abolition of Watergate Special Prosecution Task Force SI9-2 544, 815, 825

as spokesperson for CRP on Watergate break-in SIAPP1 2

statement on December 18, 1972 on Chapin continuing as Deputy Assistant to Nixon SI7-4 1621, 1709, 1710-1711

statement to press on Watergate burglary SI2 2, 22, 231, 232

statement on Schorr TW 3 507; SI9-1 11, 169, 184-236

at time of Watergate arrests SUMM I 35-36

Ziegler, Ronald L., cited testimony of

on Nixon's announcement to allow White House staff members to testify before Watergate Grand Jury SI4-1 26, 477, 480-481

on Nixon's instructions to announce his confidence in Dean SI4-1 14, 319, 320-323

on statement denying White House staff involvement in Watergate SI4-1 26, 477, 480-481

Zumwalt, Raymond

tape logs SI9-1 11, 17, 25, 169, 171-176, 289, 291-294, 351, 366-370

Zumwalt, Raymond, cited testimony of

on Bull's requests for Nixon tapes SI9-1 3, 107, 123

on Nixon-Dean tapes turned over to Bull SI4-3 1112, 1557, 1606-1607